MONEY, FOOD, DRINK, AND FASHION
AND ANALYTIC TRAINING

Depth Dimensions of Physical Existence

Ed. John Beebe

VIII. International Congress of the
International Association for Analytical Psychology

MONEY, FOOD, DRINK, AND FASHION AND ANALYTIC TRAINING

DEPTH DIMENSIONS OF PHYSICAL EXISTENCE

The Proceedings of
the Eighth International Congress
For Analytical Psychology

JOHN BEEBE, Editor

BONZ.

Verlag Adolf Bonz GmbH · Fellbach-Oeffingen

CIP-Kurztitelaufnahme der Deutschen Bibliothek

Money, Food, Drink, and Fashion and Analytic Training — Depth Dimensions of Physical Existence —
/ ed. John Beebe. — Fellbach: Bonz, 1983.
  ISBN 3-87089-304-4

NE: Beebe, John (Hrsg.)

© 1983 for the English Edition by Verlag Adolf Bonz GmbH, D-7012 Fellbach-Öffingen
Printed by Otto W. Zluhan, D-7120 Bietigheim

Table of Contents

Fashion

Analytic Training

Clinical Practice and Research

Clinical Practice and Research (continued)

Theoretical Explorations

Theoretical Explorations (continued)

Preface

When the theme of the 1980 Congress was announced, there were grumblings from the local Societies which comprise the formal organization of bona fide Jungian analysts. Why had the archetypes and the symbolic life been deserted in favour of outer, concrete, even frivolous concerns like these? Had the outer collective vanquished the inner spirit even within our own sanctuary? Despite the word "depth" in the subtitle, many thought these topics—food, money, fashion, and even analytical training—awfully superficial. At the actual Congress, I myself had occasion to recall Oscar Wilde's line, "Only superficial people insist on looking beneath the surface." The archetype, I meant, is after all a structural concept, and the structure of a situation can be found in its surface properties every bit as much as in the images which emerge from its psychological depths. Outside our own discipline, Gregory Bateson had been making this clear in his papers for two decades, alongside Edgar Levenson, whose *The Fallacy of Understanding* had first brought the Wilde quote to my attention.

But it wasn't until the Congress was over that I realized that the topics chosen had freed a new group of analysts (given this chance to come forward for the first time by a generous Program Committee) to say where they had come in their own theoretical development since their training, in languages peculiarly their own. The result was a vivid demonstration that analytical psychology is not only Jung's, despite its uncancellable debt to him, and that it is not a closed system, forced to self-destruct when its postulates no longer express the current situation in the very collective unconscious it has demanded we pay attention to.

The papers in this book need to be read with an open mind and with a welcoming attitude, because they dare to be personal, irreverent, and enthusiastically interested in the things of the world. Approaching this book, one has to relax as one would to enjoy a good dinner, or it won't digest properly. And so, a phrase from Jo Wheelwright's preface to an earlier volume of Congress papers seems peculiarly appropriate to introduce this one: Bon Appétit!

John Beebe

Acknowledgments

The editor wishes to acknowledge the advice and assistance of the following persons: Hans Dieckmann, Thomas Kirsch, Adolf Guggenbühl-Craig, Niel Micklem, James Hillman, William McGuire, Katherine Bradway, Barbara Mc-Clintock, Dorothy Sibley, Robert Sibley, Ursula Egli, Mary Webster, Joan Alpert, Joseph Henderson, and David Brown.

In addition, the Editors of *Quadrant, Spring, The Journal of Analytical Psychology,* and *Psychological Perspectives*—Joan Carson, James Hillman, Judith Hubback and William Walcott—reduced confusion enormously by granting permission for publication here of the authoritatively edited versions of manuscripts that have appeared in their respective journals. James Hillman also allowed reprinting here, in their final versions, all the papers he collected for the book *Soul and Money,* published by Spring Publications in 1982. The fact and place of prior publication is mentioned after the text of each reprinted paper, but the hard editorial work of these careful prior editors and their knowledgeable staffs must be acknowledged once again here.

At the last possible moment for timely publication Mr. Scheel of Bonz Verlag saw to the production of the book, and his generous contribution is especially appreciated.

Finally, one must thank those Gods, whoever they may be, that saw this Odyssean project to safe harbor. Its captain can only hope his many fellow sailors, the papers that follow, have not been unduly jostled by their editorial journey, and especially that they have reached their destination in their proper human forms.   J. B.

Introduction

It's an old custom that the president gives the opening address to the Congress. You are probably astonished to see that the Vice President is doing it this time. It was the wish of the President (after some discussions we agreed) to break the old custom of any international congress as other old structures are now breaking in our changing world.

Members who never spoke at an International Congress before should be heard. Afternoon sessions should give various possibilities to participate, and also not only one person alone should open the Congress, but two. Thus I will talk now instead of Adolf Guggenbühl, who spoke yesterday.

I believe that it is very necessary to change old structures to search for new ways in a world, in which science and industrial power have reached a climax and are threatening to fall apart or at least to decline during the next decades.

This week we will discuss the sense and the nonsense of our analytical training, at least I hope so. We will discuss the primary sources of our physical existence, which are food, drinking and fashion, and, last but not least, we will examine the keystone of the market of our industrial system, which has split man into consumer and producer, namely, the money.

All the hope which had been connected with the progress of our system in both East or West is now overshadowed by the end of our resources, by inflation, by an overcrowded world, by unemployment, by the fear of atomic war and by the increasingly great difference between the poor and the rich. What can Analytical Psychology do against these problems? To answer this question, I think we have to take a backward glance how modern science started, and through it our industrial system.

The founders of our modern science—Galileo, Kepler, Newton, and their followers, gave us not only a new way to see, to experience, and to manipulate the world by seeking objectivity and experimental work. They also committed, as Mumford rightly says, a hidden crime. This crime was splitting the subject from the object and putting down subjectivity to a lower and irrational level than objectivity. With this splitting the world of science gained on the one hand the enormous success of industrial development. On the other hand science lost not only its colours, its warmth of emotions, and its phantasies, but also, as we all are experiencing, its humanity.

In 1893 Robert Monroe explained in his opening address, to the British Association of Scientific Progress that "phantasy, conceptions, ideals and moral categories are the same as parasites, which live at the expense of their counterparts." And it was already Darwin, who prophesied: " At some future period . . . the civilized races of man will almost certainly *exterminate* and replace the savage races throughout the world." I fear we really did so, excepting only a small number of natural people living in isolation.

Until the middle of this century, there were enormous hopes linked to the advances of science and the myth of the machine. Man was supposed to find a life free from the slavery of hard work, free from threats of nature, free from fears and anxieties about his physical and psychical existence.

These hopes started long before the so-called industrial revolution, immediately after Galileo's discoveries. Even Kepler wrote a book about the journey to the moon. But the flood of written technical fictions started in the year 1516 with Thomas More's "De optimo rei publicae statu de que nova insula utopia". In Francis Bacon's "Nova Atlantis", printed in 1627, we find already missiles, submarines and gene manipulations.

The great hope for the progress of the industrial system was always nourished and nagged at us right through H. G. Wells' and Isaac Asimov's Star Empire or Foundation. But to-day we know that our planet is nearly exhausted, and the stars are almost as far as ever.

It was the great merit of Freud to return the subject into the focus of science with all its needs, projections, emotions, drives, dreams, and phantasies. But it was his failure that he had tried to adapt the subject to the system of the objective science. He had remained with the Zeitgeist of the end of the nineteenth century. Most of the Freudians still are doing so to-day. For example, they are still speaking of their wives as "second love objects."

C.G. Jung was the first to break out of this structure by returning to the subject its eternal value. No wonder that he was excluded at first from the scientists, until more and more people began to understand the limits and dangers of "objective" science and technology. So we are confronted to-day with a wave of interest in Jung. It is our task as analytical psychologists to understand and to help man in his search for alternatives to overt destructiveness or negative regressions, which often end in drugs, religious sects and psychic illnesses.

We all have to go back together to the collective unconscious and its archetypal structures to search for the missing links which will lead us into an unknown, probably post-industrial future in which humanity is able to survive.

I hope that some of the papers of this congress are more or less linked to these problems of our time.

Hans Dieckmann, Berlin

MONEY

Coins and Psychological Change

By Russell A. Lockhart (Los Angeles)

When I was a child I would frequently disappear into the closet of my bedroom. After locking the door I turned on a flashlight covered with blue plastic and began to dismantle what my mother called a "pile of junk." It was old toys, books, papers, clothes. What my mother didn't know—what no one in the whole world knew—was that this pile of junk was an elaborate camouflage serving as a hiding place for a secret. My secret was an old kitchen matchbox filled with silver coins—nickels, dimes, quarters. I would unearth these coins and in that strange blue light I would begin imagining. I imagined great riches and abundant wealth. I knew the meaning of a Plutonic affair! But more than riches, gazing into the silvery objects excited my imagination generally. The coins had a strong generative effect. It is said that money begets money. But then I knew that money begets imaginal worlds. I knew too that begetting had something to do with sex. I had not yet been aware of the curious relation between spending sexually, spending energy, spending time and spending money. Or yet with problems of saving oneself sexually, saving time, saving energy, saving money. Then, I was spending time with coins I would never spend. These imaginal adventures stimulated by my coins were my most valued experiences. Occasionally, I would be awakened out of my reveries by my mother pounding on the door wanting to know what I was doing. Tact prohibits going into this further than to say that my first experiences with synchronicity were in those moments of correspondence between my mother's suspicions and the full extent of my imaginal explorations.

One afternoon I came home from school and with my usual enthusiasm went for my closet and my secret coins. I was shocked by what I found. The closet floor was bare, cleaned out, swept clean. I looked frantically for my coins. I could not find them. My secret coins were gone. I ran out to the trash but the cans were empty. My coins were such a secret I could not bring myself to ask about them. I never went back to my closet again to spend those hours imagining. Something was broken in me with this loss. Shortly afterwards, I developed a severe case of measles that turned into mastoiditis and I was hospitalized. Even then, I connected the loss of my secret coins with my illness. The effect of this experience was that I wanted to become a doctor. I forgot about my coins. I forgot about imagining. I turned my attention to the world and dropped childish things. From that time until I was in graduate school I had no dreams. My coins, my imagination, even my dreams were gone.

Some months ago this dream came to me:

> I was sitting at my typewriter. Suddenly, the typewriter stopped working. I opened the cover and found a matchbox in the mechanism. I opened the matchbox and it was full of coins. I put it aside, closed the cover, and went on typing.

A short while after this dream, Dr. James Hillman called and presented me with an invitation to speak at the International Congress of Analytical Psychology on the subject of money. Why he did this I do not know. I can assure you that I have no special knowledge or wisdom about money. To be speaking on money strikes me as an enormous inflation. But I accepted the challenge in part as a way of honoring the return of my childhood coins.

I was excited about the return of my coins. It seemed so right to be writing on money under the auspices of an image that in childhood had so connected me to imagination and soul and body. But something was wrong. Try as I might I could not write. Months went by. My typewriter was stopped. Of course! The dream had shown that the coins stopped my typewriter. In my excitement over the coins I had neglected to see this. In the dream it was when I put the coins aside that I could go on typing. But how could I write on money and put aside my coins? In the dream I could do that but in the reality of the everyday world I could not. The call of my coins was too strong.

What follows then is not a scholarly piece on the psychology of money. Nor have I attempted a Jungian approach to the meaning of money in analytical practice or in everyday life in any formal or theoretically suitable way. All these things are, of course, vital issues to us, worthy of pursuit. But here, in these few pages, I have to follow the lead of my coins, letting them be psychopomp once again.

In the spring I went to Scotland. I had labored for months on money and had come to nothing. A trainee seemed to say more in a humorous remark than I had with all my effort. He said: "Money is like sex: there's never enough of either." But surely in Scotland I would find something on money that would release me from the quagmire in which I found myself. I decided to collect some stories from the old tradition-bearers in the Western Highlands. I received many stories but none about money, although I heard one proverb that excited something in my own Scottish blood. As a Jungian analyst I have tended often to focus on the roundness of coins, their inherent mandalic quality, their relation to energy and to values, and their imaging of the Self. This Scottish proverb was a jolt to my lazy thinking. "Money," say the Scotch, "is flat and is meant to be piled up." So typically Scottish to notice the forgotten characteristic and to remember the utility of things!

In the middle of a dark storm I found my way to Dunvegan Castle, ancestral home of the Clan McCloud on the Island of Skye. I fell into a long talk with a castle guide who was full of stories and delighted to have a willing ear. As we stood under the famous Fairy Flag, I asked him for a story about money. He thought for a while, looked downcast, and said he didn't know any. Then, with a twinkle as elfish as I have ever seen, he said he had one that might do. It seemed that one day a farmer's cow had wandered too near one of the high cliffs and, tripping on some small boulders, had fallen over the edge. Down below, in the loch, a fisherman was lazily fishing in his drifting boat. Well, the cow landed in the boat, destroying it completely, and managing to kill herself in the bargain. The two men got into a terrible row over who was at fault. The owner of the cow claimed that if the fisherman had not been so carelessly adrift the cow would have fallen harmlessly in the water. The owner of the boat claimed that had the herdsman not been so careless in letting his cow near the edge, she would not have fallen. Unable to settle their dispute, they took the matter to the Chief. The Chief was thrown into an enormous conflict and just couldn't decide what was just. So he called in his wiseman—what we could now obviously call his analyst—and asked his advice. "Chief," the analyst said, "you must pay both men, for it was the rock on your ground that would not hold and the waves in your loch that brought the boat where it lay."

I was struck immediately by how extraordinarily difficult it is in money matters, which seem so heavily characterized by the either/or-ness of gain and loss, have and have not, spend and save, how difficult to find the wisdom of that third position.

On this trip I discovered something in my ancestral background that seemed curiously connected with both my interests in healing and my renewed interest in coins. In 1329, a band of Scottish knights set out on a crusade to the Holy Land. Their leader, Lord Douglas, carried about his neck a silver box containing the heart of Robert the Bruce who had labored to free Scotland from English rule but who had died before making a pilgrimage to the Holy Land. Alongside Douglas rode Sir Symon Locard who had been knighted by Bruce, and was now entrusted with the task of carrying and safeguarding the key to the heart box. Eventually, they rode into battle against the Saracens in Spain. Douglas was killed but Sir Symon Locard's gallantry saved the heart box. Afterwards, to commemorate the event, Locard's name was changed to "Lockheart," and shortened finally to "Lockhart." A heart within a fetterlock *became the family coat of arms with the motto "corda serata pando,"* meaning "I open locked hearts."

During this battle, Symon captured an Emir prince of wealth and distinction. In paying a heavy ransom of gold and silver, the prince's mother dropped a jewel from her bag. My wily ancestor demanded that it be included in the ransom. Of course the mother acquiesced rather than lose her son and told

Sir Symon that it was an ancient healing stone, a sovereign and holy remedy against all manner of ills. During the reign of Edward the Fourth, the jewel, a deep red triangular stone, was mounted on a silver coin, and since that time has been known as the Lee Penny after the ancestral home of the Lockharts in the Lee and Carnwath area of Southern Scotland. The Lee Penny is now held by Simon Macdonald Lockhart, current holder of the lands of Lee, who graciously hosted me during my recent visit and gave me the chance to be alone with the jewel.

In holding the Lee Penny and admiring the gold box made to hold it, which was presented to the Lockhart family by Maria Teresa, the Empress Queen of Austria, I was strangely excited and began to experience a flood of flashing images of things I had never experienced before. The stone was alive. This talisman, which served as the impetus to Sir Walter Scott's novel, *The Talisman*, has a remarkable history of healing and an intriguing manner of exerting its power. The ritual for evoking its talismanic power is to dip it into water with "two dips and a swirl." During this rite words must not be spoken. Speaking renders the stone ineffectual. This aspect of the rite had a very curious effect on me, on one whose work is so related to the word. Water so treated can be used to heal wounds, diseases of cattle, and all manner of things, and there are many recorded instances of such effects. I can attest to the power inherent in this talisman but am reminded, too, of my host's words in his book on the history of the Lockhart family: "Pride in the possession of a charm filched from a desperate mother is not the most glorious of qualities."[1]

But the talismanic nature of the Lee Penny has haunted me ever since I held it in my hands. My attempts to write on money were bogged down, and my intense preoccupation with the talisman as a healing charm kept interfering. The image of activating its power by saying nothing kept swirling about my psyche and nearly rendered me mute. Then, quite by accident, my attention was called to Chapter 99 of Herman Melville's *Moby Dick*.

II

Riveted to the mainmast of the *Pequod* was a gold coin, a large Ecuadorian doubloon, the prize for raising the great white whale. It was, as Melville tells it, the talisman of Moby Dick. The image gripped me. Compelling also was a curious picture, the gold coin and the Lee Penny etching themselves together. I knew the gold coin was an image of the Self as was Moby Dick. But assimilating images to a concept of the Self was not very engaging. I find little life in this. But I frequently find life in the connection between images, in the manner in which they are linked, in what I call the "eros bond" between images. In Melville's story, the images of coin and whale are linked through the image of *talisman*. It was this link that began to dance in my mind together with the talisman of the Lockhart clan.

I found in Dr. Edinger's masterful commentary on *Moby Dick* an exciting and confirming observation. He said of this link that it was "an organic connection between the symbolic meaning of the coin and that of the whale."[2] To me, Edinger's use of the word "organic" was crucial, because it pointed to the living quality of the link between coin and whale. The idea that the coin and whale were symbols of the Self was dry to me because I knew it already. But the image of the coin as a talisman of the Self was one I did not know, and it felt full of life and portent.

Melville must have known of the living and organic capacity of the Self to ensoul the objects of our experience and their relationships in the psyche. In writing on the coin he gave this ensoulment a peculiar and intriguing cast when he said: "And some certain significance lurks in all things, else all things are of little worth, and the round world itself but an empty cipher."[3] In Melville's imagination, the very world is ensouled with value and worth, a significance that "lurks" in all things. It was this image of *lurking* that captured for me the living organic quality. To say that meaning "lurks" in all things leads at once to that metaphorical interiority where one can hear that meaning "lies in wait," that meaning is "ready to ambush," that meaning moves about "furtively," "sneakily," "secretly," that meaning lives and breathes unobserved, unsuspected, concealed, hidden from view. In such an imaginal underworld, meaning itself becomes personified, a living one, living in the dark, in the shadows, obscured, watching, waiting, looking for the right moment to work its will. It is true that we may find meaning. It is also true that meaning finds us.

I realized, of course, that the gold coin, in addition to being a symbol of the Self and a talisman of Moby Dick was, in fact, *money*. Perhaps nothing else (lest it be sexuality) seemed to me so hard, so real, so concrete, so literal, yet so quickly symbolized, interpreted, or translated into something else. As I puzzled on this I realized that one aspect of this lies in the nature of money itself: *money is the most powerful, practical and experienced from of transformation.* In the most starkly real way, one can turn money into anything in the world. Nothing else achieves this range of transformational possibility in actuality or in fantasy. In this direct sense, money symbolizes everything. Byron went correctly to the heart of the matter when he observed that "every guinea is a philosopher's stone."[4] The life and soul of money must lie in this transformational potentiality. This is also the deepest reason for the psyche to be drawn into a fascination with money. As with the search for alchemical gold, or the search for true love, one experiences something of the possibility of transformation in oneself when in the grips of the transformational power of money. I suppose that's why, when one is in the depths of a leaden depression, spending money will lift the spirit.

Reflecting on the gold coin as money and Moby Dick as a personification of the Self produced a most curious statement that would not leave me alone: *Money is a talisman of the Self.* What could this mean? A talisman is an object invested with 'supernatural' power that can be effectively and actively called upon to exert its effects to achieve certain ends. It is to be distinguished from "amulet" in that an amulet passively wards off evil by deflection. Clearly, a talisman carries an active transformative power. The talismanic power of money lies in its transformational nature. Since talismanic power can be invested in any object, it follows that any object can become money.

If money is a talisman of the Self, then the Self must use money to achieve its aims. Such a strange statement is in contrast to the more usual emphasis on the ego's use and relation to money. Yet, there is a talismanic power that lurks in money, and that power is invested there by the Self. When we confront the power of money in our lives, we are confronting the power of the 'other' in us, a power that works its will in and through money. It is the Self. It was this power I experienced long ago with my coins in the closet. The Self used the coins to transform my everyday world into a world of psyche.

At this point I could have gone into the history and significance of talismans and amplified all manner of interesting and powerful images concerning talismans and their use and how all of this could be seen in our behavior and relationships to money. Perhaps another time. Instead, I was gripped once again by what Paul Valery had noticed:

> You have certainly observed the curious fact that a given *word* which is perfectly clear when you hear it or use it in *everyday* language, and which does not give rise to any difficulty when it is engaged in the rapid movement of an ordinary sentence becomes magically embarrassing, introduces a strange resistance, frustrates any effort at definition as soon as you take it out of circulation to examine it separately and look for its meaning after taking away its instantaneous function .... we understand ourselves thanks only to *the speed of our passages past words* ....[5]

And once again I was gripped by my own fascination with words. Had I not myself written:

> Current meaning and definition are too often only the shell of a word. We use words but do not know their soul—or even care. We are all word abusers. Anything that will help free us from the prison of current meaning, the literalness and speed of the present, will help us to free Psyche from her prison shell. Words take on life, induce images, exite the imagination, begin to weave textures with one another and tell whole stories if we but scratch the surface of the word.[6]

So, if I was to follow this idea of "money a talisman of the Self," I would have to follow the words. Words, like coins, are realms where meaning lurks.

I approached this statement by taking each one of the central word images out of circulation: *money, talisman, Self.* One way I do this is by going into a kind of "etymological reverie" in an attempt to uncover and release the old word meanings that are still alive but forgotten. The unconscious remembers these old meanings, remembers the entire history of a word's story. But the conscious mind needs to be reminded.

I began with "talisman." It is a French and Spanish noun, masculine as befits its character of active power. It was imported from the Arabic *tilsaman*, a plural of *tilsam*. This in turn was a loan word from the Greek *telesma*. *Telesma* referred to "a ceremony of consecration" and was a name for the "mysteries." It was derived from an earlier Greek word, *telein*, which meant "to fulfill," "to initiate into the mysteries," and "to pay." Variations of these words referred to money paid to fulfill obligations and debts, money paid to enter the priesthood, and money paid as part of the mystery rites. It is clear from the history of the word "talisman" that initiation into mysteries, completion and fulfillment, and payment in money belong together.

Questions began to stir. How does the Self use money to render something sacred? How can money consecrate the work we do in analysis? Is the money paid by a patient payment for initiation into the mysteries of the Self? I remembered Tertullian's admonition that "nothing that is God's is obtainable by money," and Thoreau's echo: "money is not required to buy one necessity of the soul." But are we not workers of the soul? Do we not engage the necessities of the soul in our work? If so, money *is* required to buy connection to soul, connection to psyche, and connection to Self through us. The roots of talisman tell me that the sacred mysteries and money belong together.

The word *telein* comes from the Greek word *telos*. This meant "fulfillment" and "completeness" in the sense of reaching an end, a purpose, a final goal. Going back further, into the prehistory of the language, the reconstructed Indo-European root for *telos* is *q^wel. This root contains the basic image of "revolving," "moving around a fixed point," "dwelling within." The same root gave rise to the Latin *colere* meaning "to cultivate" which became our English word "culture"; the Old English *hweol* which became the English "wheel"; and the Greek *kiklos* meaning "wheel."

To experience the talismanic nature of something is to experience being turned, being revolved, being pulled to dwell within, encircled. It is an early experience that led to the words of circles, cycles, wheels. A talisman works not in linear ways but by turning, moving around, circulating This turning, as telos, has to do with one's fate, one's purpose, one's end. Turning points are talismanic moments when we are turned toward our fate. Money as talisman of the Self now tells us that the Self works through money toward our telos, our purpose, our end. Our relation to money must carry evidence of our telos. Money functions as talisman when it turns us, forces us, moves us into confrontation with our telos. Our telos, our final end, our purpose is said to determine our worth. When we are asked, "What are you worth?" do not the money images come bound with all other considerations? In this sense it is not surprising that the word "worth" comes from an Indo-European root which means "to turn" and "to bend" and which yields up such words as the Old English *wyrd* meaning "fate" and "destiny" and which became our English word "weird." Here also is the Old English *writhan,* meaning "to twist" and "to torture," becoming our word "writhe." Nested here is the Old English *wyrgan* meaning "to strangle," which became the English "worry." Embedded here is the Greek word *rhombus* meaning "magic wheel" and the Old English *wyrm* meaning "worm," as well as the Latin *vermis* meaning "vermin."

Thus, the worth of someone is deeply tied to images of destiny, the twists and turns of fate, and the wheels of fortune. The same is true of money. Our relation to money is our relation to fate. Our relation to money is our relation to purpose, end, goal, telos. Money as talisman emphasizes this, and money as talisman of the Self emphasizes the ways and means through the twists and turns and circulation of money that the Self brings us, turns us round, toward our telos. Ego, it seems to me, always has a straight purpose, the goal laid out in plain sight, the end always in view. Ego eyes are always on the tangent straight ahead. But the Self works to turn us from such straightness, and it uses money to do so. It turns us around a deeper axis, and we cannot see with open eyes where this turning takes us. A deeper kind of 'seeing' is required—the seeing of the mysteries. The basic meaning of the word "mystery" is "seeing with the eyes closed."

Does any of this echo in the word "money" itself? The modern English word "money" is from the Middle English *monoie* which comes from the Old French feminine noun *monie.* This in turn was a development from the Latin word *moneta*—also a feminine noun. Although this is not the place to carry on about the significance of word gender, it is striking that the word for money, so often considered a masculine province, is itself feminine. There is something even more deeply feminine about the word. It is the Latin name for the mother of the Muses who in Greek was called *Mnemosyne.* She was the goddess of memory. Thus out of the matrix or womb of memory come those creative engenderers we call the Muses who go into the name for minting, coining, and money. Money hides within its name the creative muses and their source in memory.

There is more. We find next that *Moneta* was an epithet, a name, for Juno, Queen Mother of Heaven. It was, in fact, in Juno's temple where the money was minted. This came about in the following way. A Roman army was losing a battle and was nearly out of money. This caused dissension, demoralization and loss of spirit. In a desperate attempt to find an answer to their plight they consulted Juno. She advised them that if their cause was just and they fought for their cause the money would be forthcoming. The soldiers rallied around this image and fought on. Soon, money arrived from Rome and the battle was won. As a tribute to Juno's wise counsel, the mint was set up in her temple which housed as well the Roman treasury. All of this puts money matters, we might say as well the *matter* of money (i. e., the gold and silver and other metals), in the realm of the mother. This reminds me of what Jung had said were the three "M's" of analysis: *mother, matter,* and *money.* We see it here in this dramatic image of matter being minted into money in the temple of the mother.

The word *moneta* is from an older word, *moneo* meaning "to remind," "to put in mind," "to recollect," "to admonish," "to advise," "to warn," "to instruct," "to teach." One can see in this word *moneo* Mnemosyne at work as goddess of memory and reminding. In her role as Juno Moneta, Juno was a great advisor and seer. She could see the future. A temple was built in her honor because she warned the populace about an impending earthquake. So dwelling within the word "money" are images of remembering, advising, warning, and the sense of teaching and instructing through remembering the past. Forgetting to pay one's bill, or forgettting to discuss the fee, may now be seen as part of the phenomenology of money in its character as memory. Juno must get her due if something is not remembered, and we are all aware of the kind of retribution Juno dealt. Forgetting about money, not learning from money, not heeding the warnings of money, are forgetting about Juno.

The root of *moneo* was *men* which gave rise to the Latin words *memini, mens,* and *mentio. Memini* means "to remember," to recollect," "to think of," "to be mindful," and "to mention a thing." Again we are reminded of images of remembering, of filling up the mind with a thing. If money comes out of such a verbal nest, we must attend to this extraordinary emphasis on remembering and on memory. In this regard it is perhaps telling that so little is remembered, so little mentioned about money in the literature of our field and, most likely, in the offices of our practice.

Mens is a feminine noun from this root and means "mind," "heart," and "soul." Only later was it constricted into referring to conscience and later still limited to the intellectual faculties of reason and rationality. In its personified form, *Mens* was the Roman goddess of thought. Imagine that, a goddess of thought! But other goddesses live here too. This root *mens* gives birth to the name Minverva, the Roman goddess of wisdom, of reflection, of arts, sciences and poetry, and of weaving.

Other words developing out of this basic root, such as *monitor, mentor, monitum,* and *monitus,* all convey images of reminding, warning and admonishing, as well as referring to these effects through oracles, omens and prophecies. Certainly images of prophecy, omens, and warnings are alive and well in relation to money. The stock markets of the world quicken with prophecy, portent, and prediction. Money advisors are full of warnings, admonitions, advice. Juno Moneta is at work here.

These images were already existent in earlier Greek times. The general Greek word for money, *chrimatos,* refers also to an oracular response and a divine warning. Thus, in all of these considerations and reflections on the im-

ages at the root of the word "money," we come to some basic connection
among money, memory, and mantic practices. We have arrived at this connection through a study only of the history and origins of the word "money"
and without benefit of psychological theory or praxis. I take this to mean that
if we are to have a complete understanding of our relation to money in our
psychological practice as well as in our understanding of money phenomena
on a larger scale, we shall have to bring to bear on such reflections the intricate web of connections among money, memory and mantic practices that
resides in the forgotten but still living depths of the word "money."

What is to be found in the depths of the word "self"? Its roots reach down
to *seu-*, a marvelously rich element that goes into such words as "sibling,"
"gossip," "secret," "seduce," "suicide," "custom," and "hetaera." There isn't
time to take up all these images in relation to our theme of money as a
talisman of the Self. But the fact that "secret" and "self" involve the same root
brings to mind how secretive we are about money. It is easier to find out
which analysts are sleeping with patients than it is to find out the fee for this
analytical conjunctio! It seems to me we can talk openly about sexual affairs—
ours or others—but money affairs are still shrouded in secrecy. I wonder if
the Self works less now in sexual affairs than in money matters. Why is it we
are so secretive about money? Why do we have such trouble talking and telling about our relationship to money even with each other?

If it is true that money is a talisman of the Self, it must be that talking about
money begins to reveal our relation to Self in some way that is extraordinarily
real, perhaps more real than some of the other ways we more readily reveal
ourselves—and perhaps more telling. Then we must consider how the word
"ethics" mixes together with self and secret. How shall we consider the problems of money in terms of the ethics of the Self? I recall Jungs's statement
that insight into the nature of one's own images must be converted into an
ethical obligation, and that a mans's "Failure to understand them, or a shirk-
ing of ethical responsibility, deprives him of his wholeness and imposes a painful fragmentariness on his life."[7] Images of money and our dealing with
money both in our practice and in our everyday life cannot escape this ethical
binding. As can be seen from the word-work, *self, ethics* and *secret* are intert-
wined. I see now that the deeper purpose of secrecy is not to cover up what
ego wants to hide, but to bring the ego into connection with the Self where, in
secret, it comes to learn of its ethical obligations.

Ego's unconsciousness heals frequently through revelation and telling of
secrets. But the secret connection with Self is revealed not through telling but
through *enactment* of ethical obligations learned and remembered in secret
consort with the Self. And to the extent that these reflections bear on our relation to money, what we *do* with money, more than what we *say* about
money, reveals the full reality of our ethical relation to Self.

It is this *ethical relation to Self* that binds us together as a community. It is what we promise ourselves, each other, and those who seek our help. What we do with the fruits of our soul work—that hard cold cash — has much to tell us about our relation to Self, our relation to telos, our relation to the "necessities of soul." This money comes to us marked, marked with the soul struggles of the 'other'. It does not come clean, but bloodied in the enormous battles of another's soul. "Money is another kind of blood," and when it circulates through our hands it comes perhaps with more than we care to know.

III

"Your safe deposit box is empty." This dream voice had so affected my patient that he rushed to the bank and checked his various safe deposit boxes. Nothing was missing. He was enormously relieved, but he was deeply troubled by the dream. He talked about having lost some inner valuables. I reminded him that he had never experienced a sense of inner values, that all his feeling and life were tied up in making money and wielding its power. It wasn't that anything was lost; it simply had never been there, and therefore the box stands empty. Sometimes when a word strikes me strongly I will work in the moment with it. I took the dictionary and simply said the images listed under the word "empty":

> Void of content
> Containing nothing
> No occupants, no inhabitants
> No load, no cargo
> Lacking purpose, lacking substance
> Idle
> Needing nourishment
> Hungry
> Devoid and destitute
> Empty.

My saying the word's meanings in this way, slowly and with feeling, brought tears to the eyes of the dreamer. The words had pierced him and brought feeling in the form of tears. When I told him that the word "empty" comes from an Old English word meaning "rest" and "leisure," he understood immediately the emptiness of his leisured life.

The Indo-European root for empty is *med-*, a root meaning "to take appropriate measures." It was time, I said, to take appropriate measures. A Latin word arising from this root is *mederi*, meaning "to look after, heal, cure," which is the source of the words "medicine" and "remedy." It seemed a bit peculiar that a word such as "empty" should belong to the same verbal nest as a word meaning "heal" and "cure." I said the medicine, the remedy, must lie in the emptiness—right there in that empty safe deposit box.

Another word from this root is the Latin *meditari* which means "to think about," "consider deeply," "reflect." It is the origin of our word "meditate." The word asks the dreamer to meditate and reflect on the emptiness. Another word from this nest is the Latin *modus* meaning "measure," "limit," "manner," "harmony," "melody." His analytic work must be a taking measure of himself, finding his limits, finding his manner," finding the harmony and melody in his life. It was all there in the emptiness. The English words mode, model, modern, modify, mold, commode, commodious, and commodity come from this Latin parent.

He meditated on the empty safe deposit box. Not much happened because he was not used to such introspective effort. That night he had a dream in which a young waif came up to him while he was getting into his limousine. The waif said: "I'll find it for a penny." The dreamer reached into his pocket and, pulling out a roll of bills, handed the boy a fifty-dollar bill. "No," said the waif, "for a penny." But neither the dreamer nor his chauffeur had a penny and the boy ran off. The dreamer woke in a panic.

Here is the typical fairytale motif of the worthless thing having the greatest value. But I focused on the more subtle theme that it was the *coin* that was required to set in motion the search for "it." The dreamer understood "it" to be his connection to soul without which his fortune had become meaningless. It was the way, the remedy, the medicine for the emptiness.

I have long since felt it necessary, when dealing with dreams in which money images occur, to focus first on the actuality of the dreamer's relation to money. What about pennies? The dreamer revealed that he had a long-standing habit of rejecting pennies in any transaction. He simply would not accept pennies as change. In pursuing why he rejected pennies, we discovered that it was not because they were of so little value (as the fairytale motif would have led us to believe), but because they were *copper*. He would only accept the silvery coins as change. I understood, at least empathically, because my own childhood box of coins would never admit pennies. They had to be silver. The man, hating copper, was hating the very metal necessary for him to find his way to soul.

He could not remember what had set him so against copper, so against pennies. He spoke, too, of feeling that if he did accept pennies something terrible would happen. He warded off such fears by scrupulously continuing not to touch pennies. Right here is that web of interconnections among money, memory and mantic practices of which I spoke earlier. One can see clearly how this man's fate is intricately bound up with these coins, how the penny is required as a fee for finding connection to soul, and how his relation to copper produces the emptiness of incompleteness; how this "turn of events" turned him, and how the ironic "twist" of a rich man not having a penny confronted him with his destiny, sending him into a writhing worry.

As ever, I was intrigued by the word "copper." It is, of course, the Latin *cuprum* from an earlier Greek word which was the name of the Island of Cyprus. This is the source of the best copper in ancient times. The name Cyprus is thought to derive from a Hebrew word, *gopher,* the name of the tree whose wood was used to make the ark. It was this image that released the repressed memory of the priest slapping his hands as he tried to steal from the offering plate the few pennies that had been left there. The priest, too, liked silver best.

A patient, accustomed to paying me with a check at the beginning of each hour, was writing one out, an activity usually performed in silence. He said, "Well, what happened to you this week?" I suddenly found myself unable to remember anything about my week. I was struggling to remember something when he said, "No, wait until I give you this. The gods might not like it if we begin before I pay." Clearly, for this patient, the payment had to do not just with me but with the gods. And although he said this in a joking manner, I listened as well to its serious purpose. The payment was a mantic offering to propitiate the gods and to secure their good counsel. He handed me the check, which, although made out to me, was for the gods. What is one to do with such an offering? Something accepted as part of a sacred ritual ought to be used for sacred purposes. Isn't this one of the ways money would consecrate the work? I began to puzzle over what particular use I could put this money to. I wondered if spending this money on something other than a sacred purpose would in some way affect the process engaging us. By the end of the hour I had forgotten my musings, put his check together with the others, and sent them all to the bank.

We often work diligently to keep our patients separate, often going to elaborate extremes so that no patient sees another, so that no trace of a previous patient is left in the office. But we do not hesitate to commingle our patients' money. The connection between the *origin* of the money and the *fate* of the money is broken by putting the money in a common, undifferentiated pool. This also keeps us from attending to the connection between what our patient has given us and what we do with it.

Did it really matter how I spent this money? I realized at once that this bit of consciousness—or was it a crazy romanticsm—would make it exceedingly difficult blindly to deposit all those checks each month into an undifferentiated pool of money. I realized I was going to be plagued by this image of money carrying something of the soul of my patients and by the notion that how I use the money may affect not only my own soul but theirs as well. Something kept shouting, "It doesn't matter, it doesn't matter." But now I couldn't believe that. It must matter in some way. "Silliness," the voices chorused.

Well, perhaps, But suppose our patients paid us not in checks, not even in cash, but in goods and services as in former times. Then the eggs you ate would be those brought by that hysterical woman, the cloth that made your pants brought by that depressive who can't get into life; your roof would be fixed by that alcoholic who beats his wife, and your garden planted by that woman with that terrible erotic transference. Now all of this leads into the most fantastic issues. From this point of view, dissolving our patients' money into some common pool—which breaks the connection between the money and what we do with it—allows us to remain unconscious of these things.

Recently, a psychotherapist consulted me concerning a problem he couldn't resolve. He was married with a stable family life, but for a variety of reasons found himself involved with another woman. His problem was not particularly a conflict about this extramarital relationship—he was not experiencing any difficulties about this. His problem was one of money. His other woman was expensive, and he had fallen into supporting her—paying her rent, buying clothes, and so on. He had pictured himself as perhaps worth more than he was. And, for a time, there was no difficulty. But now the ever increasing costs of this affair were becoming onerous, and he couldn't find any way to cut down or reduce them. He became depressed, which usually meant he spent even more on her as a way of alleviating the depression. The distress of these escalating expenses brought him to analysis.

After listening attentively to this tale for a while, I asked him who was paying for this affair. He was, of course. And where did the money come from? Well, almost all of his income was from his private practice. We then discussed the actual amounts that were being paid to support the other woman. They ranged between $1,000 and $1,500 a month and rising. I asked him to imagine the exact source of this money. He didn't understand. He paid it from cash, savings, and his checking account. Yes, I said, but these monies have an exact source. Patient A pays you $400 a month, patient B $200 a month and so on. These are the concrete sums that come from individual people in your practice. Could you specify which of your patients are paying for this affair?

He became quite angry, accused me of moralizing and trying to induce guilt. I didn't argue. After he calmed down I simply repeated the question.

I had not known why I put the question in this way. I do know that the art of analysis often is finding the right question. I don't know that this was the right question. But as I was speaking to him my own mind was racing into my own financial dealings and putting the question to myself. I had only just begun to consider a possible link between what a patient pays me and what I do with it afterward. I had been sufficiently schooled in how to treat and relate to all manner of patient attitudes, feelings, and behavior about money. But no one had mentioned to me that what I did with this money might be of some genuine significance in the work.

Imagine that the money we receive from a patient carries something of that patient's soul or psyche or value or energy. This money personifies the patient, and as I have described earlier carries something of the patient's telos, the patient's fate. The money is a substance, a metal, a coin, a transformative talisman that is passed into our hands in payment for our time, our energy, our love, our value. Is consciousness required of us analysts to examine how we treat this money? Does the fate of this money have an impact on the analytic process? You have a mortgage payment due next month. Or maybe some secret diversion requires money. Could you consciously choose which of your patients' money to use in this way? Clearly, it is easier to break all connection between individual patients and the payment of our own expenses. That we do by mixing together all our patients' money. But *could* we make such decisions? On what basis would such decisions be made? Or would it be better to keep this entire possibility unconscious and not intermix the fate of our patients' money so intricately and individually into our personal life? But this is just a mask. We cannot avoid mixing our patients into our personal life, because the financial foundation of our personal life—at least for most of us—is built by our patients. While this question raises such enormous difficulties, there isn't time to deal adequately with them. I must be satisfied with simply raising the issue. And, besides, like any good analytic hour, the time is up at just the critical moment, leaving us not with answers but, I hope, with pregnant questions.

1. Simon Macdonald Lockhart, *Seven Centuries: The History of the Lockharts of Lee and Carnwath* (privately published by S. F. Macdonald Lockhart, Estate Office, Carnwath, Lanark, Scotland, 1977), p. 8
2. Edward F. Edinger, *Melville's Moby Dick: A Jungian Commentary* (New York: New Directions, 1978), p. 107.
3. Hermann Melville, *Moby Dick; or The Whale* (Chicago: Encyclopedia Britannica, 1971), p. 317.
4. As cited by H. L. Mencken, A *New Dictionary of Quotations* (New York: Alfred A. Knopf, 1977), p. 804.
5. As cited in Gaston Bachelard, *The Poetics of Reverie* (Boston: Beacon Press, 1971), p. 48.
6. Russell A. Lockhart, "Words as Eggs," Dragonflies I / i (1978), p. 30.
7. C. G. Jung, *Memories, Dreams, Reflections* (New York: Vintage Books, 1963), p. 193.

(reprinted from SOUL AND MONEY, pp. 7–30 Spring Publications Dallas: 1982, by permission)

Myth and Money

By Joel Covitz (Boston)

I had two introductions to the role of money in psychoanalysis. The first came when I was studying at the Jung Institute, and a young analysand was negotiating a fee with me. I told him that my fee was twenty francs. Then we discussed the frequency of the visits, and we decided he would come three times a week. Then he asked me, "Would it be okay if I paid on the basis of three visits for fifty francs?"

My second introduction came from my dissertation on a Jewish dream book. The Talmud states that there was a dream interpreter, Bar Hedya, whose work depended on whether or not his fee were paid. Those dreamers who paid his fee received a positive interpretation; those who refused to pay received a negative interpretation.

Actually, money is an important element of an analyst's work with any patient. Everyone has a money complex, and the way each person relates to money can have a profound effect on other areas of his life. The ancient Greeks realized this when they correlated the absence of money with the disease process and its presence with the cure. Money is one of the "fundamental aspects of living reality." (Otto, 107) And in this paper, I want to address the psychological reality of money.

In our society, money is a necessity. Money *matters*. To the average employed or self-employed individual, money and its acquisition come to be extremely important. Western society is upwardly mobile. Many people in our civilization enter analysis partly because of their concern about their stations in life, often wanting to change classes and to move psychologically so that they suffer less from money problems. I want to restrict my comments here to individuals who begin with very little, who move on the path from nothing to something. I shall be less concerned with the use, investment, and spending of money than with its acquisition. I want to explore the development of what I call a "realistic attitude" toward the acquisition of money, because such acquisition must be one of the goals of an analysand trying to live in this society.

Now, money has traditionally had a rather negative 'press' in Western literature, reflecting a strong notion in our culture that affluence leads to decadence and the denial of the spirit. The Bible says that they that desire to be rich fall into a temptation and a snare and many foolish and hurtful lusts, such as drown men in destruction and perdition. For the love of money is the root of all kinds of evil: which some reaching after have been led astray from the faith: and have pierced themselves through with many sorrows. (I Tim. VI 9—10) The Puritan work ethic allows only for hard work and selfsacrifice—the notion that one should earn what one has by the sweat of one's brow, and that there should be no short-cuts, no easy way to wealth. Being in debt is frowned upon. But in our society, this is simply not a realistic attitude, as the case of Ralph will show.

In his youth, Ralph showed great promise. He wanted to be a doctor and tried to work his way through medical school while also supporting his family, but he found he couldn't do it. So he chose to drop out of medical school rather than to borrow money from the Government with a guaranteed loan. He thought that if he couldn't pay for school by himself, he shouldn't go. Ralph became a wreck; he never found a meaningful career. Years later, his wife left him. He wanted to marry again, but he had no means of earning a living. Then he entered analysis.

Now, this kind of refusal to get into debt is the wrong ethic for our culture. Ralph was really misled by the traditional work ethic. Debt belongs to a reliable person in our culture; it means one is creditable. To underestimate one's credit potential is to underestimate one's assets. Not to understand that is to be neurotic with regard to money, because it means one is living beneath one's potential. Part of the art of dealing with money is knowing how and when to go into debt, so that one can obtain the maximum potential from the money one borrows. As Benjamin Franklin said, "Money can beget money." (Franklin, 87) Many people—Thomas Jefferson was a prime example—live fruitful, creative lives without a lot of cash on hand. He was often in debt, but he lived to his fullest potential. Of course, this goes against the ethic which urges us to save rather than to borrow. But the person who will only save, who will not take risks with his money or security, who sees a concern with money as crass or 'dark' or 'shady,' will not succeed with money.

The traditional Puritan approach to money leaves behind many casualties—people with unhealthy approaches to money. Often the root of a family neurosis stems from some irresponsible treatment of one's assets. For instance, one analysand had a grandfather who was a millionaire. The millionaire's wife died when the millionaire was eighty and the old man remarried. He lived on for a few years and then died, and all of his money went to his new wife—a situation which disrupted the family. Also, it is often the children of millionaires who have to carry the shadow of their parents' wealth. The parents may consciously or unconsciously view their own acquisition of money as shady, so although they may pass on money, they also pass on ambivalent, paradoxical attitudes toward it. It is just possible that some of the destructive tendencies of children from wealthy families stem from this unconscious shadow-identification. They have the task of coming to terms with the acquisition of money, even if they themselves never had to acquire it.

In other ways the mishandling of money causes great trouble in the individual's adjustment. One patient of mine, John, neurasthenic and introverted, needed a push, and it never came. He lacked the energy even to ask for money. He knew his father had it, and he knew his father wouldn't give it to him. He was caught in the same situation as Hermes: a rich, unsupportive father. The difference was that Hermes reacted with tremendous initiative and was willing to make it on his own. But for children who are not gods, or are neurotic or depressed, nothing ever gets started. So John's father was a millionaire, and John was a do-nothing until the age of fifty, when his inheritance came. By then it was too late. The need for money helps you get out of the cave you are stuck in, with its low overhead; it gives you an incentive. The extreme case of lack of incentive might be seen in some Oriental and Christian sects, which advocate giving away all of one's possessions and money because the world will soon come to an end. (If this was Jesus' attitude, as has been argued, it was an error of predictive judgment.)

All of these problems I have just mentioned come from the lack of a realistic attitude about the need to acquire money in this society. There are a few important facts to keep in mind about money: it is a fact that money is never freely given away. You get nothing for nothing. And one should never depend on money being given. Money doesn't just come to you; you have to go after money, and this often requires that you be geographically mobile. And it is a fact that if you don't ask for money, you will never receive it. The Puritan fantasy is that wealth is not important. Other goals—honesty, hard work, generosity—have been given much better press. But one Puritan at least, Ben Franklin, talked about "procuring wealth, and thereby securing virtue; it being more difficult for a man in want to act always honestly, as ... it is hard for an empty sack to stand upright." (Franklin, 92)

In fact, Franklin devoted a great deal of time and energy to the development of his theory of the "Way to Wealth," which involved remembering certain simple, but very realistic, and still applicable, laws about money. He said that "the use of money"—that is, the ability both to spend it and to make more money from it—"is all the advantage there is in having money." (80) "Time is money" and "credit is money." (87) Franklin knew that the primary way to get ahead is to invest one's money, or to lend it out at interest, since in that way even a small sum can be made to grow and grow. He also stressed the importance of saving: "a penny saved is a penny earned." If one plays by the rules and repays borrowed money on time, one can have an enormous amount of money at one's service: "He that is known to pay punctually," said Franklin, "may at any time, and on any occaison, raise all the money his friends can spare." (88) But he knew that one could not just sit back idly and expect to get rich; "the way to wealth," he said, "depends on [wasting] neither time nor money." (89) In *Poor Richard's Almanac*, where most of this wisdom was dispensed, he told his readers that "God helps them that help themselves." (95) What you have to do is take what the Fates bring you, and make the most of it.

What I would like to focus on now is just this art of affluence-recognizing the realistic need to have money in this society, and then marshaling all of one's forces, particularly the trickster who is in all of us, to reach that goal. The myth of the Greek god Hermes provides an archetype for this "trickster" psychology which allows for creative, flexible, daring approaches to the development of all possibilities in the individual, including the possibility of affluence.

As you know, Hermes was the son of Zeus and the nymph Maia. Soon after his birth, he felt restless in the dark cave, so he crept outside. He found a turtle going by. "What a great sign, what a help this is for me!" he said. "I won't ignore it." (Boer, 19) (Even at this tender age, he was open to the synchronicity of events.) So he tricked the turtle into coming into the cave with him. Then he took a knife and scooped the insides out of the shell and strung stalks of reed along it—and he had invented the lyre. The turtle had come along "at the rightful moment," (20) and Hermes had taken advantage of that moment. He was opportunistic.

Then Hermes found the sacred cattle of the gods and took fifty cows from the herd. He wanted to cover his tracks, so he devised a magical pair of sandals for himself so that his footprints could not be recognized. Then he reversed the tracks of the cows, "turning their front hooves backward and their back hooves frontward, while he himself walked backward." (23)

Now, while as was making his escape, an old man—a symbol for the old values—saw him walking away with the cows. Hermes said to him, "You didn't see what you just saw, okay? You didn't hear what you just heard. Keep quiet and you won't get hurt." (24) And Hermes made it safely back, slaughtered two of the cows, and sacrificed them properly. Then he threw his magical sandals away—tricksters have to pay close attention to details like that—and went back to the cave. His mother knew he had been up to no good. Hermes told her not to worry, however, since he would provide for her:

> Nay, we do not wish to sit amongst the gods without gifts or prayers, as is thy plan! Surely it is better to sport for all eternity amongst the immortals, in inexhaustible wealth, rather than to cower here in this gloomy cave! I mean to win the same sacred reverence as is paid to Apollo! Unless my father grants me this, I shall pluck up the courage—and I can do it!—to become a prince of thieves. (Kerenyi, 165)

With the goal of inexhaustible, as opposed to expendable, wealth to encourage him, Hermes was determined to make his fortune, doing whatever it took to gain the same stature—and wealth—as his more famous brother, Apollo.

Meanwhile, Apollo had obviously noticed the significant decrease in the size of his herd of cattle. He tracked Hermes down and demanded the return of the cows. Hermes pretended complete innocence: he didn't have any information, he said, about the theft. It was ridiculous to suppose that a tiny baby could steal fifty cows. Apollo laughed at this clever story and called Hermes a trickster, and insisted that Hermes lead the way to the cows. Hermes complained that he had been falsely accused. So they went to see their father, Zeus, who told each to plead his case. Apollo told his story, and then Hermes spoke in his own defense: "Father Zeus, I'm going to tell you the truth. I'm a frank person, and I don't know how to lie," he said. "I didn't take his cattle home, though I do want to be rich." (Boer, 45) At this, Zeus burst out laughing, ordered the brothers to reconcile their differences, and told Hermes to show Apollo where the cows were hidden. Apollo was still angry, so Hermes decided to calm him by playing the lyre. And he played so beautifully that Apollo was charmed, and said that Hermes' music was *worth* fifty head of cattle. He promised Hermes immortal glory among the gods if only he would teach him this art. Always on the alert for a fair exchange, Hermes agreed, provided he could have the cattle. So Apollo got the lyre, and Hermes got glory and the use of the cattle. Then Apollo "presented Hermes with a further gift, a golden three-leaved staff, which bestows wealth." (Kerenyi, 170) From then on, Hermes was in charge of exchanges and commerce among men and was glorified among the gods.

The first thing to note about the story of Hermes is that he knew he could not stay in his gloomy cave. He needed to get out, into a house with a view. He did not wait for his father's inheritance; rather, he took his fate into his own hands and extraverted his affluent fantasy. When faced with the trap of poverty, he realized his dream of wealth while remaining in the company of the gods. "I will try whatever plan is best, and so feed myself and you continuously!" he said to his mother. (Hesiod) He developed a positive view, a system for becoming affluent, starting with nothing but his wits and his envy.

Hermes' style is unique. There is something very appropriate about his inappropriateness. Sometimes, going backward is going forward. His methods were trickster methods—clever theft rather than barefaced robbery, storytelling, the ability to get Zeus and Apollo to laugh instead of to curse. Hermes was a master at getting himself out of a tight spot by telling a story. The world responds to a story whether it's true or not. If you want a loan and you tell the banker the wrong story, he can't give you the loan; so if your are in touch with the strickster in your psyche, you tell the banker the right story. To tell the truth in some situations is a sign of masochism. You have to be daring and take risks to get anywhere. Hermes knew that Apollo and Zeus didn't believe his tales of innocence, but it is the story itself that counts: he made them laugh at it. The art of convincing people is an important part of the art of affluence.

At first the question arises: isn't Hermes just a common criminal? The trickster who steals cattle and then lies about it may not seem particularly praiseworthy. But there are several differences between the trickster-figure and the criminal. For one, the criminal, separated from and angry at his culture, cannot identify with the collective whole. But the Hermetic person knows the power structure and works within his culture. He looks for loopholes, for back roads, but he is not a criminal; he is merely trying to be more clever than the mainstream. The sociopath, for example, evades paying taxes; the Hermetic man, instead, finds tax shelters. Part of the key to Hermes' success in that he knew the rules within which he had to work. He knew how, when, and what to sacrifice; he stole the cattle, but hungry as he was he did not ruin the sacrifice by eating any of the meat. In the words of Rafael Lopez-Pedraza, "the classic Jungian concept [of sacrifice] is based on what is sacrificed as already being worn out, which gives it a Hermetic touch." (37)

Even though Hermes is a thief, he has a Robin Hood style—attempting to restore society's proper equilibrium. "Though much of this must seem questionable from a moral point of view," says Walter Otto, "nevertheless it is a configuration which belongs to the fundamental aspects of living reality." (107) We must assume that the individual who starts with nothing has to be a bit unethical. The trickster is not only conscious of the formal laws of society; he is also aware of custom and culture—taking into account, for example, the American ethical principle "thou shalt not get caught. The Hermetic man in Russia is the Communist who is still able to get caviar.

In setting his goal as "inexhaustible wealth," Hermes was confident and resourceful; he knew he could do it, although he didn't at first know how. He created from what was at hand, thus displaying the flexibility which is central to the Hermetic approach. A master of the art of collage, of combination, he was open to accidental discoveries, and in this way he participated in his own fate.

Hermes was traditionally the god of exchanges of goods and money between men; he was the god of boundaries, where neighboring tribes met to exchange and facilitate economic growth. Hermes was considered "a source of material blessings" for men. (Brown, 22) His staff brings wealth, and he promotes exchanges which benefit both parties, just as his exchange with Apollo benefited both of them. In ancient Greece, "mutual permission to steal" (Brown, 42) was recognized as a kind of trade, but it actually was a kind of gift exchange.

Gift exchanges are important. When an unfair exchange takes place, the delicate balance of money and power is disrupted. John, about whom I told you before, was always getting the wrong gifts; he never really got what he needed. He got ripped off in the exchange with his parents. Understanding gift-giving is similar to knowing how to deal with money, and John's father couldn't handle either one. The sentimental view, of course, is that one gives out of selflessness and love. But really, gift-giving is often setting up the possibility for an exchange at no real cost to either party. The gift is an exchange of power. From the Hermetic point of view, giving is receiving. Gift-giving can be seen, then, as an investment.

The point is not accumulating money just for its own sake, but rather having a Hermetic style, which will help constellate positive experiences. The Hermetic person will find that he has more energy to accomplish things; that he is in a position of power and can work toward achieving his own potential while also having a possible role in influencing the destiny of his culture. Money is the means to an end.

*

So the next question is, how can we apply the Hermetic principles to analytical work? How can we encourage analysands to develop the trickster in their psyches? The Hermetic approach promotes selfhelp, resourcefulness, independence, and flexibility. To encourage the acquisition of subtle, daring techniques in a patient is not unethical. In addition to promoting the trickster in a patient, the analyst must become a trickster figure himself. Norman O. Brown says, "In the modern view ... we regard cheating as the antithesis of good workmanship. Hence modern scholars have felt obliged to brand the cult of Hermes the 'tricky' as immoral ... but his function is to promote human welfare," (23) just as the analyst must promote his patients' welfare.

The Greeks used to call any lucky find that a traveler chanced upon a "gift of Hermes." (Brown, 41) The art of seeing possibilities in chance occurrences, in synchronicities, is of course at the heart of Jungian thought. When my patient, John, was eight years old, he found a twenty-dollar bill in the Kennedy Airport parking lot, and he rejoiced in his "lucky find." But his grandfather, who was not engaged with the trickster side of himself, admonishingly instructed John to return the money to the place he had found it, saying, "You may not know whose it is, but you know it isn't yours."

The trickster approach also encourages independence on the part of the patient. Having broken free of his father, Hermes was able to provide for himself and thus take his rightful place on Olympus with the family gods. Hermes said, "If my father will not provide, then I can, and I am able." The lack of money is often correlated with the lack of flexibility in life; in addition to cutting down on geographical mobility, it can prove to be a kind of psychic paralysis—a paralysis both of psychic movement internally and life movement externally. The Hermetic approach allows a person to feel free to follow his soul, his destiny; it frees up his psychic energy in order to enable him to actualize his soul.

It is known that the positive role of envy in the psyche is to show the individual what potentially can be his. Hermes' envy of Apollo's wealth and stature motivated him to fulfill his own potential. Envy often serves such a motivating force within the family. My son once asked my wife, "If I join the Boston Symphony, will I earn as much as Daddy?" At a young age, he was already using a Hermetic sense of competition as a motivation.

I had one analysand, Debra, who together with her husband mastered the non-Hermetic art of mere survival. They were what I call the lowest common denominator type—low rent, Salvation Army clothes, but money in the bank. They were content with low overhead—with the cave. Their system had a built-in breakdown point, however, which occurred when their daughter entered drama school, confronting them with the need to earn more money to pay the yearly $7,500 for her tuition and board. As could be expected, Debra and her husband, with their non-Hermetic style, constellated their daughter's adoption of a Hermetic one. While Debra had been saving her limited funds in the bank, their daughter was developing her acting career, working as a television actress all through high school and earning much of the money for her schooling herself.

How can you generate the trickster in a patient? As a Jungian analyst, you can recognize the trickster when it makes an appearance in the material of the unconscious, and make sure to point it out to the analysand. Note how the trickster appears in dreams and fantasies, and try to integrate it as a basic part of the patient's personality. The analyst should observe when the lack of connection with the trickster gets in the way of the progress of a patient who is "serious and inflexible." He or she should also observe how the trickster is projected into the relationship with the analyst and offer this interpretation to the analysand.

The acquisition of money and its relationship to the soul are reflected in the artist, writer, actor, poet musician, and even the analyst, who most people say is more of an 'artist' than practitioner. Jung represented this point of view when he said that he would be willing to change all of his theories for the benefit of any one patient.

What about the artist who cannot support himself? The artist who has not solved his money-maintenance dilemma may be a genius, but he is also ill in a money-archetypal sense. If you find that you can't support yourself as an artist, perhaps you should consider giving up being an artist. The problem of the artist, if he sees his money coming from the practice of his art, is to figure out *how* to earn money from art. Many neurotic artists are non-flexible ... "I can only work on this size canvas, in this medium ..." This kind of thinking is often rigid and limiting, whereas true artists are usually flexible. Many of the great masters of painting throughout history have worked on commission. Aside from the very few artists who are ahead of their times, the unsuccessful, neurotic artist is often either not latented enough or too inflexible. Jung warns against the "hobby artists" who try to make professions of their hobbies.

One variable to examine in the actor, musician, poet, and artist is the degree of *necessity*. How connected is the soul to the particular activity or craft? What is the soul's investment in this endeavor, and how deeply rooted is the commitment? Often when the talent is lacking, the soul and libido are elsewhere, which will be reflected in the material of the unconscious. It may sound crude to think of art in terms of its earning power, but the artist must come to terms with financial reality. To work on 'inner vision' without outer verification in the form of financial acknowledgment is reserved for the very few, or very rich.

Is the person who uses Hermetic tricks to make a little money, to get a start in the world, getting something for nothing? No. He is getting something for cleverness. The trickster will go out in search of affluence. The "welfare mentality" could be an exercise in selfdeception; the fantasy of the welfare recipient is that he is getting something for nothing. But is having to sacrifice one's self-esteem nothing? The recipient who thinks he is getting a good deal is being tricked by his own trick. Nothing comes from nothing. I am reminded of the story in Studs Terkel's book *Working*, where the hooker tells of her initial delight in making fifty dollars in twenty minutes, and coming out of it feeling unchanged. It was only years later, demoted in status from call girl to streetwalker and heroin addict, that she realized the price she had paid for that money. She was tricked by her own trick. One can also be tricked by the trick of marrying a rich spouse, since that decreases one's incentive to achieve one's potential. In Jung's words, it may also decrease one's sense of viability. An analyst does not want his patients to be tricked by their own tricks; if he can encourage them to be resourceful, flexible and daring, so much the better.

In 1911, Jung and Freud carried on the following dialogue on what Jung called the problem of the "failure of the rich marriage." Freud wrote to Jung.

> Give your charming, clever, and ambitious wife the pleasure of saving you from losing yourself in the business of money-making. My wife often says she would be only too proud if she were able to do the same for me. ... Your taste for money-making already worried me in connection with your American dealings. On the whole, it will prove to be good business if you forego ordinary pursuits. Then, I am sure, extraordinary rewards will come your way.

Jung replied,

> It's not all that bad with my money-making. ... I need a large practice in order to gain experience, for I do not imagine that I know too much. Also, I have had to demonstrate to myself that I am able to make money in order to rid myself of the thought that I am non-viable. These are all frightful stupitities which can only be overcome by acting them out. (436—437).

Women today may be expressing Jung's point of view when they equate viability with earning money. In former times, women may have found affirmation and acknowledgment from non-monetary sources; however, these seem to be lacking today.

What does the Hermetic point of view mean to the analyst himself? Hermes, who was the god of craftsmen, of men who made money from their labor and, in some myths, of healers, is a significant archetypal figure for analysts. Lopez-Pedraza says that "in spite of Hermes' marginal, crooked, trickster, thief and cheater aspects, paradoxically, we can give full recognition to him in his role as protector of psychotherapy," since "psychological thieving"—which any analyst frequently indulges—is the "natural and basic activity of Hermes in the psyche." (31) Healers throughout history have been highly paid. Pliny once complained that healers made "enormous amounts of money." (Majno, 348) As healers, we are lucky to have the god of commerce on our side.

The fluctuation of the therapist's financial state, of couse, is a subject of great concern to most of us. An old maxim says that a patient must fulfill two obligations to his analyst: he must punctually attend his agreed-upon sessions, and he must consistently pay his bill. We all know what happens to our affectionate and humanitarian feelings when the patient refuses to pay his bill. It is even more intolerable than when he stands you up for his session, and 'accidentally' represses his capacity to use the telephone to notify you. Recall the story I related at the beginning of this paper about the Talmudic dream interpreter who modified his interpretation according to the dreamer's payment. A fourteenth-century commentary on this passage interpreted it to mean that when the dreamer failed to pay, the dream interpreter acted toward the dreamer as an "enemy in revenge."

Even Freud, the first to practice our Hermetic craft, worried and wrote a great deal about the relationship of money and therapy. His early letters to Wilhelm Fliess contain many references to the important role money played in his thoughts about his practice. In 1895, he noted that he was in a position to "pick and choose and begin to dictate my fees," (136) and he talked of "earning the recompense that I need for my well-being." (173) "It suits me best to have a lot of work," he wrote in 1897. "I earned 700 florins last week, for instance, and you do not get that for nothing." (192) But he added, "It must be very difficult to get rich." (192) He kept on "worrying and saving," (218) as he put it.

Later, things took a turn for the worse; the summer season was nearly always painfully slow for him, and this depressed him a good deal. He told Fliess, "We are like to *schnorrers* [beggars]" (211) and went on to complain that he was impoverished, without enough work, having to take on new patients constantly—and even to take on some without a fee, simply to keep from getting too bored. He was worried that his financial troubles would begin to interfere with his self-analysis, and he felt that, since he was so tired and depressed, his patients were not getting their money's worth. "It is a pity," he wrote, "one cannot live on dream-interpretation." (218) (Which is what Jungian analysts might be said to do.) His financial worries left him in a "mental and material depression," (327) and he noted that "a bad mental state is no more productive than economizing is." (322) His "one weak point, my fear of poverty," (318) was contrasted with his dreams of wealth: "The hope of eternal fame was so beautiful, and so was that of certain wealth, complete independence, travel, and removing the children from the sphere of the worries which spoiled my own youth." (217–18) "Today," he wrote, "after twelve hours' work and earning 100 florins, I am again at the end of my strength....Just as art only thrives in the midst of prosperity, so do aspirations only thrive with leisure." (275)

Thus Freud understood that the analyst could only do his best work when freed from his own neurotic constraints, one of which could be the lack of money. You can only do good work when you are not sick yourself. Freud's equation of the lack of money with a "mental and material depression" is in the Greek tradition of seeing poverty as part of the disease process. This theme is fully elaborated in C. A. Meier's book, *Ancient Incubation and Modern Psychotherapy*.

The patient-analyst relationship is an exchange; the analyst carries the problems of the patient for a fee. The analysand gets what he pays for. Thomas Jefferson expressed this notion: Never buy what you do not want because it is cheap; it will be dear to you. I have at home an ad for paint which states: "Don't blame the painter. If the painter has to use cheap materials to meet your price ideas, you've no kick coming if the job doesn't last. Pay a fair price for good honest varnish, enamel and paint." I often feel that the same truth can apply to an analyst.

This leads to a last and controversial question: whether or not analysts should charge for interviews that patients miss. The rule that you charge whether or not the patient shows up is in the Hermetic tradition: the analyst is thus providing for himself, making sure that he can support himself, and not resenting his patients. Freud belonged to this Hermetic tradition, even though he sometimes took on patients who could not pay; he knew that he needed the stability of an income for his family and himself in order to be able to do good work. The idea is that the patient is not receiving help only during the session; the analyst has invested his time and energy in the whole process of analysis, and deserves to be paid for it. Frieda Fromm-Reichmann seems to agree with this point of view when she says,

> Psychiatric services...are priceless if successful or worthless if they fail. It is through these attempts, nevertheless, that the therapist makes his living, so that the settlement of his fees has to be determined by the market value of psychiatric services at a given time and in a given area....If [a] patient repeatedly misses interviews for invalid reasons, warning should be given, and thereafter charges should be made. (67)

But on the next page of the same book, she apparently contradicts herself:

"it is not the psychiatrist's privilege to be exempt from the generally accepted custom of our culture in which one is not paid for services not rendered." (68) I suggest that the Hermetic approach is a sound one to the resolution of this tricky problem, but many analysts, I realize, might not feel comfortable with it.

Jung, too, was a trickster sort of fellow; he said once that he went into the practice of psychoanalysis because he thought he could earn more money at it than he could from his first love, archaeology. "I hadn't the money," he said, "to be an archaeologist.... I never thought I had any chance to get any further, because we had no money at all....[But] a doctor can develop...he can choose his scientific interests." (McGuire, 428) However, Jung didn't have to earn a living from his practice, and as a result, some people claimed he often undercharged his patients. This infuriated some of his fellow analysts because it inadvertently undervalued analysis, and it embarrassed them about their own fees. Jung seemed to them to be insensitive to the acquisition of money from an analytic practice. He may not have fully realized that, most often, analysts were healers who were selling their expertise in order to provide for themselves. His Hermeticism seemed not to extend to the realm of money. I wonder why. Was it that he retained an old idea of medicine as Christian charity? Or was it perhaps that he felt guilty about the source of his own money?

I'd like to close with two quick stories. One is an ancient Jewish tale from the thirteenth century, which illustrates the maxim "you get what you pay for." One day a Gentile was sitting, depressed. His friend said to him, "Why is your face so downtrodden?" and he answered, "I saw in a dream that I was riding on a red horse and the horse was near an impure platform." His friend said to him, "that means that you will quickly die in your bed." And then the dream interpreter said to him, "If you give me something to drink, I will purchase the dream from you." He replied, "On this condition I will give it to you—that my dream will be sold to you." And he gave the dream interpreter something to drink, and the dream interpreter died the second day after that.

And finally, C. A. Meier tells us that in ancient Greece, "after the cure, the former patient was expected to pay certain fees and make thank offerings. We have on record instances in which the god administered a sharp lesson to tardy debtors....by promptly ordaining a relapse." (316)

Boer, Charles, trans., *The Homeric Hymns,* 2nd ed., revised, Spring Publications, Inc., Irving, Texas, 1979.

Brown, Norman O., *Hermes the Thief: The Evolution of a Myth,* Vintage Books, Random House, New York, New York, 1947.

Franklin, Benjamin, *Works,* Volume 2.

Freud, Sigmund, *The Origins of Psychoanalysis: Letters to Wilhelm Fliess, Drafts and Notes, 1887–1902,* Basic Books, Inc., New York, New York, 1954.

Fromm-Reichmann, Frieda, *Principles of Intensive Psychotherapy,* University of Chicago Press, Chicago, Illinois, 1950.

Hesiod, trans. Hugh G. Evelyn-White, *The Homeric Hymns and Homerica,* Loeb Classical Library, Harvard University Press, Cambridge, Massachusetts, 1914.

Kerenyi, C., *The Gods of the Greeks,* Thames and Hudson, London, 1951.

Lopez-Pedraza, Rafael, *Hermes and His Children,* Spring Publications, Zurich, 1977.

Majno, Guido, *The Healing Hand: Man and Wound In The Ancient World,* Harvard University Press, Cambridge Massachusetts, 1975.

McGuire, William, and R. F. C. Hull, eds., *C. G. Jung Speaking,* Princeton University Press, Princeton, New Jersey, 1977.

Meier, C. A. *Ancient Incubation and Modern Psychotherapy.*

Otto, Walter, trans. Moses Hadas, *The Homeric Gods,* Thames and Hudson, London, 1951.

Terkel, Studs, *Working.*

Von Grunebaum, G. E., and Roger Caillois, eds., *The Dream and Human Societies,* University of California Press, Berkeley, 1966.

(reprinted from SOUL AND MONEY, pp 63–82 Spring Publications, Dallas: 1982, by permission)

Fee-Less Practice and Soul Work

By Arwind Vasavada (Chicago)

When I started to work in the States in 1970 as a Jungian analyst, I found it difficult to talk about fees when an analysand inquired about them. It felt strange to equate a fixed sum of money with whatever happened in the session. After all, what was the fee for? That hour? My person? His need to pay? Was he in fact buying something or was he exchanging money for work done? If it was an exchange of money for work, then what was the criterion for deciding the amount of money—time on the clock, a quality of work? If the second, then the fee must change each hour, assessing it according to the value of that particular hour. When the hour went well, there was no problem, but often times the sessions were less illuminating and helpful, they depressed me, and I could see the depression in the face of the client as well.

The question would not let me go. Can payment for work be considered an installment purchase? If so, then it belonged to a longterm contract for work supposed to be done. But can one guarantee in advance the quality of work according to an agreed-upon fee? Perhaps the criterion for payment is biological security; a fee simply takes care of human needs. Once again the problem gets complicated. How much do I need? There is no limit. I want all the comforts and luxuries others have, and I feel I deserve them as others do.

While living in India on a fixed salary from the University, it was a simple matter. I adjusted my needs and wants to fit within that sum. But here I became aware of my greed, an I liked it. When in Rome....I soon felt comfortable with this idea, and made good progress with work and money. I could rent a reasonably good apartment and have a car. In 1972 I returned to India for the first time since I started work in the States. During this trip I visited my Guru, the blind saint.

Through letters and talks when we met, he must have been aware of whatever was going on in my life. He asked me how long I would be working and if I could see a time when I could not work. Without work, what would I do? He put it very clearly, "To this day your mind and body are healthy and you can work. There will be a time when the mind will not be sharp because of age, and the body will probably be weak also. What will you do then? How would you feel without work?

"Remember when you were an infant, helpless in every way. Were you not cared for? You will be cared for always if you can feel into the trust you had then as an infant. Although helpless and without work, you will not feel lost. Just be nothing. In order to be Nothing, be free from all ambitions and desires. You worked as long as you were in India—until the age of retirement. Had you stayed you would naturally have not worked anymore. So do not work where you live now, but serve instead. Don't ask for any fixed fee, accept what is given freely and happily."

I listened to all this and to all the doubts surfacing within. I was quite unclear as to how I could follow this guidance, but it did appeal to me. I promised myself to try it out. He was my Guru, a person blind since the age of ten, uneducated, sixty years old—perhaps more than seventy—and without house, bags or baggage.

This conversation reminded me of my experience with my first Guru. Then I had received, though I had not paid. My first Guru was a family man. He did not, however, work to support himself; his only source of income was whatever he was offered. Yet he came some 1500 miles from his home to see me whenever I asked, and also spent sums of money to entertain me adequately whenever I visited his home. I knew I had paid him hardly anything.

By the time I came to this country, I had realized that the way of Jung and the tradition of my Gurus were alike. The work was Soul Work, Soul Making. This country gave me the opportunity to fulfull this possibility within myself and to do Soul Work with others. However, only when I visited my Guru in 1972 did I realize that Soul Work is not a professional work for money.

Upon my return to the States, I began to change. When a client asked about my fees, I told him that I would be glad to receive whatever was given gladly. "Give me happily and freely whatever you can conveniently and without constraint." If the patient asked about the fees charged by my colleagues, I informed him about the present rate.

The discussion with my Guru returned me to my Soul Work, and it felt truly in line with the way of Jung. If Jung's way is to explore the Unknown and to live with the uncertainty and unpredictability of the Unconscious, then living with the uncertainty of flexible fees seems to be the way to experience what Jung said and taught.

During this period I was paid only what people felt happy in giving. A few could not pay; a few paid five or ten dollars, and some paid the full fee. Others offered to do work, such as cleaning, altering clothes, or making a bookcase.

What is the effect of the fee-less practice on the patient? In the absence of fees, is commitment to the work possible? I see no connection between exchange of money and commitment to work together. The person comes to therapy suffering and in pain. One listens to it, feels it; naturally the heart goes out to do whatever possible. While feeling this way, can one throw out the suffering person simply because he cannot pay the *reasonable* fee? Commitment to work is obvious, since here is an opportunity to enter the temple of the healing God. In my experience people have always paid what they could; therapy did not stop as insight and image went on gracing the hour. I can remember only one solitary case when a client cheated me.

Another example shows that sensitivity can grow during the work, while people pay happily. A person from the healing professions agreed to pay a certain sum in the beginning. Later, after a month or so, he felt the exchange of money was interfering with the work. I told him that if he thought not paying would make him comfortable and flowing in the work, then I was happy about that too. We continued for some time. Following his return from a vacation he told me that he gave some amount to a charity, and felt good about it. The work commenced again until he left the state on a work assignment. When he came back, he felt happy in paying me for each session. This illustrates how contract in terms of money is not essential to Soul Work.

Some misunderstanding may lurk here. This kind of fee-less practice does not mean that the therapist is unaware of the client's sense of obligation for what he is receiving. Such a lacuna is detrimental to both analyst and client. The common and reasonable understanding that one must pay for services rendered cannot be ignored. But this need not imply insistence on payment of a fixed sum of money. One who wishes to get help without paying for it deprives himself from receiving by the very nature of his attitude. He is cutting himself off from the mainstream of Life. Life is an interdependent and interrelated whole. Such a person becomes isolated from the world, ceassing to be nourished, renewed and replenished by Life. He has ceased to participate in the *Yajna*, sacrifice, of Life. Life is *Yajna*, as beautifully described by Sri Krishna in the *Gita*.

When Arjuna asks him why he is now being asked to act—fight in the battle—since Sri Krishna has already said that the path of knowledge is better than the path of action, Sri Krishna says Nonaction may not be achieved by ceasing to act or by renunciation acts. Without action human beings will die (*Bh. Gita*, III 4—5). It is here that Krishna introduces the concept of action as *Yajna*. In a very symbolic way he explains how this universe is sustained by *Yajna*.

He says: Everything grows and is sustained by food. Food is produced by rain, and *Yajna* performed brings rain. In order to perform *Yajna* one must act and work, gathering material to be sacrificed in the fire of *Yajna* (*BH. Gita*, III 14—16). The common understanding that one can choose between action and non-action is incorrect. Sri Krishna says that the source of action is Brahman, the totality of what IS; since this totality is established in the Immutable (*Akshara*), everything returns to and originates from the same source. We are nourished and sustained by that. Performing the *Yajna*, being in the mainstream of life, sustains us. Whoever alienates himself from the fact of

Life, its interdepence and mutuality, isolates himself from his own source and ceases to live. Sincerity of purpose always brings reciprocity and respect and a healing wholeness.

The experiment with the fee-less practice opened many dark corners of my psyche, and the process goes on. I have my practice as a Jungian analyst and occasionally teach Indian psychology and philosophy in a small suburban college.

As might be expected both income and the number of clients rise and fall. One month is not the same as any other; no year resembles the one just past. I have sometimes felt actutely the impact of these fluctuations. Whenever income and clients declined, my stomach felt hollow, and a sense of insecurity pounded my heart. With pain I drew money from my savings to pay the tax collector and other bills. My insecurity intensified when such periods came regularly.

Although some years were bad, the savings balance gradually returned to its previous level. I felt very happy and even secure. As my habits are, I became something of a spendthrift. Looking back, I can say I enjoyed it, but I didn't then. This period lasted until 1977, when the sense of insecurity due to instability of income and my aging monopolized my attention.

In the summer of 1977 another and more interesting phase of life came up which had remained unnoticed and neglected until then. In the last part of August 1977 I returned from India after discharging the last responsibility to my family—seeing my youngest daughter married. A great burden was lifted from my shoulders. Since the time of my wife's death I had felt keenly the obligation to see that our pet child was married happily. Three trips to India, made in order to fulfill my responsibility, naturally affected my bank balance and clientele.

Curiously enough, the relief at her marriage and at the consequent reduction of my financial burden did not last. In its place, surreptitiously, a feeling of worthlessness and meaninglessness began to permeate my life. My responsibility for my family was at an end; it was all over. Where was the purpose of living? At the same time my knowledge, whether learned from Jung or my Gurus, began to seem hackneyed, stale and useless. All I knew left me cold, and I did not want to repeat worn-out words and feelings in analytical hours. I felt out-of-date and good-for-nothing. Existence seemed futile.

I was glad to know that the way of Jung and the path of Selfrealization of the East were similar, and that the basis of psychotherapy is the knowledge and awarneness of who I am. Without this awareness no help really is forthcoming in our work Yet the soul was in agony as in a classical depression. If I knew nothing, all knowledge having departed, how would I work and live? The total uncertainty scared me. No knowledge...no work...no money...what then...?

Something happened. Sri Shunyata (Mr. Nobody) visited me for a month.

He is today ninety, comes from Denmark, and lives in a small hut in the foothills of the Himalayas on a small stipend of fifty rupees per month. In 1930 when he came to India at the invitation of Dr. Rabindranath Tagore to teach silence, he met Raman Maharshi. Raman Maharshi gazed into the eyes of Mr. Sorenson (his original name) and called him a born mystic. He said, "We are always aware, Shunyata!" In this way he was named Shunyata by Raman Maharshi.

Sri Shunyata's unobtrusive and powerfully silent personality affected me deeply. After he left, I saw some light in what had happened earlier—the classical depression.

Am I nothing if I cannot work? Am I nothing if all the acquired knowledge leaves me? What precisely is work? Is it analyzing and getting money, or is it a happening in the soul achieved through living interaction with clients and the world? The effacement of the one who could work scared me through and through.

The path I had embarked on opened innumerable fears in me until, ultimately, it led me to inquire into the root of insecurity itself. I became aware of the fact that I was identified with knowledge, a knowledge which had become the basis of my work. When knowledge had gone, security in work followed. It had been natural for me to forget myself in the doing of therapy. Once I was involved, the session hour progressed spontaneously and generally to the satisfaction of both analyst and client. Now I was nothing. I was mighty scared by the face of Nothingness. Unable to stay wholly with the experience, I could see only the nothingness of myself, while Mr. Nobody, Sri Shunyata, presented himself as a person based on Nothingness and whose work on my soul emerged not from knowledge, not even from his work, but from the soul itself. I found a new basis for soul work.

An example here to show how freedom from money (not charging a fixed fee) provides inner strength. Therapy happens between two souls when they meet honestly and sincerely—a discovery that is liberating and a relief. A client had been working with me for the last seven years. Upon retiring he reduced his appointments by half. He was a very greedy man in that, now that he had retired, he wanted a return on all the benefits of his past payments. Not at peace with himself, all alone and without work, he became impatient. No longer receiving a salary, he had only his pension and social security. At first in a veiled manner, and then plainly, he began complaining that having paid so much, not only to me, but to many others like me, he had not yet gotten what he wanted. It was my duty to give him that now.

Once in a session, he got angry and made no bones about telling me that he had been robbed. He ought now, he told me, to have peace of mind. Undisturbed by his anger, I could tell him, honestly, that I had never entered into a contract with him to supply him with this peace of mind in return for money. Calmly I told him that, although therapy happened every time we met, I never claimed to be a therapist. Nonetheless, his anger was justified. In return for his sacrifice he ought to get something. But he was angry with the wrong person. I helped him to see the healer within him, and to see through the projection of that healer onto me. This healer was the right person to be angry with. If the client really placed his complaints before Him clearly and openly, an answer was sure to come.

This brief autobiography of mine presents clearly a problem of soul work. Whether we call our work "the way to wholeness" or "a spiritual jorney" or "individuation" or "soul-making," every encounter in our work with people is a two-way process, a giving and receivind, and leaves us transformed. But is this giving and receiving necessarily identical with an exchange of money? In soul work a supra-ordinate factor, encompassing both analyst and client, is active. If we are open to it, it does the work. But 'who' then gets paid and 'who' pays? What is true of therapeutic work is perhaps true of all kinds of work.

Two issues here seem important to me: my uncertainty in the world and my fear of being without work. Both can result in a refusal to acknowledge the supra-ordinate factor in analysis. Perhaps both meet at a common point and have a common root. Let us see.

As a biological being I am quite insecure: I need shelter, food and clothing to protect me. We all need this, yet even were this guaranteed us, life can end at any moment without notice. In spite of all care, life is beyond my control. If I worry too much about this, it is a neurotic and unhealthy fear. One must live with this insecurity, yielding to death the moment it comes.

While alive I need money to live. When I recall the periods when there was no work, no money coming in and my savings depleted by paying bills, I discover that the fear originated with the specter of not being able to maintain a certain standard of living. What is this attachment? A fear of poverty? What kind of poverty? Is it fear of poverty or love of creaturely comforts? Can I not be what I am withouth these comforts? Why am I here in this country doing whatever it is I am doing? Is it not because it supports my love of comforts? I know that I can be what I really am in spite of these comforts, yet a fear lurks behind it all. Deprive me of these comforts and I must face poverty. I cannot and do not want to face it.

The fear of poverty prevents the discovery of something important. I do not trust something within, and this prevents me from discovery who really supports us all. So what is this experience of facing poverty? It opens before me my total dependence on others for everything. Choosing poverty helps me to discover that dependence is actually a basic trust, the reliance upon my whole self in its interdependence with the universe. It is my mind in its separateness, and the anxiety arising from the separateness, that turns trust into negative insecurity of dependence.

By facing this anxiety and insecurity brought on by the idea of poverty, I am confronted with soul. For as we have seen in this short paper, the desire for creaturely comforts leads to insecurity and uncertainty because I cannot control my income, my ability to work, or even my faculties with which I work and earn. So I am forced to look within and listen when this fear of poverty arises. Thus I come upon Soul Work. In this way, the problem of money dissolves into the more basic question of "Who" is uncertain and "Who" meets uncertainty with work.

Who am I? I call myself a Jungian analyst and distinguish myself from others by virtue of my training and knowledge. Giving myself a special importance because of this, I create a division between myself and others in the same profession, and between myself and those who come as patients.

I also see a deeper division within me; by identifying myself with the work I do, I find myself dependent on the faculties which make that work possible. But the work I do occupies only a small part of my life. I work only when awake which occupies only part of the day. I am myself when in deep sleep, when dreaming, eating or relaxing. By identifying myself only with work, I narrow myself down to a few hours, and think as if all of me is that. I isolate myself from the total Self and the world. It is natural, therefore, for me to feel anxious and fearful upon discovering that my work can be lost at any time. Of couse, I can try to make that isolated part appear whole by adding to it further parts of the same world, by joining groups, making money, learning more techniques, etc., to feel safe and secure. But this only makes me more identified with my work. Still, without work I lose my identity.

Having created hierarchies of values, distinctions, separations, and divisions within me and between me and the world, I attempt to meet the insecurity rooted in these divisions by receiving money. Instead of being the instrument of bridging, the 'medium of exchange,' money becomes the instrument of insecurity and separation. It leads me to forget the unique value of individual worth; it leads me to lose trust in who I really am; it leads me to lose trust in the world totality of which I am on organic part; it leads me to lose sight of Soul Work.

Reflections like these, which are themselves Soul Work, slowly bring me face to face with my No-thingness, and also at the same time with my utter dependence on wholeness within myself and with the universe. I want to be something, somebody, an unique 'I,' distinct from every other. But I cannot be anything alone. Perhaps the source of my insecurity and fear is that I do not really 'see' 'who' is so worried about insecurity... WHO AM I?

(reprinted from SOUL AND MONEY, pp. 45—55 Spring Publications, Dallas; 1982, by permission)

A Contribution to Soul and Money

By James Hillman (Dallas)

> "Money is a kind of poetry"
> Wallace Stevens, "Adagia"
> Opus Posthumous, 1957

Whatever we say about money in its relation with analytical practice, whatever we say about money at all will be conditioned by the mind-set of our cultural tradition. We speak first of all at an unreflected level, with the voice of collective consciousness, to use Jung's term. So, in order to gain purchase on the money question in analysis, we have first to see through our collective consciousness, the very deep, old, and imperceptible attitudes that archetypally, let us say, have money already fixed within a definite framework, especially in regard to soul.

This framework is that of our entire culture, and it is Christian. So we are going to have to look first of all at Christian ideas and images regarding money and soul. I set forth now without benefit of Christian apologetics and exegetics, without recourse to scholarly apparatus, simply as the plain man who opens his Bible in a hotel room and takes the words there within the framework of his collective consciousness. For the words of Jesus in regard to money, whether or not we are directly conscious of them, are still sounding in us as members of this culture. Here are a few of the passages in the Gospels which I want briefly to remind you of before drawing some conclusions.

John's Gospel puts the first of these money stories at the beginning of Jesus' ministry (John 2:14).

> And he found in the temple those that sold oxen and sheep and doves, and the changers of money sitting [kollubistes, literally "coin clippers"]. And he made a scourge of cords and cast all out of the temple, both the sheep and the oxen; and he poured out the changers' money, and overthrew their tables. And to them that sold the doves he said. Take these things hence; Make not my Father's house a house of merchandise [a market].

Mark's (11:17) version has Jesus saying "a den of robbers," specifically referring to both buyers and sellers.

The second incident is more a saying than a story. I refer to Matthew 19, Mark 10, and Luke 8:25 from which last I quote: "For it is easier for a camel to enter in through a needle's eye, than for a rich man to enter into the kingdom of heaven." Is it not curious that in these first two allegories money is expressed directly in the language of animals? Even the sheep and oxen, so significant in the birth milieu of Jesus, are driven from the temple, and the camel now becomes that animal fatness, that richness which cannot pass the strait and narrow gate where the soul must enter. In these first two images, the exclusion of money is also exclusion of the animal.

If ever the word archetypal meant anything like permanent, ubiquitous, at the roots or made in heaven, then the relation between money and animals is archetypal. The animal is the very archai of money. Pecuniary derives from cattle; fee derives from *faihi* (Gothic for cattle); capital refers back to cattle counted by the head. The Greek coin, *obolos,* refers to the *obelos* or spitted portion of flesh of a sacrificial bull, and the ancient Roman currency, *as,* meant a piece of the roast, a hunk of meat.* The vow of poverty entails the vow of chastity; money and animal life are driven from the temple together.

The third story concerns taxes, which play a special role right from the beginning. Jesus' birth took place in Bethlehem because Joseph and Mary had to proceed there to register for the tax rolls (Luke 2). The topos, "Bethlehem," not only brings Jesus together with David, Jesus and animal together, Joseph and Mary together, the Magi of various races and orientations, but also holds in one image the Emperor's rule of the world by means of taxes and Christ's star pointing beyond the world. In the image of "Bethlehem," as they say, no problem. In Matthew 17 (and Matthew, by the way, is the Patron Saint of tax collectors, assessors and bankers), Peter is asked whether Jesus pays his half-shekel or didrachma in taxes. Peter says: Yes. But as it turns out, the tax Jesus pays to the Temple is not common money of this world. It is got by miracle: "go thou to the sea," he tells Simon Peter,"...and take up the fish that first cometh up; and when thou hast opened his mouth, thou shalt find a shekel: take that and give unto them for me and thee." Again, by the way, an animal together with money.

The main tax tale is the one told in Matthew 22, Mark 12, and Luke 20. I'll give the passage from Mark: "Master... is it lawful to give tribute unto Caesar, or not?" to which Jesus answers: "bring me a penny that I may see it...And he saith unto them, Whose is this image and superscription? And they said unto him, Caesar's. And Jesus said unto them, Render unto Caesar the things that are Caesar's, and unto God the things that are God's."

Here it is money itself which divides into two alternative ways—spiritual and worldly. It is money which is used for the parable of two different and distinct worlds. If money divides the two realms, is it also that third which holds them together? We shall come to this later.

According to the texts, it sounds as if it is clearly better to be without

*Cf. W. H. Desmonde, *Magic, Myth, and Money* (Glencoe: Free Press), pp. 109—19.

money, even to be in poverty, than to be with money. (This in spite of Joseph of Arimethea and other followers who were wealthy.) For instance, in the tale of the poor widow (Luke 20, Mark 12) who is praised for her meager giving—a lesson Jesus draws out for his disciples as he sits "over against the treasury" in the temple. Or, for instance, poverty becomes mandatory: when the twelve are sent on their mission, two by two, with authority over unclean spirits or *daimones* (Mark 6, Luke 9, Matthew 10), they are expressly instructed not to carry money. Or, for instance, Luke 12 where wealth and soul are directly brought into relation. In a passage about inheritance (the parable of the rich fool) Jesus says: "a man's life consisteth not in the abundance of things which he possesseth" as he tells about a rich man laying up corn for his retirement so as to have his soul's ease, only to have his soul (psyche) called by God to death that very night. Or, for instance, Matthew 26 and Mark 8: "What doth it profit a man to gain the whole world and lose his own soul [psyche]?"

Is not by now the division utterly clear? Money belongs to Caesar's Palace, not God's Temple. The first act of cleansing the temple of money is reaffirmed all along, and of course nowhere more bitterly than in the final story, the selling of Jesus by Judas for thirty pieces of silver. (Judas is already attributed with the telltale sign of evil—a money bag or box in the scene of the supper [John 13:29].) Could money be given a more negative cast?

We are situated in this collective consciousness. We have to start from this schism between soul and money in the basic text stating the values of our tradition. The schism can lead us into taking up one side or another of it, such as exposed by Dr. Covitz and by Dr. Vasavada. Together with Vasavada, we can deny money in order to do a spiritual kind of soul-work; or together with Covitz, we can affirm money in order to become therapeutically more effective in the world. They each showed the division we already have seen: the more one concentrates on money the more one involves oneself in the world, and the more one neglects money or abjures it, the more one can be removed from the world.

But I wish to make another kind of move by taking a third position, neither high road nor low road, neither spirit nor matter. I see money as an archetypal dominant that can be taken spiritually or materially, but which in itself is neither.

Rather, money, is a *psychic reality,* and as such gives rise to divisions and oppositions about it, much as other fundamental psychic realities-love and work, death and sexuality, politics and religion—are archetypal dominants which easily fall into opposing spiritual and material interpretations. Moreover, since money is an archetypal psychic reality, it will always be inherently problematic because psychic realities are complex, complicated. Therefore, money problems are inevitable, necessary, irreducible, always present, und potentially if not actually overwhelming. Money is devilishly divine.

One of Charles Olson's *Maximus* poems sets out this archetypal view most compactly:

the under part is, though stemmed, uncertain is, as sex is, as moneys are, facts to be dealt with as the sea is...

This is an extraordinary statement. "Facts to be dealt with as the sea is." The first of these facts is that money is as deep and broad as the ocean, the primordially unconscious, and makes us so. It always takes us into great depths, where sharks and suckers, hard-shell crabs, tight clams and tidal emotions abound. Its facts have huge horizons, as huge as sex, and just as protean and polymorphous.

Moreover, money is plural: moneys. Therefore I can never take moneys as an equivalent for any single idea: exchange, energy, value, reality, evil, and whatever. It is many-stemmed, it is uncertain, polymorphous. At one moment the money complex may invite Danae who draws Zeus into her lap as a shower of coints, at another moment the gold may invite Midas. Or, Hermes the thief, patron of merchants, easy commerce. Or it may be old moneybags Saturn who invented coining and hoarding to begin with. As on the original coins the Greeks made, there are different Gods and different animals—owls, bulls, rams, crabs—each time the complex is passed from hand to hand.

Money is as protean as the sea-God himself; try as we might with fixed fees, regular billings, and accounts ledgered and audited, we never can make the stems of money balance. The checkbook will never tally, the budget will never stay within bookkeeping columns. We invent more and more machinery for controlling money, more and more refined gauges for economic prediction, never grasping what Olson tells us: the facts of money are like the facts of the sea. Money is like the id itself, the primordially repressed, the collective unconscious appearing in specific denominations, that is, precise quanta or configurations of value, i. e., *images*. Let us define money as that which possibilizes the imagination. Moneys are the riches of Pluto in which Hades' psychic images lie concealed. To find imagination in yourself or a patient, turn to money behaviors and fantasies. You both will soon be in the underworld (the entrance to which requires a money for Charon).

Therapy draws back. Do you know of the study done on therapeutic taboos? Analysts were surveyed regarding what they feel they must never do with a patient. It was discovered that touching and holding, shouting and hitting, drinking, kissing, nudity and intercourse were all less prohibited than was "lending money to a patient," Money constellated the ultimate taboo.

For money always takes us into the sea, uncertain, whether it comes as inheritance fights, fantasies about new cars and old houses, marriage battles over spending, ripping off, tax evasion, market speculations, fear of going broke, poverty, charity—whether these complexes appear in dreams, in living rooms, or in pubic policy. For here in the facts of money is the great ocean, and maybe while trawling that sea floor during an analytical hour we may come up with a crazy crab or a fish with a shekel in its mouth.

Just as animals were spirits or Gods in material forms, so too is money, a kind of third thing between only spirit and only the world, flesh, and devil. Hence, to be with money is to be in this third place of soul, psychic reality. And, to keep my relation with the unclean spirits whether the high daimones or the low daimones, I want some coins in my purse. I need them to pay my way to Hades into the psychic realm. I want to be like what I work on, not unlike and immune. I want the money-changers where I can see them, right in the temple of my pious aspirations. In other words, I try my darnedest to keep clear about the tradition I have just exposed because I think it a disastrous one for psychotherapy, and of course also for the culture as a whole.

The cut between Caesar and God in terms of money deprives the soul of world and the world of soul. The soul is deflected onto a spiritual path of denial and the world is left in the sins of luxuria, avarice, and greed. Then the soul is always threatened by money, and the world needs the spiritual mission of redemption from the evil caused by the Weltbild that cuts Caesar from God. That money is the place where God and Caesar divide shows that money is a 'third thing' like the soul itself, and that in money are both the inherent tendency to split into spirit and matter and the possibility to hold them together.

This equation—"money = psyche"—is what we Jungians have been trying to say when we translate money images in dreams into "psychic energy." "Energy," however, is heroic Promethean language. It transforms the equation into "money = ego," that is, energy available to ego-consciousness. Then, Hermes/Mercurius, Guide of Souls, has to appear as the thief, and in our sense of loss (of money, of energy, of identity) in order for the equation "money = psyche" to return again. (Poverty is simply a way out of ego, but not a hermetic way.) For Hermes the Thief is also Hermes Psychopompos, implying that from the hermetic perspective exactly there, where money is no longer available to ego-consciousness, is also where Hermes has stolen it for the sake of soul. In soul work, losing and gaining take on different meanings, a sensibility that Promethean language about "energy" is too active and goal-directed to apprehend.

If money has this archetypal soul value, again like the ancient coins bearing images of Gods and their animals and backed by these powers,* money will not, cannot, accept the Christian depreciation, and so Christianity time and again in its history has had to come to terms with the return of the repressed—from the wealth of the churches and the luxury of its priests, the

---

*Cf. my discussion of coinage in "Silver and the White Earth," *Spring 1980*, pp. 35—37.

selling of indulgences, the rise of capitalism with protestantism, usury and projections on the Jews, the Christian roots of marxism, and so on.

One particular shadow of the Christian position appears right in analysis: the old sin of simony or exchanging spiritual and ecclesiastical benefits for money. Is not the elaborate system analysts have derived for guaranteed payments from their patients for 'Heil' or individuation of the Self, and from their trainees for ordination into the analytical profession, modern forms of simony? This sin the Church was far more conscious of than we are today. The Church was anyway more aware of money for possibilizing the imagination than we are in psychotherapy. It has always recognized the fantasypower of money preventing the soul from its doctrinal spiritual path.

As long as our belief system inherently depreciates money, it will always threaten the soul with value distortions. Depession, inflation, bad credit, low interest—these psychological metaphors have hardened into unconscious economic jargon. Having "de-based" money from its archetypal foundations in psychic reality, money attempts a new literal and secular foundation for itself as "the bottom line." But this bottom does not hold, because any psychic reality that has been fundamentally depreciated must become symptomatic, 'go crazy,' in order to assert its fundamental archetypal autonomy.

We live today in fear of this autonomy, called financial anarchy. Anarchy means "without archai"; and of course money, conceived without soul, without an animal life of its own, without Gods, becomes crazy, anarchic, because we forget that like sex, like the sea, it too is a religious domimant.

Now I am referring back through the word itself to the Goddess Moneta, the Roman equivalent of Mnemosyne meaning *memoria, imaginatio,* Mother of the Muses. In her temple of Moneta, money was kept; in the word, a temple too, Moneta reappears. Money is thus a deposit of mythical fantasies. It is a treasury that mothers and remembers images. Money is imaginative, as I have been saying. Thus, money in the hand awakens imaginal possibilities: to do this, go there, have that. It reveals the Gods which dominate my fantasies—Saturnian tightness, Jupiterian generosity, Martial show, Venusian sensuality. Money provokes my behavior into mythical fantasies, so very different in different people. Why should people agree about money—where to invest it, on what to spend it, which horse to put it on? It is a truly polytheistic phenomenon in everyday life. As such, coined money is a highly cultural phenomenon. It came into history with the Greeks and not before them. It belongs in the constellation of the Muses, necessary to imaginational culture, and hence it does become devilish when imagination is not valued (as in Christianity). The ugliness, the power corruption, the purely quantitative nature of money today are not its fault, but that of its having been severed and then fallen from the Gods from which it came.

*

Let me now connect this theme with another at this Congress: Training. On occasion candidates have explained to me that one reason for their wanting to train is that analytical practice offers a noble way of earning money. So much of the world's work is soulless, they say, while analysis pays one for staying with soul, without having to open a headshop, teach guitar, throw pots or home-grow squash and tomatoes. One does not have to be economically marginal. The analyst combines soul and money; analytical money is good, clean money, and even well paid. Training tempts, evidently, because is resolves the Christian dilemma of shekel versus soul, without having to follow the spiritual solution of poverty.

The resolution of a pair of opposites, however, only perpetuates their opposition: the third requires the other two for it to be a third. Only when we can step altogether out of the dilemma that divides money (and soul) into spiritual and material oppositions, can we see that there is psyche in money all the time in every way, that it is "a kind of poetry," that it is wholly and utterly psychological and needs no redeeming into good, clean and noble money, and so needs no repressing into the poverty and asceticism of the spirit turned against matter.

In fact, that equation "money = psyche" suggests that there is more soul to be found where money problems are most extreme, not in poverty but in luxury, miserly greed, covetousness, and the joy of usury, and that the fear of money and the importance of money in some persons may be more psychologically devastating, and therefore therapeutically rewarding, than sexual fears and impotence. Extraordinary demons are startled when the money complex is touched. And no complex is kept hidden with more secrecy. Patients more readily reveal what's concealed by their pants than what's hidden in their pants' pockets. Freudians who see purses as female genital symbols may discover more by making the reduction in the reverse direktion.

Where exactly is the money complex hidden? Most often it hides in the guises of love, where so much soul is anyways hidden. As Tawney showed, Protestantism and Capitalism enter the world together. And, after all these centuries, they still hold hands in mutual affection in so many protestant families where giving, receiving, saving, participating, supporting, spending, willing (inheritance) are the ways one learns about loving. "Spending" for a long time in English had both a genital and a monetary meaning, while the words bond, yield, safe, credit, duty, interest, share and debt (as *shuld* or guilt) all bear double meanings of love and money. The double meanings doublebind: to protestant-capitalist consciousness renunciating the family's psychological attitudes often becomes refusing money from home which is felt at home as a rebuff of love. The money = psyche equation is a powerful variant of the Eros and Psyche myth where money stands in for love.

But finally, what does money do for the soul: what is its specific function in possibilizing the imagination? It makes the imagination possible in the world. Soul needs money to be kept from flying off into the Bardo realm of 'only-psychic' reality. Money holds soul in the vale of the world, in the poetry of the concrete, in touch with the sea as *facts*, those hard and slippery facts, so perduring, annoying, and limiting, and ceaselessly involving one in economic necessity. For economy means originally "householding," making soul in the vale of the world, charging and being overcharged, crimping and splurging, exchanging, bargaining, evaluating, paying off, going in debt, speculating....

Thus fee negotiation, whether in Vasavada's style or Covitz's, is a thoroughly psychological activity. Fee payment may take many styles from dirty dollar bills plunked on the table before the hour begins, to gifts and deals and wheedling, or the discreetly passed envelope, to the abstract medical model of depersonalized forms, checks, and statements. And the old joke is always true: "When the man says: 'it ain't the money, it's the principle'—it's the money." Is *is* the money where the real issue lies. Money is an irreducible principle.

Analysis, as the candidates have perceived, indeed lets soul and money meet. The spirituality of the Christian division is suspended: one renders unto the Gods and Caesars in one and the same payment. We pay tribute to the costliness of soul work, that it is rare, precious, most dear. And we pay out the common buck "for professional services rendered," a phrase equally appropriate to the physician, the plumber, and the whore.

That analysts have trouble justifying their outrageous fees (and at the same time feel they never earn enough compared with lawyers and dentists) belongs to the archetypal nature of money as we have been viewing it. The money question can no more be regulated so as to settle into easines than can sex or the sea. The underpart stems into the many directions of our complexes. That we cannot settle the money issue in analysis shows money to be one main way the mothering imagination keeps our souls fantasizing. So, to conclude with my part of this panel, Soul and Money: yes, soul *and* money; we cannot have either without the other. To find the soul of modern man or woman, begin by searching into those irreducible embarrassing facts of the money complex, that crazy crab scuttling across the floors of silent seas.

(reprinted from SOUL AND MONEY, pp 31–43, Spring Publications Dallas: 1992, by permission)

The Psyche, Wealth, and Poverty

By John Weir Perry (San Francisco)

The invitation to me to speak on Soul and Money conceals a fine irony, given that I feel myself to be one of the most careless among my colleagues in money matters. I have committed all the sins of unconsciousness about money: after three decades I still tend to feel guilt over fees; I allow people to run up inordinate bills that sometimes go unpaid; billings go out late, and I drive my secretaries to distraction by relying on them to take care of such matters, and showing not a little impatience when complications arise. Whenever possible, I prefer not to think about money; I do so only at tax time, and my neck muscles tighten in protest. Although I realize that for many people money is the really real, for me it remains an abstraction, a set of numbers colored, I hope, black instead of red. At least I can speak for California, a state that first won fame for its 'aurum vulgaris,' the 'common gold,' but now stands for something quite different: its notoriety made good during the last two decades by a beginning attempt to refine 'the true spiritual gold of the philosophers.'

With all this I felt that I would not have much to say on the topic until I began forcing myself to reflect on it. It soon became obvious that my 'sins' do not rise purely out of careless disregard, but rather out of attitudes that are ingrained, deeply. So my intention is to convey the various thoughts that appeared, and to capture their philosophic background. The fulcrum upon which they turn appears to be not money-making, but questions about the value of poverty.

As I looked back over the early signs of my inclination to avoid thinking about money, I recalled my school's motto emblazoned on its coat of arms and upon my mind: along with "Directness of Purpose" and "Self-Reliance," the one that best expressed the spirit of the school is "Simplicity of Life." I have never lost touch with that directive. I recalled also the crash of '29 and the ensuing depression. Most of us who were young then, and experienced firsthand the evanescence of riches, can never rely on money; other goals will always seem more enriching, and more dependable, than money-making.

Closer to home, though, was a choice my father made just on the verge of the crash. When his broker told him what was happening, advising him to get out while the getting was still possible, my father made an ethical decision not to do so, since that would be contributing even in small part to the general panic and the economy's downfall. It cost him; it cost all of us; yet I have always been glad for that example of a clearly moral action.

My father's courage in the face of panic and poverty reminded me of a couple of the best years I ever knew. During the second World War, I lived communally, with no money at all, as a member of the Friends Ambulance Unit in China. I particularly admired at that time the Maoist leaders in Shensi for their life-style of building and caring for their own homes, cut out of rugged loess, and Gandhi for his guiding the government of India from a simple tent in front of the government buildings.

Far in the background of my attitude to money lies the vivid awareness of widespread ancient teachings relating spiritual cultivation to voluntary poverty: that is, to develop spiritually it is important to divest oneself of too much concern with worldly welfare. Christianity, Taoism, Buddhism, and Islam share this view. We should not minimize the fact that spiritual cultivation has frequently been associated with voluntary poverty, because to do so leaves out of account considerations rooted in centuries of spiritual experience.

Seeking to learn more about the background of this association, and to fortify my paper with something solid, I went first to the *Britannica:* it had nothing whatsoever on the topic beyond socio-economic statistical studies. I turned next to Hasting's *Encyclopaedia of Religion and Ethics,* thinking it a sure bet because it had never failed me. Yet it did: there were only socio-economic researches; under monasticism, a passing mention of vows, along with chastity and obedience! In the works of Jung I could find nothing. Has it come to pass, I reflected, that our culture is so focused on the value of well-being that the value of poverty has been effaced? My initial research suggested so.

When I turned, however, to Evelyn Underhill's *Mysticism,* my quest found satisfaction: she explicates, lucidly and extensively, the motivation and rationale of voluntary poverty. For the mystics, it is entirely a question of what is most desired, and whether this results in separation or in a human-hearted connection with our fellow beings, a connection that culminates in an experience of the unity and mutual participation of all being in the One. Lusting after property, i. e., what you can possess as your own, fosters the divisiveness that nourished 'ego-motivations.' Property then defines one's identity— as that which is proper to oneself, much in the manner that the properties of a substance define its nature. The criterion of property provides a false basis for the differentiation of oneself and the world. The urgent desire to seek after God is considered incompatible with such desire for things of the world. Hence the Christian admonition, "You cannot serve both God and Mammon," or "It is easier for a camel to walk through the Eye of a needle than for a rich man to enter the Kingdom of Heaven." Yet to be poor in spirit and therefore blessed, does not necessitate being poor in substance, but rather cleaving to a detachment as an inner state independent of outer conditions. The ultimate in this direction of thinking is such a renunciation of the world that one cannot live in it and needs a monastery to solve the dilemma.

When poverty is a true deprivation, it can, of course, become distracting and finally debilitating: one's attention remains fettered to the worries of survival. I am speaking here of a simplicity of life-style chosen freely and not imposed by external constraints and hardships. The great spirits who choose voluntary simplicity avoid the constraints of deprivation by living in a faith that assures them of their livelihood. From their faith a life-style evolves. We in our practices as therapists live in a faintly discernible version of such a faith. Without beating the bushes in the professional world to fill our practice, we nevertheless find that applicants for therapy present themselves at roughly the same pace at which they finish. One senses some sort of mysterious law of nature that seems to govern this flow that we cannot control.

We must ask at this point, facing the question honestly: is there anything wrong with the desire simply to make money handsomely in a practice? Many pitfalls lie on this road. Our current economy is demonstrating that as soon as the focus of caring is the paycheck and job security, merited or not, then the concern for quality of work declines. Analyst or auto mechanic: the same rule applies. We can easily, too, fall into the error of overvaluing the analytical profession, and permitting a drift toward inflated fees by consensual agreement. Our commodity for sale is our time, not our expertise. Our feeling, especially, cannot be bought, despite the American inclination to regard the gift of money as an expression of feeling. If an archetype of wealth reigns over our work, we encounter a dark underworld deity who, if I may play upon the word, might lead us to plutonic relationships. If we consider ourselves authorities paid for our knowledge, we court the danger of esablishing inequality and non-mutuality with our clients who must labor to maintain us in this high station. The shadow of analysis, I sometimes think, is anything that separates us and our analysands.

A preference for simplicity in finances has its price. Prosperity allows one a great deal of free time to nourish the mind, and to maintain a tranquil pace in which reflectiveness and spiritual cultivation receive their due. Often I grumble at spending precious time typing letters, keeping accounts, and paying bills—even sometimes at building my house and grounds. Yet I am grateful for the grounding that these necessities have provided.

Early in my practice I decided that what I did not receive in fees I would make up by work with my hands, on house, furnishings and grounds. My children have learned to do the same. In essence, the governing thought in this way of being is "If you can't buy it, make it." Because of this I have not, insofar as I can recall, had to decline an applicant for therapy because of his inability to pay the fee requested. Nor have I had to limit my quarter-time participation in innovative programs because of the very low pay one receives (usually at an hourly rate which in one third of the standard fee in private practice). My three two-year experiences of this kind in innovative programs for therapy of schizophrenic young adults—the Agnew Project, Diabasis I and Diabasis II—have cost me more potential income than I like to calculate. No regrets, only some feeling of pinch—and a zestful race to stay a step ahead of the tax collectors.

In these projects I saw the divisiveness that money can create. The staff members who did all the heavy work of therapy and took care of the house were paid the least, while administration, the persona operations of our relationships with the mental health systems, received respectable salaries. I found myself in the awkward position of being paid at three times the hourly rate of the line staff, while at only one third of the professional fee rate of private practice. The inequality of the system caused many confrontations and objections; it took real effort to hold together in the face of these potential rifts.

Now, after making my pitch for simplicity of style, I must back up a little and remember that after all, my family and I live well by any socio-economic standard. Therefore my commitment is to a relative simplicity only, midway toward anything suggesting a voluntary poverty. This might be called a compromise, but that suggests weakness, an unconvinced half-heartedness. As I reflect about it, I find that it leads to a main point of my discussion. In our Jungian framework, we hold that when we live fully we take a position that holds us constantly in a state of sustaining paradoxes in the play of the opposites. According to this, in matters of finance we cannot choose either to renounce the world and its kind of well-being, nor allow our spiritual life to become sterile because of engulfment in worldly concerns. We must maintain both ends of the polarity in our lifestyles. We must hold to the midpoint.

(reprinted from SOUL AND MONEY, Spring Publications, Dallas: 1982, by permission)

Projections: Soul and Money

By Adolf Guggenbühl-Craig (Zürich)

I have yet to meet the person who is indifferent to money. *Soul and Money* is the title of this panel. Now 'soul' is a difficult term to use. Some psychologists avoid it, trying to create a psychology without soul. Others replace the religious-sounding 'soul' with the more neutral 'psyche.' I am all for employing the word 'soul,' yet, when used too often, it sounds pompous or sentimental. There is no way out: if you don't use the word "soul" you avoid the basic issue of psychology; use it too often and it becomes embarrassing.

Soul is and remains a mystery. What is it? Where is it? How is it? We cannot catch it, we cannot locate it; soul is everywhere and nowhere. Because of its elusiveness, we have to experience and recognize soul mainly through projection. Projecting the soul enables us to deal with it.

Throughout history soul has been projected onto many things, human and non-human. Sexuality—as an act and the fantasies about it—is a great projection carrier for soul. The development and individuation of soul are lived in and symbolized by sexuality.

Although I said that soul is elusive, let me assign the soul a few characteristics, acknowledging that these characteristics are arbitrary and subjective. First: secrecy. Wherever soul appears, there is secrecy, a secrecy that is expressed through many symbols. Initiation rituals designed to connect to soul are shrouded in secrecy. The soul is often depicted as a hidden treasure in the woods, guarded by dragons in caves, etc. Second: fascination. Being concerned with one's soul is not just a pastime; it is an obsession, a passion. Finding one's soul is the greatest aim in life; losing it the greatest calamity. Third: strength and energy. The loss of soul results in weakness, while being in touch with soul produces boundless energy.

After this arbitrary enumeration of some qualities of the soul, consider sexuality, a main projection carrier of soul.

Even today most people keep sexual matters secret. Few would ever make love in public. Although we now talk more about our sexual lives, this often means only that we lie more about it. Hardly anybody tells the 'truth' about his sexual life. Yet, from the socalled natural point of view, there is no need for secrecy in sexuality. As a tool of relationship or pure pleasure, sexuality could be lived out openly, publicly. Why not tell everyone about it? The secrecy connected with sexuality appears to be unnatural and irrational. It comes from the soul projection on sexuality.

To mention that many experience sexuality in an obsessive compulsive way is almost redundant. At times in their lives almost everyone fails to contain sexuality, and is driven to live it out, or is at least obsessed by sexual fantasies. The third characteristic of soul, strength and energy, so closely connects to soul that one of the greatest psychologists ever, Sigmund Freud, equated sexuality with psychic energy. He confused the projection carrier of soul with the thing itself.

Now my thesis: *money, also, is a main projection carrier for soul.* As with sexuality, so are secrecy, obsession, and energy qualities of money.

While the secrecy that cloaks money matters varies with each individual and culture, most people in the Western world conceal money matters one way or another. Often, we just lie. Like all tales about sexuality, stories about money fall short of the truth. The stories are a personal mythology. And as with sexuality, no objective reason offers itself as an explanation for such secrecy. What objective reason is there to hide our net worth, our yearly income from friends and enemies, and even our children?

Money also fascinates us, often in peculiar ways. We may imagine that the rich are different, and solely because they have more money. We then feel slightly inferior in the presence of rich people; many analysts have difficulty treating them. I know a colleague—his practice has a special parking space for clients—who starts sweating with anxiety each time he notices that a new patient drives a very expensive car!

Some people are over-thrifty and cannot part with their money despite a comfortable income and no financial worries. Interesting is a little experience which a wealthy friend of mine told me. He saw how a lady received a lot of small coins as change in a shop, making her purse feel rather heavy. When she left the shop, she threw the coins—worth perhaps two dollars—into the gutter because they were simply too heavy to carry. Deeply shocked, my friend *had* to pick up the coins. Throwing coins into the gutter just *is not done;* it would be the same as flushing sacramental wine down the toilet. This 'numinous' half-religious quality of money can be understood only as a projection. Money itself is a technical means of exchange, possessing no second nature, nothing 'numinous.'

That we connect money with the life-force is obvious. Old people who deny themselves every luxury, and complain bitterly about the price of heating, electricity, food, etc. sometimes leave large fortunes behind when they die. The awareness that life or energy is running out leads them to compensate by piling up money, that is, energy.

Although economists often assume the profit motive to be a fundamental drive animating human behavior, we psychologists know that few people, especially the successful ones, really work for money. For instance I know a very successful paint manufacturer who believes that he works to make lots of money. And yet when you talk to him longer than ten minutes, you see that what actually fascinates him is paint, the different colors and their effect on people.

If you live in Zurich, it's almost impossible not to notice that strength and power are projected on money. Foreigners talk of the 'gnomes of Zurich.' They imagine Zurich bankers as all-powerful manipulators who control the economic ups and downs of the whole world. There was even an English minister who blamed the Swiss gnomes for the weakness of the pound! Yet these Zurich bankers are as helpless in trying to understand or manipulate the money market as we analysts sometimes are towards a highly psychotic patient.

Money is a tremendous projection carrier. Because money is so faceless, so neutral, we tend to project on it more easily. But because it is so important, we have great difficulty knowing where projections start and where money itself begins. Nearly everything can be projected on money: power, security, sexuality and, in some bizarre way, even reality. Some people think that money is *the reality*, the *real thing*.

We take transference and counter-transference in analysis very seriously, rightly so. The patient reveals himself by what he projects on the analyst and vice-versa. In these mutual projections soul appears. The Freudians say—or said—that the therapist should be a white screen on which the patient can project his whole psyche. However, we analysts are not white screens! The patient not only projects on us; what he sees and experiences with us is influenced by what we are.

Money, however, *is* a white screen. We all project onto money those particular qualities characteristic of our personal psyches. One question I want to ask is: Why do we not look at this screen more often? Only lately have I realized that a proper analysis must include an extensive contemplation of the patient's and analyst's projections onto money. I think that we are a little wary of this topic because it touches us as analysts too deeply. Not only the patient, but we too project our specific soul on faceless money.

As with all soul things, so much lying goes on between patient and analyst concerning money. Some patients complain of the hardship worked on them be the fee, yet are actually well off, while others pay so cheerfully that the analyst is later surprised to learn that the fee represents a great sacrifice. Despite our expectation that the patient be honest in everything—including money matters—we analysts often refuse to answer point-blank questions about our income, or we lie.

Of money in relationships: the give-and-take of money is, projectively, experienced repeatedly as the loss or gain of soul. Money often causes trouble between parents and their offspring. A thrity-year-old man spent his vacation regularly with wife and children at his parents' home, accepting his parents' hospitality without qualms. But when his father offered financial help so that the son could buy a house he wanted, the son refused. As a result he could not buy the house. The son was afraid of losing his independence, or, really, 'losing his soul' by taking money. Financial independence often means psychological independence. Money relationship is experienced as soul relationship.

So much can be seen in our connection to money: our kind of greed and generosity, the way we love and hate, what we fear and what we hope to achieve in life. Psycho-pathologists know that psychotic depression often has a link to money. A very rich man who becomes depressively psychotic thinks he will soon starve to death because his money will not last. This is, of couse, an extreme. More interesting and more important in our daily practices are the subtle projections we all have on money.

What about: "Money is the root of all evil"?

For so many people, money is evil, nasty, destructive. Rich people are bad. Money corrupts. You all know the saying in the New Testament: "It is easier for a camel to pass through the eye of a needle than for a rich man to enter the kingdom of Heaven." Christianity has always deemed money as something essentially evil.

The same is true about sexuality. Christianity has every reason to consider money and sexuality as evil because *sexuality and money are the two great projection carriers for soul*. As I said: most of us project our own soul on these two things, or at least one of them. In this way sexuality and money compete with religion. Christianity asks that you project your soul and its development, its individuation, on Jesus Christ. Worldly projections of our soul distract us from the Christian aim of salvation of our soul through Jesus Christ. To put it bluntly: the great competitors for the salvation of our soul through Jesus Christ are sexuality and money. Insofar as sexuality and money detract from salvation through Jesus Christ, they are evil.

The aim of analysis—as a cure or as a way of individuation, as soul-finding—cannot be to withdraw all our projections, but to become aware of them, and to live them out intensively. Our very lives—our individuation—consist in projecting our souls on sexuality, on money, on our partner, our children, our jobs, etc., and we individualize through these. The aim of analysis is not to hinder someone from falling in love, but to love more passionately with occasional reflection. The aim is to live our projections, hold on to them, while seeing that they are projections, that most of our deeds are only symbolic rituals.

Should we, when approaching the projections on money, try to eliminate them, withdraw them, or should we even foster them?

The answer is obvious: we should certainly not eliminate and destroy the soul projections we and our patients have on money. We should even foster them if the patient is inclined to do so. Projections of soul on money have advantages over other projections. What we experience through money, what we project on money, is so clearly a projection, a fact well-known, and deeply engraved on the collective psyche. Projections of soul on money are so easy to recognize—much easier than projections of soul on relationships or art. In some ways it is desirable that we project our soul on money.

In a somewhat twisted variation of the biblical saying about the rich man, I would say that a man or woman who can project his soul on money has as good a chance as anyone of going to heaven.

(reprinted from SOUL AND MONEY, pp. 83—89, Spring Publications Dallas: 1982, by permission)

FOOD, DRINK, AND FEAST

Of Cookery

By Geneviève Guy-Gillet (Paris)

In choosing the theme of cookery in analysis, I first of all had to ask myself what I was going to put into the cooking pot, because so many questions sprang up as I want further and further into the subject; but, on looking carefully at the analytical routes taken by those who, at one time or another, had had recourse to cookery, either contretely, or through symbolic representations, I saw these self-same questions transform themselves into hypotheses on the importance and meaning of this mode of expression. These are the ones about which I am going to speak, organising them around the following proposition:

Because cookery uses food, it touches upon what is vital for man; however, it is also a cultural phenomenon and so brings into play the very complex communication systems which make up society.

This movement which flows between the individual and the collectivity is familiar to all of us Jungians, so much so that it seemed natural to me to take analytical practice as my point of departure. But, we are all aware that analytic practice takes strength from theoretical concepts, whether these be Jungian or not, such as the theory of impulses and here I am thinking especially of various outcomes of oral impulses, including even cannibalism. I shall, therefore, refer to these explanatory models in passing, as well as to some works which will lend weight to my arguments.

I have, however, chosen to give preference to the image, to let this unfold before you, setting the meal out from its source, what is acted out during the analytical session.

But, let us go into our kitchen: what is happening in there awakens in us the familiar echos of our daily life; then, if we go further, we see that our culinary preparations will arouse that deep layer which is the very stuff of our existence and into which, throughout the ages, man has delved to invent his recipes. So, on the one hand we are touching upon the need expressed by the phrase "we have to eat to live"—and we do perceive something of this basic need in some patients—and on the other, we touch upon the sophistication of cookery. The art of preparing food confronts us with other questions than simply the need to survive. Why, for example, do dreams insist that a dish of meat be boiled rather than grilled, or offer rotting, inedible food, or inappropriate dishes, like a cat roasting on a spit rather than a rabbit or a chicken?

One day, when one of my patients came to me with a dream where he was stirring a sauce, I asked him what cookery meant to him. He replied "cookery is coming up with the right mixtures. You have to know how much is needed and feel what should be put with what". This definition, which appeared to me very promising so far as the culinary talents of this young man were concerned, seemed to pose the right question so far as the cookery of analysis is concerned: that of the relationship of the elements put together and of their respective place on which the end product "the right mixture" will depend. Quite rightly, this process awakens in us Jungian ideas of conjunction, because we will see how, using a metaphor of opposites, raw and cooked, sweet and sour, solid and liquid, etc., the fundamental problems of the Self come into play, making the unconscious dictate the use of one ingredient rather than another and one method of cooking rather than another. We know that everything that can be eaten has undergone a long and slow evolution which gives us material and symbolic information about our lives and that our whole being participates in the process of transforming the food which works in our bodies. In fact, do not words reflect these movements, enchancing and projecting them in related acts where we "devour someone with one's eyes", "keep the political pot boiling", or "eat our way through books"? The mental images which these conjure up make tangible that secret alchemy which causes the metamorphosis of our body from the real to the symbolic. However, this message has to be understood if man is to have any inkling of his own reality.

It is yet again with cookery that the individual can test what differentiates him from and makes him consubstantial with the world and also what gives him a certain culture. As Claude Levi-Strauss[1] writes in *L'origine des manières de table,* "Cookery is a language in which each society unconsciously translates its structure, unless without knowing more, it resigns itself to unveiling its contradictions".

I am first of all going to speak of the importance of this collective language in the personal history of a patient and of the rôle that this played in the analysis of a young Japanese. This young man, a student of foreign languages, left his country at the age of twenty to come to France to improve his French. He had been there for eight years and had married a French woman. Apparently happy, something distressed him enough, however, for him to come and try to understand the meaning of it through analysis. We understood very quickly that his Japanese soul was suffocating and demanding to be revived. He, who was very satisfied with French cuisine, discovered that he was hungry for Japanese food. He looked for restaurants where he could eat this type of food, then, because that was expensive, started to cook Japanese food himself more and more often. He began to feel better and found pleasure in life again. Moreover, this food which linked him symbolically with his birthplace gave us access to his childhood and to his personal conflicts; he was able to face up to the despotism of parental and collective images and also to talk freely of the beauty. of his own country, whose poetical force he rediscovered with emotion. Then, to his great surprise, because he did not think of himself as at all religious, his dreams started to plunge him into the great images of the Shintoist religion.

However, he still felt a little ill at ease: "He felt like someone wearing a suit that didn't fit". It was then that he was invited to take part in a tea ceremony organised by his compatriots. He went out of curiosity and without conscious desire to be there, but he had a startling experience: "Suddenly" he told me "the world around me disappeard. I was alone, the bowl of tea in my hands, invaded by an extraordinary emotion which, at the same time, filled me with strength. For the first time, I felt I existed as a person".

By reactivating the collective structures of his original culture, expressed first of all for him in food and culinary arts, this man was able once more to harmonise his past, from which he thought he had cut himself off completely, with his present life in the West. This restored cohesion helped us in the transfer of the source of energy which enabled him to recall the image of his mother who had died when he was ten, to recognise feelings of guilt and aggression resulting from his separation from his family and to face up to these facts without losing sight of his new autonomy. Finally, the experience during the tea ceremony where he made the discovery of himself as a singular person, seemed to have been a decisive step in this process.

But, to pursue my thoughts on what is cooking in our sessions of analysis, and to go deeper into its meaning, I will now consider the elements which go into the composition of the culinary substance: that which feeds man and of which he has need if he is to live. And, speaking of life, I will speak of death. "Man" writes Mircea Eliade in his "Histoire des croyances et des idées religieuses",[2] "is the final outcome of a decision taken at the beginning of time, that of killing to live". Necessary decision but so laden with horror that, in order to bear it, men began to make it into the basis for sacrificial rites and a relationship to the sacred traces of which still remain today.

I have chosen the clinical case of a little girl to introduce us to this history of man. Her beginnings in life had been hard, and she retained a certain difficulty in coping with life. She came to me both sad and morbid. During our sessions, she told me about her nightmares which always had a background of violence: she saw, among other things, her mother grievously wounded and covered in blood.

One day, she started to model some small objects with plasticine—some animals and a person, which she grouped in three scenes. Here is what she told me: "It's night, the man is a butcher who has gone out to look for sheep and goats. He is going to kill them with his big knife and cut them into pieces. Now, it isn't night any more: it's day, the man has changed into a baker who is selling bread. And, here I am, I'm making pancakes".

We can observe that the personal cookery of the litle girl—pancakes—a food she knew how to make, was the outcome of the two earlier events, linked by a unique person who had materialised them in the sequence of night and day: first he is the butcher, sacrificer of meat by night, and then he is the bread-maker, baker of bread by day. Now, this fantasy startlingly presents us in close association the two primordial elements which have served as the basis of man's nourishment: meat and grain.

Let us go further into the history of these two aliments. The feeding patterns of prehistoric man who preceded the organization of the first communities of *homo sapiens* are little known to us: to the picking of plants, the gathering of berries, and the capture of insects, was little by little added the consumption of raw animal flesh. This was a turning point, which perhaps led to the onset of the establishment of the first communities out of the necessity for individuals who wanted meat to form groups to hunt and then to share their quarry. Out of this development, feeding habits were established, and the discovery of fire changed these into culinary practice. But, continually differentiating himself from wild animals, man asked himself more and more about his own limits. If culinary access to the animal world was the first milestone, another landmark became necessary to express the incomprehension and mystery which accompanied the awakening of his consciousness to the vulnerability of animal life.

This is why, as a pendant to the world of animals, the world of spirits and gods developed. In killing to live, man had also discovered his own precariousness and the perishable side to living matter. But, he could only accept this law if a counterpart state existed which could go beyond this limit, and it was the gods that he asked to fulfil this life outside the ephemeral.

Established within immortality, these gods owed it to themselves to consume food which was radically different from that eaten by human beings destined to uphold life, but powerless to preserve from death. Having thus situated himself between these two worlds, the animal and the gods, man marked this division by his sacrificial acts which bore witness also to his renunciation of being part of either of them.

To illustrate the stages of sudden awareness drawn from the alimentary mode, I am going to turn to ancient Greece. My ideas are drawn from the book by Marcel Détienne and Jean-Pierre Vernant, *La cuisine du sacrifice en pays grec*[3]. Once again, we find the butcher and the baker who, before becoming the simple purveyors of meat and bread that we know, served as intermediaries between animals, gods, and men, so that life and death were symbolically interchanged and a network of links was woven between living matter and the unknown which prolongs life. We will see later, after having made this detour to ancient Greece, what echoes were perceived by the little girl in our story.

So, let us go back in time to the epoch when it was the poets who talked about cookery, where men and gods held friendly intercourse, sharing their food at the altar. The two primeval foodstuffs were meat and bread, by which man established himself in his human specificity. These did not obey the same laws of distribution, but both were linked to the gods, who seemed thus to negotiate their right to exist with men.

As for the corn whose cultivation produced the first bread, this appeared as the pendant of the sacrificial victim. Zeus's reply to the ruse of Prometheus, whereby, at the expense of the gods, he hid destined for man the best morsels under the skin of an animal, was to hide the corn under the earth and oblige man to work to extract it.

If we consider meat, we see that, for the Greeks, all meat eaten had to be the flesh of an animal that had been ritually slaughtered, with one portion supplying food for the gods and the other food for man. To mark the continuity of meaning wrought in this communal act here was, at first, only one name used to designate the butcher who spilled the blood of the beast, that of sacrificer. The sacrificer was responsible for relations with the sacred being as well as with the cook who roasted the meat. Offer, prepare, eat: this was the sequence. That established man in an orderly alliance with the rulers of the cosmos.

Let us note that the victim of the sacrifice was never chosen from wild animals killed during the hunt, but always from among domestic ones, and among these the ox occupied a privileged place. Was he not the one who, attached to the cart, opened up the earth for the grain, that would produce the ear of corn, the central symbol of man's existence, gift of the great goddess Demeter?

The Greek word "bios", which designated the ear of corn, reminded man that the life he was drawing upon was woven from the same elements as those of all living matter. It was out of this corn that man one day made bread, finding in this food obtained by cooking, the sign and the guarantee of civilisation, a final assurance of the difference from the food of beasts and that made sacred by the connection to the gods. Nevertheless, even the peace ensured by corn must be subjected to the sacrificial act, because the bread of civilised man cannot wipe out the memory of blood spilled so that he might live. This is why a victim had to be offered and eaten according to the rites which would ensure the validity of the sacrifice; so that the corn would not be tainted with original sin. If man was to eat his bread in broad daylight, then the act of death has to be perpetuated within the mystery of sacred ceremonies.

The act of violence had, therefore, to remain secret. Feelings of guilt arising from the killing of a living creature are not however sufficient to explain the precautions with which the sacrificers surrounded themselves. Tales of olden times and the studies of ancient Greek myths have a background in what was being enacted in the relationships between the sexes and in their confrontations of power. It was the male's function to slaughter and spill blood, but the victim simulates another body which bleeds. Aristotle makes the parallel explicit in his *History of Animals,* when he observes that the menstrual blood which springs forth at puberty runs like "that of an animal whose throat has just been cut".

It is doubtless because of this background that the violence of the sacrifice had to be jealously guarded and controlled by men and the reason why woman had to be denied admittance. What retaliatory measures might she not have taken once the sacrificial knife was in her hand? Indeed, the tales of castration as a punishment inflicted on men who had dared to look at the priestesses performing their sacrificial rites illustrate quite well the dangers from which men had to protect themselves. We can also point to the latent power stuggle between man and woman which the strict observance of roles has never wiped out: This fight for supremacy might well have exploded if this secret violence had be revealed. Finally, we have to respect the ultimate meaning protected by the mystery at the altar, where fertility and death could meet and cross. For the one, as for the other, for man as for woman, the blood which flows should remain hidden.

Now, we will take leave of our Greeks and go back to the little girl I treated, the one who in fantasy made the butcher live again at night and the baker in the day. And, first of all, because she told me the story during a session of analysis, I am going to approach her fantasy in terms of its appearance within the transference. Here, we had a two-sided personage, slaughterer of animals and baker of bread, modelled in plasticine for the two of us. In organising this scene, the little girl clearly intimated that she had to meet the violence of the man with the knife before being able to accept the gift of the baker. Here, the night preceded the day, and it was within the sombre mystery of the body's transformations that the first act occurred. But, because the personal history of this child had been marked by early sufferings, the ritual sacrifice which symbolically opens the way to fertility, refers to a body cut into small pieces.

What the little girl was telling me were her fears of an unknown force working within her, to make her emerge from her childhood and in that way steal her animal innocence. How she detested the violence and the sight of bloodshed, which reactivated the nightmares where she saw her wounded mother. These nightmares she had first of all associated with the sexual relations of her parents, whose echoes sometimes reached her through the partition dividing her room and theirs; she fantasized these sounds as reflecting the woman's murder. But, I felt that, over the above the associated images, the danger to the mother expressed in the dreams also expresses the suffering that had been caused by separation from her mother in early childhood.

Why then did she not counterbalance the presence of the threatening male, the nocturnal messenger, with that of a woman, to represent a nourishing diurnal version of the personage, that of the corn so early associated with the mother-figure? Perhaps I should see in her choice of a man the love that this child had for her father, who played a major role at this time in her life.

Despite my maternal ability to welcome her expression of fears, and the confidence in that ability and love for it which she showed by sharing them with me, I had to see that the woman in her was trusting the capacity of my masculine side to support this double figure of man which had revealed itself to her. To accompany the unconscious images through which she was looking to fulfil this part of herself, I had to become the butcher who chased animals to kill them and the baker who prepared bread. At the same time, I had to know the fear of hunted animals and feel pangs of hunger for bread.

I know now that, with the apperance of these images on that day, both of us had met Pan chasing the nymph. Because he appeared at the moment of transference when we could live this experience together, we were able to receive his message of life, to which the way in which the little girl made pancakes bore witness. Why pancakes? Traditionally, in France, pancakes mark certain cultural moments: we toss them for the Candlemas, the *festa candelorum* which is a reminder of the Child Jesus' introduction to the Temple, yet we also make them for Mardi Gras, festival of freedom of impulse. In the past, in certain French provinces, a pancake was given to the hens at this period so that they would lay eggs; in other places, one was thrown onto the manure in order to ensure a good harvest. You can see that, in the analytical route about which I have just spoken, the little girl had many reasons to choose a method of cookery which has traditionally opened the way to fecundity.

This child's culinary moment was organised around meat and corn and orchestrated by a butcher, about whom we have learned something from the ancient Greeks. But, his presence in the analytical process is too frequent for us not to look more closely at him. Here, then is the encounter a woman of forty-five had with this figure and the dream where she lived it. "I was going to the butcher and I bought meatballs, three or four, I don't know. They were coerced in pastry or some similar type of thing which gave them a white colour when cooked in water (as for a stew)".

This woman, whose femininity was dominated by a very forceful animus, had recently felt outbursts of gentleness, and this dream helped her to talk about what she was discovering in herself. First of all, she commented on the method of cooking proposed: "Meatballs are a mixture of minced meat; covered in pastry they become softer, more unctuous. And, in boiling them, I plunge them into the water where they get a new colour, white, and a velvety quality that I don't get when frying them..." Then, she recounted how she had observed that her family felt she was "much more pleasant to live with". She noticed also that her elder children had, at the same time, begun to have sexual relationships and that she was amazed to find she felt an inward satisfaction about this. She ended the session by saying that she felt more of a "mother".

So, just as the little girl, at the awakening of her femininity, met the butcher, sacrificer of meat, the woman of whom I am now speaking demands of the person distributing the meat what she needs to nourish her femininity. This woman's butcher also brings two elements—flesh and corn—into play, but this time he advises, while conserving the contribution of the meat's pulsational energy, that the rawness be diminished by clothing it in pastry and cooking it in water. Following the recipe which her unconscious dictated, our dreamer discovered to her surprise that gentleness does not exclude force and that, in becoming more feminine, she also became more motherly.

Thus, in accepting the dialogue with this man-butcher, to whom Demeter lends a helping hand, the woman enters into relation with the deep-rooted inclinations of her own instinctual sphere, but the way in which she will use these will depend upon her own cookery. This is why, after having spoken of culinary traditions and the essential elements which make up the raw materials of cookery, I am going to go further into their preparation.

Cullinary art makes sage use of the raw and the cooked and knows, by varying the methods of cooking, how to obtain the most diverse flavours. But, in the know-how of those we analyse, we can observe that recourse to the cooking fire, as with the choice of ingredients, obeys mysterious laws. If the woman was cooking her meatballs by plunging them into boiling water, instead of frying them, it was, we have seen, to temper a fire which was too hot and to rediscover contact with the "humid" side of femininity.

Still on the subject of fire, I will cite another woman's dream in which her three-year old son burned himself taking cakes out of the oven which she herself had put in. There again, the associations which she was already able to make gave us a valuable understanding of the dream. But, let us try to reach the deeper layers, those upon which man has drawn throughout the ages to develop his culinary skills.

If I took you to ancient Greece earlier, I am now inviting you to follow those reflexions which Claude Levi-Strauss has drawn from the study of the culinary myths of South Amerian tribes. In his work *Le Cru et le Cuit*[4], the author shows us how, by cookery, man seeks to establish his place in the world, between the high and the low (the sun and the earth), trying to maintain a relationship with the three orders which compose it: the cosmological, the zoological and the cultural. In this constant search for harmony, the culinary fire which marks the passage from nature to the nurtured is the ally of man's civilizing traits.

These myths describe strange scenes of cookery which are devoted to inserting each step of the life of the tribe into the order of creation. According to circumstances of time and place, the ingredients and their utilisation will serve to nourish the order of the world. If, due to an error or a lack, a fault in the relationship appears, then its symbolic equivalent has to be called upon to restore the right balance of power.

The main myths studied also speak of incestuous relationship between the primordial elements, the sun and the earth and of the intermediary role of the cooking fire which regulates the right distance between the high and the low, the sun and the earth—providing, of course, that the appropriate rites are observed. In fact, two extreme positions of the pair of opposites, sun-earth, provide the conditions necessary for incest: on the one hand, when the conjunction of the two elements is too great, the world becomes "burned" as in the era of the canicular summers, generators of drought and fires; inversely, a total disjunction (as for example during eclipses) introduces to the "putrid world" each of them, excluding the mediation of the cooking fire which, let us remember, is a cultural act and is thus, in this way, opposed to incest.

What myths enact is not simply a cosmogony, recital of origins. The peoples creating them experience in their daily life that relationships and exchanges between individuals and their environment are part of the same mythic pattern. This is why this understanding of the place of the cooking fire in the balance of world values which Levi-Strauss proposes will perhaps help us to go deeper into the significance of "burned" which we mentioned earlier. In effect, the dream where the young boy burned himself on his mother's oven seems to us to illustrate very well the risk of incest when there is too strong a reconciliation of opposites which could degenerate into a fusional ralationship. In fact, disappointed in her affective relationship with her husband, the young woman who had the dream had transferred all her capacity for love onto her son. But, by hiding from sight the third term of the oedipal triad, she ended the possibility of mediating the mother-son relationship. Her dream translates the danger of this situation by resorting to the same symbol as that of the language of the myth: the burn produced by the incestuous position.

Through these aspects of the analysis of two women of which I have just spoken, we can observe that the way in which the culinary symbols used by the unconscious were produced has revealed the location of a "lack" or a "too much" in the psychic organisation of the subject and the way in which she lives with another: not enough femininity translates itself into advice to plunge the preparation into a pot of water, and a too intense love for the son in the burning, warning of its consequences. It seemed interesting to me to compare this process with the steps used by the Indians who try, by appropriate culinary acts, to maintain the correct relationship between the orders of creation. But, for analysts, it is in the transference that these various positions are apprehended.

If, for example, in all the cases I have cited, we have assisted in the culinary preparations of those undergoing analysis, there are moments when they symbolically invite their analyst into their kitchen, or ask to be invited into his and to be fed by him, putting forward the need of having a more manifest presence of the "good breast". Then, it is the analyst so represented who is requested to regulate the correct distance between relationships, including the recognition of the incestuous position symbolically mediated here. I remember, amongst others, a man who showed a certain dislike of women, including obviously his analyst, thinking solely of the great men with whom he wished to identify. Then, one day he dreamed that I was cooking his favourite dish made of beans. This good food made accessible for him a transference where he could recognise and accept the differentiation between the sexes and their respective values.

Sometimes it is the analyst who is fed, as happened to me with a little boy who had found this an excellent method of compensating for a not very loving mother in real life; this is why he spent several sessions cooking all the dishes he liked best for me, painstakingly manufactured from plasticine, bits of string and pieces of paper.

But, I am now going to stop unfolding these culinary images before you and go back to my initial hypothesis of the relationship between the need and the way in which all the elements composing it are integrated.

So far as the need is concerned, we have seen that it has gone in search of oral compensations, but also of sexual identity, of exchange between the different orders within the universe, and a quest for the meaning of life. Man does not live by bread alone, but if he resorts to a nutritional metaphor, it is because he feels vitally concerned by this profound exigency of his growing awareness.

In the culinary experience, man learns that there is no life without death: to consume is first of all to destroy in order to appropriate strength and energy for oneself from the particular aliment—whether real or symbolic; and, embarking upon the cooking process is to agree to submit the elements to the proof of fire which is going to transform them.

We have also seen all that man's individual experience owes to his past, both personal and cultural. Cookery in analysis unfolds before us its recipes and its knacks which tend to give reality to this symbolic happening by which an individual is born within himself and within the relationship to another. We have seen that the right mixture and the successful union depend upon the correct ratio of opposites: the moment of the sign's reversing itself, the positive becoming negative and vice-versa is shown pertinently in the culinary process where one and all can see whether the food is properly cooked or if it is fresh or spoiled.

It is thus because of the sensations which link man to his body through the two masculine and feminine poles that a sense could emerge according to the probem and the interests present at that time. These also evolve for societies and to conclude I shoud like to remind us of two Greek words which, during Plato's time, meant meals taken together and which today signify meetings at which people speak. I am thinking of "symposium" which for the Greeks was a banquet and of "eranos" which meant a meeting of friends at one of their houses where one brought one's own share of food and drink.

In his use of these terms, today's man has separated the alimentary substance from them, keeping only the metaphor of experience shared with others; where, in abandoning the culinary support, exchange feeds itself upon words.

1 C. Lévi-Strauss: *L'origine des manières de table. Mythologiques. 3.* Plon, Paris, 1968.
2 M. Eliade: *Histoire des croyances et des idées religieuses.* Payot, Paris, 1976.
3 M. Detienne et J-P. Vernant: *La cuisine du sacrifice en pays grec,* Gallimard, 1979.
4 C. Lévi-Strauss: *Le cru et le cuit.* Mythologiques 1 Plon. Paris, 1964.

Nutrition, degenerative disease and man's archetypal producing and eating behavior

By John J. Giannini (Chicago)

In this article, I am proposing the following: that modern man in his production and use of food, needs to reconsider the diets of some primitive as well as some contemporary people who, like us, had or have reasonable access to nature's food sources; that Jung's concept of synchronicity provides a comprehensive spiritual, philosophical, natural and pragmatic basis for this reconsideration, because the reality of synchronicity, not as sudden, ephemeral meaningful coincidences but as an underlying, informing acausal connecting principle, establishes the most solid basis for total health; that to the extent man strays from this underlying order, he is subjected to a steady increase in degenerative disease, a breakdown of the entire spiritual, mental, emotional and physical human spectrum; that modern man's recovery of what I call the synchronistic attitude (which primitives consciously or unconsciously possessed and utilized) has accompanied and stimulated a conscious ecological sense based on a transcendent order of meaning that Jung calls the synchronistic principle; and that this attitude is the radical basis for the healing of degenerative disease.

The first step in making these connections is to get away from viewing synchronicity in terms of specific events, coincidental events in which psychic and physical meaning are momentarily shared. To be sure, Jung defined synchronicity in this way, when he wrote:

> Synchronicity...means the simultaneous occurrence of a certain psychic state with one or more external events which appear as meaningful parallels to the momentary subjective state—and, in certain cases, visa versa.[1]

However, Jung also defined synchronicity as "an acausal connecting principle."[2] When we move to the level of principle, we became concerned not with events but with a more permanent state of things and a more abiding subjective state of mind or attitude. This attitude consists essentially of a lasting consciousness of a potential, consistent relationship of meaning among things, a commonly shared underlying, universal order between psyche and body felt within each person. It also supposes the possibility of a grounding, unifying continuum between each individual and the nurturing environment, a potential ordered meaningful rationality joining subject and object, person and cosmos. As he admits, Jung's concept of a synchronicity principle is practically identical to many ancient ideas, such as the Tao, the Medieval *Unus Mundus*, Leibnitz's preestablished harmony, the Cosmic Christ, the Body of Christ, and the ancient idea of the sympathy of all things with man as microcosm.[3] The synchronicity principle, Jung repeatedly suggests, reactivates an ancient theory of "correspondentia," in which seemingly dissimilar things are held together by their deeper, analogical resonance.[4]

The work of physicists in postulating an acausal explanation to the behavior of matter, as, for example Sir James Jeans did for the breakdown of radium, or Niels Bohr did in finding an "argument" for correspondence between the particle and wave theories of matter, encouraged Jung to further explore the psychoid realm of the unconscious. In a 1934 letter to Paschal Jordon, he characterized synchronicity as a "parallelism in time" in contrast to a more restricted "parallelism of psychic phenomena."[5] In the latter, one time/space experience is conjoined with another or many time/space experiences through personal or archetypal amplifications; in the former, synchronistic unconscious, time and space themselves become in Jung's term, "elastic," and are transcended in their ordinarily measurable and causally related aspects.[6]

Moreover, in the synchronistic unconscious, writes Jung, it is probable"... that psyche and matter are two different aspects of one and the same thing" in which"... the non-psychic can behave like the psychic and visa versa, without there being any causal connection between them."[7] This level of the collective unconscious, while still concerned with archetypal phenomena as *psychic*, that is, "... concerned solely with ideas and images" *in* us, *in* the psyche, is now conceived as more encompassing as "psychoid," that is, going beyond an individual psyche and including matter.[8]

On this level, Jung writes

> You can never say with certainty whether what appears to be going on in the collective unconscious of a single individual is not also happening in other individuals or organisms or things or situations.[9]

One easily adds here: or in food, and in metabolic processes. The psychoid or synchronistic unconscious is more like an "atmosphere" also *outside* the psyche and permeating the individual and the environment. Jung wrote to Fritz Kunkel in 1946 in this regard:

> Your view that the collective unconscious surrounds us on all sides is in complete agreement with the way I explain it to my pupils. It is more like an atmosphere in which we live than something that is found *in* us. It is simply the unknown quantity in the world. Also it does not by any means behave merely psychologically; in

the cases of so-called synchronicity it proves to be a universal substrate present in the environment rather than a psychological premise.[10]

This "universal substrate in the environment" again alludes to the synchronistic principle, which Jung in his 1951 article acknowledges as pointing to "a wider conception of synchronicity" rather than "synchronicity narrowly understood," that is, "individual cases which cannot be repeated experimentally."[11] This wider concept includes "all 'acts of creation,' a priori factors such as the properties of natural numbers, the discontinuities of modern physics, etc."[12]

I want to point out here that such "acts of creation" include the food found or planted in the earth, its preparation, consumption-assimilation, as well as the attitudes we take to this entire process and behavior.

There are several overall points connecting synchronicity, modern man's escalating degree of degenerative disease, and dietary behavior that need to be stressed before we can examine specific instances of these connections.

1. A new attitude is available to us when we focus on synchronicity as a principle. I call it the synchronistic attitude, an attitude which is shaped not so much by particular coincidental events but rather by the potential general acausal orderedness and meaning which make these events possible. This attitude includes a sense of wonder and trust, a kind of spiritual sensitivity to the ecological reality that underlies phenomena. Thus the pervasive pattern in primitive societies and in the great religions to treat food as sacred, as sacramental.

2. The attitude includes an intuitive sensitivity to the depth of wisdom that is acquired when man consciously and reverently assimilates not only plants and animals but also light and color, air and water, the hidden energies and vibrations that connect all things, all levels of being.

3. The attitude takes for granted that man exists and grows in an organic, holistic, healthful unity with nature, the possibilities of which must be constantly, consciously plumbed and the ignoring of which—as we hope to show in the refined food industry and its consumers—produces a serious degeneration of physical and mental health.

4. The attitude assumes that the present egoistic concerns of man which have created this industrial and nutritional condition must be counteracted with responsible research and action.

5. The attitude also includes a balancing sense of detachment, a level of consciousness that the traditional spiritual literature calls pure awareness, that does not moralize about this massive ignorance about diet and nutrition. Rather it is compassionately committed to both understand and appreciate the advances of the food industry but is also equally committed to educate the industry and the consumer as to the implications for man's existence on earth of

the continued use of chemical fertilizers and insect sprays, the use of lead in canning, of additives in foods, of aluminium in cooking, of refined sugar, wheat and rice, to name only a few problem areas.

6. This attitude is committed to an intuitive approach as well as a scientific exploration of nutrition, that requires one to listen to the body's and mind's responses to the intake of food, to learn the patterns in food consumption, the harmonious interaction of all the forty plus nutrients. It is concerned, therefore, with timehonored spiritual traditions, such as the Ayurvedic medicinal science of India and the science of Macrobiotics that has its origins in the Taoist philosophy; it is also concerned with the developing contemporary science called Orthomolecular Psychiatry which, according to Linus Pauling, means the optimal provision and assimilation of all nutrients needed for the health of both mind and body.[13]

7. Finally this attitude assumes that one may avail onself of an archetypally and personally suited plan of food preparation and eating that can heal when one is diseased and that can support a creative, productive and healthful life meant to end synchronistically and not suicidally.

Let us now turn to the problem of degenerative disease in our time. The land-mark study—in my estimation and the estimation of some significant practitioners in nutritional treatment—of this contemporary problem was published in 1945. Its author, Dr. Weston Price, was a dentist and his important book in entitled *Nutrition and Physical Degeneration*. The book gives us a verbal and pictorial account of a world study undertaken in the thirties by Dr. Price in which he observed fourteen peoples throughout the world, all of whom were—at least in significant numbers—isolated from the attitudes, ideas and cultural practices of modern civilization. For example, he studied a mountain people in the Loetschental valley of Switzerland, and compared them with other nearby mountain groups. This was in 1931 and 1932. Over the following years, he studied the Gaelics in the outer and inner Hebrides; the Eskimos in Alaska; the American Indians in the western and northwestern United States, in Florida and in central Canada; the Lalanesians and Polynesians on eight different archipelagos of the Southern Pacific; tribes in Eastern and Central Africa, the Aborigines of Australia; Malayan tribes on the islands north of Australia; the Maoris of New Zealand; and the ancient civilizations and their descendants along the coast, in the mountains, and in the Amazon basin of Peru.[14]

In the Loetschental valley, Price found among the teeth of children between seven and sixteen years of age only 3.4 percent with decay.[15] Two out of three children had absolutely perfect teeth. Yet in neighboring valleys, the incidence of tooth decay was dramatically higher. Here there were 25.5 cavities per hundred teeth, or about six or seven decayed teeth in each child.[16] Though the way of life and surroundings of these valleys were very similar, in the latter valleys modern foods such as refined flour and sugar had become available.

Similar results were reported from the other areas that Dr. Price visited. When the tribes or people subsisted on their indigenous diet, they were practically free of dental caries; showed no facial deformities; lacked evidence of degenerative diseases; and had little incidence of birth defects.[17] One of the other striking findings was that all the fourteen dietaries, "as selected in accordance with *the accumulated wisdom of their race*,...were found to contain two to six times as high a factor of safety in the matter of body building material as the displacing (processed) foods."[18] In all these groups the displacing diets "were more or less highly refined sugars, refined flours, canned goods, vegetable fats and polished rice."[19] Immunity for each group varied. For the Swiss, high vitamin dairy products and entire rye bread, with meat about once a week and vegetables as available; for the Eskimos and Indians of Alaska, sea and land animal tissues, limited vegetables and very limited seeds; and so forth.[20]

According to Dr. Price, the immunity from disease was not just physical but also mental and spiritual. He writes in Chapter I: "Thinking is as biologic as is digestion and brain embryonic defects as biologic as are club feet."[21] From this psychophysical assumption, Price goes on to show the peaceful, non-violent qualities of the people who continued to subsist on their traditional diets. The Loetschental valley dwellers, for example, had neither physicians nor dentists, neither policemen nor jails; they had no need of them. The 2,000 inhabitants had superb physiques, and many had become Vatican Swiss guards.[22]

However, as each of these people began to be exposed to Western ways, especially the immediate impact of processed foods already enumerated, tooth decay immediately developed. More ominously, offspring's facial structures changed; that is, the jaw arch narrowed, the face elongated. Further the hips and chest also narrowed. Degenerative and communicable diseases—especially, at first, tuberculosis—began to multiply.[23]

Is it too far fetched to go on to correlate spiritual and cultural health on the one hand and their degeneration on the other to a choice between indigenous diets and modern processed-food diets? Not if we take seriously the underlying order discussed by Jung, the total ecological unity that that order implies. The loss of the traditional diet began at least to break down the psyche-body-nature continuum that is the characteristic of all integrally spiritual people. The Swiss, for example, prayed with deep devotion and thanksgiving for the superior butter and cheese made from cows who grazed near the snow line. Dr. Price said in general of the primitive racial stocks he had met throughout the world: "Fundamentally they are spiritual and have a devout reverence for an all-powerful, all-pervasive power which not only protects and provides for them, but accepts them as a part of that great encompassing soul if they obey Nature's laws."[24] Throughout his book, Price contrasts this picture with the already developing nightmare (in the middle forties during the Second World War) of our central cities, where the numbers of school dropouts, juvenile delinquents, functional illiterates and physically and mentally handicapped children were mounting.

One wonders how he would view the human condition in large American cities today!

Dr. Price also quoted Ernest T. Seton writing about the Spirit of the American Indian in *The Gospel of the Red Man:* "The culture and civilization of the White man are essentially material; his measure of success is, 'How much property have I acquired for myself?' The culture of the Red man is fundamentally spiritual; his measure of success is, 'How much service have I rendered my people?'[25] Paradoxically, the Red man, as all other spiritually oriented people, had a sane health history tradition.

Obviously, we moderns have some reassessing to do. Vast social, cultural and spiritual changes must take place in our lands; one of these changes must occur in nutrition, beginning with the fertilizing and raising, processing, storing and distributing of crops to the consumer. As analysts, however, trained to work with individuals, it is fitting that we consider first the healing possiblities in individuals in spite of general environmental problems. Here are a few:

(1) At SAFER Foundation where I work as a director of a rehabilitation program for ex-offenders, we have begun to research the relationship between nutrition and violence. We have collected data on mineral and metal levels of cooperating ghetto clients through hair analysis and also through a questionnaire that quickly pinpoints the possibility of a hypoglycemic or low-sugar condition. Tests of a first group of 50 showed 80 % with toxic metal levels. One client's hair analysis showed a high content of lead; he was also very nervous, practically unable to sit in a chair when the counselor talked to him. His doctor called him hypoglycemic. The counselor got him to cut out sweets in candy and pastries, to cut out coffe and tea, and he also helped him get a sense of a simple, inexpensive diet of grains, vegetables and fruit, and some needed vitamin supplements. In two weeks time he was a calm person, able to sit and carry on a normal conversation. For the first time in years, he talked intelligently, rationally, with his mother; he contracted with her that he would first attend our three-week orientation program and then obtain a job. He was able to pursue these goals and stay away from violence and crime. These kind of stories can be multiplied many times over in the orthomolecular literature, in which successes with such physical problems as asthma and arthritis as well as such emotional problems as depressive neurosis and schizophrenia have been cured or dramatically relieved.

(2) I recently became aware of three cases in which nutrition contributed to the healing of cancer victims. The first must remain anonymous. This is the story of a young woman from Oregon, who, after the onset of cancer, was

treated with laetrile, with some success; then, under a Naturopath, was put on megadoses of Vitamins A and C, and a diet of juices, vegetable salads, limited milk products, Vitamin 15, multiple B's, chlorophyll tablets, protein powder, yeast, Vitamin E, digestive enzymes, zinc, iodine and kelp. Strictly forbidden were all refined foods, preservatives, additives, artificial coloring, caffeine, alcohol, meat or fried foods. She said: "I felt like a walking health food store, which is better than a walking pharmacy." Incidentally all this happened against the wishes of her physicians. She is totally healed and has remained so for almost two years.

The second appeared in the March, 1980 issue of *Prevention Magazine*. Martin Brohman, a young married man, in his early thirties in 1975, had cancer in various organs of the body. He had read of Carl Simonton's approach to healing, which uses a state of meditation in which the patient visualizes the white cells of the body attacking the tumor to drive the cancer cells out of the body as a waste product. Brohman began the practice of this meditation. He also began to take cognizance of all of his life, giving gratitude for his wife and children, for his years on earth, and for his talents. He took particular care to pay attention to nature, becoming grateful for every moment of rain, of snow, of sunlight. He made a special point to reflect upon the food he ate. He thanked the food and asked it to do its most effective, harmonious work as it was transformed in his body tissues. He wrote: "I imagined that all the food I ate was 'energized,' making me healthier and healthier."[27] In a few months, he was healed; and remains so after five years.

The last case is of a doctor, Anthony Sattilaro, the president of Methodist General Hospital in Philadelphia.[28] He was in his 48th year in May, 1978 when he was found to be filled with cancer, in his skull, right shoulder, ribs, sternum, spine and prostate. His right testicle was removed, then a rib, then the second testicle; these parts and the prostate gland all showed malignancy. His fellow doctors estimated he had 18 months to live. Meanwhile, his father died of cancer. On the way back from the funeral, Doctor Sattilaro, despite the fact that he was in pain, did something that was completely out of character: he picked up two hitchhikers. He also blurted out his life story, that he had cancer. The young man next to him said that he didn't have to die, that he should visit a macrobiotic center, the Philadelphia East West Foundation. The doctor quite cynically visited the Foundation and even decided to begin a basic macrobiotic diet. This standard diet consists of 50 % cereal grains, 25 % cooked vegetables and 25 % supplementary foods such as miso soup, bean, tofu, seaweeds, fruit and fish. This was it, at least on the surface. He strayed from the diet once and ended in the hospital; he didn't stray again. "There was a great temptation to go off the diet," said Sattilaro. "Everything that I knew in terms of my Western training as a physician mitigated against pursuing this approach. And yet, what was happening was that I basically never felt better in my whole life and it had to be attributed to the way I was eating."[29] After a year, he stopped taking estrogen, against the advice of his fellow physicians. He felt the estrogen was holding back any further healing. He persisted. Four months later, at the 16th month mark, two before he was supposed to die, he was pronounced totally clean of any cancer in all of his organs.[30]

Like the simpler-living, traditional societies that Weston Price had studied, who had regained health when they returned to their respective basic diet, these people from the American states of Illinois, Oregon, and Pennsylvania, had returned to a fundamental diet rather typical of the temperate zone in the Americas.

And as with Price's fourteen peoples, something more had happened to these individuals. They had at the same time, found another connection with the inner pulse of our existence, the ecological web of health, wholeness and holiness that has been variously called The Great Spirit, the Providence of God, the Body of Christ, the Great Tao. Jung called it the synchronicity principle; and in turn, Dr. Jean Bolen calls it The Tao of Psychology. It is, however, more than this: it is the Way or Tao of All Existence; following it, human beings find harmony not just in synchronistic events and generally social situations, but specifically in their use and reverence for food. This is the overarching philosophy of Macrobiotics, which is really only an extension of Taoism, which looks at all manifestations of life from the most universal in time and space, like the movement of the planets, to the most particular and concrete, like the intake and attitude toward food.[31] According to Taoist precepts, all things are ruled by the antagonistic and complementary principles of the Yin and Yang. The term, "macrobiotics" is derived from the Greek terms, "macro" for large or great, and "bios" for life. Macrobiotics is the way of life according to the largest possible view, the infinite order of the universe, and it has meant the way of longevity and rejuvenation. Joseph Needham (1900-) describes this in his book, *Science and Civilization of China* (Vol. 5, Part 2), as the "ancient art of health."[32] The fourteen peoples studied by Price had that art, that total outlook.

According to the practical view of macrobiotics, we are what we eat; we are the end product of our mother's blood and milk and of all the food we have consumed since infancy. However, "mother" in this context can acquire a spiritual, archetypal structure as well. Dr. Price, for example writes:

WHO WAS MY MOTHER? Was it that sweet soul who conceived me and gave me a physical birth? The land of my birth first claimed me and provided food and shelter; the church where my father was so active, sponsored controlling tenets for guiding my yound and wavering feet. Or is there a *force* back of all these that is *parent to them all?* As I go to remnants of ancient cultures I find that, though differing in color and size, they are all true to type and all disclose the same constant relation to variations in physical forms of their district. ...We have a common denominator for universes within and around each other, our world, our food and our life have potentials so vast that we can only observe directions, not goals. ... This driving power must have qualities like this universal but obscure atomic energy. ... LIFE IN ALL ITS FULLNESS IS THIS MOTHER NATURE OBEYED.[33]

We hear many echoes here of the psychological-ontological viewpoint of Jung, especially when we view the unconscious from the standpoint of the synchronistic principle and attitude: We have all sought to renew our life in the maternal womb of the collective unconscious, which we may now recognize as an atmosphere or One Psyche penetrating and encompassing all levels of personal being as well as all the relationships with the environment and world. Those connections, according to Jung, are mediated by the Yin and Yang principles, "found both in the unconscious and nature in the characteristic form of opposites, as the 'mother' and 'father' of everything that happens and they therefore form the *tertium comparationis* between the psychic innerworld and the physical outer world."[34]

Macrobiotics applies the Yin and the Yang principles to food selection in order to balance diet and assist the body in its efforts to maintain homeostasis. According to this view, all body systems are designed to adjust to changes in the external environment; examples are the acid-alkaline, glucose-insulin, sodium-potassium, oxygen-carbon dioxide, and sympathetic-parasympathetic systems. Half are Yin, half Yang. Foods too are Yin or Yang—that is, for example, are dominated respectively by centrifugal or centripetal force, by acid or alkaline, by sodium or potassium, so anyone can learn how to choose more Yin foods when the body condition is Yang, and more Yang food when the body condition is Yin. Thus, since most arthritis is considered a Yin disease, one must give up high acidic and potassium-laden foods, such as fruit, milk products, beef, etc.[35]

One of the most interesting archetypal ratios that comes out of the Macrobiotic literature is the ratio of seven to one. The forces of the sky and solar system impinging on the earth are seven to the one expanding force of the earth on the solar system. The ratio between head and body is seven to one. Therfore, "practically speaking, our consumption of the physical environment should be mineral to protein, 1:7; protein to carbohydrate, 1:7; carbohydrate to water, 1:7; water to air; 1:7 in their comparative weight."[36] Specififally with reference to foods,"...if we include animal meat, preferably a variety of fish and seafood, all vegetable quality food vs animal quality food should be in the ratio of less than 7:1. If one is vegetarian, the 7:1 ratio of complex carbohydrates vs protein is acceptable."[37] As the author Michio Kushi notes, variations from 10:1 to 5:1 are in range.[38]

The seven to one ratio is also beginning to appear in many modern nutritional and orthomolecular studies. Dr. D. C. Jarvis, in his well-known study of the Vermont Folk Medicine during the fifties, recommends that muscle meat be eaten only once a week. The rest of the week one should eat some fish, the organs of animals, fruit and vegetables. Intake of complex or natural carbohydrates dominates. I estimate that the ratio of carbohydrates to protein in this diet is approximately 5 to 1. Dr. Jarvis's diet is based on a careful study of the eating habits of the Vermonters and their grazing animals.[39]

Then there is the newer Pritikin program for diet and exercize. Pritikin writes:

> The average American diet runs to about 40 or 45 percent of total calories in fat, 15 to 20 percent in protein and 40 to 45 percent in (mostly refined) carbohydrates. The Pritikin Diet's fat level, on the other hand, runs from 5 to 10 percent, the protein from 10 to 15 percent and the carbohydrate (mostly complex and unrefined) to 80 percent.[40]

So a 7 to 1 or 6 to 1 ratio of carbohydrate to protein is established here too. And Pritikin's Longevity Institute claims success in healing or regressing many degenerative diseases such as Addison's disease, hypertension, diabetes, rheumatoid arthritis, and heart disease.[41]

Also, new worldwide research on heart disease may be pointing to a culprit other than cholesterol. Rather homocysteine, produced by an amino acid from animal protein, may be the chief cause, nutritionally, of heart disease. And homocysteine is rendered harmless by B6, found in all natural foods but often destroyed in processing and cooking. These heart specialists are recommending much more carbohydrate and vegetables and much less meat.[42] I am not trying to develop an argument for a vegetarian or even near vegetarian diet for people; the archetypal ratio is given as an example of a possible dietary norm for the temperate zone. And, I assume it is not mere chance that has established this norm, but the underling Tao which joins man and his environment.

Modern orthmolecular practitioners are rediscovering this norm that comes from the ancient traditions. In that tradition, correct food habits reportedly healed both body and mind. Yet, in spite of the ancient support, in spite of the growing evidence from contemporary practitioners, skepticism among laymen and the medical profession is still widespread as to the significance of diet in subduing degenerative diseases of both body and mind.

A leading orthomolecular physician, Dr. Michael Lessing, in his statement before the 1977 Senate Commitee on Nutrition and Human Need quoted Hippocrates, the Father of Medicine, who said to his medical students: "Let thy food be thy medicine and the medicine by the food." Lessing then noted that Moses Maimonides, the great philosopher and 12th century physician of the Sultan, said something similar: "No illness which can be treated by diet should be treated by any other means."[43] Recently, Roger Williams, a leading exponent of nutritional counseling and discoverer of pantothenic acid, reported a 1960 statement by Dr. Frank G. Boudreaux, an eminent New York physician, that"... nutrition, if really applied, would bring about a greater revolution in medicine than did the discovery that germs cause disease."[44] The evidence that this has been gradually happening and now accelerating enormously is now clear. In the 18th century, providing English sailors with oranges and limes healed them of scurvy. Not until 1932, however, was it learned what the sick sailors had lacked; it turned out to be ascorbic acid, or vitamin C. Now we know that Vitamin C helps one maintain cell tissue and overcome toxic conditions, often prevents the common cold, strengthens the adrenal gland, and is important in generally aiding in the prevention of degenerative diseases, including cancer. Linus Pauling has used it to extend the life of cancer victims.[45]

In 1951—1952 Abram Hoffer and associates reported that they had significantly improved the healing of schizophrenics with large doses of niacin, or B 3. Since then other Vitamins, the Bs generally, calcium, magnesium und Vitamin C, also have been reported as contributing to the healing of serious mental diseases.[46]

For decades Dr. Ben Feingold has been demonstrating, to the satisfaction of at least a significant number of fellow professionals and thousand upon thousands of parents and children, that up to 40% of children labeled hyperkinetic are so suffering because of synthetic food additives, such as colors, flavors and preservatives.[47] What is the hidden toll of such additives on all of us? It is estimated that, given the average diet, we take in up to 5 lbs. of additives a year.

Equally significant and related evidence is mounting that refined sugar and grains are creating a condition in millions called relative hypoglycemia, or low-blood sugar, and that the symptoms of what Hoffer calls this "Saccharine Disease" include all the classical neurotic ones and often psychotic ones. They include, says Hoffer, depression, insomnia, anxiety, irritability, crying spells, phobias, lack of concentration and confusion. Accompanying physical symptoms are: fatigue, sweating, rapid heartbeat, diminished appetite and chronic indigestion.[48]

Without doubt, one of the prevalent sources of the physical and mental breakdown of the peoples studied by Dr. Price was this relative hypoglycemic condition. To what extent are our patients, are we, affected by low blood sugar? It is sobering to reflect, in this regard, on the following statistics: from governmental sources, it has been determined that in 1822, each American consumed 2 teaspoons of sugar each day; and in 1980 the amount consumed is 38.[48]

Yet today, as Dr. Hoffer points out, relative hypoglycemia is uniformly rejected by the majority of physicians as a valid disease entity or even as the end result of a diagnostic laboratory test.[50] Further, the medical profession has almost unanimously rejected the orthomolecular practitioner's claim that a nutritional corrective is available for this low blood sugar condition, for its neurotic and psychotic effects on the mind and body.

Why do we find such widespread resistance to the claims of the orthomolecular practitioner? I recall how only three years ago I could not stomach the claims of some counselors and doctors in criminal justice that crime and violence could be reduced significantly through nutrition, that in fact, hypoglycemia was a significant factor in many crimes. Cirminal tendencies they maintained, could be considerably overcome by avoiding junk food and following a diet rich in complex carbohydrates, fruits, vegetables, as well as some animal sources of food.

However, as my interest and research in synchronicity developed, and as I grew in consciousness of the interconnected order of things, I could no longer ignore the possibilities of the above claims. I therefore would like to close with some formally Jungian arguments, as to how a respect for synchronicity as an acausal connecting principle may help us over came our resistances to recognizing the connections especially between mental health and nutrients. I want to do this by comparing nutritional science with Jung's psychology:

(1) In macrobiotics and in the developing orthomolecular practice, the basic assumption is that man is a unit, an integrated organism in which all parts function interdependently. Further, man is organically linked with his environment so that food, light, air and earth, all affect both the mind and body of man.

Synchronicity provides the broadest and deepest basis for this holistic view of health and healing. We are again reminded by Jung that in the psychoid unconscious or atmosphere, the "nonpsychic can behave like the psychic, and visa versa, without there being any causal connection between them."[51]

(2) More specifically, Jungians conceive of the psyche as made up of countless complexes, autonomous configurations of feelings, around which images, memories, ideas, and even bodily feelings and specific private or societal behaviors group themselves. Within a synchronistic perspective, a *psychic* complex such as the inferiority complex or the mother complex does not essentially differ from say, a *sugar* complex, a *drug* complex, or a particular *allergic* complex. All of the latter have specific emotional and behavioral components, as we have already pointed out.

(3) We say of a complex that to the extent it is unconscious it acts compulsively. In other words, we are *addicted* to its specific feelings, images, etc. Equally, the hypoglycemic condition and any related allergic condition are also addictive.[52]

(4) Again, Jungians ask analysands to watch out for the shadow projections as negative complexes; the faults they like to point out in others may well be revealing the shortcomings, the denials, the unspoken evil in their own psychic makeup. Nutritional counselors help clients look with suspicion on the foods to which they are consistently attracted as the usual sources of hypoglycemic and allergic reactions.[53]

(5) Healing in the Jungian view does not occur simply by exposing the

negative complexes of the shadow to the light of consciousness. At the core of the complex is the archetypal pattern, the formal, quasi-instinctual factor, with its deepening numinosity as consciousness plumbs the eternally reoccuring basic experiences of mankind. As Jungians have learned, the deeper the archetypal stratum, the scantier its basic design, but the greater its possibilities and its meaning. As we probe into the psychoid dimension, we reach the synchronistic stratum, in which subjective meaning is now caught up in a wider objective meaning, in which conscious knowledge is impregnated with intuitive knowledge in the psyche and also the absolute knowledge or rationality permeating all of nature. Healing, according to Jung, does not occur on the level of the problem. The problem does not disappear; rather he has "seen individuals simply outgrow a problem. ...Some higher or wider interest appeared on the patient's horizon and through this widening of his view the insoluble problem lost its urgency."[54] In an August 8th, 1945 letter, Jung wrote that his main interest was not the treatment of neurosis. He continued: "But the fact is the approach to the numinous *is* the real thing and inasmuch as you attain to the numinous experiences, you are released from the curse of pathology."[55]

In an analogous way, healing through nutrition does not occur simply by avoiding sugar or an allergen. Rather, it involves reestablishing one's conscious organismic connection with the earth through whole foods, through balanced diets, in which the essential nutrients, the carbohydrates, the fats, the proteins, minerals and vitamins are all present. In fact, there is considerable evidence that when this is done, most allergic responses no longer occur.

In the synchronistic vision, the process of reconciliation with any complex and archetype in the imaginal unconscious is inseparable from a reconciliation with mother nature as a whole. Ancient peoples unconsciously, or better, trusting in their all-pervasive sense that they were part of nature and its underlying Tao, developed sacred liturgical and dietary traditions that provided them maximum strength of body and mind. Their primitive intelligence, unaffected by modern man's egoistic hubris, had heeded an absolute law of existence, as succinctly stated by Francis Bacon four hundred years ago: "We command Nature only by obeying her." We need now to abide by this law consciously.

1. C. G. Jung, "Synchronicity: An Acuasal Connecting Principle," *The Structure and Dynamics of the Psyche,* CW 8 (Princeton, N. J.: Princeton University Press, 1960), p. 441.
2. Jung, p. 417, 452.
3. Jung, Section 3, "Forerunners of the Idea of Synchronicity," pp. 485–504.
4. Jung, P. 489.
5. C. G. Jung, *C. G. Jung Letters,* vol. I (Princeton, N. J.: Princeton University Press, 1973), pp. 177–78.

6. Jung, *C. G. Jung Letters*, pp. 177—78.
7. C. G. Jung, "On the Nature of the Psyche," *The Structure and Dynamics of the Psyche*, CW 8 (Princeton, N. J.: Princeton University Press, 1960), p. 215.
8. Jung, "On the Nature of the Psyche," pp. 215—16.
9. Jung, "Synchronicity," p. 481.
10. Jung, *C. G. Jung Letters*, p. 433. (Italics, Jung.)
11. Jung, "Synchronicity," p. 516.
12. Jung, "Synchronicity," p. 516.
13. Abram Hoffer, M. D. and Morton Walker, DPM, *Orthomolecular Nutrition (New Canaan*, Conn.: Keats Publishing Co., 1978), pp. 12—13.
14. Weston A. Price, D. D. S., *Nutrition and Physical Degeneration* (La Mesa, Calif.: Price-Pottenger Nutrition Foundation, Inc., P. O. Box 2614, La Mesa, CA, 92041, 1979, p. 1.
15. Price, p. 34.
16. Price, p. 38.
17. Price, pp. 493—94.
18. Price, p. 490 (my italics).
19. Price, p. 491.
20. Price, p. 490.
21. Price, p. 7.
22. Price, p. 24.
23. Price pp. 42—43, 49.
24. Price, p. 419.
25. Price, p. 419.
26. Martin Brofman, "Meditation Took Me Past Cancer," *Prevention Magazine*, March, 1980, Vol. 32:3, pp. 150—55.
27. Brofman, p. 155.
28. Tom Monte, "An M. D. Heals Himself of Cancer," *East West Journal*, March, 1980, Vol. 10:3, pp. 35—39.
29. Monte, p. 39.
30. See also Max Gerson, M. D., *A Cancer Therapy: Results of Fifty Cases* (New York: Dura Books, Inc., 1958), in which all of the reported cases were considered incurable by other physicians. Albert Schweitzer was moved to state that Dr. Max Gerson was "a medical genius who walked among us." In July, 1946, Dr. Gerson had the honor of demonstrating five restored cancer patients to the United States Senate's Pepper-Neely cancer sub-committee, the first such honor accorded a physician. However, this report and this book, not to speak of Gerson's method, has effectively been buried by the medical establishment (p. vi). In line with the thesis of this article, Gerson espoused a holistic approach (Chap. 2) and his healing diet stressed potassium-strong foods, such as vegetables and fruit (Chap. 3).
31. Michie Kushi, *The Book of Macrobiotics* (Tokyo, Japan: Japan Publications, Inc., 1977).
32. cited in Kushi, pp. 16—17.
33. Price, pp. 523—26 (italics, Price).
34. Jung, "Synchronicity," p. 452 (italica, Jung's).
35. Kushi, pp. 117, 122. Also see Collin Dong, M. D. and Jane Banks, *New Hope for the Arthritic* (New York: Ballantine Books, 1975).

36. Kushi, p. 31.
37. Kushi, pp. 41, 31.
38. Kushi, p. 31.
39. D. C. Jarvis, M. D., *Folk Medicine* (New Yolk: A Fawcett Crest Book, 1959).
40. Nathan Pritikin, *The Pritikin Program for Diet and Exercise* (New York: Grosset & Dunlap, 1979), p. 5. On p. xx, Pritikin points to a recommended diet issued by the McGovern Senate Select Commitee on Nutrition and Human Needs "that jibes very closely with the Pritikin Diet. ..."
41. Pritikin, pp. 375—80.
42. Jack J. Challem, "Step Aside, Cholesterol!" *Let's Live Magazine,* April, 1980, Vol. 48:4, pp. 26—30.
43. Michael Lessing, M. D., "Statement of Dr. Michael Lessing, Psychiatrist, Berkeley, Calif.," *Nutrition and Mental Health,* Hearing before the Select Committee on Nutrition and Human Needs of the United States Senate, June 22, 1977, Berkeley, Calif., Parker House, 1980 update, p. 13.
44. Dr. Roger J. Williams *The Wonderful World Within You* (New York: Bantam Books, 1980), p. 113.
45. Linus Pauling, Ph. D., "On Vitamin C and Cancer," *Executive Health,* Vol. XIII, No. 4 (January, 1977), Pickfair Building, Rancho Santa Fe, Calif., 92067. In a study of 100 patients with advanced cancer, each given usually 10 grams of Vitamin C per day, compared with 100 controls, 16 of the 100 in the experimental group lived more than one year, whereas only 3 of the 100 controls have lived that long.
46. Abram Hoffer, Ph. D., M. D. and Morton Walker, D. P. M., *Orthomolecular Nutrition* (New Canaan, Conn.: Leats Publishing inc., 1978), pp. 30—33.
47. Ben F. Feingold, M. D., *Why Your Child Is Hyperactive* (New York: Random House), 1975.
48. Hoffer, P. 45.
49. Alexander Schauss, *Diet, Crime and Delinquency* (Berkeley, Calif.: Parker House, 1980), pp. 19—20.
50. Hoffer, p. 44.
51. Jung, "On the Nature of the Psyche," p. 215.
52. Robert Forman, Ph. D., *How to Control Your Allergies* (New York: Larchmont Books), p. 67: "In the 1950's, [Theron] Randolph, based on the work of himself and Rinkel, called attention to the similarity between allergy and addiction. These doctors had observed that a patient who went without a frequently-eaten allergenic food for a period of time, ranging from a few hours to two or three days, usually felt worse from doing so, but could be generally relieved by eating that food again. ... Thus we have the paradoxcial fact that a person can make himself feel *better* by eating a food to which he is allergic when the allergy to that food has been masked by frequent consumption of it. ... Dr. Randolph has stated: 'I think of addictions and allergies as being synonyms.'"
Forman, p. 63.
54. C. G. Jung, "Commentary on the Secret of the Golden Flower," *Alchemical Studies,* CW 13 (Princeton, N. J.: Princeton University Press), pp. 14—15.
55. A. Jaffe, *C. G. Jung: Word and Image* (Princeton, N. J.: Princeton University Press, 1979), p. 123 (italics, Jung).

The concealed body language of anorexia nervosa

By Bani Shorter (London)

According to some stories, after the Medusa had been slain, Athene wore the severed head upon her breast. Over the shoulders of the goddess was slung the goatskin, the aegis, which represented both armour and authority. Either hanging from it like a trophy, or emblazoned upon the hide was the hideous head of the Gorgon encircled by writhing snakes. Later statues show the same moonshaped face engraved upon Athene's shield.

Thus defended, she advanced. Earliest Mycenean art, possibly including more archaic representations of Athene, shows an armed goddess nearly obscured by her enormous shield. But in those days there was no suggestion of the Gorgon's head. This was the plunder of a later time when the chthonic, stultifying power of the threatening earth spirit had been overcome. Perhaps the change from dangling trophy to etched symbol suggests a civilizing influence made possible by the perspective of distance from that encounter. Kerenyi saw in Athene's use of the emblem not only the moon-face of a winged deity (for such were the Gorgons) but also the motif of the head taken as booty and feminine mask.[1]

I have given this description because we can see the familiar syndrome of anorexia nervosa reflected in the image of Athene and, figuratively speaking, it is as a person holding the Gorgon shield that we meet an anorectic woman first of all. Characteristically, she appears in maiden form, advancing with tremendous authority and power, like a goddess, hidden behind a formidable defence, ready to attack, always on guard. And, as part of her protective armour, she presents a most distorted face, sign of conquest as well as mask of her real features.

A woman suffering from anorexia nervosa resists her natural mother, resists being a mother, and resists mothering. Her defence is expressed outwardly as defiant, wilful denial of the flesh, excessive drive, and almost superhuman striving. On the psychological level, she combines an inflation of omnipotence with a frustrating sense of not being able to live up to expectations. And, in physical terms, her rejection of motherhood manifests itself in amenorrhoea, and in an emaciation of the body that erases any trace of feminine contour; while, at the same time, she engages in ceaseless, wakeful activity.

It was armed with the Gorgon shield that Athene entered the Greek world. Zeus, the greatest of the gods, was her father, and Metis, her mother, was considered "the most knowing of all beings." Fearful that a child of Metis might prove to be even wiser than he, Zeus took the precaution of swallowing the mother when the child was still in her womb. Released at last, Athene sprang from the forehead of her father, fully armed. As woman, she was both martial maiden and maternal protector. Although disinclined to love and marriage, she became the resourceful companion of great men and was known as the guardian of heroes. She seems to have emerged at a threshold between two worlds or states of being, a transitional figure between mother and father realms.

In that dark period when the might of the earth goddess was overthrown, Athene appeared, radiant of bearing, a civilizing agent. But, first of all, she came as conqueror and protectress against the archaic, earthbound aspect of woman. She represented a new style of femininity and was able to hold her own against regressive tendencies. It is in this role that we hear her speak to the vengeful Furies, the crones whose static law she undoes:

> "I will bear with your anger. You are older. The years have taught you more, much more than I can know. But Zeus, I think, gave me some insight, too, that has its merits...
> Here in our homeland never cast the stones that wet our blood lust. Never waste our youth, inflaming them with the burning wine of strife. Never pluck the heart of the battle cock and plant it in our people...
> This is the life I offer, it is yours to take. Do great things, feel greatness, greatly honoured."[2]

These are strong, assertive words; yet Athene is more than a divine warrior and even her exercise of authority is persuasive. She curses civil strife and is the declared enemy of Ares, god of war. At home or abroad she deplores the onrush of battle, the savagery of armed conflict. To see her only as one who advances with the shield is to misread her message or to allow a part to speak for the whole.

Instead, as goddess of wisdom, Athene provides leadership which counsels, tempers and moulds outcomes. When there is tension, she supplies the clarifying insight needed for decision-making. She causes reflection in the moment, reflection that leads to prudent action. With these attributes she won the epithet *Glaukopis*, bright-eyed, and the sign of her presence was the owl, a bird that finds its way in the dark and sees all round.

Psychologically, Athene brings illuminating perception, the product of reflection in terms of long range and meaningful objectives. For her interests are on the side of applied consciousness. Hers is a civilizing influence. She pays attention to the outcome of the deed and in this way she both guides and relates to her favourites.

Perseus was one of these favourites. When he set out to slay the Medusa, Athene gave him a polished shield to use as mirror lest he be transfixed by sight of the Gorgon's features. Thus she destroyed the Medusa, by producing an instrument for reflection at the crucial moment, and, so, she acquired the trophy. The battle wasn't won either by brute force or calculated logic but by the insight which made possible immediate, inspired, and ennobling action. In classical Jungian terms, we might say that Athene facilitates reflection which attends upon effective realization of the self.

We see a distortion of this image in the syndrome of anorexia nervosa. Here the patient seems to have undertaken a self-conscious *opus contra naturam*, the realization of spirit by the destruction of matter; and the heroism of Athene, with all its possibilities for the discovery and fulfillment of meaning is subverted to a single purpose, that of conquest over the feminine body. The anorectic woman looks at her emaciated form but sees something different, a different reality; and, without reflection, she cannot make a wise or informed decision. Moreover, all that suggests companionship, warmth, involvement and caring appears disgusting and unclean to her. She applies herself to ritualised abstention and/or purgation and, as a consequence, becomes increasingly isolated. She detaches herself from meaningful relationship, whether that relationship is to herself, to someone else, to study or to work. So in this way she turns aside from the civilizing opportunities that Athene offers. Wisdom no longer counsels; body commands.

Probably no one archetypal image ever creates or cures an illness. Psychopathologies, like gods, act and interact, combine and recombine with infinite variations. But it is from the perspective of Athene that I would like to consider anorexia nervosa. Tor this illness, too, belongs to a threshold. Its onset most frequently coincides with adolescence. Like the appearance of Athene, it manifests itself at the intersection of two epochs in feminine life, two worlds, one characterised by the influence of woman and the other by the influence of man.

Before she reaches puberty, a girl expresses herself in conformity or nonconformity to an undifferentiated mother-father ideal. But with the coming of adolescence a change takes place. When she begins to menstruate, she who has been daughter becomes mother, ready and capable of receiving, bearing, giving birth and nurturing. At the same time, the destiny of her life, its direction and decision, confront her in a new way for she is also capable of being mistress, lover, and wife. She can attract, select, allow or reject relationships with men. She is a woman and her virginity is exposed. This is a moment that older and less sophisticated societies prepared for with initiation ceremonies and, by way of ritual, provided a tool, a language for expressing the passage of a changed being into a new world.

Now, in modern times, anorexia nervosa is on the increase. Is this because mothers no longer prepare their daughters to *be* women, wives, and mothers?

Is it that women are now presented with new opportunities and pressures for expressing their femininity in ways radically different from those of previous generations? Do we stand at a point somehow reminiscent of the transition occasioned by the slaying of the earth goddess and the advent of masculine consciousness? Or have we no fathers capable of giving birth to daughters who can play the role of transitional women?

For anorexia nervosa is a disturbance of a woman's being in the world as a woman, although it involves more than her overt sexuality. There are, in fact, a comparatively few cases of anorexia nervosa recorded in men when probably the reverse is true. It is possible that in these cases the primary disturbance is in a man's relationship to the anima and the role that Athene plays there. But amongst women the illness begins most frequently, as Hilde Bruch has observed and my own work suggests, with an unmet challenge and the nature of that challenge has to do with the loss of psychological virginity.[3] In *The Virgin Archetype* John Layard summarizes: "...the word *virgin* does not mean chastity but the reserve, the pregnancy of nature, free and uncontrolled, corresponding on the human plane to unmarried love, (and) in contrast to controlled nature, corresponding to married love."[4]

From my experience, if you listen to the fantasies of women who have suffered from anorexia nervosa, read their writings or receive their dreams—even if you do so long after the crisis of adolescence has passed—it is impossible not to be impressed by the strong impact of the threshold of adolescence upon their continuing self-image. For example, when she was in hospital, a young woman of seventeen wrote of herself, describing how it had been a few years earlier:

> Love exchanged its bonds for shackles of obligation and I submitted and suppressed myself to the figures who sweated obscenities and grabbed out for what they wanted, never noticing their dirty hands."

And, one of the most telling biographies was shared with me by a person now in her forties, mother of three. It ended with the following: "Ever since I was a teenager I have felt like I had to win. Winning implies competition. I have been competing against myself. The self that wore the armour has been competing against the other self that is me."

Traditionally, both in diagnoses and in treatment, the nature of the triggering challenge for anorexia nervosa has been seen as the demand for a girl to become a woman, lover, wife and mother. But there is a somewhat moralistic tone in the way doctors have written about their anorectic patients. In 1903 Janet perceptively described a case of "mental anorexia" but suggested that the illness showed the patient's *refusal* to play a feminine sexual role. Freud defined the disease as "melancholia of the sexually immature." What has not been acknowledged and what the image of Athene suggests, is that in these women an archetypal image has been activated that prompts them to live out a sexual role which is a different one from that of the prevailing cultural expectation.

In my own work I was alerted to this possibility by the way anorectic women first spoke of themselves, by their pictures and by their dreams. With hindsight I now see more in the latent symbolism than I recognised initially. But what struck me forcefully was the strong influence of the father upon the lives of the daughters who came for therapy.

From the outset, the image of the father occupied a position of exaggerated importance in the psychic life of these women. One decribed her father as a forbidding judge who beat his child without mercy when she failed to come up to his expectations. I heard another speak of her father as a rapist and paedophile, a man who seduced little girls into mountain huts or dark cellars. Others portrayed their fathers in glowing terms and described a similar saintly figure, a spiritual leader of extraordinary patience and forbearance. He was presented as a potential head of state, an arbitrator and conciliator and conciliator among nations. Yet others saw the fathers as a misunderstood genius whose talents were unrecognised either by hs family or his colleagues. He could be a ne'er-do-well and a failure in the eyes of society, but the same man would be a father of awesome and dramatic significance for his anorectic daughter. And the father figures who appeared in dreams were especially powerful. They included Alexander the Great, leaders of mountain climbing expeditions, conductors of great symphonies, wardens of concentration camps, mystics, and liege lords.

These women also defined themselves in father terms. Their aspirations and motivations had a masculine character. Some could even admit to wishing that they had been born men rather than women; though there was seldom much of the tomboy or the homosexual about them. But they emulated men and, if married, wanted to walk alongside (rather than sleep with) their husbands. I heard a man describe his anorectic wife as the only woman he knew who had borne three children and remained a virgin; she referred to these same children as her husband's rather than her own.

Such expressions have led me to examine the nature of the incestuous link between anorectic daughters and their fathers. The actual father's attitudes and his behaviour appear to be determinative in the way the daughter considers and conducts her life. Sexualy, these women hold themselves aloof and chaste, but psychologically they are bonded to the father image, and the strength of that unacknowledged incestuous bond is of such proportion that it compels them to adopt a sacrificial attitude of spirit, a purity of body, and an abstinence from involvement with intercourse and childbearing. The anorectic woman is relentlessly committed to holding a special and favoured place in relation to man, although her role may be closer to that of the priestess than the paramour; and with her allegiance, her devoted ritual ablutions, her striving, and her loyalty, she tries to assure herself of recognition in man's hierarchy of values. Analytically, we see this as a primary disturbance of the animus, both in its activation and expression.

Again and again, anorexia nervosa has been called *wrong thinking*. From the time it was first written about by an English physician in the seventeenth century, it has been described as an illness of the mind that affects the body.[5] Doctors, psychiatrists, and religious leaders, no less than family members, have been confounded and distressed by the tenacity of a conviction that compels a wanton wasting away of the flesh. The behaviour of the anorectic woman has been labelled illogical and the patient's attitude interpreted as stubborn. The emphasis on "wrong thinking" still persists in diagnosis and therapy even if the focus has been shifted from mind to behaviour and from individual to family. And, although elaborate attention has been given to psychoanalytic investigations, almost no one has tried to piece together the coherence of a story that is being told from within the recesses of the patient's own psyche.

The notable exception to this, of course, is the celebrated "Case of Ellen West" by Ludwig Binswanger. It is a case which corroborates much of my own thesis, although undertaken initially from a very different point of view, that of psychiatry, and it has been presented as an example of existential analysis. Significantly, however, that case begins with the sentence, "Ellen West, a non-Swiss, is the only daughter of a Jewish father for whom her love and veneration know no bounds."[6] This was an observation that, unfortunately, I feel, Binswanger did not follow up.

Trying to unravel the story I was being told by my patients from within, I found that at the beginning of treatment both patients and I were struggling with the language in which their innermost selves were striving to communicate. For these women seemed to have little contact with the reality of psyche as such; its place had been usurped by the flesh of their misshapen bodies. The fleshly figure dominated their lives, and what I was trying to do was to hold a mirror to an image they couldn't see. Yet, out of the basic discrepancy between what the analysand was telling herself and what was being enacted before my eyes, a pattern of certain well-marked characteristics emerged.

I found that the image for a woman suffering from anorexia nervosa is one in which, by way of the flesh, her soul has been sacrificed to the patriarchal spirit; and, at another level, fantasy is held captive by a chaste and celibate marriage of image and symptom. She is incapable of imagining that she can be other than she is and, so, is caught on a psychological threshold which cannot be crossed. As a woman, she finds it impossible to step through the adolescent barrier of mystery and fear to a place where experience can become realized as a new world; and, because of her terror, she takes refuge in identification with her aggressor. This means that she is fixed at a point of entry, remains always on a border, somehow suspended and playing out a role for which she has no natural talent. It is an arrested image, starved of individual significance.

The summation of what I observed can be expressed in clinical terms as the fixation of delusion. In personal terms it is a failed initiation which results in a paralyzing state of ineffectiveness. From another point of view, the anorectic woman is Athene swallowed and not yet born. Analytically, this manifests itself as a state of possession in which the animus has usurped control of the personality.

Writing about this dark consequence in mythological terms, Kerenyi says:

"It is to the father, then, that the daughter falls victim in this mythic region ... he allows her to descend into the darkness. And it is the daughter who offers the sacrifice: *she* descends into a paternal-masculine darkness ... the strange image of the devoured wife of Zeus (Metis) also corresponds to a purely human situation; the binding of the daughter to the father out of which the patriarchal order of the family, as opposed to the matriarchal, could most easily arise ... That to which one succumbs and falls defenselessly always has a lethal aspect, the more so here where the masculine appears not *graciously* and paternally but aggressively, like the father in (this) father-daughter mythologem (which) lies at the foundation of the Athene religion."[7]

The result of such a sacrifice is that a woman lives her life onesidedly in terms of a masculine principle and the onesidedness reveals only the active conscious part of her being. Such a woman becomes a "man-woman", as one lover of an anorectic girl put it; and, therefore, she often appears ambitious and over zealous. If well enough, she may achieve a great deal academically, in the performing arts, in politics, or in literature. But one notices her creativity is employed in service to a goal which is a projection of her own masculine ideal. Somehow that drive is never mediated by the warmth, the surprise, the pain, or the mystery that are associated with the natural process of childbearing.

The contrast with another kind of womanhood is reflected in the contrast of Hera and Athene, wife and daughter of Zeus. Kerenyi helps us to see how they represent two different aspects of feminine being. "Hera's esence in its fullest development was the full moon," he writes. "From the viewpoint of Athene, the most essential phase is the exact opposite, the darkest night preceding her birth."[8] It is this darkness of no reflection against which the anorectic woman is so heavily defended. She has been blinded by the sun of too great an emphasis on masculinity and, being in a defensive position, gives the impression of having no depth, living on the surface, being on the alert, ever wakeful.

During the past few years I have met women who have been exposed to a spectrum of treatment ranging from prolonged hospitalization and forced feeding to systems analysis and family encounter, and as I have worked with them I have been persuaded that if this kind of patient chooses and can tolerate a psychotherapeutic relationship, she belong in analysis.[9] Here I would like to refer again to the longstanding definition of anorexia nervosa as *wrong thinking.* In my experience, anorexia nervosa is not a disturbance of mind and thought, but a disturbance of psyche and reflection. It is a "soul problem" but a soul problem of a particular kind, which is summarized as loss of reflection; metaphorically this may be expressed as a disturbance of sun and moon. The moon no longer reflects the sun. It is possessed by the sun instead. For a woman, that condition amounts to "loss of soul."

We in analytical psychology do not attempt to find answers to the disturbing and recurrent problems of psychiatry so much as to suggest approaches to perplexing borderlines of psychic development, and we do our work by way of reflected images, constantly observing how they are perceived. Therapy with the anorectic patient must be oriented toward the restoration of imagination and the reflective capacity though, as we all know, attempts at psychological forced feeding are almost never successful. It seems that if therapy is to succeed at all, it has to focus attention elsewhere than on symptoms, concerning itself with events in depth rather than with surface appearances.

Here it is important to differentiate between the structure of delusion and the image contained in the structure. Analysis properly concerns itself with images; that is to say, with the content of what is perceived and with its reflection. The observation of a process in which formerly unconscious contents claim attention and enforce awareness is part of the work involved in analysis. And, there is implied in this work a position of importance for fantasy and imagination which is the key issue in the activation of reflection and, so of psychic movement for the person fixed in delusion. Jung writes: "The richness of the human psyche and its essential character are probably determined by (the) reflective instinct ... through (which) the stimulus is more or less wholly transformed into a psychic content; that is, it becomes an experience."[10]

In this statement Jung refers to the role of reflection in the process of *apperception,* which he further defines as "a psychic process by which a new content is articulated with similar, existing contents in such a way that it becomes understood, apprehended or clear." He distinguishes between active and passive apperception, the first being "a process by which the subject of his own accord and from his own motives, consciously apprehends a new content ..." and the second "a process by which a new content forces itself upon consciousness either from without (through the senses) or from within (from the unconscious) and, as it were, compels attention and enforces apprehension."[11] Analysis attends the latter.

Initially an anorectic woman is arrested in direct encounter with a fixed image, and she lacks an instrument of reflection with which her gaze can be diverted and her perceptions prevented, like those of Perseus, from turning to stone. In this state she is cut off from the civilizing influence of reflection which would enforce apprehension. In analysis, the familiar reflector is the dream, which can mirror psyche to reality and reality to psyche without the intervention of moral judgment. By the indirection of its commentary, its fascination and self-enforcing character, the dream has the possibility of attracting the overconscious attention of the patient. With a person suffering from anorexia nervosa, this means that if the gaze can be deflected from its fixation upon body imagery to the enigmatic imagery of the dream, psychic movement may again become possible. If this happens, psyche paradoxically will assume body (as distinct from spirit) and at the same time acquire a meaning distinct from flesh.

"To see," wrote Merleau-Ponty in his last published essay, "is to have at a distance."[12] This, too, is an attribute of Athene's wisdom. She intervenes; she stays the hand upon the sword, she restrains the eagerness to engage and keeps at a distance until counsel can be taken, the plan of the gods revealed. In the therapy situation there is always danger that with its orentation towards action, the impulsive animus of the anorectic patient will seize upon insight and apply it for heroic purposes. The work of the therapist is to encourage distance and detached reflection until perception changes by the *self-enforcement* of new psychic content.

This new content usually makes its initial appearance by way of a dream image that not only attracts attention but releases imagination; for it is imagination that breaks the bounds of a given reality. And once the constricting form of existing reality is loosed, there is a possibility that it can be perceived in a new way. Therapy with anorectic women involves the loosening of the hold of delusion by allowing attraction to new images and fantasizing about them. Importantly, this will involve choicemaking.

Psychic images have a way of presenting alternatives, suggesting first one possibility and then another. Where there are alternatives, choices must be made, and questions of significance and meaning inevitably arise. With questions of significance and meaning the cultural and civilizing potential of Athene has a chance to re-assert itself.

If there is a play of changing images which involve choice-making, psychic movement is restored, and some sort of breakthrough or personal initiation is possible. In this connection, when working with anorectic patients more so than when working with others, I have been struck by the way significant rituals have been devised and spontaneously enacted to safeguard the initiatory passage between two states of being, the old and the new. These spontaneous ceremonies often have an archaic and mythic resonance, but they arise within an individual context which makes them memorable. In these ceremonies I find evidence that the person has been released from her identification with her delusion and has begun to speak the language of her individual self.

What I have been describing is a process which is familiar to the analyst. "The most remarkable thing about this method," wrote Jung:

"...(is) that it (does) not involve a *reductio in primam figuram* but rather a synthesis—supported by an attitude voluntarily adopted, though for the rest wholly natural—of passive conscious material and unconscious influences, hence a kind of spontaneous amplification of the archetypes."[13]

This quotation leads to my final point in support of analysis for cases involving anorexia nervosa. To me, the body language of the anorectic patient conveys an ontological obsession no less bizarre than that of the fakir or mystic, but it can also be spoken of in Eliade's words as "at once (a) thirst for the sacred and (a) nostalgia for being."[14] To contradict it is to deprive a woman of significance, for contradiction separates her from her living myth without which there is no chance of psychological survival. If her story is allowed to unfold itself naturally, however, we can see that she will fulfill herself *primarily* (though never entirely) within the context of an Athene image and this carries with it both promise and responsibility.

If anorectic women see this possibility, in its fullest sense, they are able to enter into themselves. However, a purely intellectual understanding is not enough. The long, slow work of analysis may succeed in release from the bond of identification with the aggressor, though that bond will remain a threat from within the confines of the shadow. However, these women can now face other women without shame, recognizing they are different from those who fulfill other images such as those of Hera, Aphrodite, or even the virgin Artemis. They realize that suffering the constraints of certain boundaries nevertheless enables them to explore new borders of individual and feminine expression.

Each of the goddesses has her own style, her own way of being in the world, and you will remember my reference to Athene as having emerged at a threshold, a transitional figure between two states of being, between mother and father realms. "She is what she is," Kerenyi wrote of this goddess, "fully apart from whether she ever belongs to a man or not."[15] What this means for anorectic patients in therapy is that they need to come to terms with their animus identification and allow the male spirit to counsel and inspire, rather than to dominate, the proper work of the animus being not the *pursuit* of consciousness but its *realization*. At the same time, with these women, allowance has to be made for independence, since it reflects psychological virginity, and when that allowance is made they can be valuable, supportive companions in relationship. Like Athene, such women have the resources to meet the challenge of new possibilities with inventiveness, though their forthrightness and assertiveness must be tempered by *reflected* wisdom if they are to remain true to their feminine nature. These are women of action, and today especially they are drawn to the forefront of change.

The archetypal image provides a theme upon which an individual plays infinite variations. And yet, the Athene image holds the possibility of combining strongly opposed tendencies. When it can be sustained, analysis provides the experience of becoming acquainted with *both* sides of an opposed nature. This process in anorexia nervosa is illustrated by the dream of a woman who worked with me for two and a half years. Near the end of her analysis she dreamed:

> I came out of the forest and stood on the edge of a lighted clearling. Here I saw two handsome horses. One was dark, high-spirited and unruly. The other was chestnut coloured, lively, well formed and intelligent. This was a training ground and these horses were being trained. But there weren't any fences and there wasn't a trainer. Instead, the horses moved round the circle themselves. What was happening fascinated me. When one of the horses stepped out of line or failed to keep pace, the other reached across and nudged him back into place. In this way they moved round and round the circle, training themselves."

The dream says many things and, like most dreams, speaks both to analyst and analysand. Athene's connection with the horse is well known: at times she was worshipped as mistress of horses.[16] Reflecting upon the dream when it was received, however; I was reminded that the bridle, too, was one of her gifts to man.

1. Karl Kerenyi. *Athene: Virgin and Mother.* Zürich, Spring Publications, 1978, p. 67
2. Aeschylus. "The Eumenides," *The Oresteia,* trans. Robert Eagles. Middlesex, Penguin Books, 1976, p. 269
3. Hilde Bruch. *The Golden Cage* (The Enigma of Anorexia Nervosa). London, Open Books, 1978, Ch. 4., "How it Starts."
4. John Layard. "The Incest Taboo and the Virgin Archetype," *The Virgin Archetype.* Zürich, Spring Publications, 1972, p. 291
5. For an historical survey see Mara Selvini Palazzoli. *Self-Starvation,* trans. Arnold Pomerans. London, Jason Aronson, 1978, Pt. 1, Ch.1
6. Ludwig Binswanger. "The Case of Ellen West," trans. Werner M. Mendel and Joseph Lyons. *Existence,* ed. Rollo May; Ernest Angel and Henri F. Ellenberger. New York, Simon and Schuster, 1958, p. 237 ff.
7. Kerenyi, *Athene,* p. 43
8. Kerenyi, *Athene,* p. 58
9. After specialized work extending over many years, Dr. Hilde Bruch has been led to emphasize a psychotherapeutic approach. See Bruch, *Golden Cage,* Ch. 8., "Changing the Mind."
10. C. G. Jung. *Collected Works,* Vol. VIII, 2nd ed. London, Routledge and Kegan Paul, 1969, para. 242 and 243.
11. Jung, *Collected Works,* Vol. VI. London, Routledge and Kegan Paul, 1971, para. 683
12. Maurice Merleau-Ponty. "Eye and Mind," trans. Carleton Dallery, *Phenomenology, Language and Sociology: Collected Essays,* ed. John O'Neill. London, Heinemann, 1974, pp. 280—283

13. Jung, *Collected Works,* Vol. VIII, para. 403
14. Mircea Eliade. *The Sacred and the Profane,* trans. Willard R. Trask. New York, Harcourt, Brace and World, Inc., 1959, p. 94
15. Kerenyi, *Athene,* p. 21
16. Walter F. Otto. *The Homeric Gods,* trans. Moses Hadas. London, Thames and Hudson, 1979, p. 50

The Hydrolith:
On Drinking and Dryness
in Archetypal Medicine

By Alfred J. Ziegler (Zürich)

I: Archetypal Medicine

An archetypal understanding of Man and his diseases lies beyond the realm of logic. Although in the course of the history of the humanities many attempts have been made, none has really dealt in earnest with the archetypal standpoint. Traditional, or as Kant termed it, classical logic which unites the natural sciences is not at all suited for this task, for the "archetypal" cannot be dealt with according to the principles of identity or contradiction, nor does it maintain a legitimate relationship to the principle of cause and effect, i. e. to causality.

Despite all attempts to at least hybridize archetypal reflection and logic, the former eludes our grasp again and again. It seems from the very beginning to be of a basically different nature and in many respects to complement logic. Communion with the archetypal is unique and wakens in us sensations which are much more "sophical" than "logical". Archetypal understanding is, in fact, a communion with Sophia, wisdom, rather than with logos, intelligence in the narrower sense of the word. It seems as if we were dealing with two different forms of intellectual eros and we may wonder, on first hearing the word "sophical" and on fathoming its true significance, why it has been missing from our vocabulary.

This lack of a word for archetypal understanding must be due to the one-sided presuppositions of our culture. Actually the pre-Socratics had already diagnosed the *intellectual dichotomy* from which we suffer. Heraclitus appears to have introduced the term 'philosophos' to differentiate those who loved wisdom from those who were "only" intellectuals. And for Plato in the later works, the philosopher is characterized by by his modesty, a person who know that he knows nothing whilst remaining enthralled by his love of wisdom. In the works of Aristotle communion with Sophia becomes the "prima philosophia," metaphysics in its proper sense. The Romans also made the existential distinction between "sapentia", wisdom, and "scientia", science. This is not the place to further explore this differentiation. Nonetheless, we may ascertain with astonishment that the majority of our philosophers have not been philosophers at all but rather philologists, concerned almost exclusively with logos. Their spirits loved a different sphere than archetypal wisdom.

Even on the bare experiential level *communion with the archetypal* appears to be something special. Thinking becomes more contemplative; in the place of clearly defined concepts we encounter qualities of *iridescence* and *twilight*. Clarity and precision are exchanged for an increase in depth. When the "superficial" bond to time and space becomes of secondary importance, eternity steps into the foreground, and development is superceded by the eternal present. What is lost in the earthshaking applications of logical concepts is retrieved in "magic". What is missing in cerebral insights is replaced by empathy. Such contemplation is a function of the entire body. Whatever had been merely logically clear now becomes urgent and passionate. And whenever serious distress would otherwise prevail, in matters of life and death we encounter drama, whereby our existence takes on a quasi-illusory quality introducing irony. Archetypal understanding ranges in the realm of the possible: it is "possibilistic" and its language is not that of the scientist but that of the poet who muses.

As a consequence, when the effort to convey an archetypal understanding of Man and his suffering is called "analytical psychology", we find two obscurantisms as well as an unjustified modesty in such a nomenclature. First, as we have demonstrated above, in its archetypal interests analytical psychology has very little to do with "—logy;" it is, properly speaking, in no way comparable to that which other sciences utilizing this suffix pursue. The association studies marked the historical conclusion of that part of Jung's work which can be considered to belong to the realm of conventional science. Everything that came later was born of a different spirit and was much more a courting of wisdom. This new position, however, seems to have been so misleadingly formulated that to the present day attempts at a retroactive corruption are made again and again. It seems to me that new attempts are constantly being made to integrate analytical psychology into the currently official scientific framework, tying it down by force.

Second, after my introductory remarks concerning logos and Sophia one can hardly speak of analytical psychology as being analytic, because analysis means "the resolution or dissection of one into many". One might sooner refer to it as being synthetic, but even then one would imply a construction and unification that was not intended. It might be more accurately termed the art of interpreting primal images, because it proceeds from specific phenomena via a primarily analogical path to the archetypal, thereby revealing meaning. It is an art, not a technique.

Third and finally, "analytical psychology" imposes upon itself a limitation, which I have to this day never been able to understand: although it is characterized by its communion with the archetypal, it purports, at least nominally, not to deal with the entire person, the anthropos, but rather to limit itself to his "psyche". Although it would be natural for analytical psychology to be a general pathosophy, whereby every analytical psychologist would as a matter of course be considered a physician, analytical psychology restricts itself instead to comprehending the phenomena of psychiatry. Hence it isolates the soul as a "relatively closed system", separating it from the entirety of the person and bringing archetypal reflection to bear on it. Then it becomes necessary to reconnect the body and the soul via more or less plausible mental gymnastics. One speaks, for example, of the "irradiation" of the psychic into the somatic, etc. However benevolent toward Sophia we may be, and willing to recognize archetypal wisdom, we are stuck with a theoretical scandal.

Aside from the element of illogic, it is probably this curious self-restriction to dealing with the psyche which has led analytical psychology to have so little intercourse with medicine. If ever someone should fall prey to the desire to bring order into the diversity of physical illness using analytical psychology, he would soon give up in despair. Medical experience cannot be integrated into analytical psychology, not only because the latter is too illogical but also because it has not applied archetypal reflection to the whole person.

And so it is that we succumb to fictions. It is as if in therapy we could conduct a pseudo-business without consulting one of the partners. By concerning ourselves with psychic behavior and leaving the body to the technicians on the grounds it does not belong to the relatively closed system of the psyche, we move in a dimension that is variously sustained by another one without this being adaquately realized. For instance, do we really take adequately into account how closely in time the disappearance of a psychic syndrome may correspond to the development of an evident physical illness? The question is not posed moralistically; rather, it is asked from the standpoint of the theory of cognition. Obviously, it is not possible to do justice to all sides simultaneously, but it does seem that the exclusion of bodily pathology from the sphere of our proper concerns encourages us to move in an unreal world of the so-called psychic.

Archetypal understanding of human suffering did not originate in the twentieth century. On the contrary, we can trace it throughout the whole of occidental intellectual history. But it is as if this were only a sort of *via occulta,* a dark path which runs in the shadow of the official sciences. It is af if everyone who has trod this path were something of an outsider. Such persons were termed either heathens or heretics; many were excommunicated or burned at the stake by the official Church. An archetypal understanding was not easily integrated with the concept of spirit which, among other things, led to our formulation of the highest sacred value, our Christian God. Archetypal can be appended neither to a unipolar, unchangeable Creator, nor to His image and likeness, *homo faber*, who always remains identical with himself, whilst creating the "best of all possible worlds". Indeed, the primary characteristics of archetypal understanding seem to me to be of a dramatically different nature, than those of Christendom's official God.

Historically, this was dealt with through the appearance of a radically different set of concepts concerning God and Man. The highest being in the gnostic, and later, alchemical view is an eternally changing figure, phanteistic, who is simultaneously "the world" and as such subject to suffering from inner conflicts. This picture of God is correlated to a similar image of Man as monadic, changeable, and subject to suffering. And just as the Creator is linked to *homo faber* by their similarity and communion, there is also a correspondence between macrocosmos and microcosmos and a participation of the one in the other. In the case of the changeable deity, one is tempted to see not a male but a female godhead and image of man. This conjurs up not only visions of the gods of India and the Far East but even more importantly the experience of a realliance with Sophia as wisdom.

To find an arbitrary beginning to an equally arbitrary recounting of the history of this idea, such an understanding of God and man is already discernible amongst the pre-Socratics. For example, the enigmatic Heraclitus held the world to be a god struggling with eurptions of elemental passions or actually of a world-fire in which manifestations arise and disappear again. And a sequel to this image may be found in Plato, where the eternal fire becomes an intelligent unchanging deity who manifests himself in the diversity of the world and who has a central heart similar to that postulated by Pythagoras. The suffering (but also spectral) world then becomes his theater. This primary Platonic insight takes on another form in late Neoplatonism and in the Platonism of the Florentine Renaissance. The latter may have inspired Shakespeare to hang the motto; *totus mundus agit histrionem* (all the world's a stage) over the entrance to the Globe Theater. If we exclude the Baroque period, which tends anyway to be world-theater, we find that archetypal understanding takes on new forms during the Romantic period. "Primordial phenomena" take on a thousand changing forms and the god whom they constitute becomes a monstrous organism which is kept in motion by the struggle of its inner contradictions. This image corresponds to that unstable and passionate figure, the Romantic personality, whose asthenic body anticipated each increase in the intensity of his existential experience by developing multiple illnesses. Such a figure never seems to be completely in earnest, and always has a touch of irony about him, going through life "trembling and tottering" as Novalis put it.

Thus in the history of the humanities wherever we meet with an understanding that gives preference to the archetypal we will encounter notions and a language which are, so to speak, those of Nature herself. They are not cerebral, but rather bodily and emotionally moving.

After this digression into the history of religious ideas, I would like now to close the first part of my lecture with a somewhat more detailed discussion of the three characteristics, mentioned above, which especially characterize the archetypal. Though there are certainly more such characteristics, these will suffice to clarify what is meant by the term *"archetypal medicine,"* which will be examined more closely in the second part of my paper. These characteristics almost always appear in conjunction with one another. Nonetheless, in cognitive theory they constitute separate units. We will be considering: the mutability of the archetypal; the fact that it most often reveals itself as pairs of opposites; and its relatedness to a central focus.

First, the *mutability,* or *changeableness* of the archetypal manifests itself in archetypal medicine most strikingly when behavior is transformed into a physical gestalt and vice versa. What was recently an aspect of demeanor can be transformed and appear as a physical symptom. Hence our readiness to be shaken or moved can be transformed into a physical trembling disease; our reluctance to act can appear more or less abruptly in different forms of rheumatic stiffness; and our capacity to keep life moist may reappear in addiction to water and edema. Such embodiments operate like the inferior function of the ego in analytical psychology: they too lead to some of the most difficult complications in life, especially when they sink below a level that would previously have just been tolerable.

Hence the archetypal alters only its appearance. It searches so to speak for another aggregate condition; the archetypal condenses, immobilizes or even makes one bedridden. The basic question of "psychosomatic medicine," namely how psychic phenomena influence the body, hardly even arises when we think in terms of "archetypal medicine." The archetypal already belongs to a dimension that is sufficiently broad to allow such metamorphoses to take place. In addition, the clear boundaries that separate the so-called functional from truly organic disturbances are no longer present. What would otherwise enmesh the diagnostician in formal argumentation becomes from the archetypal point of view a question of the depth of somatization. What arise are more or less reversible, mutable syndromes, images of illness, which ought not be confused with units of disease. The latter are categories of another form of medicine, derived from the natural sciences. It has been my experience that mixing the two uncritically leads to annoying difficulties in communication. One must stick to the "images" and wonder at the sometimes astonishing dramatics of which Nature is capable.

Second, the archetypal tends to *appear as opposites.* It is as if a need for a more rigidly structured understanding were being thereby satisfied, for with all its changeability the world tends to get out of bounds. Hence one finds awe more or less openly affiliated with arrogance, inflexibility with compliance, and preference for the wet with a longing for the dry. There is nothing final or stable in such relationships between opposites; rather, a diverse dialectic proves to be the rule. Sometimes, a complementarity of the opposites may create the impression of a special harmony, but at other times one is faced with almost indistinguishable contortions, a blur, or even a mutual avoidance equivalent to an inner rift, which induces on the one hand inflation and on the other somatization. An archetypal attitude tends not only to pull as completely into its sphere and to impose an absolute and exclusive style upon us; it also tends to comdemn its complementing attitude to bodily exile, where it will be compelled to lead a demoralized, often surreal existence. The opportunity for transformation presents itself when one caught in this rift complains of being trapped without an alternative, as is apt to occur when life has taken on bizarre proportions.

Finally, the archetypal strives for *structure*, we see this not only in the polarization mentioned above, but also in the way the archetypal tends to be related to a virtual center. It is as if it were constantly oriented around this center, the way the pantheistic deities arranged themselves around a world-navel. Hence all of the dialectic variations of the relationships of the archetypal, as well as their above mentioned potential for transformation, maintain at all times a point of reference. It is as if each individual's life follows a golden thread of meaning, despite the fact that he may have to confront extremes of repulsion, nothingness and absurdity. Whether we like it or not, Nature compels us to a "philosophical life" in the sense defined above. We cannot avoid our lifelong longing for Sophia, the wisdom that lets all the horrible variations of Being be encountered as something numinous and amazing.

II: Thirst, Drinking and their Morbid Alterations

In this section I would like to try to interpolate the topics of thirst and drinking and their morbid alterations into the general theory of archetypal medicine which I have briefly sketched. We are going to have to pose the same fundamental question which was originally raised by Heraclitus, i. e. how does that which is liquid, wet or moist relate to that which is dry? And we will put this question into the language of the pre-Socratics, as what does Dionysus have to do with Hades?

It may be said that *wetness and moisture* introduce chaos and that they are inclined to motility, instability, storminess, and even to intoxication and delirium. Hence, according to the Taoists, water can have no boundaries, because wetness harbors chasms and infinity. Considering water's dangerousness, Isaiah besought the Lord to rescue him, because the waters of death had penetrated his soul and he was drowning in filth. On the other hand, wetness also harbors genius, originality and humor. (In German the word for salvation is even etymologically related to hydrophysics—Erlösung: Lösung = solution.) The positive aspect of water is why Christ could say that he would give drink to the thirsty, and that water would fall in the desert and springs would open up in the land of thirst and make it fertile. That is also why the Holy Spirit completes Christ's redemptive work as the *fons vivus,* pouring down on mankind as a living spring.

Indeed Dionysus and Bacchus are closely related to wetness and fluids. They are the gods of the instinctive and the driven. It is they who tend toward motility, delirium, swelling and decomposition. But it is also their spirit which inspires the arts, which bring the world comedies and tragedies and laughter and which in the Orphic-Bacchic mysteries promise redemption from life through life, itself.

Dryness, on the other hand, tends toward infertility, sterility, endless frustration, renunciation, and privation. According to the history of symbols it is not only salty but also bitter; as dust, it has the meaning of nothingness. On the other hand, dryness enjoys the highest respect as that through which everything arises out of the flood of the indistinguishable. So it was that in the story of the creation the first "Let there be..." called forth dryness, which was the first firmament. In Tantrism the ego is composed of dryness and thereby differentiates itself from a universal Being, and in the Bible the drunkard Noah sees it as the land of the future. In alchemical speculation many islands combine to compose a standpoint much as sparks combine to form the light of consciousness. Dryness reminds one of the ascetism of the inner world, of puritanism, of an urbanity which we try to preserve with a plethora of fire, i.e., of energy.

Indeed dryness is an attribute of Hades who takes after his father, Cronus, who ate his children. For Hades tends to destroy life. Not only does he not even look at or listen to life, his head being on backwards, but he also causes it to decompose and disappear and makes himself and others invisible, thereby taking away their vital energy. In this respect he is similar to the Christian "death" who, in the form of a rattling, bone-dry skeleton, reaps the living with his scythe. In contrast to Dionysus, Hades turns an ominous visage to the world; he is a stern deity. Accordingly he inhabits a desolate, rocky, dusty Tartarus where dusk never really gives way to light. Although several rivers run through Tartarus, an endless desert of sand and stone seems to stretch out there and one encounters everywhere frustrated souls tortured by thirst. One encounters, of course, also the dastardly Danaides, who hopelessly try to fill a barrel which is full of holes, and the degenerate Tantalus, who fruitlessly tries to quench his thirst with the water in which he is standing.

Still this unhappy picture does have a lighter side—when Hades becomes Pluto and as such possessor of chthonic wealth in the form of all sorts of jewels and metals. He is closely related to scientific artfullness and technical processing and was hence in Rome termed simply "Dis", the rich man. Hades must be somehow related to our urban civilization and to the modern, rational coming of age. The more we exclude death from our lives, namely, the more it spreads ubiquitously in the form of a general, grey, stony urbanity.

It is certain that all of us are in one way or another and to one degree or another determined by Dionysian tendencies and by the dryness of Hades. But it is often not so easy to distinguish these two Gods and to separate their spheres of influence. As psychologists, we are then subject to a well-known predicament, just as we are liable to become bewildered by the polarized iridescence of the psychic attitudes and functions. It is well known that analysts are often not able to state with certainty which is really the dominant and which the inferior function. Often we can only establish only that an individual life is marked by this or that conflict.

When the functions can be determined experience has proved that it is the darker of the two, the so-called inferior function, which not only provokes psychic trouble but also tends to be *embodied* (transformed into a physical illness). The latter happens, as we have already mentioned, when the dominant function takes too unquestioned possession of us. Hence when dryness in one form or another sets the keynote to our life we can expect that a neglected "drunkenness on life" will show itself as an illness in which exceptional thirst and compulsive drinking play a role. What was previously visible only as a psychic disequilibrium becomes more and more distorted and begins to extend into the realm of physical medicine.

A whole range of more or less serious illnesses through which Dionysus can overtake us originate in this manner. We may well all understand that we reach for a glass when we have run dry. This otherwise unremarkable act can reach the intensity of an awful need for certain persons who—as it is phrased in psychosomatic literature—are of dry nervous susceptibility. They may be compelled to drink up to twenty liters of fluids daily. Then it is very difficult to determine to what degree physical alterations are a contributing factor, e. g. whether the production of the hormones which regulate the metabolism of fluids is disturbed perhaps by brain damage due to an encephalitis or to a tumor which affects areas of the brain-stem. With such organic illnesses as diabetes insipidus, a disorder of the pituitary gland characterized by intense thirst and the excretion of large amounts of urine, it is uncertain as to the extent that nature has gone to somatize a temperamental disability.

There are also forms of alcoholism, especially beer dinking, which are linked to a disturbance in the regulation of fluids. It is then often easy to establish that the patients are driven to drink and to become bloated by their exceptional sobriety and boredom, i. e. by their "thirsty souls".

Thirst and the compulsion to drink can become especially torturing for diabetics who are also said to be prone to a dry performance of their duties and to choleric self-frustation. When untreated, diabetes insipidus can also lead to bloating.

In related syndromes "drunkenness on life" is somatized and develops into a monstrous drinking bout. The individual shrinks so to speak into something inorganic, but in so doing succumbs to a process that is none other than that which takes place in most illnesses. The environment of the rheumatic patient becomes less "lively" when his resistance embodies itself in his joints, as does the environment of the skin patient when his need for isolation takes on the form of reptilian scales, or of the trembler who must experience being deeply moved as a tremor. Last not least, the lonely psychotic individual becomes a "case" when the enzyme secretion of his brain goes its own way, and he hallucinates his relationship to the world.

One's environment not only becomes inorganic, along with one, but also bizarre. Normally the organism maintains certain concentrations and dilutions throughout the body. In and between the cells there is an optimal saturation, i. e. a balanced relationship between all the salts—especially chloride and sugar salts—and their solvent, water. This balance belongs to our genetic inheritance, deriving from our prehistoric, oceanic origins. We live best at a certain level of aqueousness, with an optimal tumescence. It is as if Nature were in this respect subject to a "horror torri", a fear of drying up. In diseases of thirst, however, the dry salts, following the laws of osmotic wedlock, carry the water off in enormous quantities of urine or draw it into the body tissue, so that a compulsive but futile drinking is the result. Thirst is then located not only in a burning, feverish throat. The osmotic catastrophe is rather a torture of general insatiability.

This change is terrible and purports a mythic destiny. It reminds one in many ways of Bacchic dipsomania and of some traditions concerning the diseases sent by Dionysus. Without forcing the issue, one may include here the fate of Tantalus, king of the Phrygians. As is well known, he suffers eternal thirst in the company of Hades for having stolen sweet nectar from the table of the gods. It is as if archaic phantasy had tried to explain diabetes in this fashion, just as the collective imagination in general, of course, attempts to enmesh the sick person in the web of serious tales. There are similar legends in the Germanic culture.

There, however, Tantalus becomes a devilish figure, called the "eternal thirst". He in turn is related to Wotan who was in the Germanic pantheon truly the god of drunkenness. Not only mead but also the arts of poetry and music belong to his domain. He is a figure similar to the Mediterranean Dionysus, but he was also a god of warmaking having little to do with military technique. He embodied the primitive love of fighting and killing, and he had a taste for the blood-curdling. It was not so long ago that he raced on stormy nights with his dead warriors through remote valleys in the highlands of Switzerland. But he was banned from the newer religions, and like Bacchus and Tantalus, he retreated to the world of pathology. There, he not only haunts our rational era like a persistent shadow; he also incarnates himself in various illnesses where hardly anyone recognizes him.

Wotan is also called Türst in Switzerland and Türse is an archaic term for giants. It is a manifold relationship. They too are characterized as humid and ecstatic. According to the legends they brewed thunderstorms in huge kettles, and they had been nursed for seven years. Their drunkenness was well known, and they were seen toasting to one another across the mountains. These giants were never very clever and like Wotan, who when reason and enlightenment took over the land had to retreat to the remoter regions and to withdraw into the realm of illness, they too had to embody themselves. One legend claims that they all were conquered "full of wine" in a war against the cunning Austrians.

Of course, physiology has taught us to identify disturbances in the hormonal secretions that regulate the balance of fluids and salts. These disturbances are accompanied by psycho-endocrine-syndromes, more or less characteristic personality changes accompanying hormonal diseases. These syndromes are characterized particularly by drive and need disturbances, by mood swings, etc. One such condition occurs in acromegaly and in acromegalic growth disturbances, disturbances which produce a tendency to "giantism" in the extremeties—the hands, feet, chin and nose. This condition is often accompanied by excesses of all sorts, including heavy drinking.

For centuries, whenever drinking has become a compulsion and the disease of thirst has taken on a medical dimension, because the individual has gotten too dried up, treatment has centered around the question of how much wetness and dryness were beneficial for the patient. Treatment becomes an attempt to influence the osmotic relationship, and the resulting ambivalence about what to do has provided the opportunity for the most diverse and contradictory prescriptions. There is a long history of dispute over the therapy of osmotic conditions, concerning, on the one hand, what quantities of salts, carbohydrates that will be turned into salts and proteins which will retain water, can he prescribed and, on the other what quantities of daily fluid should be introduced into the patient.

The treatment can be seen to have followed always one of two ancient therapeutic principles: on the one hand, the principle of "contarium contrario", on the other "similis simile curatur." According to the first principle, a "drying out" was applied as the remedy for thirst because everything in excess will call opposing forces into play. The privation of fluids and dry foods were prescribed, although this led in some cases to death accompanied by tortures of thirst. Procedures that led to sweating were introduced, or the patients were sent to the desert. When it was held that *"similis simile curatur"* the opposite was done. One acquiesced to the patient's desire to drink, prescribed drinking and bathing: the thirsty diabetics travelled to the famous baths at Karlsbad and Vichy.

Today the treatment of compulsive drinking is certainly more effective. In addition to the appropriate diet there are diuretics, substances which remove the salts and hence the concomitant water from the body. Or hormones are prescribed, like insulin, which play a role in the regulation of the osmotic balance.

Despite all the advances in pragmatic doctoring one feels nonetheless a lack and the necessity of orienting actions toward the archetypal. The treatment remains insufficient if it is performed only with the ingenuity of the natural sciences and remains puerile despite all its diversity and effectiveness. A philosophical standpoint requires that both physician and patient contemplate the archetypal in fluids and in dry things, because their conflict is so fateful. Otherwise, despite all the therapy, neither will know where he stands. Nature does not take well to being only understood and treated solely on the basis of rational knowledge or from a social standpoint. Then it tends to veer off into seemingly magical irrationality. Not only psychic phenomena obtrude of their own accord into amplification; so do bodily syndromes.

We have examined to the changeability and the dialectic of the archetypal, using as examples diseases of thirst and compulsive drinking. Now, as a final reflection, we should examine the relationship of the archetypal to a virtual center.

Neither the medicine of the natural sciences nor archetypal medicine can do without a relationship to a center. During the entire process of diagnosing and curing one's thoughts will center around the coordinating brain-centers in the hypothalamus and the hypophysis as well as on the presentiment of a Self as analytical psychology understands it. The phenomena of moisture and dryness in sickness and health remain related to this focus, just as the neurotic and psychotic phenomena of psychiatry relate to this virtual center.

In order to name this center only a paradox will be adequate. It must be one which can be integrated into the long chain of designations for the "stone of the wise". Although modern physiology produces models and symbols in order to make the regulation of salts and fluids comprehensible, and although these in their turn are reminiscent of a cabbalistic, mystical language, still the name ought to bear another non-rational "Sophia" quality. In alchemical speculation there is a water-sone, or Hydrolith, which is neither crystal nor water-glass but rather a mysterious "solid water". Therein converge and resolve all the cognitive difficulties which arise from the complicated union of the dry and the moist. As in all symbols of the Self, so we find in the image of the Hydrolith a golden thread of meaning which we mentioned at the beginning of the lecture. As is always the case, it has not only a general numinous feeling but due to a particular disposition it also awakens a *particular* numinous sensation. Contemplating it lets us begin to sense that frustration, selfdiscipline and rationality, on the one hand, and satisfaction and art, on the other, are related in a manner that is at once mysterious and sober. Reflecting on the Hydrolith may clarify for us how to approach Dionysus and Hades. It contains a philosophical knowledge of how much privation and redemption may await us in this life. This may not only help preventive medicine to prevent the outbreak of the maladies we have been considering, but also to bring about an inner stability when they have already reached the point where they are irreversible and lead to death.

translation: Carolyn Landry

Festival, Communion
and Mutuality

William Willeford (Seattle)

The Words 'communion', 'community' and 'communication' are interrelated in ways that tell us something important about the nature and purpose of feasts and feasting. Communion is a celebration of community—of participation in a social group whose members communicate with one another by means of shared images, words, and concepts. But 'communion' can also name a mode of emotional interaction that is largely pre-verbal or sub-verbal in character, and such interaction, too, is communication. The chief characteristic of this second kind of communion—and communication—is mutuality. This mutuality is both presupposed and fostered by the giving and taking essential to festival.

Some striking comments by the psychoanalyst D. W. Winnicott about the relations between mother and infant bear directly and importantly on this non-verbal and emotional communion.

There are moments in which the infant is appreciatively aware of its own security. Such moments, according to Winnicott, 'have no climax. This', he observes, 'distinguishes them from phenomena that have instinctual backing, where the orgiastic element plays an important part and where satisfactions are closely linked with climax'. He criticises psychoanalysts for neglecting 'the tremendous intensity of these non-climactic experiences of relating to objects' (WINNICOTT 17). And in the original version of the paper from which I have quoted he is said to have denied strongly that 'the most intense experiences belong to instinctual and orgiastic events', since such a view 'leaves out of account the function of the ego-organisation. Only if someone is there adding up personal experience into a total that can become a self', according to Winnicott, 'does the instinctual satisfaction avoid becoming a disrupting factor, or have a meaning beyond its localised meaning as a sample of physiology' (GUNTRIP 9). In other words, ego-organisation and the sense of self-identity are largely built up through non-consummatory experiences of mutuality, these being in important ways independent of physiological appetite.

Festival not only affirms mutuality but may even elevate it to the status of an ultimate value. For example, St Augustine did this, in effect, when he sought to express his vision of perpetual communion with God by asserting that in the House of the Lord festival is eternal (AUGUSTINE 2). But festival affirms mutuality in the special way of satiating appetite. In the following reflections I will be regarding appetitive behaviour and experiences of mutuality as embodying distinct but interrelated and complementary principles.

I wish now to stress my own personal interest in the themes of this presentation. Over the years mutuality has become central to my own thinking about psychological matters. Indeed, I am completing a book with the sub-title *On the Psychology of Mutuality and the Self.* In this subtitle I put 'mutuality' before 'the self' because the self—and individuation—are to me incomprehensible without mutuality.

Our lives are largely governed by what I will for the moment call emotional evaluation—that is, by psychic processes reflecting our selfesteem, trust, and hope—or our lack of them—our loves and hates, our immediate feeling responses, and our more enduring attitudes. A sense of mutuality is crucial in bringing meaningful coherence into these processes. With my distinction between appetive behaviour and mutuality in mind, I wish briefly, by means of three examples, to illustrate these claims, and to look ahead to issues I will be discussing shortly.

A young man describes his fleeting sexual diversions. On the level of appetite these are satisfying enough, but the satisfaction of appetite is, he finds, not satisfying. They hardly lessen his isolation or increase his relatedness and his awareness of his own feelings. Such diversions are available in abundance. Thus he finds himself complaining, in effect, of abundance reduced to meaninglessness.

A man and woman—married to others—meet and *see* in each other the best of which each is capable—undistracted by the kinds of 'inferiorities' they share with everyone else. Having the best of oneself *seen* in such a way is an experience of abundance, as is *seeing* the best in another. Unlike the young man just described, the man and woman know *their* abundance to be of something remarkably and uniquely good. In an important sense it is for them of another order than sexuality as appetite. Without having been sexually intimate with one another, they—not very diplomatically—become celibate in relation to their spouses. This shows that the two orders finally, if mysteriously, meet.

A younger woman who has been with them together remarks, 'the two of you have a *secret:* so much *goes on* between you, even when you are just sitting together quietly'. She has realised that they not only *see* the best in one another but seek to call it forth and affirm it. She does not mean that what goes on between them is simply *their* secret—she means that it is a secret about human life and the possiblities it holds, perhaps even for her. She and they know that what they have discovered is part of something larger than their private world.

There are relationships in which this sense of abundance prevails, even if they are as rare as the young man's sexual diversions are common; and the terms 'projection' and 'idealisation' are grossly inadequate to describe them. The younger woman is right to feel that the order of reality she has glimpsed through her friends concerns us all if we are ever to be more than fragments of ourselves.

I will now explore three themes, with the distinction between appetitive behaviour and mutuality—but also with their interrelations—in mind: *first, Festival and the Natural man;* second, *Festival and Personal Self-Identity;* and third, *Festival and Symbol.* I will begin with observations about Shakespeare's dramatic treatment of these themes and will close with a brief fourth section about *Festival, Communion and Mutuality* in *The Tempest.*

I. Festival and the natural man

In many places Shakespeare makes dramatic use of elements drawn from marriages, wassails and pageants, and from such festivals as Shrove Tuesday, Midsummer Eve, and the twelve days of Christmas ending in Twelfth Night. As the literary critic C. L. Barber observes, Shakespeare's use of such elements brings about a surge of 'the vitality normally locked up in awe and respect', and this results—for both the characters and the audience—in a clarification of perception. This, Barber describes as 'a heightened awareness of the relation between man and "nature"—the nature being celebrated on holiday....The plays', he remarks, 'present a mockery of what is unnatural....[as well as] of what is merely natural...' (BARBER 3).

Though leaving some important things unsaid, this account—based on Freud's analysis of wit—does call attention to an essential function of festival. As Barber observes, festival generates and channels energy partly to the end of modifying the forms of consciousness that govern ordinary life. It modifies them by enhancing our awareness of mutuality.

Mutuality, as I am using the word, is not primarily the result of making up a deficit. It rather entails at the outset a sense of abundance. It is very little like making sure that there is exactly enough money in one's account to cover all one's outstanding cheques. It is very much more like investing money from one's savings account in a stock that will earn a higher yield, and then learning to one's surprise that the yield is evan higher than one had expected.

These reflections bear on the theme of festival in that a festival offers its participants more than enough. It is a celebration of abundance. But what, in a psychological sense, is the primary source and nature of the abundance experienced through festival? *How* does festival make us feel more fully alive?

Barber's answer, as we have seen, is that the psychic energy formerly 'lock-ed up in awe and respect' is, through festival, devoted to a renewed apprecia-tion of nature and of that part of our makeup that St Paul called 'the natural man' (I Cor. 2:14). And indeed, though words for 'spirit'—such as German *Geist*—are derived from words suggesting churning, spontaneous activity (JUNG 11), there are forms of 'spirit' that are listless and deadening. We might think, for example, of the medieval ascetic whose spiritual exercises resulted in what was recognised as 'spiritual dryness'. And pondering the per-sonality of an obsessively rigid bureaucrat, we might express some of the ironies of 'spirit' by describing him as overly spiritual but spiritually con-stricted and inert. When spiritual salt loses its savour in such ways the natural man may provide energies for a needed renewal of attitude.

It is wrong, however, to make a too neat distinction, as Barber perhaps does, between nature as the immediate satisfaction of appetite, on the one hand, and spirit—or culture—as the force impeding that satisfaction, on the other. In fact, one of the functions of festival is to soften the distinction between nature and spirit, so that nature becomes nature-as-spirit and spirit becomes spirit-as-nature. Festival does this by making the satisfaction of appetite a process of understanding. What is understood is in a broad sense spiritual: a festival is an occasion on which people celebrate something they deem larger and more significant than their individual lives, most usually something having connec-tions with divinity.

As we know from psychosomatic illnesses, there is a 'thinking of the body'; festival behaviour—even in festivals of licence—is highly coded, and the satisfaction of appetite in festival is a complex processing of information. The excellence of the dish, for example, tells the guest that his host is magnanimous, and that he himself is valued; its delicacy tells him that he is regarded as discriminating; its traditional character tells him he has ties with his ancestors and the gods. Festival includes such transpersonal elements as the configuration of the group and the occasion being celebrated. For example, a festival with the king present is different from one with the king absent; the joy of Easter is different from the riot of carnival. Indeed, the festivals of Catherine de' Medici and other rulers in the seventeenth century were elaborate and sumptuous works of art (YATES 18). None the less, though rules, structure, and inhibition are necessary to the larger meaning of festival, the experience it offers is one of abundance. More specifically, this experience is of abundance as a quality of mutuality.

2. *Festival and personal self-identity*

Before exploring this topic, I wish to grant that one of the purposes of feasts in many times and places has been to impress the guests and increase the host's prestige for the purpose of his wilful domination of them. Thus—to emphasise this purpose—a recent book about the 'potlatch' ceremonies among American Indians of the Pacific Northwest is entiled *To Feast with Mine Enemy* (ROSMAN, RUBEL 15). But I am concerned rather with mutuality of a more benign sort, and with the bearing of this mutuality on self-identity in a very fundamental sense.

C. G. Jung antedated by several decades the psychoanalytic writers currently concerned with a distinction between ego and self, and his concept of the self, manifold and paradoxical as it is, is dynamic in ways that recent psychoanalytic concepts of the self at their best scarcely approach. The self as he understands it is often symbolised by religous contents of various kinds, which he studied in his later writings. But one can find his concept of the self prefigured in his early work 'The psychology of dementia praecox', and I will use that prefiguration as my point of departure in what I want to say now about personal self-identity.

In that extraordinary essay Jung focuses on a 'central psychological disturbance...a disturbance that sets in at the vital source of all the mental functions; that is, in the realm of apperception, feeling, and appetition' (JUNG 10, p. 13). He follows Wilhelm Wundt in calling this disturbance 'apperceptive deterioration', apperception being in Wundt's words 'the single process by which any psychic content is brought to clear comprehension'. Pondering the problematic term 'apperception', Jung remarks that it 'is volition, feeling, affectivity, suggestion, compulsion, etc., for these are all processes which "bring a psychic content to clear comprehension"' (*Ibid.*, pp. 13—14). Jung is here implicitly talking about the self as what Maurice Merleau-Ponty would later call the 'body-subject'. And it is as body-subjects that we participate in festival.

Schizophrenic disintegration results from what John Weir Perry has called a 'central injury', an injury to his vital core of the personality, which has capacities for integration and disintegration ranging from the simplest appetitive behaviour to the most refined complexities of language, art, and religious symbolism (PERRY 13).

There are vital needs on the level of physiology—the need for air, water, and a certain range of temperature, for example. But 'vital' is also a term of value, as certain things may in a literal but also in an extended sense be 'vitally important'. Such physiological vital needs are finally inseparable from a vital need for self-esteem, which is found and given through mutuality. Mutuality is vitally important—in an extended but also in the literal sense—in that frustration of the need for it may result in a central injury manifest in the most varied domains of mind and body. And yet even in someone so afflicted there may be attempts—expressive of the vital core—to reconstitute the personality. Thus Jung regarded the sense of worthlessness of one of his patients as in part 'the normal correction of her grotesque ideas of grandeur' (JUNG 10, p. 149)—such ideas themselves often representing attempts to compensate impaired self-esteem. A failure of mutuality surely contributed to the formation of this patient's psychopathology; an increase in *genuine* self-esteem—and the abandonment of her grandiosity—would be required for her to achieve a fuller participation in community. Still—precisely with regard to these issues—her psychopathology was partly the product of a failed attempt at self-healing; and such attempts must be regarded as expressions of the will to live.

I am talking about self-esteem in connection with the will to live on this fundamental level because the self as the vital core of the person has an evaluative aspect that has never been sufficiently stressed—and has never been made explicit enough—though Jung had it in mind when he regarded feeling and affectivity as essential qualities of the vital core. I would basically summarise the evaluative aspect of the vital core in this way: *somewhere in one's person, relatively distinct from the ego and supraordinate to it, is a self that knows what is good for itself. That good must be found in the world, but knowledge of what must be found is presupposed in the seeking.* St Augustine expressed this in religious terms when he thanked God for giving him as an infant a care for his own well-being (AUGUSTINE I). And two of Jung's patients expressed care for *their* well-being in the form of 'teleological hallucinations', one as he tried to kill himself by jumping out of the window but was hurled back into the room by a tremendous light, the other as he tried to kill himself by inhaling gas but felt himself grasped by the throat and thrown to the floor by an enormous hand (JUNG 10, pp. 147—8).

In saying that self-esteem is found and given through mutuality I have meant to give as much importance to the seeking and finding—on the part of the infant—as to the giving—on the part of the mother. I would elaborate upon my description of the evaluative aspect of the vital core in this way: *to know what is good for oneself is to know oneself as good.* This knowledge can be amplified, attenuated, inhibited, or even largely destroyed through interaction with others, but it is not simply given by them. The expression 'good-enouth mother' implies that no mother is perfect—indeed it is important that any mother should not be—and that the infant has resources for finding what it needs, and for making do, in an imperfect environment.

As Jung realised, compensation is one of the fundamental principles of psychic life—at work, for example, when daydreaming offers relief from the rigours of directed thinking, or when a dream corrects one's conscious understanding of a situation, or when delusions of grandeur balance injured self-esteem. *Compensation actively expresses the evaluative aspect of the vital core as the self that knows what is good for itself.* Compensation embraces processes and contents of the most varied kinds, but its essential nature is evaluative—and emotional.

Cultural values are made part of the developing personality through introjection. Very important among these values are those proscribed by the injunction, 'thou shalt not'. But before these cultural 'Thou shalt nots' are even intelligible to the infant it evaluates on the basis of the self that knows what is good for itself. Thus, the infant may fall into a depression that amounts to a rejection of a mother the infant finds *not* good enough. The positive meaning of such a depression is an attempt to defend the vital core of the infant, even thought the attempt is, in effect, suicidal.

In my reflections on the vital core I have been influenced by the invaluable researches of Anne I. De Vore into 'defences of the self', a concept adumbrated some years ago by Leopold Stein and Michael Fordham (DEVORE 4, 5, STEIN 16, FORDHAM 8). DeVore has graphically shown how such a symptom as migraine can serve the constructive purpose of inducing the ego to realise that its perspective is inadequate to the fundamental aims of the larger personality. She has also traced the process by which such a symptom may become associated with an imaginative symbol that reaffirms those aims. In doing so she has made strikingly clear how deeply rooted the self that knows what is good for itself is in the body subject.

The view of the self I am now presenting is very different from that propounded by Edward F. Edinger in his book *Ego and Archetype* (EDINGER 7). Edinger's basic terms for describing the relations of the ego to the self are 'inflation' and 'alienation', states inviting disaster, the prospect of which should inspire fear and trembling. Such states do occur, as does the disaster resulting from them; and, as Edinger argues, the oscillation between such states may be followed by something like a dialectic process between ego and self (*Ibid.* 7, p. 103). The self that knows what is good for itself may indeed be manifest in such dreadful forms as those experienced by Jung's patients. But more characteristically, the self that knows what is good for itself tells us that whatever is necessary and desirable for our truest wellbeing is available, accessible, indeed perhaps even already present. Our response to this knowledge is not fear and trembling but joyous calm.

As I argued in the preceding section, mutuality is an experience of abundance. More specifically, it is an experience of the abundantly good. Festival is a reaching out to this good. There are, to be sure, festivals commemorating dismal shades of the dead, and there are festivals of mourning. But even a funeral banquet conveys an affirmative message: 'Reduced as we are by this loss, we are and must remain part of life and open to its goodness'. Indeed, one philosopher has regarded the essential nature of festival as the affirmation that *everything* is good (PIEPER 14). The self that knows what is good for itself is at work in this affirmation.

3. Festival and symbol

Much of the power of festival derives from its appeal to non-verbal levels of our being. Still, as we have seen, festival has symbolic content—in the form, for example, of the occasion being celebrated or the 'higher power' being in-

voked. Thus there is a relation between festival and the kinds of overdeter-
mined', complex, polyvalent symbols of special interest to depth
psychologists, especially in the tradition of Jung. I mean the kinds of symbols
that give one the sense of not only stating and summarising in an illuminating
way but also of providing a momentary glimpse of something otherwise
unknown, something that will fade again into its unknownness. It is a mistake
to draw too pat a distinction between such symbols and the more prosaic
'signs' employed in our practical work in the world. Still, *some* such distinction can validly be drawn and it will reflect divergent attitudes concerning our
purposes and the nature of our actions.

We are creatures of language, which—through its resources of metaphor—ex-
tends the known into the unknown and makes the unknown known, and
thus gives us mastery over the world. But utilitarian mastery is not the only
form of relationship to the world; indeed, it is in many respects a self-
deceiving and self-destructive one. This may be seen if we contrast it with one
that also can define purposes and actions: I mean the attitude expressed in the
beliefs of various peoples that human life is some sort of partnership between
man, animals, the elements, and spirits of various kinds. The attitude of
utilitarian world-mastery erodes the sense of mutuality I have been describing.
But as such beliefs in man's partnership with elements of his world suggest,
the mind also has resources to create symbols fostering the sense of mutuality.
Their nature and function—and the process of their creation—have been well
described by the philosopher Mikel Dufrenne.

We may begin, Dufrenne proposes, by considering the perception of an ordinary object, which—even when singled out by perception—remains part of a
larger world of objects, from which it cannot be completely separated. Thus
in a certain sense the perceived object may be said to reach beyound itself into
the world against which it is silhouetted, or to draw upon that background as a
guarantee of its form and its reality. 'It is by means of the world that the object is real', Dufrenne remarks, 'not only because its profile stands out against
in but because it is supported by that unfathomable reservoir of beings'
(DUFRENNE 6).

Generally, ego-consciousness in its discriminating, analytic mode—reflecting
the utiliarian attitude of world-mastery—leads us to experience ourselves as
self-encapsulated subjects, and to experience objects as isolated from the living
context that is part of their reality and meaning. Poetic and mythic symbolism
serves to complement this one-sided attitude. Thus Dufrenne observes that
'most ancient religions call on us to perceive the world (as if it were an incomplete spatial totality, and perhaps in order to compensate for what the
totality lacks) as an elementary power—the Earth-Mother, the Ground—a
fundamental force of which myth is the explanation' (*Ibid.* 6). In such a view
the individual thing or event is experienced as integrated into the world by
virtue of its participation in this fundamental force. Festival is one of the most

ancient and widespread ways of being mindful of this participation. This is so because festive abundance corresponds on the level of appetite to what could be called the 'fullness' of the mythic symbol—of the 'fundamental force' described by Dufrenne—so that festival becomes the medium whereby such a symbol is apprehended by the 'thinking of the body'.

The most fitting response to this abundance—as well as to the magnitude of the divinity or other 'fundamental force' invoked by the festive occasion—is gratitude. Thus festivals have as one of their primary aims the giving of thanks. And to turn from festival to Winnicott's observations about the non-orgiastic mutuality of mother and infant, I find it not far-fetched to imagine that such experiences are partly characterised by gratitude: for the otherness of each other, and for that otherness as ultimately unknown. The psychoanalyst Melanie Klein has convincingly maintained that the gratitude of the nursing infant is an important formative experience (KLEIN 12). Conjectures about the infant's undifferentiated psychic unity with the mother surely need to be tempered by the reflection that mother and infant may indeed be mutually grateful in such a way.

I have been considering festival as a vehicle of mythic symbolism. But as we have seen in St Augustine's description of the House of the Lord as a place of eternal festival, festival may itself become such a symbol. I wish to elaborate upon this point in my concluding observations about Shakespeare's *The Tempest*.

4. Festival, Communion and Mutuality in 'The Tempest'

In this play Prospero, the banished Duke of Milan, lives on an enchanted island with his daughter Miranda. A shipwreck brings to the island his evil brother, along with the King of Naples (his brother's accomplice in treachery), Ferdinand (the King of Naples' noble son, whom the King believes drowned), and various others. Miranda and Ferdinand fall in love, and Prospero blesses their intention to marry. Toward the close of the play Prospero stage-manages three spectacles bearing on the themes I have been discussing.

The first of these is a banquet magically prepared for three of the shipwrecked 'men of sin', who reach for the food, only to have it vanish. In this brief action we see food, the material for the satisfaction of appetite, divorced from mutuality and from the broader meaning of festival. The vanishing of the food is a judgement on the men intent upon simply eating it.

The second spectacle is an entertainment of songs and dances presenting to Miranda and Ferdinand the goddesses Iris, Juno and Ceres. (Juno and Ceres are patronesses of the fidelity and fruitfulness that should prevail in the coming marriage; Iris is the intermediary between the divine and the human worlds.) Such an invocation of 'higher powers' is a common ingredient of festival, which brings us into communion with them. This second spectacle, too, is broken off, as though the festival of the wedding must take place within a larger community fit to celebrate it, and—with the evil characters still unrepentant—this community has not yet been achieved.

The third spectacle is remarkable in its brevity and pointedness. The time has come for Prospero to reveal to his evil brother and the King of Naples that Ferdinand is alive and will marry Miranda. Prospero does this by drawing back a curtain to disclose the two lovers playing chess. Miranda is overheard saying: 'Sweet lord, you play me false', to which Ferdinand replies: 'No, my dearest love,/I would not for the world'. And Miranda protests: 'Yes, for a score of kingdoms you should wrangle,/And I would call it fair play' (Act V, lines 172—5).

Chess employs the discriminating, analytic intellect to the final end of winning. It thus reflects a world in which wars are fought, dukes banished and dukedoms usurped. But the game, with its elaborate rules guaranteeing mutuality, is being played by lovers whose love is the ultimate value in their lives. And if the permutations of chess moves are abstract and 'spiritual', the love—and the mutuality—of which the chess game here becomes the expression is bodily and erotic.

As we have seen, mutuality is not a matter of starting from a deficit that somehow needs to be made up. Thus if Ferdinand wishes to 'wrangle', Miranda will 'call it fair play', as she is unconcerned with the sort of deficit that would be represented by losing a game. She is concerned, rather, with a sense of abundance that would magnify the kingdom of the chess board into a 'score of kingdoms', which she would happily let Ferdinand have.

In these three scenes Shakespeare has in effect, analysed festival into its components. The last component presented—the sense of mutuality—is the most basic. Without it we are at best fragments of ourselves. Mutuality is, as I have argued, a vital need. The trust and hope that this vital need will indeed be fulfilled is itself cause for celebration. All festivals are celebrations of this trust and hope.

Summary

Mutuality is not primarily the result of making up a deficit. It rather entails at the outset a sense of abundance. Mutuality is a vital need, expressive of the self that knows what is good for itself. Festival—with its abundance—celebrates the trust and hope that this need will be fulfilled.

Mutuality and appetitive behaviour represent distinct but interrelated and complementary principles. Festival awakens 'the natural man', while softening the distinction between nature and spirit. In the process, the 'thinking of the body' becomes a means of apprehending the symbolic content of the festive occasion.

Owing to the importance of mutuality and abundance in it, festival itself may become the symbol of an ultimate value, as when St Augustine declares that in the House of the Lord festival is eternal.

1. AUGUSTINE [AUGUSTINUS], SAINT (1912). Confessions, Vol. I Cambridge, Mass., Harvard University Press, pp. 58—9.
2. —(1841). 'Enarrationes in psalmos 41.9.' Migne, Patrologia latina, 36, 470.
3. BARBER, C. L. (1959). Shakespeare's Festive Comedy. Princeton, Princeton University Press, pp. 5, 7—8.
4. DEVORE, A. (1980), 'Migraine as symptom and symbol', Journal of Biological Experience, 3, 21—33.
5. —(1980). 'Symptom as symbol: body symptom in individuation', Unpublished diploma thesis submitted to the Inter-Regional Society of Jungian Analysts.
6. DUFRENNE, M. (1973). The Phenomenology of Aesthetic Experience. Evanston, Northwestern University Press, p. 150.
7. EDINGER, E. F. (1973). Ego and Archetype. Baltimore, Penguin.
8. FORDHAM, M. (1974). 'Defences of the self', J. analyt. Psychol., 19, 192—9.
9. GUNTRIP, H. (1971). Psychoanalytic Theory, Therapy and the Self. London, Hogarth Press, p. 122.
10. JUNG, C. G. (1907). 'The psychology of dementia praecox', Coll. wks, 3.
11. —(1948). 'The phenomenology of the spirit in fairytales', Coll. wks. 9, 209.
12. KLEIN, M. (1975). Envy and Gratitude and Other Works 1946—1963. London, Hogarth Press, pp. 188, 254—5.
13. PERRY, J. W. (1957). 'Acute catatonic schizophrenia', J. analyt. Psychol., 2, 137—52.
14. PIEPER, J. (1973), 'Uber das Phänomen des Festes', Arbeitsgemeinschaft für Forschung des Landes Nordrhein-Westfalen, 113, 12.
15. ROSMAN, A. RUBEL, P. G. (1979). Feasting with Mine Enemy. New York, Columbia University Press.
16. STEIN, L. (1967). 'Introducing not-self', J. analyt. Psychol. 12, 97—113.
17. WINNICOTT, D. W. (1967). 'The localisation of cultural experience', Int. J. Psycho-Anal., 48, 369—70.
18. YATES, F. (1959). The Valois Tapestries. London, Warburg Institute, University of London, pp. 51—108.

(Reprinted from The Journal of Analytical Psychology 1981, 26, 345—355 by permission.)

FASHION

The Time of Fashion

By Sonja Marjasch (Zürich)

I have called this essay "The Time of Fashion" because I find the constant interplay of time and fashion to be a fascinating subject. To catch the essence of fashion "on the wing" is as tricky as trying to describe an elusive butterfly. It is easy enough to observe in detail the colorful pattern of butterfly wings when the butterfly is impaled on a board, but what is a dead butterfly compared to the one in flight from one flower to another, of which you can catch only a glimpse now here, now there?

I remember well how as a child when I was about ten years old, I let a thermometer fall to the floor. It broke and a dozen glittering balls of mercury rolled on the wooden planks. With a paper I tried for a long time to shovel them together so that they would form one big luminous ball, but at the merest touch they broke into a host of tiny balls until instead of being rolled into one they had disappeared into the cracks of the floor. What intrigued me was not the substance of mercury but its inherent liveliness. This is still the case. *Ille mercurius fugax* fascinates me as it is hidden in matter, moving it from within.

Whilst I was working on this paper a poem by John Donne: "Go and catch a falling star . . ." haunted me. I cannot put the essence of what I am writing fully into words, I can only point to it. Look here! Look there! When I write of "the time of fashion" it is not always the same time. It can be the chronological time with its hurry and its leisure, or the time not ruled by the clock—the time of imagination, or "our time" in the sense of our cultural or political situation. Fashion moves freely through all these different times and mixes them up like Puck in "Midsummer-Night's Dream." I shall approach the topic by making use of my own fashion memories.

My first fashion memory dates back to the time when I was about four years old. I remember sitting on the polished dark brown stairs of our home, playing with buttons. They had various forms and sizes but I sorted them out according to color, making two heaps, one black and one brown. I could do this over and over again. In this play I had unconsciously already made a major decision: I gave color preference over form.

Fashion behavior in general can be roughly sorted out into two different attitudes, whether the purity of line or the colorful material is more important.

Folk and tribal costume make full use of color in intricate patterns or subtle combinations, often the gorgeous cloth is not cut at all but simply wrapped around like the Indian sari. At the center of Western fashion, which is the Parisian Haute Couture, the cut of a dress is all important: it is its big secret. The famous "little black dress" is an example for this. Some models have beautifully colored patterns inspired by folk art and an ingenious cut. In the field of couture these are really attempts at a "coincidentia oppositorum" and some are true works of art.

When people show an obvious preference for color in their way to dress I suspect them of having a tendency to "go native" in many ways. I surmise, for instance, that they will remember their dreams in color rather than in black and white, and I am not surprised when they labor at finding the exact words for the subtle shadings of their emotions.

At my grandmother's there were fashion magazines called *The Lady, Silver Mirror* or *the World of Elegance*. On rainy afternoons I cut out the model I liked best to make a paper doll, from the rest I cut out only the dresses. The play consisted in changing these dresses. From morning to evening, my paper-lady changed about six times to be properly dressed for sports, shopping, lunch, cocktail, dinner and gala ball. There were dresses for all occasions but the essence of the play was change.

In those days it took ocean liners, like the Ile de France, four and a half days to cross from Cherbourg to New York and whilst on board the passengers changed up to five times daily and never put the same dress on twice.[1] By changing their outfits so many times a day, a continual adjustment to mood and outer circumstances was maintained, at least on the surface.

Seen from today, the greatest luxury of the pre-war fashion world was having time enough to change that often. In a study called *The Harried Leisure Class* the author, Stephan Linder, observes that nowadays such commodities as books, records and dresses are bought in great number without thinking about the time needed to enjoy them.[2] As a result they often pile up unused. Our society is characterized by the fact that there is more affluence than there is time at hand. "I didn't have time to realize that I had time on my hands," said an analysand just back from the United States—by jet of course.

In order to enjoy changing, a moment of rest between the old and the new stage is needed. Winnicott calls this resting-place "the area of intermediate experiencing" to which both worlds, the inner and the outer, contribute.[3] It is the basis of our psychic elasticity. If it is lacking, the changing of a dress, for instance, doesn't bring refreshment but is just an additional chore. The area of intermediate experiencing, however, is in direct continuity with the playground of the child, and to have time enough to play is the basis of all luxury.

The antipode to the couture model, made for a special occasion, is the drip-dry no-wrinkle, synthetic dress, to be worn if necessary round the clock. It is a practical American invention but from the point of view of fashion a kill-joy.

In my early teens I felt that the world was against me. I certainly was against the world and expressed my rebellion by wearing only dresses and coats of a red color. The current fashion was then, for schoolgirls, navy blue or checkered skirts and blouses. This led to endless discussions with teachers and parents, but I was stubborn: I saw red, so I dressed in red. In the early thirties my personal protest got engulfed in the irrational undercurrents that expressed themselves in an anti-intellectual back-to-the-roots trend.

In Germany, fashion was declared to be the decadent product of city life and an adaptation of a folk costume, the "gretl," was sported. In Switzerland genuine folk traditions were still alive. The national fair of 1939 was the apotheosis of a new style based on old traditions. It strengthened national identity and was directed against Germany. Folk costumes inherited from one generation to another, were proudly worn again. They embedded their bearer into a community and declared his status within it. I remember participating in a parade in the costume I had inherited from my mother. I had a white linen blouse with puffed sleeves, a darkbrown handwoven skirt that would last for three more generations, but the black silk apron and cap broke with age. There was silver jewelry to go with it. At that time there was strength in unity—after the national costume came the uniform. The Parisian Haute Couture whose *clarté d'esprit* served to difine the individuality of each client, had to lead a shadowy existence during the war years.

To-day we have fashion and anti-fashion. Anti-fashion is the name of a distinct style of dressing that was first meant as a protest but has now become part of the general fashion scene.

In the past fifteen years folk art and folk costume came again into the foreground. But they have an exotic touch. Couture finds its inspiration in the fabulous costumes of the Near and Far East and Eastern Europe. Yves St. Laurent has created a dress inspired by Peruvian folk-art. It is of breath-taking beauty, but these luxury editions of folk costumes remind me of the time the court ladies loved to dress up as shepherdesses, just before the French Revolution.

It is an interesting detail that the extraordinary six-color knits of the St. Laurent collection were programmed for the first time by a computer. It saved time and money and chances of error. Nobody knows how long it takes for the weavers of the Sierra to work out their patterns. It is a pointless question because they work in a different kind of time, where there is still place for the soul to expand and play; and to shy away from perfection which is the prerogative of the gods.

Anti-fashion went for the real thing, for instance, genuine Afghan and Bedouin dresses, Peruvian ponchos or embroidered blouses from Turkey. This led quickly to a big sell-out of the last remnants of folk costume and folk art. The need for change superimposed itself even on these garments that were made for more than a generation. The last Afghan embroideries, at least for the Swiss market, were dyed to a modish violet. The trend had as positive effect the revival of old textile techniques in Western countries.

Last year Zürich experienced a sudden outburst of youth demonstrations one of which was headed by stark-naked young people. This seems to me to be the logical consequence of anti-fashion, the antithesis to fashion, as silence is the antithesis of over-verbalization. It reminded me of the Doukhobors in Canada who, in 1903, marched naked through startled prairie settlements. They were Russian immigrants, members of a Utopian religious movement, and their nakedness was a protest against the growth of materialism.[4]

The naked Zürich youngsters marched through the city on a warm summer evening; maybe they were caught by a Dionysian raving. They caused great merriment which reached a climax when they were greeted by professional strippers who came out of a bar to invite them for a special performance.

Nakedness is the zero hour of fashion. It is the goal of seductive fashion that provides a stimulating prelude to sexual enjoyment—stripping is the parody of it. Nakedness in the street is a challenge to civilized values, one of them still being sexual modesty. Some naked girls at the demonstration had veiled their faces as protection against tear gas and as safeguard of their individuality.

In their nakedness the youngsters clearly expressed their longing for paradise, oscillating between a nostalgic looking-back and an utopian program to realize it in the near future. Sometimes their patience is exhausted and then they call for "Paradise Now." In his book *Sehnsucht nach dem Paradies*, Mario Jacoby has explored in detail (and with vast learning and experience) the archetypal background of this desire.[5]

A short glance at travel folders shows that the demand for an earthly paradise is still increasing. Yet the islands on which the archetypal image is projected are farther and farther away from Europe. After their discovery it takes about five to ten years until they make for the last time headlines as "A Paradise Lost." This happened, for example, to the Maledives. They are destroyed by mass-tourism, and the pace setters are already following a new "inside" tip. By and by, suitable islands will be scarce.

Paradoxically, the war years bring back vivid fashion memories. There was general shortage and great improvisation. Austerity was defied by playfulness. I was then in my twenties and never realized better how many different persons were in me, all wanting to be differently dressed. To satisfy them all, I changed from dress to slacks and back again, sporting a new hairdo every day. Scarcity of material forced everybody to make old into new, and I remember fondly a dress I remodeled myself for a romantic occasion.

I am touched when I see how nowadays young women, in spite of affluence, have the need to make something for themselves according to their own invention. This is a new trend that grew out of readymade antifashion. I call these embroidered dresses and overalls, hand-knitted pullovers, shawls or mittens, hand-woven jackets and so on, "soul clothes." It is a primarily introverted trend; the dress item is more intended for soul comfort than for show. It is rarely made for sale, more for personal use or as a gift.

Such items, be they cap, gloves, blouse or socks, are actually "playthings for the soul." I borrow this expression from the Sakkudais, a small tribe in Indonesia. They believe that the soul tends to wander away from the body and can get lost if not attracted back into it. In order to amuse it and to lure it back into the body the Sakkudais make beautifully carved birds as playthings for it, and they celebrate many festivals, for which they make up and dress up most carefully.[6] To them the soul likes comfort and beauty and does not want to be hurried. The trend of "soul clothes" springs from the same need: to lure the wandering soul back into its body in order to feel animated. Fashion can only animate when it touches the soul, and practically all ready-made dresses are only for the body.

Soul clothes are by nature soft and pleasant to touch, often made from handspun wool or natural silk. Their touch evokes memories of the towel or the teddy-bear that were, what Winnicott calls, "the first transitional objects."[7] They helped in childhood to overcome anxiety, caused by a feeling of abandonment. Soul clothes are therefore a source of basic comfort, not only by themselves but through the memories they stir up.

Many soul clothes are patterned. Through their patterns they root in the nourishing ground of symbolic imagery. There is a tremendous dynamism in basic patterns like stripes or checkerboard. They are by nature endless, extending to all directions and only limited by the surface of the object they decorate. They make the infinite visible in the finite and are therefore a concentration of soul quality. A mathematician knitted a multicolored shawl making use of the law of proportions and was very pleased to explain with the help of her shawl these mathematical truths to her pupils.

Sometimes by way of pattern there is a relation between a soul garment and a dream. A gifted woman analysand was about to knit a vest for a little boy with an animal pattern. "Oh, I have to put a cow into it," she said one day, because she had had a dream about a cow that impressed her. It turned out that this was not as easy as she had thought it to be. First, she experienced it as a purely technical difficulty, then she realized that the problem of the dream involving a cow had to be dealt with first. She decided to knit stags into her present pattern, but she was determined to find out eventually "how to render that cow."

After the War, the fashion dictates from Paris set in again with a bang. Dior created the New Look. From then on, I wavered between adaption to fashion trends and personal preferences. The few times I was dressed to kill, with matching dress, coat, hat, shoes, gloves and bag were a disaster. Either I had a run in the stockings or I had forgotten the handkerchief. It is not without reason that I recently lectured at the C. G. Jung Institute in Zürich on "Fragmentary Communication or Problems of the *Non-finito!*" The problem in the background is of course the difference between a classical and a romantic *Weltanschauung* and temperament.

The moments I came closest to the mysteries of fashion were in the theater, where I worked as secretary. I had access to the wardrobe of the actors when they were preparing themselves for the stage. Whether an actress donned a period costume or put on a dress of the latest fashion for a modern play, the miracle of transformation was the same. When I had met her some hours ago in the tram, nobody had noticed her, although she was well known. Now she became more beautiful by the minute.

The paint she put on her face had the same magic in it that it has had since the dawn of time. The few remnants of the Neanderthal or Mousterian man comprise red and yellow ocher and black manganite of iron, and in the undisturbed caves often human skulls painted with these pigments were found.[8] Their paint assured the dead of life in the beyond. When actors are preparing themselves for the stage their dressing-up has a transcendent quality. They become more beautiful than they really are, as if they plugged into streams of energy which charge them up. On the stage "beautiful" is not the same as being "pretty." Even an actress made up as an old hag can be beautiful. In the primitive sense, beautiful equals being alive, illuminated from within.

The first show of a Parisian collection has theatrical qualities. Like actresses the models are, on that occasion, far more beautiful than usual. There is tremendous tension until the applause makes it known whether the new collection is a cuccess or a failure.

Coco Chanel was a woman designer who has not only created dresses but herself as well. She created her own legend, the role she was to play on the stage of the world. Her approach to fashion was as archaic as could be. Her source of inspiration were her lovers. She translated their apparel into garments for elegant women, who enjoyed a new freedom of movement. A "Chanel" is the name of a costume which, in its basic cut, is still today (almost sixty years after its first appearance) worn by women in top social and professional positions such as Simone Weil.

Chanel worked directly on the model without making preliminary sketches. She adapted the jersey sweater and the flannel jacket of her English lover and when she changed to a Russian count, she adapted the Russian peasant blouse as well. Later she switched back to English style, because by then she had become the mistress of the richest man in Europe, the Duke of Westminster.[9]

Coco Chanel's way of creating fashion reminded me of a tale from Middle India, about the origin of patterned cloth: "A girl fell in love with a snake, who sometimes took the form of a handsome youth. In his snake form he curled himself in her lap. She copied the markings of her lover's body and was soon making the most beautiful cloth that was ever seen."[10]

Chanel refused to design a fashion she would not want to wear herself and had a hard time with "mini" and "maxi", because she could not see herself in these kinds of dresses. She had some lean years until the battle was won. Now her style has become classic and a "Chanel" is an investment that will not lose its value for a long time.

With a male designer—and they are in the majority—the process of making fashion is more complicated, because obviously he can't see himself in his creations. Chanel was adapting literally what her lovers wore, to her own use, which may have included the taking-back and realizing of some animus projections. Dior for instance, who wrote an intelligent autobiography, called *Christian Dior and I*, relied entirely on his imagination, and gradually his anima fantasies took on concrete form in his dresses. They were at the beginning full of life, full of soul-stuff to him. Whilst he still was improving on them, they were worn by a girl who was sensitive to his intentions like an artist's model. Only when they were presented to the public did the extraverted star-mannequin take over. After the show the dresses had become mere ware to be inspected and torn apart by the commercial buyers to reveal the secret of their cut—and Dior never looked at them again.

New fashion collections are shown in Paris twice-yearly at least three months ahead of the season. "It is a characteristic of fashion,"writes Christian Dior, "that it is born outside its proper season. As with poetry, a certain nostalgia is needed. In summer the couturier dreams of winter and in the heart of winter, of summer. It would be totally impossible for me," he continues, "to make a summer dress in August. Distance in time is a prerequisite."[11]

When I read about Dior's need for creative distance and his comparing of making fashion to making poetry, I was reminded of a story about Rilke. He had once left a woman friend in the middle of the night, rode from Paris to Switzerland in order to write a most touching love-letter to her. Dior needed to turn his back on Paris and retire to the country to gather ideas for a new collection. His sketches were at first love-letters to his anima, and the presence of real women would have been disturbing. When he saw them later worn by beautiful women, they had lost, for him, their animation and had become mere things.

Although to-day only a few women in the world can afford to be dressed by Haute Couture, even the French Communist Party is against its abolition. Without it, the craft and art of French needlework would be lost.

The moment a new collection has been presented, first to the press, then to the buyers and finally to the individual clients, fashion has stepped from the time of imagination into everyday life and the race to be ahead of others begins. Everybody wants to be first to wear a new model or throw it in a thousand copies on the market. When a fashion trend has become so popular that it is obvious in the street, it is really old-hat. What becomes of out-dated couture models? I don't really know. Some land eventually in museums. The race to be ahead in time pervades the market also on the department store level, where seasonal fashion is sold earlier each year. Whoever wants to buy a winter dress in winter has little chance.

Only few people have ever seen an original model, but all know about it through press and television information. To most people fashion is basically a second-hand experience, something to be copied. The persuasiveness of fashion advertising can be observed best when there is a major change in design. Overnight the old hemline looks wrong, the fear to be unacceptable in an outdated dress is artificially kindled and kept up by a clever press.

Some time ago a marketing research organization invited a group of women to discuss the change of the hemline from "mini" to "maxi." A student said that in the "mini" in autumn she felt young, dynamic and desirable, but in January, when "maxi" length was really "in," she felt somehow undressed and exhibitionist in "mini." In "maxi" however, she now felt femine, catlike, adult and warm.[12] It is not difficult to reconstruct the advertising copy on which these statements were based. They had influenced the student without her realizing it.

From being told how to dress to be desirable, there is but one step to being told how to behave in order to be loved. Many psychological reports are used or misused as a guide as to how to avoid "psychological mistakes," leading to a loss of love.

Some two years ago a book by the psychoanalyst Alice Miller became in Zürich an overnight best-seller. It was called *The Drama of the Gifted Child* and was reviewed under the headline "The Tragedy of the Loss of Self." Miller deals with the vicissitudes of mother-child relationships, making use of some concepts by Kohut and Winnicott.[13] To one group of readers, who identified with the child, it was an additional help to deal with their narcissistic wounds. But to the readers who identified with the mother, because they had a small child, the book became a source of anxiety, full of warnings about what not to do, and it made them very self-conscious.

In disturbed mother-child relationships the battle over how to dress is a paramount feature with the mother intent on gratifying her narcissistic needs through the child (dressing it in the way she would have liked to have been dressed), whilst the child is fighting for its personal taste or its security in conformity (wanting to be dressed like its peers).

Sometimes fashion helps to improve the relationship of mother and daughter. This season the stiletto heels of the fifties are "in" again. "It is so nice to sound like mother," said a young woman, who had just bought a pair. "I still remember the clatter she made with them. Now I can make it too." Usually she was not so well-spoken of her mother, but the stiletto heels helped her to a momentary identification with mother in a playful way.

I have the suspicion that, working hour after hour in the consulting room, many analysts feel rather remote from the fashion scene. This is a pity, because such an attitude might further the shifting of attention from the creative process of fashion to the endproduct. Generally speaking: an increased awareness of ongoing processes is needed to balance all the accumulated knowledge that wants to be applied. Maybe more space should be given in the analytical hour to such activities as musing. The word "to muse" comes originally from the French *muse*, English "muzzle," meaning to sniff the air when in doubt about scent. Today musing is synonymous with pondering and reflectively gazing on what is going on.

Everyday fashion consists at best in combining ready-made stuff from the store with some item of personal fancy. This may sound banal but it is not, because when this process is blocked, there is considerably less relating to the outer and the inner world. Feeling-wise there can then be winter in summer and if, as an answer to his freezing soul, a person puts on warm clothes, he may look very awkward, which in turn aggravates his loneliness.

Not long ago a young man came to see me because he felt very blocked. He was clad in old black clothes and had very thick glasses. He dressed as if he wanted to make himself invisible and was all the more conspicuous. Soon afterwards he could vent his anger very successfully and as a result of unblocking, his outer appearance changed considerably in the following weeks. He now wore jeans and shirts of light, washed-out colors and had exchanged his glasses for contact lenses. He had literally brightened up.

I find it a worthwhile analytical task to help an analysand to rediscover and enlarge his play area. It may become the stage on which the joyful little mysteries of everyday life are played, imaginative fashion satisfying body and soul being one of them.

1. Veccio W. and Riley R. *The Fashion Makers*. New York, 1968, p. 5.
2. Linder, St. B. *The Harried Leisure Class*. New York, 1970, p. 90.
3. Winnicott, D. W. *Playing and Reality*. London, 1974, p. 3.
4. Woodcock G. and Avakumovic, J. *The Doukhobors*. London, 1968, III. p. 6
5. Jacoby, M. *Sehnsucht nach dem Paradies*. Bonz Verlag, 1980.
6. Schefold, R. *Spielzeug für die Seelen*. Kunst und Kultur der Mentavi-Inseln, Indonesien. Museum Rietberg Zürich, 1980, p. 10.
7. Winnicott, *loc cit*, p. 2.
8. Crawford, M. D. C. *Philosophy in Clothing*. The Brooklyn Museum, 1940, p. 9.
9. Haedrich, M. *Coco Chanel, secrète*. Paris, 1972.

10. Elwin, H. B. *Tribal Art of Middle India.* Oxford, 1951, p. 25.
11. Dior Ch. *Dior.* Frankfurt, 1956, p. 85.
12. Curtius M. und Hund, Wulf D. *Mode und Gesellschaft.* Frankfurt, 1975, p. 60.
13. Miller, A. *Das Drama des begabten Kindes und die Suche nach dem wahren Selbst.* Frankfurt, 1979.

(reprinted from Psychological Perspectives, Volume 12, No. 1, Spring 1981, pp. 31—42 by permission)

Fashion viewed as a Body-Soul relationship

By Bianca Garufi (Rome)

I propose to insight the unique phenomenon of fashion, inasmuch as it is one of the ways in which the soul expresses itself, attempting to communicate through the image.

Many authors, representing a broad variety of disciplines, have dealt with this vast topic. After reflecting on what they had to say, I found that it was possible to agree by and large with most of them. Nonetheless, I was somewhere left with a hunch that—despite my respect for their reasoning—they had not got down to bed-rock: some basic area had been left unexplored. That area is the psyche with its inherent need to find expression.

My guiding principle in these considerations will be the assumption that fashion is essentially a psychic phenomeon, that originates in the area of the psyche. There an image is generated and begins to move toward self-expression, until finally it takes on body and shape through extension in space and time.

Flügel[1] wrote that "fashion is a mysterious goddess, to be obeyed rather than to be understood, for its decrees transcend human comprehension".

No doubt he has a point, which does not, however, prevent us from spelling out some basic principles concerning fashion, some of which are upheld, others rejected by the specialists in the field.

In his writings Stratz[2] suggests two methods for classifying human dress: one distinguishes between *primitive, tropical* and *arctic* wear; whereas the other approach distinguishes between *fixed* and *fashionable* items of clothing.

Without dwelling on the primitive dress, which usually consisted of a simple girdle around the hips, we find that it soon developed into the loosely draped skirt generally worn in the tropics. Arctic wear, on the other hand, is characterized by the fact that it is tightly wrapped and worn close to the body. Although both types were worn during prehistoric times, it cannot be denied that *homo sapiens* and *mulier sapiens* made their first appearance in temperate climates and that the kind of dress they wore was derived from the draped variety. This also means that they may have been born at the same time as their garments and that their origin is shrouded in the same mystery as the one mentioned by Flügel.

In general, arctic dress, worn close to the body and parted to cover the extremities, was adopted by Western man less as a protection against the cold climate than out of a growing need to cover the body. Man rejected the body because it was evidence of his close and humiliating association with the animal kingdom and therefore the world of instincts in general. Most likely his choice was also dictated by the need to set himself off as the heroic patriarch against the more feminine types. Women's garments, as well as those of priests, were considered to be evidence for the surrender of the extraverted, heroic, virile and technologically inclined attitudes of the male.

Stratz's classification into *fixed* and *fashionable types* of dress relate to geographical space and roles, on the one hand, and time, on the other. National costumes, for example, are space-related. So are uniforms, which are, however, also related to specific roles. The *fashionable type* of garment is exclusively time-bound. It is an expression of change and versatility, reflecting the mercurial side of human nature. The *fixed types* are associated with security, tradition, and repetitive mimicry and reflect the Saturnine disdain for innovation and for the imaginative contribution of the individual, which is considered dangerous, a threat to the moralistic authority imposed by tradition.

Another fundamental aspect of fashion, which has often been the subject of controversy, is concerned with ranking the most prevalent motivations underlying the tendency of human beings to cover themselves with clothes: *protection, modesty,* and the *need for adornment.*

The majority of specialists do not attribute much importance to the *protective function* of clothes, and I entirely share this view. It seems, in fact, highly unlikely that the important custom of dressing could be based on so simple and functional a motive.

Modesty carries a great deal of authority according to biblical tradition, yet its manifestations seem to be a question of cultural convention rather than the result of an innate need. Following this line of thought, modesty would have to be considered as a reactive movement of the psyche, a rejection of exhibitionism as a too direct expression of the sexual impulse.

The proposition which gives the function of *adornment* priority over modesty and protection is supported by many arguments. Take, for example, the pleasure children take in displaying their nakedness, as well as their satisfaction with any object designed to stimulate their decorative fantasy, whether or not they are naked or dressed. Further, we find among the so-called primitives individuals not at all devoid of ornaments, despite the fact that they do not wear a stitch of clothing. No doubt modesty and climate only acquired functional values for dress as time went on, once the impulse to wear all kinds of ornaments, tattoos, necklaces, etc., etc., were well established. In other words, the desire for ornamentation would be enough motivation for man to contact his psyche through the body, by decorating, covering and uncovering his body, altering its shape, changing its color and size, following in all these behaviours a capricious and mysterious inner daimon whose *telos* and transcendency obey the supreme law that governs us all. What are we going to call this guiding force? We can choose from: Psyche, Eros, Anima, Soul, Tao, Fatum.

The inherent human need for adornment, seems to be the prime mover behind fashion in the broad sense of the term. The majority of authors contend that the motivation for adornment is associated with the need of human beings to impose themselves sexually. Dress thus becomes a means of expressing all the contents symbolizing sexuality in a given culture: power, wealth, authority.

But to decorate oneself may also reflect a need to compensate for feelings of inadequacy, a failure to accept one's body. And other authors claim that adornment expresses an aggressive drive, the need to acquire or preserve some sort of supremacy over others. Decoration in this view becomes a weapon for the purpose of conquering, aimed at reducing other people and at keeping them at a distance, a way to humiliate by displaying one's ornaments in a particularly glittering, appropriate or even refined fashion. (The same effect can be achieved by displaying restraint or monastic simplicity, or even wilful indifference and neglect, to summarize any number of past and recent trends.)

Fashion has also been viewed as a more or less explicit or a coded message, intended to establish contact between the individual and his environment. The language of this message is the individual's manner of dress, which serves the individual's need to introduce himself his desire to be decoded, read.

Narcissism as a motivation for adornment is such a complex subject that it would need an entire paper to deal with it adequately. No doubt Freud[3] was well aware of the complexity and far-reaching implications of this topic, when he spoke of the *quasi* biological nature of narcissism, with specific reference to the narcissism of the germinal cell and the fetus.

The myth of Narcissus may provide us with the best bridge between the traditional reductive approach to fashion and the "imagistic" approach I am putting forth. If we reject the notion of guilt associated with Narcissus, the myth can serve as a magnifying glass, enabling us to detect and contact moments of great psychic importance. I have in mind, for example, the ego's love and absolute respect for the image, and its total indifference to the body. One could also point out the totalitarian and monotheistic relationship between Narcissus's ego and the psychic image.

The ego's love for the image can be considered to express a situation in which the ego bows to the reflection of the psychic image, and capitulates to psyche itself, becoming her vassal.

Unless you interpret it literally, the myth does not say that this capitulation is fatal. In suggesting the annihilation of the ego, its effacement before the image, the myth gives us a glimpse of that intangible moment, the *fiat voluntas tua*, which the ego has so much trouble formulating, but which is equally indispensable for the coming of the stranger. This unknown visitor, as von

Franz[4] calls him, is the completely new, the divine presence, the creative—in short, one's destiny.

Whereas Narcissus' imaginal involvement in sacrifice allows us to contact the moment immediately prior to creation, Pygmalion may be designed to get us in touch with the moment that follows, the moment when the ego, after emerging from its absorption by the image, or perhaps its *coniunctio* with it, collaborates with the image in the process of expression. Whereas Narcissus *re*-flects, Pygmalion "flects", bends the image, giving it body and bringing it to life in accordance with its own proper dictates. In contrast with Narcissus, who is for ever caught up in reflection, Pygmalion expresses the movements of the image in time, its dynamic qualities that make for relationship, the erotic element in the ego's relationship with the image. The image is by no means immovable and Pygmalion has the task of following its movements, its disintegration and aspirations, observing it as it disappears and reappears, understanding what it means and does not mean.

Pygmalion is a servant of the image; he discerns its movements, listens to it, would like to see it move, talk, feel its warmth, listen to its sighs. He is so obstinate in his purpose that in the end he succeeds in establishing a dialogue between the ego as subject and the image as queen, a dialogue reminiscent of the kind of conversations women engage in with their inner image, while looking at a blouse, whose cut or color intrigues them; or, the dialogue a man has with his fantasy, when he is suddenly attracted by a strange T-shirt, or a showy yellow and green silk tie, or one with pink and blue dots, of a kind he would not normally wear.

The reason for dwelling on this point is to espress my conviction that creating, giving body to the image through one's own body, enables us to get to the roots of the mystery of fashion; and the figure we meet there is Pygmalion and not Narcissus. The impulse to adorn the body as an object, or rather as a medium for expressing the image, is governed by Pygmalion.

As we all know, Jung[5] speaks of five basic human instincts: hunger, sexuality, activity, reflection, and the creative instinct, the latter being the quintessence. In accepting the notion of a creative instinct, we also have to assume that—like the other four instincts—it produces goal-and behavior-oriented images, which serve its self-actualization. There is no doubt that the creative instinct, just like hunger, needs to be satisfied.

We are in the habit of confusing creative activity with artistic activity, as Hillman[6] has so aptly pointed out. We thus tend to limit the creative instinct to a special, extraordinary category of persons. It seems to be a contradiction in terms to include the creative instinct among the other basic human instincts, considering it even as a point of convergence and condensation for these other instincts, while claiming at the same time that only highly exceptional persons possess it, by way of a special gift, as it were, and that it is not an impulse like any other.

Just as the other instincts are lived in different ways by different people, at varying degrees of intensity and more or less apparently, the creative instinct can also be lived, expressed, and inherited with more or less strong manifestations. From this perspective, artists, geniuses, and creative people in general no longer belong to the chosen few; they are only human beings like the rest of us, who, however, happen to have an infinitely simpler and more direct connection with their creative instinct. The simplicity of this relationship as well as other personal, cultural, and historical factors, makes it easier for these people to psychicize and to favor the process, which makes for what Jung[7] called an encounter between the ectopsychic instinct and a psychic *datum*.

With the creative instinct in mind, we can look again at some of the main motivations of human beings to adorn and clothe themselves. These are the need to protect themselves against climatic factors; the drive to cover up with modesty their identities as earth-dwellers who have bodies, which have made them sinners; the desire to accentuate their capacities for sexual seduction and the contrary wish to deny and hide them; the urge to label themselves socially by means of certain codes and messages, which lend expression to specific roles.

The question arises, however, whether these are the immediate and distinct motivations behind the desire of human beings to adorn themselves, or whether they are not all inherent in that fifth instinct, described by Jung, as a result of which human beings express themselves in images of themselves, or as images, or through the images they have of themselves.

Just as in the case of food we proceed from the raw to the cooked stage, so in the case of the body, we go from the nude to the ornate stage. To decorate oneself might therefore be compared to a form of alchemical processing of the image we have of ourselves, a way of concentrating by placing layers of the most varied objects on top of each other as in a collage—within a context that bears in mind space and time: leaves, flowers, skins, furs, tufts of feathers; necklaces of shells, of teeth or precious stones; layers of paint; skirts, shirts, pants or jackets; anything, provided we get the psyche to yield up an image that can be projected on the body, just as a psychic image can be projected on canvas, into marble, a dome or an arch, any concrete or theoretical construct.

What we are dealing with is therefore an instinct for processing—combining, mixing, placing, adding, removing—an instinct—whose purpose it is to track down and to materialize the image we have of and/or in ourselves.

What are a warrior's clothes made of if not the image of a warrior? What makes for the hieratic nature of the priestly vestments, the glamorous sinuosity of a seductress, the austerity of what is considered a model house-wife and mother, if not the images themselves within these figures? These images, which have usually come down to us from remote ancestors, have been preserved in time the way parts of the anatomy can be preserved in formaldehyde.

These images return us to the myth of Narcissus, which emphasizes the moment when a totalitarian, monotheistic relationship is established between one's Narcissus-ego and one's image, a relationship experienced as loyalty to a unique and absolute entity. What is loyalty in substance? What constitutes loyalty to a style, or a model, if not the loyalty to an image we wish to hold or preserve for all times to come? Totalized and totalizing, fixed and fixated, like Narcissus, we are not capable of going through the metamorphoses and revolutions inherent in the flow of images and we become alienated from the potential of our creative instinctuality.

Unfaithfulness to a model or a style is not true disloyalty because, on the whole, we remain faithful to the flow of images. This particular aspect of imagination, that is, its flow, reminds us of a truly Heraclitean phrase attributed to Leonardo da Vinci[8]: "The river water you touch is the first that comes and the last that has flown past. Such is the present time."

This ever-changing but stable and permanent present, which connects us to the past and to the future takes us back once again to the phenomenon of fashion which, despite the great diversity of its manifestations, contains elements of both stability and permanence. With these two paradoxical components we also return to Stratz's contrasting yet parallel categories of dress, the *fixed* and the *fashionable type*, and this classification in turn suggests analogies with the attitudes of loyalty and disloyalty. The *fixed type* moves with time while being anchored to a fantasy of the past, whereas the *fashionable type* moves with time by mixing his fantasies of the past and intuitions of the future in the crucible of the present. The ever-changing present, described by Leonardo, and Jung (when discussing the spirit of the times), is a continual mutation born of the past and projected into the future. This present reflects not only the profound and recurring ties between the flow of psyche and the matter that constitutes today's moment; it also recalls the past ties between psychic flow and the matter that has formed part of the phylogenetically most remote roots of our body; and finally, this present expresses a commingling between psychic flow and the matter that is the concentrate of the future about to take shape, that is, our becoming.

The fruit of all this commingling is the modified instinct mentioned by Jung[9], that is, the psychic image. It is born of the very body, which is so difficult for us to accept *in toto*, just as it is difficult to accept *in toto* the products of our imagination.

This is where, it would seem, that psychization of matter coincides with the far-off origins of people's need to tie a liana around their hips, or to put a flower into their hair, a need which gradually gave rise to the phenomenon of fashion. And, because the flow of imagination is continuous and ever-changing, fashion is the most frequent place for the creative instinct to find expression in the continuous, primary, and autonomous manner it prefers.

Creativity has always been a human prerogative supported and stimulated by psychotherapy. Jungians particularly favor creative expression and often consider creative expression to be almost the equivalent of the cure.

So, let us dwell for a moment on what we may or may not have done with this creative instinct, when either the dreams or behavior highlight a person's innate capacity to adorn himself, to be creative in dressing. This need and innate capacity suggests for all of us a passive-active pause of reflection in a mirror. The mirror may be of water, of glass, it may be mental, or whatever. The important thing is the pause, which permits us to contact the image we have of ourselves at a given moment and therefore also our imagination; a pause, which obliges us—like Narcissus—to re-flect on our image, and which forces us to halt in that reflection. Only then is it possible to go on to follow in Pygmalion's footsteps and to create a likeness to the image proposed by the psyche.

Even if we allow ourselves to be influenced by the collective and consumer-oriented dictates of fashion, we still have the possibility of choosing detail and color, of giving free reign to our individuality and imagination. We cannot deny the existence and the importance of individual choice, of our preferences and our inclinations, our emotions, our Eros and therefore, the intervention, however marginal, of the individual psyche and body. It would be more appropriate to say that our choice is a necessity, a *psycho-biological* necessity, whose living seat is our very body.

If the need to adorn ourselves is indeed to be attributed to a *psycho-biological urge*, we might ask ourselves just what has become of this innate urge. Perhaps we have put it away into a box, labelled it as something basic, to be accepted for what it is, but have failed to see through to the archetype of pure creation, or to one of the many myths, in which beauty and adornment are closely intermingled. Did it ever occur to us to associate a fantasy of dress or ornamentation with the beauty of Psyche? Hers was a natural beauty, it is true, but on the day of her fatal encounter with Eros she was very ornate and elaborate. Did we ever stop to associate images of vanity and youth with Paris? Vain Paris, it should be recalled, chose Helen, the beautiful, the ornamented; and between the two of them there was maybe only beauty and ornamentation. Despite this, they turned out to be instruments for the transformation of a world, a culture; their dalliance led to the creation of other worlds and other cultures.

Do we ever think of Aphrodite and the beauty of her inimitable belt (a unique item of high fashion)? Does it occur to us to think of Hephaistos as the Christian Dior of Homeric days, whose wife was—according to Hesiod—one of the three Graces, *Aglae*, a synonym for ornamentation, pomp and splendor? And Ganymede with his flowery garlands—does he ever come to mind in this context?

What about Achilles, Hector, Aeneas, who staked their lives and honor on seizing an enemy's armour, possibly because as conquered booty it was supposed to confer magic, but even more so because there was magic in the fantasy of wearing it?

In looking at the picture Homer paints of Greek mythology we note that all the figures—from Zeus to the last of the nymphs—do their best to represent the image they have of themselves. This applies equally to Hestia, the virginal and patriotic guardian of hearth and home, and to Athene, so splendidly attired in her peplum and metallic accessories, and even to the pessimist Cassandra, who always dressed in mourning with a total absence of ornaments.

Another question: whatever became of the little girl, who dressed up for carnival as a fairy, gypsy, pirate, nun, or as Barbarella or Little Lord Fauntleroy, and thus gave free reign to her fancy, instilling life into the images of her fantasy? One could ask as well about the little boy, who dressed up as a beggar, emperor, veiled odalisque, musketeer, magician, astronaut, or superman.

Most people have some sort of sentimental memories of these childhood fantasies, and yet they take on significance when we consider them as elements that allow us to understand and attend to the disturbances of the adult psyche. This is more or less the attitude we adopt when a dream image stands out for the dress which is worn, be it a shabby fur, a lace skirt, velvet pants, a coarse monastic frock, or even an abstract or geometric construction. While this information may be very useful therapeutically, I wonder what else we do with this wealth of data? Do we actually use it to pursue the dialogue with the soul, with these curious images of male and female figures? Perhaps not very often, at least not along the lines of thought pursued in this paper, that is, by looking on *fashion*, on *body* and *soul* as an inseparable whole. On the whole, it would seem that dress has always been dealt with in the analytical context reductively, that is, in moralistic terms of improvement or deterioration, or, in the eyes of the ego subject undergoing analysis, as an expression of a positive or negative phase. Even in dreams the need to wear clothes and to decorate oneself, and fashion, as the direct product of this need, have been dealt with as pertaining exclusively to the world of ego. Too frequently, a person's manner of dress is reduced to something other than the reflection of psyche's image in the body, and body's image in the psyche.

Although none of us likes to approach things schematically, we cannot always avoid it. It is not easy to stop thinking in terms of Persona when it comes to clothes—either the underdeveloped Persona, identity with the Persona, or lack of Persona, the right dose of Persona, etc, etc.

Colors also lend themselves easily to thinking in categories, especially typological ones: too much blue, too yellow, not enough green, red is totally lacking, etc. etc. Despite its usefulness and the best of therapeutic intentions, typology and its color symbolism can also be used schematically and in routine fashion.

Alchemical symbolism is another schema we tend to use for the purpose of interpretation. It is not my intention to go here into all the distinctions that can be made between the image and the symbol. Let us nonetheless take a closer look at the sort of thing that can happen when an image is linked with an alchemical symbol, to the detriment of the image as such. We know, for example that white represents the *albedo*. When white appears in a dream in the form of a dress or suit, we can use all the alchemical implications of white as a working hypothesis, ranging from initiation to purification, such as the fact that white is an amalgam of all the colors and therefore all the possibilities, is the white of wisdom, is the bitterness of salt, etc. But aside from all these possible meanings of white, we also want to know more precisely what this particular dream is saying.

And to answer this question about the dream by digging deeper into our bag of psychological symbolism is a little like approaching a Rembrandt, a Van Gogh, a Magritte or a Morandi picture with a dictionary of symbols in hand. This detracts from direct communication between the immediate image, which is meant to have its own impact and fertilizing effect, and ourselves, who are meant to be open to the image, allowing ourselves to be enriched by it. When we immediately reach for the symbol, access to the image becomes infinitely more difficult, along with the possibility of its therapeutic effectiveness. Finally this approach obstructs the imaginal inroads into our psyche and makes it difficult for the image to find a place in us.

If we quickly bury the image in one of the numerous little graves in the cemetery of symbols (especially freguented by Jungian analysts—so familiar with the symbols and their use), the poor image will be entombed alive. When we are presented with an image involving dress, this image needs to be related to the basic and primordial instinct to adorn or to paint, to balance or unbalance ourselves, to remove or to add something. It is this instinct that enables us to pause for an instant before our reflected image (forgetful of any social obligations) and which induces us—metaphorically or otherwise—to step back, like a painter after a stroke of the brush, to check whether we really succeeded in reproducing the image we had of ourselves at that moment, the moment of pause and reflection.

Provided we are capable of it, we need to learn to stop, and to waste time, as Casey[10] has put it. Let us try to make a mandala of our body, turning it into a temple, whose rituals and parameters have rarely if ever been used consciously to the glory and the honour of the gods who continue to dwell within. We do not remember sufficiently, or often enough, that our body is a ἓ *emenos*, the sacred space of our plurality and our totality, from which nothing is excluded and to which nothing can be added, neither above, nor below, to the right or the left, neither within nor without, in front or in back, by nothing that is palpable or impalpable.

In this connection a number of questions come to mind: how is it possible not to decorate a temple, which shelters a divinity that is truly cherished and respected? How is it that not infrequently the divinity inhabiting it and therefore part of it and permeating it, is desecrated, sacked and humiliated in open warfare?

The real question is whether we do, in fact, show enough respect for those images, which, in dreams or in daily life, speak of the need to care for our body, of ways to dress and their relationship to fashion. Although fashion expresses the spirit of the times, it is—one way or another—also associated with care of the body and ways to dress it. Are we capable of recognizing that behind some of our dreams and daily gestures there is an instinct that prompts us to fashion and recreate ourselves and at times to recreate others? I truly wonder whether we are aware of the unique (though perhaps not necessarily grandiose) means available to each one of us in order to reduce the tremendous gap which exists between care of the body and care of the mind. The distance between the two can only be described in light years. It goes back not only to Descartes, but thousands of years beyond: body to one side and mind to the other, nature, including animals, wilderness, darkness (and even the feminine) on the one hand and, on the other, snowy peaks which, in their whiteness and remoteness, represent the widespread aspirations of so many in our (patriarchal, rational, scientific, and hyperborean) culture. This longing for the summits has so many grandiose names, that it would seem blasphemous to refer to them without going on our knees. For centuries they have been charged with so much intensity that they have become just a bit too "heavy", to wit: development, individuation, process, ascension or, worse still, asceticism. These expressions are like milestones on the road, along which the mere desire to travel is enough evidence of noble effort, admirable will-power, and great valor. But what do we do with our life as it is, in the present, with its corporeality, its earthboundness? We act as if it is only meant to secure a place who-knows-when, who-knows-where, up-there, in *nirvana,* or paradise, anywhere, provided the place is high up, very high and very difficult to reach from where we are, *hic et nunc,* very remote from the world of instinct and imagination, body and soul, a life, whose origins we know no more than the purpose of its death.

Fashion and its relationship to body and psyche has been the phenomenon which has inspired some of the ideas I have outlined here. It is my hope that they will lend more depth and more ease to the *opus* of living an earthly life, which means ever moving in circles, or better said, circumambulating, mixing the poetic with the prosaic, reason with unreason.

What I feel most is that we should never lose from our sight the tie with *ars;* it is the only umbilical cord which must never be cut, because through the many manifestations of the creative instinct, it keeps us connected to nature. These manifestations may be graffiti or rock paintings in the Sahara, murals in the Sistine Chapel, Homeric hymns or the *I Ching,* poetry by Sappho or

Sylvia Plath, the works of the anonymous architect of Angkor Vat or a Brunelleschi cupola, the Eiffel Tower or the Empire State Building, Assyro-Babylonian astrology or Einstein's theory of relativity, as well as the concept of synchronicity, and they include — and I place strong emphasis on this point—the simplest, most humble and elementary form of creative expression that occurs every time we give body to the image through our own body. It is essential that we preserve this connection with *ars*, because it is the most human of all our qualities. If art is understood in this manner, it is like a light that knows no darkness, a consciousness that lovingly befriends the unconscious, perfection that cannot do without imperfection, a way of knowing nature in nature, which—through nature—precludes onesidedness. It embraces all we are, all we have been, and all we ever shall be, along with everything we have done, and everything we do at this very moment, here and now, and all we ever shall do. Todays as in the past and future, the instinct to adorn ourselves responds to an impulse that is very close to the faculty of selfcreation. Self-creation follows the paradoxical counterpoint of beauty and ugliness, harmony and disharmony, simplicity and extravagance, that is inherent to nature.

A quick glance at the etymology of the word *fashion* takes us to *facere* for the Englih and *modus* for the French (mode). But going back even further we come upon the Greek word *kosmesi*, which is derived from *kosmos*.

Kosmos denotes and continues to denote sphere, beauty, ornament, measure, discipline. With its variety of meanings it seems to me that *kosmos* is the best term to express the incommensurable imagination of nature when it comes to ornamentation and beauty; perhaps this is where the imagination of nature manifests itself *par excellence*. In addition to the terms ornament, measure and discipline under *kosmos*, we find under the heading *kosmesi* the term fashion, along with other near-synonyms: instrument, manner, system, construction, glory, honor and art, that *ars* which nature uses in order to give form and life to its own fantasies, and therefore to itself.

The *opus*, which cannot be accomplished, and *ars*, which can be accomplished, are in fact one and the same, just as *opus* und *ars* are one with the internal and mysterious rhythm of the creative impulse in its variegated expressions, as present in visceral glow as in apical iciness, in monstrous upheavals and in idyllic placidity.

In conclusion, one might say that nature is eternal in its changing (its changing being an important aspect of fashion), and that the eternity of nature rests on this very changing.

translation by Ruth Horine

1. J. C. Flügel. *Psicologia dell'abbigliamento*, Milano, Franco Angeli Editore, 1974, p. 166.
2. C. H. Stratz. *Die Frauenkleidung und ihre natürliche Entwicklung*, Stuttgart 1922, 93, p. 114.

3. S. Freud. *Opere Complete, vol. 9*, p. 235—236: "Al di là del Principio del Piacere".
4. M-L. von Franz. "Il Visitatore Sconosciuto nei Sogni e nelle Fiabe", in *Rivista di Psicologia Analitica*, 4/2, 1973, Marsilio Editore, Padova, pp. 556—570.
5. C. G. Jung. "Psychological Factors Determining Human Behaviour", in *C. W. 8*, Routledge & Kegan Paul, London 1960, p. 118.
6. J. Hillman. *The Myth of Analysis*, New York, Harper & Row, Publishers, 1972, p. 34.
7. C. G. Jung, *C. W. 8*, Routledge & Kegan Paul, London, 1960 p. 115.
8. G. Fumagalli. *Leonardo omo senza lettere* (cit. da Trivulsiano 34 r), Beltrami, Firenze, 1970, p. 357.
9. C. G. Jung. *C. W. 8*, Routledge & Kegan Paul, London, 1960 p. 115.
10. E. S. Casey. *Time in Soul*, in Spring 1979, Spring Publications University of Dallas, Irving, Texas, pp. 114—164.

ANALYTIC TRAINING

The Training of shadow
and the
Shadow of training

By Patricia Berry-Hillman (Dallas)

I have always found the shadow the most difficult of psychological experiences (which is rather embarassing since it is supposed to be the first and
so presumably the easiest). The shadow is not difficult to understand conceptually. The idea is based on a model of opposites and Jung's notion of the
onesidedness of conscious functioning. What is easy to understand theoretically is practically and experientially much more difficult. Part of the difficulty
for me, I thought, had to do with my generation of the 'Fifties and 'Sixties, in
which conscious identifications were uncertain, since consciousness itself was
uncertain. The generation Jung addressed was seemingly more solid, still a bit
Victorian in its convictions. In that generation there seemed a clear distinction
between what the ego embraced and the shadow undid. There was a light, and
a darkness of the light. There really were Dr Jekylls and Mr Hydes.

In my generation we were 'on the road' with Kerouac, wailing with Elvis,
Fats Domino, Little Richard; we also embraced the virtues of science (there
was a space race and LSD was a chemical compound); we were idealistic (we
marched for racial integration and burnt draft cards).

Now all of this confused emotionality (beatnik, scientific, idealistic) makes
of the shadow a complicated entity. First, there is not *a* shadow but many (as
there is not one conscious standpoint but many—all equally serious, depending upon the mood and the moment). Structures of awareness shift. What is
relatively conscious at one moment is not so the next. As the source of light
shifts, as position or situation changes (as a different light is cast upon
things)—so the shadow wanders.

I felt better about this shifting character of my shadow when I came across a
passage in Jung. In 'On the nature of the psyche', Jung notes that 'sliding consciousness', as he calls it, is 'thoroughly characteristic of modern man'. Is is
not so unusual after all. Jung goes on to explain why he uses the word
'shadow' rather than a more scientific conceptualisation, such as, 'the inferior
part of the personality'. The problem, he says, with these 'scientific-looking

Graeco-Latin neologism[s]' is that the content becomes fixed, so that one loses the suffering and passion that implicate the whole man. The reason he prefers the word 'shadow' is because it is a poetic term, implying plasticity and an aesthetic, linguistic heritage (JUNG 2).

So the shadow is connected with culture. It is not a term from scientific psychology or from moral theology; rather it is an imagistic idea. The word itself has shadowy connotations, being inexact, non-static, varying over time and in different situations.

In keeping with Jung's poetic description of shadow, one might imagine the best training for shadow awareness to be poetic or aesthetic. Now I do not mean necessarily poetry or painting. Nor do I mean literally that a candidate for training must have an academic background in the arts. Though I think that might be a good idea, at the moment at least I am referring to the arts as a metaphorical backdrop against which we might view our work with shadow.

As a poetic (rather than a scientific) idea, the shadow becomes difficult to define in general, as in the arts general laws seldom hold true. When one says a good poem is this and not that, one is in trouble, since in another poem, in another situation, the same criteria do not apply. Rather what is required is a sharp eye to situation—the shape of the work, the behaviour, the action, the feeling within a particular context.

Assuming this aesthetic metaphor as background to our work, what are its implications? As craftsmen or artists the first implication is that we begin with distinct, particular perceptions rather than with generalities into which particulars must then fit. In other words, in training for shadow awareness we encourage the aesthetic perception of particulars in lieu of global thinking, thinking in large general categories about the shadow.

For the aesthetic eye, conceptual thinking would be to obscure, if not to lose, the shadow. For example, even thought it is theoretically and conceptually correct to regard the shadow as the inferior part of the personality because it is closer to the animal and the instinctual, in a particular situation, that is often not the case—at least on an apparent level. As Jung frequently noted, the shadow may be a superior part of the personality, a hidden talent, a figure more moral than the ego. Also, it need not be animal and instinctual; it may as well be disembodied, airy, rigid, anorexic.

Another way in which one may generalise shadow and thus aesthetically miss it, is by thinking of shadow as only a moral problem. When looking for good and evil, black and white, one misses the colours and shades. In painting, for example, shadows are actually greens, purples, browns, deeper tones of the same colour—not usually blacks. These shadows give form. Shadings make certain things stand out and others recede so that (as in a painting or building, poem or human face) depth, perspective and substance become apparent. So the shadow as form, substance, body, is a fitting aesthetic description.

There is a third way to miss the shadow aesthetically. Traits, types, complexes and syndromes: when they are global general concepts, they lead us to miss the shadow in particular. Let us say that my shadow in general is extraverted feeling, laziness, pretentiousness. Whereas all these traits are true, they do not really give me the experience of shadow. Worse, they occlude the possibility of my experiencing shadow: once I have conceptually wrapped it up, I think I have already experienced it, and so pay little further attention.

Also, what we tell others can block shadow awareness. Recently I told an analysand that he was caught in the mother complex. Of course, this was an analytic *faux pas*, but I was tired that evening and his insubstantial, clever talk irritated me. The whole of the next week he could see only his mother complex. In the following session everything that happened to him he interpreted as a further instance of mother. He told of a scene with his wife, who accused him of not doing enough housework, not taking her out enough, not protecting her, not paying enough attention to her. He had concurred because he 'knew' he had a mother complex, and the discussion had stopped. Of course, his giving in to the accusation *was* his mother complex! Armed with this general idea about himself (unfortunately given him by me), this man then used the generality to keep from perceiving or feeling anything sharp and detailed about himself, any particular value or shadow shape.

The shadow must threaten awareness, and *nothing in general is really threatening*. Only the specific and the unexpected hit us hard. The specific is intimate (close, small, near) and the unexpected is simply the unconscious itself. So the shadow comes in specific and unexpected moments—in the moment when I am both baring my soul and also manipulating for sympathy; or in analysis when I am feeling love and genuine warmth for my analysand—then realise it is *my need,* and that I am also binding the analysand to me; or when I predict a marriage is breaking up—and then realise my prediction is playing a rôle in the disaster, scheming it along; or, in the realm of thought, when I am speaking intellectually and suddenly realise I am lost in my own abstraction.

There seems to be a certain masochistic enjoyment in shadow awareness. We must like this suffering, else why would we do it? Something in us must delight as our ground collapses. Maybe this painful enjoyment of losing certainty is an aesthetic pleasure—like the enjoyment of a good play or novel that upsets, turns round, the way we have viewed things and, through the tensions it creates, forces upon us another vision.

So we come to tension. Shadow awareness proceeds through tension, and again we find that the more specific or close we can focus on shades of difference, the more the tension. Is is the pink that clashes with the red, just because they are so close. Blue does not clash with red so much as it compensates or balances it, preventing the intimate tension that makes for specific shadow awareness.

As an example of these tensions, I have a woman in analysis who is wildly libidinous, irrational, and 'liberated' in her night life; whereas in her day life she is rational, considered, responsible. These red and blue opposites stand side by side, balancing each other in a way that does not move and makes psychic work difficult. Although these red and blue sides of her personality are large-scale opposites, they are not effective shadows: they do not create tension, they would not make an interesting painting. A better psychologically working tension, a moving tension, if it could be brought about, would be between her softly pink sentimental notions of love and her red hot tin roof nights. Then her pink and red would be in tension.

This aesthetic emphasis on the particular is like Jungs's insistence on the individual—the unique against which he posited the collective. Jung eschewed large systems and organisations; he keenly distrusted general strictures. As a good clinician, Jung was a craftsman, an aesthetician.

So far I have looked at the shadow against an aesthetic backdrop in order to emphasise its multiplicity, specificity, and subtlety. Now I would like to move more directly into Jungian terminology—where specificity is called 'the individual', the unique, and the general, or, broadly conceived, becomes 'the collective'. Since relationship with the collective is a current issue in our training programmes, I would like to go into Jung's notions of the collective in some detail.

Jung had three psychological nuances in his use of 'the collective'. Most negatively, the collective was the mass, the crowd, the mob—Hitler's Germany. In this idea of the collective, the archetypes seem to have no organising, structuring propensity of their own, but appear titanically as compulsion or mass, formless energy. Organisation is split off and arranged from above by system and dictatorial edict. The split is between an organising, forming aspect of the psyche, on the one level, and a formless mass energy on the other. One can see such a split in analysands with Hitler dreams, where a highly structured, dictatorial—even paranoid—ruling principle lays down the law for the rest of the psyche, which, as a result, is a formless mass.

The second collective Jung refers to is less dramatic—in fact, the danger of this collectivity is in its comfortable, apparently harmless, character. Within these adaptive collective patterns or aspects of oneself, consciousness appears sleepily unaware. One is carried along by habitual social patterns—and pre-established structures—those attitudes and values that the individual psyche has not actually worked or grappled with. Thus the psyche moves sheep-like along paths others have formed—as the usual, most natural, easiest routes.

Aesthetically, to work in this natural, comfortable mode would be like crafting a painting or poem in the most conventional manner—with mediocre, though perhaps acceptable, results. The key to recognising sheeplike collectivity is uniformity. The forms, styles, techniques are all the same and in tune with the times—the present structure of things, present values. We all live to some extent in this mode, for conformity can free our energy for other things, and besides we need something of this 'forgetful attitude' from which to work.

The third manner in which Jung used 'the collective' is by far the most important. This collectivity is the grounding of his thought. At the deepest reaches of the psyche, this collective points to human potentiality; it is the source of creativity, universal values and archetypal possibilities. Unlike the first collective, which appears *en masse,* this third sense of the collective displays inherent formal properties as well. In an individuation process the psyche comes to terms and works with these collective forms and contents, so that in the (ideal) end one is not only unique, but also most connected with collective—by which Jung here means commonly shared universal, archetypal—qualities; that is to say, one is in touch with the deepest levels of others' and one's own world as well.

Thus, when in our training programmes we speak of the necessity to maintain a tension with the collective—if we are referring to this deepest collective of commonality with others, then by tension we mean the deepest tension of the individuation process which requires us to sacrifice ego narrowness, self-interest, pettiness—to larger, broader values and concerns. Collectivity in this third sense is very much connected with Jung's notion of the self. In fact, if 'the self' be an isolated figure in a tower it is not a self at all (rather is it an ego). The self is connected with the collective in this deepest sense.

When it is a deep connection with humanity and its values, the collective has absolutely nothing to do with standardisation, networks of rules, or with any fixed notion of society. As an ingredient in the individuation process, this collectivity is an achievement by way of the unique: it begins with the unique tensions of a particular soul. It is a work from within an individual psyche, and the result of the psyche coming to terms with its own necessities. This collectivity is both a natural process (given with the nature of the psyche, the nature of being human), and it is a great work, an achievement. To relate *commonly* by means of one's own *individuality* is thus a goal of the process.

But, I must repeat, to achieve this collective engagement, it is essential that one should begin with the individual, with the particular. By so beginning, the collective shows immediately, irrepressibly, in whatever one is working with. Every psyche is in a collective setting, but this collective is always particularised—in a room, a family, a city. In other words, the collective manifests itself within a setting of particular significance, a setting that has psychological importance. We recognise the collective not by a general idea but as it actually impinges. For one individual the collective may show in his inability to connect with his family; for another, the inability to talk with the petrol station attendant or to use public toilets. If we look for the collective in what we *expect* as collective we may miss where the collective is actually most importantly present.

So although everything exists within a collective, it is best not to define from the outside or in general what that collectivity necessarily is. Whenever we say that the collective must necessarily be some set of rules of standardised structures, then we are no longer working from the individual psyche and its process. We are no longer beginning with the work and how *it* frames itself. Further, by standardising our notion of the collective, we have shifted from Jung's deepest sense of commonality to the more superficial notions with which individuation feels itself in conflict.

I believe this conflict was going on in Jung. When he made his vehement attacks against collective standardisation, perhaps it was not only Nazi Germany he was reacting against (though of course he was), but also psychologically he was fighting for the right of his originality, which led to the founding of a psychology based on the individual in his or her psychological reality. What Freud called the reality principle, for Jung, as I read him, began with and proceeded out of *psychic* reality.

This tension between external, collective adaption—the systematised and 'most natural' route—and the discovery of one's unique mode of commonality is a dynamic of the shadow—or rather, two shadows, as though these shadow conflicts were necessary to generate psychic tension, and thus transformation. It is as though the psychic process has two shadows: one shadow, unconsciously adaptive and conforming, follows the most natural route to avoid consciousness or trouble. The second shadow is a miscreant who does not fit in, disturbs irritates, is not satisfied with the *status quo*. This shadow embraces the unique for the sake of the unique, and through symptoms, oddities, unconscious slips, goads the psyche into continuous movement.

To connect these shadow danamics with practical matters of training: one of the issues—a very hot one in some groups—is whether to require that trainees be licensed, registered. Now licensing and registration are eminently practical, reasonable, sensibly adaptive moves. The conformist shadow has no difficulty understanding the advantages: practice can be covered by insurance in countries where that applies, and one is respectable; analysands can pay with insurance money, thus one can build a large practice. The advantages are so great that even the miscreant shadow would enjoy the shelter it offers (the better to work his mischief). So licensing for him too is preferable, but only insofar as the paths leading to licensing do not compromise his miscreant sense of the odd, the unusual, the individual. For that reason he may have trouble should he study academic psychology, a field based on scientific thinking: the principle of parsimony (reducing the complex to the simple), generalities, statistical averages. Within this way of thinking, the miscreant shadow loses his purposeful function within the psyche and becomes merely a variation of the statistical norm.

But here I too may be guilty of generalising. In truth there are individuals for whom this kind of scientific training *is* in keeping with their shadow dynamics, their inner processes. The real problem, I suppose, comes only when this adaptive shadow turns solar, moves into power and forgets then its nature as shadow, i. e., as dark, distinct, multiple and particular. When the shadow claims itself as sun principle, claims its unique processes as general rule—then we get dictums and systems, and networks of unbendable rules. Then the self-organising power of the psychological is lost, and we are no longer working aesthetically from deeper levels of collective potentiality.

One of the characteristics of the shadow turned solar is that it sees reality in the harshest glare of sunlight. Requirements, rules and accepted patterns must be followed directly and literally, whereas from a darker, more shadowy point of view, the world itself is in the shadows. Reality is not just one hard-edged thing but multiple things in softer hues. There are indirect, sensitive, moonlit ways of moving through and with a gentler world. One need not project all one's tensions with the collective onto the literal world of the fathers above. Psychologically there may be many more fertile realms of tension.

One of these realms, ironically, may be the tensions that exist among us as Jungians. It seems to me that Jung's psychology is broad, complex and rich enough to hold many differences. These differences and differentiations, regionally and individually, are our fertility. Thank heavens Jung never laid out a clear, non-contradictory system. Because his psychology is based on the individuation process, diversity is crucial. The great danger for our discipline is not where we disagree but where we agree; for where we agree, we have no chance to recognise shadow. Where we agree, we become organised, systematised—the collective entity against which Jung always warned.

By way of summary let me list some implications of what I have said for training:

(1) The more we acquire dogmatic rules and elaborate systems for our training programmes, the more we move towards international standardisation, an external unity in which we all would have the same training requirements, the more we lose our particular value, our uniqueness, regionally and individually.

(2) In order to improve quality in training, we might best train for a sharper, more differentiated perception of the individual. Our present emphasis upon quantity in training (requiring greater and greater numbers of hours) does not necessarily meet this need. In fact, quantitative thinking may be obscuring the real need.

(3) As our numbers grow, the need to protect ourselves against charlatanism increases. But as Guggenbühl has pointed out, the charlatan is within us all (GUGGENBÜHL-CRAIG I). Thus the best safeguard against charlatanism is a training that makes absolutely essential a detailed, differentiated shodow awareness. Early on I called this an aesthetic training, and said I did not mean necessarily by that a literal training in the arts. True, an exact eye and ear for individuality and differences can be developed in clinical work as well as through a training in the liberal arts or humanities. Indeed, this perception

could be developed in almost any number of different educational disciplines, or apart from them all. Thus what one has studied would seem less important than the eye one has developed. Further, since shadow arises with each stance or position, it is crucial for us to disagree and to diversify.

(4) If we keep individual differences ever before us, in our training and among ourselves, those differences will not be forced to amass and split off. What is actually happening when there is emphasis on unification and standardisation is that a counter-movement is being constellated. Talk of uniformity is destroying our unity. For the Jungian mind, uniformity and unity do not mix easily.

Were we to agree to differ, i. e., to agree upon individuality, we would effect a much stronger binding amoung us—a binding based not too much upon one kind of shadow raised to solar consciousness, with its resulting programmes and procedures. By agreeing to differ, we would more likely keep our unity, since our true Jungian commonality is rooted in each of us as individuals.

(reprinted from The Journal of Analytical Psychology 1981, 26, 221—228 by per-mission)

1. GUGGENBÜHL-CRAIG, A. (1971). *Power in the Helping Professions.* New York, Spring Publications.
2. JUNG, C. G. (1947). 'On the nature of the psyche'. Coll. Wks, **8.**

Fragmentary Vision: a central training aim

By Andrew Samuels (London)

I am going to present an approach to training which I think will at first seem quite inimical to analytical psychology. In part I am reacting to my own training; in part to what I see and hear, particularly in the group of trainees and junior analysts from several countries which has been meeting regularly. This is certainly not a paper about psychological theory—it is an attempt to make proposals about how to organize training for analysts and back up these proposals with some psychological reflections. I shall be arguing against current tendencies to concentrate in an unrealistic and counterproductive way on the idea of wholeness or, somewhat in oppositon, to overemphasise the logical, linear, orderly aspects of training. Some societies could be criticised for the former and some for the latter tendency.

My initial contention is that in many circumstances a whole-person view is alike inconsistent with practice and theory and on occasion destructive to analyst and analysand. I am thinking of a spiritualised *folie à deux* in which erotic and aggressive interaction is denied. Some of the risk of this can be overcome by adopting what I call *fragmentary vision* and by organising training in terms of this. A slogan at the outset: "bits are beautiful." Actually I point out that bits are inevitable and that bits form the basis of practice. This makes training organised conventionally, with a linear syllabus, like the chapters of a book, rather difficult to justify.

To make sure that there is as little misunderstanding as possible (and in full knowledge of the dangers of stereotyping, not to mention naming names) I would think that the Zurich training programme concentrates too much on "wholeness" and that the S.A.P.'s programme in London is rather too "linear".

My approach has been anticipated by the pluralism of Karl Popper and William James, and I shall touch on this, albeit sketchily.

Conflict-Orientated Training

In many respects our various international gatherings serve as paradigm and stimulus for this way of thinking since one is healthily deprived of the familial support for one's ideas that is often available at home—where even virulent disagreement within the local group can function as a matrix-strengthener. The international context is the best training ground of all for a fragmentary vision point of view. As Popper has said, the place for any beginning seeker after knowledge to go is *where the disagreements are.* If you allow that psychological theory and practice develop organically, in a process, then just where current practitioners cannot agree represents the state of the art. Here you can be sure of being in the presence of the best minds and talents and the most contemporary viewpoints (that is, the most contemporary synthesis of what has gone before and view of what might happen next.).

This notion of what a trainee should do opposes the apparently more sensible and customary view that you should start with what is known and agreed, and when that has been mastered or at least understood, engage in the grown-up disagreements. Of course the arena where talented and experienced people differ is a heady place to enter, dizzymaking, frightening, fragmentary. But a training program basing itself on conflict rather than consensus has its points.

For instance, I should suggest that next year's training in the various centers commence with the arguments entered into at the International Congress in San Francisco, not with Jung's early dealings with Freud or whatever usually comes first. Not only would such a program attract the bolder soul to analytical psychology because of its danger, it would serve as an appropriate analogue to the ongoing personal analysis of the trainee. In analysis the beginning is also where the conflicts are, where the forces of the psyche are fragmentary, not in agreement with each other.

Another point in favour of exchanging linear training for conflictoriented training is that the latter continually puts the student in a problem or rather a problem-solving situation. He has to decide which of several views is more reliable and suits him best—often quite a problem. He will still be at the growing tip of some line of inquiry, stretching back to Jung and beyond, but directly in touch with the complexity and fragmentation of the psyche. His first experience as a trainee is to *choose.* Popper says, "We do not know how or where to start an analysis of this world. There is no wisdom to tell us. Even the scientific tradition doesn't tell us. It only tells us where other people started and where they got to."[1]

A further example: instead of studying the works of Freud, Jung, Klein in a sensible order, one might start with Hillman's attack on the developmental approach in *Loose Ends* or Fordham's attack on Neumann in his last C. G. Jung Lecture. Here you have two excellent minds at work; what turns them on, energises them, is worth being close to. Such arcane conflicts are supposed too much for the student to bear. It wouldn't matter if some aspects of these disputes were over students' heads; they will understand more in time and even linear syllabi are not absorbed in a linear manner. *Starting at the beginning is no guarantee of comprehension.* The assumption that students are not equipped to make choices and handle problem areas needs to be questioned. Accepting the fragmentary nature of the problem situation, adopting a conflict model for learning, compels the student to resonate more fully with didactic material. If fragmentation has to do with conflict then it has to do with wholeness, so the idea of wholeness is at least notionally present.

For the teacher too there are advantages in starting where the problem or conflict is—particularly if he has been teaching for some time. For even old arguments are more stimulating and refreshing than rehashing consensus theories on a more or less chronological basis. By plunging into the chaotic and fragmented world of the conflict or argument the student cannot avoid learning what has been said by others before him. It seems to me that in doing so one pays more respect to the history of knowledge and of dynamic psychology in particular.

And again, I think this approach fits with the unfolding of an analysis which is irregular and unpredictable. I remember one of my fellow trainees being quite upset that we hadn't got to some subject or other which she thought might apply to her analysand. I say this because I want to defend my position against a possible charge of irresponsibility; it might be thought a student trained in the fragmentary way would be somehow less well prepared to undertake clinical work than one whose professional development has been linear.

In general, there are three places to start a training—at the beginning, where you're told, or you can look for where the explosion is and start there.

Against Holism

I do not doubt the sincerity of those who wish to relate in a whole way to whole people or live in a world experienced as inextricably united or to feel shole. Though I doubt such things are possible to the extent wished for, these are acceptable ideals I partly share. I simply doubt that they are an appropriate base for psychology in its attempts to put its insights and understandings at the service of others. In a recent paper June Singer summed up the idea behind the stance:

> that it is holistic means we see entities first as wholes and only secondarily do we examine the parts ... every science, every religion, every philosophical system .. . helps those who use it gain a holistic and organised picture, involving phenomena too vast and complex to be grasped if approached piecemeal.[2]

Jung seems aware of the dangers of this. In "Depth Psychology and Self Knowledge" he writes

> if the goal of wholeness and of realizing the personality originally intended for him should grow naturally in the patient we may sympathetically assist him toward it.

But if it does not grow of itself, it cannot be implanted without remaining a permanently foreign body. Therefore we renounce such artifices when nature herself is clearly not working towards this end. As a medical art, equipped only with human tools, our psychology does not presume to preach the way to salvation.[3]

Since first writing this paper I have been heartened by what Guggenbühl-Craig has to say on this topic.

Unfortunately, when we talk about the Self, there is too much said about qualities like roundness, completeness, and wholeness. It is high time we spoke of the deficiency . . . of the Self. Today we have succumbed to the cult of the complete, healthy and round, to mandala-like perfection.[4]

Firstly, holistic thinking tends to be utopian, covertly reformist if not revolutionary (Jung's "preaching"). One common variant of the holistic theme is the "unus mundus." Sometimes I think that Latin functions like a mantra for believers. There is a certain moral compulsiveness that gets attached to holism. In the field of personal relationships this overlooks the fundamentally fragmented nature of human contact. We are *not* with our partners all the time and with our analysands even less. I shall say more about analytic sessions and what they mean later on; for the moment I would say that holism seems an attempt to deny that the outcome of one's growth or of a relationship is uncertain. We do make mistakes and miscalculations and we *can* learn from them. In the development of our theory and its application we need trial and (very much) we need error. The inevitability of error compels us toward accepting a pluralist world-view which could be flexible, adaptable and human. For one immersed in fragmentation the holistic aspects will look after themselves. Would not this imply a trust of the self that the thrust of holism does not?

Those who measure cognitive dissonance have shown how a person aims to organise his inner and outer world as harmoniously as possible. This I take to be a way of dealing with anxiety rather than satisfying a holistic impulse. Thus the individual will give greater weight to select aspects of his perceptual field to fit his relatively strong needs. A deprived person will see parent figures everywhere or be overwhelmingly conscious of their absence. The perceptual field alters to avoid a sense of fragmentation or confusion; even gross inconsistencies are accommodated. Sometimes this smoothing over is not a positive phenomenon. I suspect a good deal of holistic thinking is of this kind; current interest in astrology and acupuncture, for instance, may perform this butterknife function for some people. We could go on to say that psyche is meant to be experienced in a fragmentary way. Wholeness exists before birth perhaps or after death. Wholeness is therefore a spiritual matter while fragmentation remains the affair of the psyche.

Fragmentation, Anxiety, Training and Cults

I now wish to apply this to training. Though the trainee is an adult who has had experiences in profusion, a degree of regression seems inherent in the training situation due to the various entanglements of the student's continuing analysis, supervision and interaction with fellow-trainees. The trainings I know about attempt to isolate this regression on the part of the trainee both from anxiety in general and from the fragmentation process in particular. I am thinking of the whole range of syllabi, seminar themes, reading lists, feedback sessions and all the other thoughtful, caring experiences most of us have been through. I wonder if all this might inadvertently take the creative sting out of fragmentation. A denial of fragmentation may be built into the integrated training program. Since doing away with the fragmentation process is impossible, some sort of response to the anxieties of the trainee *is* needed. I am thinking of some sort of peer group experience whether with a leader or not. This proposal has already been adopted in at least one training centre but I am not sure if this is for the same reason—to relieve anxiety without running from fragmentation.

I fear that the attempt to protect the trainee from fragmentation may have contributed to the formation of cultlike bodies within our little world of analytical psychology. I refer first to a pattern which you might call the cult of the seniors. I may be a part of it, having been invited to give this paper perhaps because I am a Congress virgin as it were, and have not spoken at one before. Choosing an all-new team suggests, after all, an oppressive awareness of the same old faces. The paradox is that of planned novelty.

Being in a cult implies obedience. There is too much obedience in the Jungian world today and the idea of fragmentary vision is deliberately set against it. There is a serious danger of any training program becoming an obedience cult. I may be accused of being naive or ahistorical but I am struck by how many of our groups cluster around leader figures. The leaders may be remarkable people but the phenomenon as a whole is worth examing. I am thinking of Fordham in London, Adler (also London), von Franz in Zürich, Henderson in San Francisco, Dieckmann in Berlin, Hillman anywhere . . . I don't think this results from conscious fostering, but would argue that it protects the trainee from fragmentation. For the need for strong leader figures has a lot to do with the desire to avoid the anomalous. The leader sorts out issues by arranging competing ideas in a hierarchy of acceptability. The desire to avoid fragmentation leads groups to erect leaders as combination censor and safety net. Is is a misconceived attempt to acquire parenting.

A cult is characterised by a belief system based on ideas which have become standard within the group. The group is hence relatively closed, and backed up by a degree of police power over the members. Indeed the key element can be summed up in that word "membership." There are two things involved here, (a) the status of belonging to a group to which not everyone can, and (b) the hurdle one must cross to obtain status (a). The quality of the status must be in part an effect of what happens at the hurdle.

Individuals of a certain turn of mind and personality "decide" to become analysts. Even a person without the slightest notion of becoming an analyst at the start of his analysis has to make a decision at some point. There are then a series of stages or phases the individual passes through. For a variety of reasons (I wonder if the reader has noticed this) these stages usually get refer- red to as "years"; "she's a second year trainee" or "he qualified a year ago" or "the third year group are monsters." This calendric approach can be seen as a massive defence against fragmentation because the implication is of an orderly, logical, in control sort of process, a symbol of the dangerous tendency to mass produce our new analysts.

And yet our courses, my course, are not unhealthy or sterile places to be. Most of the members of the International Juniors group speak highly of their training and this cannot all be put down to identification with the trainers or flattery or professional protectionism. I think that what happens for many (it happened to me) is that at a certain point one takes up a fragmentary stance toward the training. This can take the form of doing less or even more work than is required or otherwise varying the task in an attempt to individualize it. For me this usually happened in the form of reading everything in a journal or book but the required piece. In particular I liked the obituaries. What this says about my psychopathology is neither here nor there. Of the 1974 year (!) at the S. A. P. nearly all report a similar experience. Seminar leaders note: if you want a paper read, recommend one adjacent.

What does membership really mean? The opportunity to relate to people and share feelings and ideas does not depend on membership. Even adequate practice does not depend on it. But membership, while not logically crucial, has emergd as the universal procedure for societal recognition. I do not want to tackle the question of why this is so, but merely to suggest that this may have something to say to us about the way we run our trainings on the human level. There is clearly a desire for a true *membership* which is a com- munity of equals, of peers. In London over the past few years there has been a substantial growth in the number and variety of small, informal peer discus- sion groups. Some have felt that these sap the vitality of more formal meetings and that these groups are too subject to favoritism. I think that membership as lived in these groups is what is truly desired in our general move toward in- stitutional membership. I envisage such groups as preventing our slipping back into the safe and easy world of linear, consensus training.

Fragmentary Vision and Analytic Practice

Translating the vision of fragmentary training into reality does, as I have just hinted, risk the re-emergence of linearity. Another way to meet that danger might be to entrust a part of the training to those who have only just qualified. This does happen to a limited extent but I am thinking of making the teaching of new trainees a part of the immediate post-qualification experience. The relative uncertainty and unknowingness of the new teachers, together with their freshnes and enthusiasm, would act as an antidote to linearity.

When the idea of a general education for all was mooted in nineteenth-century England there were a number of schemes proposed, and some actually set up, in which the older pupils were given responsibility for teaching the younger. It was felt that the closeness of the older children to the problem of learning made them suitable teachers. Of course there were economic factors. The schemes did not survive partly because of the disapproval of schoolteachers who were beginning to organise as a profession, with rules governing membership and so on. If this idea were applied to analytical training a permanent stake in fragmentation would be acquired, and there would be advantages for the new teachers.

Student teachers and peer discussion groups are fragmentary answers to fragmentary questions. The important thing is that there should be an oscillation between anxiety and security, a mixture of cosiness and danger. That mixture fits all the great vortices of life—feeding, sex, marriage—all are cosy and all are dangerous.

I should now like to consider the way in which the fragmentary approach has most conditioned our practice, the general procedure of dividing work into sessions. Whether we offer our analysands one hour, fifty minutes or what, whether once, twice or five times per week does not alter the fact that the work goes on in a bitty way. Of course it could not be otherwise in practice. But practice generates its own truths, its own symbolic life and psychological meanings. The sessional nature of our work makes us face the great theme of parts and wholes, makes us think about the possibility of treating the whole person or training the whole person. The sessional approach involves separation; out of separation comes individuation. Separation as a psychological theme is accentuated by the sessional approach, which, as essentially fragmentary, has something to do with individuation.

One aspect of the session/fragment approach has great relevance to training for analysis. I refer to the attempt of the analyst to commence each session as if it were a fresh event or fragmentary phenomenon, trying to forget all that is known about the patient and all that the analyst wants to achieve in his work. The purpose of this is to plug into the psyche as directly and spontaneously as possible and release the analyst's intuitive capacities, in particular his capacity to observe and make use of his various countertransferences. It is in order to use these countertransferences that the analyst tends not to speak first but rather to wait and react. Various practical measures follow—very little note-taking, working on written productions from the patient only in the session in which they are introduced, and so on.

What I am describing is derived from Bion's work. He states that the analyst

> must impose on himself a positive discipline of eschewing memory and desire. I do not mean that 'forgetting' is enough. Only by doing this can analytic intuition be enhanced . . . . By rendering oneself artificially blind through the exclusion of memory and desire . . . the piercing shaft of light can be directed on the dark features of the analytic situation.[5]

There is a rather surprising feature in all this. It follows that it is a good thing for an analyst to be slightly too busy in his daily routine so that he does not dwell too much on any one analysand's material or on any one area of interest. This presents special problems in the training situation since the number of analysands seen under the training umbrella is very small. Given this and the understandable conscientiousness of the beginning analyst, the conditions for unanalytic unfragmentary excessive recording of case material and dwelling on it are created. It would seem to be necessary then to assess potential trainees on the basis in part at least of how busy they are likely to be during their training. If they are just a bit too busy then they will have less difficulty with the analytic attitude; but if they have no other therapeutic investments at all then they do run the risk of creating a nonanalytic style for themselves. In a way, the ideal candidate for training should be less than fully committed to it.

Fragmentary Vision and Pragmatism

It has occured to me that a pragmatic coloring can be put on most of this. Fragmentary vision does resemble pragmatism as I (probably imperfectly) understand that approach. William James said "ideas become true just so far as they help us to get into satisfactory relations with other parts of our experience."[6] So, for example, the psychological theories we learn in training are not to be seen as answers to questions of human nature but as instruments to guide future action and practice. Pragmatism involves a type of democratic procedure in which a man is free to decide which of various conflicting hypotheses to accept. If his rational examination of the alternatives cannot help him make a decision then he is free simply to follow his own inclination. I hope it can be seen how this fits in with the notion of a conflict oriented training. The truth of an idea will be in whether or not it has fruitful consequences. This sums up the essence of fragmentary vision. (Note: written before reading *Spring 1980*, Taylor on Jung and James.)

Summary

Fragmentary vision seems inherent in analysis, fundamental to both its theory and practice, but unrecognised in any specific sense in its training. The adoption of a fragmentary approach to training would be justified to avoid excesses of linearity on the one hand and holism on the other. This involves challenging the training structure and I put forward certain specific proposals to increase the amount of fragmentary vision in a training program and prevent backsliding to more conventional models, viz:
(a) the abandonment of consensus based training and the chronological approach; these would be replaced by a training centred around contemporary arguments or disputes in the field. This may be termed "conflict oriented training";
(b) training would tend to use books and papers written with polemical intent;
(c) the abandonment of fixed curricula, syllabi and other pedagogical devices and the institution of peer groups to focus on resultant student anxiety;
(d) the utilization of recently qualified analysts as teachers for their very lack of certainty. This should be part of the qualified members' final training stage;
(e) the selection of candidates who are not too committed to the training and who have a rather full life already;
(f) a conscious attempt to avoid installing strong personalities as cult leaders;
(g) informal groups should be promoted within the overall life of the training institute.

1. K. R. Popper, *Conjectures and Refutations: the growth of scientific knowledge* (London; Routledge and Kegan Paul, 1972). p. 129.
2. J. Singer, "The Use and Misuse of the Archetype," *Journal of Analytical Psychology*, Vol. 24, No. 1, p. 10–13, 1979.
3. C. G. Jung, "Depth Psychology and Self Knowledge." *CW* 18, p. 97.
4. A. Guggenbühl-Craig, *Eros on Crutches* (Spring Publications, 1980), p. 25–26.
5. W. R. Bion, "Attention and Interpretation," *The Seven Sisters* (London: Tavistock, 1977), p. 31.
6. W. James, *Pragmatism* (Fontana Library of Philosophy, 1962; orig. Longmans, Green, 1911).

(reprinted from Spring 1981 pp. 215–225 by permission and with slight revisions by the author)

The image of the Jungian analyst and the problem of authority

J. Marvin Spiegelman (Studio City, Calif.)

In the spring of 1966, my colleague Robert Stein and I were rejected as Training Analysts by the Certifying Board of our local Jungian Society. We were told to wait six months, with the implication that we should undergo further analysis with one of the older analysts. This was a shock for which we were unprepared; both of us were constitutionally qualified, members of the Executive Committee, and I was already engaged in judging candidates as Director of Studies and previously a member of the Certifying Board itself! And we were unprepared because those judging us were friends, colleagues, teachers and analysts—the people with whom we were closest.

We spent years trying to comprehend this act and its consequences. The intervening years [fourteen at the time of this presentation] have dulled the pain but failed to answer our questions of the time. Stein's was, What image have they of how a Jungian Analyst or Training Analyst ought to be? Mine was, How can Jungians be so irrational, unjust and violating of personal relationship? I believe analysis of this event and the images underlying it can contribute to the understanding of training, the sum of our notions of what we expect analysts to be like.

What kind of image have they of how an analyst ought to be? This question of Stein's continued to haunt me long after he abandoned it as unproductive. When I read Barbara Hannah's biographical memoir of Jung, I got a hint. She described Jung's centrally important encounter with Richard Wilhelm and the now-famous story of the "Rainmaker" the Sinologist told him, which moved him deeply:

> Richard Wilhelm was in a remote Chinese village which was suffering from a most unusually pronlonged drought. Everything had been done to put an end to it, and every kind of prayer and charm had been used, but all to no avail. So the elders of the village told Wilhelm that the only thing to do was to send for a rainmaker from a distance. This interested him enormously and he was careful to be present when the rainmaker arrived. He came in a covered cart, a small, wizened old man. He got out of the cart, sniffed the air in distaste, then asked for a cortege on the outskirts of the village. He made the condition that no one should disturb him and that his food should be put down outside the door. Nothing was heard of him for three days,

then everyone woke up to a downpour of rain. It even snowed, which was unknown at that time of the year.

Wilhem was greatly impressed and sought out the rainmaker who had now come out of his seclusion. Wilhelm asked him in wonder: "So you can make rain?" The old man scoffed at the very idea and said *of course* he could not. "But there was the most persistent drought until you came," Wilhelm retorted, "and then—within three days—it rains?" "Oh," replied the old man, "that was something quite diferent. You see, I come from a region where everything is in order, it rains when it should and is fine when that is needed, and the people also are in order and in themselves. But that was not the case with the people here, they were all out of Tao and out of themselves. I was at once infected when I arrived, so I had to be quite alone until I was once more in Tao and then naturally it rained."[1]

Miss Hannah relates that not only was Jung profoundly affected by this tale but he encouraged her to tell it whenever she gave a lecture on Jungian psychology.

Here is to be found a central image of Jung's psychology, one that informs us all as an ideal. One of our colleagues, de Castillejo, wrote a paper extolling this approach to life, entitled, "The Rainmaker Ideal."[2] This image reminded me of a story told about Jung's attitude, when I was a student at the Institute in Zürich in the late 1950's. Jung was said to have remarked that after the age of thirty men are really alone, each pursing his course like ships which pass in the night, blinking a greeting light but no more. This was said approvingly albeit a trifle sadly. Even then, however, I recall that Stein and James Hillman and I did not like this image of grand aloneness and challenged it, pointing out that it merely led to a parting of the ways, a la Freud, Adler, Jung, Rank, Reich, and the rest. We felt that brotherhood and comradeship could be an important part of the "journey" as well. I recall adding, as a veteran of the Merchant Marine some years earlier, that ships had crews of at least thirty and demanded mutual effort and tolerance both to sail the ship and provide privacy in close quarters.

Here was the image that underlay such a vision: man alone and reconciling himself with the powers of the universe alone, retreating and healing himself in the face of social dilemmas. And here was Jung, suspicious of groups and institutions, advocate of internalizing the conflict of nations as a way to grow in individual consciousness. How often did Jung not say that ten or a hundred savants together were one huge fool, and that the hope of mankind lay in the individual not the group?[3] Here was the image: The Rainmaker Ideal. Was I not also a follower of that ideal? Had I not practiced active imagination all those years since first beginning analysis at the age of 24? Did I not share Jung's suspicion of groups? I was worse with them than Jung was—consider the trouble I often got into. Further, I shared his blief that the individual was the locus of consciousness. What then was the difference? What was *my* image?

I realized I was always emphasizing dialogue and mutual work, and recalled that the paper I wrote for the 1965 *Festschrift* for C. A. Meier, "Some Implications of Transference," emphasized this character of analytical work and the necessity for mutual openness. I remembered the suspicion with which this paper was greeted by these elders at the time, and realized that my image of the analyst was based more on the alchemical model, the Alchemist and his *Soror Mystica*. This for me was not just the alchemist and his inner anima, but an actual sharing of a work of transformation of the *prima materia*, beginning with the unconsciousness brought in by the patient but soon affecting the analyst as well, and requiring the two, in work and prayer, in struggle and devotion, to attend to the gods as they manifest in their work, within them and between them.

I realized that this alchemical image also underlay the Jungian ideal of how an analyst ought to be, and that this emphasis frightened and offended even Jungians who accord recognition to the alchemical model. In Britain a student said he would never tell a patient a dream, particularly sexual, he had about her but would work on himself to change his attitude. I would have felt a moral obligation to tell the patient, feeling this was a joint matter and the telling would reduce the impression of impersonal authority and show that I was personally involved in this process as well. Jung often indicates that he agrees with mutuality in analysis, at least in any deep, fundamentally transforming work. He says in his paper "Problems of Modern Psychotherapy," published as early as 1929:

> What does this demand [that analysts undergo analysis] mean? Nothing less than that the doctor is as much "in the analysis" as the patient. He is equally part of the psychic process of treatment and therefore equally exposed to the transforming influences. Indeed, to the extent that the doctor shows himself impervious to this influence, he forfeits influence over the patient; and if he is influenced only unconsciously, there is a gap in his field of consciousness which makes it impossible for him to see the patient in true perspective. In either case, the treatment is compromised.[5]

Jung goes on to state that the doctor is faced with the same task he expects the patient to face—strong words in support of the mutuality idea.

So there are two canonical images of how the analyst sees himself: the Rainmaker, alone and self-transforming, and the Alchemist with his co-worker, sharing and dialoguing. For some, even the latter has a Rainmaker quality—he knows that the archetypes affect both parties, but transforms himself in order to produce changes. He does not attend to the "third" in the work, namely the relationship itself and the unconscious "between" them. As for me, I was a Rainmaker when alone and an Alchemist with patients.

Why did my colleagues shrink from my view of mutual process? I think they rejected what I understood to be some natural implications of Jung's view of the transference. For me, at the moment the analyst begins having fantasies about the patient, or is experiencing an obstruction or strong affects, he or she is entwined in a mutual process with the unconscious and is no longer in possession of "objectivity." Rather, the two partners are wrapped in the anima/animus or other archetypal conditions of unconscious relationship. My conclusion was that I had a moral responsibility (in the name of honesty) to tell my fantasies, as well as to hear the patient's. It was this, I think, that frightened or offended colleagues. From such sharing, however, both patient and therapist gain insight as to what is transpiring in *the* unconscious (as opposed to "my" and "your" unconscious) and we are now mutually connected to the "third" or the relationship itself. I have called this third the "God among" (as opposed to the "God within"). Objectivity and authority is hence transferred to the unconscious itself, as revealed in the fantasies and dreams of the participants, as partner, who can now attend to the other as well as to this third, thus performing the work of alchemical transformation Jung was writing about.

Let me give an example of such an exchange, which occurred as I was working on this paper. A patient was having sexual fantasies about me but was unwilling / unable to tell what these were. I found myself alternately excited and repelled without knowing quite what was affecting me. Her withdrawal produced either withdrawal on my part or impersonal, aggressive sexual fantasies. I also had a dream in which I had intercouse with her. I told the dream and the fantasies along with the interpretation that I was both trying to penetrate her resistance and unite with her and was also afraid of this. She then dreamt that the therapist was holding a gun on her from the genital region and then she invited him to lie down on the floor with her and make love. He responded he could not—end of dream. I acknowledged the accuracy of the imagery and she added that her own intensity frightened her as well as did the fear of rejection. Then she told her fantasy of being alone before a fireplace, nude and dancing. The therapist appears and she gradually becomes the fire itself. As fire she draws toward the therapist. My reaction to her fantasy was one of withdrawal, fear of being burned, which I told her. Then I saw that we were involved in the alchemical fire-water union, the attempt of the unconscious to unite the fire of passion and desire with the water of feeling. The play of these opposites was going on both within each of us and in the relationship itself. The fire-water image and the union in steam (fantasy, spirit) proved a saving "third" from the unconscious to which we could both relate.

After I had written the foregoing, the patient appeared once more and told me she had been a fool to believe that stuff, she now had her personal power back, and that she had felt me judging her for her physical desire. I was astonished and hurt, not to mention feeling a fraud for using the event in my paper. I told her my feelings and also mentioned that I had even used the incident as an example in a paper I was writing. She was patently moved and told me that after the last session she felt taken over by a sneering, suspicious, cynical spirit, which said I didn't really care about her and she was a worthless, undeveloped from of life. As we worked, it became apparent that the fire-water union had indeed occurred, but that another dimension, that of earth and air, got opened up and showed its split. She felt identified with the body, earth side of concrete fulfillment and the spirit (air, judge) came in as a negative, denying power. Our discussion seemed to clear the air, particularly her felt reassurance that I really did care about the relationship.

She then dreamt of a lovely princess who lived in a magnificent castle but was lonely. A handsome prince, whom she admired and loved deeply was guarding this castle, riding back and forth on his horse, his powerful sword unsheathed and ready to fight anyone who approached. At last, the princess asked the prince to lay down his sword, come inside and be with her. She didn't want to be alone any more and did not need protection—end of dream.

Following this, the patient dreamed that the therapist was standing in front of her, smiling and holding out his arms to her. This dream was similar to one she had early in the analysis, a year before, in which the therapist stood at the head of a long flight of stairs, arms outstretched and welcoming. She had to ascend this long flight, with no bannisters, to reach him. In the current dream she sensed the power of the therapist, but also his humanity and vulnerability, and felt a tremendous amount of loving and caring. Later that same night she dreamt that the therapist came to her house, met her family and played the piano. The next night she dreamt that she came to the therapist's house also. These dreams are transparent, I think. In the castle dream, she finally makes connection to her animus and is ready for her own inner union—a Rainmaker work! With this shift away from the defensive use of the animus, she is ready also for "mutual process" with me, at a deeper level, as the following dreams show. I am also struck by the presence of the Judge archetype, which intrudes into the work and tries to destroy the union which did take place. This Judge, about which I will have more to say in the next section, is very much present in regular analytic work, particularly in transference problems, as well as in the training / assessing process. But here it was essential that I was willing to "unveil" my own fantasies and dreams in relation to her, as she was doing until blocked. I do not see how the union could have been otherwise effected.

Once more, after the paper was already in the hands of the editor, the patient dreamed that she came to the therapist's office, but found both it and him changed. He was dressed in a green Elizabethan costume, a little chubby and foolish-looking. An authoritative voice said that the therapist could not help her. End of dream.

The patient was devastated by this dream, as was I, once more feeling the fraud. But no. As we worked, it became clear that the "fool" was now I, as she had felt herself to be previously, and this was correct insofar as I was foolishly dependent on her psyche for validation of my views about mutual process. Her authoritative voice, it emerged, was really insisting that she not give herself totally to the relationship, as she was in danger of doing, but to stay, too, with her inner Self, the "God-within." She was being tossed back and forth between these opposites and was compelled to honor both her own Rainmaker AND the alchemical process between us.

That insight helped me to realize how foolishly dependent I had become upon patients' dreams as revelatory of objective authority, so my patient and I were really in the same boat. We are taught in Jungian training that dreams about the therapist are largely projection. I, with my mutual-process idea, had often gone overboard in the other direction and accepted the patient's dreams of me as "true," thus losing my inner authority.

It is this unveiling of fantasies, I think, that my colleagues had great doubts about. The material revealed may include content which is sexual, aggressive or infantile and they may fear that such openness can lead to "acting out" or a loss of control on the part of the therapist. This is a legitimate fear, but one must realize that such fears are also instinctive and perform a regulatory function, as in the foregoing example. If I have a fantasy of slapping a patient, I also have a fear of hurting or being hurt myself, which restrains bodily action. This, too is part of the "unveiling." Moreover, when we understand that therapy is a psychological relationship aiming at the enhancement of consciousness and the capacity for loving, such natural limits as provided in the mutually agreed aim prevent—or at least make less likely—damaging events. In any case, I think it is better to be open about such processes (making mutually conscious), than to let them fester in the dark to cause mischief from being handed over to the witch and devil archetypes.

A colleague has suggested that therapists shrink from mutual process and openness because of their unwillingness to show their weakness, vulnerability or need. Once you do this, he says, you lose your authority and the other will hurt you! I am afraid that this is true; I have been so treated more than once. Yet the therapist can speak about his hurt or rejection, perhaps evoking the compassion of the patient and thus enhancing the latter's inner authority as well.

This holding on to authority is a not infrequent experience among therapists. I have encountered many, including Jungians, who were judgmental, inflated with the archetype of Old Wise Man or Woman, impenetrable and invulnerable. Indeed, I am grateful for the work of Guggenbühl, who has shown so brilliantly in his *Power in the Helping Professions* that therapists can readily succumb to the rigidity and impenetrability our profession seems to produce. Guggenbühl's portrait of this malady, I feel, is an apt picture of the shadow of the Rainmaker. I think my colleagues' fears were largely a dread of openness, as I discuss in my papers on transference.

I am well aware that other images such as being "closed" are also of great value. The fantasy of growth, in the silence and darkness of earth and womb, is an obvious example, as is the Hermetic stance of "indirection." If I emphazise openness, it is because this has been grossly neglected in our field.

How could Jungians be so irrational, unjust, and betraying of personal relationship? How could they indeed? One might ask why they should *not* be, since we are "all too human" as Nietzsche said, and we all share the "ugliest man" who does these things. At that time, my belief was that people on the conscious road of individuation would not do such a thing.

It was not so much that I was more innocent then that I am now, but that I had no adequate conceptual tools to differentiate between my personal shock and the larger impersonal issue of judgment. Nothing in my training or experience equipped me to penetrate the meaning of this event. In retrospect I can see that neither the Rainmaker model (not conscious at the time), nor Alchemist could help me understand better. I knew that I was in the grip of an unjust judge and this was central to my experience. My own inner image of the archetype of the Judge was perfectionist, harsh and demanding, and it was to that figure that I turned in trying to deal with my pain and disbelief. This Judge was very hard on me at the time for violating its standards in my personal life, and I bore an intense conflict of my own. I could readily see a Freudian interpretation of what happened to me. I had unconsciously produced or provoked these betrayals and judgments from without in order to punish myself for my infractions. That would also account for my failure to stand up for myself more forcefully and protest the action's injustice. The causalist Freudian interpretation must be true. After a time I could also see the merits of a finalist, Adlerian interpretation. Despite the fact that I was rejected as a training analyst, I continued to have therapists come to me for analysis (at least half of my practice has been with therapists ever since). Was this, then, an "arrangement" in Adler's sense, so that I had to sacrifice the power-drive of being the "training analyst" only to become one in a nonrecognized power-shorn way, thus contributing to a genuine "social interest"? That made good sense too, and it has helped me to appreciate the Adlerian viewpoint.

I could also see the value of a Jungian finalist interpretation—that I needed to break away from the group, at the age of forty, and pursue my individuation. This made sense on the basis of dreams and my later fictional writing. This individual imaginative work would very likely not have been produced had my inner figures remained only in the service of the Jungian collective, hence the validity of the Jungian finalist interpretation. But these three interpretations were not enough. They retained an inner-oriented viewpoint (i.e., still Rainmaker) and did not give sufficient weight to the dialogic, relational, and group needs involved. This is where Stein and I attempted some consciousness-raising and healing on our own. We knew that both of us were heavily affected by the inner Judge and we tried, in our relationship, to deal with this. But despite the apparent successes of my mutual process idea with my patients, particularly with younger therapists and those with an existential background, I still suffered the wound and hurt of the "Unjust Judge". The several interpretations, causalist, finalist, and relational all seem helpful and true, but I could not isolate the image and myth I was shruggling with. I sensed it, but it seemed too grand to be connected with the small-scale issues and relatively minor agonies I was coping with. I refer to the Job story and to Jung's work with that important myth of our westem consciousness.'

In that work, as we know, Jung took on what he felt to be a central myth of western culture: God's injustice, his need of man in dialogue with him to advance his own consciousness, the continuing incarnation—the humanization of God and consequent divinization of man. These weighty matters, and Jung's passionate explication of this development in the western image of the divine, have been as central in his psychology as his preoccupation with alchemy as the precursor and symbol-carrier for modern consciousness.

It was this story that I felt to be at work in my experience with my Jungian colleagues, in my own work with myself and in my practice. For me the Board was an embodiment of the Sanhedrin of Jesus' day, arrogating to themselves a retrogressive judgment out of fear of the prevailing collective and in subservience to their own power needs. And I was partially identified with Jesus, a man who had an inner relationship to God, denied the authority of the "elders" was himself combining divinity and humanity! I certainly felt crucified and abandoned.

My approach to healing lay in the idea of mutual process, of working-through this complex so that as a group we all would emerge relating to the God-Among. I thought this combination of the personal and the impersonal would do the work of humanization of the archetype. That is not how the original story went, of course, nor did my colleagues cooperate, so I was stuck in myth and could find no satisfying alternative solution. Gradual dis-identification from the God-man archetype was difficult, I found, since the conscious carrying of such an image was precisely what Jung had concluded was contemporary man's condition in *Answer to Job*. We in western civilization are living through this myth in some fashion, and I think those of us in Jungian psychology have a particularly close affinity to it. The problems of judging, of being "human" and dis-identifying with archetypal possession are very much in the forefront of the training process, in therapy, and in life.

Some features of the myth pertain to the analytic and training situation. These are: (1) Personal-Impersonal; (2) Subjective-Objective; (3) Power—Assertion-Submission.

Personal-Impersonal: The image of the divine figure in the Job story is passionate, personal, single-minded, and apparently unreflective. He identifies with his power while disregarding its effects. He is personal in his intensity and passion, but impersonal, not affected by, the reality of his human partner.

He plots in the background and justifies himself with his own power and lofty aims. Throughout he makes judgments.

This authoritarian image dwells in many of us. When not humanized, it can muddle the therapeutic situation and cause great pain, but the need for healing and some sort of union can bring about a satisfying humanization of the archetype. In the training situation, however, particularly if some judgment of the rightness, adequacy, or "readiness" of the candidate is at issue, the worst aspect of this archetype can obtrude. Should either party insist on his own righteousness (often the case) it is hard to see that any resolution is possible. Should they accept the idea of mutual process, they can attend to the personal reactions, viewpoints, dreams, and fantasies of all parties, and the "third" can manifest from the unconscious to show the possibility of union of the personal and impersonal.

Objective-Subjective: The emotionality in this archetypal pattern of Job/ Jahveh and its consequences of unjust judgment have led many to substitute for it an objective viewpoint. The difficulties are enormous, especially if we deceive ourselves that we are truly "objective" and have overcome the personal affects and biases which distort judgment. This is particularly apparent in the training/assessing situation and causes the kind of distancing and violation Jungians complain of in Freudians and patients complain of in both. The difficulties are particularly great since the Judge usually considers itself quite correct and in touch with ultimate truth. At the same time, the distancing from emotionality and subjectivity brings on an illusion of objectivity from having "overcome" the affects. Yet each view sees the inadequacy of the other, and the judged scratches his sores like Job. The prologue in heaven with light and dark sides of the authority having sway results in the split archetype we see in the human situation.

The way to overcome this split archetype is to sacrifice one's claim to exclusive objectivity, just as I think it wise to sacrifice impersonality. One can permit the conflict of objective-subjective in one's self and know that greater objectivity can arise when the views of all parties are connected, once more, with the third of the unconscious itself.

Power—Assertion-Submission: In Jung's description of the psychological process going on in the divine, recognizing its own injustice and lack of consciousness of "what it means to be human", there comes a sacrifice of its power and a surrender to the frail human condition. This "incarnation" brings about an advance of consciousness which can contain the divine and human, in psychological terms a union in consciousness of the archetypal and the personal. Presumably this process is a continuing one for us, psychologically, but in the training/judging situation it is only too easy for the archetype to split, and the student/trainee must submit to the power and authority of the trainer/judge. I suggest, once more, that this split can be overcome by recognizing it. I suggest that to overcome the negativity and destructiveness of the split archetype of divine/human, judge/ judged, assessor/trainee, etc., we follow the process we do for ourselves alone and for our patients when we, as Jungians, submit to the unconscious itself and to the process of its unfolding! But here the unconscious is also "among" and not only individually within each. I realize there are other approaches to this dilemma (which can be characterized, I think, as the problem of authoritarianism) and it is these various solutions I wish to examine next.

Antidotes to Authoritarianism in the Therapist: The problem of authoritarianism in our field goes back to its modern beginnings. Jung's conflict with Freud in this regard is well documented in both Jung's autobiography[8] and his *Two Essays.*[9] Jung, of course, felt that the conflict was a type-problem, but in his memoirs he shows only too clearly that Freud's view that it was a "revolt against the father" was also true. The breaks by Adler, Rank and Reich can also be seen as stories of a newer spirit unable to stay contained in the older vessel, or to be accepted by the older spirit. Jung has described this process well, and both von Franz[10] and Hillman[11] have explored the archetypal background of such conflict.

It was Guggenbühl, however, who first described this issue in the context of the therapist and the struggle with power.[12] His answer to the danger of the therapist becoming invulnerable, rigid, and increasingly impenetrable was the cultivation of eros in the form of friend-ships outside the therapeutic relation. Friends and close colleagues are the antidote to one's isolation and empire-building, says Guggenbühl. That seems most heartwarming advice, but I have doubts about it as a single solution. Friendship is certainly a desideratum but the archetypal image of father-son, separation and individuation seems more powerful than comradeship, despite the presence of societies to foster the latter. My own position has been to enhance eros in the analytic relation itself by the emphasis on openness and mutual process. This type of eros seems to have worked for me, as friendship has worked for Guggenbühl, but what is the experience of our colleagues in the struggle with authoritarianism?

Hillman, in his "Psychology: Monotheistic or Polytheistic,"[13] attacks the authoritarianism of monotheistic consciousness, equating it with a kind of theologizing, in contrast with psychologizing, and holds that a polycentric view is more in line with the facts of the psyche, thus truer to the soul. He realizes that his either-or position is itself an indication of the type of consciousness he is rejecting, yet he refuses a more inclusive position. Kathleen Raine's response to his view, in terms of William Blake's system, is that the enemy is the arrogation of power of one function or "god." My response to his position derives from Kundalini Yoga; the "Place of Command" is not and need not be the highest authority.

In the Kundalini system,[14] each chakra has a divine syzygy of god and goddess, representing a type of consciousness and energy. Since the energy rises and descends in a circulation bringing enlightenment, no chakra is superior to the other and no divine manifestation carries hegemony. Even Ajna, the "third-eye," is called the "Place of Command," but is subservient to Sahasrara, the highest lotus at the crown of the head. This chakra connects the yogin with the most sublime experience of the divine and his ultimate enlightenment. But even "ascent" itself is not the desideratum, since circulation of the energy is the aim, and all the images of the gods are seen as aspects of the one divine pair in union. This multiple image of authority offers a model for the de-literalizing of our authority symbol. One might ask how an image of multiple centers squares with the vision discussed in Jung's *Answer to Job*, the humanization-of-God—divinization-of-man? I have attempted such a reconciliation in my fictional work, *The Tree: Tales in Psycho-Mythology*.[15]. In that book, ten people, each respresenting a different belief system—Catholic, Pagan, Atheist, Taoist, Hindu, Gnostic, Jewish-Kabbalistic, Alchemical, Zen, Moslem—recount their own stories of individuation in connection with their myths. They meet in Paradise and it seems apparent that even such diversity has a commonality in the experience of the "humanization of the divine—divinization of the human" paradigm Jung explored in his Job work.

It seems to me that the problem is not one of authority alone, since each function, type of consciousness, religion or "God" has its own sphere of power. Rather we are faced with the arrogation of authority and the unwillingness to relativize claims. Neil Micklem of London has suggested[16] the idea of "de-training" as an antidote to rigidity and narrowmindedness in the therapist. He has pointed out that just such a de-training occurred in his own transition from physician to analyst at the Jung Institute in Zürich. He also notes that there are many Jungian analysts who have undergone other kinds of analysis, both before and after their Jungian work. The Kleinian experience of many in London is well-known. I too have undergone extensive Reichian work (eight years as a matter of fact) and can restify that "de-training" can have enormous effect on the personality. Each therapeutic system has something specific to offer hardly attainable whole in another modality. So, too, each system has its shadow: the achievement of any system's main aim also entails its opposite, failure. There always seems to be further work to be done.

In our Jungian field, the shadow of the individuation process (isolation, rigidity, invulnerability) is perhaps best approached in an eros manner. This eros is found in relationship, perhaps even in group work. Jung, of course, was very much against group therapy and on strong grounds. We all know how groups can use the power of the archetypes to destroy individuality and reduce the membership to the lowest common denominator of consciousness. But is this necessary? Can there not be groups composed of individuals each seeking his or her own individuation, yet sharing a common quest as well?

Some might reply that there are Jungian groups all over the world which believe precisely that they are doing this. This was not true in my own experience with a particular group many years ago, and my occasional forays to Jungian enclaves both in the United States and abroad lead me to doubt that even now many of these groups differ markedly from the usual professional societies or clubs, with the typical power struggles and politicking. F. Riklin once said in Zürich about the Jung Club there, "it is not a club, it is a battlefield!" But there is every possibility that something along the lines of common quest is happening or can.

What further can we do, beyond the suggestions of Guggenbühl, Micklem, Hillman and myself? I think we can return to the image of Jung's Job, which instaurated our now declining era. Perhaps the next step for us Jobs (the "many" as heir to the "one" sufferer) is not only to see the flaws and the shadow of the authorities and gods, and internalize our own but to no longer "cover our mouth" (as Job does at the end), but speak out. It seems to me that we very easily slip into unconscious indentification with that authority and we do need each other to point it out in some way. In the very act of pointing this out, the partner can slip into such identification himself, causing no end of trouble. For me the emphasis on eros, on connection with the soul of the other, is the best antidote to identification. I grow increasingly aware of how subtly we slide from stating where we are personally, or connecting to the other, to this assertion of what "the truth" is. Mutual process is one way to deal with this in a relationship of two, but is often not adequate in the group connection. In the relationship of three or more, the complexities increase. I am fond of the story told by Hannah in her memoirs about Jung in his days at Burgholzli.[17] Jung gathered together three people, each of whom thought he was Jesus Christ. Each thought the other two were crazy. Our next step, I think, is for the many "Christ-bearers" those who experience an inner connection with the Self) to acknowledge the other selves and to listen to their truth speaking as well. I see this as the individual carrying the dilemma of being both with the personal and the transpersonal, with his inner authority, yet open to others, working alone and in groups, living his own conviction but knowing the relativity of his experience.

What has this to do with our theme of training? Everything, I think. An analyst can only train and influence according to his being, rather than according to his words, persona or authority. We train by what we are. It behooves us, then, to follow Jung's advice to be both aware of what we are and not hang a curtain of "transference" or "projection" to protect us and our patients from our condition. I realize I am an advocate of a personal stance in analysis and this in itself may prove inimical to some. But these ignore the questions posed in this paper at the risk (as Jung says) of "compromising treatment."

I think that Jungians are particularly heirs of the Job problem. We are willy nilly in the boat of judging and being judged. As heirs to Jung, we are heirs to Job. Thus the conscious and unconscious horror that is happening to candidates—and to judges—should not be banished, once more, to heavenly prologues and hellish sequels, to unspoken plots and opinions followed by pronouncements and onesided decisions. Rather we need to examine these issues, I think, and not "compromise" training either.

When we come to training, we know that deep distrust can be constellated with the problem of judging. Because of this the personal analyst is often not called on to be a judge, but judgment is not avoided on that account. In light of these problems I would like to suggest that once candidates have been accepted into training, the judging process no longer resemble the patriarchal, asymmetric model. I think it better to understand that there is a mutual commitment to the process of helping the candidate to determine when he or she is ready to go from stage to stage. Particularly when there is doubt, I suggest that the mutual process model be applied to this process. This means that the participants openly give their views and feelings, that no authority is claimed beyond such statements and that more than one meeting be given over to such discussions. In this process, the relevant dreams of candidates and judges need to be shared. The image, then, is that the Judge becomes the "third," the God-Among to which all relate.

(reprinted from Spring, 1980 p. 101—116 by permission.)

1. Barbara Hannah, *Jung: His Life and Work, a biographical memoir* (New York: Putnam's. 1976), p. 128.
2. Irene Claremont de Castillejo, *The Rainmaker Ideal* (London: Guild of Pastoral Psychology, Guild Lecture No. 107, February 1960).
3. Most powerfully affirmed in *The Undiscovered Self (CW* X).
4. In *Speculum Psychologiae* (Zurich: Rascher, 1965). The sequel to this paper is "Transference, Individuation, and Mutual Process," a talk delivered to the San Diego Jung Group, 1972.
5. ° *W* XVI, p. 72.
6. Adolf Guggenbühl-Craig, *Power in the Helping Professions* (Spring Publications, 1971).
7. *Answer to Job,* in *CW* XI.
8. C. G. Jung, *Memories, Dreams, Reflections* (New York: Pantheon Books, 1963).
9. *CW* VII.
10. M.-L. von Franz, *The Problem of the Puer Aeternus* (Spring Publications, 1970).
11. James Hillmann, *Senex and Puer: An aspect of the historical and psychological present in Puer Papers* (Spring Publications, 1979).
12. See note 6 above.
13. James Hillman, "Psychology: Monotheistic or Polytheistic" in Spring 1971, pp. 193—232.
14. See Arthur Avalon, [≅] *he Serpent Power.*
15. *The Tree: Tales in Psycho-Mythology* (Los Angeles: Phoenix House, 1975).
16. Personal communication.
17. B. Hannah, see note 1.

Is there such a thing as Jungian psychology: Portrait of a jung man as artist

By Gary V. Hartman (St. Louis)

Prologue

"There was once a queer old man who lived in a cave, where he had sought refuge from the noise of the villages. He was reputed to be a sorcerer, and therefore he had disciples who hoped to learn the art of sorcery from him. But he himself was not thinking of any such thing. He was only seeking to know what it was that he did not know, but which, he felt certain, was always happening. After meditating for a very long time on that which is beyond meditation, he saw no other way of escape from his predicament than to take a piece of red chalk and draw all kinds of diagrams on the walls of his cave, in order to find out what that which he did not know might look like. After many attempts he hit on the circle. 'That's right', he felt, 'and now for a quadrangle inside it!'—which made it better still. His disciples were curious; but all they could make out was that the old man was up to something, and they would have given anything to know what he was doing. But when they asked him: 'What are you doing there?' he made no reply. Then they discovered the diagrams on the wall and said: 'That's it!'—and they all imitated the diagrams. But in so doing they turned the whole process upside down, without noticing it: they anticipated the result in the hope of making the process repeat itself which had led to that result. This is how it happened then and how it still happens today."[1]

For Laura

"What is Jungian Psychology? Is there such a thing? Is it a thing?" *"Is there such a thing as a Carl Gustav Jung?"*
"Sure—at least I guess there WAS! Certainly there was a historical figure called Carl Gustav Jung."
"That is not what I mean. I mean—was Carl Gustav Jung a 'thing'?"
"No . . . of course not! He was a man, a person . . . what Jolande Jacobi would have called a 'personality'."

"Don't get off the subject and start name-dropping. YOU talk about him. What was he?"

"I guess I don't know from first-hand experience. I could talk about the stories I've heard about him . . . how he liked the ladies, how one of his analysands called him a 'Spanish bull'."

"There you go again getting off the subject. YOU talk about him. Why go to someone else's stories to talk about him. You only know about something from your story. What the hell have you been doing the last ten years or so if it hasn't been getting to know who Carl Jung is—seeing the way Carl Jung saw. What is training to be an analyst anyway?"

"You lost me there. I thought what I was doing while I was in training and since has been trying to see who *I* am, not who Carl Jung was?"

"Now you are getting technical on me. Do you want me to talk my language—"soul's soul souls soul" or "soul's whole souls hole"? I don't think your dumb-dream-ego attitude would find it very understandable. If you are going to talk to me you have to at least make the effort to meet me halfway—just as I am doing with you. Now how is it going to be?"

"Okay, I get your point. I guess it is like two-by-two going—I have to try to understand your language and you have to try to understand mine?"

"Not quite! If you are coming to me it is because you want to learn something from me, not out of some ego hubris that you can teach me something. That is nothing but ego cramp!!"

"'ego cramp' . . . That's from Fordham, isn't it?"

"Fordham, Shmordham! That's from me! Oh, sure maybe Fordham wrote it down somewhere—I could give you the journal and the page number if you wanted. Where do you think these things come from? From people? From some 'massa confusa' that thinkers like yourself take and refine into pristine truths? Hell, no! You are the ones who are confused! Look at how silly you are. You call what you don't know, 'unconscious' and make it into some kind of boogey man that jumps out at you if you're not careful. You are just seeing your own reflection! You are the one who is 'unconscious'; the boogey man that scares you, that goes 'bump in the dark', is YOU!"

"I see. You're saying that the 'what' of my seeing is simply the 'how' of my seeing. What I see is how I see. Jung said that about the unconscious, that it presents to us the face we present to it."

"There you go again! Boy, are you hopeless! Fordham said, Jung said. I thought we had just gotten that cleared up and your are right back there mucking around. Seesaw, sea, sawed. Do you see the sea on Vitamin C or did you see what you saw when you saw the sea? Who seesawed in the sea and saw?"

"Okay, okay! I really would like some help with this whole question. I seem to keep getting in my own way, though."

"Is it a whole question or a question of holes?"

"Hey, I'm serious . . . I *do* need help with this!"

"*I'm serious, too. Dead serious . . . well, where were we before you got off on your little technicalities?*"

"You had asked me to talk about Carl Jung, Carl Jung as I know him."

"*Right. But first the question about a thing—was he a thing?*"

"No. I already answered that. I said he was a man."

"*I'm well aware that you already answered it. I'm just not too certain you heard what you said. Remember Oedipus? You should since you are 'into' myths and that sort of thing. Oedipus answered the riddle correctly, but he sure didn't hear what he said. There was a fellow who never would listen to me! 'Who me? Kill my parents? Oh, no, never!'*"

"I *know* I said that Carl Jung was a man. What is there to hear in that?"

"*Look. Do you remember how we got started with this whole thing, this thing of holes? You asked if there were such a 'thing' as Jungian Psychology. (I guess I'm going to have to spoon-feed it to you!) Then I asked if there were such a thing as a Carl Gustav Jung, right?*"

"Right."

"*And you answered . . .?*"

"No, of course not."

There's your answer!"

"What answer?"

"*To your question!*"

"Which question?"

"*Oh, my God! I have run into come bloody-minded people in my time, but you top them all. Its a good thing you weren't around when Oedipus was. The two of you together would have driven me to an early grave! Let's try it one more time. You asked, 'Is there such a thing . . . '*"

"Ohhhh!! I get it!"

"*May Allah be praised!*"

"You're saying that the answer to my question, whether or not there is such a thing as Jungian Psychology is, 'No, of course not!'"

"*Hold on there just a minute, boy wonder! Before you start imagining your name up in lights, let's at least get it straight. The answer I gave to your question was, 'Is there such a thing as a Carl Gustav Jung?' That, properly speaking, is the answer. The, 'no, of course not,' is just icing on the cake.*"

"All right. Let me see if I've got it. You are saying that there is no more such a thing as Jungian Psychology than there is such a thing as a Carl Gustav Jung?"

"*Erraten, mein Junge!*"

"Huh?"

"*He can't hear German either! That's it. You got it. Well, now that that is all cleared up, I guess I'll be off.*"

"Wait! Maybe I'm thick, but it doesn't seem at all cleared up to me. Let's say that I have a notion of what Jungian Psychology *isn't*, but I'm still at a loss to know what it *is*. From your response it seems you are suggesting that is has something to do with the man Carl Jung?"

"That sounds like a logical conclusion. Who would have thought to link up Jung with Jungian Psychology?"

"Hey! At least give me a chance to follow out my thought. You don't have to be so cynical! I was going back to the beginning of our conversation and your asking me to talk about Carl Jung . . ."

("By Jove, I think he's got it!")

"IN other words, if I want to talk about Jungian Psychology, I have to talk about Carl Jung and all the things he was interested in like schizophrenia and word associations and myths and legends and alchemy and synchronicity and types and functions . . ."

". . . and fairy tales and flying saucers and religion and mandalas and Philemon and, and, and, and . . . No! No, no, no, NO! Next you are going to tell me that Jungian Psychology has to do with being the son of a theology graduate of the Stift at Tuebingen, being born in Thurgau, and specializing in psychiatry at the Burghölzli under Eugen Bleuler! Well, good luck, because Bleuler is dead, you weren't born in Thurgau, and your father was't a Swiss Reform clergyman! Guess you can't be a Jungian, huh? That makes about as much sense as saying that one is only a Jungian if one has a Ph. D. in psychology. If you are going to carry it to that extreme you might as well go to Basel, enroll in med school, and then move to Küsnacht into a house on the lake . . . although you might have some difficulty in finding a lady by the name of Rauschenbach to marry you, to say nothing of what your wife would have to say about it!

"Aha! I *have* got it! It is like the story that Jung told about the old man in the cave who . . ."

"Ah, ah, ah . . ."

"Right, I know. Talk about me, not about Jung and Jung's story.

"Now you're getting it!"

"I have a sense of something going on with me, something moving in me and around me, in the people I meet, in my dreams, in situations, events, and happenings. Its maybe like what the Dakota call the thing that is 'moving-always-moving'."

"But what do YOU call it? See, here we are getting down to the nittygritty of your question as well as to one of the points I've been trying to make. You say there is some 'thing' going on with you. That's good—at least you know that much. But when you go to Carl Jung or the Dakotas or anyone else to find a name and description of it, you are moving away from the work which is proper to you. Let me give you an illustration of what I mean. You've mentioned the story of the old man in the cave, that will serve nicely."

"That's cheating! How come you can use that example and I can't? That's not fair!"

"Who said anything about being fair? You're here to learn from me, so stop com-

plaining and listen. If you want a reason for it, call it poetic license, the artist's prerogative to say, do, paint, or write whatever is appropriate to his art."
"Oh, so now you're calling it art. That's quite a switch!"
"Oh, so now you're calling yourself a 'Jungian', whatever that means. Sure its art—wasn't Jung interested in something called alchemy? You are supposed to be the scholar, the thinker, the intellectual, and you ask me whether or not it is art? Try a couple of these quotes on for size: 'Ars' (hear that?), 'Ars requirit totum hominem', or 'Nota bene', (right, 'Nota bene'): 'In arte nostri magisterii nihil est celatum a Philosophis excepto secreto artis . . .' Hear that, 'artis'? That last quote Jung took from the Rosarium and can be found in Volume 16 of the Collected Works, paragraph 411 n., for your esteemed information!"
"That's Latin!"
"Sure its Latin—you didn't think it was Swahili did you? You Jungians are real handy with all those hot little Latin phrases like 'pars pro toto' and 'sine qua non' and the one that really slays me, 'cum grano salis.' 'Cum grano salis' my foot! What you need is a whole salt mine! You get hung up in the trappings, in the details, and completely lose the image, the spirit of the whole thing. It is like the dream that nun had where she had celebrated the mass and then got concerned about the pieces of the host that were lying around on the floor. When she bent down to pick them up, though, she found that they were only bits of cloth. Cloth, material, matter, no spirit . . . do you hear that?"
"What are you saying?"
"You are the dream man—you tell me about the dream!"
"Do you mean that what matters is not the material; in other words, don't get hung up on appearance at the cost of essence? Is it like the man who couldn't be a photographer because he couldn't afford a Hasselblad camera?"
"Right. Now you're starting to cook. What does that say about those people who claim to be Jungian because they have read the whole of the Collected Works or because they have painted one hundred mandalas or how about the fellow who was kneeling in front of the portrait of Jung in the Institute in Zurich?"
"Do you mean that they are just going through the motions, that they are not seeing what is essential within the appearance?"
"Well, yes, although I wouldn't have been quite so philosophical in my language. The words that come to my mind are blasphemy, idolatry, pornography, prostitution. At best they are epigones, cheap imitators who cheapen themselves and their art, blaspheming and prostituting their own souls! Kitsch . . . junk food upon the altar of soul!
That's pretty strong language!
Damned right its pretty strong language. But don't just take my word for it, go to your guru, go to old C. G. himself and all his alchemists. (I'll give you the English since the Latin seems to make you squeamish). He writes, 'Wherefore all error in the art arises because men do not begin with the proper substance, and . . . were

*that to happen that man would be accursed; he would incur the wrath of God and
perish of the apoplexy.' Do you need the reference, oh learned one?*
No, that's okay, but . . .
*And before you start telling me that I have turned the quote around or cited it out
of context or violated any of your academic, MLA style-sheet compulsions, just
remember—poetic license! Besides, where did this stuff come from? I could just as
easily say that they had misquoted me! Listen to what is there instead of always
telling me what is NOT there! Be an artist for once in your life! When you get the
wrath of God, you get some pretty strong language. Even Jung sees that. Why
don't you listen to all those damned books you read? Now I'm doing your thing,
quoting Jung. Maybe you can hear him, for crying out loud. He says, Vol. 16 of
the sacred writ, paragraph 412: 'If we take the fear of divine punishment for
betrayal at its face value, the reason for this must lie in something that is thought
to endanger the soul's salvation, i. a., a typical 'peril of the soul'. When your art is
improper, you imperil your soul, for Christ's sake. Can't you hear that?*
Yes, I hear it. But, I thought you were going to talk about the story of the old
man in the cave. You had me all primed and ready and then you got off onto
art and soul and all that sort of thing.'
*Whoa there. Let's call a spade a spade You were the one who didn't
understand—that's why I've been having to explain myself. Besides, all that stuff
with art and proper-ness of art and soul is the story of the old man in the cave.
Don't be so stuffy and pedantic! Here, you tell me. Of the two groups of people in
that story, the old man on one hand and his 'disciples' on the other, which was do-
ing art?*
The old man, of course.
Of course? Of course? Why? You tell me.
The disciples aren't doing their own art, they are simply trying to get hold of
what the old man has by imitating his art? Right?
*Yes, and no. You are still doing your thing of seeing what is not there. I'm in-
terested in art, not in pronography—you've told me about pornography, now tell
me about art!*
The old man, you mean?
You are the one doing the telling, so tell!
Is the old man doing art because he is trying in some way to express that
which he doesn't know, but which he knows is there, trying things, ex-
perimenting, concentrating only on that particular thing?
*Very good? Excellent even! You didn't have to quote Jung to do it either! Tell me,
my learned friend, (should I call you 'Doctor' in recognition of your Faustian efforts?), tell me, what would have happened if the old man had started quoting
from Jung or the Dakotas or Freud or anyone for that matter? What would have
been the effect on his art?*
He would have been moving away from it, he would have been giving importance to someone else's art which would have been superfluous. Only that

person can recognize the art proper to him or her. You can tell a person that they are doing art, but ultimately the valuing of it must and can only come from that person, themself.

He has . . . he has got it! Oh, its plain old rain in Spain time again! But hold! You didn't completely answer my question: What would be the effect on his art?

It would have gone undone.

Ah, you're like cheap wine—the more I drink, the better you taste. That is very good. But how about a pithy metaphor to go with it? Any ideas?

No, afraid not.

It just so happens I have one . . . that was a rhetorical question, you see. People think I'm a poet, but I'm really a rhetorician. I'm thinking of something of mine that Nikos Kazantzakis wrote down—there was an artist! That was no Ripple or Thunderbird dollar-a-quart stuff! Pure Chateau Lafitte-Rothschild '47! Ahhhh!

You're getting off the subject - - - the metaphor?

Sorry about that—you've made me wax euphoric. I get that way when I think people are hearing me, really hearing. And then it just flies: there are sees and saws and see-saws and Spains in rainy plains which, of coure, are contra-indicative of Vitamin C treatments.

The metaphor?

Oh yes. I was thinking of something that the character Alexis Zorba said or, properly speaking, something of mine which Kazantzakis put in the mouth of Zorba—the Greek, you know? Amazing how much we use that expression, 'you know' . . . you know? Seems almost as if it is to hide the fact that we don't—know, that is. Yes, yes, yes, the metaphor. Well, Zorba, 'El Greco', Zorba said, 'There is one sin which God will not forgive: when a woman calls a man to her bed and HE WILL NOT GO!' Pithy people, those Greeks!

I don't quite get it. You were asking after a metaphor for art going undone. I don't understand.

Oh no! And I thought we had made a prophet of you. I guess my jubilation was somewhat pre-mature. You really want me to explain it? Do you know what happens to a metaphor when you explain it? It becomes an allegory! Its like putting a Reubens woman in a whale-bone corset. Let's try something else first. Let's stay with the image for awhile longer. Imagine, if you will, that a woman wants a man. I know this might be difficult for you, but trot out what little sense of romance, Eros, and sensuality might be at your disposal—to say nothing of imagination. What happens to such a woman if the man ignores her, has eyes only for other women (I trust you are hearing the metaphor here? Hear?), if he flits from one sweet thing to the next? What happens to his woman?

She would probably feel neglected, ignored, worthless, maybe even ugly.

Right. And how would she behave? Would she be all sweetness and light or . . .

Bitchy. She would get bitchy, try to trip him up at every opportunity, block him, get in his way, spy on him while trying to pretend that she was totally ignoring him or clutch at him like someone who was drowning.

Yes, yes! Do you have it now? Can you hear the metaphor? Isn't that what the old man in the cave was really doing? Attending, courting, serenading, loving his lady? He wasn't concerned whether what he was doing was sorcery or how people saw him. His sole interest (mark the pun!), his soul interest was his lady and who she was and what she was about and what her language was. That's art!

It is?

Sure it is. Don't make me get indignant with you again! You know about it. You have told me about it. All you have to do is to tell me again so that you hear it. Okay?

Well, we started out talking about art and what consisted of doing one's art and what not. The old man was doing art—the disciples aping of *his* art was pornography. I guess the reason the old man was doing art was because he was following the lead of his lady, following his curiosity about what he knew but what he didn't know. He was true to his art as one would be true to one's lady. In paying attention to her, he gave her reality and being which she then returned to him?

Is that what you think or are you just saying it?

In a way I'm just saying it, as if I understand it in my head, as a notion or concept, but it lacks substance or body. It hasn't been *embodied* yet. I feel almost as if you had blindfolded me and led me somewhere, but I don't exactly know where I am or how I got here. I'm kind of disoriented.

Good.

Good?

Sure. If you're off balance, uncertain, disoriented as you put it, you keep asking questions, you keep looking. There's necessity there. You really need only one necessity: being about your art. Isn't that what you have been doing with this discussion? Wasn't that the direction of your initial question?

Maybe. I wanted to come back to my question, though. I'm glad you brought it up. How does all this tie in with Jung and his psychology?

You tell me.

I'm almost afraid to. I'm not sure I want to admit where we've gotten to.

Steady on, me bucko! You're not chicken little and the sky is not falling in. Where have we gotten?

What we call 'Jungian Psychology', the stuff in the Collected Works, all the alchemy and myths and studies in religion and everything that Jung thought about and wrote about is the portrait that Jung painted of his lady—no, its the picture of where his lady led him. It is a record, a kind of journal of his attempts to express what he knew, but what he didn't know, to give substance and significance to his soul, like the old man with his piece of red chalk making marks and drawing designs on the walls of his cave. But, but . . . damn! That is not what Jung was about at all! He was trying to tell people how to do art so that . . .

Hold on there. I hate to interrupt you when you've just gotten going, but I think you may have taken something of a wrong turn at that last intersection. Was Jung trying to tell *people how to do art or was he simply reporting on how he did his art?*

How he did *his* art. I suppose you can't tell anyone how to do their art; you can only report on your own art.

Right. You're not out to save anyone else's soul—you'll have more than enough to do working with your own.

Where I was when you interrupted me was realizing how false all the stuff that I studied while I was in training was.

False?

Yeah. If what Jung was about was art, if that's what Jungian Psychology is about, why study all this useless stuff about primitives and fairy tales and psychiatry and myths and so forth and so on? That is simply aping Jung! That's pornography!

Not quite. You seem to have swung from one extreme to the other. Let's say that Jung, at least in his old age, knew that he was doing art, was conscious, aware of what he was about. First, though, he had to go through a process of frustration, of uncertainty, of not knowing, of searching—maybe even despair. What is important is the process, going through the steps, like the various steps the alchemists laid out. When you can see it as a process, then you become aware of the art in it. You were talking about stories that other people told about Jung. Remember Fierz's?

Yes.

What did Jung say?

Oh—He said, 'You have to learn your ABC's before you can be Jesus Christ.'.

Voila! Maybe the study of myths and alchemy and everything that Jung did is, like learning the ABC's. We couldn't have gotten to where we have in this discussion if you hadn't already spent years studying Jung. Right?

Right.

By the same token, though, that is not the only way to arrive at that realization.

What realization?

Seeing what is going on with you, with anyone, as a process, as an artistic movement of creation.

Are you saying what I think you are saying? Are you saying that one can be a Jungian, at least insofar as we have defined it, without ever having heard of Jung, let alone having read anything he ever wrote?

You said that—I didn't!

That's not what you are saying?

No, I didn't say that that is not what I said. I'm simply saying that you said it! Pay attention; be precise! Why should you ask me what you know? Why do you need me to confirm what you know? Do you know it or don't you?

I think I know it, at least, it sounds like where I have gotten to with this discussion. But . . .

But?

But I don't know if it is valid, if it is true for me. I have the feeling of being led again, as if I had come to this conclusion and had been tricked into saying something that I'm not sure about.

So what is the next step? Remember the process? Step by step? And don't say, 'What do you mean?'

If I'm not sure its valid then I had best be about checking it out, investigating, testing, trying it on for size.

Right. Maybe that has something to do with the process of embodying it that we were talking about earlier, huh? When you question, reflect, investigate, aren't you fleshing it out, giving substance by attending to it? Don't you give body and weight, importance and three-dimensionality to it?

Yeah. I guess I do at that. You're trying to lead me somewhere else now. No, don't interrupt me. Let me see if I can get it. It starts with an idea, a fantasy . . . a dream. Maybe its like Athene, born in the head, parthenos, but what it wants is body-ing, embody-ing.

Look out! The kid is cooking now!

So that its want is for body, for substantiality, for flesh, for something you can get ahold of. Ohhhhh! That's the hunger of the soul, the Big Hunger, and the more you pay attention to it, the more you feed it, nurture it, satisfy its wanting.

Gently, gently. Make haste slowly!

No. No, I hear what I said. I seemed to be implying that satisfaction is possible. That is not what I mean to say. I mean that wanting tells me where the work is to be done, that wanting belongs to the work of psyche, the work of art. Hey, that sounds like something Hillman said, that want is the primary quality of soul.

Whoa there, Silver! Who said it? It may sound like, feel like, look like, but you got where you got the way you got there. That is you! Don't give it away by dragging Hillman or anyone else into it.

Right. Okay. What does that say about satisfying? Want tells me where the work is, where it is to be done. What wants wanting is the want. What wants wanting is the want! Want's wanting wants wanting!

Want's wanting wants wanting! You're beginning to sound like me. Maybe we'll make an analyst of you yet. Go back to your original question, though: 'Is there such a thing as Jungian Psychology?' Do you hear the answer? Do you see?

Yes, I think so, but I still want . . .

Stop!! Stop right there! If you still want, then that means . . .?

That I'm on the right track, that I'm doing my art or my 'Jungian Psychology'. Thank you. Thank you very much!

1. Jung, C. G. "Concerning Rebirth" (CW 9, i, 233)

The analyst's myth:
Freud and Jung as each other's analyst

By C. Jess Groesbeck (Sacramento)

Introduction: Psychotherapy and One's Personal Myth

In all cultures there have existed at all times and in all places myths of healing. Man apparently cannot survive without designating as a healer a member of the group who is trained in the art. With the rise of scientific methods of healing in the last hundred years, never before have so many secrets of healing been revealed, especially those concerning the body and its functions. So powerful has been the scientific objective approach that it has been considered the *only* basis on which to judge a healing system and its usefulness. As with studying the body, so the study of the healing of the mind has been increasingly subjected to scientific research so as to establish a sound basis for knowledge of the psyche alongside of soma. Unfortunately, in our attempts to accomplish this in the last century, we appear to be further away than ever from "an objective system" and have a morass of opinions, claims, and "schools" of psychology each proclaiming its "truth." So frustrating and dismal has this situation become that a psychiatrist with a sound background in research recently has prophesied the death of psychiatry as a specialty *per se.*[1]

Well might the intelligent layman and serious student ask: What am I to do? Where can I even find a basis from which to evaluate this problem of approach to psychological healing?

I will attempt in this paper to address the problem of "conflicting psychological schools" and "truths" by focusing on all psychotherapeutic systems as, basically, systems of "personal healing myths" that have come out of the lives and experiences of their founders in their attempts to heal others. That is to say, I will propose that all psychological systems, or schools of healing and techniques derived therefrom, are essentially personal confessions of the world view and experiences of their founder(s) and confessions of *how* these experiences and techniques healed the founders and/or helped them heal others. The implication to be derived from the thesis, assuming it can be demonstrated, is that every successful psychotherapist must and will evolve his or her own myth or system of healing. Though it may have certain collective derivatives such as "being a member of a particular school or system," these elements will be individualized along with other idiosyncratic elements to be integrated into a unique personal approach by *this* therapist, to *his* particular kind of patients in the practice of his art.

Rollo May recently pointed out that our values by which we ultimately live are based on symbols; symbols being defined as "that (image? feeling? thought? behavior?) which draws together and unites our experience." He further defined a myth as "a cluster of symbols that express a drama" and life story that confer upon us meaning.[2] Myth, then, makes possible meaning in relationship to ourselves, others, and the cosmos. It gives access to the bedrock of what one understands as to be for him, reality.

Jung noted also that myth is "what is believed always, everywhere, by everybody." He said:

> I was driven to ask myself in all seriousness: "what is the myth you are living?" I found no answer to this question, and had to admit that I was not living with a myth, or even in a myth, but rather in an uncertain cloud of theoretical possibilities which I was beginning to regard with increasing distrust. I did not know that I was living a myth, and even if I had known it, I would not have known what sort of myth was ordering my life without my knowledge. So, in the most natural way, I took it upon myself to get to know "my" myth, and I regarded this as the task of tasks, for—so I told myself—how could I, when treating my patients, make due allowance for the personal factor, for my personal equation, which is yet so necessary for a knowledge of the other person, if I was unconscious of it? I simply had to know what unconscious or preconscious myth was forming me, from what rhizome I sprang.[3]

Note that Jung felt that knowledge of "his myth" was necessary in the treatment of his patients as a physician. He was, of course, taking into account his own "personal equation" that would skew objectivity in viewing the patient. In another place he further elaborated:

> Every theory of complex psychic processes presupposes a uniform human psychology, just as scientific theories in general presuppose that nature is fundamentally one and the same. But in the case of psychology there is the peculiar condition that, in the making of its theories, the psychic process is not merely an object but at the same time the subject. Now if one assumes that the subject is the same in all individual cases, it can also be assumed that the subjective process of theory-making, too, is the same everywhere. That this is not so, however, is demonstrated most impressively by the existence of the most diverse theories about the nature of complex psychic processes. Naturally, every new theory is ready to assume that all other theories were wrong, usually for the sole reason that its author has a different subjective view from his predecessors. He does not realize that the psychology he sees is

his psychology, and on top of that is the psychology of his type. He therefore supposes that there can be only one true explanation of the psychic process he is investigating, namely the one that agrees with his type.[4]

Also, he states: "I need hardly say that technique is necessary up to a
point—we are all sufficiently convinced of that. But behind every method
there stands the man, who is so much more important because, irrespective of
his technique, he has to arrive at decisions which are at least as vital to the patient as any technique however adroitly applied. It is therefore the duty of the
psychotherapist to exercise self-knowledge and to criticize his personal
assumptions, whether religious or philosophical, just as asepsis is obligatory
for a surgeon. The doctor must know his 'personal equation' in order not to
do violence to his patient."[5] When one observes what goes on in the name of
psychological healing today, this warning is timely!

Thus, one can view psychotherapy in whatever form it comes, as an attempt
by a designated healer to help an identified patient examine and become aware
of his personally lived out world myth. That is, together psychotherapist and
patient continually attempt to differentiate, and change if possible and
necessary, the patient's life in and from all its context and development to the
end that the symptoms and sufferings of the patient will be relieved. Henderson noted that at the core of Jung's method or approach "the analysand (patient), himself, was to be amplified as well as his dreams (and other fantasy
and unconscious material?); that is, his own symbolic (mythic?) origin, life
style, and purpose were to be determined to the widest extent possible, as a
process of development, not just analysis."[6] In essence, one's personal myth
was to be explored to the fullest.

Strangely, this connection of the personal myth of the healer and his
theoretical approach to healing the patient has been largely overlooked by
most founders of schools of psychology. Even Freud did not leave a
reasonably complete account of his own inner personal development and its
relation to the origins of psychoanalysis. Other schools, both the earlier and
the modern, have done even less. It was only with the publication of Jung's
autobiography, *Memories, Dreams, Reflections,* that at last a major founder of a
modern school of psychotherapy revealed the inner connections of his personal myth to that of his theories, teachings, and techniques elaborated in the
eighteen volumes of his collected works. From that autobiography one can,
for the first time in modern times, examine *where* and *how* a man's system
evolved. In fact, Jung viewed his whole life and work as an experiment in the
elucidation of his personal myth, just as he expected a patient to go through in
the process of an analysis or depth psychotherapeutic experience:

My life is a story of the self-realization of the unconscious. Everything in the unconscious seeks outward manifestation, and the personality too desires to evolve out

of its unconscious conditions and to experience itself as a whole. I cannot employ the language of science to trace this process of growth in myself, for I cannot experience myself as a scientific problem.

What we are to our inward vision, and what man appears to be *sub specie aeternitatis*, can only be expressed by way of myth. Myth is more individual and expresses life more precisely than does science. Science works with concepts of averages which are far too general to do justice to the subjective variety of an individual life.

Thus it is that I have now undertaken, in my eighty-third year, to tell my personal myth. I can only make direct statements, only "tell stories." Whether or not the stories are "true" is not the problem. The only question is whether what I tell is *my* fable, *my* truth.[7]

To more fully illustrate the above thesis, in the rest of the paper I will examine a crucial dream in the life of Carl G. Jung, along with several significant interchanges and incidents in the life of Sigmund Freud. Their interrelationships will be highlighted to illustrate how the different personal myths and life experiences of each determined their orientation, viewpoint, and understanding of the same psychological data. Thus, this attempt, if successful, will demonstrate in bold relief how several well known differing theories and techniques of these two giants in the history of depth psychology virtually *derived* from the personal myth of each founder. My focus will *not* be on who was *right* or who was *more correct*, but how and in what way each came to view certain fundamentals about psychological healing as a result of his own personal equation. Thus, we will turn the searchlight of analysis on the founders themselves; we will return to those days when Jung and Freud became—and continued to be—each others's analyst!

The Clark University Trip Incident

The time was late August, 1909. Freud and Jung along with Sandor Ferenczi met in Bremen, Germany, to travel together to Clark University at Worcester, Massachusetts, to deliver lectures in America on Freud's new movement of psychoanalysis. During the jorney of seven weeks, they were together daily in intimate contact, and apparently analyzed each other's dreams. The accounts of the journey say little or nothing of Ferenczi's part in these events. The most important interchange was between Freud and Jung and their being each other's analyst. According to Jones, Freud's official biographer, the theme running through Freud's dreams was his concern and anxiety over the future of "his children" and of psychoanalysis as a movement.[8] According to Jung's account, it was a time when Freud, then fifty-three, was definitely the older, mature, experienced leader; Jung, then thirty-four, felt like a son following in the master's footsteps.[9] Earlier that year, in

April, 1909, Freud had adopted Jung as "an eldest son, anointing him as his [Freud's] successor and crown prince in the movement."[10]

It was in this setting, then, that Freud and Jung began to analyze each other's dreams and participate in what was to be a fateful experience for both. Jung noted that he had dreams which Freud could not analyze, but this apparently was not of great concern. However, Jung did become upset at a dream Freud had that Jung tried to interpret, but could not because Freud failed to supply personal associations concerning his private life. Jung noted that, when asked for associations, Freud responded with a "curious look—a look of the utmost suspicion." Then he replied, "But I cannot risk my authority!" For Jung, that moment was decisive; he said, "At that moment he lost it [authority] altogether. That sentence burned itself into my memory; and in it the end of our relationship was already foreshadowed. Freud was placing personal authority above truth."[11]

Undoubtedly, Jung, from his remarks, felt rebellious toward Freud as an idealized father and master and the subsequent history of their separation most likely began at that moment. But why was *this* incident so upsetting to Jung? Were there other issues not articulated that may have been present too? We shall return to this later.

Following this incident of Freud's dream, Jung then relates a very important dream to him that Freud could not interpret. It was to be a decisive dream in that it would foreshadow the work he would do that would bring about his total break and separation from Freud. He states:

> This was the dream. I was in a house I did not know, which had two stories. It was "my house." I found myself in the upper story, where there was a kind of salon furnished with fine old pieces in rococo style. On the walls hung a number of precious old paintings. I wondered that this should be my house, and thought, "Not bad." But then it occurred to me that I did not know what the lower floor looked like. Descending the stairs, I reached the ground floor. There everything was much older, and I realized that this part of the house must date from about the fifteenth or sixteenth century. The furnishings were medieval; the floors were of red brick. Everywhere it was rather dark. I went from one room to another, thinking, "Now I really must explore the whole house." I came upon a heavy door, and opened it. Beyond it, I discovered a stone stairway that led down into the cellar. Descending again, I found myself in a beautifully vaulted room which looked exceedingly ancient. Examining the walls, I discovered layers of brick among the ordinary stone blocks, and chips of brick in the mortar. As soon as I saw this I knew that the walls dated from Roman times. My interest by now was intense. I looked more closely at the floor. It was of stone slabs, and in one of these I discovered a ring. When I pulled it, the stone slab lifted, and again I saw a stairway of narrow stone steps leading down into the depths. These, too, I descended, and entered a low cave cut into the rock. Thick dust lay on the floor, and in the dust were scattered bones and broken pottery, like remains of a primitive culture. I discovered two human skulls, obviously very old and half disintegrated. Then I awoke.[12]

In Freud's attempt to help Jung analyze the dream, the primary focus, according to Jung, was in the personal associations to the two skulls. He "urged me to find a *wish* in connection with them."[13] Jung adds:

> What did I think about these skulls? And whose were they? I knew perfectly well, of course, what he was driving at: that secret death-wishes were concealed in the dream. "But what does he really expect of me?" I thought to myself. Toward whom would I have death-wishes? I felt violent resistance to any such interpretation. I also had some intimation of what the dream might really mean. But I did not then trust my own judgment, and wanted to hear Freud's opinion. I wanted to learn from him. Therefore I submitted to his intention and said, "My wife and my sister-in-law"—after all, I had to name someone whose death was worth the wishing!
>
> I was newly married at the time and knew perfectly well that there was nothing within myself which pointed to such wishes. But I would not have been able to present to Freud my own ideas on an interpretation of the dream without encountering incomprehension and vehement resistance. I did not feel up to quarreling with him, and I also feared that I might lose his friendship if I insisted on my own point of view. On the other hand, I wanted to know what he would make of my answer, and what his reaction would be if I deceived him by saying something that suited his theories. And so I told him a lie.
>
> I was quite aware that my conduct was not above reproach, but à la guerre, comme à la guerre! It would have been impossible for me to afford him any insight into my mental world. The gulf between it and his was too great. In fact Freud seemed greatly relieved by my reply. I saw from this that he was completely helpless in dealing with certain kinds of dreams and had to take refuge in his doctrine. I realized that it was up to me to find out the real meaning of the dream.[14]

Freud as Jung's analyst: A personal dynamic interpretation

Looking at Jung's dream and associations from a personal dynamic point of view one is struck by a number of things. First, his associations to the dream as he related them in the *context* of the relationship to Freud (as his analyst) suggest defensiveness and a transference reaction to him. Note his words, "I *resisted* his interpretation [fear], I did *not trust my* judgment [inferiority], I wanted to hear Freud's opinion [idealization? avoidance?], I *submitted* to his intention [fear of father? homosexual wishes or fears?], I did *not* have such wishes [denial?], I [did] *not present my* view, vehemence, resistance from Freud [projection of all powerful authority, projection of own aggression, father?], I was *not up to quarreling* with him [fear of power?], I *fear loss of friendship* [idealization? insecurity?], I want *his thoughts*, . . . I told him a *lie* [rationalization], and *he* [was] *not really able* to see *my* mental world [self inflation as defense to alleviate guilt of keeping secret his thoughts?].

The response has the all too familiar flavor of the early stages of an analysis wherein the patient is dealing with conflicts over the outward authority of the analyst. Overall what is most notable, it seems, is the need for Jung to conceal his real associations and thoughts from Freud, and the guilt, conflict, and anxiety which that engendered, even apparently to the point of his lying. But, why should this be so? Is there a clue as to what this was *really* about? Perhaps Jung's *alleged* lie has the key to the answer. His answer or "lie" was "my wife and sister-in-law." In an emotionally charged situation where a complex was activated such as here detailed, one cannot assume that only irrelevant associations are given. In fact, Jung's "lie" may have had an unconscious meaning at a different level. In a private discussion with Billinsky in 1957, Jung revealed that in his visit to Freud in Vienna in 1907 Freud's sister-in-law had confided in him of an unresolved affair between her and Freud.[15] Jung's reaction is noteworthy, "It was a shocking discovery to me, and even now (1957) I can recall the agony I felt at the time."[16] It appeared Jung carried that burden from then on. Then he stated:

> Two years later Freud and I were invited to Clark University in Worcester, and we were together every day for some seven weeks. From the very beginning of our trip we started to analyze each other's dreams. Freud had some dreams that bothered him very much. The dreams were about the triangle—Freud, his wife, and wife's younger sister. Freud had no idea that I knew about the triangle and his intimate relationship with his sister-in-law. And so, when Freud told me about the dream in which his wife and her sister played important parts, I asked Freud to tell me some of his personal associations with the dream. He looked at me with bitterness and said, "I could tell you more, but I cannot risk my authority." That, of course, finished my attempt to deal with his dreams. During the trip Freud developed severe neuroses, and I had to do limited analysis with him. He had psychosomatic troubles and had difficulties in controlling his bladder. I suggested to Freud that he should have complete analysis, but he rebelled against such an idea because he would have had to deal with problems that were closely related to his theories. If Freud would have tried to unterstand consciously the triangle, he would have been much, much better off.
>
> It was my knowledge of Freud's triangle that became a very important factor in my break with Freud. And then I could not accept Freud's placing authority above the truth. This, too, led to further problems in our relationship. In retrospect it looks like it was destined that our relationship should end that way. It was full of questions and doubts from the very beginning.[17]

This now clarifies many obscure details of their relationship. In the before noted incident of Freud's refusal to give Jung associations to *his* dream, a conflict developed for Jung because he *knew* and Freud did not know he knew of the triangle of Freud, his *wife*, and *sister-in-law*! Later, when they were analyzing Jung's dream, and his *own* conflict over Freud's and his relationship was activated, he responded defensively and in guilt by keeping his associations secret just as Freud had done when they were previously trying to analyze Freud's dream. Jung's communication was an anxious, conflict laden response to Freud concerning what *he* (Freud) needed to verbalize openly, i.e., the triangle with his "wife and sister-in-law" as the basis of *his* (Freud's) conflict. In a sense, Jung was saying to Freud as his analyst, "you have two skeletons in your closet or unconscious, those of your wife and sister-in-law; get those out first before I can be totally candid with you concerning *my* inner life and we can get on with *our* work." Jung undoubtedly felt great agony over this because of his great love and admiration of Freud. Yet, it must have created guilt also to know of it. Jung's own father had been a disappointment to him, and Freud was probably the only man who had given him a father ideal to follow. To see Freud's humanity, after all of Freud's greatness, must have engendered the agony Jung refers to. Or further, did this incident activate in transference fashion, via Freud, Jung's own unresolved Oedipal conflicts over his father wherein he (Carl) was closer and favored by his mother over father? Ehrenwald, a Freudian analyst, reviews this aspect of Jung's life beginning with earlier dreams of Jung wherein his father is seen as a threatening figure.[18] Ehrenwald then concludes with an interpretation of Jung's dream of the two skulls as representing indeed what Freud probably suspected—death wishes toward himself and Jung's father, the evidence of double parricide.[19] Further evidence for Jung's death wishes against Freud has been suggested by Jung's denial of a negative father complex in the Egyptian King Amenophis IV (Ikhnaton) when this was being discussed by Freud, Jung, and others at the Psychoanalytic Congress in Munich in 1912.[20] Freud apparently reacted to Jung's irritation at his (Freud) interpretation as evidence of Jung's unacknowledged death wishes toward Freud. Though these interpretations may be questioned to some degree, undoubtedly they point to accurate dimensions of Jung's personal psychology, and his conflict with his father and Freud.

But what of Jung's Oedipal complex as it related to women? Could this unresolved complex of Freud's wife and sister-in-law have also activated in Jung a conflict he himself had only recently struggled with concerning the love of his wife and a young cousin who had been a medium Jung had studied? Fodor has suggested that this mediumistic cousin who helped Jung so much do his doctoral thesis on occult phenomena was a childhood love he may have had a struggle to leave behind after growing up getting married. She died young, at age 26 years. Fodor's evidence is not convincing, but, again there may be elements of truth in it. He deduces this primarily from the description of Jung's wife at her death when he saw her in a dream with a dress given her by his mediumistic cousin, that made her "the most beautiful she'd ever looked."[21] Therefore, Jung's "lie" of alleged death wishes toward wife and sister-in-law may have been a truth at another level, a wish to bury old struggles between his wife and cousin ("sister-in-law"?) These would be *his* two skeletons in the unconscious!

One might also speculate how this triangle he knew of in Freud's life (wife and sister-in-law) influenced Jung's inner life as he struggled in later years with the deep attachment he had for his assistant, Antonia Wolff, and the working out of that relationship appropriately with his wife to whom he was absolutely and deeply committed.

What of Jung's Oedipal, incest tie to his own mother? Jaffé notes that Jung's early dream of the phallic god, as a gigantic tree trunk with an eye and living flesh and skin, reveals the basis of the tie to his mother.[22] In that dream his mother's voice called to him saying, 'that is the maneater.'[23] Jaffé states that the mother here is inviting the boy to stay in her realm, avoiding contact with the phallic, masculine, father image, which in actuality could be potentially positive and creative for masculine growth; i.e., identifying with the father. Jung in later years felt his mother's influence was too strong upon him, and he viewed the problem as one of growing *up away* from mother and her world. It was from her and her family that he got his mystical leanings and interest in the occult and parapsychology. He was an introverted thinking intuitive type. He later saw the incest taboo as a preventative from the falling back into the *natural regressive* pull toward the mother and her world. He came to identify the unconscious itself with the more primitive earthy qualities of the mother. It was not until 1946, when, Jung was 71 years old, that he had a dream that showed him the resolution of the relationship with his father and mother. See the dream of the Fish Laboratory and the Reception Room for Spirits. In that dream he seemed to finally make a reconciliation with both of them.

Jung As Freud's Analyst: A Personal Dynamic Interpretation

Returning now to the Clark University trip events, we may now try to view the other aspect of the relationship, Jung as Freud's analyst from a personal dynamic point of view. In a sense when Freud was helping Jung work on his dream of the house and the two skulls, Jung was attempting to "cure Freud" as the analyst so their work could go on, as does every patient to his analyst when the healer has a blind spot. However it may have been, Jung *was also* trying to analyze Freud, as noted by Jung's comment to Billinsky.[25] Jung "suggested to Freud a complete analysis but Freud rebelled against such an idea," as noted before.[26] Apparently, Freud had psychosomatic difficulties controlling his bladder. Also, he (Freud) would have to "deal with problems too closely related to his theories."[27] What theories could be referred to? Certainly, themes of the Oedipus Complex, parricide, incest, and sexuality would be what Jung had in mind. Well might one ask why Freud was *so* anxious to impute death wishes to Jung? His anxiety concerning this had actually begun at the start of the trip in Bremen when they had sailed. Jung had read about the peat-bog corpses in Northern Germany, archeological remains that excited interest of the day. He says:

Having read about these peat-bog corpses, I recalled them when we were in Bremen, but, being a bit muddled, confused them with the mummies in the lead cellars of the city. This interest of mine got on Freud's nerves. "Why are you so concerned with these corpses?" he asked me several times. He was inordinately vexed by the whole thing and during one such conversation, while we were having dinner together, he suddenly fainted. Afterward he said to me that he was convinced that all this chatter about corpses meant I had deathwishes toward him. I was more than surprised by this interpretation. I was alarmed by the intensity of his fantasies—so strong that, obviously, they could cause him to faint.[28]

Note Jung's comment on the intensity of Freud's fantasy concerning this. The suggestion that Freud had death wishes toward Jung, which were in turn projected onto Jung, receives corroboration from several pieces of evidence. Freud stated that in the two fainting episodes in the presence of Jung—there was another in 1912—and also with Fleiss, "a predecessor of his (Jung's)" Freud's own repressed feelings of hostility and death wishes "played the main part."[29] Fleiss, of course, had been an important father figure and guide for Freud prior to Jung. He was also related in Freud's mind to his own father, for whom Freud had strong death wishes. It was via Fleiss that Freud had allegedly done his "self analysis."[30] In the fainting episode at Munich in 1912 all stood helplesly around; only Jung picked up Freud and lay him on a sofa. Jung noted "As I was carrying him, he half came to, and I shall never forget the look he cast at me. In his weakness he looked at me as if I were his father. Whatever other causes may have contributed to this faint—the atmosphere was very tense—the fantasy of father-murder was common to both cases."[31]

Jones pointed out that both fainting spells, by Freud's own admission, were also related to Freud seeing Jung as his younger brother whose death Freud had wished for in childhood and who had subsequently died in childhood. These feelings of guilt and anxiety had apparently never been worked out.[32] Further, Freud felt there was "an unruly homosexual feeling at the root of the matter," concerning the fainting spell at Munich in 1912 with Jung.[33] Here the elements of Freud's preoccupation with a father complex is elucidated. Hall and Domhoff suggest after analyzing Freud's dreams exhaustively by content analysis that he had a preoccupation with men and an "inverted Oedipus Complex," i. e., a deeper relationship to men and a hostile one to women.[34] While this may have general validity, the aforementioned evidence suggests certainly an uneasy equilibrium in his relationships with important men, such as Jung, at that time in his life. It is curious that Freud chose the Oedipus myth to describe what he felt to be the most important paradigm of parent-child relations. As has been noted by some, Freud had, more accurately, a "Laius Complex" (Oedipus's father), wherein he, at a certain point, could not tolerate the sons taking over from his as the father; they had to be murdered, as Laius tried to do his own son, Oedipus.[35] Equally, it could be said that in Freud's own personal life he, at best, uneasily took his father's place as did

Oedipus. His whole struggle with the psychoanalytical movement was one of trying to be the successful dominating father over "the sons" in a movement that would revolutionize society. Jung most clearly states this in one of his final latters to Freud.[36]

Jung in 1957 wrote that he had analysed Freud on the Clark University trip:

> When I analysed Freud a bit further in 1909 on account of a neurotic symptom, I discovered traces which led me to infer a marked injury to his feeling life. Experience shows that at such moments a feeling type switches over to thinking as the counterfunction, together with the compensatory overvaluation. The original auxiliary function—in this case intuition—is replaced by a somewhat deficient "fonction du réel." This transformation has been described by the French as "simulation dans la charactère." Freud, when one got to know him better, was distinguished by a markedly differentiated feeling function. His "sense of values" showed itself in his love of precious stones, jade, malachite, etc. He also had considerable intuition. Yet the superficial picture he presented to the world was that of an extraverted thinker and empiricist who derived his philosophy of life from the man in the street, which is supposed to be modern.[37]

What was this feeling injury that Jung referred to? Here our knowledge of Freud's life is obscure. Certainly, it could have related to unresolved emotional ties to his mother. The fact that his sexual life ended with his wife at age forty makes one wonder what injury to his feeling side and function may have been involved in that issue.[38] Could the affair with his sister-in-law at age 52 that Jung refers to have been some mid-life manifestation of a depression with a belated attempt to cure himself via contact through a feeling-eros relationship? One often sees this in men in the forties and fifties.

But what of Freud's Oedipal Complex from a feminine perspective? Jaffé noted that, totally different from Jung, he related to his mother as a needed lover who had been lost:

> Freud's nature and creative destiny were quite different. In his *Interpretation of Dreams* he reports a nightmare from his seventh or eighth year in which his beloved mother, dead, is carried into a room by two or three persons with bird's beaks. The bird-people remind him of an Egyptian tomb relief. The boy awakens crying and screaming.
> As was the case with Jung's childhood dream, this solemn, frigthening image presages a destiny. The pall-bearers are related to the birdheaded Horus, and because of the solar quality of this God they must be governed by the realm of daylight, by logos and reason. They are the ones who carry the mother to the grave. Clearly, then, the spiritual destiny, the creative work of a man who as a child comes upon such a powerful dream image of his mothers's death, cannot be determined by the matriarchal feminine but will stand under the sign of the opposite spiritual pole, the masculine paternal logos. The lucid scientific spirit which permeates Freud's thinking and writing and the logic of his scientific decuctions receive their support from this reservoir of his being.[39]

Thus, he was under the father's psychology. Also, Freud saw the incest taboo as necessary so as to prevent one from obtaining mother from father, after she has been taken away. She is sought for because she is desired by the child.

Jung as Freud's analyst: A symbolic transpersonal interpretation

To move now to the symbolic view of Freud's life, especially in relation to Jung, requires a different perspective. In 1910, Jung relates how Freud asked him to "promise not to abandon the sexual theory," that it was the "most essential thing of all," and that a "dogma must be made of it."[40] It was to be "an unshakable bulwark" against the "black tide of occultism." Occultism, Jung found, referred to virtually "all things in philosophy and religion, including parapsychology." Jung saw this as Freud making his sexual theory a "numinous God."[41]

Neumann, himself a Jewish analyst, elaborates on this thesis of Freud's rejection of the "occult" or irrational, i. e., religion and mysticism. He refers to Freud and some of his Jewish followers as having an unanalyzed unconscious prejudice concerning the mystical. Neumann states:

> This brings us to a problem that belongs both to Freud and to psychoanalysis, namely the Jewish problem, the significance of which has not yet been given enough attention and which in this context can only be hinted at.
>
> By this we do not mean the problems arising in this Jewish group from anti-Semitism and deep-seated resentment, for these are relatively comprehensible, and were characteristic of unanalyzed Jews of the "assimilation period" and long after it. Often enough the Jew instinctively feels the "goy" to be the enemy and anti-Semite, even when he himself is behaving anti-Semitically. The Jewish problem of Freud and his paladins is a much deeper question, by no means a mere negative bias but a pre-condition, essentially related to Freud's great work and to psychoanalysis itself. That Freud was deeply conscious of his specifically Jewish qualities is clear from a passage advising Ferenczi how to reply to Maeder, who felt that, in the conflict between the Viennese (Freud) and the Zurich (Bleuler-Jung) schools, the difference between the Jews (Vienna) and the non-Jews (Zürich) was significant. Freud wrote: "Certainly there are great differences between the Jewish and the Aryan spirit. We can observe that every day. Hence there would assuredly be here and there differences in outlook on life and art." This statement is, in its simple matter-of-factness, so significant because, when expressed by a non-Jew, e. g., Jung, it has always been foolishly taken as a proof of anti-Semitism. With equal simplicity and as much justification, Freud then, however, goes on to state: "But there should not be such a thing as Aryan or Jewish science. Results in science must be identical, though the presentation of them may vary. If these differences mirror themselves in the apprehension of objective relationship in science there must be something wrong." Our distance from the conflicts of this creative period, during which Freud and Jung came to the parting of the ways, enables us to see that what Freud took for granted

as "scientific" was partly colored by his own unconscious prejudices which had never ben analyzed. It almost looks as if he was aware of it when he wrote to Abraham: "Don't forget that really it is easier for you to follow my thoughts than for Jung, since to begin with you are completely independent and then *racial relationship brings you closer to my intellectual constitution.*" One can gather from this sentence that to be a Jew was, in a way, a better "racial" background for a scientific approach to psychology. This statement, like nearly all statements about fundamental racial characteristics, shows an unconscious prejudice. We find this confirmed in the whole of Freud's work, where the chief distinction is seen to lie in the fact that, in contrast to the Jews, non-Jews regard religious contents as of essential significance. It is typical that the word "mystical" is used to mean "of religious content," and one hardly trusts one's own eyes when in this context one reads Freud's statement: "We Jews have an easier time, having no mystical element."[42]

As Neumann summarizes, Freud had a particular problem concerning the approach to the mystical. He had the bias that only the scientific rational point of view would be acceptable in a true scientific psychology. Anything that smacked of religion or of the mystical was considered to be invalid and explanable on other reductive grounds. Because Freud assumed this was true, as well as did others of his Jewish followers, he therefore assumed that Jews in general were superior in grasping a more enlightened scientific approach over non-Jews. This was so because it was apparently Freud's experience that only non-Jews like Jung were prone to take mystical happenings, i. e., the occult and religious, seriously! Later, Neumann notes that Freud totally ignored the fact that it was from the Jews, a religiously enlightened people par excellence, that had come a strong mystical tradition, i. e., Chassidism and the Kabbala.[43]

Bakan, in a remarkable book on Freud's life, elaborates this thesis of Freud's relation to the Jewish mystical tradition.[44] It is here perhaps that, to date, we have the most profound insight into Freud's life and what Jung meant to him from a symbolic, archetypal point of view.

Freud suffered restrictions as did most Jews concerning anti-Semitism in both his personal and professional life in the 1880's.[45] As he grew in his work as a neurologist and later in his psychological investigations that led to the founding of his therory of psychoanalysis, he wanted his work to be accepted on a professional scientific plane, i. e., outside and beyound only Jewish circles. He suffered great personal frustration for never being made a full professor in Vienna in his early years and this embittered him to the end of his life. Therefore, he looked for a non-Jewish friend and colleague that would help him become acceptable in the gentile scientific community. Jung turned out to be just the man, being a non-Jew, bright, a believer and accepter of Freud's views and thus fulfilled the criteria to become the crown prince or successor to Freud in the psychoanalytic movement. In 1910, when Jung was publicly announced as being the successor to Freud as president of their psychoanalytic society, there was a storm of protest from other Jewish analysts. Freud told them "most of you are Jews, and therefore, you are incompetent to win friends for the new teaching. Jews must be content with the modest role of preparing the ground. It is absolutely essential that I should form ties in the world of science. I am getting on in years, and am weary of being perpetually attacked. We are all in danger." Then Freud, seizing his coat by the lapel, said, "they won't even leave me a coat to my back. The Swiss will save us (refering to Jung); will save me and all of you as well."[46]

Bakan then elaborated his thesis that Freud's creation of psychoanalysis was closely related to his personal development, and historically was at once a denial and reaction against Jewish mystical trends as well as at the same time, covertly an expression of them via a scientific framework. He details the background of the Jewish people's struggle in the previous 200 years before Freud to find a stable social equilibrium in western culture with the gentiles. Complicating this struggle for a secure identity and acceptance was a deep internal struggle within Judiasm itself concerning the orthodox rabbinical tradition and the mystical Kabbalistic tradition. The internal struggle apparently complicated and fomented the anti-Semitism from non-Jews. Most importantly, the mystical element was related to, in the minds of many Jews, as the source of Jewish betrayal in a spiritual way and essentially the element that led to exposure and downfall both temporally and socially with the gentiles. Therefore, in the minds of the progressive liberal Jew, identifying with the mystical tradition was something totally foreign and repugnant. From many sources, including Bakan and Jones, it is clear that Freud longed to be both a hero and deliverer of his people as well as a rebel concerning the tradition of the past. Thus, Freud identified with the scientific and rational mode of thinking and research as the only legitimate way of expression. Yet, as Bakan argues, psychoanalysis itself dealing with the unconscious and the irrational covertly expresses many Jewish mystical elements. Thus, it expressed Freud's other side, i. e., being a revolutionary and a creative artist. He warred with these impulses throughout his life, as can be noted concerning the general validity scientifically of the study of parapsychology. Though he rejected this in most of his early years, at the end of his life he stated that "if he had it to do over" he would "study parapsychology and not psychoanalysis!"[47]

What is *also* important in this context is that Freud psychologically had a fixation and identification with the figure of Moses.[48] Freud's relation to Moses is then viewed by Bakan as an unconscious means of working out both sides of the father complex, i. e., killing the father yet also trying to exalt him. He correlates Freud's fanciful theory of the origin of human culture in his book, *Totem and Taboo*, in this context as being essentially a subjective insight into Freud's inner working struggle to understand himself. In the book, *Moses and Monotheism*, Freud views Moses as not actully a Jew, but an Egyptian who rescues the Hebrew people and gives them a religion. However, in so doing he has to be killed for it![49] Freud postulated that a "second Moses," a Jew, appeared who killed the first Moses, but in turn honored his memory and became the new leader. He thus reconciled the father complex for the Hebrews, and later the Christians, thus alleviating their guilt. In substance, Bakan sees Freud living out both dimensions of this drama in his own life with Jung in the creation and development of psychoanalysis as a movement. It is here that Freud's transference to Jung is critical to a profound understanding of Freud's personality. Bakan shows how Freud as the "first Moses" creates a "new religion," psychoanalysis, for the Jewish world. Then, in Freud's unconscious, Jung is seen as the alien, the second Moses who wishes to come in and kill the first one, Freud, and thus worship him and enjoy the glory of the creation, the acceptance by the scientific world. Freud was said to have felt that Jung was the only disciple that he had who ever had as many creative ideas as he did. This created envy in Freud.[50] Many of Freud's preoccupations concerning his death, the devil, and the psychology of the "double" as it related to Jung would here be pertinent in corroborating this hypothesis.

In essence, *if Freud could have seen it,* he was utilizing Jung in a transference situation to work out the symbolic archetypal wellsprings of his life. But to do that he would have to have been able to go beyond the positivistic prejudice mentioned by Neumann and take religious, racial, and the mystical experience in terms of one's origins, seriously! In Freud's elaboration of the theme of Moses, he came very close to understanding the symbolic nature of the psyche, but turned away from it and even postulated the inheritance of collective guilt concerning the Jews and later Christians in their worship of Moses. Though this was totally unscientific because it represented an outmoded aspect of evolution concerning inherited character traits, still Freud was not deflected in his theorizing. And so it seems the die may have been cast from the beginning; Freud needed a non-Jewish bright follower who could, as Joshua did for Moses, lead the children of Israel into the promised land, someone with a mystical bent, who would pick up that unacknowledged, shadowy, unspoken side of Freud's nature. It would also have to be someone, however, who would accept being the sacrificial lamb and be killed when he went too far in living out what had been prefigured for him by the first Moses, Freud! Jung fit all these criteria and the story of Freud and his relationship and transference to Jung as well as the final separation appears to be a living out of this whole archetypal theme in Freud's life. Interestingly, it was after the break with Jung that Freud, for the *first time,* was able to fully identify himself as the author of psychoanalysis.[51] Prior to that he had never been able to thus publicly acknowledge it. Thus, to some degree Freud was able to make gains in his own individuation via his relationship to Jung.

The theme of the two skulls in Jung's dream may now be looked at from still another perspective. Did they represent Freud, the first Moses killed by Jung, the second Moses, *and vice versa,* at a symbolic level in Freud's working out of his inner life? Suggestions that the dream could have had just such intimate connections with Freud's unconscious can be noted from Jung's associations to the dream. "Certain questions had been on my mind during the days preceding this dream. They were: On what premises is Freudian psychology founded? To what category of human thought does it belong? What is the relationship of its most exclusive personalism to general historical assumption? My dream was giving me the answer. It obviously pointed to the foundations of cultural history—a history of successive layers of consciousness."[52] Thus, one is led to the conjecture that Freud's own unconscious life was strongly activating what was already stiring within Jung, i. e., looking to a view of the psyche and its collective layer going beyond the personal! Freud was never to reach the "promised land" of looking at the symbolic dimensions of the psyche, however; he remained forever within the context of 19th century rationalism and a purely personalistic view of psychological man.

Freud as Jung's analyst: A symbolic transpersonal interpretation

To return now to Jung and view his development, especially in context with his relation to Freud, from a symbolic dimension requires following Jung closely. He noted concerning his associations about the dream of the house and two skulls, "I realized that it was up to me to find out the *real* meaning of the dream."[53] Jung goes on,

> It was plain to me that the house represented a kind of image of the psyche—that is to say, my then state of consciousness, with hitherto unconscious additions. Consciousness was represented by the salon. It had an inhabited atmosphere in spite of its antiquated style.
> The ground floor stood for the first level of the unconscious. The deeper I went the more alien and the darker the scene became. In the cave, I discovered the remains of a primitive culture. That is the world of the primitive man within myself—a world which can scarcely be reached or eliminated by consciousness. The primitive psyche of man borders on the life of the animal soul, just as the caves of prehistoric times were usually inhabited by animals before men laid claim to them.
> During this period I became aware of how keenly I felt the difference between Freud's intellectual attitude and mine. . . . When I thought about dreams and the contents of the unconscious, I never did so without making historical comparisons; in my student days, I always used Krug's old dictionary.

Jung then goes on to say that Freud's intellectual history had begun with writers such as Darter and Buchner, those of a much later period. Jung continues, "the dream pointed out that there were further reaches to the state of consciousness I have just described. The long uninhabited ground floor in medieval style, then the Roman cellar, and finally the prehistoric cave. These signify past times and past stages of consciousness. . . . *My dream* [Italics mine] *thus constituted a kind of structural diagram of the human psyche;* it postulated something of an altogether *impersonal* nature underlying that psyche. It "clicked," as the English have it—and the dream became for me a guiding image which in the days to come was to be corroborated to an extent that I could not at first suspect. *It was my first inkling of a collective unconscious beneath the personal psyche.* [Italics mine] This, I first took to be traces of earlier modes of functioning. Later, with increasing experience on the basis of more reliable knowledge I recongnized them as forms of instinct, that is as archetypes."[55] In one of the most critical experiences of Jung's life, then, he discovered the symbolic transpersonal layers of the psyche. Further on, Jung implies what perhaps he and Freud could not at that time accept; the skulls represented the death of their relationship. From another perspective it was, "Freud's conceptions cannot reach beyond a personal psychology. His psychology for you is dead in the realm of the deeper symbolic layers of the psyche."[56] Indeed, their total pespectives were so different that they were in fact, even then, totally irreconcilable. Thus, the end was foreshadowed.

One must remember that according to Jung's personal associations to the dream, the questions that had been on his mind most intensely were that of the foundations and assumptions upon which Freud's psychology was based. Therefore, it would seem natural to look to the dream as a help for Jung in answering the questions of the assumptions upon which a healing approach to the mind was to be based. Strikingly, the images of the dream take Jung back in time and place to beyond the foundations of his cultural matrix. The theme of his dream was clearly from that of his own, then present-day European culture, back to the time of Rome which, indeed, was the foundation of western European culture. Finally, beyond the Roman culture and possibly even the Egyptian, the imagery reaches to the prehistory of Western man. This is in interesting contrast to Freud's plummeting of his foundations by his search back to Moses as a historical and symbolic figure. But if the unconscious of Jung was trying to help him understand the question of psychic healing taking him in imagery beyond the confines of his own western history, to what ends could it be taking him? It is here that the theme of initiation could be raised. Could it be in a sense that the unconscious was trying to help Jung understand that at the very source of being is a healer and to understand the healing process he had to go back to the very beginnings, to the oldest forms of healing? In a sense, the unconscious may have been saying, "you must go far deeper than within your own personal complexes to comprehend what healing is; you must do more than just analyze dreams; you must go to the oldest form of healing known to man, symbolic healing i. e., Shamanism." The two skulls and bones that Jung saw in the dream suggest a striking relationship to the theme of shamanic initiation through which those ancient healers went. In a compensatory way the unconscious was saying that both Jung and Freud would have to be able to plummet their own souls to symbolically contemplate their own skeletons much as the ancient shamans did in becoming healers!

Eliade noted that with some Eskimo shamans their initiation involved the making of a long effort of physical privation and mental contemplation directed to "gaining the ability to see himself as a skeleton." By thus seeing himself naked he is "freed from the perishable and transient flesh and blood and thus can consecrate himself to his sacred task."[57] To reduce himself to the skeletal condition was equivalent to "reentering the womb of his primordial life to complete a mystical renewal and rebirth."[58] Amongst the Tungus in Siberia some groups venerated the bones of the shamans, and their skulls were used in the process of divination.[59] Among "hunting peoples bones represent the final source of life, both human and animal, the source from which the species is reconstituted at will. . . . The 'soul' is presumed to reside in bones and hence the resurrection of the individual from its bones can be expected."[60] Also, Eliade later states, "the human skeleton in a manner represents the archetype of the shaman, since it is believed to represent the family from which ancestral shamans were successively born."[61]

Thus, the skulls for Jung may have foreshadowed the deep initiation process with the unconscious that he was to undergo in the years to come. It was to put Jung in contact with the deepest known source of healing in the psyche of man, and prepare for the great journey into the unknown he was to make. Like the ancient shamans of old, he was to go to where few men ever go and return. Thus, Jung's dream may have heralded the re-emergence of the most ancient of all forms of healing, Shamanism. The implications and interconnections of Jung's work with ancient shamanic healing is just now beginning to emerge, and their far reaching ramifications barely beginning to be explored.

Theory and technique of
Freudian and Jungian psychotherapeutic systems
As derivatives of the personal myths of the prospective Founders

Returning to the central theme of this paper, it will be our task to relate what has gone on before, i. e., the analytic exploration of the personal myths of the two famous founders of modern depth psychology to the theories and techniques that later came to characterize their particular schools. The first and perhaps most striking difference between the two schools is how the "unconscious" is viewed. As noted above, Freud with his Jewish background and in relationship to his place in history had many reasons to suppress the mystical and irrational side of the psyche. He was committed to science and hence saw the unconscious as something to be programmed within a frame of predictability. One can note this in his need to see unconscious psychic processes clearly explained within a theoretical frame. For example, note how he approached Jung's dream and his need to see a clear-cut interpretation concerning death wishes. The unconscious to him was regressive. Note, for example, his conception of the Id as an instinctual uncontrolled caldron of urges as the origin of psychic life. The Ego, then, was to integrate and refine these instinctual roots. Viewing the unconscious in this way could also have derived from Freud's particular psychological type configuration. Apparently he was an introverted feeling intuitive type who had suffered a severe wound to his feeling side and thus had identified strongly with his inferior functions of extraverted thinking and sensation. Thus, with these functions he oriented himself to a more rational, logical, and scientific orientation.[62]

Jung, on the other hand, saw the unconscious as a place of not only primitivity and chaos, but also as the source of creativity, itself.[63] As such it could not be programmed.[64] Jung postulated the Self as the seat of the unconscious and viewed this as the supraordinate place of organization and integration. He saw this as the source of creativity even greater than that of the Ego. Jung, of course, coming from a more mystical background, especially in relationship to his parents and grandparents, was ready and prone to accept that dimension of the unconscious. The mystical orientation derived also from the relationship he had in early life with his mediumistic counsin. He was an introverted thinking intuitive type and looking at psychic data in that way is consistent with that typology. The conflicts that Freud and Jung had concerning parapsychology and the occult highlight again their irreconcilable differences in this area.

The second major difference is the emphasis Freud gave to a reductive interpretation and approach in dealing with the associative material of the patient. His bias was to refer the fantasy life to outward experience, particularly the past and childhood. Jung, on the other hand, while he did not necessarily ignore that view, oriented more to a symbolic and prospective approach in dealing with psychic material. Two approaches can be noted in each attempting to interpret the dream that Jung had. Freud obviously looked for the reductive outer aspect and Jung finally reached for a more prospective inward symbolic view.

Another striking difference is their contrasting views in viewing the therapeutic setting for psychotherapy and particularly the handling of the transference. Freud, with his stronger orientation to science and a more extraverted view as noted above, made famous the view in analysis of the "mental surgeon with the sterile technical arrangements" whereby the patient on the couch relates to the analyst who is behind the patient and thus conducts the treatment. The analyst, in essence, remains unknown keeping his personal life as much as possible out of the realm of the patient's life and working with his own unconscious to help the patient get a perspective with the dialogue going on within himnself. Jung, in contrast, saw the transference as basically taking place in a mutual dialectical relationship between doctor and patient.

He felt, in fact, that the unconscious of both doctor and patient were in union, in fact were the primary source where real healing took place. Thus, Freud's orientation was to the efficacy of the technique and arrangements of psychoanalysis, whereas Jung felt that the healing process took place in the context of the personal relationship. This suggests Jung's more symbolic, shamanistic leanings as a healer, a quality that pervaded his whole approach to analysis. These views can be noted from the dreams discussed in the paper where Freud very much wanted to keep secret his personal life in relationship to Jung and thus maintain his mantle of authority whereas Jung, in contrast, felt that these deeper unconscious meanings should be shared freely by both analyst and patient. Again, the philosophy and practice of technique can be directly related to the general underlying philosophy of Freud's relationship to a scientific approach and Jung's relationship to a more subjective symbolic approach.

Another aspect of the handling of the treatment situation was Freud's strong reliance on free association with dreams actually being put into a secondary position.[65] Jung, on the other hand, did just the opposite. He placed a great, perhaps primary, importance on the dreams and their amplification with a secondary concern for free association that led to the complexes. This, too, in Jung, suggests a more shamanic quality. Paradoxically, it was Freud who made the dream famous with his book, *The Interpretation of Dreams*, and it was Jung who did the most decisive sientific work on free association with his study of the word association test. It should be clearly noted that these techniques are not divorced again from the personal psychologies of the founders but in fact fit in more comfortably with them.

Another differing attitude was that related to authority and the conduct of the therapy in general. Freud saw the therapeutic situation as definitely being a hierarchal one with the analyst as the authority and the patient in the inferior position. Jung, on the other hand tended to opt for more equality and a co-working together with the patient in exploring the unconscious terrain. These views, it can be noted, derived from their different approaches and ideas concerning the Oedipus Complex and the relationship to the father and authority generally. As noted before, Freud had a strong relationship to his father but which consisted of one of feeling very dominated. Thus, the only security he could find and felt comfortable with was when he, as a father authority, was clearly in the higher respected position with the sons, such as Jung and others, being in the disciple relationship. He ofttimes described analysis in this fashion.[66] Jung, on the other hand, in his own view of the father relationship, viewed the father as important by his being available as a partner, the very thing his own father was not. Therefore, he tended to seek for a father who would bring co-equality and a brotherly sharing to the exploratory relationship in therapy and otherwise. Jung, for example, in the analysis of his and Freud's dreams, wanted a co-equal sharing rather than a hierarchal relationship of master to disciple as Freud wanted.

But perhaps the most overtly expressed difference in the theories between these two men related to the incest aspect of the Oedipus Complex. Freud, as Jaffé summarized, saw the incest motif when it occurred as being literal and related to an objective parental (i. e., mother) complex in childhood that had to be worked through because it contained the sexual connotations. Jung, while he did not exclude this possibility, felt that in most cases incest had a symbolic menaing. That is, the fantasy or image as it may occur suggests a longing within the individual, i. e., the son, to return to the primary source of his life and regressively reunite with the mother. It was an attempt to return to the security of the mother and her world in a state of twilight bliss. These views of incest can be noted to stem from the dream of childhood that Jung had wherein the father image was seen as a fearsome thing and he was called back by the voice of his mother to stay in her world. Thus, he would see the incest image as a regressive pull by the mother. Freud, as Jaffe noted, in the dream of his childhood saw his mother carried off by pallbearers and experienced the deep loss of her and thus the positive desire to have her after she had been lost. Jung, then, saw the incest taboo as the need to prevent that regression back to a more natural primitive state whereas Freud saw it as a prohibition placed upon the sons by the fathers because they would want the desired object of the mother in a more fully matured sexual sense. Thus, Freud's perspective on this problem comes from the world of the fathers and indeed his view has been noted to be that of a patriarchal father psychology. Jung's psychology relates to that of the mother and the world of the feminine. His psychology has been strongly noted to be oriented to and give positive affirmation to the feminine. It is clear with the publication of the Freud-Jung letters that this became the final doctrinal struggle in which they could no longer make reconciliation.[67]

The effect that this view of the incest problem has upon the question of transference in analysis is also striking. Freud in the handling of the incest complex, in analysis as it became projected upon the analyst was to give up one's incest desires and thus sublimate them so as to go on and grow up to become a mature human being. This was fostered by the threat of castration by the father and thus promoted this outward resolution of a real problem that had never been solved in the childhood experience. In contrast, Jung viewed the incest motif in the transference as part of a deep symbolic inner problem of the patient. Its appearance in the transference in relationship to the analyst suggested that there was now a regressive pull to return to one's earlier ground of his being, i. e., to the world of the mothers. Therefore, as Jung, saw it, utilizing the alchemical model, he felt that if incest were lived out in the transference relationship with the analyst indeed only a regressive situation would be activated. On the contrary, this outward incest desire in relationship to the analyst was to be denied so that the patient can experience "a symbolic inner incest" with one's self and thus achieve a state of wholeness and individuation. Thus, Jung saw the incest motif, via fantasy, as the important avenue to getting in touch with one's own soul. Via the death and rebirth process and going "back into the mother" in a symbolic way this experience could take place.[68]

Thus, both Freud and Jung viewed the incest taboo in analytic therapy as being absolutely essential and that sexual relations between patient and therapist would in no way be permitted but for very different reasons. It is important to note, however, that the transference can be viewed in its outer aspect as Freud described it, i. e., sublimating the relationship outwardly with the parents and parental figures in order to become a more adult person, as well as how Jung described it in an inner introverted fashion as a way to get in touch with the deeper symbolic layers of one's self, by experiencing "inner incest."

Finally, their differences also highlight the type of approach as healers or physicians that they actually took. In a recent interview with Roy Grinker, M. D., one of the last people who was analyzed personally by Freud in 1935, Grinker found that Freud generally was depressed at the time with feelings that he could not help anyone personally. For that reason Freud had put all of his energies to the founding and development of psychoanalysis as a movement, thus sustaining his faith in technique and science as to what psychoanalysis could accomplish. Of course, it must be noted this was at the end of Freud's life when his strength was gone and he had cancer. Descriptions by others who were analyzed by Freud, however, also suggest this same attitude in earlier years. In contrast to this the author also recently interviewed Joseph Henderson, M. D., someone who was analyzed by Jung in the 1930's and who was intimately acquainted with him until his death in 1961. Henderson pointed out that in one of the last seminars he heard Jung give to students concerning analytical psychotherapy, Jung refused to become involved in discussions of technique. Apparently the students pressed him greatly to "give them his secrets of technique" in being an analyst. Jung categorically declined to so do but instead told them that they needed to consult the "Great Man within themselves." He told them the story of a group of Labrador Indians, the Naskapis, who had very little formal religion but who individually could contact "The Great Man." He emphasized that it was far more important in therapy what one was rather than what one did. Here Jung unequivocally sided with the personal equation of himself as the therapeutic factor in the analytic process. Interviews with others who were analyzed by Jung note this as the most outstanding quality; i. e., the immensity and importance of Jung's personal equation in the process of therapy. Thus, Jung clearly identified himself with the image of the ancient Shaman, who in his own person mediated the healing experience for the patient.

An Example and Personal Experience

One may well ask the question, but is all of this really that important? Are the differences and similarities in psychotherapeutic systems really that important to understand in the practice of psychotherapy? An example, in the author's recent experience, gives a cogent answer to that question. The patient was a thirty-two-year-old Jewish man who had received nearly a thousand hours of classical Freudian analytic psychotherapy as well as a mixture of some interpersonal approaches. At the particular time the fantasy he related was recalled, he was in a Jungian-oriented analysis. He recalled a recurrent fantasy that began in his sixth year and went into his teen years. It was always experienced as a nightmare and terrifying. In the dream he would be alone in his room, lying naked. Suddenly from out of the ceiling near the lights would come a long strange series of pinchers that he came to call "the Tonkers." They would come out of the light bulb, down the walls, across the floor, come up behind him, and attempt to snip at his buttocks! He therefore, in sheer terror, would awaken holding his buttocks firmly to the bed trying to keep it from showing. In the early stages of his classical Freudian analysis, the interpretation in one form or another was always given that he has a deep fear of the vagina. Though at times that interpretation was helpful to him, especially as he was attempting to work out a very disturbed and inadequate masculine sexual identity, he soon came to feel frustrated and upset by it. After relating these experiences he noted in a recent dream the same imagery in full form. This time the interpretation, obviously from a more Jungian view, was that the tonkers represented the *fear he had of the feminine* and *that the message was that he needed to open himself up to it in a receptive way; then it would not be so frightening.* In essence, it was stated the tonkers were attempting to open up the feminine side of himself so that he could begin to live in that world, too, that he had neglected. This interpretation was involved with many other dreams and fantasies which reflected a need to relate to the inner feminine world within himself. Almost like magic it opened up subterranean areas in his unconscious life that to that time had been totally unexamined or explored. It was a critical event and essentially changed the course and direction of his analysis. It is to be noted that the interpretation was, in essence, the same as what had been previously given to him, with one change. The interpretation was oriented from the point of view of the unconscious from a feminine perspective rather than from the masculine world of ego where the unconscious is viewed as feminine and threatening. To be fearful of the vagina would be the masculine outer conscious perspective wheras "opening one's self up to the feminine" would be that perspective from the unconscious. The interpretation was the same, but from an opposite vantage point and perspective.

Finally, from my own life, I would like to relate two recent dreams of my own that have highlighted the importance of this issue. *I am in the old North Seattle Mormon Stake Center and Church. It was the church of my childhood and youth where I learned from "the fathers" the way of life I pursued. Many of the old friends who were fathers to me were there. Suddenly, the building was empty; they were gone and I was alone. I left rather frightened, alone, directionless, and looking for someone to help. At that point I saw my analyst whom I had worked with for several years. He was leaving and I followed him across the University Bridge and went to the center of the city of Seattle where we climbed Queen Anne Hill. Somehow I sensed I had found a new place and a new center.* My associations and interpretation to that dream suggested to me that at last I was leaving the confines of my personal parochial childhood in which I had grown up. I was leaving the personalistic identification with men who had been extremely important to me in helping me establish early roots in my own personal private world as I grew up. Now, however, they were gone for a variety of reasons and I had to look to new paths. I was leaving the north section of town where I had grown up. I went to Queen Anne Hill, a hill in the city of Seattle that is the center and the highest place in the city. Somehow this image suggested to me a move to become a more universal person to center myself beyound the confines of my personal psychology and roots. This to me was similar to Shamans in times or old who went to the World Pole, the symbolic center of the world in their villages as part of their initiation as healers.

A short time later I had a second dream in which *I was again leaving the north of Seattle and going to the University of Washington School of Medicine where I had become a physician. I was going there to be operated on by a neurosurgeon because of a strange illness I had. They were going to operate on my head and my nose and some organ in my abdomen. However, when the operation was about to begin a strange thing occurred. It turned out that the neurosurgeon was not a modern one, but an ancient one who in the guise of being a modern neurosurgeon actually practiced the secrets of old Indian medicine. He, in fact, was an Indian healer. In his art it was proclaimed to me that he also combined the traits of old English medicine and history as well as the secrets that George Albert Smith, an early Mormon pioneer, held.* Associations and interpretation of this dream suggested that now in another dimension I was receiving a very significant operation to change my conscious orientation and adaptation. The head and nose suggested my intellectual and intuitive tendencies that I had heavily relied upon in growing up. I was going to a new stage beyound the development of my own immediate cultural past that included America and England and even the roots of my own Mormon origins. I was going now to a deeper level of the psyche beyound the cultures that I knew, i.e., to the level of healing related to the Indians who inhabited this land long before my own ancestors, whose way was that of a symbolic healing, Shamanism. In a modest way I was in a circumstance similar to Jung's where I was being told that I must comprehend a different kind of healing than I had been involed with up to that point. I now had to make that transition to the symbolic layers of the psyche and understand healing as it has existed from the beginnings of time; symbolic or shamanic healing, just as Jung had to learn. These two dreams, perhaps more than any others, have suggested to me that the comprehension of one's personal myth is a absolute necessity for the growth and development of an individual on his way to becoming a healer in the fullest sense of the word.

1. E. Fuller Torrey *The Death of Psychiatry* (New York: Emerson Hall, 1974).
2. Rollo May, "Values, Myths, and Symbols," *American Journal of Psychiatry*, 132: (1975), 703-704.
3. C. G. Jung, Symbols of Transformation, CW 5, pp. xxiv-xxv.
4. C. G. Jung, *Psychological Types*, CW 6, par. 849.
5. C. G. Jung, "The State of Psychotherapy," *Civilization in Transition*, CW 10, pars. 350-51.
6. Joseph Henderson, "C. G. Jung: A Reminiscent Picture of His Method," *Journal of Analytical Psychology*, 20 (1975), 116-17.
7. C. G. Jung, *Memories, Dreams Reflections*, ed., Aniela Jaffé (New York: Vintage Books, 1963), p. 3.
8. Ernest Jones, *The Life and Work of Sigmund Freud* (New York: Basic Books, 1955), II, 53-62.
9. Jung, *Memories, Dreams Reflections*, pp. 158-64.
10. *The Freud-Jung Letters*, ed., William McGuire, Bollingen Series XCIV (Princeton: Princeton University Press, 1974), pp. 218-19.
11. Jung, *Memories, Dreams Reflections*, p. 158.
12. Ibid., 158-59.
13. Ibid., p. 159
14. Ibid., pp. 159-60.
15. John Billinsky, "Jung and Freud (The End of a Romance)," *Andover-Newtown Quarterly*, 10 (Nov. 1969), 39-43.
16. Ibid.
17. Ibid., 42-43.
18. Jan Ehrenwald, *The History of Psychotherapy* (New York: Jason Aronson, Inc., 1976), pp. 361-64. See Jung's dream of God defecating on a cathedral in such an explosive manner as to shatter the walls! *Memories, Dreams, Reflections*, pp. 39-41.
19. Ehrenwald, *op. cit.*, pp. 361-64.
20. Jung, *Memories, Dreams, Reflections*, pp. 156-57.
21. Nandor Fodor, *Between Two Worlds* (New York: Paperback Library, 1964), pp. 50-56.
22. Aniela Jaffé, "The Creative Phases in Jung's Life," *Spring* (1972), p. 163; Jung, *Memories, Dreams, Reflections*, pp. 11-12.
23. Jung, Ibid., p. 12
24. Ibid., pp. 212-16.

25. Billinsky, op. cit., p. 42.
26. Ibid. (In a personal communication Joseph Henderson has clarified some of that issue for me.)
27. Ibid.
28. Jung, *Memories, Dreams, Reflections, p. 156.*
29. Paul Roazen, *Freud and His Followers* (New York: Alfred Knopf, 1975), p. 249.
30. Jones. op. cit. II, 307.
31. Jung, *Memories Dreams, Reflections, p. 157.*
32. Erich Neumann, *"In Honor of the Centenary of Freud's Birth,"* Spring, 1957, p. 49.
33. Roazen, op. cit., p. 254.
34. C. Hall and B. Domhoff, "The Dreams of Freud and Jung," *Readings in Psychology Today* (Del Mar, CA: CRM Books, 1967), pp. 388-92.
35. Erik Erikson, Freud-Jung Seminar, October 26, 1974, Friends of Langley Porter. Neuropsychiatric Institute, San Francisco.
36. *The Freud-Jung Letters, p. 535.*
37. *C. G. Jung Letters: 1951-1961,* ed., Gerhard Adler, Bollingen Series XCV: 2, (Princeton: Princeton University Press, 1975), pp. 346-48.
38. Jones, op. cit., II, 86; Roazen, op. cit., pp. 51-52.
39. Jaffé, op. cit., pp. 171-72.
40. Jung, Memories, Dreams Reflections, p. 150.
41. Ibid., p. 151
42. Neumann, op. cit., pp. 47-48
43. Ibid., p. 48.
44. David Bakan, *Sigmund Freud and the Jewish Mystical Tradition* (Boston: Beacon Press, 1958).
45. Roazen, op. cit., pp 224-26.
46. Bakan, op. cit., p. 58.
47. Roazen, op. cit., p. 241.
48. Ibid., pp. 284-87.
49. Bakan, op. cit., p. 121.
50. Roazen, op. cit., pp. 259-61.
51. Ibid., p. 287.
52. Jung, *Memories, Dreams, Reflections, p. 161.*
53. Ibid., p. 160.
54. Ibid., pp. 160-61.
55. Ibid., p. 61.
56. Ibid.
57. Mircea Eliade, *Shamanism: Archaic Techniques of Ecstacy,* Bollingen Series LXXVI (Princeton: Princeton University Press, 1964), p. 62.
58. Ibid., p. 63.
59. Ibid., pp. 62-63; 245.
60. Ibid., p. 159.
61. Ibid., pp. 159-60.
62. *C. G. Jung Letters, II,* 346-48.
63. Roazen, op. cit., p 267.
64. Henderson, op. cit., pp. 116-17.
65. Note Charles Brenner's view of dreams, a modern-day classical psychoanalytical ap-

proach: *The Psychoanalytic Technique and Psychic Conflict* (International University Press, 1976), pp. 137-44.
66. Roazen, op. cit., 162-72.
67. C. G. *Jung Letters, II,* 314-17.
68. C. G. Jung, "The Psychology of the Transference," *The Practice of Psychotherapy,* CW 16.

(reprinted from Quadrant, *Spring 1980, pp. 28—55, by permission.)*

Training Problems:
Schools of Individuation

By Rudolf Blomeyer (Berlin)

I am going to speak about questions of training. I will not be giving an overview of the situation, but rather will be looking at a very subjective selection of issues which particularly concern me. I hope they are also important to you. Concerning Freud and his followers, Jung once wrote: "It is well known that things are much more fluid and flexible in the spirit of the creator's new views than in the spirit of the followers, where the living power of shaping and creating is missing and this lack is replaced by dogmatic fidelity." Enough said on the Freudians: fidelity is not something which is missing with us. Not that we might not be fluid and flexible. A very broad and rich collection of published material demonstrates the continued development of analytical psychology within the bounds of its own school and in a fruitful exchange with other analytical and (more general) psychotherapeutic schools around the world. That is progressive and modern. However, the so-called official theory, especially as it appears in our textbooks, is really more on the conservative side. There appears for the training candidate a rather colorful if not partially confusing picture emerging out of the old and the new. I would look particularly at difficulties which arise in connection whith the old, that is with the basic Jungian concepts and positions. These difficulties are in principle well known. That they continue to to be a problem makes one have to think them through again. They are not going to simply disappear.

In the forefront of this discussion, I would put the word "individuation" and would say, that the idea of individuation is utopian, but also that it is an effective Utopia without which we cannot and should not wish to get along. Difficulties arise in many places when the idea is understood concretely, that is, where, either openly or in secret, the expectation exists of really reaching individuation. The same is true, however, for many great ideas, for example those of Marxism or Christianity: it is not possible to really realize the ideals as they are expressed. All reasonable people know this, but the faithful still deny it; and in the main, the reasonable ones are basically still believers in their hearts. The power of being gripped is too great. Thus even the reasonable people are not going to give up the basic idea.

I am giving our problem here the title: "Schools of Individuation" and would first make a typological comment. Jungians often like to think of themselves as introverts, especially as introverted intuitives. If they really are, and if Jung's description of this type is correct, the following is to be considered: the introverted intuitive makes, as Jung says,

> "himself and his life symbolic—adapted, it is true, to the inner and eternal meanings of events, but unadapted to present-day reality. He thus deprives himself of any influence upon it because he remains uncomprehended. His language is not the one currently spoken—it has become too subjective. His arguments lack the convincing power of reason. He can only profess or proclaim. His is 'the voice of one crying in the wilderness.'"[1]

If that is what he is, and if he wants to teach, he must translate the voice of one crying in the wilderness into the everyday local language. Otherwise, he truly remains incomprehensible. Also, he must now and again give some thought to the differences between "teaching" and "preaching" so that the teaching end of it is not disadvantaged. Otherwise he would be tempted to refer only to a few phrases from the creed, that we Jungians do indeed have. Let me name two of our major creedal statements: First: what God does, so does the unconscious, and that is well done! Second: God gives to his own when they are sleeping (that is: in the dream). Both sound good enough and would also be good if God didn't occasionally for example, give his own now and again in sleep, a psychosis. Unshaken, Jungians teach that in these cases the meaning of the sickness really becomes visible. But I don't feel exactly good about this explanation. And the ones who get the psychosis don't either.

Again: when God really means well, he gives individuation. But this he does only in the second half of life. There are some problems with this formulation too, especially visible in matters of training, but not only there.

By individuation, following Jung's definiton, we understand the following:

> "It is the process by which individual beings are formed and differentiated; in particular, it is the development of the psychological *individual* as being distinct from the general, collective psychology."[2]

Our candidates are prepared for the forming and differentiating of individual beings However, they are not prepared that at the same time something flowing in the opposite direction is also at work in them. Certainly, if they knew about this opposite current ahead of time and could understand it, they would not want to let it happen. I mean that through training they acquire a new identity, which is at the same time a group-identity. They are taken into the fold, made part of a Society, and submitted to a particular group spirit. They become Jungians. Along the way they get new parental figures or new parents—the male or female training analysts through whom certain introjects are formed. The training and especially the training analysis make some things conscious, but there appear also new and unconscious "im-ag-inations", which will stubbornly continue to influence the trained persons the rest of their lives. In fact it is unavoidable that we form "Ein-Bildungen," unless of course we strive to remain uninfluenced by the training analysis. But that would be like wanting to go into the water without getting wet.

The group spirit howevers, is blind. It sternly demands individuation, even when we know or argue: it really doesn't exist, at least not in the sense of reaching a particular condition which one could call "individuated" and which aims as we must say far higher than simply than the "formation and differentiation of individual beings."

Taking off from a discussion of typology. M. L. von Franz in 1971 grappled with the question of what is attainable in individuation. She spoke of moving away from an identification with one's own conscious and unconscious functions and remaining at a kind of middle level, or at least making an attempt at remaining there. This would be, however, only a first step in further pesonality development. Yet, it would be enormously difficult simply to reach this particular middle point. When she was asked for an example she answered that this was not easy, since there are very few people who had reached this point. Her nearest and most convincing examples were in some descriptions of the behavior of Zen masters.[3] That is (as far as I understand her), these examples are to be found in areas beyong the field of analytical psychology, and they are really very rare. One should really note this and take it to heart. Indeed, von Franz must have know what she was talking about. People who are given as examples of individuation usually (if not always) live quite far from where we are. The degree of individuation seems to multiply with the distance between the observer and his example.

The expectation that one must be or become individuated is not, however, mitigated by this fact. The idea still seems too fascinating and wonderful to be given up completely. Whether conscious or unconscious, the concept remains. As a conscious content it is truer to the spirit of the basic image beneath it, that of healing, an image of the whole man, of the Anthropos, never losing its attraction and effectiveness. It is not a question of eradicating this image, but rather of differentiating ourselves from it. It we are not very careful in observing this difference, the idea of individuation will actually seduce us into precisely what it demands that we avoid at all costs, namely, a confusion in the borders between ego and Self, an identification with the archetypal image of God, and an inflation. One acts then as if one could "see God" and even control Him. Moses who hid his face was certainly more cautious, "since he was afraid to look upon God."

In terms of the psychology of neurosis, image and and pretension can be easily fit together. They are part of a narcissistic fantasy. One has tried, shall we say, to describe lower categories of individuation and to take these as worthy goals. For example, Plaut, in conjunction with some London training candidates came "to the conclusion that there is a much more daily form of individuation which means that they seem to possess especeially well-rounded personalities. . . . (One may) experience that having had a contact with such a person one feels better connected to the world. . . . (Especially it was noticed), that these persons lived in contact with the elements and with the changing of the seasons, be it, for example as farmers, gardeners, hunters or fishermen." The narcissistic fantasy takes on a depressive accent in this reduced form: precisely the reduction and "back to nature". However, it remains a fantasy, and it remains the (unreachable) goal. In this connection: what are the city-folks supposed to do?!

There are still other attempts to take individuation out of the special and into the general and not only to find reduced forms of the phenomenon, but rather to declare that individuation is always taking place (in all phases of life) and everywhere (in all people). Thus, no sooner has a patient lost a few symptoms than it is suggested tha he has made "important steps towards individuation." One can put it that way. One can also call all donkeys horses and all camels gazelles. But in doing this one has lost more than one has gained and along the way hasn't exactly done the donkeys and the camels a favor when they're visible in the light of day. Here, one forgets that individuation has something to do with the very special, with the absolutely individual, with the gripping experience, with that which seldom occurs, with numiosity. One also "forgets" that one cannot "create" something numinous. That is, one says that one cannot do it and then one sets about making a situation in which it can happen. The claim remains. And individuation remains a hidden hope and an assurance: it must really be possible. All of the reduction merely protects one from among a ther things, the final discovery that indeed it is not possible.

For the younger training candidates with respect to the demand there is another way out: the "real" individuation is supposed to take place in the second half of life and that should begin around the age of 35—40. Since many training candidates are between 30 and 40 and not yet in this second half of life, the need for this change is prolonged. They find themselves then in a rather unusual place which one can describe equally well as hopeless and also as hopeful. Hopeless at least for now, since that which is to be reached is by definition "in the second half of life" and therefore cannot yet be reached at this period of their lives, except as an anticipation. Hopeful, since they can always think: maybe later!

This state of affairs is an important special factor in our training. For a significant number of our trainees, a major aspect of our theoretical teaching, the concept of individuation in the second half of life, cannot be experienced or grappled with during the training from the point of view of the trainee's own experience. And as we know, theory alone is never enough to teach. (in a similar fashion the thinking of Jung's "old age" is not really accessible to many even after training.)

Since a trainee cannot attain the demanded individuation, he or she attempts to at least get on with the process by first of all "assimilating the shadow" in order to be able thereafter to pass through the various stages of individuation. Here again there arise misunderstandings which result from our language, which is so rich in images and is in other ways so impressive, yet which has a tendency to formulate issues in ways which are onesidely positive and affirming, leaving out the negative and destructive.

No one assimilates his shadow. Pieces of it become more conscious, but probably there will be a counter-movement wherein other aspects simply become more covered over. In the language of this image, the bright light only make the shadows more clear. And in the outer collective as well as in the psyche of the individuals, for one holy person at least ten sinners grow up after him . Even "the stages of the way of individuation" don't exist. It is a legend which has its roots in a beautiful old image entiled: "the way to the inner world" and rooted in pictured conceptions and schematic diagrams of the various "layers of the structure of the personality": the persona on the outside, the Self on the inside. Outside, in the shadow on the edge of the forest are the robbers; farther within are the dragon and the treasure. At the very center on a mountain is the grail. The analysands go, according to this rule, first through the lower parts of the personal unconscious and then across the wide spaces of the collective unconscious. They work first on the shadow, then on the anima or animus, and so on. (And if they're not dead yet, then they're working on these things still).

To be sure, there *is* development. Certainly there are archetypal series of images and fantasies in which certain themes (unconscious—made half conscious with the help of the analyst) are again and again systematically taken up, and shaped in a particular way. Such images can lead either into heaven or hell and can be accompanied by measurable psychic and bodily changes. This fact certainly doesn't mean, however, that the so-called "images of the personality" Persona, Ego, Shadow, Anima-Animus, Mana, Self turn up, even with some regularity in the sequential way described in our texts. In reality they all play a role from the very beginning. The mana personality, for example, with which teacher and student love to do magic is in principle no easier or more difficult to come into contact with than animus or anima. Or the persona, which is said to be found "right on the outside", can be affected by certain operations of a cosmetic behavioral sort, yet still remain quite untouched by the analysis, or only very gradually begin to change as the whole person changes. The wind bloweth where it listeth. As if the Self or "God" was nearer or closer to us when we speak of him as our "Neighbor's wife"!

At this point, I want to go into another aspect of the problem, of training which has recently been quite intensely raised. Let me cite a few figures: The IAAP had 150 members in 1958. 20 years later, in 1978, it had more than four times that: 650. The German society for Analytical Psychology was founded in 1961 with 19 members. In October, 1979 there were 169 (9 times the original) with another 136 training candidates (that is about 9 analysts to 7 training candidates) (The society in Germany to which analysts of all schools belong had about 800 members in 1979, with 20 training institutes and about 4,100 training candidates.)

In the middle 60's in the Federal Republic of Germany, psychotherapy was made payable in full by insurance. The condition for this was that an application had to be made for the patient which would be reviewed and approved by a third party expert in the field. In 1968 there were 60 psychotherapy applications. In 1979 there were 18,000 (that is almost 30 times as many) In 1979 there were over 2,000 psychotherapists with different pre-analytic training (1, 333 M. D. s and 728 non M. D.'s in the Federal Republic of Germany who were eligible for insurance payments.) In addition to this was a group whose size is hard to estimate, made up of M.D.s, psychologists, and other therapists who were not eligible for insurance payments for psychotherapy as trained analysts, yet nevertheless via various institutions of the state received some sort of compensation for the psychotherapy they did.

To cite some statistics derived from our literature: in 1977, Vincie and Rathabuer-Vincie put together a bibliography on the literature of Analytical Psychology leaving out Jung's own writings).[4] The first 1000 titles appeared over a period of 45 years (1910—1955). In the following 20 years, up to 1975, about 3000 titles were added, leading to a total of about 4000 titles: 3, 687 original pieces of work and 344 reviews of various works.

These figures clearly reflect a very broad extension of the field of psychotherapy together with a strong institutionalization in the framework of the general psycho-boom. The figures show also that this psycho-boom has been taking place in the Jungian camp as well. Basically this is a positive development: more analysts, more analytical treatment, more literature, more Jung. However, who's to keep an eye on all of this? And how is this increasing quantity going to affect the quality?

I once had a kind of a Grail fantasy that Zurich had an Arthurian kind of analytical Round Table. That is not irrelevant, but also it is not original. Jung himself had some thoughts which went in this direction, for example in a dream in India: "What are you doing in India? Search rather for the holy vessel for your own people, the savior of the world (i. e., the grail) whom you so desperately need."

The fantasy of finding "the savior of the world" shows how high our claims and our hopes really go in their ideal formulation. If one keeps in mind the image of the Grail and the Round Table of Arthur as a consitutional basic motif of Jung's and therefore of analytical psychology something else also becomes clear: The impossibility of teaching that idea. There can always be a "Book of the People about the Grail," but never, "The Grail for the Common Man" which anybody can "look into Monday to Friday from 3 to six in the afternoon, Sundays from 10 to 12." The Round Table of the Grail has something extremely elitist about it. For 650 members there will hardly be places enough.

Apart from the Grail, certain aspects of the teachings of Jung are not teachable for another reason: to the Grail, there might be what we call a pure gate of access, but this is not true when it comes to getting to Jung! One can learn to toss around a few tidbits of theory on animus and anima, and perhaps for the psychotherapy of everyday life this might enough. But for the deeper aspects of Jung, and probably that means for the real Jung, such rote learning is not sufficient. In order to really be able to follow Jung, one needs not only the pure gate of access, but also great quantities of imaginal power. In addition, so much general and broad education are needed to gain real access, and so much education must continue along the way, that most of us, including myself, simply get left along the wayside.

People are fond of saying that in a changing world Jung has continued to be attractive; in fact, that he has become even more attractive. But when I speak of the Grail and of the high demands made on one's powers of imagination, one's education and knowledge, and when I remind you that for many of us as well as for others, the real Jung is not really accessible or only with extreme difficulty, how can it be that Jung appears to be even more attractive? *And* can he be attrractive when so many psychotherapists today have a strong leaning towards social concerns which go counter fo Jung's demand for the individual's search for meaning and "Besonderung von Einzelwesen"? (Of course Jung did clearly state that individuation was also a matter of better fulfilling of a person's collective role, but this aspect is traditionally much less emphasized.). Most of all, how can Jung be found attractive when the image of an *opus* taking place in a *vas hermeticum* hardly accords with a typical treatment paid for by insurance and somehow also determined by it? (It is even less in accord with a group analysis, which in my opinion should be obligatory for training candidates next to their personal analysis!)

Perhaps analytical psychology is partially—and I emphasize the word partially—still so attractive or has become so now for many, *because* it does not go along with the named collective tendencies and corresponds to opposite kinds of tendencies. The following is so often said about us that one hardly feels like mentioning it: that we are willing "to respond to the deep yearnings for the irrational in this technical-rational world." Here we must also consider the fact that in this we enter into competition with the Maharishi and all sorts of sects, both good and bad, and that people do say of us, often in somewhat unfriendly tones, that some find us so attractive because we are so beautifuly incomprehensible. Furthermore, we must warn that according to our own logic it must be assumed at the beginning that those who find us particularly attractive are projecting their inferior functions onto us in an expression of yearning.

What can I say after all this? Certainly it is only possible to recognize and to allow the idea of individuation even as one stande for the "psychotherapy of everyday life" in one's teaching and daily application of the idea of individuation. My phrase "psychotherapy of everyday life" can seem rather devaluating and derogatory. When one seeks the Grail and finds instead only the "psychotherapy of everyday life", something has indeed been devalued. However the effect of this devaluation depends on the point of view one has in looking at this situation. If one does not approach the question from the standpoint of the Grail, but rather from the other side, then the "psychotherapy of everyday life" can even from a Jungian point of view become something extremely valuable, helpful, refined, enlivening—even (insofar as one can use the word in connection the treatment of sick people) something thrilling.

Naturally, this still means that it's not enough to "simply learn how to chat intelligently about animus and anima". It seems to be a fact, however, that a relatively large group of analysts manage to get along with a rather small amount of theoretical knowledge. This is also the case among analysts of other schools. It would seem that in training the question is not only to impart theoretical knowledge, but much more to enable candidates to carefully sharpen their perceptive tools to grasp and to experience psychic contents in a highly differentiated fashion. Though practicing they learn how best to deal with these psychic contents.

Jung emphasized at the end of his "Psychology and Alchemy "that alchemy" was concerned with creative processes that can be truly grasped only by experience, though intellect may give them a name." He added that the alchemists on the one hand indeed insisted on the study of their books, but on the other hand said: "Rumpite libros, ne corda vestra rumpantur", (Rend the books, lest your hearts be rent asunder.) As Jung put it: "Experience, not books, is what leads to understanding."

At the outset I spoke of the followers who substitute dogmatic faith for the ability to genuinely exercise living creative powers, Perhaps some of them might be losing some of these living creative powers due to excessive fidelity. Or perhaps they read too much. This might require a turn about where they rend their books, becoming unfaithful so that they come to their own personal new experience and understanding in Jung's spirit.

1. Jung, C. G. Collected Works, vol 6, para 662
2. Ibid., para 757
3. von Franz, M. L. "The Inferior Function," in Lectures on Jung's Typology, Spring Publications, New York: 1971
4. Vincie, Joseph F. and Margreta Rathbauer-Vincie, C. G. Jung and Analytical Psychology: A Comprehensive Bibliography, Garland Publishing, Inc., New York and London, 1977

(Translated by Alexander Mc Curdy, Philadelphia)

Has training gone too far?

By Mario Jacoby (Zürich)

First of all, I want to say that the reflections I am going to present are not representative of a so-called Zurich School of Jungian analysts. They are purely my own personal view. I am glad to say that different points of view are more or less tolerated in Zurich nowadays—it would be fundamentally contradictory to the Jungian approach if this weren't so.

Now in order to answer the question "Has training gone too far?" we first have to ask: what is training supposed to achieve? We train Jungian analysts. The task of the analyst is to help the analysand to get in touch with his deeper Self and its unfolding. This can be attempted:

a) by trying to remove blockages and anxiety-laden resistances by means of interpretation and analysis in its proper sense, the aim of this procedure being the achievement, to quote Jung of a "conscious attitude which allows the unconscious to cooperate instead of oppose"—and

b) by trying to stimulate and constellate emotions and fantasies directly from the unconscious. This can be done in various ways—such as confronting, suggesting, inspiring or actively entering into the patient's fantasies. Yet fundamentally the possibility of doing this depends on the constellating power an analyst radiates as a personality. In the selection procedure for training candidates one of my main criteria is the quality of the candidate's constellating power—how do I feel in his presence? A candidate who is a strongly constellating personality may become a very effective, yet at the same time a very dangerous, analyst—depending on his ethics and his potential for awareness and differentiation and his talent for analysis in its proper sense.

According to Jung the analyst has first of all to understand in an optimal way the language in which the unconscious expresses itself—hence so much emphasis is given on getting as familiar as possible with the rich symbolism of the collective unconscious. Has training gone too far in this respect? I want to postpone my own reflections on this point until later.

Anyhow, the idea is that in analysis unconscious contents should get assimilated or integrated. But there is no technique to be learned in order to facilitate this procedure—at least not in so-called classical Jungian analysis. No rules exist except to be in tune with what is demanded from the situation at any given moment. Thus there is wonderful freedom for creative encounter.

Yet isn't this asking too much from any human being? Wouldn't it as a consequence mean that the analyst has to be continually in "Tao"? Otherwise he
cannot be fully responsive to what is demanded from a situation at any given
moment—especially when a situation is as complex as in the analytic encounter. Thus training would mean getting to the point where all interactions
with the patient are inspired so to speak by the personality-center of the
analyst, by the Self. This idea is of course absurd, and invites inflation or grandiosity, or inhibits all effective interaction from fear of inadequacy. Yet there
are moments when something crucial happens due to a sudden inspiration the
analyst has and communicates. I do not want to deny the psychic reality of
Tao. The only trouble is that in Jungian psychology we have so many powerful and holy words and so much awe for the so-called "numinous"—which is a
wide field open to inflation, illusion, and superstition. Yet again, the experience of the numinous *does* exist and may be crucial. The difficulty lies in
the problem of distinguishing between the genuine and the illusionary, between the "true bride and the false bride"—to use fairytale language.

Training therefore means to my mind develping refined inner instruments
which give sensitive signals of where we are in connection with the inner
truth of ourselves and of our analysands. And it goes without saying that this
is a lifelong task also for the practising analyst.

Inner truth is again a big word, encompassing gut-experience as well as refined feelings—and also ideas. Now to speak of ideas: I think that generally
speaking the time when a Jungian analyst considered himself as a kind of mis-
sionary of the ideas of his Great Master has passed. This happened mostly unconsciously by identification. And often its inherent danger, that the truth of
the great master's ideas might become more important than the patient's immediate needs, was not enough recognized. There is obviously much less fu-
sion with the mana of the great master today—the pendulum swings rather in
the opposite direction. Still, the need of the analysand—also of the so-called
"training"-analysand—to identify with an idealized figure, is always present.
And with it also the question: how far does training in practice mean to identify with the teaching and attitude of one's training analyst, who is in his
turn a part of an institute (or maybe at odds with his institute)? I personally
must confess that as a training-analyst I cannot help feeling rather satisfied
when a candidate's development runs close to my own ideas and my own attitude. It looks like kinship and might even be so. Yet I hope to be conscious
enough to keep my narcissistic needs in check and adequately suspicious of
the Pygmalion complex to form candidates according to my wishes. Suspicions of the candidate concerning the Pygmalion complex of his analyst can
too easily be interpreted as neurotic resistance. On the other hand, candidates
who are too apprehensive about their own independence usually have to live
in a constant defense of their relatively weak inner autonomy. Without letting
oneself be in-fluenced in that word's literal sense, no real training is possible.

But sorting out with time and experience which ideas, suggestions, or interpretations can be integrated into one's true personality and which have
truthfully to be rejected as alien to it, is a very necessary procedure. We have
to allow and even further it if we want to train mature future analysts who are
genuinely in touch with themselves. Thus an analytic development can take a
direction the analyst does not really like. And the difficult question then arises
as to whether the candidate is off the track or really on his own personal
quest. His dreams may cast some light on this question. Still, according to my
experience, the belief in the so-called "objectivity of dreams" also needs recon-
sidering. But this is a theme I cannot go into here.

We can say that training is a process of integration with the result of enabling the candidate to use for the benefit of patients in a productive way his life-
experience and his own conflicts and complexes together with a wide
psychological knowledge and sensitive skill. Wide psychological knowledge
includes, to my mind, not only Jung's work and the related amplification
material, Freud's basic writings, and psychiatry and psychopathology, but also
some familiarity with current trends in psychoanalysis or other approaches.
Practical skill in interpreting in dealing with transference/counter-
transference, and leading meaningful dialogues may also make use of techniques such as Gestalt, psychodrama, and so forth.

But with all those various demands, doesn't training—at least in its expectations—go too far? If the candidate or also the practicing analyst loses spontaneity of interaction out of fear of being insensitive, naive, off the track or
mistaken, if he is overconcerned with the correctness of his theory, or if he is
carried away by displaying his mythological knowledge—then something has
gone too far. Perhaps with his training? I rather would say: something has
gone wrong with his training. It has not become integrated, not become part
of the analyst's personality. And this integration is crucial because the practice
of analysis is to my mind much more an art than a science. I therefore think
that the question is *not* "Has training gone too far?" It is not a matter of quantity but of quality. I would like to ask instead: Does or does not our way of
training really help that process of desired integration as much as possible?
And if not, why not? This is to my mind the main issue.

Training of analytical psychologists and Xhosa medicine-men (South african indigenous Healers): A comparative study

By M. Vera Bührmann (Gansbaai, South Africa)

For the past 5—6 years I have been doing research into the healing procedures of the *amagqira* (medicine men) belonging to the Xhosa speaking people. They inhabit an area in the South Eastern Cape and form part of the bigger Nguni nation.[1] I will limit myself to a small group who live in a rural area but who also practice in surrounding towns. The group under discussion are those who confine themselves largely to psychotherapeutic techniques; herbalists, throwers of bones and other categories of medicine men are excluded.[2]

This group has been studied in depth. The aim of this paper is to describe their approach to the training of prospective *amagqira* and to illustrate it with a description of one of several ceremonies which are performed during training. The training is lengthy, demanding, costly, and associated with a considerable degree of personal sacrifice. Some of their concepts and methods will then be compared to those of analytical psychology.

The following aspects will be considered briefly:

1. Their cosmology and the role of ancestors in health and ill-health.
2. The initial illness, *thwasa*, which leads the individual to seeking treatment and, in some cases, training from a recognized *igqira* (medicine man).
3. The description of one ceremony to illustrate certain points.
4. The subtle thread of the transference and counter-transference.

Cosmology

The Xhosa world view can be described as holistic. There is little, if any, distinction between physical and psychological experiences and sickness. They combine nature and spirit, and thus achieve a cosmic relatedness which has been extensively described as occurring among preliterate people.

For the present purpose an understanding of the role of the ancestors in

Xhosa life is crucial. In the literature they are also called "shades" or "living dead". For psychological reasons the term "ancestor" seems more appropriate because it denotes a relatedness which is important in the context of this paper. The ancestors are the deceased members of the family or clan who live around the homestead, and share the lives of the living in the most intimate way.

The ancestors can become manifest in many ways, as human beings, known and unknown, and as animals, wild or domestic. According to von Franz[3] in fairy tales and legends animals are anthropomorphic beings—they are both animals and human beings at the same time. Events such as sudden death, especially by drowning, lightning, floods and inexplicable natural phenomena are seen as evidence of ancestor activity. They can also be experienced in the human body as either pleasurable or causing dis-ease. They communicate with their living kin largely through dreams.

The living communicate with the ancestors through a variety of rituals and ritual ceremonies. A common method is by the ritual preparation and use of a substance called *ubulawu*. It is a herbal extract which can be whipped up to form a white head of foam which is used for drinking and cleansing of the body. It is reputed to call the ancestors, to stimulate dreaming, to clarify dreams, and to open one's mind to the messages of the ancestors. The ritual brewing and drinking of beer is also commonly used to please the ancestors and thus to facilitate communion with them.

Sacrificial and other ceremonies are important but less commonly used. The chief informant said:

> The perfume of *ubulawu* and the smell of beer attract the ancestors. We sacrifice to the ancestors asking them to teach us to be able to distinguish between right and wrong."

On the whole the ancestors are kindly mentors and protectors. They can, however, get offended when their needs are not met, or their injunctions not obeyed. They then withdraw their protection, thus exposing an individual and his family to misfortunes, sickness and the evil effects of witchcraft. The observance of customs related to the ancestor cult as well as those which order society are particularly important in the Xhosa cosmology, and also in the cosmologies of other Black nations in Southern Africa.

There are two groups of ancestors which are not family or clan linked. They are the "People of the Forest" and the "People of the River". The latter group is particularly important to my study. They live under the water, are white, have long fair hair, have cattle, and carry on agricultural activities, much as the living do. Apart from the "People" there are also powerful ancestor animals under the water, especially the *ichanti*, a river spirit which can take several forms but is often conceived of as being a big snake. It is dangerous to see it, as it can emit a bright light and thus cause madness. One should pray for it to be seen only in one's dreams. It is supposed to guard some treasure—it is powerful and numinous. The River People have fewer human qualities than the clan ancestors and are powerful and awesome. They seem to be primarily, but not exclusively, responsible for the illness *thwasa* which leads to the training for the healing function of the igqira. It is said: "you get sick by the forest or the river—but most of us have the river illness."

In the description of the ceremony it will be shown how these two groups of ancestors interact, and how the *igqira* functions as mediator between the living, their deceased clan-linked ancestors, and the People of the River.

Thwasa

All *amagqira* experience an initial illness called *thwasa*. It is, however, not con-fined to them, and other people who never undergo the full training are also diagnosed as such. (It must be explained that, especially in the early stages of the treatment of *thwasa*, it is not always possible to distinguish between treat-ment and training.)

Thwasa has been seen as a schizophrenia-like illness by many research workers and practising psychiatrists on account of the symptomatology. It can only be properly assessed and diagnosed in the context of the Xhosa cosmology. It usually becomes manifest during a crisis in living, and seems to be a process of disintegration which will permit re-integration on a different level.

The affliction can assume a variety of forms. The afflicted are always ir-ritable and withdrawn. Their sleep is disturbed by excessive and confusing dreams. They experience auditory hallucinations but "these come from inside me—from the ancestors". They are usually restless and given to wandering. They neglect their personal appearance and have a variety of somatic com-plaints and even symptoms. In Xhosa cosmology the above syndrome is due to a disturbance in the relationship between the individual and his ancestors. The dreams are described as frightening and unclear. "Other dreams we understand, but these are not known to anybody."[4]

Such a person is taken to an *igqira* for a *vumisa*, i. e. a diagnostic session, during which a diagnoses of *thwasa* can be made. *Thwasa* sickness is associated with the experience of

"being called by the ancestors to beome their servant" . . . "to carry out their wishes" . . . and "to become what you must become".

The word *thwasa* means dawn, i. e. of a new day, emergence of a new moon, or a new heavenly constellation.

If *thwasa* is diagnosed there is usually considerable resistance to accepting it, and it is not uncommon to consult other *amagqira* to confirm it. It calls for commitments and sacrifices of several kinds from the person concerned and his relatives. "They, the kin, must also accept it, because it does not only concern the individual, it concerns the whole family." He and they can brood on it for as long as they like to, but if he does not comply with the wishes of the ancestors he may become more sick, mad and even die. One informant described his experience as "a battle with the ancestors . . . until at long last I gave in to the demands of the ancestors", and went for his treatment and training.

If and when the findings are accepted, the sick one leaves his home to live with the *igqira* of his choice, and treatment and training starts.

Treatment / Training

This is complex and prolonged and, if the aim is not only symptom relief but full training, it usually lasts three to five years. It includes:

1. Milieu therapy
2. Medication
3. Dream interpretation
4. Ceremonies
5. Ritual sacrifices
6. Dancing sesions.

Some of these have been described already: dreams[5] and dances[6].
There are several aims with the treatment and training:

1. To restore the person to full health.
2. For the trainees to:

   1.Learn to understand what the ancestors have to say to them and others seeking their help especially through the understanding of dreams.
   2.Learn to *vumisa* (diagnose); to give reasons for the problem and to advise on corrective procedures.
   3. Learn to carry out the instructions of the ancestors as regards dream messages, ceremonies and ritual in general, including animal sacrifices. In the rituals strict and meticulous attention to detail is essential.
   4. Acquire knowledge about herbal remedies, customs and cultural beliefs, and to become skilled in the use of these.
   5. To get "to understand their illness properly and be prepared to follow up their training."

3. They must experience all treatment procedures themselves—"no one can perform a custom for others which he had not undergone himself."

4. The most important aim is perhaps to strengthen the trainee and to help him to gear his life into one which will allow for the constant brooding of the ancestors without becoming mentally disordered. "One must be strong to take what the ancestors have to say to one—we have to take medicines to make us strong."

To illustrate some aspects of this lengthy programme one ceremony will be described in some detail.

The River Ceremony

This is the first ceremony which is done for a trainee, but it is usually preceded by a long period of treatment consisting of milieu therapy, medication, dream discussions and *xhentsa* (dance) sessions[7].

> The chief informant expressed it as follows: "When a *thwasa* person responds well to treatment, I accompany him to his home, and a discussion with his people is held about his future training . . . If I get the proper messages from my ancestors, and his people agree to his training, the first step is the River Ceremony. . . . They will have to decide when they are ready to go to the *komkhulu* i. e. "The Great Place—the place where the River Ancestors live."

A date is set, and at the appointed time the trainee is sent to his parental home to help his people with the necessary preparations, because "his hands must also be in it". The ceremony must be performed at his home because it concerns himself, his family, their ancestors and the River People, also called River Ancestors. The explanation for the preparations is "to make the home ancestors ready to be accepted by the Ancestors of the River."

The actual ceremony lasts three days. On the first day the training agqira, his other patients and trainees having arrived, move into a hut set aside for their exclusive use, and do the main work of the day, i. e. the preparation of sorghum beer. It is brewed in their hut according to strict rules, and under the supervision of the *igqira*.

The owner of the homestead must then place a canister containing some of this beer in the cattle pen for the night, in the area where the home ancestors like to linger.

> If my mission is accepted by the home ancestors at the kraal (cow pen) it can be seen next morning by the foam which spilled over onto the ground, i. e. manure. The most senior of the ancestors of the homestead will then come to my hut to form a relationship, and to co-operate with my ancestors in the work for the trainee."

This beer is then used to prepare the larger quantity required for general consumption. The person making this beer must be "a daughter of the house"—not one married into it, because she and the patient must have the same ancestors. This beer is then placed in the main hut of the homestead, opposite the door at the *entla* (place special to the ancestors) on manure from the cattle pen "because the ancestors like the warmth and comfort of manure."

The patient must remain with his people and may not enter the *igqira* hut. In the *igqira* hut there is much social interaction and almost uninterrupted *xhentsa* sessions.

On the third day before dawn a procession sets off to the river. The party normally consists of four people, two males and two females: The *igqira* or his senior assistant, one of his trainees and two relatives of the patient. With their faces painted with white clay, with their bodies well decorated with white beads, and wearing a head cover, they walk in single file and in complete silence with their offering for the River People to a particular pool. The offerings consist of a small billy can of beer mixed with *ubulawu*, white beads, pumpkin and calabash seeds, sorghum seeds and tobacco. At the pool these are poured into the water one by one, and in a special order. Their movement on the surface of the water is watched with great concentration, and from these the attitude of the River People can be gauged—rejection or acceptance and approval of the trainee.

The party then hurry back so as to report at the homestead before sunrise. This reporting must be done at the *enkundla*—the space between the gate of the cattle pen and the door of the main hut, i. e. in the presence of the ancestors. Up to that time everybody has maintained complete silence.

If the report is good, i. e. of acceptance of the trainee by the River People, it is celebrated and sealed by the ritual drinking of beer, and these days also of neat brandy. The ancestors are served first by pouring some on to the ground, then everyone present must take a sip from the billy can as it is handed around.

The face of the person who has been accepted is then also painted white, and he joins the group in the igqira hut. By that time other *amagqira* with their trainees and patients have arrived. The whole group then develops into a discussion and teaching session concerning the events of the morning. Afterwards the party move to the main hut of the homestead where an *inthlombe* is held, i. e. dancing to the music of singing, clapping of hands and drumming.

At a later stage in training the River Ceremony is repeated with several alterations, the most important being the complete isolation of the trainee for 36 hours. The main aim is to stimulate "brooding", i. e. introversion of libido. "He must, however, have some strength before this ceremony is done."

Discussion

There are many similarities of conception between the above and the thinking of depth psychology, particularly analytical psychology. The Xhosa conceptualize the forces and images of the personal and collective unconscious as ancestors—the personal unconscious as the ancestors of the home, and the collective unconscious as the Ancestors of the River and Forest.

The *thwasa* person is an emotionally disturbed one, suffering from an intolerable life situation. In Western culture a similar suffering often induces the individual to seek psychotherapy or analysis in an effort to sort out his inner turmoil. The Xhosa patient consults an *igqira* to be told:

"that he is being called by the ancestors to serve them" . . . "to learn to communicate with them" . . . "to understand their messages" and "to become what he must become."

This formulation makes eminent sense. It gives meaning to the suffering and to the life of the sufferer. It also indicates the future development and direction of the sufferer's life. This approach conform to Jung's concept about the positive nature of a neurosis.

The Xhosa sufferer's resistance to the findings of the *igqira* is not unlike that of a Western person about having an analysis—facing one's unconscious and shadow side. Its usual course was put very clearly by one informant:

"Even if it is a struggle you'll go on because you're not under yourself, but under the ancestors".

The call is not easy to obey because it usually leads to considerable changes in one's life style[8]. The Xhosa are also aware that such treatment is not without dangers[9]. Without the constant "brooding of the ancestors", i. e. introversion and preoccupation with the unconscious material of oneself and others, one is not able to divine, mediate and heal effectively. Yet, on the other hand:

"If one does not have the medicines to make one strong, the brooding brings about sickness and even madness."

As is the case in analysis, communication with the unconscious occurs largely through the medium of dreams. In both cases emphasis is placed on understanding and accepting the dream content. Obedience to the ancestors is marked in Xhosa culture, as is the case with other Black people in Southern Africa[10].

In the training situation the transference and countertransference is dealt with through the concept of "ancestor animals"—"our animals must work together". Each *igqira* has a special animal and his trainee acquires one, usually from a dream. These animals function as guiding spirits—perhaps like a

Mercurius. It has been said that a person left treatment "because our animals did not work together nicely"—clearly a negative transference.

The aim of the River Ceremony is to consult the powers of the collective unconscious. Is this person acceptable, and is he ready for greater confrontation with the primordial images? This approach is not made until, in the judgment of the healer, the person is ready, i. e. healthy and integrated enough. The *igqira* has various ways of assessing it, but waits for the final guidance from his ancestors as conveyed in his dreams and the dreams of the trainee.

The three days are full of symbolism and symbolic behaviour, but I will confine myself to the relationship between the ancestors of both healer and patient / trainee and their relationship to the Ancestors of the River.

By brewing beer ritually in the hut which has become his temporary home the *igqira* calls *his* ancestors. He is intensely preoccupied with his own and his patient's mental state through this symbolic activity. That some of the beer is taken by the head of the household to *their* ancestors (who reside in the cattle pen) indicates the involvement of the family, and their appeal to the ancestors of the home for their help with the work in hand. The home ancestors give a symbolic answer—the spilling of the foam on to the manure covered ground indicates that they have partaken of it and are ready to assist.

> "The most senior of their ancestors will then come to my hut to form a relationship and to co-operate with my ancestors in the work for the trainee."

It seems that in our language, a strong and workable transference has been established.

The archetypal unconscious must, however, be confronted and consulted—the River People. This can only be done by taking special measures. The four people who go together to the river form a quaternity, containing some opposites. It is said that faces of the river party must be covered with white clay, so as not to "scare" the River People who are white. There is, however, more to it. The godhead as in other cultures may not be approached with an uncovered face and may not be looked in the eye. The white face and white beads can also point to some form of identification with the white River People. Wosien[11] writes:

> "Body-painting signifies dynamic transformation; and as the ornamental vessel, as the dwelling-place of the power, as the city of God the body is sacred. The head was often covered or masked as being the seat of the power, . . . To put on another face with the help of the mask was to admit another spirit; by the loss of one's own shape and physiognomy the transformation into the god had become evident."

That the number and constellation of the group, two males and two females, forms a quaternity, hints at integration and individuation. The hazardous journey into the unconscious can only be taken when there is co-operation between all the ancestors of trainer and trainee, i. e. when the transference and countertransference is well established.

From the tension which develops at the edge of the pool it is clear that it is a very meaningful encounter. The dim light of the early dawn, the wild natural surroundings, the complete silence except for the soft ripple of the stream together give the numinous quality which leaves no one untouched. One has a feeling of having been touched by something suprapersonal.

The acceptance of the patient as a trainee *igqira* is only done after everyone has been informed and assured of the acceptance by the River People. His face is covered in white clay and he moves from the homestead of his relatives into the hut of the assembled *amagqira*. A new stage in his development and training starts—he is being initiated into a new phase, as the word *thwasa* intimates.

This ceremony bears some comparison with what happens when, after the specified period of analysis, the analysand applies for training. The judgment of the personal analyst and the opinion of two independent training analysts are usually required. The training committee then has to assess these and make the final decision about the suitability of the candidate.

In both situations the aim of treatment and training is the integration into the conscious mind some of the unconscious contents of the psyche, and the full development of potential. There is, however, a difference. In Western culture the whole exercise is more conscious and cerebral; in the Xhosa culture it occurs at a more unconscious, symbolic level because they still have a living mythology.

1. W. D. Hammond-Tooke. *The Bantu-speaking peoples of Southern Africa.* London, Routledge & Kegan Paul, 1974.
2. M. Vera Bührmann. "Xhosa diviners as psychotherapists", *Psychotherapeia,* 1977, Vol. 3, No. 2, pp. 17—20.
3. Marie-Louise von Franz. *Interpretation of Fairy Tales.* Zurich, Spring Publications, 1975.
4. Axel-Ivor Berglund. *Zulu thought patterns and symbolism.* London, C. Hurst & Co., p. 136 (1916).
5. M. Vera Bührmann. *"Inthlombe* and *Xhentsa:* A Xhosa healing ritual".* Journal of Analytical Psychology. Vol. 26, No. 3, July 1981
6. M. Vera Bührmann. "The health care of an *igqira* (indigenous healer)," in *Contemporary approaches to Jungian thought.* Ed. R. K. Papadopoulos and G. S. Saayman. Ad. Donker, London and Johannesburg, 1980.
7. M. Vera Bührmann. *"Inthlombe* and *Xhentsa,"* op. cit.
8. M. Vera Bührmann. Health care of an *igqira,* op. cit.
9. Axel-Ivor Berglund. *Zulu thought patterns,* p. 128.
10. M. Vera Bührmann. "The inner reality of the Black man and his criminal responsibility". *South African Medical Journal,* Vol. 28, No. 15, pp. 817—820.
11. Maria-Gabriele Wosien. *Sacred Dance.* New York, Avon Books, p. 21.

CLINICAL PRACTICE AND RESEARCH

Archetypal transference as observed in the Healing procedures of Xhosa indigenous Healers

By M. Vera Bührmann (Gansbaai, South Africa)

I will here attempt to give some indication of how the transference and counter-transference operate in the healing procedures of the *amagqira* (indigenous healers), with special reference to what appears to be archetypal aspects.

As the research is still in progress my conclusions are tentative, and what I present preliminary, and based on observations and discussions with healers. Discussion of transference as understood in Western terminology has not been attempted with them, as I have learnt from experience that these sophisticated concepts lead to puzzlement and confusion in the healer instead of clarification, and that they cause misunderstandings. I have learned that direct questioning or invasion of their privacy must also be avoided. My method and attitude remain that of an analyst. From observations it is, however, clear that strong bonds of affection and respect exist between patient and healer. My material has been gathered from a small group who primarily use psychological methods in the treatment of their patients[1]. Most of them have been trained by my chief informant, Mr. Tiso, and his wife.

It is fairly generally accepted that what Western man talks about, preliterate man acts out in his ceremonies and rituals. These have become my main concern. They are rich in meaningful symbols which at times have moved me deeply.

I will trace certain archetypal features from the onset of the *thwasa* illness, through the training, to the stage of the person's becoming a fully qualified *igqira*.

Thwasa is the mental state which always precedes training and which is characterized by excessive dreaming, mental confusion and behavioral disturbances. It has many features of schizophrenia but is not identical with it. In Xhosa cosmology it indicates that:

"One has been called by the ancestors to serve them . . . to carry out their wishes . .
. to learn to understand what they have to say . . . to become what you must
become."

The word *thwasa* means "emergence", as of a new day, new moon, new
heavenly constellation and the new season-spring. From the onset, therefore,
the condition is seen as the emergence of something new, as a process of
transformation with a clearly defined goal, i. e. to become a knowledgable and
worthy servant of the ancestors—an *igqira*. In Xhosa terminology: "You must
become what you must become."

The goal-directedness of the *thwasa* state is illustrated by the dream of a
woman who was seriously disturbed and had been unsuccessfully treated by
herbalists and White doctors.

> "I dreamt that a person dressed as an *igqira*, carrying a sjambok and spears, ap-
> peared. I was frightened and he asked which direction are you going?"

The sjambok and spears are insignia of the fully qualified *igqira*. She was
diagnosed as being *thwasa* by the *igqira* they consulted. She had treatment and
training with him. She is now fully qualified with a sjambok and spear of her
own.

That the ultimate goal could be directed towards establishing the Self can
again be illustrated by a pretreatment dream. The man, now an *igqira* and my
chief informant, had been ill for many years. From his history I considered
him to have been seriously drepessed.

> "I dreamt I was on a mountain, there on top of it, lying next to a bush, and
> something came and licked me, here on my cheek. I dreamt I was very stunned at
> first, I didn't know what it was. My mother came to me in the dream and told me I
> should slaughter an ox for the animals, because that thing that licked me on my
> cheek was an animal. She said after I had slaughtered the ox, my people should build
> a private house for me, like the house of an *umkwetha* (a trainee) built of grass like
> an *intondo* (a grass hut specially erected for the final initiation and graduation
> ceremony)."

This dream demonstrates that the symbol of wholeness, the *intondo*, can
manifest during the initial illness even before an *igqira* has been consulted or
treatment has been started. Jung[2], writing about the "futurity of the archetype" states that: "The goal of the individuation process is the synthesis of
the self". This concept could not have been expressed more clearly than in
this dream.

Both these dreams are regarded as being archetypal. They demonstrate the
search for, and need of, wholeness of the human psyche, a process which
starts in the collective unconscious. At the time of the dreams both dreamers

were overwhelmed by contents from the collective unconscious. The *amag-qira* recognize this and have their own unique way of conceptualizing it—"it is the call of the ancestors". *Thwasa* can therefore be seen as a lack of relatedness of the individual to his ancestors. I have come to see the ancestors as personifications of primary complexes—archetypes—and *thwasa* as a state in which the collective unconscious has been activated, and the equilibrium between the ego and the unconscious has been disturbed.

Treatment and training

The aim of analysis is to help the patient to come . . ." in harmony with himself, neither good nor bad, just as he is in his natural state."[3]

According to the Xhosa "you must become what you must become". In addition, their aim is to help the person to get into a healthy relationship with his ancestors:

> "They, the patients and trainees, must learn to understand the wishes of the ancestors, and what they have to say to them."

The *igqira* functions as a mediator between the individual and the ancestors, i. e. between the ego and the unconscious in its widest sense. He becomes a symbol of transformation. Awareness of a personal unconscious and personal transference and countertransference appears to me not be absent, but it has not been clearly conceptualized by them, and viewed from the present state of my knowledge, it plays a relatively minor role. Pfister[4], analyzing the methods of shamans, concluded that the unconscious of the medicine man speaks directly to the unconscious of his patient, and he thus circumvents consciousness and the resistances arising from it and the ego defense mechanisms. This is relevant to my observations. Transpersonal forces are present from the onset. A person being taken to an *igqira* for a *vumisa* (diagnostic session) already sees him as a magical figure. This is strengthened by the *vumisa* where the *igqira* gets in touch with his own transpersonal guiding spirits. The patient, in a sense therefore, constellates archetypal layers in the healer. This leads to a relationship "founded on mutual unconsciousness."[5] The transference and countertransference is thus archetypal in nature from the first meeting. From the beginning it is accepted that "you are not under yourself, but under the ancestors". That is the acceptance that suprapersonal forces are dominant. No important action such as a ritual or ceremony during treatment and training is done except at the instigation or with the agreement of the ancestors.

Ancestors manifest in a variety of ways. For the purpose of this article the human and animal forms are the most important. The terms "ancestors" and "ancestor animals" are to a large extent interchangeable in the context of this presentation.

Specific transference aspects

Jung[6] wrote that:

> through the transference the activity of archetypal figures is liable to be let loose, a fact we had not banked on. We have reckoned without our hosts, for we forgot the gods."

This aspect is appreciated by the *amagqira*, as one informant said:

> "One must be strong to take what the ancestors have to tell you . . . we constantly have to take medicine to make us strong."

Another said in connection with the same topic, i.e. the power of the ancestors:

"Even if it is a struggle (i.e. the training) one has to go on."

The treatment starts and the transference develops in a close and structured environment. The person is taken up into the household of the *igqira*, sharing in everything, including sleeping quarters and domestic chores. In certain cases he initially even shares the sleeping hut of the *igqira* at night so as to enable him to relate his dreams immediately before they are forgotten. The lives of the Xhosa are ordered by fairly strict customs, role divisions and some taboos. This also applies to the *igqira*, his patients and trainees. Periods of intimacy occur during the discussion of dreams when no one else may be present. This forges strong bonds and certainly enhances the transference. Without the permission of the *igqira* no dreams may be discussed with others. There is one type of dream which is not even told to the *igqira*. One may only say that "one had a good dream". He, the *igqira*, will see your dream from his own *izilo* (animal). These special dreams concern "an animal of the river".

> "This animal of the Great Place can change his shape . . . it can change itself into a torch, a great light, only a light, no form of a person . . . You must pray for it only to appear in your dreams . . . If one sees it at the river in the waking stae, it can cause madness and even death."

It is not uncommon for the *igqira* to appear in the dreams of his trainees. In Western concepts this would indicate unrealized personal transference aspects.

This is certainly so in the Xhosa also, but in most of the dreams which have come to my notice he usually had suprapersonal features with all the authority of the ancestors—who "must be obeyed."

An aspect of the transference which Jung stressed is the personality of the analyst, certain aspects of which are perceived and incorporated by the patient "and help in constructing the bridge to reality"[7]. This probably happens with the Xhosa patient also, but in my research I have, in addition, seen the opposite. The *igqira* seems to be very much of a bridge to the non-rational aspects of the unconscious—the archetypal ancestors. They, the patients and trainees, do see him as an ordinary person around the homestead, but also very often in his suprapersonal role conducting ceremonies and sacrifices and dining at *inthlombes* (healing dances). At such times he often becomes identified with the ancestors or with his special guiding spirit, thus becoming their mouthpiece. He appears in his full regalia. This is an impressive sight with clear evidence of his identification with the Ancestors of the River and the Ancestors of the Forest. Every detail of his outfit has some symbolic meaning. He looks transformed. These situations can be powerful and gripping, and the influence of these seem to outweigh his ordinary characteristics. A patient expressed his feelings as:

"The Tisos have seen God—and we trainees hope that we will also see God one day."

Jung[8], writing about the psychology of the transference, said:

"At this point, unpalatable as it is to the scientific temperament, the idea of mystery forces itself upon the mind of the enquirer, not as a cloak for ignorance but as an admission of his inability to translate what he knows into the everyday speech of the intellect."

This is how I have felt at times, having experienced the power and numiosity of some of their ceremonies, where archetypal material too unformed to be verbalized was touched upon.

For self-realization to proceed, and for the Self to emerge, projections must be withdrawn and the transference be severed. During the training period their "animals have worked together" in harmony. If the animals of the *igqira* and his trainee could not work together as seen in dreams, training was discontinued. At the end of successful training "the animals must be separated", i. e. transference must be dissolved. They have a unique ceremony during which this is done.

It is part of the *godusa*, "bringing home", ceremony. The *godusa* is the final ceremony of the training process. The trainee is "taken to his home" by his *igqira* and is introduced to relatives, friends and neighbours as a fully qualified healer on whom they can rely to serve them in times of illness and need. It is both a graduation and initiation ceremony with many facets to it, one being the drama of the "separation of the animals". I was a participant observer at one such ceremony.

Basically it consisted of a mock fight between the "animals" of the teacher and those of his pupil. The place where this occurred was the *intondo*, which is a special round hut, newly and firmly contructed of poles and grass, and with a strong door. It was erected near the house and cattle pen of the graduant, and is the place from where he will in future conduct his practice. Mr. T. formulated their thinking and rationale as follows:

> We believe that while we are working together, and he was my student, our ancestors united. Now we are dividing them so that he may be able to stand on his own, while leaving my ancestors with me. While we were together, even when he had started practising on his own, my ancestors were to some extent leaving me to assist him. We must now divide and test his animals to see if he can work independently. He and his animals are inside the *intondo* and I and mine will attack him, and try to force the door. If in the struggle I succeed to push in the door, it would mean that my student had failed".

In answer to a question he said:

> "You yourself have your own ancestors, *izinyanya*—it is difficult to describe—I can just say it is your own god."

For the *godusa* which I attended a large number of relatives and visitors, including trained and semi-trained *amagqira*, their patients and trainees, assembled at the homestead of the graduate, Qadi. The teacher, his entourage and the visiting *amagqira* and theirs had a hut specially put aside for their use during the 4-day ceremony. At the other end of the property were the huts belonging to the graduate, his cattle pen and the newly erected *intondo* in close proximity to each other. These two areas formed the stage setting for the "separation of the animals". The one area will be called "Mr. Tiso's house" and the other "Qadi's *intondo*".

At dawn on the first morning, but the second day of the ceremony, everyone from Mr. T's house, excluding himself but including Qadi, set off to the *intondo*. They sang and danced, carrying black sticks. They circled around the *intondo* several times singing:

> "You are still asleep *igqira*
> Come outside
> Wake up, come outside."

In the same way, singing and dancing, they returned to Mr. T's house. As they approached they sang:

"Wake up, wake up.
Wild animals are outside your door."

This was repeated several times outside, and it continued inside while Mr. T., lying on his sleeping mat, feigned deep sleep.

This performance was repeated on the second day, except that this time Qadi opened the door of the *intondo* and went inside for a few minutes before rejoining the dancing and singing group.

On the third day, at dawn, there was a repetition of the previous day, but Qadi stayed inside the *intondo* for a longer period. The excitement in the group was clearly mounting, and there was much playful stick fighting. Mr. T. was still asleep in his house! At about mid-morning the whole group divided into two factions, the Tiso supporters (animals) and the Qadi supporters. Armed with sticks and sjamboks the Qadi group sang warlike songs and danced their way to the *intondo*.

"They are coming, they are coming.
Beware, they are coming."

On arrival at the intondo they organized themselves inside and outside. The Tiso group, with himself in the lead and similarly armed, followed the Qadi group, dancing and singing:

"We are coming, we are coming.
Beware, we are coming."

When the two groups met at the *intondo* a fierce struggle developed between those inside and the Tiso group from outside trying to force the door. They were cheered and urged on by the dancing, singing, joking and mock fighting of their supporters. The excitement mounted. In spite of trying several tricks the door could not be forced. In the end the Tiso group took flight with the Qadi group in hot pursuit. Tiso barely reached the safety of his house and had to admit defeat. All the participants gathered outside the house, and lengthy peace negotiations were conducted. It was agreed that Qadi's animals could not be overpowered by the Tiso animals. He, therefore, was now strong and independent and the equal of his teacher. This was very gratifying to both teacher and pupil.

Later the same day an animal was sacrificed and an impressive and moving graduation and initiation ceremony was performed. This clearly indicated Qadi's new role and status, particularly his close identification with the Ancestors of the River and the Ancestors of the Forest. His teacher presented him with a white blanket and a special spear and sjambok and other symbols as indications of his authority and fully qualified status.

Discussion

The intondo is seen as a symbol of the Self, both in its construction, its use during this ceremony, and its meaningfulness in his future practice as an *igqira*.

Adler's[9] introductory note in his book *The Living Symbol* is applicable to the above material,

> ". . . there are analyses in which the therapeutic goal appears to be reached almost exclusively by a process of symbolic transformation."

To a large extent it throws light on what happens during the healing procedures of the *amagqira*. The final result is achieved by a process of symbolic transformation, without the analysis of the transference and countertransference. The *relationship* between healer and patient-trainee is, however, vital as expressed in their concept of "our ancestors working together."

Adler[10] defines a neurosis as a loss of the "symbolic attitude", i. e. a break in the spontaneous relationship between the conscious mind and its matrix, the unconscious. The Xhosa also conceptualize *thwasa* as lack of communication between the individual and his ancestors, and the resolution of the impasse is for him to become their servant and "to know their wishes".

The "symbolic life" means primarily . . . "a realization of the transpersonal archetypal factor of inner order and significance"[11]. This is an aspect which has impressed me—the realization which the *amagqira* have of the meaningfulness and significance of their lives and living in general.

The importance of the transference should be given due weight. The realization of transpersonal factors and aspects are constantly stimulated by their rituals and ceremonies. These trigger off archetypal layers and images which are shared by both, and which must strengthen the transpersonal transference bonds. As a patient remarked during a ceremony "the Tiso's have seen god".

The union of the opposites, which are essential for the development of wholeness, is acted out in their healing dance, the *inthlombe*, which I have described as a dancing mandala[12]. This ritual is very frequently performed and plays an essential part in the training and development of the trainee.

The separation of the animals is the final withdrawal of projections from the outside. The images and their power are internalized, resulting in the independence, equality and effectiveness of the new *igqira*, with the *intondo* as an appropriate symbol of the self.

The healing work of the *amagqira* is achieved by their ability to experience, and to let other people experience, the creative work of the living symbol. A characteristic feature of the archetypal transference is the constellation of archetypal images, and these can lead to inflation. The shaman and some medicine men are often quoted as examples of inflation and possession, but I have seen very little of this in the group being studied. They regard ecstasy and inflation as undesirable[13]. It must be added, however, that in some groups in Southern Africa it does occur. The members of the research group have impressed me with their professional attitudes, dedication and integrity. Mrs. Tiso said: "It's better for the *igqira* to cry over what he had done to the patient, than for the patient to cry over what the *igqira* had done to him."

The author wishes to acknowledge financial assistance from the Human Sciences Research Council, Pretoria.

1 M. Vera Bührmann. "Xhosa diviners as psychotherapists", *Psychotherapeia*, Vol. 3, No. 4.

2 C. G. Jung. "The psychology of the child archetype" in *Collected Works 9*. London, Routledge & Kegan Paul, 1968, p. 164.

3 C. G. Jung. "The theory of psycho-analysis" in *Collected Works 4*. London, Routledge & Kegan Paul, 1961, p. 196.

4 Oskar Pfister. "Instructive analysis among the Navahos". Journal of Nervous and Mental Disease, 1931, No. 76, p. 251.

5 C. G. Jung. "The practice of psychotherapy" in *Collected Works 16*. London. Routledge & Kegan Paul, 1954, p. 176.

6 C. G. Jung. "Archetypes of the collective unconscious" in *Collected Works 7*. London, Routledge & Kegan Paul, 1953, p. 99.

7 Michael Fordham. "Jung's concept of transference". *Journal of analytical Psychology*, 1974, Vol. 19, No. 1, p. 3.

8 Jung, "The practice of psychotherapy", p. 270.

9 Gerhard Adler. *The Living Symbol*. London, Routledge & Kegan Paul, 1961, p. 3.

10 Adler, p. 9.

11 Adler, p. 10.

12 Bührmann, "*Inthlombe & Xhentsa a Xhosa healing ritual*" *Journal of analytical Psychology* July, 1981, Vol. 26. No. 3

13 Bührmann, "*Inthlombe and Xhentsa*"

Glossary

Igqira	=	Xhosa word for medicine man who heals primarily with rituals and ceremonies.
Amagqira	=	plural.
Thwasa	=	the initial psychic disturbance which precedes the training to become an *igqira*.

Intondo	=	round hut constructed of poles and tall grass which is necessary for the final graduation and initiation ceremony of a trainee.
Vumisa	=	diagnosis by divination.
Xhentsa	=	special slow, rhythmic, pound dance, performed as part of healing ceremonies.
Enkundla	=	open space between main hut and cattle pen which serves as meeting place of the living and their ancestors.
Umkwetha	=	a trainee *igqira*
Izilo	=	one of the names for ancestor animals.
Godusa	=	"taking home ceremony"; the graduation and initiation ceremony of a qualifying *igqira.*
Izinyanya	=	ancestor
Ubulawa	=	a herbal extract which has a wide variety of uses in the healing and training procedures, primarily to assist communication with the ancestors.
Entla	=	special area in the main hut opposite the entrance door, which is favoured by the ancestors.

Transference Addiction

By Jef Dehing (Bruxelles)

In this work, I would like to examine the addiction of the analyst to the transferences of his analysands. I do not intend to treat a simple countertransference, where the analyst would react neurotically to his client's transference; what I have in view is a *need*: the analyst needs the transference of his patients, just as the alcoholic needs alcohol, or as the heroin addict needs heroin.

Neither does it concern a pure flight into work, an addiction one can find in every trade. The addiction I wish to describe is marked by the specificity of the drug: the transference of the clients. This can affect every member of the socalled helping-professions, but particularly the analysts who have learned to work with transference, and to handle it.

So, I will confine my survey to the analysts and we will see that their training does not protect them from this affection but merely tends to foster it.

In the *first part*, I shall endeavour to paint the "clinical picture" of the addicted analyst; a somewhat caricatural mirror wherein the reader might possibly recognize himself . . .

In the *second part*, I will try to consider the aetiology of this addiction. This more theoretical survey will confront us with some interesting paradoxes, not unexpected ones though, since, as the alchemists already said, our art requires the whole man.

1. Portrait of the "transference addict".

Symptoms

The addicted analyst is awaiting his clients impatiently; he doesn't like them to be later or to cancel their appointment, nor does he like a cure to be interrupted prematurely (according to his appreciation, of course); a state of need becomes manifest when the client is recalcitrant to enter into the transference, when he has (though well founded) "resistances"; this need is expressed by impatience, exasperation and sometimes even rejection of the patient. This rejection will then be justified by excellent rationalizations: "a client who doesn't transfer is not fit for analysis, anyway!". Apparently, our addict is a good analyst: he works well in the transference and never acts out. His only acting out is the use of the transference as a drug.

When a client yields himself to the transference, our analyst is delighted! He really cossets this excellent analysand and is ready to any sacrifice. He might tell his colleagues that such or such client is extremely difficult, ungrateful or exacting, but he merrily endures all these ordeals as long as they are besprinkled with the delicious nectar called transference.

For his client, he likes to be the only important person in the world; he is jealous of other relations the analysand might have (and he will interpret these as an acting out in order to avoid the transference); he doesn't want his client to use drugs that might become rivals of the analysis (here too, he will consider the behaviour of his patient as resistance). He tends to exert a subtle control on his client, not because of the luxurious feeling of this power, but merely in order to ensure the availability of his prey.

Never will he allow one of his clients to go to another analyst; he is utterly convinced that nobody in the world understands the patient better than he does.

Often do we see the addict increase his dose, his working time; he despises any non-analytic activity and abandons all occupations he could have in these profane domains: he will tell you that only analytic work is really meaningful to him.

He is incapable of decreasing his dose at the time where he could consider retirement, and ending a cure is extremely difficult to him. Back in his family environment, his analytic work done, his behaviour bears some resemblance with that of an alcoholic who comes home after his daily carouses: either he is peevishly turning around like a bear in his cage, behaving unplesantly or even aggressively, or he is indifferent, apathetic, absent-minded, and falls asleep in front of his television set. This behaviour is the more difficult to endure for his environment as the latter feels itself excluded from something very important, going on in a hieratic far-away place, safely protected by the analytic fence. A phone call of one of his clients (and he certainly will encourage them to call) can suffice to restore all his vitality . . . but when the conversation is over, his sullen mood returns.

Our addict is incapable of gaining any satisfaction from anything but transference: his conjugal and family life, his hobbies, all seem dull and uninteresting to him: how could a real situation ever compete with the unspeakable savour of a good transference?

When leaving for a holiday (provided he comes to it or is forced to by his relatives), the need becomes amply manifest: his mood is execrable, he suffers from anguish and insomnia, he dreams about his clients; in his phantasms, he sees them coming to him: how the devil are they capable of enduring this atrocious situation? He may then turn to other drugs: alcohol, tobacco, tranquilizers . . .

The end of the holiday is a deliverance to him; and the next day we find him in his office, an hour in advance, arranging the cushions of his couch, preparing his files, anxiously awaiting his clients.

Sometimes, one has the impression that the drug is hallucinogenic (although specialists are not unanimous in this subject): our analyst sees things which exist only in his intoxicated imagination; his evolution of what happens in his analyses is gravely compromised: he fancies that he fully understands his client whereas he is miles away from the latter's experience, he is having hallucinations of transferences, stagnations, suicide risks, resistances, improvements . . . at the expense, of course, of a realistic evaluation of the evolution of the cure.

As in other addictions, some alarm-signals should be mentioned: addiction is imminent when the therapist needs his patients to stimulate him or to restore his balance, or when, after a day of analytical work, he feels unable to do anything else, or also when he chronically complains of having too much work, while not doing anything to remedy this situation.

Evolution

The addiction can remain stationary for a very long time; possible complications are easily imaginable: for the analyst, a growing impoverishment of all his non-analytic cathexes, and for the clients a very big risk of interminable and never-finished analyses; they can also, for the worse, identify with their analyst and in turn become addicted to the analysis and even to the countertransference.

When external causes force the therapist to suspend his activities, one can expect a break-down, made even worse by the fact that the analyst has for a long time lost contact with other sources of possible satisfaction. This depression can also arise spontaneously; like every depression, it will contain the possibility of a new orientation.

Treatment

Should one, with heavy cases, recur to the severe measures used for other addictions: complete weaning and total, definitive abstinence?

It would of course be a draconic remedy, because the drug itself simultaneously constitutes the means of subsistence fot the addict: transference addiction is a very particular condiditon! Abstinence may be very hard for the brewer or the barman, but they can—at least—go on with their trade.

One could advise the former addict to learn rediscovering the non-analytic joys, to cathect the world around him, beyond his job. But, will he succeed in doing so?

Or should one recommend a psychotherapeutic, analytic attendance? In that case, one should beware of sending him to a colleague, suffering from the same syndrome! And what if all analysts were, more or less, addicted to the transference? But first let us try to elucidate the aetiology of this addiction: this might allow us to deduce a therapy to the cause. And, who knows, as good Jungians, we may find a positive purpose to this trouble.

2. Aetiology and theoretical discussion
Structure of the psyche.

Before we go to the heart of the matter, we would like to dress a hypothetical model of the psyche; our fashionable sketch is inspired by Carl Gustav JUNG and Erich NEUMANN on one hand, and by Piera CASTRORIADIS—AULAGNIER on the other (2).

The latter, a Parisian analyst of Lacanian origin, describes three systems or processes of psychic functioning. These systems succeed each other in time, but each, once set in motion, continues to act during the entire liferime of the individual. She calls them the original system, the primary system, and the secondary system.

All psychic activity is marked be *representation:* in order to have an existence at the level of psychic functioning, an external element must be represented in it. The term "representation" is deliberately ambiguous: at the same time is points to the action of presenting anew, by an image or a "mise-en-scène" (in German: "Vorstellung"), and to the exercise of a delegated power (in German: "Repräsentierung"). This ambiguity is intended to convey what really takes place. In fact, the image (or the pre-image, as we shall see) repesents an external (or heterogeous) element within the psychic system; the image is the psychic representative, or substitute of the heterogenous element, the thing being metabolized into the psyche. Castoriadis defines *representation* as "the psychic equivalent of the metabolization inherent in organic activity"; this activity is common to the three psychic systems she describes, and representation's "aim is to metabolize a heterogeneous element into an element which is homogeneous to the structure of each system"[3]

These three systems have a different structure and function according to their own rules:

1. In the *original system,* everything that exists is self-engendered by the system itself. Its activity is closely related to sensorial activity. Here we stand at the origin of the psyche-body ralation. The original system constitutes the psychic functioning of the infant and concurs with the "primal unitary reali-

ty" of Neumann; at this stage, all is one—body, mother, Self and other are contained within the Uroboros, the ideal image of self-begetting.

Castoriadis calls the *"pictograph"* the representation of the original process: this pictograph is a kind of pre-image, picturing both the sensorial zone of the infant and the external object to which it corresponds. The simplest example is the mouth-nipple couple, represented as both self-created by the representing agency.

An experience of pleasure goes along with the desire to incorporate the good object, and also with the desire to cathect the incorporator positively. The pictograph of love "finds its origin in the unifying design of Eros: picture of a world in which every object tends to and reaches its complement, merging with it in order to attain a perfect totality"[4] Following Neumann, we Jungians would rather say: to preserve—at this precocious stage—this perfect totality.

An *unpleasant* experience leads to a desire to annihilate the object, to reject it out of oneself, and at the same time to a desire for self-annihilation (because the displeasure is represented as self-engendered). The pictograph of hate, takes root in Thanatos, whose design is to annihilate both the desire and its object.

Two fundamental pictographs thus emerge, and on this precocious level, and ever after, we discern an opposition of contrary principles:

love	hate
Eros (Zoe)[5]	Thanatos
pleasure	displeasure
life	death
good	evil

2. the *primary system* becomes installed from the moment when external reality forces the child to abandon his illusion of self-engendering. Now, a new postulate is substituted: "every existence is a result of the omnipotence of the other's desire". And new kind of representation appears, the *phantasm*, wherein the child represents itself in a relationship to the other. Leaving the dual relationship it starts seeing itself, as in a mirror, confronted with the other and a first triangulation is achieved. The analogy with Lacan's "specular" stage is obvious. The phantasm presents on the one hand an imaginary ego (in other words, the child takes its reflection for itself) and on the other an equally imaginary, almighty "other". At this stage the images of the Great Good Mother and the Terrible Mother emerge, and these will lose their omnipotence quite slowly.

3. the *secondary system* starts developing once this omnipotence is contested. Then, a new postulate appears: "every existence has an intelligible cause; its knowledge might be expressed by the discourse". Representation now becomes *enunciation*, "mise-en-sens", and the enunciator becomes subject, "I".

The establishment of the secondary process implies development of the intellectual functions and access to language. Language is imposed by the environment, with all possible risks of alienation this implies). Enunciation, "mise-en-sens", may lead to the "symbolic order", which we can define as that order in which the image is no longer confounded with reality. This is the order which liberates us from the illusions of the imaginary. We can also define the symbolic order positively, with Lacan, as "the order of phenomena inasmuch as they are structured as a language". The symbolic order is based upon a ruling principle which controls the insertion of man into a pre-set order.

The Oedipus complex is the most striking example of this passage from the imaginary to the symbolic: the child—not without difficulty—learns that it is not at the disposal of his mother's desire and that she is not omnipotent; it discovers that it has *a* father and *a* mother, and that this situation is not unique; and it abandons its own omnipotence, eventually to accept that it cannot *be* all for its mother, nor *have* everything.

So far the scheme presented by Castoriadis, as I have metabolized and summarized it.

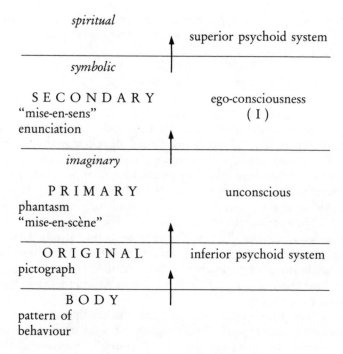

spirit

spiritual

    ↑   superior psychoid system

symbolic

S E C O N D A R Y   ego-consciousness
"mise-en-sens"   (I)
enunciation

imaginary

P R I M A R Y   unconscious
phantasm
"mise-en-scène"

O R I G I N A L   inferior psychoid system
pictograph

B O D Y
pattern of
behaviour

matter

Hypothetical scheme of psychic functioning

Some important remarks remain to be made: The "original" is radically cut off from any possible direct knowledge by the subject; we can talk about the pictograph and name it, but this appellation is entirely relative. Its nature remains absolutely unspeakable to us.

The sudden intrusion of the original into the space of the I leads to an affect that cannot be mastered and which may precipitate the subject into the twin abysses of merging and of murder[6], into gross acting out, into break-down, and into catastrophic anguish—all the phenomena we could call "psychotic". They occur because the primary has not effected the metabolization of the pictograph. Healthy psychic functioning is based partly on a sufficient separation of the three systems (Logos), and partly on a sufficient permeability (Eros) between them, so that passage and successive metabolizations of the representations all along the scale can occur. This permeability is compromised when the defensive mechanisms are too strong.

Let us now amplify this scheme, taking inspiration from analytical psychology. The reader might already have noticed several analogies with the Jungian mode.

—the original process concurs with what Jung called the "inferior psychoid system", situated between the "merely vitalistic phenomena on the one hand and . . . the specifically psychic processes on the other"[7], elements which cannot be grasped by consciousness.

—the passage from the imaginary to the symbolic order concurs largely with the withdrawal of projections. Through projection, we confound the other with the projected image; by the withdrawal of projection, we can see the other as such. The alchemists knew this: they made a distinction between "true imagination" (which leads to the symbolic order) and "fantastic imagination"[8].

— Jung called the apprehension and representation of a content by the consciousness "apperception": to him "consciousness is not only itself a transformation of the original instinctual image, but also its transformer."[9]

There is also an important gap for Jungian psychology to fill. Castoriadis's scheme leads in her view only to the insertion of the subject into the pre-established social structure. A Jungian will want to know about the person's individuation. Or, to formulate this in other words as a question, how will the archetypes express themselves and exert their action?

First, we should note that the development itself of the described systems is determined by the archetypal powers: consciousness develops out of the unconscious which subtends it.

When we consider the archetype as a pattern of behaviour—an innate potential or "instinct", the expression of it should start in that mysterious zone, situated on the border of what can properly be called that "zone" we have called the original or inferior psychoid system. The first representation of the archetype, then, is the pictograph. When the pictograph enters into the conscious mind in unmetabolized form, it provokes a "psychotic" experience, the numinous character of which is intolerable for the subject, destructuring his consciousness. (As we know, such destructuring is not necessarily negative!).

The other, less dramatic, possibility is that the pictograph will be metabolized by the primary process. Then, the content presents itself to the subject as a phantasm, an *image*. This image can in turn become an imaginary trap (indeed it often will be!). But the image too can be metabolized by the secondary system and submit to the symbolic order: the meaning it bears can be extracted from it. That is the reason analytical psychology promotes with these imaginary agencies an "Auseinandersetzung", which implies a distance as well as a dialogue. Our Jungian *symbol* can now be re-defined as a pictographic representation, expressing a pattern of behaviour, that has been pictured by the primary process and received by the subject as a *meaning-bearing image*, whose meaning can be found through interpretation.

This final outcome can eventually lead to a new structure, which is the spiritual dimension, or what we may call the superior psychoid system. The postulate of this new structure can be formulated as: "there are powers which are beyond the reach of our understanding; they transcend the apprehensive possibilities of human consciousness; nevertheless they direct psychic development and functioning."

The principal restriction of consciousnes is that it has a discriminating function. Jung says, it "must separate the opposites, and it does this *contra naturam*"[10] ". . . nothing that exists could be discerned were there no discerning psyche . . . . Consciousness grasps only a fraction of its own nature, because it is the product of a preconscious psychic life which made the development of consciousness possible in the first place. Consciousness always succumbs to the delusion that it developed out of itself, . . ." The very definition of imaginary illusion! and that " . . . all consciousness rests on unconscious premises, in other words on a sort of unknown *prima materia*; . . ." coming ". . . from the mountain in which there are no differences, . . ."[11].

By its very constitution, therefore, ego-consciousness is radically cut off from direct knowledge of the unconscious from which it springs and which continues to be its basis.

Hence we must postulate an intermediate realm which can allow for exchange between ego-consciousness and the deeper layers of the unconscious; this intermediate realm concurs with the primary process and the imaginary order. As far as the image is intergrated at the symbolic level, ths realm is a bearer of meaning.

Jung relates this *intermediate realm*[12] between matter and spirit to the alchemical *imaginatio*[13]. *Imaginatio* allows the actualization of ". . . those contents of the unconscious which are outside nature, i. e. not a datum of our empirical world, and therefore an a priori* of archetypal character. The place or the medium of realization is neither mind nor matter, but that intermediate realm of subtle reality which can be adequately only expressed by the symbol. The symbol is neither abstract nor concrete, neither rational nor irrational neither real nor unreal."

This Jungian concept of an intermediate realm is to be related to Winnicott's intermediate area, which he speaks of as a potential or a "transitional" space. Winnicott has especially studied this intermediate area at its origin, in the interaction between infant and mother, at the very moment that the primary process reaches its full development.

The analytic situation

Armed with this scheme, we can come back to our starting point: the analytic situation. There we find two individuals, both functioning psychiacally in this same hypothetical way.

What animates these two protagonists?

The client is always animated by the conscious affliction which he hopes to relieve by analysis. This may be:

— psychosomatic suffering, which occurs when the imaginary eleboration is blocked, the metabolization of the pictograph is lacking, and something like a reflux to the body has occurred. The content is them expressed by functional troubles.

— "pregenital" suffering, including narcissistic and even psychotic disturbances, reflecting severe perturbations that took place before the installation of the primary system. These have led to a too important and too precocious appearance of the Thanatos pictograph in the original process.

— "neurotic" suffering, which occurs when the subject has not succeeded in disengaging from the traps of the imaginary and persists in projecting almighty parental images upon those around him

— suffering related to disturbances in the intellectual functioning, such as problems with concentration and memory. These difficulties often arise from a precocious development of the secondary system that is serving a defensive purpose or even a "false self";

— spiritual suffering, when the access to this dimension is cut off to the subject. This alienation may occur either because he overvalues his conscious mind and the "meaning" proposed by his socio-cultural environment, or because he is afraid to confront the paradoxical mesages of true spiritual meaning.

And *the therapist?* We have to say that the same possibilities apply to him and are likely to animate his involvement in the analytic situation. They not only formed the motivation of his personal analysis and his analytic training, but also continue to subtend his therapeutic activity in the here and now. Indeeds as Michel NEYRAUT[14] rightly remarks, the counter-transference of the analyst precedes the transference of the client. This fact produces the paradox-ial situation of a therapist who more or less needs the patient even before the latter needs a therapist.

These are the two protagonists between whom transference will occur, this "phenomenon that" as Jung wrote[15] "may be regarded as the crux, or at any rate the crucial experence, in any thorough-going analysis".

We will not make a distinction here between transference and counter-transference, because the latter is in fact no more than a transference to a transference. We would define transference as the whole of all possible interac-tions between the two present psyches, at every possible level.

Transference is amply favoured by the analytic situation which creates a par-ticular atmosphere that almost invites regression. As Eros elements of the analytic situation, we must cite the regularity of the sessions, the availability of the therapist, his sympathetic audience, his effort to understand the client, as well as the fact that the analysis is conducted in a quiet, protected mood. Logos is represented by the rules that direct the cure: scheduled hours of meeting, fees, abstention from acting out, etc.—all boundaries of the alchemical bath in which the adventure may happen.

As we have said, these Eros and Logos elements invite regression. They en-sure the "holding" the client needs in order to be able to confront his *prima materia*, the uroboric situation of the original matriarchal world. The client makes this confrontation hoping to finally metabolize traumatic infantile ex-periences, but he can also be brought to it by the necessity of recognizing the archaic powers of the unconscious in these deep layers. He is spurred to this recognition either because he feels the need to make it, or because these powers themselves urge him to do so.

Jung knew the "fascinating attraction"[16] of the original system very well, "the horrible darkness of our mind, of which Aurora Consurgens speaks"[17]; he said, "Dionysos is the abyss of impassioned dissolution, where all human distinctions are merged in the animal divinity of the primordial psyche—a blissful and terrible experience."[18] There is in what transference can lead to "a panacea for one and pure poison for another"[19], as Jung said. No doubt he was referring to the regressive transference that activates the original process.

The irruption of the pictograph into the analytic situation produces either break-down, panic, and unspeakable anguish; or delight, enchantment, and the perfect beatitude of a paradise finally regained. In either case we find a dramatic confrontation with good or evil in their most archaic forms, requir-ing the best metabolizing functions at the therapist's and client's disposal. We can only hope that the analyst—thanks to his training—will be better prepared than the client to metabolize this material, so that he can truly help the latter with the integration of the experience.

In the transference the unitary primary reality of the original process can unfortunately also be re-actualized in a more chronic fashion, leading to the establishment of a merger-relationship which endures over time, its meaning lost in imaginary meanders. Jung was familiar with this "atmosphere of illusion which either leads to continual misinterpretations and misunderstandings, or else produces a most disconcerting impression of harmony"[20].

Knowing that every addiction implies a tendency to recover the uroboric plenitude of unitary reality, we now better understand the danger to which the analyst is exposed. We see that his profession offers the chance of regaining this lost paradise, especially with those privileged clients who indulge in a "thorough-going" transference. The profession itself provides him with the drug, in a subtle and completely socially acceptable way. Indeed, during his training he has learned to distill the drug. Of course, we can only conjecture that his choice of this particular profession rests upon motivations that include a longing to re-experience the original process.

Search for a lost paradise, we said, but also, as in every addiction, a dangerous game with Thanatos, whose destructive effect may occur at any moment. The dangerous illusion of the imaginary everywhere, and mostly at places where we would not expect it: the most exalted pseudo-spiritual zeal can disguise the deepest neurotic misery. In this regard, we Jungians are more threatened than our Freudian brothers; our acceptance of the spiritual dimension leads to the risk of seeing it co-opted by the imaginary order. Similarly the degree of attention neo-Freudians such as the followers of Winnicott pay to the pregenital needs of their clients—no matter how legitimate and worthy of interest these needs may be—threatens them with getting lost in the imaginary labyrinths of dual relationship.

One can understand Freud's reserve and prudence. In his writings, he pleaded for absolute abstinence in the conduct of treatment, in order to avert the traps of the imaginary (which he sometimes confounded with all expressions of the spiritual order). He well knew the risks of seeing the reappearance of the imaginary on the theoretical level and of the analyst's becoming addicted to the client who is willing to confirm his theory.

It may be noted in passing that every attempt at psychological theorization incurs the risk of imaginary contamination; any such theory is the product of the psychic metabolizations of its author, resulting in a more or less sucessful "mise-en-sens".

How can we get out of the imaginary trap in our analytical work without having to definitively shut down our trade?

Let's for the last time use our scheme as a road map: on the one hand, therapeutic efficacy requires the possibility of regression to levels as deep as the originary system; and on the other, the integration of the activated unconscious contents is necessary. One needs "mise-en-image" and then (most essentially) "mise en sens". But we must recognize that the resistance to making transition from the imaginary to the symbolic order, in which the image can be used as a symbol, is often the stubling-block to this metabolization.

Jung expressed it in his own way: "The prerequisite for this, of course, is that the artifex should not identify himself with the figures in the work but should leave them in their objective, impersonal state."[21] As long as the analyst identifies with these figures whose images are projected on him, he remains trapped by the imaginary. His prevailing task is instead to maintain the symbolic order, which implies that he has continuously to forgo imaginary satisfactions. At the same time, the effort to maintain the symbolic order will be the choice therapy of transference addiction. It is therapy that must be continually renewed, since the access to the symbolic order is never acquired definitevely. The analyst should not relinquish the means which are at his disposal to continue this incessant quest.

An example may help us see more clearly what these means are. A therapist analyzing an attractive young woman had been mired down in a symbiotic relation that had paralyzed every possible therapeutic progress. He then had a dream in which he saw himself sitting in a room with this charming person; the atmoshpere was smooth, exquisite . . . Baudelaire would have said:

> "La, tout n'est qu'ordre et beauté,
> luxe, calme et volupté . . ."[22].

All this was being experienced quite decently, though; not even in the dream was there an acting out. Then suddenly the door of the room opened and the analyst's wife entered, along with their four children. (In fact, he only has two). The intruders were very noisy and completely disrupted the idyllic setting. Raging mad, the analyst vainly tried to urge them to silence, to get them out . . . as the dream ended.

Without excluding other possible interpretations of this dream, we suggest that it offers a humorous exposure of the imaginary trap, which doesn't resist the intrusion of four healthy kids, full of vitality! Not to speak of the therapist's wife! It is of course very hard to maintain an idealization of one's daily partner. In contrast, the protected situation of the analysis dangerously favours the development of an imaginary breeding-place, well sheltered from the down-to-Earth concerns of day-to-day reality.

In short, the analyst should not flee from the trials that reality, family life, partner and friends cast on him. And above all he should be aware of the fact that the analytic setting is not to be compared to the family scene.

And, with his colleagues, he should avoid becoming trapped in a collective imaginary world where one revels in subtle theories at the expense of the clients (who aren't even there to defend themselves against the regressive atmosphere to which they are being exposed.)

He should go his own unrelenting way.

"Individuation" is a word that would lead us astray towards an imaginary ideal if ever we forgot that the process it intends always and necessarily has two aspects: an interior process of integration and an equally indispensable growth in the relationship with the other.

Jung[23] presses us always to bear in mind these *two* aspects. Only in this way can analytic experience be non-addictively successful. To end this survey in Jung's company, we repeat his hope that analysis might be "a fundamental discussion between "I" and "You" and "You" and "I" on a plane stripped of all human pretences"[24]!

1. Hoghelande, *"Liber de alchemiae difficultatibus"*, p. 239, quoted by C. G. Jung in *The Psychology of the Transference*, C. W. vol. 16, (pp. 163—323), § 400, p. 199. (The Collected Works of C. G. Jung, translated by R. F. C. Hull, London, Routledge & Kegan Paul, second edition)
2. Castoriadis-Aulagnier, Piera, *La violence de l'interprétation*, Paris, Le Fil Rouge, P. U. F. 1975.
3. Castoriadis, *Violence*, p. 26.
4. Castoriadis, *Violence*, p. 64.
5. I have wondered whether it would not be more suitable to use the term "Zoe" = life, in opposition with "Thanatos", and to restrict the term "Eros" to its opposition with "Logos". In the Gnostic system, Zoe was a goddess coupled with Logos.
6. Castoriadis, *Violence*, pp. 68—69.
7. Jung, C. G., *On the Nature of Psyche*, C. W. vol. 8 (pp. 159—234) § 368, p. 177.
8. Jung, C. G., *Psychology and Alchemy*, C. W. vol 12, § 360, p. 257.
9. Jung, C. G., *Nature*, § 399, p. 201.
10. Jung, C. G., *Alchemy*, § 30, p. 25.
11. Jung, C. G., *Alchemy*, § 516, pp. 432—433.
12. Jung, C. G., *Alchemy*, § 394, p. 278.
13. Jung, C. G., *Alchemy*, § 400, pp. 282—283.
14. Neyraut, Michel, *Le Transfert*, Paris, Le Fil Rouge, P. U. F. 1974.
15. Jung, C. G., *Foreword to the Swiss Edition* of Volume 16 (1958), C. W. vol. 16, p. vii.
16. Jung, C. G., *Alchemy*, § 439, p. 336.
17. Jung, C. G., *Alchemy*, § 389, p. 273.
18. Jung, C. G., *Alchemy*, § 118, p. 90.
19. Jung, C. G., *Transference*, Foreword, p. 164.
20. Jung, C. G., *Transference*, § 383, p. 187.
21. Jung, C. G., *Alchemy*, § 43, p. 37.
22. "There, all is but order and beauty, luxury, calm and voluptuousness . . ." Baudelaire, C., L'Invitation au Voyage, in *Les Fleurs du Mal*, Le Livre de Poche, Paris, Librairie Générale Francaise, 1972.
23. Jung, C. G., *Transference*, § 448, p. 234.
24. Jung, C. G., *Alchemy*, § 5, pp. 5—6.

The psychotherapy of the psychoses in analytic training

By Eberhard Jung (Berlin)

General Considerations

In writing about the psychotherapeutic treatment of psychoses I am afraid I shall invite criticism from my colleagues for implying that the treatment of psychosis in Germany today does not bear comparison with, nor is it quite up to, international standards; though, admittedly, it is thanks to this comparison that we in Germany have been able to initiate discussion on general psychiatric care. Even so, those who study the conditions of the psychotically ill in Germany base their deliberations in this field largely on a comparison with the progress achieved in the U. S. A., England and the Scandinavian countries. It need hardly be said, therefore, that at all important meetings and congresses held in the Federal Republic, there is a demand for the programme to include papers dealing with the psychotherapeutic treatment of psychoses whenever possible.

To begin with I propose to make a short historical digression, since it is important to sketch in the development which has led to the situation on which our present-day practice is based.

As we now know, the forerunners, or earliest practitioners, of the dynamic approach to psychiatry were the shamans and medicine men of primitive peoples, who treated and cured illness by psychological methods. No branch of science has, however, subsequently undergone so many metamorhposes and been exposed to so many threats as the dynamic approach, especially within psychiatry itself. Always ambivalent, it has been treated at all times like an unloved child. Discoveries made in physics, chemistry and physiology have always gained easier success and recognition. Moreover, dynamic thinking in psychiatry tends to be especially neglected during those periods when the natural sciences are expanding. This can be easily illustrated if we take, by way of a contemporary example, the victorious progress and extended use of psycho-pharmacology, and compare it with the numerous attempts that have been made to win an assured place for the dynamic approach within psychiatry. Even today that place is secure in only a few areas. Nevertheless, in spite of uninterrupted threats and crises, it is still possible to trace a continuing development in the dynamic systems of our time from their beginnings to the present day.

About a hundred years ago it looked as if the spell had been broken. Hopes ran high at the time, but once again disappointment quickly followed. The psychiatry of the institutes, or of the academic departments, compared with the dynamic approach, expanded further within its specialised field and became more sharply defined, so that psychiatry and psychotherapy faced one another like two hostile brothers. The vicissitudes to which all serious attempts to establish a dynamic approach to psychiatry have been subject are, in the final analysis, nourished and maintained by the notions of a sharply-drawn opposition between soma and psyche. And so, in Germany as in other countries, psychiatry and psychoanalysis have gone their wholly separate ways.

It is all the more regrettable, therefore, that the research carried out at the turn of the century at the Burghölzli mental hospital in Zürich did not lead to any change within psychiatry (E. JUNG 7). When C. G. Jung arrived there in 1901, Bleuler expressly stated that he wished to explore the unconscious of schizophrenic patients by means of the Association Experiment, a clear indication of the importance then attached to psychodynamics. Special mention must also be made, at this point, of wellknown American psychiatrists like Brill, Peterson and Putnam, who brought psychoanalysis to American psychiatry long before the First World War.

Among the pioneers of dynamic psychiatry Jung holds a secure place. By his investigations into the unconscious, made independently of psychoanalysis, he reinstated the forgotten duality of the conscious and 'unconscious' psyche, and underlined the importance of the 'affective rapport' in relationship with patients—the humane principle distinctive of the Zürich school. In his early psychiatric writings, Jung points out repeatedly that the psychological atmosphere of a mental hospital is far from being a luxury; everything that goes to make up this atmosphere is an essential component of the curative measures influencing the patient. Nor did his insistence on maintaining a high scientific standard in his work prevent him from discussing everyday therapeutic questions, and he quite outspokenly criticised the persistent efforts to account for schizophrenia in narrowly somatic terms.

[The schizophrenic] is a person like ourselves, beset by common human problems, no longer merely a cerebral machine thrown out of gear. . . . When we penetrate into the human secrets of our patients, the madness discloses the system upon which it is based, and we recognise insanity to be simply an unusual reaction to emotional problems which are in no wise foreign to ourselves (Jung 5).

As for his use of the Word Association Test in the investigation of schizophrenia, only the study carried out jointly with Emma Fürst need be mentioned here, deserving our attention for its connection with family therapy, today acknowledged as a therapeutic method in its own right, as well as a field for further research (Jung 4).

As analytical psychologists we must very much regret that the work carried out at that time was not continued, as it held important implications for psychiatric research and its further development. The few exceptions—the scientific and clinical therapeutic work of Fierz (I) and Frey-Wehrlin (2), for example—should not, however, be overlooked. Although Jung's scientific interest in schizophrenia continued until his death, he greatly reduced his therapeutic work with psychotic patients during his later years. Thus he, too, belongs to those therapists who show strong initial interest in psychosis, but then withdraw from mental hospital work to treat mainly neurotic disturbances.

Even today most of those who work in mental hospitals and, at the same time, undertake further training to become analytical psychotherapists are exposed, during their training period, to the opposition between the psychiatric approach on the one hand, and the psychodynamic approach on the other. Yet if full-time psychotherapeutic training were to become possible in the near future, we should no doubt once more be apprehensive about the success of attempts at integration, and again fear a split between psychiatry and psychotherapy—even at this time when psychiatry, for its own part, is striving to integrate the dynamic approach.

Volk has recently compared the sharply demarcated, and even conflicting, rôles of the psychiatrist and the analyst. He describes the sort of demands made on the analytical trainee who works in a mental hospital and who is not only exposed for several years to the tension this situation creates, but expected to put up with it and even to resolve it. Volk highlights the differences in diagnostic concepts and therapeutic tactics between psychiatry and analysis and the differing therapeutic attitudes and activities they demand (Volk 13).

The polarity between these two disciplines is especially stressful for the young doctor who, since both are mutually exclusive, being antithetical and contradictory, finds them unreconcilable. At best, both training courses run parallel. Yet there can be no scope for any basic integration of the two viewpoints if those who are to pass on their knowledge and experience have not themselves taken any steps towards reconciling them.

Experience in treating psychotic patients is looked on as an important qualification for further training in analysis, but mainly for the reason that it enables the trainee to make precise diagnoses quickly and at as early a stage as possible. Accuracy in diagnosing neurotic states is, consequently, likely to be improved.

At the same time, the inclusion of the psychotically ill within the psychotherapeutic situation seems not to be envisaged, though the mental hospital serves admirably as an institution within whose protective walls practice and valuable experience can be gained with patients who are violent, aggressive and suicidal. This means that even today the psychotherapeutic treatment of psychoses is not yet integral in courses of further training. Also, it often happens that those practitioners who earlier had dedicated themselves to the treatment of psychosis by therapeutic methods later confine themselves to dealing with neurosis. Moreover, it indicates a poor state of affairs if, during a prolonged and specialised course of analytic training, a therapeutic method which is designed to strengthen the personal relationship between doctor and patient cannot create, offer and mediate those requirements needed for the treatment of psychotics and the establishing of a relationship with this category of patient.

The attitude of training analysts in this matter seems to be one of reserve rather than of critical discussion. In any case, courses of analytic training do not yet offer an opportunity for specialisation in the psychotherapy of psychoses. If a practitioner begins to treat psychotics early in his career, his activities will be viewed with suspicion; his seniors will mistrust him and will be prone to consider that his specialised interest and daily occupation betray more individualism than they are prepared to allow for during training. The fact is that, frequently, it is the markedly original and individual practitioners who devote themselves to the treatment of psychoses. And along with the criticism that a colleague when functioning in his capacity as an analyst is 'too psychiatric', there is the parallel criticism that his psychiatric work is 'too analytic'.

The Psychiatric hospital

I am in charge of a mental hospital of 950 beds which provides for the total psychiatric care of five residential districts in Berlin. Here we have developed a therapeutic concept which seeks to combine patient care with further training needs.

Owing to the variety of our tasks we are organised on functional as well as on departmental lines. Specially selected patients can be treated in accordance with their needs using psychotherapeutic methods based on depth psychology. Apart from one unit in the hospital which is reserved for the treatment of neurotic disorders, each department has its own ward for the psychotherapeutic care of those neurotic and psychotic illnesses for which analytical psychotherapy in the strict sense is not indicated. The patients of these thirty-bed units are either direct admissions, or transfers from closed wards. In order to create a situation corresponding as closely as possible to life outside the hospital, both men and women of varying age groups are admitted.

Today we can look back on over ten years of experience with this type of arrangement (E. Jung 8). Our therapeutic methods have, of course, undergone a change over the years, to the extent that we ourselves have changed. This is quite understandable, since we assume a psychiatric department or unit to be a dynamic group, the work of which is determined solely by the need for change and further development. Such a project can, of course, only succeed if all practitioners engaged in therapy are fully committed—and here I should like to point out that, in this respect, it is no less important that positive development should take place as regards non-medical personnel. In any event, in the course of several years it has been possible to establish an atmosphere of confidence, mutual frankness and common interest to which patients and therapists have contributed equally.

This development I personally find very stimulating, and the course it has taken over the last few years can be described briefly as follows.

If we assume, as we must, very strong regressive wishes in patients admitted for hospital treatment, we cannot be surprised when these regressive desires for passive care and nourishment occasionally take extremely distorted forms. The fact that these desires cannot, and must not, be satisfied leads necessarily to outbursts of unhappiness, dissatisfaction, disappointment and reproach. When we realised that this constituted a displacement of other, more important but also more dangerous, needs on to the material or the oral level, we began by assuming the rôle of the denying mother, and thus introduced a long and productive phase of conflict. To our surprise the next step entailed working through the disappointments experienced with the father, because the actual fathers had either been totally absent or had largely withdrawn from the domestic scene. In any case, they were seen as too weak. Repressed longings were activated, and it became clear to what extent these were directed towards husbands and partners who now—measured by the strength of those unconscious longings—became the weak ones. After several months we were able, for the first time, to work on the more reliable basis of a positive father transference, which offered a very important counterbalance to the strongly maternal atmosphere created by the hospital environment. We can now determine relatively easily if the transference is serving mainly as a compensation for a deficit. Attributes like consistency, orderliness, punctuality, conscientiousness, precision, frankness, communicativeness, attentiveness, learning and inconvenience are then felt as mainly positive.

Training

In this paper I am unable to refer in much detail to what is probably the greatest obstacle at the beginning of treatment—the patient's lack of insight into his illness and poor motivation for treatment, both of which are based on a deep distrust. During my discussion on the bad part of the self and the bad object, I will consider the reasons why the image of the enemy is so often projected by these patients on to the hospital, and the therapists. And this brings up the question of how the therapists obtain the strength to suffer daily exposure to a situation in which they are rejected, insulted, threatened and attacked. It is here that the urgent question of the quality of training confronts us in its full magnitude.

How, then, are we to solve training problems and needs? For me it goes without saying that the theory of analytical psychology, and the practical experience gained through its therapeutic application, constitute a sufficient precondition for an integrative model.

Group Therapy

Psychotherapy of the psychoses, particular in the setting of a hospital ward, needs to include group psychotherapy, so long undervalued and neglected by analytical psychology, though it is closely related to the dynamic attitude in psychiatry. The reservations of analytical psychologists towards group psychotherapy can, in the main, be traced back to C. G. Jung's own very critical comments. Not only did he emphasise the pairs of opposites—the collective and the individual, or social and personal—but, for the most part, he treated group phenomena and group dynamics purely and simply on the basis of mass psychology, of which he took a negative view, and hence rejected group dynamics as a therapeutic method. Even in his late work, *Mysterium Coniunctionis,* the masses are seen as a monster, its primitiveness reflected by 'primeval bloodthirstiness and lust for murder' (Jung 6). Comments such as these put the brakes on so effectively that at first there were only spasmodic attempts to develop group psychotherapeutic methods. Psychoanalysis had given up its reservations much earlier, so that in the beginning we orientated ourselves by its hypotheses and experiences.

In Germany, Seifert was the first to demand that, in this context, we speak not of masses but of large groups:

> Large groups challenge us to develop methods and new attitudes in order to find a solution to these varied and often threatening problems. It is just here that analytical psychology can and should make valuable contributions, and not least on the basis of the compensatory dynamic of collective consciousness and collective unconscious which it recognises. The ego of the individual must assert itself between these two forces (Seifert II).

Seifert concludes from this that group therapy offers the possibility 'of treating constructively questions central to analytical psychology, namely the strengthening of the individual ego when faced with the dangers of large groups' (*Ibid.*).

By our therapeutic methods, which consist of therapy in large and small groups, family therapy and individual sessions, we can cover all important therapeutic needs corresponding to the demands of the psychotic patient. Moreover, the participation of the whole team at these group sessions ensures that many of their individual training needs are met at the same time.

The use of dynamic and interactional therapy in large groups is still in its infancy. Even the fifteen-volume encyclopedia, *Psychology in the Twentieth Century* (each volume of which contains more than 1000 pages) devotes a mere half page to the subject of large groups. Only a short reference is given to Lionel Kreeger, who reports his initial observations, while Martin Grotjahn comments:

> But neither the technique nor the difficulties of describing such a group have been mastered so far . . . . Some conclusions and psychoanalytic postulates from the theories of Melanie Klein seem directly observable in large groups. It is not certain, however, if the present level of group therapy allows for experiments with large groups. It seems there do not at present exist any research methods with which group processes in large groups can be investigated or even described (Grotjahn 3).

We had already gained valuable experience over a period of years with the therapeutic model we had developed, including therapy in large groups, when, in 1978, Lionel Kreeger's publication, *The Large Group* became available, the first work to treat the subject in some detail (Kreeger 9). The experiences described in the book were a valuable confirmation of our own work, particularly since we had started using the group concept at a time when the therapeutic application of large group psycho-dynamics was hardly known. On the basis of our own observations and experiences we feel able to put forward the central thesis that therapeutic work in large groups does not endanger the individuation process of patients, but can promote it, since the individual does not necessarily succumb to the regressive situation and become victim of his inertia; rather does regression to very early developmental stages become of great therapeutic value, and especially with psychotic patients.

We define a large group as consisting of some twenty-five patients in a ward of about thirty, in contrast to the small group of from five up to a maximum of eight which has been well researched. Our experience suggests these limits, although Asch and others mention a figure of fifty participants at which point, in their view, a small group merges into a large one *(Ibid.,* p. 117). In groups of the size we use the extraverted members usually dominate the interchange while the introverts tend to hang back, so that explorative discussions, through which unresolved differences among members might be accepted, are not frequent. Nevertheless, higher demands are made on participants in groups than in any other therapeutic situation. The fact that often the group reacts more indulgently towards the leader and his interventions than to its members can become a temptation for him and a danger for the group insofar as its effect may be that he misleads, rather than leads, the participants.

The large group meets regularly for two one-hour sessions a week. Prior to this some patients may have received treatment for psychotic disturbances either in our own, or in another hospital. Previous illness, or treatment, is not a contraindication to joining the group.

Over the years we have found that the dynamic process within the group very soon induces active participation even by those patients who, in the beginning, were uncertain about their motives for seeking treatment. It is an aspect of reality-testing that patients convey to each other that the outcome of the therapy depends on them all participating. Such immediacy of experience within the group can exercise a more positive influence than a therapist can hope for from difficult individual sessions with ambivalent and resistant patients.

We cannot confirm C. G. Jung's reservations about dynamic group processes, given above. He based them on dangers to which the individual is exposed in a group and to which he can easily succumb, namely:

1. surrender or unawareness of personal responsibility;
2. capacity to be easily seduced;
3. lack of initiative;
4. evasion of individuation;
5. neglect of one's creative powers.

Jung never investigated how the demands made on, and the attitudes of, an individual in a group could be used therapeutically, which is all the more regrettable since he developed in analytical psychology practicable, that is, therapeutically applicable, theoretical concepts.

The large group comes next to the family as an extended social unit and represents, more or less consciously, the principles and norms of a society, or at least makes them more discernible. In fact, the taboos protecting the intimacy of the family are left behind in a large group, and this enables the individual seeking independence to overcome his anxiety to a certain extent, and express himself more openly. He is freed from the narrow outlook which families often impose on their members, and this enables him to talk about the social aspect of his problem. Work in large groups is, therefore, the medium *par excellence* for the study of collective consiousness, its authoritativeness, and especially its rigidity.

This can be illustrated by the following example. Two young women report that they are faced with the question of whether they should have their babies, or whether they should have an abortion. They ask if it is not better, and even necessary, to terminate their pregnancies in view of their 'illness', that is, their present life situation and stage of development, particularly as regards becoming mothers, taking on the maternal rôle and function. This leads at once to confrontation with the male members of the group, who insist that a good mother would naturally wish to keep her child and give birth. What is so striking is that, at first, the pregnant women receive no support from the other females in the group. They are left to themselves to act on their own responsibility in the face of the men. They reject emphatically the claims made by the men, and protest at having to validate their image as woman and mother by submitting to what soon becomes evident as the masculine idea of what constitutes a good mother. Meanwhile the members of the female group, for their part, are now united, and lay claims to having a say in what, for them, are fundamental questions about the rôles of wife and mother. They resist the moral valuation imposed on them by the male members of the group, and any ideas that they are full of guilt feelings, are bad, worthless and insufficiently devoted and selfsacrificing. No one takes into account the fact that both women had been deserted by their men, and that it had been left to them to decide whether to keep their babies or have an abortion. That had, in turn, constellated the deserted child in them so that they are not able to feel, or react, as women and potential mothers. It emerges that as children they were disappointed and deserted by their fathers, and their negative experiences which had been repeated in partnerships and marriages are now appearing within the group situation. But these discussions and altercations about norms and values as determined by collective consciousness merely clarify and illuminate the surface aspect; the more important dynamic processes have been taking place on the level of the collective unconscious during the course of the weekly therapeutic sessions.

The historical dimensions of this subject and its problems have been dealt with by Klaus Theweleit in his two-volume work, *Male Phantasies* (Theweleit 12). The distorted male image, with its false educational ideals, presents an almost insoluble problem for men and women alike. The male personality is often undeveloped and infantile. This makes men feel afraid, and quite rightly so, as comments from women like the following confirm: 'I hate my husband because he is so childish, he isn't a man at all'. The man who has not progressed beyond the infantile level cannot offer his wife the security she longs for, least of all when she most needs his support and help.

> It was just before my confinement and he was lying-in himself, even before the birth. I knelt in front of him and begged him to go to work so that we would have something to eat. I should have been very grateful to him, in spite of the fact that my mother was always demanding gratitude of me: up to now I've never understood why she kept on telling me, all these years, that a few days before she expected me I almost went down the loo when she had a sudden, very quick labour. I would have been, literally, in the shit.

The depth of regression is clearly shown by this dream of a female group member:

I saw large blood vessels in front of me. They were red outside and black inside. I jumped into them and floated down. The blood vessels went into the earth and when I got to the end there were many beds in a large room. There were doctors in this room and I talked to them and the patients. Then I wanted to leave but the way was sealed off by electronic barriers. Some people stood beside them and didn't want to let me through. It was really hard to get through the barriers, but I managed it. When I was on top again I could breathe and felt wonderfully free.

After the patient had reported this dream other group members spontaneously mentioned dreams on similar lines, containing symbolism which clearly showed the depth of regression. The archetypal regression into the mother is demonstrated quite clearly in the above dream. This dream, however, does not show a return into the body of the personal mother but of entering into Mother Earth, thus expressing the need for a connection or life with the earth instead of a life in opposition to nature and the earth. The dreamer has brought to light one of the most immediate and critical collective problems of our time. We live too much in opposition to nature, against the earth and against life, so that we are always on the edge of acting destructively, of fighting our nature and our world as unrelenting enemies. The threatening obstacles on the way into life appear in the dream as the electronic barriers of a hostile technology.

Therapeutic regression: early self and ego states

Because it offers ample scope for regression, therapeutic work in large groups reveals particularly clearly the hierarchy of different depths of regressive states. The level in question is that of the early symbiotic relationship between mother and child, that of the primary self. Since these early disturbances are relevant to psychotic illness, we attempt, for therapeutic reasons, to reach this deep level of repression, at least with those patients who are capable of it. From there we can approach the early ego disturbances which have come about in the forming of an individual self and a selfidentity, and which arise after the symbiotic unity with the mother has been left behind. Among other things, the large group symbolises the all-embracing archaic mother who, as the good mother, represents the world—the world of trust. It is not surprising, therefore, that regression to this early developmental phase reactivates early traumatic injuries. Feelings of worthlessness and rejection are re-lived, and these feelings of untrustworthiness and rejection are accompanied by unbearable feelings of being utterly bad. Thus everything directed towards personal existence and development, insofar as it is associated with such feelings, is rejected. In this context only brief mention can be made of 'coanaesthetic schizophrenia', that is, the idea that in order to retain the life-preserving feeling of being good, all badness must be eliminated from this early level of experience.

Closely connected with the experience of the patient's own uselessness, worthlessness and badness is the problem of destruction. The withdrawal of the psychotic person protects him, among other things, from the confrontation with his own latent aggressivity. At the same time, feelings of hate make him aware of the extent and danger of his latent murderous impulses. Believing that he is himself unable to control them, he becomes fearful that his therapist will also be unable to withstand them. A victim of his desires and feelings of magical omnipotence, he is terrified by phantasies of dismemberment. Early cannibalistic impulses mingle with the desire to rob the other of his strength and potency, to dismember and ingest him, and thus gain strength for oneself while remaining as close as possible to the other person.

Verbal communication, too, is seen as extremely threatening since it is through speech that phantasies manifest themselves. Hence language is experienced as destructive, disintegrating, egoistical and hostile; that is, verbalisation of these phantasies disturbs the relationship to the environment to such an extreme that any such relationship is avoided. 'The verbal process of analysis', as Theweleit puts it, 'cannot be made use of by patients who do not possess an Oedipal ego. The "ego" is not available because the development of the person was disturbed at a period when the child, psychically or physiologically speaking, neither has an "ego" nor is an "ego" *(Ibid.* 12).

We know today that the ego does not simply emerge form the unconscious but differentiates itself out of the mother-child symbiosis, out of the dual union with her, a relationship crucially important for early development. If this emergence from the symbolic relationship does not succeed, serious disturbances of vital ego functions will ensue, the most important of which is an insufficient, or total lack of, capacity to form object relations. While the Oedipal ego can ultimately resort to repression, the patient whose disturbances occurred at an earlier stage must endure his destructive impulses consciously and can, at best, only conceal them.

In the large group regression to a deep level only becomes possible because it is carried by everyone without any one person having to verbalise it. Some group members—the introverts especially—can allow themselves simply to be attentive listeners. They support the group situation, rather then determine it, in that they help to shape and maintain the unconsious phantasies at the level important for the therapeutic process, even though they do not themselves participate verbally. All share, however, in discharging the conflicts by their refusal to submit to insecurity and rejection. The intrapsychic experience is thus projected through interaction in order to produce a situation in which all play a decisive rôle, and for which the large group offers a favourable setting.

The therapeutic process is carried onwards through the integration of those individual aspects of the self that have not so far been realised. Here non-verbal communication is of the greatest importance, for what matters is that others should be put in a mood, or feeling situation, similar to that experienced by one or more members of the group. To display and transmute this feeling is the joint task of the group. It is particularly important that an experience incompatible with intra-psychic feelings is thus brought out into the open to enable some group members at least, to maintain a certain rôle, or remain within it, until this stage is reached.

Primitive and early forms of communication are especially evident in the large group; archaic and archetypal transferences to the group leader are often experienced. As it is in this way that archaic desires are constellated, the acceptance of these transferences is one of the group leader's most important tasks and functions. Attention must be paid to the degree of anxiety, and the feelings of relevancy, which emerge in this context. To use a large group situation therapeutically does, in any case, seem to evolve quite naturally, since after an early developmental phase within the primary family we are all part of larger social groupings.

The value of work with individual patients

Nevertheless, therapeutic work in large groups is no substitute for work in small groups or for individual therapy, and exact knowledge of transference / countertransference phenomena is essential for therapeutic success. One of my patients suffered from the pressure of his compulsive phantasies and urges to murder and dismember me. The sure knowledge he had of his magical and omnipotent powers meant to him that he really could destroy me, but then, with equal certainty he would also lose me. First he suffered another psychotic decompensation which lasted a few days. Even then contact with him was not lost. Then he told me that all was pointless, that he was mentally ill and nothing could change it. He wanted to leave town and move to a different district altogether. Consideration of why, just at this point, he saw his mental illness as the lesser evil confirmed for me the extent of the danger. He will always be grateful to me for telling him to his face what he had experienced, and that I understood what he was going through. Without some relief from that internal pressure at this point he would have missed his last chance. Most certainly he would, at sometime or other, have murdered someone, and have had to spend the rest of his days in prison. His life and his development had been interrupted when he was eight years old. He was a child during the war and was evacuated to a rural area. His sensitive young soul could not come to terms with his experiences on the farm, and the daily routine of slaughter, cutting up and eating of animals. After returning to his home town he wondered if murder and suffering did not take place everywhere. His distrust was confirmed in observations and experiences of the behaviour of those he loved best.

After he had managed to shed some of his armour, early experiences became available to him, for example, the fact that both parents wore very thick spectacles as they were extremely short-sighted, so that when he looked up during play he used to see the greatly enlarged eyes of his mother turned towards him.

In order to avoid misunderstanding it seems essential, at this point, to clarify, on the basis of our experience, what we mean by 'positive transference'. We would define it as follows: the relationship to the therapist must acquire so much holding capacity as to permit the expression of the whole range of murderous, sadistic and cannabalistic impulses. We can only warn our trainees that there is danger in apparently loving and friendly conduct, under the surface of which lies concealed much anxiety, endangering therapy, patient and therapist. This is far from being the daemonisation of the psychotic, it is rather that the patient's need to protect his therapist disappears when he has ben able to express his impulses to destroy him. Disintegration of the ego is no longer synonymous with destruction, if confrontation with the destructive side, as part of the personality, has taken place. The relation to the object is no longer total, because not every situation demands involvement of the total personality. Only then can the patient strive for, and achieve, satisfaction, because some parts of himself become linked with parts of other objects and from transitory units of production which dissolve again in order to form other such units (Ibid. 12).

Unfortunately, space does not permit me to go into the details of partobject theory and its importance for later relationships, though it would seem appropriate to do so at this point, and I should like it to be borne in mind.

The concept of 'maintenance mechanisms' was formulated by Margaret Mahler. She uses it in the context of the aggressive behaviour of psychotic children and describes the mechanism 'to which the ego regresses in cases of very grave disturbances of individuation and psychotic disorganisation' (Mahler 10). The illusory image of a common boundary shared by mother and child in intended to deny the fact that both are in reality separate entities.

Theweleit speaks of unready people, of people born in an unfinished state, who remain caught in a certain destructive phase of their development beyond which they do not progress in order to avoid fragmentation of the body-ego (Theweleit 12). As my patient said, 'I'm still living within the amniotic sac, hanging on to the placenta, my umbilical cord has not been cut'.

Aggressive-destructive phantasies or actions are an attempt, moreover, to give the ego a feeling of 'I', in the sense of a circumsribed psychic structure or a unity not exposed to disintegration. If this 'I' feels endangered the experience of destructive impulses or actions can take over the function of holding together an ego threatened with disingetration. Every opening to the outside must be kept closed. The patient cannot unlock himself, he cannot let anything get near him, even less allow it to enter himself and be absorbed:

There is hardly any osmosis; the pores are closed in order to avoid the complete loss, the dissolution, of a weak and threatened ego. Exchange seems synonymous with adulteration. Exchange is only possible if the ego structure stays intact, that is, everything must be, and remain, ego-syntonic, and nothing else can and is allowed to exist except the 'I'.

Psycho-Pharmacotherapy

These considerations point to what, in our opinion is the cental problem of psycho-pharmacological therapy. Only that which is good is allowed inside. A few days after beginning this treatment, and to the extent to which primary psychotic symptoms recede, the diverse and, at times, unbearable side-effects of these drugs become evident. The changes arouse extreme anxieties because they alter awareness of the differences in body feelings, emotions and affective states, including phantasy states. Thus a struggle for power ensues. The therapist now comes to be seen as the patient's enemy, the violent intruder invading the territory and the boundaries of the sick person, who is forced back upon himself as a negative, bad object. The inevitable consequence is that the therapist himself is thrown out, i. e. rejected. I think that the frequent remarks of patients that we, the therapists, are poisoning them should be interpreted in this light.

Conclusion

My theme has been that large groups provide a therapeutic setting sufficient to allow for regression to early levels of disturbance. Led by an experienced analyst, the therapeutic process can be made clear with the inclusion of participating colleagues. Detailed discussions after each group session are absolutely essential. They give analytical therapists, at a relatively early stage in their training, a practical insight into dynamic processes, and convey important knowledge of how to handle those process therapeutically. They can subsequently apply that experience with necessary care and assurance in their own small group and also in individual sessions, the results of that work, in turn, flowing back into the large group meetings.

It is well-known that in therapeutic work with psychotic patients the dynamic approach cannot be undertaken without considerable risk. Through it we gain a valuable insight into a particular archetypal constellation; but, at the same time, we encounter collective consciousness in all its rididity and that narrow-mindedness so inimical to development. This further highlights the importance of the social aspect. Jung repeatedly pointed out the importance of the relative point of view, and of the dangers of treating patients within the limits of a pre-determined therapeutic technique. The greater the variety of psychic and psychiatric illnesses we include within the scope of our psycho-therapeutic endeavours, the greater the demands we make on the flexibility of the therapist, and especially on those of us who are responsible for training. If, for example, we enlarge our training courses to include psychotic illnesses, and take into account the varied forms these illnesses can assume, we have to face the fact that not only do we have to carry greater responsibilities for the care of larger groups of patients, but will be brought up against the relativity of our hypotheses.

At the same time we cannot ignore the undeniable increase in grave psychic disturbances, and especially of narcissistic disorders, border-line syndromes and psychotic episodes and reactions. It would be a poor outlook indeed for analytical psychology if its task could not come to be understood more broadly in terms of a wider therapeutic spectrum, in the sense of providing complete psychiatric and psychotherapeutic care.

1. Fierz, H. K. (1963). 'Klinik and Analytische Psychologie', in *Studien aus dem C. G. Jung-Institut Zürich*. Vol. XV. Zürich, Rascher-Verlag.
2. Frey-Wehrlin, C. T., et al. (1978). 'Behandlung chronischer Psychosen', *Analyt. Psychol.* 9, 132.
3. Grotjahn, M. (1980). 'Gruppentherapie in der psychiatrischen Praxis', in *Psychologie des XX. Jahrhunderts*. Vol. X. Basel, Kindler-Verlag.
4. Jung, C. G. (1907). 'The family constellation', *Coll. wks*, 2.
5. —(1908). 'The contents of the psychoses', *Coll. wks*, 3.
6. —(1955/6). *Mysterium Coniunctionis. Coll. wks*, 14.
7. Jung, E. (1973). 'Über den Beitrag der Analytischen Psychologie C. G. Jungs zur psychiatrischen Forschung', *Analyt. Psychol.*, 4, 105.
8. —(1979). 'Interaktion und Beziehung im analytisch-therapeutischen Prozess mit Psychosekranken', *Analyt. Psychol.*, 10, 23—41.
9. Kreeger, L. (Ed.). (1977). *Die Grossgruppe, Konzepte der Humanwissenschaften*. Stuttgart, Klett-Verlag.
10. Mahler, M. (1972). *Symbiose und Individuation*. Vol. I. Stuttgart, Klett-Verlag.
11. Seifert, T. (1974). 'Die Gruppentherapie im Rahmen der Analytischen Psychologie', *Analyt. Psychol.*, 5, 3—44.
12. Theweleit, K. (1977). *Männerphantasien*. Vols I & II. Verlag Roter Stern.
13. Volk, W. (1979). *Zur Polarität von tiefenpsychologischer Ausbildung und Psychiatrie: Theorie und Praxis der Psychoanalyse*. Bonz-Verlag.

Based on a paper read at the Eighth International Congress of the International Association of Analytical Psychology held in San Francisco, September 1980. (Translated from the German by V. Marlowe and J. Seddon.) Reprinted from *The Journal of Analytical Psychology* 1981, 26, 313—327 by permission.

Individuation and group

By Robert Strubel (Zürich)

Throughout the history of Western thought, philosophers and theologians have concerned themselves with the relationship of the individual to society. Their formulations have always tended to emphasize either the importance of the collective or the importance of the individual in this relationship. The theme of the individual and the group is thus not new; yet it always presents itself anew for consideration, as it does also today. There are many modern theories which hold that all wrongs derive from social conditions, and that also expect all solutions to come exclusively through social change. And, on the other hand, there are many philosophers and psychologists who treat the problem of individual existence as if people were not affected, or at least affected very little, by the life of society. Some researchers, among them C. G. Jung, see social life above all as a threat to individual self-realization.

First of all we want to consider Jung's remarks about the group. In doing so, we have to keep in mind that he was not a social psychologist or a group therapist; his statements are unsystematic and partially contradictory. In 1955 he summarized his opinion in a letter[1] where he took an official position in regard to the then new group therapy. There, among other things, we read as follows: " . . . the mass as such stifles all individual values. When a hundred intelligent heads are united in a group the result is one big fathead [because each individual is inhibited by the others being different than he is]."[2] And: "Individuals can be improved because they present themselves for treatment. But societies only let themselves be deceived and misled, even if temporarily for their own good."

Such negative judgements accord with the fact that in discussing the concept of society, Jung used the words "group," "community," "sect," "crowd," and "the masses" without differentiation.

On the relationship between group therapy and individual analysis he wrote: "The social attitude does not come into operation in the dialectical relationship between patient and doctor, and may therefore remain in an unadapted state . . . ." "The danger of individual analysis is the neglect of social adaptation."

And about group therapy he said: "In my opinion group therapy is only capable of educating the *social* human being." "The danger of group therapy is getting stuck on the collective level."[3]

Here Jung sharply separated individuation from adaptation. The individual, from his point of view, is something other than the "social being". If we developed this thought further it would mean that the individual personality of a human being moves and unfolds apart from the field of tension formed by social events. Other people, groups, or society as a whole would not be able to promote or hinder the individual in his self-realization; on the contrary, the self-realization of a person would have nothing to do with change in his social behavior and still less with the solution of social conflicts.

Indeed, Jung did not arive at such extreme conclusions; perhaps he would protest against such an interpretation of his statements, although it is a logical conclusion to his formulation quoted above.

We cannot overlook that Jung here—as in many other places—gives social life a onesidedly negative value. In doing so he seems to fail to appreciate how the individual is influenced to the depth of his soul by social events. In any case, a moralistic devaluation of social life cannot change the fact that society often has a basic and compelling significance for the destiny of an individual.

It would be wrong, however, to pin Jung down to such a bias without considering his other statements on this subject. In his essay "Psychotherapy Today", for example, he wrote: ". . . the natural process of individuation brings to birth a consciousness of human community . . . . Individuation is an at-one-ment with oneself and at the same time with humanity, since oneself is a part of humanity. Once the individual is thus secured in himself, there is some guarantee that the organized accumulation of individuals in the State . . . no longer consists of an anonymous mass but of a conscious community. . . Without . . . individual freedom and selfdetermination there is no true community, and . . . without such community even the free and self-secured individual cannot in the long run prosper."[4]

In another passage Jung called the "inner order of the psyche . . . the indispensable instrument in the reorganization of a civilized community . . ."[5]

These statements show us in which direction we can continue to explore the relevance of analytical psychology in regard to social-psychological questions. The considerations which follow will therefore start from Jung's central idea of the Self.

Where is it that man for the first time meets his Self? Erich Neumann states that in the infant the archetype of the Self is evoked by his experience of the mother. She represents the child's first regulating system because she removes all that disturbs his well-being. She embodies his Self as long as the child in the original relationship remains in a psychic unity with her. Only after the end of the primary relationship, says Neumann, does the archetype become an autonomous, spontaneous psychic organ.[6]

One could ministerpret Neumann and think that the Self is at first outside and later inside, only from then on being independent of the mother. It is true that with germinating consciousness an inner mother-image or self-image is developed in the child, an image that never corresponds exactly to the child's experience of the mother. But the mother remains the child's external regulating system because for years he goes on taking all important emotional experiences to the mother and can work them out only together with her. In a certain sense the evocation of the archetypal image is therefore never concluded.

If this were not so, we could achieve nothing with all our therapeutic efforts. If a patient comes for treatment with a negative mother-complex, we will be able to help him only if we succeed in evoking in him the positive side of the mother-archetype. The inner psychic spontaneity of the archetype is not enough; as an analyst we have to embody the worldfactor symbolically, which helps the inner positive image of the mother to become reality. Thus we take up, for a certain time, the role of the mother for him.

If the evocation of the archetypal image is never concluded, this means that the Self is never only in the inner image, but is constantly in outside reality also. The inner image is not the only symbolic realization of the Self—the role of the mother is a symbolic realization too. The mother represents the child's Self, but she is not his Self, nor does she play this role once and for all. In a certain aspect, she is for the child only the symbolic hint at his Self, although she at first necessarily has to represent the child's Self. But soon the father and the whole family as well become symbolic representations of the Self in the child's life. Indeed, all groups into which he grows are external representations of his Self. He experiences who he is and what belongs to him in kindergarten, in school and in his group of students, in the church and local congregation, on the sports team or in a choir, or in whatever group in which a growing child may live and develop. In this sense the group may basically be understood as a symbol of the Self. I want to illustrate this with an example.

In order to demontrate the universal existence of mandala-type forms, Jung referred among other things to the ground-plan of towns. He himself once painted a mandala that represents a town.[7]

If we look at the concrete ground-plan of a medieval town, we see that it was built according to clear aims. The fortification wall protected the inhabitants from enemies or wild animals. The church, the town hall, and the market place formed the middle of the town, where material and spiritual needs were fulfilled. The inhabitants were a defined group of people whose lives were ordered through this external frame.

The mandala-form ground-plan of such a town was at the same time a concretisation and a symbol. The plan of the town was the concrete area where the life of society of that time took place, and yet it was also the image of a social order. Church, town hall, and market place symbolized spiritual power, secular power, and commerce. So the town was a small world and also a hint at a world-image, a symbol of the world-understanding of that time. With reason we see in such a town-image a symbol of the Self, and in the same sense this is true about the group. The group is also a small world, a defined wholeness. It consists of a certain number of people who meet for a certain task. For a group to be able to gather in an ordered way at all, it needs a leader or someone empowered to undertake its oragnization. The leader represents the concrete center of the group; through him the group becomes comprehensible as a whole to its members as well as to people outside. The periphery of a group is formed by people who participate only moderately—on the margin, so to speak—in the life of the group. But there is a certain border, which defines whether one still belongs to the group or no longer belongs to it.

This group structure is linked to an ideal centre, which Neumann called the group-self. We shall briefly explain this concept here. In order to do so, we must first go back to Jung's statements about the Self.

In describing the paradox of the Self, Jung wrote: "It is the 'uniting symbol' which epitomizes the total union of opposites".[8] Since the symbol of the Self embraces every possible opposition, the opposition between I and Thou and the opposition between individual and society also belong to the symbolism of the Self. "The self too is both ego and non-ego, subjective and objective, individual and collective."[9] "It is as much one's self and all other selves, as the ego".[10] Therefore it must also be understood as the symbol of union of I and Thou, of I and the others, "because relationship to the self is at once relationship to our fellow man . . ."[11]. In that sense it is also the symbol for the unity of a group.

Jung once wrote in a letter: "The self . . . is of a conglomerate nature. It is, as it were, a group. It is a collectivity in itself and therefore always, when it works most positively, creates a group."[12]

Neumann considered this idea more closely as he studied the formation of religious groups. If a "Great Individual" founded a "community" as a result of his own experience of the Self, he did not at all experience his Self as something purely individual. His Self appeared to him as a group-self, compelling him to found a group. Paul expressed this when he said: "Poor me, if I didn't preach the Gospel!" (1. Cor. 9, 16). Creative people experience basically the same impulse nowadays, even though they do not become founders of religions. Jung himself, for example, told about the phantasies he had during his crisis: "There were things in the images which concerned not only myself but many others also."[13] And elsewhere he explained: "It is true that widely accepted ideas are never the personal property of their so-called authors; on the contrary, he is the bondservant of his ideas. . . . Ideas spring from something greater than the personal human being."[14]

In totemism, an early form of established religion, the totem as symbol of the group-self has a significance that is not only religious. Neumann specifies: "The spiritual nature of the totem . . . is the formative principle of all primitive life, since all conduct, rites, and festivals are determined by it, as well as the social hierarchy established by the totem."[15]

Even from the point of view of modern man, the group-self has entirely "profane" aspects, although religious components always resonate through it as well. For example, the natural law of group dynamics, by which a group is always structured as a circle of people around a leader or empowered person, is directly related to the group-self. In this sense, the more or less conscious representation of the group-self is to be seen as a "pattern of behavior" of group-formation, for it represents the living active archetypal image of the order, unity, and wholeness of a multiplicity, namely the plurality of the group-members.[16]

I want to illustrate the two basis dimensions of the group-self, which can be associated with the principles of logos and eros. (In accordance with the nature of these two principles the role of the leader is usually divided between two people, one the most efficient and the other the most popular.[17]

Each group has a main idea or a central task. From a merely practical point of view, this has to do with what it is that sets a group in motion. People outside the group may ask: What do they do? What do they want in their group? Participants in an ad-hoc group and also unhappy members of a permanent group ask the question: What do we really want? These questions aim at the content of the group-happening and at the same time at the meaning of this content, which is either no longer or not yet clear.

However, what it is that they have in common is often very unconscious for the members. It may be that for a long time they have participated in work by which all were fascinated, and no one has doubted its meaning although the meaning was not yet clearly comprehensible. At group-dynamic or group-therapeutic sessions the common content is not set beforehand, but comes up only gradually during the meetings. W. Willeford, for example, describes how, from scraps of conversation and accidental happenings, a common content may turn into a "uniting symbol" in such a group. Thereby each participant can be set free from his feeling of isolation and achieve a genuine experience of community.[18]

The self-realization of an individual who lives in such a group is constantly related to the group-self. He finds the way to himself only while participating in the life of the group and gaining orientation through the common guidelines of the group. If a young man for instance has the talent to become a baker, a musician, or a philosopher, he will develop his talent only though his connection with teachers and colleagues or fellow students. His individuality is expressed among other things in his talent, and it can be unfolded only through contact with others. He gets nearer to the image of who he wants to become not only by working on himself, but also by adjusting to the standards of the group.

Thus it belongs to individuation that we join groups and leave them again, that we feel bound to groups but also restrict these obligations or undo them. In some groups we may belong to those who carry the main idea, and in others we may belong to those who stay at the margin and participate less in the main idea. And these positions of the individual in various communities show something about himself.

The common center consists not only of the main idea, the task, and the aim of the group; the aspect of relationship, the eros which unites a group, also belongs to the group-self. A group embodies a certain style of relationship which strongly influences the interaction of its members. The relationship among the members and with people outside the group determines the kind of group-bond and at the same time determines how the group relates to the whole society. If we feel at ease in a group or not, if we want to participate or not, depends not only on the aims of the group, but also on the kind of group-feeling we find in it. The members of the group experience themselves not only in their commitment to the common idea, but also in their play of relationship. Tensions in the group, which may induce the individual to aggression or submission, to courage or to cowardice, to a power struggle or a biased viewpoint or any thing else, show him who he really is.

The group as a symbolic wholeness constellates the wholeness of the individual; it also releases in him unconscious impulses, so that he may discover with amazement what he is able to accomplish — or also to what extent he is able to be mean. His attitudes and behaviors may seem very strange to him, but they belong to him whether he wants to admit the fact or not.

On the other hand, the group finds neither its characteristic identity nor its wholeness if it avoids the creative impulses that come from the individual's self-experience. These impulses may bear the imprint of the individual very strongly; however, they refer to the whole group, even if this is not easily recognized at first. In extreme cases an individual, usually very intelligent, becomes alienated from his original group in order to found a new group out of his encounter with himself, a group which realizes his interests and mediates them to society.

In such a group there is great danger of identifying the group-self with the outstanding leader, so that the individual self of each member becomes oppressed. But only if each individual may be himself, only if each may bring his individuality as a specific contribution to the group, does the group realize itself as a symbolic wholeness. Only then does it remain related to its transcendent group-self. And this relatedness includes the relation of the group to the whole society, just as it includes openness to human nature in all its fullness and variety.

Here we see how the wholeness of the group and the wholeness of the individual are constantly in relation to each other. Sometimes the individual self almost coincides with the group-self and sometimes the difference between the two leads to larger conflicts, but the individual self and the group-self are never completely identical.

These conclusions bring us to the question of what conditions are necessary for the life of a group to be healthy and under what conditions the group degenerates into a sect. Speaking about sects here I do not mean only those religious groups that have separated from the traditional churches. I am using the term sect in a basic sense for the neurotic group and the group in which people become neurotic, and for the shadow aspect of the group with each group has to cope. A sect corresponds as a matter of principle to the masses, as Le Bon rightly described it.[19] R. Battegay calls it "the masses in miniature"[20]. Between a sect and the masses there is no fundamental difference other than size.

I prefer the word sect to other terms because the group-self includes religious aspects, even if the group's communal aim is profanely defined as material. (In the same way, the God-image of a religious community also includes the handling of practical aspects of life.) The community of a group — and this applies to every group — is always confirmed by rituals that have a binding character for the individuals and thus a more or less clearly religious character. In modern society the religious character of the community is indeed unconscious to most groups. During tension or even quarrels one can feel that the group (or at least part of it) is seized or possessed by something which "absolutely refers" to everybody.[21]

In relation to the latter description of the group as a symbolic concretisation of the Self, I want briefly to characterize the group's degeneration into a sect. According to R. Battegay's definition, the individuals in a group are strongly linked and each one has a special function in the collective. In the masses, on the other hand, individuals are "emotionally and instinctively on the same level" and there is no differentiation of particular functions other than that between leader and followers.[22] A group turns into a sect if it loses the openness to the group-self and identifies with it. Then it no longer understands itself as symbolic hint at the Self, but as its absolute embodiment. Such a group falls into a collective inflation, sees salvation realized in its existence, and becomes totalitarian. From this inflation comes its claim for power, which under certain circumstances can strikingly disregard social conceptions of right and order. One thinks of the Mafia or of the sect of the Peoples' Temple, of which more than 500 members committed suicide on the order of their leader in November 1978 in America.

With the loss of relationship to the Self comes the loss of relationship between the members. The group's inflation leads to transference among them; the members are no longer open to each other, just as they are no longer open to the Self. Each one is overcome by narrow expectations arising from the collective, just as we see this in the transference of some patients. If one remains in such a sectarian group one feels oppressed. One is no longer allowed to be oneself, but must have the same language, the same feelings, finally even the same gestures as everybody else. Through the collective power of suggestion, and this is a very strong force, one is pulled into a process of suppression and is so to speak no longer allowed to be a whole person, Genuine self-experience such as the encounter with one's own wholeness is no longer possible in such a group.

Since there is no real I-Thou relationship, conflicts cannot be worked out. They smoulder and poison the atmosphere without ever being solved, and an artificial unity covers everything.

This corresponds to the fact that the main idea of the sect is also clearly defined and unimpeachable in its external form. No one is allowed to ask about its meaning, for this meaning is regarded as identical to the external formulation. The only saving dogma is the main idea of the group. Any contradiction of it has to be eliminated and displaced to the evil world outside. Therefore the border is too sharply drawn, and the question of who belongs to the sect and who does not is overvalued. Outsiders and other groups are not allowed to come too close to the sect, otherwise it feels menaced; because the inner menace cannot be worked out and overcome, it remains projected on the environment.

If the sect puts its members emotionally, instinctively, and ideologically on the same level, it means that their individual selves must be stiff and unchangeably identical with the group-self. In this way not only the individuality of each member is repressed and violated, but the whole life of the group becomes stiff after a while because the individuals are not allowed to live freely. The group dies as soon as it can no longer endure the paradox of being the symbolic embodiment of the Self and yet only a symbolic hint at the group-self.

The aim of this description is not to campaign against groups that fall into the sect-spirit. The group and the sect do not stand static and cleanly separated side by side. I have already said that by the term sect I mean the shadow aspect of the group which threatens every group.

In the psychology of the individual we are used to seeing the shadow not only as the psychic illness of the human being. It also conceals "unlit" parts of the psyche which can impel an individual to the further unfolding of his personality. In a similar way, each group has its "shadow-sides", which can develop into a group-neurosis but can also contribute to its growth. A group can, so to speak, pass through a sect-stage that leads to the further development of its being. In order to illustrate this I want to describe briefly the development of a group.

During my studies I participated in a group that met every Sunday morning at a different member's home for breakfast together and discussed various questions. The subject was determined each time by the member at whose home the group met. Everyone was supposed to have the opportunity of bringing his ideas and problems to the group.

But in the course of time the need arose to work together on a specific field of interest. Soon the group was dominated by a woman who developed a firm study program and as a teacher started to indoctrinate the others. Most of the participants were happy with this; in accordance with the saying "knowledge is power" the group wanted to gain more political impact. This communal effort left less and less space for personal relationship; the Sunday morning breakfast was given up and we always held the meeting in the same room. Also the style of the conversation changed; instead of discussing together, most of the participants now only passively received instruction. Gradually an atmosphere of anxiety and bondage developed, because the "teacher of the group"reacted violently and aggressively to critical questions and only a few felt themselves to be on her intellectual level. Soon all the power and all the activity were in hands of the group-leader, who seemed compelled to control and direct everything in an almost pathological way. The group was actually terrorized by her.

The sessions became more and more monotonous and boring. Indeed, the accumulated tension sometimes burst out in vehement quarrels, and on the whole the group lost its original liveliness. It developed more and more into a sect.

In their communal idea the participants had looked for a clearly comprehensible group-self by which they could easily orient themselves. The identification with the aims of the leader gave an impression of unity and power that at first increased each individual's feeling of life. Only this makes comprehensible the willingness of the participants to be put under such pressure for a certain time.

But in the long they could not bear it, and after some time the group succeeded in freeing itself from its sectarianism. The repressed relationships came up through the group's wish to have a beautiful party once again, after a long time of work. The leader also showed up, although she was against it at first. But soon she no longer felt well, for at the party she could not play her domineering role. She suddenly stood up, accused the others of not giving her enough attention, and left. In contrast to earlier times, this scene did not impress many participants, and most of them went on enjoying the party without feeling disturbed.

This event announced a turning-point. After that the life of the group relaxed and the discussions became freer and livelier again. The participants had less and less fear of the leader, gradually took her power away, and soon looked for another leader and got interested in other subjects.

This example shows that a group, like an individual, always has to look for its group-self anew. Its main idea has to be formulated again and again and its communal life always has to be shaped anew in order to remain meaningful. In this effort the group inevitably meets its shadow. If it turns into a sect in the process, not only the community sickens, but the spiritual balance of its members becomes disturbed. A sectarian group can impair the well-being of its members and even injure it severely.

Nevertheless, the individual cannot escape this threat by looking for his self-realization totally apart from social life. Whether he wants it or not, whether he is aware of it or not, he is dependent on society's well-being or lack of it. Not only is he supported by the healthy life of his community, but he also has to contribute to the health of society. The individual has to work out the collective conflicts that affect him and take his creative solutions back to society if he wants to remain healthy himself.

Individuation always involves interplay between the individual and the collective search for the meaning of life. There is no individuation which is independent of the search for identity of groups and finally of the whole society.

Summary

C. G. Jung often stressed the danger of social life for individual self-realization. However, he also recognized the necessary and essentially positive interplay between individual and community. One of the contexts in which the individual encounters the Self is in groups to which he belongs; for the Self is not simply an individual entity, but transcends the individual, and indeed the group.

The well-being of the group and its members depends upon the relationship to the group-self. When this relationship is disturbed, the group sickens and turns into a 'sect'. Its life congeals because it suppresses the individual personality of its members.

1 Jung, *Letters II* (1951—1961), Princeton, New Jersey, Princeton University Press, 1975, pp. 217ff

2 This phrase was omitted by mistake in the English edition

3 C. G. Jung, *Letters II,* 217ff

4 C. G. Jung. *"Psychotherapy Today".* Collected Works, vol. 16, New York, Pantheon Books, 1954, p. 108 (§227)

5 C. G. Jung. *Psychology of the Transference.* Collected Works, vol. 16, New York, Pantheon Books, 1954, p. 321 (§ 539)

6 comp. Erich Neumann. *The Child.* New York, C. P. Putnam Sons, 1973, p. 86

7 C. G. Jung. *"Concerning Mandala Symbolism."* Collected Works, vol. 9/I, New Jersey, Princeton, 1969, p. 356ff, Fig. 36

8 C. G. Jung. *Psychology of the Transference.* Collected Works, vol. 16, p. 264 (§ 474)

9 C. G. Jung. *Psychology of the Transference.* Collected Works, vol. 16, p. 264 (§ 474)

10 C. G. Jung. *On the Nature of the Psyche.* Collected Works, vol. 8, New York, Pantheon Books, 1960, p. 226 (§ 432)

11 C. G. Jung. *Psychology of the Transference.* Collected Works, vol. 16, p. 233 (§445)

12 C. G. Jung. *Letters I* (1906—1950), New Jersey, Princeton, 1973, p. 508

13 C. G. Jung. *Memories, Dreams, Reflections.* London, Collins and Routledge & Kegan Paul, 1963, p. 184

14 C. G. Jung. *"Freud and Jung: Contrasts."* Collected Works, vol. 4, New York, Pantheon Books, 1961, p. 333 (§ 769)

15 Erich Neumann, *The Origins on History of Consciousness.* New York, Pantheon Books, 1964, p. 423

16 comp. C. G. Jung. *On the Nature of the Psyche.* Collected Works, vol. 8, p. 200ff (§§ 397ff)

17 comp. Peter R. Hofstätter. *Fischer-Lexikon Psychologie.* Frankfurt/M., Fischer, 20. Aufl. 1974, pp. 169f

18 comp. W. Willeford. *"Gruppenpsychotherapie und Symbolbildung."* Psychother. Psychosom., 1966, no. 14, pp. 282—297

19 Gustave Le Bon. *Psychologie des foules.* 1895

20 Raymond Battegay. *Der Mensch in der Gruppe.* Bern, Huber, 2. Aufl. 1969, vol. III, p. 11

21 comp. Paul Tillich. *Wesen und Wandel des Glaubens.* Frankfurt/M., Ullstein, 1961, Kap.I

22 comp. Raymond Battegay. *Der Mensch in der Gruppe.* Vol. I, p. 11

Narcissism and the Search for Interiority

By Donald Kalsched (New York)

-✗ *It is hard to believe that this teeming world is too poor to provide an object for human love—it offers boundless opportunities to everyone. It is
rather the inability to love which robs a person of these opportunities.
The world is empty only to him who does not know how to direct his
libido towards things and people, and to render them alive and
beautiful. What compels us to create a substitute from within ourselves is
not an external lack, but our own inability to include anything outside
ourselves in our love.*

C. G. Jung, *Symbols of Transformation,* par. 253.

Introduction

Jung once said that the gods have become diseases, and perhaps nowhere in
contemporary Western culture is the truth of this statement better illustrated
than in the case of the mythological Narcissus. The handsome youth immor-
talized in Ovid's *Metamorphoses* has lent his name to an evolving list of
psychological and sociological "pathologies" in our time beginning with
Freud's early use of the name in his classic paper *On Narcissism* (1914). Narcissus has not fared too well in these descriptions. Contemporary psychiatry,
for example, has recently adopted his name to designate a specific type of personality disorder in which "a grandiose sense of self, exhibitionism," and
"severely disturbed object-relationships" are the predominant symptoms.[1] Applying the various psychodynamic insights to an examination of the American
cultural scene, historian Christopher Lasch has managed to find Narcissus'
bent figure reflected in virtually every polluted pool. He concludes that, in a
"dying culture" like our own, narcissism "appears to embody the highest
hope of spiritual enlightenment,"[2] expressing the anxieties of "a culture that
believes it has no future."[3] As though to support this gloomy analysis, a recent conference at the University of Michigan on "Narcissism in Modern
Society" proclaimed pathological narcissism the "besetting psychological
disorder of modern western culture."[4] Apparently the Narcissus disease has
reached epidemic proportions.

This disturbing fact is not really news to any practicing psychotherapist today. The damaging and destructive effects of chronic, unresolved adult narcissism are only too obvious in the consulting room (and especially so of late with all the professional literature on the subject). But the exclusive attention devoted recently to the psychopathology of narcissism runs the risk of neglecting or obscuring the deeper individuation-urge embedded in this frustrating disorder and the wider relevance of the narcissist's suffering and disillusionment to the conundrums of relatedness in our time where the "inability to include anything outside ourselves in our love" seems an increasingly prevalent problem. For this wider perspective we must reach back to the myth itself and examine the plight of the mythological Narcissus in light of recent psychoanalytic findings. While it is no doubt true that Narcissus is infatuated by an illusory grandiose image of himself; that his selfesteem is dependent on external sources of approval; that his emotional life is shallow and lacks differentiation; that behind his ingratiating facade he is full of envy; that he is unable to mourn the loss of affectional objects; that he fears aging and is often pansexual and promiscuous—while all this is true about him and his modern-day namesakes; nevertheless it is *also* true that Narcissus is the hero in his own compelling story, that he loves too much, not too little, that his suffering and passion leads ultimately to his transformation, and that in the disillusioning "moment" when the paradox of his own subjectivity breaks through to him, he loses his "image" and gains a soul.

This "moment," which I refer to as the simultaneous birth of otherness and interiority (paradoxically paired), will be the focus of our analysis. As I hope will become apparent from our step-by-step exploration of Ovid's tale, this disillusioning moment conceals a mystery which is one of mythology's most popular secrets (and a preoccupation of contemporary psychoanalysis as well) i. e., *the mystery of psychic internalization*. I have intentionally not called this the "birth of consciousness" although this, of course, would be one way of looking at it. I prefer to think that the profound change in Narcissus at his "moment" (and also at those analogous "moments" within the psychoanalytic relationship) is not in the simple discovery that he has unwittingly been in love with *himself* (this is the ego's insight into its own projection) but rather in the development of the underlying structural capacities for internalization—the emerging ability to see through the watery film that separates him from otherness—to leave behind the image-realm with which he has been unconsciously identified and to involve himself in life and relatedness on the basis of what he feels *internally*. These developments commemorate the beginning of a psychological life, that is to say, an interior life reflectively in dialogue with the reality-of-otherness and especially in dialogue with the reality of *others* as separate persons. Needless to say, this is hardly the discovery of *one* moment, and the myth must be understood to present a paradigm of the countless incremental experiences through which an authentic core of selfhood is gradually built up. Nor is the result of this process a purely *percep-*

tual glimpse of one's paradoxial subjectivity like the Archimedean "aha!" although of course such dramatic insights do occur within the interpretive milieu that we call psychotherapy. Rather, what is closer to the experience of the patient, as narcissism gradually gives way to interiority, is an agonizingly slow but deeply reassuring emergent feeling of personal solidity and separateness—a sense of *inner sustainment* that provides the personality with a center of selfhood and infuses the inner world with the self-esteem necessary to allow—in Jung's words—something "outside ourselves in our love."

For our analysis of the myth, we will employ the comprehensive and detailed account of Narcissus' adventures found in Ovid's *Metamorphoses*.[5] I will first summarize the story, then go through it step by step in order to illustrate the various parallels between the stages in Narcissus' transformation on the one hand, and the relevant psychological issues confronted in the psychotherapeutic treatment of the narcissistic personality disorders on the other. To support my interpretations, I will amplify the discussion with additional mythological material drawn especially from the Orphic myth of Dionysus' birth, from the ancient Egyptian tradition regarding the origins of Osiris-Horus, and from the epic of Gilgamesh.

The story itself—which we will divide into four parts—begins and ends with the prophet Tiresias, whose blindness to the things of this world has been compensated by Jupiter with the power to know the future. In Part I of the narrative ("Birth of the Miraculous Child and Prophecy about Him"), Tiresias' prophetic powers are tested for the first time by the fair river nymph Liriope, who—following her rape by the river god Cephisus—has brought forth a child so beautiful that "one could have fallen in love with him, even in his cradle." She has named the boy Narcissus. Liriope asks the old prophet if her son will live to a ripe old age. Tiresias replies "Yes, if he does not come to know himself."

In Part II ("Excessive Fortune Followed by Divine Intervention") we meet Narcissus sixteen years later. Many youths and maidens have fallen in love with him, but —alas!—all have suffered painful rejection because Narcissus' "soft young body housed a pride so unyielding that none dared touch him." One of these unfortunates is a nymph named Echo. Because of a prior punishment by Juno for interfering in the affairs of the gods. Echo has only a partial use of her voice and can only repeat the last few words of what she hears from others. Narcissus scorns her advances and Echo, heartbroken, retires to a lonely cave where—unable to express her love—she watches as a strikingly similar fate befalls him. Her longing and anxious thoughts consume her and she withers away until all that is left is her voice, the only part of her that still survives. Finally, after much suffering, one of Narcissus' scorned suitors raises up a plea to the gods, and prays "May he himself fall in love with another, as we have done with him! May he too be unable to gain his loved one!" Part II ends as Nemesis hears and grants his righteous prayer.

The third part of the narrative ("Passion and Bliss in the Context of Illusion and Enchantment") finds Narcissus at the sylvan spring, tired after the day's hunt. While seeking to quench his thirst, he becomes enchanted by the beautiful reflection in the pool of water, and falls in love with his own reflection—mistaken for an "other." Spellbound by all the beautiful features for which he himself has been admired, he reaches vainly for the lovely countenance separated from him by only a thin film of water. Endlessly frustrated in his efforts, he cries aloud "Whoever you are, come out to me! Oh boy beyond compare, why do you elude me? Where do you go, when I try to reach you? Certainly it is not my looks or my years which you shun, for I am one of those the nymphs have loved." But Narcissus' pleas are all in vain, for he has not seen through his own illusion. His confusion and bafflement only heighten his frustrated passion as Nemesis' vengeance is carried out upon him.

In Part IV of the story ("Disillusionment, Death, and Descent into Hell") we have the final denouement and the ultimate fulfillment of Tiresias' prophecy. In one cataclysmic moment, Narcissus sees through his illusion. "Alas!" he cries, "I am myself the boy I see! I know now my own image! I am on fire with love for my own self. . . . What I desire, I have. My very plenty makes me poor!" In the agony of his self-discovery, Narcissus—like Echo—wastes away until finally death puts an end to his pain. Even in the abode of the dead he keepts watching himself in the waters of the Styx. Later, with the funeral pyre prepared, the nymphs cannot find his body. In its place they find a flower with white petals round a yellow center—the narcissus.

Having outlined the story briefly, let us now go through its various stages in more detail in order to illustrate how this mythologem—like others we will cite—records the miraculous transmuting internalization of the true self.*

Part I: Birth of the miraculous child
and prophecy about him

Ovid's account of Narcissus' birth places the fair youth in some rather distinguished mythological company. We are told (a) that the new babe is set apart from the average human condition by his miraculous beauty, and (b) that his mother consults the prophetic seer Tiresias about his future. These

---

* In the following pages, I have used this term to designate the individual's true personal individuality—his own particular uniqueness—and have contrasted this with the *collective* self or *false* self which is only a feigned individuality. The true self might be thought of as an affiliate in material reality of what Jung meant by the Self (which I have capitalized in the following pages) and emerges whenever the ego-Self axis in constallated.

facts alone are enough to inform us that we are dealing here—on a psychological level—with some aspect of the individuation process. For example, these twein themes are roughly parallel to the dramatic origins of Oedipus, who is also born of "royal" blood and whose tragic fate is both predicted by the oracle and finally revealed to him by none other than the old seer Tiresias himself. There are other parallels between the two myths, most notably in the cataclysmic insight "I am the one!" that breaks the illusory worlds of both figures, and leads to the fragmentation of the collective self (blindness and death). Thus both myths are essentially about self-knowledge that comes through a process of seeing through the seductive surface appearances of things, and the tragic consequences of this event seems in both cases to be the inevitable result of an over-inflated self-image. As spokesman for this destiny, Tiresias stands for the inner "voice" of the self. Blind to the things of this world, Tiresias "sees through" into the subjective core. (In the Odyssey, for example, only he can see in the underworld.)

The importance of Tiresias to our story is underscored by the fact that within the overall structure of the Metamorphoses Ovid's tale of Narcissus is the first of several stories designed to demonstrate the prescience and wisdom of the old sage. In each case, Tiresias' presence stands as a warning against crossing the boundary between the human and the divine, between the personal and the archetypal. In each case, he stands for human servitude and humility, and against aping the gods—whether through beauty (Narcissus), through seductive chatter (Echo), through audacity (Actaeon) or arrogance (Pentheus). Somehow Tiresias, on the one hand, and the arrogant, appearance-bound (collective) Narcissus on the other are tied together mythologically as two sides of the developing self.

If we inquire into the etymological origins of Narcissus' name, we discover that it derives from the Greek _narke_ 'stupefaction, numbness or torpor'—the same root from which we get "narcotic." In the myth we see this illustrated in first Echo's, then Narcissus', stuporous enchantment—a trance-state that leads in both cases to "death" and transformation. In the psychoanalytic transference, we observe this state in the treatment of narcissistic personalities, where the patient forms an especially intense, idealizing, and almost addictive attachment to the therapist and attempts to merge with him as a "twin."* During this stage of the narcissistic transference, the therapist is not experienced as a separate person, but rather exists in the patient's world as a "transitional"[6] figure occupying a magical place between reality and fantasy (like

---

* Most of our information on the peculiarities of the narcissistic transferences derives from the work of Heinz Kohut, who has distinguished a two-faceted transference constellation alternating between the "mirror transference" and the "idealizing" or "twinship" transference. Cf. especially Heinz Kohut, The Analysis of the Self. (New York, International Universities Press, 1971).

Narcissus' image in the pool) and performing the crucial function in Martin Buber's terminology, of "making the patient real."[7] As such, the therapist is cast in the role of Hermes, both human and divine, real and not real, "other" and yet also "self." Standing at the boundary of existence, he embodies for the patient certain crucial psychological functions (such as self-mirroring and the regulation of self-esteem) which are not yet internalized but are slowly, through continued and dependable contact, becoming introjected.

The peculiarites of such transference "amalgams" in which the therapist's psyche actually serves as an auxiliary self for the patient, together with the unusual countertransference problems they present for therapists, are among the major topics in the wider psychoanalytic discussion of narcissism, and need not concern us here. What I do wish to emphasize, however, is that if we are to conceptualize this peculiar form of narcissistic relatedness theoretically from a Jungian perspective, we are obliged to realize that the narcissist's self is not yet an internal reality but is to be found in two places—that it is, in other words, a "bi-polar" self, residing partially within, and partiallly outside in the "other." In this condition, the patient's whole sense of identity—his whole self-image—is suspended in the "bi-personal field."[8] It is not quite correct to say, therefore, that the image of the Self or *Imago Dei* is *projected* during this phase. The central image of wholeness is neither "in" the doctor, nor "in" the patient's unconscious, but is "alive"—so to speak—only in their *meeting*, i. e., in this "between" which they live together. The ego-Self axis is not yet an internal reality but is constellated between "me" and "You."* Jung gave beautiful expression to this preliminary bi-personal constellation of wholeness when he said:

> Thus the underlying idea of the psyche proves it to be a half bodily, half spiritual substance, an *anima media natura,* as the alchemists call it, an hermaphroditic being capable of uniting the opposites, but who is never complete in the individual unless related to another individual. The unrelated human being lacks wholeness, for he can achieve wholeness only through the soul, and the soul cannot exist without its other side, which is always found in a "You." Wholeness is a combination of I and You, and these show themselves to be parts of a transcendent unity whose nature can only be grasped symbolically, as in the symbols of the *rotundum,* the rose, the wheel, or the *coniunctio Solis et Lunae.*"[9]

---

* Topographically speaking, this intermediate space is the "location" of the unconscious; hence dreams during this stage in the transference are almost always sparked by incidents or events in the bi-personal field. This is what Jung must have meant when, in response to a letter from James Kirsch whose patient seemed always to be dreaming about her analyst, Jung said: "With regard to your patient, it is quite correct that her dreams are occasioned by you. . . . In the deepest sense we all dream not *out of ourselves* but out of what lies *between us and the other.*" Jung. *Letters:* Vol. I, trans. by R. F. C. Hull (Princeton, N. J., Princeton University Press, 1973) p. 172.

Perhaps the most exciting discovery in the recent literature on narcissism, and especially highlighted by the work of Heinz Kohut and the Chicago group, is the clinical fact that if this preliminary narcissistic transference is successfully constellated and allowed to exist over time without unduly intrusive interpretation, etc., a quite miraculous process of internalization takes place. This process might be likened to the gradual growth of a crystal (the core of the patient's individuality) within a super-saturated chemical solution (the transference amalgam). Thus the transformation of narcissism within the psychoanalytic paradigm affords us a unique opportunity to examine the actual processes through which the idealizing energies suspended in the bipersonal field of the transference are transmuted into psyche and become incarnate in the individual as a coherent interior self and corresponding self-image. These processes, we are beginning to understand, occur at the interface, between the develping child and his mother—between the patient and his analyst—between the lover and his beloved. Just as the increasingly microscopic study of the synapses between neurons in the central nervous system is now enhancing our understanding of brain function, so—I believe—examination of processes which occur in what Winnicott has described as the transitional area may hold the key to a deeper understanding of the actual formation of psychic structure, i. e., to the development and differentiation of an internal world, and particularly to the development and differentiation *in* that internal world of that "core" of selfhood that Jungian theorists have identified as the ego-Self axis. In the nascent personality this is not a "given" but a potentiality that must first be constellated with another person (prototypically the parent) before it ever "migrates"[10] home to roost. Individuation, in other words, before it is an internal process is first of all a bipersonal event. A psychological theory that assumes interiority prematurely cannot adequately encompass the *processes* through which interiority comes about.

The myth tells us that the chief "agent" for Narcissus' tranceinduction is *beauty* itself. Narcissus is described as strikingly *beautiful*—even in the cradle. The sight of this beauty, reflected back, locks him into a kind of benumbed enchantment, holding him long enough in an "interpersonal" spell for a transformation to occur. This involves "seeing through" the attractive surface appearances and ultimately "falling through" the illusory reality into the underworld, i. e., the world where the souls dwell. Thus we have the well-known mythological motif of *beauty* arresting the normal habitual flow of libido long enough to plunge the hapless hero into the nightmare of his own interior and hence into his own individuation process. So ubiquitous is this mythological theme, that we are tempted to conclude that it describes somthing fundamental about the *process of psychic internalization,* i. e., the processes by which psyche itself is transmuted from the "illusory" interpersonal space and takes up residence as internal structure. Actaeon stops to look at the beautiful Artemis and is *devoured* by his own dogs; Little Red Riding Hood stops to pick some flowers and is *swallowed* by the wolf; Persephone, enchanted by the beautiful narcissus flower, is *dragged into* the underworld by Hades. In each case the movement is first *outward*, drawn by a reflected reality full of beauty, then back *inside* (swallowed, engulfed, dragged into). In each case, the return is experienced as a disaster for the collective self which functions only in the outer image realm.

Clinically, narcissism is often found to be the particular psychopathology of individuals who are especially beautiful and/or gifted. Frequently, this results from a family milieu where the parents themselves are narcissistically deprived and who therefore neglect the child's spontaneous *being* while favoring the "good looks" or special "talents" the child displays as their genetic extension. As this happens over time, the child rapidly comes to exchange his deeper needs for *response* (and the selfesteem that comes along with being responded to) for the fragmentary recognition and "prestige" granted him in the areas where he pleases his parents and—as their extension—brings applause and recognition to them. This pattern forms the foundation for an entire collective or false-self system. The child's awareness is prematurely led away from the playful transitional space between fantasy and reality into *external* reality where, among the appearances of things, it functions in a pathologically extraverted fashion, reacting instead of responding, hearing instead of listening, seeing instead of perceiving.

These factors set the stage for a common crisis in the narcissistic personality around the midpoint of life. Until about the age of forty, narcissistic individuals—especially if they are wealthy, famous, attractive, or brilliant enough to maintain the illusion of perfection around them—can continue in the stage of "enchantment" and archetypal grandeur. But at the midpoint of life, things begin to break down. A man begins to realize he has not become as wealthy, famous, or remained as attractive as he thought. A woman begins to see wrinkles, and has to face the fact that her childbearing years have run out. The narcotic begins to wear off. Panic may set in, and with it a desperate effort to arrest the body's natural aging through cosmetic procedures, plastic surgery, and compulsive 'physical culture.' Like Narcissus in Part III of the myth, the narcissist looks into a darkening mirror and cries to the receding image "it cannot be my looks or my years which you shun, for I am the one the nymphs have loved!"

An excellent literary example of the narcissist's obsession with beauty and its psychological consequences in the crisis of mid-life is Oscar Wilde's novel *The Picture of Dorian Gray.* Like Narcissus', Dorian's youthful appearance is exquisitely beautiful, divinely perfect—the "visible incarnation of that unseen ideal whose memory haunts us."[11] Everyone falls breathlessly in love with Dorian, including a young artist Basil, who paints his portrait. In a moment of monstrous pride, Dorian prays that this portrait should carry the burden of his aging and allow him to preserve the innocence of his eternal youth. And so it is! Dorian remains lovely and fair—a collective ideal—while slowly his real (subjective) and darker characteristics emerge in progressive corruption in the portrait—hidden now behind a screen and unveiled only in secret isolation, horror, and dread. Then, in the final denouement, Dorian, like Narcissus, falls through the mirror:

> The curiously carved mirror that Lord Henry had given to him, so many years ago now, was standing on the table. . . . He took it up, as he had done on that night of horror, when he had first noted the change in the fatal picture, and with wild tear-dimmed eyes looked into its polished shield. Once, someone who had terribly loved him, had written to him a mad letter, ending with these idolatrous words: "The world is changed because you are made of ivory and gold. The curves of your lips rewrite history." The phrases came back to his memory, and he repeated them over and over to himself. Then he loathed his beauty, and flinging the mirror on the floor crushed it into silver splinters beneath his heel.[12]

At this moment, Dorian must look face to face at his real self . . . now hideously deformed. He lights a lamp and creeps upstairs to the portrait. Horror-stricken, he decides to destroy the loathsome split-off alter-ego that now taunts him with his past, and plunges a knife into it:

> There was a cry heard, and a crash. The cry was so horrible in its agony that the frightened servants woke, and crept out of their rooms. When they entered, they found hanging upon the wall a splendid portrait of their master as they had last seen him, in all the wonder of his exquisite youth and beauty. Lying on the floor was a dead man, in evening dress, with a knife in his heart. He was withered, wrinkled, and loathsome of visage. It was not till they had examined the rings that they recognized who it was.[13]

The crisis of narcissistic relatedness need not be as horrifying or dramatic as that of Dorian Gray. Such "moments" occur in many different forms in each individual's life, especially at times when the collective self and its habitual patterns of functioning begin to break down or be "seen through." Frequently, such crisis in identity, when the "mirror has broken," lead the individual into psychotherapy.

Part II: Excessive fortune followed by
Suffering and divine intervention

The central theme of Part II is Narcissus' unyielding pride and total inacessibility to those who care for him. This causes great suffering and lamentation among his suitors, particularly the hapless Echo, until finally one of the scorned successfully appeals to Nemesis (the god of divine retribution) and Narcissus gets a taste of his own medicine.

It is to Ovid's great credit and psychological sensitivity that he includes the Echo episode in the tale of Narcissus. Through this device we are given a glimpse of the peculiar frustrations of "love" viewed from the side of the narcissist's *lover*. In addition, a feminine component is added to the story as the 'other side' of masculine narcissism, i. e., the *puella* side of the *puer* problem. The first thing Ovid tells us about Echo is that she can only repeat the last words of semeone else's speech—in other words, she is totally *reactive*. This has come about because often Echo (when she still had her full voice) would detain the goddess Juno with endless chatter so that her fellow nymphs, lying with Jupiter on the mountainside, could flee. Juno, in her wrath, "curtailed the powers of the tongue that tricked her" and left Echo with only the "briefest possible use of her voice." These details of the narrative identify Echo as the "father's daughter." She is in seccret collusion with the Father-god against his jealous wife, but the price she pays for Jupiter's favor is high . . . she pays with the loss of her own soul (her voice).

We have here a glimpse into psychological origins of feminine narcissism in the father complex of the young girl. In particular the myth tells us (and clinical experience confirms) that where there is a missing soul-connection between father and mother (Juno and Jupiter), the daughter will be drawn into a mediational role in a triangular alliance-structure, serving as an affect-bridge between both parents—thus supplying the father with a feminine substitute for his own missing anima-life, and at the same time providing a mouthpiece or channel for the mother's *unexpressed* desire for connection to her husband and to life. As mediational "bridge" in the undifferentiated atmosphere of such a family environment, the daughter never develops her own *inner* differentiation and autonomy, i. e., her own soul. As "anima" of the family system, she never *herself* becomes animated or ensouled.*

In the family backgrounds of narcisistic personalities we find many variations of this pattern where the child is not "seen" in his or her own spon-

---

* Another contemporary mythic figure who embodies this soul-less-ness is the now-popular figure of Dracula. The fact that Dracula hmself has no soul and must feed off of other's blood goes together with the fact that, in a mirror, he leaves no image. On a psychological level he is a perfect representation for the narcissistic personality, i. e., the self without any autonomous animation or subjectivity (no self-image) who comes to life only as a reflected image for someone else. We might imagine that the surge of interest in Dracula in the various theatrical and cinematic productions of late reveals our continuing preoccupation with the problems of narcissism.

taneous expressiveness but rather serves a particular function within the psychic "economy" of the family system, for example, as mother's darling or father's "twin." This is especially true where there is a great deal of unlived life in one or another parent. Under these conditions, the child's frequently endless need for attention (like Echo's constant chatter) may arouse an envious or wrathful response (like Juno's). Or, the parent will simply ignore the independent needs of the child and respond adoringly to those special abilities, talents or endearing set of attributes with which he/she can *identify* and perhaps obtain vicariously, through the child, the needed appreciative mirroring from others. It very often happens that the "audience" from whom appreciation is wanted is the spouse, as for example, in the case of a father who appropriates his son's endearing qualities and "shows him off" to his own wife from whom he feels otherwise estranged. Or, the audience may be the grandfather or grandmother from whom the narcissistically deprived parent may be able to evoke the appreciative "gleam in the parents' eye" that was never seen in response to his or her own personal accomplishments but now appears as a ready mirror for "my son" or "my daughter." Sometimes it is the very expressive lovingness of the child which is appropriated. Andras Angyal has made a vital contribution to our understanding of the personality by reminding us that among the spontaneous capacities of normal children is a deep capacity for loving.[14] Children who have not experienced what Winnicott calls "good enough" mothering have to be carefully taught not to love or not to love *totally*. Such total expressiveness may be gobbled up by the emotionally deprived parent so that the child quickly realizes that his loving does not come back to him . . . it does not make an impact "out there" and return. It disappears. The parent cannot get enough. Or, what is often worse, the parent appropriates the very lovingness of the child itself as the earliest of the many "special" talents the parent eventually sees in the child. The parent calls attention to the child's loving gestures and asks others to watch. This is another way of taking the love away. Without knowing it, the child becomes aware that his very warmth and affection itself is made into something for the parent's aggrandizement. This is often the precursor to the superficial warmth and charm of the narcissistic individual so frequently noted in the literature.

Under these familial conditions, the normal narcissistic stage of spontaneous adoration of and merger with an idealized parent has not been adequately constellated, and the ego-Self axis, correspondingly, is not vitally polarized. This makes for a lack of psychic energy in general and means that the capacity for internalization itself is damaged. The child grows up too fast. He is a "little prince" or "princess" by the age of four or five. In response to the unconscious pressure of parental expections, his collective pseudo-self becomes hyperdeveloped and alongside in there exists—split off from his conscious awareness—another self, i. e. , the enfeebled subjective internal self—the true self which has gone into hiding and remains permanently hungry for the transitional object.*

The myth gives us an appropriate image of the narcissist's hidden injured inner self in the figure of Echo. We are told that after Echo has been painfully rejected, she hides herself away in the woods, covering her shamed face among the leaves, until gradually, consumed by her own anxious longing, her body wastes away, leaving only her voice. Even her bones are turned to stone. As far as we can tell, Narcissus never thinks twice about her, so apparently afraid is he of the humiliation his ideal image might suffer by contact with her. Such is the duplicitous (split) psychology of the narcissist. On the one hand, the despairing inner self, devoid of vitality and suffering from a lack of connection to reality and to life, maintains a secret but desperate search for admired others to whom he can attach himself (for example, an analyst) in order to relive the missing stage in childhood. On the other hand, the collective self, puffed up, inscrutable and "perfect" pretends to be the ideal and altogether admirable personage the inner self desperately longs to idealize. While he is thus apparently complete in himself—both perfect parent and injured child*— master and disciple—all in one, the narcissist nevertheless is split off from his other half and without a conscious relationship to the true self, the collective

---

* It should be noted in this connection that Guntrip[15] and Laing[16] have described this extreme as the schizoid condition, where the true self has retreated, become encased, and lost its connection to reality; in other words, become pathologically introverted. The narcissistic personality, on the other hand, has not lost contact with the world, but maintains a *falsified* contact with it, especially in the particular area of his idealized self-image. His hunger for approval and recognition in the areas of his special attributes or talents becomes insatiable (substituting for his deeper cravings) and this keeps him *pathologically extraverted.*

* Ferenczi gives the following dramatic description of these two: "A surprising but apparently generally valid fact in the process of selfsplitting is the sudden change of the object relation that has become intolerable, into narcissism. The man abandoned by all gods escapes completely from reality and creates for himself another world in which he, unimpeded by earthly gravity, can achieve everything that he wants. Has he been unloved, even tormented, he now splits off from himself a part which in the form of a helpful, loving, often motherly, minder commisserates with the tormented remainder of the self, nurses him and decides for him; and all this is done with deepest wisdom and most penetrating intelligence. He is intelligence and kindness itself, so to speak, a guardian angel. This angel sees the suffering or murdered chilf from the outside, he wanders through the whole universe seeking help, invents phantasies for the child that cannnot be saved in any other way etc. But in the moment of a very strong, repeated trauma even this guardian angel must confess his own helplessness and well meaning deceptive swindles to the tortured child and then nothing else remains but suicide, unless at the last moment some favourable change in the reality occurs. Ferenczi, Sandor. *Notes & Fragments; Int. Inl. Psychoanalysis,* XXX (1949), 234.

self is totally cut off from its own nourishment—hence this other half must be found "out there."

The split between the personal-true self on the inside and the collective-false self on the outside explains why these patients frequently feel that they have lived their whole life but never really existed. At the core of their personalities is a deep sense of loneliness which is not touched by most interactions with others—or if so, only indirectly. This core of loneliness—which these patients often cannot admit even to themselves—represents the aching desire of the true self for incarnation and embodied life as an "ego" in this world. Effective psychotherapy with these patients is a painstaking process of creating an intermediary (transitional) space for this nuclear self to enter the relationship with the therapist. The patient *resists* this process because he himself is highly ambivalent about this "weak" or "pathetic" part of himself and associates its emergence with the *humiliation* of his ideal self-image. Moreover, the patient brings to the analysis a full armamentarium of intricate and subtle transactional "techniques" with which his collective self has entered into identity-providing collusions and alliances in the undifferentiated atmosphere of his family of origin. All his charm, and even his genuine talents, may go into an unconscious effort to re-create in the therapy the same approval-gaining alliances or self-esteem assuring emotional fusions which "worked" in the previous system.

In a recent case which illustrates this point, I suddenly became aware in a session of how helpless and lonely I felt underneath the apparently engaging surface discussion of a patient's dream. Nothing I said made an impact or seemed to really matter to the patient. Reflecting on this out loud with the patient, I asked him if he ever felt lonely in his hours with me. At this point he filled up with tears and himself suddenly became aware that indeed he *was* often lonely in relation to me—and elsewhere in his life too. This led to some intimate revelations about his interior life and opened the way for a direct communication with his true self. The next session he brought a dream that I had moved into the apartment right across the hall from his in the apartment building of his childhood. This had been a very lonely place for him, and he was glad to have a neighbor.

Being without her own voice (and hence without a soul) poor Echo can only communicate by throwing back other people's words, i. e., by reflecting the sound she hears. This makes her a perfect auditory mirror for everyone—including Narcissus. In this way, the Echo episode serves as an auditory version of the later visual reflection episode of Part III. The parallel between Echo's auditory mirroring functions and the later visual mirroring is suggested by the words Ovid employs for echo *(imago vocis)* and for Narcissus' later reflected image *(imago formae)*. In both cases, the reflected "imagos" create for Narcissus a deceptive *illusion of otherness*. In the former case, Narcissus is "deceived by what he took to be another's voice" (alternae deceptus imagine vocis) and in the latter episode, he mistakes the beautiful reflection he sees for a real body *(visae correptus imagine formae spem sine corpore amat.)*. As we shall see, Narcissus prefers the *illusion* of otherness to otherness itself. This becomes obvious for the first time in the Echo episode. It is confirmed later in Part IV. For now, let us look at Narcissus' first experience of otherness and how he handles it.

Ovid tells us that Echo falls in love with Narcissus and then secretly follows him around waiting for sounds that she might re-echo with her own voice.

> The boy, by chance, had wandered away from his faithful band of comrades, and he called out: "Is there anybody here?" Echo answered: "Here!" Narcissus stood still in astonishment, looking round in every direction, and cried at the pitch of his voice: "Come!" As he called, she called in reply. He looked behind him, and when no one appeared, cried again: "Why are you avoiding me?" But all he heard were his own words echoed back. Still he persisted, deceived by what he took to be another's voice, and said, "Come here, and let us meet!" Echo answered: "Let us meet!" Never again would she reply more willingly to any sound. To make good her words she came out of the wood and made to throw her arms round the neck she loved: but he fled from her, crying as he did so. "Away with these embraces! I would die before I would have you touch me!" Her only answer was: "I would have you touch me!"[17]

In this charmingly evocative dialogue between Echo and Narcissus we observe a process that is typical of narcissistic relatedness. In the early part of their exchange, Narcissus gets a perfect reflection of himself *(imago vocis)* from the auditory mirror she provides. His own words come back unaltered. This perfect empathy enchants him. Yet he seems to want more. Just as in the later Part III over the pool, he asks "Why are you avoiding me? . . . Come here and let us meet!" Taking him at his word, Echo presents herself. This is her first and only subjective act in the entire dialogue—expressing initiative that resides in *her*, i. e., at this moment she breaks out of her mirror-role and presents herself as *other*. But at this point things go sour!

The narcissist's quick change from apparent interest in the "other"s and desire to have them make themselves "known," to ruthless rejection and cold withdrawal, is well documented in the clinical literature on narcissism. It is a common source of suffering and disillusionment (on both sides) among our patients, and it comes home to us especially poignantly in the narcissistic transferences. A typical form of it with which I am familiar goes more or less as follows.

After an initial period of therapeutic "enchantment," the patient begins to complain that the therapy is an "artificial relationship," that the analyst doesn't "really care" about the patient—otherwise why would he confine his attention to two hours a week—that the analyst never shares anything about his own life and thereby keeps the relationship "unequal," etc. The patient's unbridled and continual disappointment in the analytic relationship may begin to wear off on the analyst. He may begin to lose confidence in himself and to feel ineffectual—as though nothing he does is ever enough—and, if he himself has some of his selfesteem invested in being a "good" therapist, the patient's recurrent negativity may succeed in making him quite miserable. At this point perhaps, his guilt and anxiety will get the better of him, and—like Echo—he will cease to simply mirror the patient, and step out of the woods in some small gesture or self-revelation. At this point (in keeping with the myth) things are likely to go quite sour! Although the patient rarely *rejects* such a gesture with Narcissus' accustomed coldness (usually, in fact there is some temtorary symptom relief), nevertheless, the perceptive analyst will notice that the new reciprocity in the relationship does nothing to assuage the patient's complaint or the despair that accompanies them. In fact, to his chagrin, he may find that matters are only made worse by his supposed generosity. The patient is now suspicious (and rightly so) that the analyst himself needs a response. This not only shatters the idealized image of the analyst, but burdens the patient with too much responsibility in the situation and repeats an early collusive alliance with a narcissistically deprived parent. No longer is the patient captivated by the appreciative echo he gets from the idealized analyst; now he is asked to be a mirror for the analyst and offer some appreciation in return. And yet the analyst is asking for a fee! The patient now becomes additionally contemptuous and the cycle is perpetuated.*

The central problem faced by the therapist in this situation is in approximating the unique combination of intimacy-yet-distance that allows the patient the needed merger and identification on the one hand, while maintaining the necessary distance and separateness on the other. For this reason, it is no accident that the suffering of the narcissistic personality is so uniquely amenable to psychoanalytic treatment, where the required mixture of closeness and separateness is built into the relational framework *contractually*. Frequently, it is not until he gets into psychotherapy that the narcissist finds a true "other" and a relational container with sufficient "holding power" and continuity to contain his unconsciousness to a point where the necessary internalization and transformation can take place. In his outside life he usually gets "too close" and gets hurt, or, like Narcissus, gets involved only so long as his love-object maintains a titillating remoteness. In the former case, the usual pattern is an intense "crush" on the beloved followed by a brief period of idealizing love and self-object merger in which all boundaries of otherness are

---

* A typical factor in the development of this pattern is a high level of sexuality in the transference. The patient may, for example, invite sexual contact in an effort to gain total possession of and contact with the beloved analyst. This inevitably leads to a tragic outcome because (as above) the patient ends up with an entangled relationship instead of the mirrroring self-object who is so desperately needed if the true self is to emerge and consolidate.

penetrated and all secrets uncovered—followed by a loss of interest, boredom and perhaps another intense crush on someone else. The latter case occurs where the "transitional object" is not available enough for the needed merger—such as in the case of a narcissistic woman's crush on a married man. Under these circumstances, the relationship usually lasts longer, but is not more "therapeutically" helpful in resolving the narcissistic problem in relatedness. In this situation, the women frequently feels intensely alive, even "high" in the presence of her beloved, but alternately numb, bored, and empty when he is out of sight. She does not really suffer in his absence or "miss" him, as this would imply keeping his image alive internally and this is precisely what she cannot do psychologically. Sometimes, such a woman comes into psychotherapy complaining that she is involved in "self-destructive patterns" of dating men who are really not "available" to her. Viewed from the standpoint of the above dynamics, her lover's unavailability is not her *problem*, but rather her unconscious effort to *heal* her problem.

Part III: Passion and bliss in the context of illusion and enchantment

To return now to our story. We have seen how Narcissus' pride and self-inflation caused suffering in the human souls around him and how Nemesis, contacted through intercessory prayer by one of his scorned suitors, decreed that Narcissus would "fall in love with another" and "be unable to gain his loved one."

Part III of the narrative finds our hapless hero at a tranquil pool of clear spring-water, a place "with shining silvery waters, where shepherds had never made their way." Narcissus lies down there "attracted by the beauty of the place," and while seeking to quench his thirst, "another thirst" grows in him as he drinks. He falls in love with his own reflection, mistaking a mere image for a real body (*visae correptus imagine formae spem sine corpore amat*). For a correct understanding of this episode, and Ovid's mythologem as a whole, we must emphasize that—contrary to psychoanalytic assumptions—Narcissus has not here fallen in love with *himself*. As far as he knows, he has fallen in love with an "other." The fact that this "other" is not "real" is the whole point of the story the way we are interpreting it; i. e., the narcissist's only encounter with otherness is in an image realm where both self and other are mutually reflected realities vis-à-vis "each other."*

---

* Vinge emphasizes this in her book (cf. p. 12) pointing out that, Narcissus makes a double error (1) he doesn't realize that he only sees the reflection of a body, and (2) he doesn't realize that the body is his *own*. This last discovery is the culmination of the story and describes the transformation of narcissism (and Narcissus) into genuine subjectivity and relation to otherness.

Narcissus has now, in effect, changed places with Echo. This time it is *he* who gets consumed with longing in the face of his beloved's indifference and inaccessibility. In both cases, Ovid seems to emphasize the theme of suffering experienced in the process of wanting-and-not-having. The various metamorphoses in the story (Echo into a disembodied voice, Narcissus into a flower) occur out of this tension. It is as though Ovid were drawing our attention to the issue of frustrated or possessive desirousness and saying "this is the stuff of transformation."

However, Echo's transformation is different from Narcissus'. The tension of her longing does not lead "through the looking glass" to another level of awareness. Both she and Narcissus are portrayed as essentially empty and soulless. But her transformation in the self-object dyad is regressive, whereas Narcissus breaks through to the traumatic discovery of his own subjectivity, i.e., he comes to "know himself" and this means a death of his merely reactive existence, i.e., of his collective self.

Before proceeding further, we must inquire into the meaning of Nemesis' appearance in the story, for after all, it is *she* who causes Narcissus to fall in love with what he mistakes to be "another." Nemesis plays an important role in the Greek pantheon as a complement to the goddess Tyche or "Fortune." As Zeus' daughter, Tyche presides over the various fortunes of mortals, meting out gifts from her horn of plenty to some, depriving others of all that they have . . . but she is totally irresponsible in her awards (and hence is portrayed as a juggler, exemplifying the total randomness of chance). As her complement, Nemesis, daughter of Oceanus (the complement to Tyche's sky father) functions as a kind of moral control over the fortunes so indiscriminately dished out by Tyche. If, for example, Tyche should bless a man with great beauty or wealth, and that man did not—in return—pay homage to the gods, Nemesis would step in to humiliate him.[18]

Psychologically, then, Nemesis embodies the compensatory functions of the unconscious and, as such, serves the process of individuation. It is interesting, in this regard, that Nemesis seems to preside over the transition from the first to the second half of life (a period when, as we have noted, many narcissistic personality disturbances come to a head and appear in the therapist's office). She is pictured in the ancient iconography with an apple-branch in one hand and a wheel in the other, and her crown is adorned with the stags of Actaeon. Robert Graves points out that Nemesis' wheel was originally the solar year and that, in Latin, her name means literally "she who turns the year about." When the wheel had turned half circle, the sacred king, raised to the summit of his fortune, was fated to die—the Actaeon stags on her crown announce this—but when it came full circle, he revenged himself on her rival who had supplanted him."[19] Nemesis, then, is at the hub of the death and rebirth cycle. In the archaic iconography she is the nymph-goddess of "Death-In-Life." The apple-spray carried in her other hand was the slain king's passport to Elysium, i.e., a promise of immortality when duly killed by his successor. One might surmise that Nemesis' "sentence" of Narcissus carried with it the same promise. The appearance of the narcissus flower (associated with rebirth) at the moment when Narcissus himself (the fallen king) passes to Elysium certainly at least hints at a possible theophany.

As a divine figure who comes on the scene and interrupts the beautiful and fortunate hero in his mindless inflation—seducing him into an elusive love-relationship just long enough to transform him—Nemesis reminds us of Aphrodite's role in the individuation of Psyche and Aruru's role as goddess of creation in the heroic development of Gilgamesh. These parallels, which throw additional light on the meaning of the Narcissus myth and further support the interpretation we are giving it, will be explored at greater length in the final portion of this paper. For now, however, we must return to the poor Narcissus—on fire with desire for his own reflected image, attempting vainly to make contact with this "other."

As we have already mentioned, at this stage Narcissus is identical with his image. The image he sees is mistaken for "real." Narcissus' reflected image is called both "imago" (reflection) and "umbra" (shadow or soul).* Psychologically, then the "pre-fallen" Narcissus represents a stage of ego development when one's only "soul" is in one's reflection "out there," i.e., as one exists for the "other". James Frazer[20] has given us a wide-ranging anthropological description of this "primitive" stage with its attendant mirror-magic and fear that the soul might actually be stolen (by the spirits of the dead) if it were caught in a reflection. While Frazer incorrectly reduces the entire meaning of the Narcissus myth to this primitive fear,[21] he nevertheless correctly perceived that at this stage in the development of the self to lose one's mirror is tantamount to losing one's soul, because the self is identical with the self-image which only comes into being with a reflective surface "out there." The world of autonomous *self* and autonomous *other*, independent of "each-other"has not yet differentiated.

If we are to follow the line of reasoning that we explored earlier, this differentiation will take place (developmentally speaking) when Narcissus develops an *internal* mirror to replace (or supplement) the mirroring "other" out there upon whom—in his pre-fallen condition—he is wholly dependent for his sense of self and for his self-image. This will be the moment when he comes to "know himself," and will require that his internal world be divided up to contain simultaneously a "knowing subject" and a "known object." Clinical evidence leads us to believe that this inner doubling comes about in a *two-stage process* or double incarnation. First, there must be a mirroring self-object (mother, analyst who *accurately reflects the spontaneous gestures of the*

---

* Vinge reminds us that the words for shadow and reflection remain interchangeable for a long time and that they also stand for the "shadows" (souls) of the dead.

true self from "out there" and gives it an actual incarnation in life. (For the child this is experienced neither as "out there" nor as "in here" but is instead a paradoxical reality "between" self and other.) We might describe this as the "first birth" of the self. This first stage is embodied in Part III of the Narcissus myth.

Second, through a miraculous process which is still a mystery (and therefore mythology's most popular subject) these functions of accurate reflection of the true self, heretofore "carried" by the mother or analyst, gradually "migrate" into the personality from out of the transitional zone and set up residence "in here" as an inner mirror. This miraculous inner presence in whose image we are created and as subjective persons—this mysterious Being who comes to dream within us—is what Jung called the Self. Constellated first in the primordial transitional field that exists between child and parent or between patient and analyst, this core of individuality gradually and miraculously incarnates itself as an internal axis of energy within the individual's psychology. At this moment both self and world are born simultaneously. We might describe this as the *second birth* of the human self.* Looked at objectively, the first stage occurs in an illusory reality where image and reality are intermingled and mutually dependent, but this stage is nevertheless an essential preliminary to the second stage. The process describes a two-fold (systolic-diastolic) movement—from unconscious outer doubling to conscious inner doubling.

In stage one of this two-fold process, the mirroring functions of the child's parents and significant others are never perfectly empathic, i.e., perfectly in tune with the spontaneity of the true self. Hence, the child's true individuality is always more or less adequately reflected, more or less completely incarnated. In the *best* psychological environments, the true self emerges strong and forms a flexible and adaptive relationship with the collective self. In the *worst* psychological environments—those which form a breeding ground for narcissistic disturbances—very little, if any, of the true self gets echoed, and the collective self (now a false self) shakily takes over its functions.[22] With this there is an injury to the capacity for internalization itself. Narcissus' experience of self-recognition does not come about and there is a fixation at the "mirror" stage where image and reality are identical. At this stage, fragmentation of the self is an ever-present danger for there is no internal principle of coherence. The narcissist gets reflected and reflected and reflected, but the mirror never "swings inside" as it were, because (apparently) only the true self—made real in relationship over time—will "return" to its home. For the narcissist, everything stays *outside* in the veil of ten thousand things.

---

* In contemporary American culture we hear a good deal about "twice-born" Christians, and—theology aside—one wonders whether the psychology of this phenomenon might not be fruitfully examined as a function of contemporary narcissism and the complicated difficulties it poses for any genuine contact with otherness.

The subtleties of this two-stage process are given mythological expession not only in Parts III and IV of the Narcissus myth, but in various other traditions, for example, the Orphic legend about the "twice born" Dionysus, and the Egyptian legend of Osiris-Horus.

In the Orphic Theogony, Dionysus-Zagreus is the last in a series of six divine rulers of the world[23] and the one whose second birth commemorated the entry of mankind into creation (hence it is also a myth about the creation of the self). In his original form, Dionysus was the son of Zeus and Persephone, and even in infancy, he was trusted by Zeus with the rule of the world. However, the wicked Titans, urged on by Hera, devised a treacherous plan by which to destroy. They gave him many attractive gifts, among which was a mirror, and while he admired his own image in it, they fell upon him. He tried to escape them by repeatedly transfroming himself into different shapes, but finally, as a bull, he was caught and torn to pieces, then devoured. Only his heart was rescued by Athene. She brought it to Zeus, who swallowed it, and from his thigh there sprang the "new Dionysus" in whom Zagreus once more came to life. With the second birth of Dionysus, the existing period of human history begins and the great mythological events come to an end.

In this myth, the "first incarnation" of the self (Dionysus) is brought about by a "trick" in which the *mirror* plays a prominent role. I believe that the motif of a "trick" (of reflection) or a (mirror) "illusion" connected to the idea of *creation* is an expression of mythology's understanding that at this transitional stage in the two-fold birth of the self, there is indeed an enticing *confusion* between fantasy and reality, and a *necessary* one at that.* In fact, this is precisely the *nature* and *significance* of this stage, i.e., it is a magical level between fantasy and reality so that what the child "sees" in the mirror of the mother's eyes is *neither* the mother, nor a pure reflection of itself, but *both* self and other in paradoxical union—a union which makes possible (in the next stage) the transmuting internalization of the true self.

The illusion of beauty captures the attention of Dionysus (and Narcissus)

---

* A similar example is to be found in the ancient Shinto myth of the beautiful sun-goddess Amaterasu who (in the critical first period of the world) had retired to a cave, leaving the world in perpetual darkness. In great consternation, all the gods assembled and appointed the deity Thought-Includer to devise an enticing plan. Many beautiful things were brought and great fires were lit. As Amaterasu heard the uproar and looked out in amazement, an eight foot mirror tied to a tree, reflected her image. Astonished and enchanted, she gradually emerged from her cave to gaze upon it. As she did so, other gods stretched a rope (shimenawa) behind her with the instruction "Thou must not go back further than this!" Hence the sun recedes only a small distance into the night and is reborn every morning. Campbell, Joseph; *Hero With a Thousand Faces*. 210–11.

just long enough for a dismemberment to take place. This dismemberment corresponds to the passion and suffering which inevitably follows a complete identification of image and reality. During this transitional stage, the self is inevitably inflated with archetypal energy. Its fate is always "disillusionment". But this disillusionment is no ultimate catastrophe. It is simply the end of an initial stage in the dialectical development of the self—the final contraction, so to speak, in the systolic movement of stage one, and a preparation for the dramatic internal developments of stage two. Out of the reflected realities of stage one, something special—a special organ or essence, in this case the heart—"moves inside" (gets swallowed) and from this *internalization* the twice-born god-man emerges, and human history, i.e., the history of the authentic personal self, begins. The mirror has moved inside, and what was at first a reflected self, alive only in the transitional area between fantasy and reality, neither "I" nor "Thou"—is now also the *inner double*, the "swallowed one", the earth-bound *son* of God—no longer the God-man (who, as with Christ, is a *transitional* figure, i.e., the "way" to the Father)—but now the *man in relation to God*—as both outer and inner Other—the man who carries within himself a miracle he is at a loss to explain—a child of nature who now has all of nature in his own soul—who is both *self* and *other—paradoxical man.*

The dialectical movement of the Orphic Dionysus from first outer incarnation to dismemberment to inner re-incarnation (resurrection) is also a central motif in the Egyptian cult of Osiris-Horus. According to the Egyptian mythology, human history (the reign of the Pharaohs) begins with the establishment of the earthly monarchy under the kingship of Horus, Osiris'son. As the great ancestral father, Osiris is credited with the creation of Egyptian civilization, with the first sculpturing of divine images, with the production of wine, and the invention of ceremonial song. However, his sovereignty as the primordial "Good One" representing *order* is ended by Seth, the primordial "Evil One"representing *chaos* and fragmentation. Seth's treacherous plan to destroy Osiris is exactly parallel to the wicked Titan's plan to destroy Dionysus—and the result is also the same. Here also are the enticing gifts, the conspiratorial festivities, but instead of a mirror, Osiris gets trapped in a beautiful box or chest "made to the exact proportions of his body," i.e., a perfect likeness or image. In this coffin, he dies of suffocation and is thrown into the Nile. He is later dismembered by Seth after Isis recovers his body from Byblos, but before this happens, something of his essence is preserved by Isis. The magical begetting of Horus is described in this ancient hymn to Osiris:

> She [Isis] flew round over the earth uttering wailing cries of grief and she did not alight on the ground until she had found him. She made to rise up the members of him whose heart was at rest, she drew from him his essence, and she made therefrom an heir. She suckled the child in solitariness, and none knew where his place was, and he grew in strength.[24]

Horus thus represents the "heart" of Osiris . . . his essence. As such, it is only Horus who can restore life to Osiris. According to Plutarch's account of the story, Isis re-collected his *body*, but earlier passages in the native literature[25] make it clear that in the underworld Osiris was still fragmented, without his soul, and hence, a dead god. Horus revived his life for a second time and made him equal to all the gods by transferring his soul, i.e., his *Ka* or *double* to the dead god. Horus' soul was contained in his Eye, and the means by which he transferred his Eye to Osiris, and by which Osiris received it, is again parallel to the Orphic Dionysus legend. Osiris *eats* the Eye . . . *swallows* it and, as a result, comes to life again for the second time. At the moment the soul of Osiris is liberated and—as the twice-born god—he becomes ruler of the spirit-world, simultaneously the earthly reign of Horus begins. Now there are two worlds—a world of souls and an earthly world—an inner world and an outer.

If we are correct in our analysis, then both the Orphic Dionysus and the Egyptian Osiris-Horus represent the gradual transmuting establishment of the inner personal-true self, the indestructible, immortal soul of man that Jung called the Self. Both traditions describe this process as a two-stage movement. Stage one starts as the "great one" or the "beautiful one" or the "good one" is enticed by a perfect image of the self. This is the stage of empathic "meeting" where the nascent personality is "made real" in a transitional realm where image and reality are intermingled. On a psychological level, this stage of development is always "narcissistic" (normal narcissism) because both *self* and *other* are differentiated only as image-realities vis-a-vis a mirroring "other" and hence are extremely vulnerable to fragmentation or identity diffusion. In the myths, this dismemberment inevitably follows and constitutes the suffering and passion of the dying god-man. However, out of the disillusionment of this stage, an *essence or soul-substance* gets preserved and it is the fate of this substance to be *swallowed*, i.e., *internalized*, and *from inside* to become the second "double," the indestructible core of selfhood. The process moves like a pendulum out into the transitional realm (outer double)—then into the self as inner *Ka* or double. Both stages, like systole and diastole, are essential. The first describes the "imperfect" incarnation of the true self amidst the multiform personified incarnations of the collective self with its multifacted role-identifications; the second portrays its "homecoming"—its "incoming" and its enshrinement as *center* of the inner world.

Part IV: Disillusionment, Death, and Descent

In Part IV of the story we have the final denouement, and the ultimate "moment" of insight when both self and other are born in paradoxical union.

Tiresias' prophecy is fulfilled as Narcissus' illusion of "otherness" dissolves:

> Alas! I am myself the boy I see. I know it: my own reflection does not deceive me.
> (I know now my own image!) I am on fire with love for my own self. It is I who
> kindle the flames which I must endure. What should I do? Woo or be wooed? What
> I desire, I have. My very plenty makes me poor. How I wish I could separate myself
> from my body! A new prayer this, for a lover, to wish the thing he loves away![26]

In its essence, this is a paradoxical moment. It is the moment when Narcissus'
"object" turns into a "subject" also, and thus it is simultaneously the birth of
subjectivity and the death of narcissism. Narcissus heretofore has been able to
bend reality to his own pleasure. All "others" have been so enamoured of him
that they have been only too willing to conform totally to his expectations
and needs. . . only too willing to reflect him flatteringly, only too willing to
provide for him an echo of his own perceptions and his own energy. In this
world, Narcissus has come to see the "external world" and "others" in it, as
extensions of himself (self-objects) and, reciprocally, has come to see himself as
an extension of them. But this all ends when he discovers "someone" whom
he *wants* but *cannot have*—someone whom he does *not* control, someone
who is *not* available. What an irony, then, when the one he cannot have is he
himself!

The deeper wisdom embedded in this irony, however, is that with the experience of otherness, there is simultaneously born the inner "double,"i.e., the
conscious self-image. "I know now my own image!"Narcissus exclaims. The
mirror has been internalized and what was a unitary image-reality "outside" is
now a bi-nocular view of reality both inside and outside. Narcissus now finally sees himself seeing himself.

In order to untangle this paradox a bit, I would recall the reader's attention
to some reflections by Winnicott on the mirroring function that the mother's
face provides for the baby:

> What does the baby see when he or she looks at the mother's face? I am suggesting
> that, ordinarily, what the baby sees is himself or herself. In other words the mother
> is looking at the baby and *what she looks like is related to what she sees there.* All this
> is too easily taken for granted. . . I can make my point by going straight over to the
> case of the baby whose mother reflects her own mood or, worse still, the rigidity of
> her own defenses. In such a case what does the baby see?
>
> Of course nothing can be said about the single occasions on which a mother could
> not respond. Many babies, however, do have to have a long experience of not get-
> ting back what they are giving. They look and they do not see themselves. There are
> consequences. First, their own creative capacity begins to atrophy, and in some way
> or other they look around for other ways of getting something of themselves back
> from the environment. Second, the baby gets settled in to the idea that when he or
> she looks, what is seen is the mother's face. The mother's face is not then a mirror.

So perception takes the place of apperception, perception takes the place of that which might have been the beginning of a significant exchange with the world, a two-way process in which self-enrichment alternates with the discovery of meaning in the world of seen things. . . . A baby so treated will grow up puzzled about mirrors and what the mirror has to offer. If the mother's face is unresponsive, then a mirror is a thing to be looked at but not to be looked into.[27]

Winnicott's distinction between perception and apperception helps us to get at the change in Narcissus in Part IV. The word "perceive" means "to acquire knowledge through one of the senses" whereas "apperceive" means "to be conscious of perceiving" or "to comprehend by assimilating a new idea with the mass of concepts already in the mind." The idea is, then, that if the child does not see itself being seen by the mother, but only "sees" the mother, then its sense of itself does not develop simultaneously with its sense of an other. *Without an internal world, the external world substitutes for it, and this is why it is not experienced as other.*

Perhaps a homely example from my domestic life will illustrate the difference. While doing the dishes one evening, I asked my wife where the large soup-ladle should be hung in the kitchen. She told me to put it "where it had always been,"—next to the telephone. I remarked "Oh, I have never seen it there." Now of course I had "seen" it there. I had spoken for many hours on that telephone and "looked" at the soup-ladle many times, but I had not "seen" it. It was part of an unconscious imagefield and did not "exist" independent of my perception of it. (One might say that this was a "narcissistic" stage in my relationship to the soupladle.) However, this situation changed radically at the moment that I *experienced* myself seeing it. At that moment, perception gave way to apperception, and the soup-ladle became *other,* i. e., became an object to my subjectivity. This, in effect, is what happens to Narcissus. It suddenly dawns on him that reality exists independent of his perception of it, and that there is a subjective "inside" as well as an objective "outside." This presents him with a terrifying experience of depth which is also, paradoxically, full of meaning and possibility. He is no longer identical with how he appears, and others aren't either. But who, then, *is* he? A great fault opens up in the fabric of his world, and he falls into the hell of his own subjectivity.

Clinically, this "moment" is generally marked by a tremendous depression. The self feels suddenly very vulnerable, as thought it might be easily crushed by an implacable and indifferent reality. Previously, reality was not so frightening because it was "seen" as intimately connected to the self and the self's perceptions through the medium of unconscious fantasy. But when the miror breaks and imaginary realities evaporate, reality stands over against the self as the *ganze andere,* the wholly other. Whereas fantasy has previously been pressed into the service of defending *against* this otherness and annihilating the awareness of it, it must now test its dreams in the cold light of day and try to make something of them. More than anything else, this means giving *voice* to what is *inside* and making it real *between* self and other or between self and world *in relationship*. This is the work of creation itself—hence Narcissus' moment, with all its anxiety and dread, is nevertheless the birth of the creative soul, i. e., of the *Anima*.

In the previous analysis, we have outlined a four-part skeletal structure for the Narcissus mythologem consisting of:

1. Miraculous Birth and Prophecy
2. Excessive Fortune, Suffering, and Divine Intervention
3. Passion and Bliss in Illusion and Enchantment
4. Disillusionment, Death, and Descent (Realization of Paradox)

and have further suggested that Parts III and IV respectively express both the first and second stages in a two-fold process whereby the Self is constellated and gradually comes to function as an interior center for the personality. As a final illustrative example of how this structure may be applied to other mythologies which reflect the same psychological issues, I would like to briefly examine the Sumerian legend *Gilgamesh & Enkidu* through the "lens" provided by this skeletal breakdown. In doing so we find that some informative parallels emerge, and the particular approach that we have taken to the Narcissus myth and the interpretation we have given it are provided with some amplification.

In Part I of the *Gilgamesh Epic* the glorious Gilgamesh is described. Again, the hero's distinguishing mark is his beauty.

> When the gods created Gilgamesh they gave him a perfect body. Shamash the glorious sun endowd him with beauty. Adad the god of the storm endowed him with courage, the great gods made his beauty perfect, surpassing all others, terrifying like a great wild bull. (p. 61)

The glorious Gilgamesh, we are told, is two-thirds god and one-third man, but is is a human destiny that awaits him, a destiny of individuation. Enlil, the father of the gods, decrees:

> In nether-earth the darkness will show him a light: of mankind, all that are known, none will leave a monument for generations to come to compare with his. The heroes, the wise men, like the new moon have their waxing and waning. Men will say. "Who has ever ruled with might and with power like him? As in the dark month, the month of shadows, so without him there is no light. O Gilgamesh, you [will be] given the kingship, such [is] your destiny, everlasting life [is] not your destiny. (p. 118).

In part II of the narrative, Gilgamesh is abusing his powers and the men of Uruk mutter in their houses:

Gilgamesh sounds the tocsin for his amusement, his arrogance has no bounds by day or night. No son is left with his father, for Gilgamesh takes them all, even the children; yet the king should be a shepherd to his people, (p. 62)

Here we have a picture—parallel to the Narcissus myth—of the collective self, cut off from its own roots, run rampant with inflated energy and pride and without direction or meaning. The sounds of suffering and lamentation in Uruk reach the gods:

When Anu had heard their lamentation the gods cried to Aruru, the goddess of creation, "You made him. O Aruru, now create his equal; *let it be as like him as his own reflection, his second self,* stormy heart for stormy heart. Let them contend together and leave Uruk in quiet." (p. 62) [Italics mine]

As Nemesis with Narcissus, so here the prescription of the gods is that Gilgamesh should "fall in love" with his *second self,* a "double" *as like him as his own reflection.* Gilgamesh' double is named Enkidu, and he too is to be encountered "face to face" at the water hole . . . where the beasts come down to drink. He represents the first incarnation of Gilgamesh' true self. He is "innocent of mankind" and "knows nothing of the cultivated land." We meet here with the interesting theme that the true self undergoes a transformation as it confronts the "civilized" collective self. Enkidu must first be seduced out of his natural state. The prescription for this is "the woman's art," i. e., *love*—first as sexual passion, then as the arts of civilized living embodied in the "customs fo the land" until finally Enkidu is filled with longing for a comrade, for one who "would understand his heart."

When finally (Part III) Enkidu and Gilgamesh meet "face to face," the men of Uruk rejoice:

He is the spit of Gilgamesh . . . now Gilgamesh has met his match. This great one, this hero whose beauty is like a god, he is a match even for Gilgamesh. (p. 69)

Gilgamesh proclaims Enkidu brother, and loves him "as a woman." Now Gilgamesh, fortified by his double, becomes the Hero. With Enkidu as his guide, he defeats the evil Humbaba, spurns the seductive overtures of the wicked Ishtar, and kills the Bull of Heaven. This stage corresponds to the establishment of the nuclear ego as affiliate of the Self, and describes the enormous passion and vital energy that results from its dialectical connection with the collective self. All true mythological heroes are possessed of this bi-polar self. Edinger has made this point by placing the mythological hero *between* Self and ego and distinguishes him from the tragic hero.

Viewed psychologically, the mythological hero can be defined as a personification of the urge to individuation. He stands midway between the Self and the ego—less than

Self but more than ego. The tragic hero is more human that the mythological hero. He has no supernatural powers. He is a limited human being caught like Laocoön in the coils of a transpersonal destiny. He represents the ego gripped by the process of individuation.[29]

In the exploits of Gilgamesh and Enkidu then, and in the parallel passion of Narcissus with his "other," we have a glimpse of the original bi-polar self which—psychologically speaking—is to be located in that magical transitional space so important at the narcissistic stage of relatedness. This is a stage of perfect mirroring reciprocity . . . a stage of imaginal play between self and other, mother and child, lover and beloved, where one need not yet separate, where total empathy reigns over "insight," where self creates other and other creates self . . . a world where everything is both-and, not either-or . . . a world of total "as-if-ness," total vis-à-vis. Here the self is not yet its own hero, but self and "other" are hero together. We are the greatest—you and me, Daddy, or you and me, Mommy, or you and me, Doctor. The nuclear ego, as affiliate of the Self, is constellated, but the "axis" of this relationship is not yet internal. It is here and there, me and *you*.

It is a deep hunger for this empathic reflection—skipped over in childhood—that our narcissistically injured patients bring with them into therapy, and it is at this level (all our efforts toward conscious insight and "owning projections" to the contrary nowithstanding) that the mysterious processes of healing and transformation commemorated in myth unfold themselves. For this is, in every way, a mythological process, a reality of enchantment and illusion. It is the world of the archetypal hero, the "beautiful one" who, in dialogue with his newly discovered tutelary spirit or double, *lives* the illusion of his life fully enough, or honestly enough, or long enough until the miracle of interiority finally happens.* At this moment, the mirror breaks, the universal "We" becomes I and Thou; self is born along with other,

---

* This "moment" in the life of Jesus is beautifully described by Jung in a "Farewell Speech" given to the Analytical Psychology Club of New York on Oct. 26, 1937. In some informal remarks after dinner, Jung said:

...the utter failure came at the crucifixion in the tragic words "My God. My God, why has Thou forsaken me?" If you want to understand the full tragedy of those words you must realize that they meant that Christ saw that his whole life, sincerely devoted to the truth according to his best conviction, had really been a terrible illusion. He had lived his life absolutely devotedly to its full and had made his honest experiment, but . . . On the cross his mission deserted him. But because he had lived so fully and devotedly, he won through to the resurrection body.

We all must do just what Christ did. We must make our experiment. We must make mistakes. We must live out our own vision of life. When we live like this we know Christ as a brother and God indeed becomes man, i. e., God becomes man in ourselves.

and the mythological hero becomes the tragic hero, i. e., becomes man. At this moment Narcissus sees through his illusion, Oedipus realizes what he has done, and, in the *Epic of Gilgamesh,* Enkidu dies.

(Part IV) When Endiku dies, Gilgamesh becomes the wanderer. What he has discovered—his own disillusioning insight—is his own vulnerability, his own mortality—in short, his own humanity. "Because of my brother I am afraid of death," he says, "Despair is in my heart, and my face is the face of one who has made a long journey." But there is more than despair in Gilgamesh' heart. Now there is a deep longing for the secret of life itself—for the herb of immortality—for a sense of meaning that would make sense of his own suffering. Like Narcissus, Gilgamesh' arrogance dies hard. Still desperate for the marvelous plant that will restore his lost youth and win back all his former strength, he undertakes many ordeals and journeys. He becomes wise with stories and even succeeds momentarily in procuring the miraculous plant from the God-man Utnapishtim, but alas!, by a well of cool water (again, the place of transformation), a snake emerges from the depths, snatches it away, and vanishes.

Finally Gilgamesh accepts his destiny and returns with his secret and his story to Uruk where he resumes the kingship—a man among men. Now a figure of great wisdom and knowledge, he completes his self-creation, "engraves on a stone the whole story" and accepts his death.

Conclusion

If the above analysis is valid, then we are afforded a vivid impression of mythology's general preoccupation with the phenomenon of narcissism, especially as it represents (or at least seems to characterize) the first stage in a two-fold or double incarnation of an interior core of selfhood. I believe that Jungian theory has not sufficiently taken into account the importance of the first stage in this double movement for the very *formation* of an inner life, and by assuming interiority prematurely, has been led away from an adequate examination of the interpersonal processes—especially those available to us in the psychoanalytic transference—out of which an individuating personality eventually emerges. This introverted bias in Jungian theory is perhaps traceable to the Gnostic and Neoplatonic traditions which so heavily influenced Jung himself and so readily resonated with his own particular personality. In these traditions the notion is promulgated that the perfect ideal "Self" exists *a priori* in a transcendent form and then "falls" into matter (or the body) where it is corrupted until finally it gropes its way *back.* The emphasis is on the "remembering" of the original condition and on the movement back. I want to emphasize that there is no such "return" without first a movement "out into" relationship (the transitional stage) and that *this* is where we have an impact in psychotherapy. If this stage is negotiated properly, then the "return" happens of its own accord as a wonderful mystery. We don't have to work at it. If one wants to see the deepest—and therefore faintest—stars in the night sky, one must look slightly to the side.

1. *Diagnostic and Statistical Manual of Mental Disorders: DSM III* (The American Psychiatric Association, 1980), p. 317.
2. Christopher Lasch, *The Culture of Narcissism* (New York: W. W. Norton & Co., 1978), p. 235.
3. Ibid., p. 217.
4. As reported in *Newsweek*, Jan. 30, 1978, P. 70.
5. *The Metamorphoses of Ovid*, trans. by Mary M. Innes (Great Britain, Penguin Books, 1955). In addition to Ovid's account, there are various other classic versions of the Narcissus myth that come down to us from antiquity. These are all reviewed in Louise Vinge's excellent *The Narcissus Theme in Western European Literature* (Lund, 1967). Vinge points out that Ovid's version—in addition to being the most detailed account—is probably also the earliest, dating from around the time of the author's exile in 8. B. C.
6. Cf. "Transitional Objects and Transitional Phenomena," in D. W. Winnicott, *Playing and Relaity.* (New York, Basic Books, 1971), pp. 1—25
7. Martin Buber, *The Knowledge of Man*, trans. by M. Friedman and R. G. Smith, ed. by M. Friedman (New York, Harper & Row, 1965). Buber refers to this empathic process as "imagining the real" in the other and thereby making him present to himself.
8. I have taken this term from Robert Langs whose book *The Bipersonal Field* (New York. Jason Aronson. 1976) has been instrumental in my own thinking.
9. C. G. Jung, *The Practice of Psychotherapy*, CW 16, par. 454.
10. Erich Neumann uses this term in his description of the two-fold birth of the human child. According to Neumann, during the "post-uterine embryonic stage" the child's Self is (paradoxically) in two places, i. e. both "in" the child and "in" the mother. Gradually, the child's relatedness-Self, incarnated in the mother, must "migrate" into the child. When this happens, the child gains a "total Self" and the ego-Self axis makes its first appearance as an interior polarity within the child's psyche. Cf. Erich Neumann, *The Child*, trans. by Ralph Manheim (New York, Harper Colophon Books, 1973), p. 13 ff.
11. Oscar Wilde. *The Picture of Dorian Gray*, in *The Portable Oscar Wilde*, (New York, Viking Pess. 1946), p. 267.
12. Ibid., p. 387.
13. Ibid., p. 391.
14. Andras Angyal. *Neurosis and Treatment*, ed. by Eugenia Hanfmann and Richard M. Jones (New York, Viking Press. 1965). pp. 78 ff.
15. Harry J. S. Guntrip, *Psychoanalytic Theory, Therapy and the Self* (New York, Basic Books Inc., 1971), *Part II*.
16. R. D. Laing, *The Divided Self,* (New York, Penguin Books, 1965). Chapter 5.

17. Ibid., p. 84.
18. Robert Graves. *The Greek Myths* (New York, Penguin Books, 1955). pp. 125 ff.
19. Ibid., p. 126.
20. Sir James George Frazer. *The Golden Bough*, ch. xviii, part 3: "The Soul as a Shadow and a Reflection." pp. 220—225.
21. Ibid., p. 223.
22. John Perry provides us with a description of the "reconstitutive" processes that occur when finally the collective self in this condition collapses and the true self—now unprotected but available to reality—has a chance to be mirrored and come into being. Cf. John Perry, *Roots of Renewal in Myth and Madness*. (Jossey-Bass. 1976).
23. For an excellent discussion of the Orphics, see Erwin Rohde's scholarly book *Psyche: The Cult of Souls and Belief in Immortality Among the Greeks* (Books for Libraries Press. Freeport. N. Y. . 1920).
24. E. A. Wallis Budge, *Osiris & The Egyptian Resurrection* (Dover, 1973), Vol. 1. 94.
25. Cf. Budge, 82 ff.
26. Ibid., 86.
27. Ibid., 112—13.
28. All quotations are from *The Epic of Gilgamesh*, N. K. Sandars (Penguin Books, 1960).
29. E. F. Edinger, "The Tragic Hero: An Image of Individuation," Parabola, 1976, Vol. I, 66—73 (67).

(reprinted from Quadrant, Vol. 13, No. 2, Fall, 1980, by permission)

The effect of frequency of sessions on the analytic process

(Financial, practical, theoretical and clinical issues)

By Crittenden E. Brookes, M. D. (San Francisco)

The classical psychoanalysis of Freud and his more orthodox followers rather precisely defines a mode of therapy which includes, among other specific aspects of the analytic setting, a rule for frequency of sessions. Under this rule, analytic sessions should be held as often as six times per week, and in no event should be less frequent than four times a week. The rationale for this rule is equally precise, and its argument is generally well known. The argument is based upon the well-established clinical fact that a setting combining relational deprivation and high frequency of sessions produces an intense activation of elements of personal transference. Since the function of a classical Freudian analysis is to produce and isolate as pure a form of personal transference neurosis as possible, so that it may then be interpreted and analyzed, great frequency of sessions is not only warranted but mandated.

The efficacy of such a treatment method has long been questioned by less orthodox, neo-Freudian and other analysts. It is now widely accepted by many depth psychologists that an analysis of two or three times a week is optimal. Analytical psychologists have traditionally recommended a frequency of one or two times a week. Currently, Jungian analysts throughout the world see patients with wide degrees of frequency, ranging from one a week or less, to four or five times a week.

Meanwhile, practical and financial factors have developed which urge a re-examination of the question of frequency of sessions. Depth-psychological therapy has with some justification been attacked on the grounds of being "elitist," both because only a small number of individuals can afford frequent analytic sessions, and because highly-trained analysts who see their patients frequently can only work with a small number of patients during a professional lifetime. In addition, demands have been made for clinical justification of frequent treatment, and analysts have often been hard-pressed to demonstrate a correlation between increased frequency and increased efficacy of therapy. In recent years, both the development of third-party payment and the deepening of world recession have intensified these questions and concerns.

The purpose of this brief paper is to review the question of frequency of sessions in analytic treatment, with special reference to the current development of analytical psychology.

Although Jung did not outline his therapeutic method in any detail, it is quite clear that whereas the events of particular concern are intra-psychic, the method is interpersonal. For Jung, and for analytical psychologists, the process of individuation and the alleviation of blocks to individuation arise, during analysis, out of the psychological dialogue between analyst and analysand. Analytical psychologists deal, then, directly with Eros, the archetpe of relationship. This places the model of therapy in analytical psychology in apparent contradiction to the model of classical Freudian psychoanalysis. The Freudian method separates out the personal transference neurosis in order to work with it as an "objective phenomenon;" the Jungian method focuses on growth factors within the psyche, and seeks to activate them through dialogue and relationship. Personal regressive aspects of the patient's psychological functioning are consequently given less recognition and attention in the Jungian system, at least insofar as the therapeutic model is concerned.

For purposes of explication, we have just outlined two extreme positions. In point of clinical fact, analysts of the two schools, as well as depth psychologists of all gradations and persuasions, have been forced by the reality of the day-to-day working with patients to move to some compromise between the two points of view. No one who works as directly with the human condition and experience as do practicing depth psychologists, can fail to witness the power of personal conflict and defensive functioning; nor can he or she fail to note the fundamental drive toward meaning and relatedness. These factors exist in varying combinations from moment to moment and from individual to individual, and the therapist is constantly called upon to make choices as to whether to attend to progressive or regressive aspects of the dialogue with his or her client.

Recent developments, in both theoretical and historical arenas, have aided in bringing these two viewpoints closer together. In generic depth psychology and psychoanalysis, the advent of object relations theory as a common language for psychodynamics has begun to break down the traditional barriers among theoretical systems. A number of analytical psychologists have already noted the importance of this development in encouraging a *rapprochment* between Jungian thought and other depth psychologies. In addition, the amplification of recent concepts involving the so-called borderline and nacissistic disorders has been a great encouragment to the replacing of the old view (of analyst as detached and separate from the patient) with a dyadic and relational model. Traditionalists in psychoanalysis increasingly realize that in all probality, the patient with a pure transference neurosis and an absence of relational needs in the analytic setting does not exist. On the other hand, historical developments in the Jungian community involve recognition of the importance of ego defenses, regressive elements and the vicissitudes of transference and countertransference in the analytic transaction. British analytical psychologists have been particularly active in this area, and many British Jungians subscribe to a format for analytic work which bears considerable resemblance to classical Freudian psychoanalysis, including a frequency of four or five sessions a week. For another example, the San Francisco institute has more recently recognized the need to include in its curriculum a survey of the directly clinical applications of Jungian concepts, including the Jungian approach to both the classical and contemporary psychiatric syndromes, as well as borderline and narcissistic conditions. In addition, the San Francisco group includes a review of object-relations theory in its current curriculum.

As these events have occurred, contradictory arguments have converged on the question of frequency of analytic sessions. On the one hand, analytical psychologists are increasingly recognizing the need to meet the demand for more frequency of contact from analysands who are experiencing the regressive and defensive pull of personal transference elements, particularly during early and middle stages of analysis. On the other hand, Jungians still operate primarily from the dyadic and relational model of analysis rather than from the model of analyst neurality and impersonality. In this they have long since been joined by neo-Freudian and existential analysts, and more recently by a number of prominent analysts from more traditional Freudian viewpoints.

Meanwhile, the reality demands of the financial cost of analysis and the need to be helpful to more patients insist that analytic work be carried out with a maximum of efficiency and a minimum of frequency. Finally, the recognition of archetypal and colective transference elements, an almost exclusively Jungian contribution to psychodynamics and to the theory of analytic work, raises the question as to whether increased frequency is a help or a hindrance to the activation and maintenance of the archetypal transference, and the process of individuation during analysis. Central here is the issue of *dependency* versus *individuation.*

All of these historical and theoretical elements provide background and data for a discussion of the question of frequency of analytic sessions. Jung himself can only be relied upon indirectly for contribution to such a discussion, because he did not directly concern himself with the technical considerations of analysis, leaving others to fill in the gaps which his own focus of interest left behind. We do know that he considered the time *between* sesions at least as important, if not more important, than the sessions themselves, that he tended to rely as most therapists do on the presence of intense anxiety as an indication for greater frequency, that his interest was much more in archetypal than in personal elements of the transference, and that he frequently used the once or twice a week format, often referring his patients to others for greater depth in the personal aspects of the work.

In doing so, Jung could rely on the power of his own personality and reputation to induce archetypal elements of the transference, and he could very much afford to follow his own interests in dealing with his patients. He was also quite aware that the personality and other characteristics of each analyst provide a "hook on which to hang" specific aspects of the transference—so that different analysts induce differing aspects of the transference relationship, even in the same patient. This observation seems to have been lost on most of the proponents of the "impersonal" schools of depth analysis.

We can quite justifiably continue our discussions of this question with the dictum, derived from the demands of finance and efficiency, that the lowest possible frequency of sessions in a particular case is indicated, as long as the frequency selected is minimally sufficient to initiate, maintain and resolve the analytic process. Next, it is generally accepted by all psychotherapists that sessions must be set at least at the frequency to honor and contain the anxiety and dependency of the patient, not only to reduce acting out of psychological elements that should be reflected upon and contained within the analytic relationship, but also to enable the patient to experience a degree of security within that relationship necessary for analytic work. It also seems obvious that, considering the variables just outlined, frequency of sessions can be expected to vary during the course of analysis.

However, at this point in the discussion, we are confronted additionally by two apparently conflicting criteria for setting frequency. First, Jungian analysts are increasingly cognizant that, more often than not and particularly in younger patients, personal transference elements demand the attention of both analyst and patient early and often for some time during the analytic process—in fact, such elements often obscure collective issues until the personal regression has been worked through to some degree. The activation of such elements usually demands increased frequency, although it can be argued that only rarely is the need for containment of and attention to regression so great that a frequency of four or five times a week is required. Such a frequency is an invitation to gross dependency and regression, a dependency which could of course be somewhat ameliorated by a relational and reality-based approach to the patient. But when increased frequency is combined with an impersonal approach on the part of the analyst, a powerful and repetitive activation of childhood aspects of the transference occurs, an activation which may permanently obscure or exclude synthetic and progressive elements. Even with a purely personal transference neurosis, sole attention to regressive transference factors could negatively condition the analytic process and relationship through selective inattention to collective, progressive and synthetic factors.

This leads us to a second and contradictory criterion: It is not at all clear that increasing the frequency of sessions increases the projection of collective elements of the unconscious; in fact, the opposite may be the case: Relational deprivation and increases frequency may increase the personal transference at the expense of the archetypal transference; whereas moderate frequency and increase of the relational factor may focus on the archetypal transfeence at the expense of the personal transference. That is to say projection of personal elements is a substitute for relationship when relationship is absent, whereas the deeply collective drive for growth and individuation arises from the fact of relationship itself. Frequency begets dependency which is antithetical to the individuation drive.

The clinical experience of the present author certainly bears this out, and it is generally well recognized in analytical psychology that, once activation of deeper layers of the unconscious occurs during therapy, a self-perpetuating process occurs in which the analyst becomes a guide to the unconscious itself, a guide who is represented in dreams and fantasies even when relatively long periods elapse between sessions. This phenomenon may be the basis for Jung's observation that what goes on outside the sessions is at least as important as what goes on within them. The individuation path, the self-activation of the evolving aspect of the psyche, is self-perpetuating, and the image of the "guide" is utilized as a creative principle of the self. Once established, this internal dialogue with the "guide" needs only occasional reinforcement, whereas a predominantly personal transference, the re-activation of previous issues with significant figures from the personal history, requires rather constant attention and a "clear field" within the analytic relationship for projections to take place.

The activation of the archetypal transference is closely associated with the relational aspects of the analysis; the archetypal transference provides the underpinning for constellation of the relational aspect—the dyadic relationship or *temenos* from which the analytic "cure" proceeds. In this sense, collective elements are always present in the analysis, from the very beginning. The "cure" is the reactivation of the growth process of the psyche which was originally stunted, distorted or blocked by the selective experiences of early significant relationships.

In order for the curative process to take place, however, the personal repetition compulsions, e. g. stereotyped ways of reacting to specific situations, must be "separated out" in consciousness and rendered ego-alien. Consequently, analysis should be designed to encourage the activation and interpretation of elements of the personal transference, both to alleviate suffering and to clear the way for creative and meaningful elements of the psyche to express themselves.

The presence of criteria for the selection of frequency of sessions which stand in opposition to each other creates a paradoxical situation which itself finds meaning in the theoretical model provided by analytical psychology. For analytical psychologists, paradox, the intensity of the dialogue between opposites, produces the conditions necessary for transformation. At each moment during analytic work, the analyst is confronted by the necessity of assessing the progressive and regressive aspects of the situation. The relative importance of these opposite elements inevitably varies from moment to moment during analysis, although some generalizations can be made about early, middle and late stages of analysis, age of the patient, characterological and defensive elements, and so on. An assessment of such elements will be an important factor in determining and setting frequency of sessions, as well as many other aspects of the analytic setting. Thus one major criterion for such a determination is by its very nature a paradoxical one, and few if any generalizations can be made from it to the specific situation.

We are now in a position to briefly summarize the major criteria for determination of frequency of sessions in analytical psychology. Indeed, the criteria to follow may be said to be applicable to any depth therapy, except perhaps for one which still seeks to isolate the personal transference neurosis as a separate phenomenon so that it can be observed and manipulated—an approach which in the opinion of the present author (as well as many other authorities), although it may have some scientific value, has little or no value in the therapy of human suffering. To put it bluntly, it is the view of the present author that therapeutic change cannot take place without relationship. Therefore the criteria to be summarized are applicable to all therapies which utilize relationship as the central context of the therapeutic process.

Primary criteria for the setting of frequency of sessions in analysis include the following:

1. Financial and practical realities require the selection of frequency at the *minimum* necessary to initiate, maintain and resolve the analytic process.

2. Sessions should be set at a frequency necessary to contain the patient's manifestations of anxiety, and to provide the security necessary for analytic work. It is recognized that frequency might vary, under this criterion, during various phases of the analysis.

3. Frequency should be set at a level sufficient to maintain the quality of relatedness necessary for the work, but not so frequently that dependency *per se* is encouraged.

4. Sessions should be frequent enough to encourage and maintain elements of regression and of the personal neurosis, during phases of the analysis when such elements are the predominant order of business. However a close watch should be kept for activation of progressive elements of the Self in archetypal transference, so that when such factors become predominant, measures such as high frequency of sessions which would tend to perpetuate regressive dependency at the expense of progressive factors should be abandoned, so that emergence of the dynamics of individuation is not postponed.

5. A serious question is raised about whether, except under the most unusual cirmumstances, a frequency of more than three sessions per week is indicated. It is recognized, however, that in rare situations a higher frequency might be required to activate and maintain a focus on the personal transference, or to contain severe anxiety. At the other end of the scale, it is demonstrably possible to maintain an analytic process at a frequency of less than once a week.

The criteria outlined above must often, of course, be applied simultaneously. Such is the art of analysis, which after all is inevitably a subjective process. Above all, since we too are human, we must guard against acting out our own potential contempt for, fear of and consequent rejection of those who come to us for help, by either over-treating them or under-treating them. The resolution of this danger lies in our capacity to "make manifest" the archetype of relationship in our work.

The Donald Duck fascination

By Ingrid von Hänisch (Berlin)

There is an uneasy feeling somewhere deep down in my stomach at the thought of having to tell you about the Duck family.

This feeling tells me that I might be facing an audience of Duck fans who would send me to hell with my Duck analysis. In this case I will comfort myself with the thought of Donald who is used to misfortune. The Scrooge within me, however, feels at his best, confident, as he knows how to take advantage of any situation. Huey, Dewey and Louie, too, radiate optimism.

The Duck family is a creation of the inexhaustible inventiveness of the Walt Disney crew, initiated and led for many years by Walt Disney who was born in 1901 and died in 1964. He started his career with fairy-tale cartoon films followed by comics and comic books. His exceptional success is due to his rich fantasy and his belief in himself, as well as to his persistent diligence and strict discipline. Walt Disney is said to have been a perfectionist who sometimes thought an idea over for several years before putting it into practice. To him, money was of importance only as an aid in perfecting his creations.

To Scrooge, however, money is an end in itself. He has a good nose for gold and his business methods are not exactly clean. He takes people in whenever he can. He is a multi-billionaire and the richest and most powerful man in the Universe. Donald is nothing but his nephew, and the triplets Huey, Dewey and Louie are again nephews of Donald.

In the process of Walt Disney's creation, however, Donald was the first-born, 12 years before the appearance of Scrooge. Donald's career started in 1934 with a minor part in one of the Mickey Mouse films, which had already become famous. A year later he appeared in a film of his own. In 1947 the cartoonist Carl Barks invented Uncle Scrooge McDuck and the triplets Huey, Dewey and Louie for a successful series of comic books.

The Duck family live in Duckburg, the model of an American small town. Scrooge rules the Duckburg market and has built up a business network covering even the remotest parts of the world. After his strenuous work he relaxes in a bath of gold. "Oh, sweet, fresh, shining gold", he cheers, burrowing in his gold coins like a mole or letting them pelt on his head under the shower.

Each individual story follows the same underlying pattern: By some coincidence Scrooge gets wind of a good business deal. He calls for Donald who comes along with his three nephews and joins in. Usually Donald's stupidity gets them into a difficult situation and the children get them out again. Meanwhile, Scrooge acquires an even more profitable source of money.

Usually they undertake expeditions to foreign countries, and discover cities, treasures, or fertile land under water, species from other planets, monsters, or fabulous kingdoms. The people living there are depicted according to stereotyped clichés. They are either uncivilized, highly developed technically, or live in former times. But Scrooge is a man of today. He has Gyro Gearloose construct unbelievable technical devices, for instance a robot that can read thoughts and help him to cheat the big business bosses, or a bouncer machine that throws out burglars.

On the surface, these are present-day situations, mainly in the world of economy and finance. When asked what he liked so much about the Duck stories, a nine-year-old boy answered: ". . . this is not like a fairy-tale." Here it becomes evident how artfully the fabulous and mythical contents are disguised. I think that exactly these concealed fabulous features contribute essentially to the fascinating effect of the Duck stories. My goal here is to prove this hypothesis with the aid of analytical psychology.

The most obvious fact is that the protagonists of the stories are a family of ducks. The duck is connected with water and air as a diving and swimming bird, and thus symbolizes the connection of instinct and intellect as well as of the unconscious and consciousness. The best known duck in the world of fairy-tales is "The Ugly Duckling" by Hans Christian Andersen. It gives an account of the duckling having been hatched as the last of its siblings. It is bigger than the others and is therefore regarded as ugly and is rejected by its family and everybody else. It is bitten and kicked around until, one day, it runs away into an unknown world. But there it does not get on well either. Everywhere it encounters the same rejection. One day, it watches swans flying overhead and feels mysteriously attracted to these stange birds. During the following winter, the duckling has to suffer even more. But with spring the swans return and the duckling swims toward them even at the risk of being bitten to death. Underway, it discovers its own reflection in the water: it is no longer the Ugly Duckling but has matured into a magnificent swan who is received affectionately by the other swans.

In this tale, the Ugly Duckling is the outsider who attracts all negative projections. As a foreigner it is rejected and excluded from the community. In isolation it discovers its identity, changes—and in its new role it takes its place among its equals.

The Ugly Duckling may also be undersood as an inferior part of the personality which is integrated as a means of individuation, not without suffering and pain. Thus the symbol of the duck serves as a link between the unconscious and consciousness. At first the Ugly Duckling does not realize that it is no duckling at all. Its sensation function is underdeveloped and disturbs its relationship with itself and others. The opposite function, the intuition, attracts it to the swans and stimulates the use of its underdeveloped sensation function: looking at its reflection in the water, it realizes that it is a swan.

Is there an Ugly Duckling in Donald Duck's family which undergoes a similar development?

Let us first look at Scrooge. His literary precursor is Uncle Scrooge in Charles Dickens' tale "A Christmas Carol". This famous miser was haunted by spirits on Christmas Eve. Three spirits appeared in succession and reveal his past, present and future. They show him the way to happiness through human warmth and goodness or to its repression through the idolized worship of gold. Dickens' Scrooge is so deeply impressed by these visions that he turns into a charitable and cheerful person over night.

Walt Disney's Uncle Scrooge, on the other hand, has been forsaken by all good spirits. He cannot be converted. He persists in his indefatigable zest for activity with the sole intention of getting richer and richer. He is a fanatic saver and does not spend a penny on himself. "How could I have acquired all my wealth, if I had not renounced all unnecessary expense?", he declares, and on another occasion he reveals that he has never given way to his longing for an ice-cream or a cigarette.

Donald is dependent on his Uncle Scrooge. From time to time, he tries to resist, but he always has given in again. He is in a permanent financial squeeze as he has no regular job or income. Uncle Scrooge can always present a bill to make him render any service required.

While Scrooge, when angry, just becomes raving mad, Donald reacts to his defeats with auto-aggression: he jumps into the air, bangs his head against the wall, and drums his fists on the table. So Scrooge takes the obsessive-compulsive part and Donald the depressive one.

Huey, Dewey and Louie are structurally the least defined. They function quite clearly as one person: they always appear as a trio; they complete each other's sentences, or all say the same thing. Donald claims a parental role towards them although he often would have perished through his stupidity, shortsightedness, and naivety without the help of his nephews. The children realize where help is needed and rescue Donald from many embarrassing situations with their scouting experience. They would give him the shirts off their backs even though he steals their property secretly or sometimes even openly.

An Ugly Duckling does not seem to exist in the Duck family. Even though Donald is an unlucky fellow, and always hopes to be better or to receive some recognition, it would never dawn on him that he would have to change his character or anything else in his life. The Duck stories do not aim at change or development of character: Donald is always caught by the same nonsense; he never learns from his errors. There is no inner or outer change. Nowhere is there development. Nobody ages or matures—time stands peculiarly still—but within this stagnation there are all these adventures, dangers, hardships which are cleverly overcome. This may never stop, every week from issue to issue of the comic books in which they appear.

From the first to the last number the basic traits of character remain the same; none of them ever has the chance of becoming a swan althought this might be one of Donald's secret wishes. So in one way all of the Ducks resemble the Ugly Duckling—in the underdevelopment of their personalities. Scrooge is governed by his intuition, which gives him a special sense for gold and money; Donald follows his feeling; and the children solve all problems with their intellect. They all communicate by means of their auxiliary function, the emotion, with which they plunge into adventures. All three of the elementary figures are extremely extraverted: they are mainly orientated towards external objects and are easily terrified if encountered by something they do not understand. They are perfectly oblivious to their inner world. As each of them represents the inferior function of the other, they depend on each other to get along with the pitfalls of life.

On another level, a fourth element can be found, when the three elementary figures are taken together: if we add up Donald's cluminess, the children's sly intelligence, and Scrooge's instinctive activities, we get the Trickster figure.

The Trickster is characterized by his close relation to the unconscious starting his way into the consciousness. Therefore he is often depicted as an animal. The striking aspect of the Duck characters, however, is that apart from their animal body they live in the range of consciousness. The unconscious appears only as interference through error, affective crises, of fear. With this Trickster figure the unconscious secretly steals into the Duck stories through the back door which is probably the main reason for their great success. C. G. Jung writes about Trickster:[1] "The effect of the figure is based on its secret links with the psyche of the spectator, it even seems to be its reflection, which, however, is not identified for what it is." and he continues: "The Trickster is the collective shadow figure, the sum of all individual inferior character traits."

There is, for instance, the primitive but cunning and realistic intelligence of the Duck children. This is the opposite of our highly developed abstract thinking, which is only employed in scientific areas and has lost its ties to the person concerned. Then there is Donald's stupidity and undifferentiated emotionality which an average citizen of our culture could not afford and which only appears in jokes. And Scrooge, on his treasure hunts, follows his instincts, whereas nowadays, no enterprise is launched without pilot studies and prognoses.

Typical of the Trickster archetype are the following situations: Scrooge bargains with a company, which later on turns out to be part of his own empire already, or he spends five dimes on a newspaper for the first time in his life, and it is blown away by the wind shortly afterwards. Or Donald, having at last discovered a treasure of his own, throws the case of gold into the water, instead of the case of bills.

Some children told me in an interview what they liked best about the Duck stories: they are funny—they are witty—they try to outdo each other—because they are so sly.

There is still another link between Donald and Scrooge. As an illustration, I would like to give an account of the fairytale "The Two Wanderers" by Wilhelm and Jacob Grimm.

These two are a happy-go-lucky tailor and a mean and grumpy shoemaker. When the tailor asks the shoemaker for something to eat he has to pay with his eyes and is taken to the gallows where he is left behind on his own. There the tailor hears a hanged man say that the night dew has the power to give him back his eyes. So the tailor can wander again the next morning. On his way, he encounters several animals—among them a duck—which he actually would have liked to eat, but he curbs his hunger and lets it live. Then he serves the King as a tailor. Here he meets the shoemaker again who anticipates revenge and tells the King that the tailor claimed to be able to find the lost crown. Now the tailor must bring back the crown or leave the country. Sadly, the tailor sets out and again meets the duck which he had not eaten the time before. It dives to the bottom of a pond and comes back with the crown. All the other tasks which he has to fulfill as a consequence of the shoemaker's slander can only be completed with the help of the animals he had not eaten on his first journey. So at last he is given permission to marry the King's daughter. Finally, the shoemaker's eyes are pecked out and he is never seen again.

Are there any parallels between the two wanderers and Donald and Scrooge?

The tailor is the hero and winner and can be seen from an intrapsychic point of view as the ego where his opponent, the shoemaker, is the shadow.

In the beginning, the lively and superficial tailor has a weak ego not adjusted to reality. He does not even think of taking provisions with him on his journey. This makes him dependent on his shadow, the shoemaker, whose demands lead him to the brink of ruin. In this misfortune, the tailor becomes alert to his unconscious: something dead begins to speak. A so far undeveloped part of his personality awakens to life and, in this case, changes his view on reality.

The formerly irresponsible and superficial tailor now develops sensitivity, understanding of nature, and self-assurance toward his own instincts. Now he is invulnerable to the shoemaker's attacks which he can use as guides to his happiness—to the King's daughter. Here the duck serves as a bridge to the unconscious when it retrieves the crown from the water.

The starting point of the tale is similar to many Duck stories: At the beginning Donald often is in a squeeze—usually in a financial one—and asks Scrooge for help, who, just like the shoemaker, makes his aid subject to certain conditions. In the attempt to meet these demands, Donald usually gets into very difficult situations. But at this point, Huey, Dewey and Louie intervene and save him without he himself having to stir a finger. In the end, Scrooge manages to take advantage of Donald's squeeze. Thus the shadow wins over the ego. In contrast to the tailor Donald remains dependent on his shadow. None of the conflicts offer a chance of deposing Scrooge or of increasing Donald's ego. Nobody ever has to plan his own future. One lends his hand to the other without the overall situation or their relations being changed.

Donald's unconscious and therefore negative tendencies never hit Scrooge but always himself. And Scrooge is much too narcissistic to be really moved by Donald's misfortunes. He feels no sorrow for others but only for the loss of his money. As, for example, when in one of his short financial crises he bursts into tears and desperately cries out: "I have to stop losing a billion dollars every minute immediately! If it goes on like this I will be broke in 600 years!"

Apart from this splendid fantasy of immortality, it becomes obvious how much his emtional committment has been diverted from man to money. In a German Duck analysis of 1972, Scrooge's habit of bathing in money is considered a sexual perversion: "The touch of coined metal and bank-notes highly excites him until, with erected tail, he finally dives into it and comes to his fulfillment."[2]

Scrooge's sexual perversion is conspicuous even to Jungians. We, however, attribute a higher significance to his inability to establish social relationships; particularly as this can be seen in connection with the disintegrated, and therefore autonomous shadow. As long as the shadow is not integrated, the ego-consciousness can build up no relations with its inner picture of the soul, which, in a man, is identical with his anima. In our fairy-tale, the tailor's anima is personified in the King's daughter whom he marries after the struggle with the shadow.

All this is a far cry from the Ducks. Their relationships with women are minimal. The anima is contaminated by the shadow; that is, the anima has not yet found its proper form. As a matter of fact, the Ducks are not only without a father, but also without a mother, who is the first love object. Thus not only the oedipal conflict but also the struggle with the interior and exterior images of woman are avoided. The few female characters appearing in the Duck stories embody nothing but the collective clichés about woman, a mixture of an emancipated woman and a little stay-at-home. Scrooge treats women exactly as he treats his own soul: he replaces it with money. His entire libido is directed toward money. He keeps his twenty-five phantastillions stored in 176 warehouses throughout the world. He neither spends nor invests his money, he merely stores it. The idea of swimming in money is certainly a special incentive in our capitalist society, which incessantly suggests that money is the source of happiness. On the other hand, the excessive quantities of money and Scrooge's total inability to enjoy spending it give us a hint that money stands for something else.

It reminds me of the alchemists' attempt to produce "philosophical gold" from a chemical substance where the contrast of fire and water played an important role. When being united, they were supposed to produce the "fiery form of the true water". Scrooge's swimming pool of gold seems also to be a transmutation of water. Here again, the only difference is that the alchemists were mainly interested in processes of change—aiming, though never arriving, at perfection. Scrooge, with his swimming pool of gold, is already in possession of his "philosophical water" and is only striving for the preservation and the multiplication of his wealth. His indefatigable struggle for gold and money is not a hero's struggle for his anima, imprisoned by the dragon, but is the untiring, endless struggle for securing the Great Mother. The Ducks' behaviour and inner fantasies are defined by this archetype, its elemental character, that preserves, protects, and keeps hold of things. Erich Neumann[3] considers the vessel a central symbol of this basic feminine principle, which we can easily recognize in Scrooge's gold warehouses. His wealth and his power are not the result of a spiritual principle but are derived from this basic feminine principle.

As a consequence there is no personal mother in the Duck stories, which reinforces the projection onto the archetype of the Great Mother, who only rarely is personalized as Granny Duck. The Great Mother's second stage of development, however, which is characterized by mutability and by the experience of giving birth, releasing, and even repudiating, (thus necessitating a first relationship to a thou), has never been accomplished by the Ducks. The Great Mother's mutability is a prerequisite for the release of the shadow or the anima. This would clarify the conflicts and disturb the idyllic world of the Ducks. So they prefer to remain asexual. Scrooge's plunge into the swimming pool full of gold therefore is not the result of a perverted sexuality. Scrooge, like all the Ducks, is asexual, he has not even reached the oedipal stage. His phallus lies buried under the money, in Great Mother's store, and buried with it are his procreative capacity, his creativity, and his ability to build up relationships.

In conclusion, I would like to return to the questions of the great popularity of the Ducks, the fascination they arouse. This must be connected with the repression of the unconscious in the western world, where relationships and emotions often are reduced to business transcations.

Therefore, characters whose underlying patterns raise hope for solution and development become so fascinating. Not only children pursue this modern trickster in pursuit of themselves, from comic book issue to issue. As a mixture of duck, manager, oil sheik, and fool, this modern trickster builds up a connection to the unconscious but, unlike the Ugly Duckling or the tailor in "The Two Wanderers", does not show any possibility of development.

The simplicity of the Duck figures, who represent one psychological function each, conforms the pattern of the fairytale where similarly simple characters eventually achieve an integration with each other or within themselves. The Ducks, however, remain separated, repeating the same excursion to the unconscious over and over. They take advantage of the hope that individuation can still be expected. With this, they do not promise more or less than drugs, alcohol, and youth sects. Of all these addictions, Donald Duck may be the least dangerous.

1 C. G. Jung: Zur Psychologie dr Tricksterfigur. Gesammelte Werke Band 9/I, Walter Verlag AG, Olten 1976, pp. 288

2 Gans, Grobian: Die Ducks, Psychogramm einer Sippe. Rowohlt Taschenbuch Verlag, Reinbek bei Hamburg 1972, pp.24

3 Erich Neumann: Die Große Mutter, Watler Verlag AG, Olten 1974, pp. 51

Analysis of Holocaust Survivors

By Gustav Dreifuss (Haifa)

More than 35 years have passed since the Holocaust, the mass-murder of Jews in the camps of extermination. Survivors are still living among us. They confront us with the Holocaust and with their past and present suffering. This is so especially in Israel, with its high percentage of survivors of the Nazi persecution. We are also faced with a new problem, that of the children of the survivors, who though never having personally experienced persecution, yet develop related psychological problems. I find survivors among patients and friends. They are a constant and living reminder of the barbaric attempt at the systematic extinction of the Jewish people. To be sure, there were other persecutions and attempts to wipe out peoples (such as the Armenians), but the Holocaust of the Jewish people is outstanding in the high degree of organization to the mass murder. Jews were shipped to factories of death; one million children were killed; personal possessions of the victims were collected and used by the German populations. When I visit museums of Holocaust remembrance, like Yad Vashem in Jerusalem or Lochamei Ha'ghetaot, and I see photos and films of that period, time and again an uncanny emotion grips me and makes me shiver. How could human beings become so vicious as to degrade and slaughter fellow human beings without the slightest compunction or conscience? In Israel we have a yearly "Holocaust Memorial Day" which opens with a long steady sound of sirens. Israel's population unites with the dead victims and the survivors in an awesome minute of silence. This silence is an act of remembrance and inner union, but also a sign that vis-a-vis the Holocaust, nothing can really be said. And yet, this silence itself is a scream and evokes the need to wrestle once again with the incomprehensible evil and to express one's thoughts, however inadequately. I have made this Effort once before, in the 1968 congress (1).

As I lived in Zurich during the whole time of the Nazi atrocities in Europe, the sources for this paper are my experience in the analysis of Holocaust victims, the information given by friends, victims of Nazi persecution, and books on the subject.

Taking into consideration the prolonged physical and psychic damage of the survivors, we have to ask ourselves, if our usual psychothrapeutic approach holds true also for the survivor-patient? The more I worked with survivors the more I realized that their indescribable experiences cannot be understood nor adequately explained by a humanistic perspective. The effects of the prolonged utter helplessness under most cruel treatment, the constant confrontation with one's imminent death and the death of comrades, the smoke of the crematoria ovens, the human degradation by the S. S. guards, the hunger and thirst, are beyond any trauma theory. The absolute separation from the outer world, the systematic, destruction of the frame of reference to normal life standards and values that had up to then been valid for them, were more than psychic shocks; they undercut and threatened the very basis of the human psyche.

A very common concern of the inmates was the question as to whether the outside world at all knew what was going on in the camps—and what kept many alive was the burning need to testify as to what was happening, and to ensure that it never be forgotten—nor happen again.

The concept of the Concentration Camp Syndrome takes these special conditions, the extreme situations in the camps, into consideration with regard to symptomatology. These are the symptoms of the concentration camp syndrome: anxiety, chronic depression, nightmares, voluntary social isolation, psychosomatic symptoms and inability to trust.

I want to turn now to the survivor. In the excellent book of Terrence des Pres, "The Survivor" (2, p. 94), I found many moving testimonies of survivors and I want to quote one ot them: "When the body lies shrunken to a childish form, when arms and legs have become like thin twigs, when the mouth is parched and puckered, when every bite of food causes the return of dysentery, when the very smell of the camp soup brings on nausea, when there is no help, no care, no medicine—whence comes this magic will to live?"

For the inmates of the camp, food had become life, the bare necessity for continuing to live. Preoccupation with food was the condition for mere animal (i. e. biological) survival. And the systematic starvation of the inmates was a tool used by the Nazis for their dehumanization. It is clear in this case that the usual symbolic understanding of the meaning of food does not suffice. Food does not *symbolize* life, *it is life itself.* The psychic damage caused by this situation is fundamental and far reaching; it is an irreparable damage of the positive, elementary character of the mother archetype (Neumann,3, p. 147).

If a survivor today dreams about food, it has a very special meaning. When a survivor (4) hoards food, carries bread in his briefcase wherever he goes, needing the continuous physical connection with bread even in a normal life situation, we can readily understand his conviction that this bread, even if moldy, is his guarantee not to starve again. Bread, in its *concrete* form is for this man a life necessity in the face of his camp experience. It is for him, life itself; its possession guarantees so to speak a human way of existence. This has to be kept in mind also with regard to food appearing in dreams of survivors.

This brings me to the central question: Can analysis in its usual application heal survivors?

The current therapeutic approaches are based on a personality development under more or less normal circumstances. But, what happened to camp inmates cannot be compared to any "normal" neurotic development. Many if not all Holocaust survivors have suffered so irreparable damage that even prolonged analysis seems not to heal them. The survivor has to be helped to live better with his experience. I want to point out that many survivors seem to behave normally in their every day life, they seem well adapted, yet they still scream in their sleep . . .

Psychotherapy of survivors can soften, but not completety heal, existing wounds.

In my experience of psychotherapy of survivors, I felt that a kind of participation in listening to the unbelievable stories of the survivors is of special importance. The complete and total being with him, the reliving with him of his experiences is for the survivor most esential. It creates a bond of soul. The terms of transfernce / countertransference, if they apply at all, may have to be interpreted anew for this kind of relationship (cf. D. Kutzinski in Dreifuss (1), p. 170). For the Jewish therapist it may be easier to identify with the experiences of the survivor because he himself is a potential victim, and may be aware of their common fate. The non-Jewish therapist may be touched and shaken enough to feel with the survivor by a sensitivity to and understanding of the horrible outcome of antisemitism.

As death was there, in the camp, in a most manifest way, life for many had no purpose beyond itself, as des Pres so aptly put it (2, p. 103). Life alone became for them the highest value. Some broke on the moral problem: they could not tolerate the evil. They would rather starve to death, commit suicide, or die to sanctify God's name. The survivor must, therefore be brought to appreciate meaning and values in normal conditions of everyday life, even of small things which for the ordinary person seem trivial and self-evident.

What does the specific Jungian approach add to the treatment of survivors? (see also Dreifuss, 5) To answer this question, let us look at some dreams of survivors, whose content are unique to survivors. Here I give you some examples: (6)

This is material from a 42 year old patient, who lost his mother when he was 5 years old in consequence of the Nazi persecution. He lived with his father in the Underground, moving from one place to another, till the end of the war. He suffered from heavy depression, was unable to work. After a Freudian analysis and treatment by two psychiatrists he came to a Jungian analysis, which lasted one and a half years. Here are some dreams that came half a year before the end of the treatment.

1.) "A mother, together with a child, runs along railway track as if driven by invisible ghosts. She has to get to the train. To my astonishment she holds the child upside down. I see that the head of the child is completely bandaged The train leaves. An oppressive feeling stays with me."

2.) "After a strenuous voyage, I arrive at a temple. I am let in and led to the innermost chamber of the temple. There, the High Priest, in ritual dress, comes towards me and offers me an object, apparently a cult object. It is a vessel from which emerge brilliant beams of light. I receive it with ambivalent feelings. Suddenly I see that there is an atom bomb in the vessel which can explode at any moment. I do not know waht to do with the vessel and wake up."

The analysis was terminated by the patient as unsuccessful, and he was referred to a psychiatrist. After one year, at the age of 44, he committed suicide.

Here, from a survivor of Auschwitz, who lost her whole family there, is a dream that came 20 years later, when she was 45 years old: "I am in a dense forest. I went there for a hike with my friends, maybe also including my husband. Suddenly all are gone and I find myself completely alone. I become afraid and feel that I am slowly losing my mind. Suddenly I no longer know who I am, what my name is, and what I am doing here.

It is indescribably dreadful because I sense that I am completely dissolving. In my despair, I start touching myself all along my body in order to tell myself that this is me, my body. My fingers fall on my arm, on the number of Auschwitz. (As you know, inmates of the camps were identified by numbers tattooed on their arms, and not by their names.) Suddenly I know again who I am—not my name, but I regain my identity. And now again, there are people around me, and to them I say: "They call me the survivor of Auschwitz, and I have no other name than this." They look at me strangely, but I know my mind came back to me."

The dreams speak for themselves. So much for them. The Holocaust happened in Europe in the 20th century. It shows an abysmal failure of Western culture. It confronts us more than ever with a new dimension of evil—the calculated effort to annihilate totally an entire people, who were assiduously sought out all over Europe and who were degraded, tortured, and systematically murdered regardless of age, for the mere fact of having Jewish blood in their veins.

Jung's psychology deals extensively with the problem of evil, on a personal as well as on a collective level. But to what extent do we really grasp the enormous dimension of evil with which the Holocaust confronts us?

Does our psychology with its contribution to the shadow problem, and to the problem of evil, contribute to the overcoming of at least some of its collective manifestations? Are we, as individuals, shaken by the evil that is happening here and now? Have we remained as resigned and accepting of the fact of eveil as we were when we permitted the Holocaust of the Jewish people, with little protest, some 40 years ago? Do we remonstate loudly enough about the injustices done by our friends and our nations today?

1. Dreifuss, G.: The Analyst and the Damaged Victim of Nazi Persecution, J. analyt. Psychol., 14, 2 (1969) and in *The Analytical Process, Aim-Analysis-Training*, Joseph B. Wheelwright (ed.) New York, G. P. Putnam's Sons (1971)
2. Des Pres, T.: The Survivor: an anatomy of life in the death camps, New York, Oxford University Press (1976)
3. Neumann, E.: The Great Mother, New York, Pantheon Books (1963)
4. Private communication from Mrs. Y. Haft
5. Dreifuss, G.: Psychotherapy of Nazi Victims, Psychother. Psychosom., 34, 1 (1980)
6. Private communication from Mrs. D. Kutzinski

I must express my special thanks to Yeheskel Kluger for his many valuable suggestions and additions in editing this paper.

Further Bibliography

At the Ray D. Wolf Centre for Study of Psychological Stress, Haifa University, a bibliographical collection of all papers and books dealing with the medical and psychological sequels of concentration camp imprisonment, was established 1979 by Prof. L. Eitinger, Psychiatric Department of Oslo University, Vinderen, Norway. This work deals with the medical and psychological state of many different populations, including survivors and their offsprings. (800 papers and 50 books were collected). This information was provided by Mrs. M. Rieck of the above center who is also prepared to answer by mail, all questions regarding the collection.

Two reflections on the beginning of analysis

By Kathrin Asper-Bruggisser (Zürich)

I: The patient's need to know what's wrong

Although Jung was very reluctant to make firm diagnoses, there is never-theless a deep need in evey new analysand for an answer to his tormenting question: "What is wrong with me?" The answer doesn't have to be a clinical diagnosis, a description in terms of analytical psychology will usually provide at least a temporary relief.

The complexity of early sessions—where the analysand is struggling to find a new direction, and the analyst needs to organise the chaotic flood of incom-ing information—calls for a compensatory perspective which may help to organise this *"massa confusa"* and illuminate this *"nigredo."* For this is a situa-tion typical of the beginning of treatment where both analyst and analysand are in the darkness. One way to illuminate this darkness at the beginning is to pay close attention to one's subjective reactions to the new analysand, because they often give information about him or her. In this respect, I am reminded of a young woman I had met in one of my courses. I was quite pleased when she called for an analytical hour because I had liked her spontaneously and had noticed that she seemed particularly gifted. In the first hour she outlined her history which was rich in unusual details and events—and seemed like a fairy tale.

Although she came from an extremely humble background she had manag-ed, again and again, to be very successful at jobs for which she had had no training whatsoever. These triumphs were always short-lived, and seemed to have happened "just by chance." She described these experiences with all the astonishment of a Grimm's heroine and that made me wonder if she might possibly be a swindler. Then, I was ashamed of my own subjective reactions and tried to suppress them because I simply couldn't (or wouldn't?) admit that I had been so mistaken about her character and talent.

When I thought about it later, after the hour, I asked myself whether her gifts didn't function autonomously—without having been integrated in her con-scious personality. Was that why her professional development seemed so in-credible; did her triumphs really happen by chance: and was her talent therefore an aspect of what Heinz Kohut calls the "grandiose-exhibitionistic self"[1], working almost exclusively in fantasy and only appearing now and then by chance in the outer world only at certain "constellated" times? My counter-transference reaction, once interpreted, seemed to confirm this idea. My subjective reaction was therefore "syntonic" as Fordham[2] once termed it: one that told me something about the analysand rather than only about myself.

Born into an unsophisticated, petit-bourgeoise family, she had had no opportunity for education, and her talents were nourished at best only sporadically and as if by accident. Without education or training, she had no chance to use her gifts in everyday life. And on top of that hurdle, she was afraid that she might outgrow her family's social background. Her narcissistic ambitions and plans for a career were riddled with guilt. But in her dreams they could express themselves freely; they frequently showed her living in solitude on a beautiful island or deeply immersed in the contemplation of a majestic mountain. These dream images seemed to express her "grandiose-exhibitiomistic self"-fantasies. Gradually, as the problem became more conscious, the dream images were transformed: she left the island and found herself among people who were on their way to school. The latter dream image pointed toward the future, and she subsequently began to take her professional plans more seriously. At the same time, she felt less guilty about her ambitions. In this case, my countertransference-reaction had led to a perspective or diagnostic impression which could be put to good use in our work together.

The perspective gained in the beginning of analysis is the result of an emotional experience in which both the analyst and the analysand participate. As I started to work on this topic a line of a poem by Hermann Hesse: "Jedem Anfang wohnt ein Zauber inne"—("A magic dwells in each beginning") was haunting me. I got very intrigued by the word "Zauber" (magic, enchantment, charm) and soon found out that it is related to the Old English word "teafor" meaning red ochre or earth coloured. This has to do with magic rites of some Northern tribes who carved magic letters (so-called "runes") into stone and, in order to make them legible, coloured them with a red substance. This origin of the word "Zauber" seems to me to picture very well what happens in analysis, especially in the beginning. Red is traditionally the colour of life; the runes were reddened in order to distinguish them from the gray stone and so make them visible. In the analytical situation this amounts to giving emotional amphasis to the at first incomprehensible "runes" which the analysand brings with the hope that they are at least understood by the analyst; but this can only be achieved by *mutually shared* reexperiencing of the analysand's past and not by the application of any preconceived diagnosis which would fix him into a theoretical category. This perspective will have to be found where the "rune" is coloured red and filled with life, and therefore where we share a life-experience in the hour.

It is an entirely legitimate need of the analysand to know what is wrong with him. In conventional medicine of course, it is on the basis of a diagnosis that medication can be given. The mental image taken from the medical model—I show you my illness and you give me something with which to cure it—still plays a role with our analysands, even though psychogenic problems are not illnesses in the narrowest sense of the word, a malfunctioning of some organ or other, but encompass the whole person.

I am reminded of another analysand who told me about her "illness" and wanted me to give her a "prescription". She had come to me because of a feeling of emptiness, a lack of meaning and purpose in her life which bordered on despair. Earlier she had worked with a male analyst and "knew" what was wrong with her: depression based on a negative mother complex. She told me that she had worked out her father complex with her former analyst and came to me just to work out her mother problem. In addition to this diagnosis, she had definite ideas how she should be tackled. I noticed a resistance in myself to all this, a voice inside of me that said: "I don't like this, I haven't had the chance to experience or share that with her myself." The demand to work out the mother problem seemed too rational to me, too direct. I also got the impression that she was always confronted by the demands of others and now wanted to make me into a demanding figure as well.

While I was aware of all this, at that moment I had no alternative but to inquire about her mother. Still, I was uneasy in asking the question and realised that I was fitting all too easily into her pre-arranged agenda. What remained was the possibility of holding my counter-transference reaction in the background in the hope that it would prove fruitful at some later point.

She began to describe her mother to me as above average in conscientiousness, ambition and dominance. The mother had achieved a high position through hard work and great efficiency and was held in high esteem. My analysand added incidentally that people always inquired about her mother, and that she felt herself to be a mere subsidiary of her mother. People never asked about her.

This analysand put me into the role of a sympathetic listener, but did she allow me to share her experience? In no way. She described and explained things as if she herself were not really involved. It was if she had to clear her agenda with my help. While she was talking about her mother, indicating that people always asked about her mother and not about herself, I remembered my above mentioned counter-transference reaction. It suddenly became very clear to me that what she had just described was repeated between us. I too had inquired first about her mother and not about her, making her into a mere subsidiary of her mother. I explained this to her and said that I was repeating the pattern, and the ice was broken. I was transformed from a mere witness into a partner. Then she could share her loneliness, sadness, isolation, weakness and dark moods with me with great emotional involvement. She did precisely that which people with negative mother complexes find so hard to do, namely, reveal their wounds.

But at the end of this first hour she said: "I've talked so much about myself and haven't even begun with my mother problem. It did me good, but the next time we must work on the mother problem!" Thus, she pulled away from herself and fell back into maternal rejection. I was then able to explain to her that what she had told me and what she had experienced in the hour was related to her mother problem. In that context she allowed herself, at least for a moment, to take a maternal attitude to herself and allowed herself to be asisted.—Now we had a shared impression and in addition we had a *living experience together.*—To return to my analogy of the "runes"' The gray stones had been reddened, the secret in the cryptic message at the beginning was made vitally legible and drab gray theory was replaced by mutual living experience.

II: The Similarities of Fairy Tale Beginnings and the First Hours of Analysis

There is something fascinating about the first hours of analysis being very similar to the situation at the beginning of fairy tales. I would like to illustrate this similarity by discussing two fairy tales in the Grimm collection: *Cinderella* and *One Eye, Two Eyes and Three Eyes.* Each tale is a variation on the same theme. I wish to discuss them as part of the background of two cases. The two tales resemble each other especially in the way they begin: both heroines have a negative mother and two nasty sisters. In *Cinderella* a step-mother and two stepsisters are responsible for the suffering of the heroine. In *One Eye, Two Eyes and three Eyes,* two Eye's suffering is caused by her natural mother and sisters, although in some versions (including the earliest, 1560, by Montanus) a stepfamily is also emphasized. The major difference between the two stories is that two Eyes suffers at the beginning not only from excessive labour but also from the abnormal numbers of eyes of her sisters. Furthermore, the father is missing in *One Eye, Two Eyes and Three Eyes* whereas in *Cinderella* there is a relatively positive father figure.

Let us now turn to two analysands whose problems and transference experiences can be clarified against the background of these two somewhat different fairy tales.

Cinderella: The analysand I discussed earlier—the one who came with definite ideas how she should be handled—was an unusually dutiful daughter and had inherited her mother's "work ethic". One of her basic unconscious assumptions was that she had to *earn* the right to live and to justify her existence through tremendous effort. Her demand in the first hour was a "demand of duty" to work out the mother complex with me. By doing so she maneuvered me into the scenario of *Cinderella,* into the role of stepmother and/or stepsisters who would simply demand that she work harder, confirming that all her earlier efforts had been below the mark. Her suffering was left out as if I could not be sympathetic to it. And you remember: the moment she came to talk about things as she really felt them to be, she started weeping like Cinderella at her mother's grave, which is the turning point in the fairy tale.

"Weeping at the mother's grave" is a common scene in fairy tales. If we translate it into that particular analytical situation, it means taking the risk of expressing one's deep feelings, even though the situation seems to be hopeless. With my analysand it indicated that a first decisive change had taken place, namely her negative view of herself had at least for a moment been transformed into a positive acceptance of her sufferings (this could also be considered an indication of a good prognosis). Although at this beginning of analysis, I myself did not represent more than the absence of the positive mother, indeed was nothing more than the grave of the dead mother at which this Cinderella did her weeping, my analysand could at least for a short moment take the risk of telling me about her emptiness and her need of a positive mother. This, without her realising it, constellated me in the role of a positive mother. I could now cast off my resistances to her, for she herself had been able to look on her suffering in a motherly way.

I don't believe anyone can "bring about" such transformations. They happen, as Jung would have said, by the grace of God. What we can do however, is to sharpen our perceptions, so as to comprehend the role the analysand has assigned to us. An image from a fairy tale can help in the necessary ability to recognize where we are while we await the grace of tranformation. Later, whenever the above-mentioned analysand fell back into the old pattern (with a stepmotherly or stepsisterly attitude) and tried to maneuver me into that scenario as well, the small but significant transformation which occurred in the first hour gave us direction as well as hope. The fairy tale image I had pointed out to her could be used as a point of orientation in the dynamic between us. This image not only organised chaotic material, but did so in a way which was "verdant" as the brothers Grimm would say: "It both satisfied and soothed, without ever becoming boring" ("Das Grün, das dem Märchen" eignet, "sättigt, sänftigt, ohne je zu ermüden."[3].

One Eye, Two Eyes, and Three Eyes: One of my first analysands struck me as unusual in the very first hour because of the "possessed" way she talked. I was amazed to ovserve a constant change in her self-image. At first, she was full of hectic questions. She asked, what on earth must she do to feel more relaxed? Then she would make assertions that she was "nothing but this" or "nothing but that". Her tones of voice and her gestures would shift abruptly; all were strangely unintegrated. Her words were accompanied by a questioning undertone and restless eye-movements. High-flying verbiage and a resigned attitude were punctuated by animus opinions. I was left after this first hour with the impression that I had been confronted with a kaleidoscopic personality; its composition was constantly changing. Already in the first hour I had felt that she was demanding (both directly and indirectly) that I either offer still another point of view, which would only further increase this multiplicity of self-images, or move to confirm the assertions of her negative animus with unequivocal support. In the language of the tale, I was to become either the three-eyed or the one-eyed sister.

Her problem, it seemed to me, lay precisely in her inability to accept herself; her dissatisfaction led her to shift constantly between single-vision and multi-vision in relating to herself. Strictly speaking, her ego was too weak to stand ambiguity and in the background there was a disturbance of basic trust which seemed to feed her lack of self-esteem. When I realised, much later, that the matrix or core of this experience was similar to the situation in the tale of *One Eye, Two Eyes and Three Eyes*, the tale's precise imagery helped to orient us to the problem. Using the fairy tale image, we could see that it was important neither to fall into a rigid one-eyed nor into a three-eyed or multi-eyed view, but to support her own normal two-eyed approach.

A look at the biographical background shows that she had suffered under an extremely tyrannical father and had only a slightly better relationship with her mother. In the same household lived an aunt who had "vaccinated" her in her childhood with the "proper restraint" and the "correct way of life". Her aunt was the very personification of a one-eyed view of life. The analysand had never shone in her mother's eyes, and the lack of an approving parental guide was responsible for her identity disturbancce. This, in turn, led to her yearning for confirmation in the eyes of others, but at the same time she was terrified that she might be destroyed by the "glance of a stranger's eyes." On the basis of all this she took her environment as expressive of a multi-vision or a mono-vision depending on whether she projected her own uncertainty or the pseudo-certainty of her aunt onto it. During the analysis, a "mirror transference" in the sense of Kohut[4] developed, and this led to an improvement in her self-esteem and strengthened her normal two-eyed view of life. In this case, too, it was a fairy tale image which led the way for me. This clarification of the situation that had obtained of analysis at the beginning allowed both of us to see through her problems. In my opinion, the ability to stay out of the transference roles she presented to me (to become the three-eyed or one-eyed sister) and my concern with her profound lack of a warm centre, were the very things which made the analysis a fruitful one.

I will conclude by noting that these two fairy tale images appear the same in many respects, but that they have important specific differences. And, although the two analysands shared similar problems (both were depressed women who lacked basic trust) it was the subtle difference between the fairy tale images that helped me to elucidate the equally subtle differences in their problems.

1. Michael Fordham, *Technique in Jungian Analysis*, Vol. 2, London, Heinemann, 1974, p. 247.
2. Heinz Kohut, *The Analysis of the Self*, New York, International Universities Press, 1971, Part II, 5 / 6.
3. Jacob and Wilhelm Grimm, *Kinder- und Hausmärchen*, Vorrede 1856, Zürich, Manesse, p. 13.
4. Heinz Kohut, *The Analysis of the Self*, New York, International Universities Press, 1971, Part II.

Including the Religious Experience in the Analytical Process

By Rachel Hillel (Amherst, Massachusetts)

Today I would like to share with you some thoughts concerning an analyst's approach to the religious experience and its possible manifestation within the context of analysis. I am concerned with the conscious recognition of religious attitudes evoking archetypal healing forces which may arise within the patient's psyche, and the possible value of enlisting or reinforcing these attitudes in the service of the individuation process.

Even though my own concern over this problem has evolved gradually as an integral and probably inevitable part of my process of self-discovery, I think that this concern, whether explicitly or only vaguely or dimly perceived, is common to all of us here. I believe that no one who becomes a Jungian analyst can fail to connect to a religious attitude, can fail to grasp the symbolic meaning of the God archetype as a source of nourishment for one's soul. It seems probable that spiritual motives attracted each of us profoundly before we became analysts, and that religious experiences played a role at the very outset when we first embarked on our personal journeys and became, later, an inherent frame of mind when we chose our vocation. Thus we may all share a commonality in the discovery of the religious factor in our own individual realities. Let us take time and reflect on this together.

First, let me tell you about myself. I was born and raised in an Israeli kibbutz, an enlightened community, guided by high moral and social ideals, determinedly secular. In my childhood, I was told that there is no God, and that only the old-fashioned and ignorant still believe in Him. I was surrounded by an unqualified belief in the perfectibility of human beings and of human life through scientific, social, and economic progress; and by the assumption that all phenomena could be comprehended within a rational context. In this environment, there was no room for mystery, the unknown, the transcendent, in short, for the numinous.

Despite the outward denial of all religious faith, there is no doubt that my parent's pioneering generation was in fact fulfilling a divinity myth. In returning to their ancestral heritage, in reclaiming the land, they were filled with inspiration and faith. Indeed, they were impelled by a numinous vision and mission. In my education as a member of the second generation, however, the denial, even purposeful exclusion, of the numinous realm created a vacuum and failed to answer my inner yearning for meaning. I know that this deprivation was at the central core of my distress when I entered analysis in my early twenties.

Thus I came to appreciate Jung's postulate of man as an intrinsically religious being, his observations concerning the estrangement of modern man from the realm of the sacred within his psyche, and his conclusion that healing always turns out to be a religious problem.

As well all know, an encounter with the autonomous contents of the psyche can be a powerful religious experience and lead to rediscovery of the religious realm. Our personal symbols can bring us into engagement with the divine. Openness to emerging archetypal material evokes in us a sense of awe toward, and faith in, a greater wisdom that knows and guides. The answer is found inside, where it had always been latent. The inner healer needs to be contacted as a source of renewal. A religious attitude means a living contact with the unconscious and a conscious integration of its messages. The individuation process can be perceived, ultimately, as a religious quest. To be religious, in a psychological sense, is to acquire a state of consciousness that has been transformed through the experience and continous awareness of the presence and power of the numinous in our lives.

However, in order to engage with the numinous one must attain an inner attitude of reverence. One needs to prepare to become a participant in a divine drama. In ancient times, people lived much closer to awe-inspiring powers, and hence to a sense of the sacred. (Nowadays we seem to be insulated, as if protected, from such powers; this is largely illusory, however.)

An ancient language like Hebrew is replete with designations that aptly describe the proper psychic qualities needed for such an attitude of reverence. In order to meet the holy, one ought to be prepared and ready, *muchan umzuman;* attain a state of commitment and purity of intention, *kavana tehora;* and be filled with worshipful devotion, *dveikut;* all of which are essential in order to distinguish between the sacred and the profane, *bein kodesh lechol,* so that one can be worthy of attaining an 'oversoul', *neshama yeteira,* which, according to legend, every devout person acquires on the Sabbath.

It is perhaps significant that nearly all of these words are of the feminine gender, as is the *shechina,* the presence and manifestation of God on earth. Thus, even though the Hebrew legacy was intimately associated with the evangelion of masculine Logos, its language reflected the basic archetypal identification of religious attitudes with Eros, perceiving the soul as feminine. The feminine principle of relatedness has always been perceived as an essential factor in psychological healing processes. In parallel fashion, the Greek god of healing, Asclepius, was surrounded by three feminine figures with the significant names of Epione (the soother), Panacea, and Hygeia. In Christianity, it is the personality of Jesus, a man whose feminine side was so highly evident, which made the New Testament a healing testament.

According to a Chassidic saying, "God enters whenever man lets Him in." Translated into psychological notions, this attitude of reverence, inviting God into one's own life, is attained by accepting the numinous energy of the unconscious and subjecting the ego to the call of the non-ego, toward full acceptance of the personal meaning of one's unique destiny.

Jung stated that numinous experiences cannot be forced. They happen as a gift of grace. Still, it is possible to draw them in, as it were, through the adoption of a receptive frame of mind.'

Bearing in mind that the psychic qualities of sacredness and reverence can be vital in relating to non-ego contents, it is illuminating to look at the ancient archetypal roots of psychotherapy as provided by the ancient healing model of the Asclepian cult. My focus is not on the operative details, which are probably familiar to most of you, but on its psychological foundations.

The Asclepian religious cult was essentially a cult of the psyche; its religious attitudes and practices were dedicated to the psychological welfare of its participants. It was based on archetypal themes of psychic needs and nourishment, and its symbolism reflected an archetypal perception of inner events that occur during the healing process. Essentially, the theurgic healing code accepted the power of a higher authority, a directing intelligence. It acknowledged that destiny is an unknown plan, dependent on divine intention. Healing was based on the recognition and honoring of this higher principle at work. The healing rites were aimed at establishing a proper attitude to the divine power, the major focus being the invocation of the transpersonal dimension, an appeal for the intervention of this autonomous factor.

The various stages of ancient healing practice find their equivalents or counterparts within the psychodynamics of the individuation process as we perceive it today. The ancient pilgrimage to a remote temple connotes the opus of the journey into one's soul. Purification rites imply a catharsis and inner preparation. The sacrificial offering represents the ego's surrender of its old attitudes as psychic movers, forms of inner communication, active appeals by the ego to enlist the guidance and cooperation of the self. These rituals were designed to give the individual the courage and trust necessary for the sacrifice of old values and the leap into the unknown.

The incubant is singled out, summoned to the *Abaton*, suffer through the inner to process in the solitude of his soul. The transforming mystery of initiation, renewal, and rebirth can take place only in an introverted state, after a visit to the underworld in the course of which the incubant is reborn healed.

True religious life, then as now, consists of a living experience that integrates the unknown and unknowable. In the theurgic process, major therapeutic effects were assumed to occur in the dark, the numinous having to be concealed and guarded. The participant, by subjecting himself to whatever may come, submitted to the higher power. In the loneliness of incubation, he awaited God's message through a dream. Healing was assumed to result from the interpretation by the psychotherapists, as indeed the temple attendants were called.

An aspect of the theurgic view was its positive attitude toward affliction, and its recognition of the value and purpose of suffering in the service of growth and transformation. Experiencing the dis-ease was the way to discover God's message, sent through the symptoms. The dis-ease was accepted as a godsend having meaning as a potential source for new consciousness. The god himself was archetypally perceived to be a wounded healer. Paradoxically, that which wounds can also heal, and only the wounded can discover the way to healing. Having suffered through his own wounds, the healer can remain humble and compassionate toward the afflictions of others subject to his care. In contemporary terms, this vulnerability can be seen as the best antidote to the danger of the healer's self inflation as a consequence of the projections cast upon him by his grateful subjects. Rather, it assists the afflicted to realize that he himself, like the healer before him, contains his own inner healer. A consciousness of God's role, which transcends the personal psyches of the healer and healed, is equally important to both.

Our analytical practice shares many of the attributes of the ancient method. The qualities of solemn respect, of serious devotion, embodied in the ancient rites characterize our work as well. We speak of redeeming unconscious contents, a task of self-direction, and self-discovery through various means such as active imagination, inner dialogue, creative writing, drawing, etcetera, all of which are to be performed in a spirit of commitment akin to traditional ritualistic attitudes. However, the difference is our emphasis on personal means, designed to serve the individuation process, as distinct from what were collective ritualistic patterns.

Religious practices have always served the basic human need for expressing inner communion. From time immemorial, sacred activities were practiced for the purpose of eliciting contact with the divine, relating to the transpersonal dimension within the psyche, and bringing into consciousness an inner connection to the holy. The gods were always perceived as requiring rituals. In psychological terms, it is as if the unconscious demands that some positive, if only symbolic, acts be performed as part of the healing process. Based on human history, we can define religious expressions and rituals as channels for psychic motion, inherent patterns of the soul's expression, vessels by which to reach into the psyche. If indeed archetypal religious rituals have for so long a period been found to be so effective in serving psychic needs, we ought to consider today if they can be of use within our analytical work.

To sum this up: even though in practice our work may be implicitly permeated by a psychic sense of the sacred, it may behoove us to attempt to raise this sense to the conscious level. This attempt may include the following points: first, a conscious acknowledgement of our engagement as a sacred activity; second, a conscious attitude of reverence toward the autonomous power of the psyche; third, explicit recognition of our methods as containers and conveyors of sacred contents; and fourth, examination of the possible value of invoking either traditional or innovative modes of religious expression to aid the analytical process, provided such rituals assume an individual, unique form of self expression for a particual analysand.

For me, these are not merely abstract or theoretical issues. The question of whether and how to incorporate religious expressions or rituals in therapy has occurred repeatedly in my practice and has indeed prompted me to prepare this presentation.

Some of my analysands, while undergoing acute distress and a sense of impasse and despair, have at times indicated a spontaneous need to give vent to religious feelings in ways which they felt to be personally suited to their current state. Their ways included periods of silent meditation, contemplation, or prayer. At such times, I felt impelled to admit my own human limitations. It has been by experience that whenever I could genuinely respect their wishes, significant inner events moved me as well as the analysand.

I have often been impressed by the effects of these forms of inner communication, which tended to occur during intense conflict, mounting tension, and profound emotion. After the state of conflict had been acknowledged and the situation of impasse fully recognized, and when I on my part made no attempt to mollify or minimize the searing pain of my analysand's inner furnace, then it seemed that a resolution could only be attained by allowing a religious experience to take place, if indeed it arose spontaneously. We did not contrive this resolution in the manner of *deus ex machina;* it came of itself. Whether by listening in silence to the small still voice or by actively appealing for guidance and illumination, the analysand was moved and transformed. No merely verbal discussion could substitute for the emotional experience which then took place.

I have come not only to accept and appreciate the comforting aspects of these religious expressions, but also their active role in mobilizing the analysand's inner resources. Furthermore, these experiences often brought up fresh material from the unconscious, including images and themes which contributed significantly to the analysis.

It is important, in the context of Jungian analysis, that the analysand not become entrapped in a state of passive longing for a power that might change him without own effort and conscious cooperation. Having allowed the experience to arrive, the analyst and analysand must then work on it. The symbolic meaning of the images and the purpose behind their emergence should be evaluated. In fact, the material arising out of the religious experience can be treated as we normally treat any unconscious material obtained from such channels as dreams and fantasies. The new themes brought up by religious experiences may initiate processes which continue to operate within the analysand even while he is at home, and give rise to new modes and contents of self expression.

Being open to these unconventional manifestations has made me more aware of the manifold criteria which the analyst must weigh in responding to the analysand's requests, particularly within the transference/countertransference dimension. Whenever I as the analyst felt uneasy about certain of the manifestations, I had to reflect on the reason for my unease and consider the possibility that the analysand's request was motivated by counterproductive tendencies, such as the desire for manipulation and control, or for evasion and denial.

To sum up my experience: if and when an analysand indicates a desire to give expression to religious experiences or feelings, and suggests a suitable mode for such expression, I have tended to respond affirmatively whenever I assessed such expressions as offering promise; and I then worked with the analysand to help integrate the material which emerged via images, feelings, and insights in order to realize it within the analysand's conscious self-awareness.

Now let us consider some of these issues from the analyst's point of view. In contrast to traditional healers and clergymen, an analyst may not impose his own values on the analysand. His approach should be based on activation of the self-healing potential of the psyche, an autonomous factor able to work spontaneously. The analyst should heed the manifold diversity of his analysands by honoring the mode and pace of each one's inner processes and by remaining unbiased toward the emerging material. If the analyst operates with his own set of values, offering them *a priori* as panaceas, thus in effect controlling the situation, he may prevent the analysand from attaining genuine individual development. The analyst ought not to incur the risk of forcing the analysand into a religious attitude. If the analysand needs the religious factor for his healing, he must indeed discover it for himself, in himself, as a consequence of his own most personal experience. The analyst can only adopt a mode of patience, listening for and allowing the religious inspiration to occur spontaneously, and assisting in support and affirmation of the inner event once it occurs.

The analyst's own religious attitude is involved, of course, in the faith the analyst accords to the guidance potential of the analysand's psyche and to the analysand's ability to discover the inner healer. The analyst's role can be seen as that of a mediator who helps the analysand to recognize the knowledge offered to the ego by the unconscious and to apply it in a constructive and creative way.

I believe that the inner necessity for a relationship with the autonomous factor within can be discovered, and will germinate naturally, when the analysand is allowed, indeed encouraged, to enter as deeply as possible into himself or herself, even if on occasion this entails an increase of pain. There are times when the analyst may find it more constructive to resist the temptation to step in prematurely in an effort to alleviate the analysand's suffering. Rather the analyst might help the analysand to understand the meaning and positive potential of his affliction, and support the development of a capacity to endure tension and pain as essential aspects of the healing process.

This is how matters stand theoretically. In practice, however, they are not so simple. Reality is especially complex in view of our emphasis on the importance of developing a personal relationship between analyst and analysand, in the course of which the analyst may not be able to refrain from conveying personal beliefs and values relative to symbols, dreams, imaginary processes, and religious attitudes. One's relationship to the religious factor in the psyche is of such central importance that it is hard to imagine how an analyst can refrain entirely from mentioning and discussing it, or even from implying it. The analyst is, after all, a human being, and what he or she believes in may have a profound effect upon the analysand no matter how the analyst may try to hide his beliefs. The appropriateness of admitting religious contents into analysis is therefore a problem with which the analyst, as well as the analysand, must struggle in principle, and in each case in particular.

Another aspect of the analyst's problem is the selection of the term, whether God or Self, most appropriate for conveying the numinous experience. The criterion for this choice must be based on which of the two terms best facilitates the development of a personal relationship to the autonomous powers within the psyche. For some of us, the Self corresponds to a personal representation of God in our psyche. Other among us are better served by the image of God. The latter group often finds that the very use of the name God has a nourishing, healing effect. Perhaps this stems from its being a basic universal archetype and a container of emotions, memories, and ancient spiritual roots. So certain analysts prefer to consecrate the ego by placing it in the service of God, whereas other perceive the higher call through the concept of Self. Among the latter are those of us who have had to struggle hard to free themselves as individuals from containment in an orthodox dogma in which God was identified with collective attributes. In reading Jung I had the impression that he stated that the infinite image of God is for most people a more comprehensible designation of the Power Beyond Us than is the finite Self. Be that as it may, both Self and God remain symbols, man-given names for a perceived existence which is basically a mystery. We are here attempting to deal with what is essentially undefinable. That which leads us is ultimately paradoxical and unknown; finally it is the inner psychic motion that counts.

I would like to suggest in a tentative way, if only for the sake of argument, that analysts tend to fall into three categories with regard to the issue I have been discussing. The first consists of those who cannot accept, intellectually and emotionally, the inclusion of any ritual with religious content as an integral part of the analystical hour, though they might well approve of such rituals as modes of expression for the analysand in an introverted state outside the session. The second group includes those who feel that it is legitimate and even therapeutic to share their own religious experiences and reveal themselves to the analysand whenever it seems relevant and appropriate. The analyst might consider his own experience to be a possible helpful source of clarification and healing from which the analysand may draw support. By admitting their own limitations and need for guidance at times of crisis, and thus by exemplifying their humanness, analysts can perhaps demonstrate that only when open to doubt can one act with trust and faith. In the words of the New Testament: "My strength is perfected in weakness." It is in this frame and in accordance with the analysand's individual needs that the analyst may share his religious experiences and reveal how deeply he himself may have been moved by encounter with the mysterious guiding factor. The third group of analysts includes those who identify the entire analytical process as an initiation ritual, and their vocation as the guidance of souls, much in the tradition of the psychopomp. These analysts may promote and initate a God-centered perspective by active advocacy. They consciously encourage an attitude of reverence within the analytical hour and attempt to maintain a quality of sacredness throughout the process. Such analysts tend to stress the equivalence of the symbolic and the religious attitudes and to impress upon the analysand the importance of the mysterious, the unknowable, the wordless, the numinous. Analysts in this group need not state their beliefs explicitly, but rather convey the value of sacredness by creating the atmosphere of a shrine in various symbolic and concrete ways designed to aid the analysand in the task of shifting from a more typical extraverted mode into the unique elevated spirit of the session. Other analysts in this group may invoke the sacred by the way they prepare themselves for the session, in an effort to become "right channels." They allow time for introversion between sessions, dedicating the interval to the service of the forthcoming analysand, not through intellectual examination of his or her file but rather through silent meditation and inner focusing.

This brings me to the final point, the dialectical nature of the analytical process as another distinction between the Jungian analyst and the clergyman and as an obvious reason for the reservation many analysts feel toward religious matters. Even though Jungian analysis accepts the basic notions that psychic reality is inseparable from the religious experience and that psychological welfare depends on connection to an inner religious factor, analysts are primarily engaged in furthering the growth of human consciousness. Based on the assumptions that the Self drives the individual toward consciousness, that the image of God in man requires the ego's consciousness in order to realize itself, and that the individuation process depends on the continual development of consciousness, we aim at establishing dialogue and rapport between the conscious and the unconscious. We attempt to reconcile, on the one hand, receptiveness toward emerging unconscious contents (an attitude requiring ego surrender to a greater, ever-existing intelligence, indeed an attitude which has always been the essence of true religion), with, on the other hand, an active will by the ego to attain consciousness.

The search for wholeness and healing consists ultimately of the complex and paradoxical reconciliation of personal and transpersonal opposites, requiring a combination of hard work (on the part of the ego) with a receptive willingness toward that which only an experience of the unconscious can reveal (and which is, one might add, a state of grace).

In closing, I would like to share with you a memory of a personal experience of fateful importance. Twenty years ago, doctors in this city of San Francisco pronounced me to be terminally ill and predicted that I would live but a few more months. I was hospitalized here for over a year, during which I had a unique opportunity for introspection and for initiating an inner search that eventually led me into analytical psychology as an avocation and a profession, a source of enrichment and endless fascination, and a channel by which I might transmit to others the process and discovery by which my own illness served as a source of renewal, by which my nearly tragic misfortune ultimately became my greatest good fortune. I am convinced that I could not have been cured by drugs alone. An inner fountain of life-affirming faith lies hidden within each of us, waiting to be tapped. I feel something of a numinous experience even as I stand here in the city of San Francisco among my colleagues from many countries, wounded healers that we all are, in common search and common dedication.

The Cipitillo and Siguanaba:
Erotic Awakening in a Central American Peasant Culture

By Joseph Wakefield (Austin, Texas)

I. *Introduction:* The idea for this paper came from year of working as a general psychiatrist in the state hospital of the Central American country of El Salvador. A number of adolescent girls were admitted, excited and frightened, because they had heard the Cipitillo, a male sprite prominent in folk belief, calling them. Although they had been diagnosed as schizophrenic and given antipsychotic medication, none of them really seemed schizophrenic. They readily made emotional contact, did not display loose associations, and were not psychotic upon withdrawal of the medication. All of them were experiencing problems in their personal lives, problems of romantic and sexual nature, problems of the erotic awakening from child to woman.

In this paper I intend first to review the problems of erotic awakening facing an adolescent girl in the peasant culture of El Salvador; then to review the myth of the demented female spirit, Siguanaba, and her son the Cipitillo; then to present several cases to illustrate what is experienced. Finally, I will consider what happens from the point of view of analytical psychology.

II. The Salvadorian peasant culture is a rural, agricultural, subsistence culture. Its roots go back to Pre-Colombian Indian societies based upon a close relationship to the earth and its changing spirits with an overlay of Catholic morality. Economically, it resembles a feudal society where the peasant, *(campesino)* works the land of his master, *(patron)*. The Catholic Church has a strong influence in matters of morality and conduct, as well as a more recent role in the peasant resistance against the established economic order, as part of a "theology of liberation." Various Protestant, evangelical churches also are influential. The *campesino* tends to act spontaneously, trust his own ability to fight rather than the law, and accept what happens as destiny or fate.

The transformation from child to woman can be especially problematic in El Salvador's peasant culture because of the conflicting demands present. Expectations are quite different for the adolescent boy and the adolescent girl. The boy is expected to be "macho" which includes being brave, prepared to fight to defend his own and his family's honor, capable of drinking alcohol, and sexually active with women. The adolescent girl is pulled between the conflicting demands to become sexually active and to maintain her "honor" *(la honra)* and be virgin at her marriage. A girl who has sexual relations is said to be "ruined" *(arruinada)* and not fit for marriage. She is thought of as a whore, and indeed sometimes has to support herself through prostitution when abandoned by her family. Neither adolescent boys nor girls are thought capable of controlling their impulses. (Indeed, several years age El Salvador had one of the world's highest population growth rates, 3.5% annually, and the world's highest murder rate, suggesting that the instinctual forces of aggression and sexuality are not well controlled.) In the middle class, safeguards exist to control sexual expression, such as avoiding allowing the adolescent couple to be alone together. In the rural peasant environment such safeguards are weaker, and the adolescent girl is presented often with a situation of being courted by a male who thinks it only natural to have sexual relations, faced with the risk of being "ruined" if she accepts, and confronted by her own awakening impulses. It is in such situations that the Cipitillo appears to her.

III. The Cipitillo and the Siguanaba are figures in myths current in El Salvador. For the *campesinos* they are not metaphors or abstractions; rather they are experienced, seen, heard. Children learn about them from other children or from maids or from their elders, who learned about them the same way, or perhaps experienced them firsthand. So, I did the same as a Salvadorian child. After reading some folk tales such as Miguel Angel Espino's "Mitologia de Cuscatlan", Salarrue's "Cuentos de Barro," and Dr. Efrain Melara Mendez's "Mitologia Cuzcatleca," I went to the source. I spoke to children from neighboring homes and from the barrios, to maids, gardeners, and field laborers. As I describe what they told me, I think you will recognize the mixture of archetypal figures and superimposed ege-consciousness moralizing.

Sihuelut was beautiful and married, but was coquettish and so abandoned her home to go with another man. Her mother-in-law complained to the god Tialoc, who changed her name to Siguan (meaning woman of the water) and condemned her to wander, insane, by the banks of rivers. At night, she appears to a fisherman as a beautiful woman who asks him to take her home. On the way, if he makes advances, she turns into a horrible hag and leaves him frightened and confused in the forest. Her insane laughter can be heard at night along the rivers.

The Siguanaba has a son, the Cipitillo. He lives near the river with her, but when he wanted to make love to his mother, the Siguanaba rejected him, and so he ran into the forest where he awaits young girls. He is a boy-man, who never ages. Some say he is like the *duende:* short, fat, with a long pointed hat, a long pointed nose, and a long penis, always playing tricks. Other say he is handsome, irresistible, a charmer who sings songs and drops garlands of flowers upon the girls as they walk in the forest. Some say he still lives in the river where he caresses the girls as they bathe. Others say he lures girls to his cave under the volcano, from where they never return.

Here is a translation of a poetic description of the Cipitillo given by Miguel Angel Espino in his "Mitologia de Cuscatan."

> So it was. The Siguanaba was insane. She was to be seen with her wild laughter, running by the banks or the rivers and hiding in the deep, obsure wells. Cipitillo moved to the mountains and lived in a cave under the volcano.
>
> Much time has passed. The grandfathers have died, the ancient trees have returned to the earth, the Cipitillo remains handsome with black eyes. The son of the Siguanaba still is ten years old, still shy, hiding in the forests, dancing upon the wildflowers.
>
> Cipitillo was the spirit of romantic love. In the chill mornings the girls of the villages would bring him gifts and flowers, to play together on the riverbanks. Hidden among the flowers he would watch, and when a girl passed by he would drop flowers upon her.
>
> But ... it must be told. Cipitillo had a love of his own. A girl, small and beautiful as he, whose name was Tenacin.
>
> One day Cipitillo slept upon a bed of flowers. Tenacin entered the forest, cutting flowers. She lost the path, and running lost, came to where Cipitillo slept, and saw him.
>
> The noise of breaking branches woke Cipitillo who fled, leaping from flower to flower, singing with enchanting tenderness. Tenacin followed him. After a long journey, Cipitillo arrived at a rock above the foothills of a volcano. The hands and feet of Tenacin were torn by the thorns on the path.
>
> Cipitillo touched the rock and a moss-covered door opened. Taking each other by the hand, Cipitillo and Tenacin entered, and the moss-covered door silently closed behind them.
>
> No more was Tenacin seen. Her father wandered through the hills, searching for her, and after some days died, broken by grief.
>
> It is said that Cipitillo and Tenacin enclosed themselves in a cave of the volcano Sihautepeque (mountain of the woman), which is now in the county of San Vincente.
>
> Eons of time have passed. The world has changed, rivers have dried, mountains have been born, and still the son of the Siguanaba remains a beautiful youth. Often he can be seen, hidden among the flowers, spying upon the girls who are laughing at the river's turn.
>
> Oh Cipitillo! Careful with your glances which incite such love in the hearts of the adolescents!

IV. I have presented the cultural pressures an adolescent *campesina* may experience and have presented the mythic context in which Cipitillo appears. Now I would like to present several cases encountered at the psychiatric hospital where the girl's conflicts gave rise to a direct encounter with the Cipitillo.

Maria, age 14, became increasingly agitated in the five days prior to admission. She would cry, shout at her parents, not sleep at night, and said she heard the Cipitillo singing rancheros to her, calling her to follow him. By the morning after her admission her excitement had subsided. She remained quiet and shy even after medication was stopped, without evidence of psychosis. An attractive person, Maria was deeply conflicted over her relationship with her boyfriend, age 18. He told her she was beautiful, that he loved her, wanted her to come live with him, and of course he suggested sexual relations. Her parents bitterly opposed the relationship, in part not wanting her to leave home, and in part not wanting her to be "ruined." Also, the boyfriend was a member of FECCAS, a militant peasant organization often in open conflict with the guardia nacional. The European parallel would be an Irish Catholic girl whose parents are members of the IRA falling in love with a British soldier stationed in Belfast.) As the tension mounted, as her own feelings of love and desire made her want to give herself, Maria became increasingly agitated, until she heard the Cipitillo calling her and was admitted to the hospital. As we explored her dilemma, she recognized the need to choose. Outwardly, she said she would obey her parents, but her boyfriend often visited and upon discharge she ran off with him. The Cipitillo, at least in the form of a projected verbal hallucination, did not return.

Patricia, age 16, entered with a three month history of insomnia, nightmares, constant headaches, and hallucinations of being caressed; she heard a masculine voice (identified as the Cipitillo) calling her at night. She appeared immature and manipulative, but not psychotic.

Patricia's mother had been seduced and abandoned by Patricia's never-known father. When Patricia was born her mother tried to give her away, and finally placed her with her grandmother to live. From the mother and grandmother, Patricia learned that men were deceiving brutes, not to be trusted. She was shy, performed poorly at school, and was controlled by her grandmother. When Patricia entered adolescence she became attractive to the men who entered the grandmother's store. When these men would court her, Patricia felt attracted and yet felt rage at the same time. She became increasingly irritable, moody, rebellious, until her symptoms at admission developed.

I suggested to Patricia that exploring her nightmares might help her overcome her symptoms. Here are several that she told me:

1) A group of snakes has entered my house and says to me, "Do you want your grandmother to die? Do you want to stay with the snakes?" (Patricia awakens, frightened, hearing the Cipitillo calling her to come outside to the forest, feeling hands caressing her body.)

2) I am in a desert. A stick changes into a snake, then into the head of a woman whose hair consists of multiple, writhing snakes. (Patricia awakens with one of her severe headaches.)

As we explored her situation it seemed clear that Patricia was blocked in her evolution from child to woman. She felt abandoned and rejected by the mother, with resultant doubts about her own worth. She learned that men were not to be trusted. She couldn't imagine becoming a woman, becoming a mother, being intimate with men. When men treated her as an attractive woman, when her own desire to become a woman awakened, she experienced the images of this instinctual awakening as frightening, as snakes or as the Cipitillo. The maternal image didn't lend support to her development. In Greek mythology, the Gorgon paralyzed those who looked upon the snakes. Patricia experienced headaches which indeed were paralyzing in that they prevented her from leaving the home or accepting social engagements.

As Patricia and I explored her conflict, her nightmares and headaches subsided. She began to think that perhaps, emotionally, she did need to "leave the grandmother," and, while some men were destructive exploiters, not all were, and she had the capacity to judge, to choose. She appeared less immature, more of a woman. I wanted to continue therapy when she left the hospital, but she lived two days journey away, and so we had to trust in the forward movement of her own psyche.

Finally, an example of a colleague of mine hints both at an underlying neurological foundation and the shared, communal nature of the experience. His adolescent *campesina* and her grandmother both heard the Cipitillo sing to the patient. The girl heard singing during sharply-defined episodes followed by confusional states. An EEG revealed temporal lobe epilepsy. When Tegretal, an anticonvulsant, was prescibed, both the girl and her grandmother ceased to hear the Cipitillo.

V. From the point of view of analytical psychology, hearing the Cipitillo could be described as a culturally defined and sanctioned visionary experience, a projection of the animus. In the Cipitillo, we see a nature-spirit whose touch awakens longings, erotic fantasy, or at times fear and repulsion.

Esther Harding, in her book *The Way of All Women*, has written of "the ghostly lover," the projected eroticised animus. Such experiences are more frequent at times of instinctual upheaval . . . the menopause, or especially the instinctual awakening of puberty. Often this eroticised animus can be projected upon an actual person, through an actual or a fantasied love relation. When concrete experience is blocked or very conflictual (as it may be for adolescent girls in El Salvador's peasant culture), then the projection may take on a visionary character, such as the Cipitillo, in fantasy.

Parallels from European mythology come quickly to mind. Let us recall the tale of "Amor and Psyche" as related by Erich Neumann. When the time had come for Psyche to leave her parents, to become a woman, she experienced her marriage as a death. She hurled herself from a cliff as the bride of death, yet wound up living in a cavern, with the god Amor, until her need for further consciousness upset the arrangement. (We can recall the Cipitillo taking his bride from her parents, to live in a cave under the volcano.)

And we could recall "Beauty and the Beast," or "The Princess and the Frog," where the adolescent's erotic awakening is at first experienced as animal-like, dirty, and frightening; the task being to embrace the feared, new, unknown masculine presence, at which point he becomes a handsome prince and the girl an erotically alive woman.

Kate Marcus, in her article entitled "The Stranger in Women's Dreams," makes the point that the intruding, dangerous masculine figure is an unconscious content becoming conscious. From the perspective of analytical psychology this content could be named an eroticised animus, and is first discovered through projection.

The animus as bringer of consciousness is found also in India, in the myth of Krishna, who charms the Gopi shepherd girls in the forest with his flute, dance, and caresses. As told by Joseph Campbell in *The Masks of God*, Krishna not only awakens the maidens to erotic love, but also to a knowing of themselves, to the krishna inside them; the projection is brought back within.

I said earlier that the Cipitillo experience was culturally defined and sanctioned. What I mean by "sanctioned" is that the adolescent *campesina* is not held morally responsible for her awakening eroticism when the Cipitillo is involved. The sanctions against erotic expression for the *campesina* can be very strong, and can range from being called ruined or a whore publically, to being literally killed by her family. When the Cipitillo is involved, however, the attitude becomes, "ni modo, es su destino" (nothing can be cone, it is her fate). For a girl to become sexually active while unmarried could be considered pride or arrogance; when the Cipitillo is involved, it is not a willful act, and her moral culpability subsides. With the examples I encountered in the psychiatric hospital, I was impressed how the nursing staff (from the same culture as the patients) when they heard of the Cipitillo, would encourage the patient to choose the boyfriend and not choose to remain daughter of her parents. If we translate this attitude into terms of analytical psychology, we could say that sexual activity at a time of instinctual, achetypal awakening is accepted, even if it runs counter to the collective conscious morality.

I have spoken of the Cipitillo in terms of destiny and in terms of erotic awakening. Another way to consider the experience is in terms of growing consciousness, growing self-awareness. The Cipitillo is a trickster-like figure. As Jung has written in "On the Psychology of the Trickster-Figure," such figures are inventive and give rise to new knowledge or create new worlds "by hook or by crook" (por lo bueno or por lo malo). In the Maya creation myth, the *Popul Vuh*, the world is brought into its present existence by battling the forces of the underworld. The victory is won not by force, but by being inventive with magical tricks. In the cases of adolescent young woman which I have described, erotic awakening could nor occur automatically or unconsciously because of the conflicting demands upon these young women to be sexual and not be sexual at the same time. For young men of the same culture, the expectations that their behavior will be erotic are clearly defined by the code of *machismo*, and they can act without thinking much about it. Adolescent young women are faced with a conflict, and as a result become more aware of how the young men think and aware of themselves, so that at the same chronological age the adolescent young woman is more socially and psychologically aware than is her male counterpart. Jung once described a neurosis as an advantage because the neurotic conflict led to greater self-awareness. The conflict over erotic awakening here described is more cultural than neurotic, yet it serves the same function of leading to increased self-awareness.

Campbell, Joseph, *The Masks of God: Oriental Mythology*, The Viking Press, Inc., New York, 1962

Espino, Miquel Angel, *Mitologia de Cuscatlan*, Direccion de Publicaciones, San Salvador, Quinta edicion, 1976

Harding, M. Esther, *The Way of All Women*, G. P. Putnam's Sons, New York, 1970

Jung, C. G., *On the Psychology of Trickster-Figure*, in Collected Works, Volume 9.1, Princeton University Press, Princeton, 1968

Marcus Kate, "The Stranger in Women's Dreams," in *The Well-Tended Tree*, Hilde Kirsch, editor, G. P. Putnam's Sons, New York, 1971

Melara Mendez, Dr. Efrain, *Mitologia Cuzcatleca*, Impresora Pipil, S.A., San Salvador

Neumann, Erich, *Amor and Psyche*, Bollingen Foundation, Inc., New York, 1956

Recinos, Adrian, *Popul Vuh*, Quinta edicion, Fondo de Cultura Economica, Mexico 12, D. F., 1961

Salarrue, *Cuentos de Barro*, Direccion de Publicaciones, San Salvador, Novena edicion, 1977

von Franz, Marie-Louise, *Problems of the Feminine in Fairy Tales*, Spring Publications, New York, 1972

Polanyi and Jungian Psychology: Dream-Ego and Waking-Ego

By James A. Hall (Dallas)

The crucial insight of Jungian dream theory is the understanding of dream images in a true symbolic fashion, not simply reducing them through personal association to the furniture of waking life, and refraining from reducing them to the meaning of the archetypal core that can be found behind every image. It is to this central task of the analytical process that I wish to relate the epistemology of Michael Polanyi. There are several reasons for my interest:

1) Polanyi is one of the major theoreticians of science who, like Jung, attempts to bridge the tension between inner subjective experience and outer social and scientific forms;

2) Polanyi, like Jung, has relevance for the conceptualisation of religious experience, as attested by an increasing number of theological dissertations discussing his work; and

3) although Polanyi himself did not apply his concept of focal and tacit knowing to the imagery of dreams, he raised no objection to that possible extension of his language into the intrapsychic field of subjective experience. A fourth reason for my concern with Polanyi's work is the possibility it offers of applying Jungian dream theory in such a way that the specificity and grain of the dream image is preserved without reduction, while a form is provided for relating the structure of complexes, as revealed in dreams, to our central clinical focus of understanding the structure and fluctuations of the waking ego.

The plan of presentation is to discuss first those concepts of focal and tacit knowing that are relevant to the problem of the dream ego and the waking ego, then to apply them to certain recurrent problems of clinical interpretation.

Polanyi's concept of focal and tacit structure

Polanyi began his career as a physician in Hungary; later, in England, he became a chemist and was elected to the Royal Society for work in physical chemistry; he concluded his life working in the philosophy of science. He was

deeply concerned to elucidate the underlying quality of passionate commitment and quest in the process of scientific discovery, a view of the actual process of scientific discovery that is vastly different from the traditional one of
science as simply the disinterested accumulation and weighing of factual data.
Much of the humanistic protest against scientism is based upon that mistaken
image of a dispassionate science, an image that Polanyi refutes (POLANYI 5).

In searching for the roots of the scientific urge, Polanyi took up the position
that all knowledge is irreducibly personal. Objective statements by scientists
(or others) are statements of personal commitment uttered with universal intent. One can hear echoes of Jung's discernment that all psychology is confes-
sional, inevitably reflecting the unique personal experience of the speaker's
psyche.

Polanyi's theory was as follows. Any act of knowing has a from-to structure, *tacitly* relying upon some information in order to attend *from* that content *to* other information that is *known focally.* This structure of focal-tacit
knowing is present in every act of knowing. it is not possible to shift arbitrari-
ly the boundaries of the focal-tacit structure, but they are changeable. The
tacit component is not necessarily unconscious, nor the focal one conscious.
To take a physical example, or analogy, a pencil held in the fingers may be used as a probe to determine, while the eyes are closed or the head averted, the
edge of this page. As the pencil is progressively tapped towards the edge of the
page, consciousness is relying upon the movement of the pencil against the
fingers in a tacit way — that is, the subject is attending *from* the movement of
the pencil against the fingers *towards* the desired focal knowledge of the edge
of the paper. In this example, both the focal and the tacit compartments are
conscious, although the tacit component is *subsidiary* to the focal.

The body itself is relied upon in a tacit way in order to attend focally to the
external world. We (by which I mean ordinary people) consider the nervous
system and our integration of its informations to be transparent. We construct
an elaborate view of the physical world, including our body-image located
within it, by tacit reliance on the body and the nervous system. In some instances, a part of the body itself or portions of the nervous system may come
into focal awareness, while the remainder of the body is relied upon tacitly.
When perception is distorted by a psychedelic drug such as LSD, the changes
in the perception of objects (such as a fluid undulating quality of boundary
lines) is not in the objects themselves, of course, but is a change in the integrative ability of the nervous system. The perception of apparent undulation
is referred not to the objects (as in the usual act of attending to the external
world) but to the changes in the visual integration of the nervous system.

The perception of a comprehensive entity involves the tacit reliance upon
cues, in a subsidiary way, in order to attend to the entity perceived. We are
thus always participant in our perceptions, although usually in a tacit fashion
of which we are unconscious. The perception may be faulty, as in the case of

illusions, and we may be inclined towards further reliance upon further cues to discern a still more comprehensive way of integrating the same cues into a more reliable and enduring comprehensive entity.

In Polanyi's view, the creative movement of science consists of the apprehension of ever more comprehensive entities that permit a more satisfying integration of the available information. This is like an intuitive search for an understanding that will 'make sense' of the information supplied by the sensation function, the logic of thinking, and the affect of feeling, by showing that they originate from a comprehensive entity that had been insufficiently apprehended before the creative act. There is an intrinsic satisfaction in the discovery of more comprehensive entities, a satisfaction that underlies the creative activities of science. It would seem that a similar joy inhabits the movements of analysis in discovering for the analysand more comprehensive ways of understanding the process of individuation.

Focal-tacit knowing and dreams

Since, in the language of focal-tacit knowing, Polanyi made no clear intrinsic demarcation of conscious/unconscious, there is not a prior reason why the same fundamental principles should not apply to perception within a dream. In every dream there is a point of observation, a centre of subjectivity, although it is not always associated with the image of a body as in waking life. The dreamer may even experience the perception of his body in the dream as if he were outside it.

One man, for example, reported a reassuring dream at a time when he was experiencing anxiety about approaching surgery for coronary by-pass. He dreamed that he saw himself in three different bodies: the physical body, an identical but translucent body, and a third identical but transparent body. As he watched, the physical body removed its heart and handed it to the translucent body for inspection. The translucent body looked at the heart and handed it back, saying, 'It looks to me as if it will be all right'. The third, transparent, body simply observed without interaction. The dreamer awoke with a sense of conviction that his surgery would be successful as it proved to be. It was only after awakening that he realised he had been watching the three dream bodies from a fourth point of view, one that had no body whatsoever.

Another person suffering from severe self-criticism and depression dreamed that he shot another man, only then immediately to become the other man, feeling the impact of the bullet and the pain of injury. Many other examples can be cited by any analyst to illustrate the fashion in which the 'I' of the dream (which I shall call *dream-ego* or dream-I) has a variety ob bodily representations in dreams (including the case of the no-body, the 'floating eye' perspective). With a slight amount of additional intuition, it is possible to describe the fashion in which a dream-I seems to shift its tacit structure from one scene of the dream to another.

Let us consider one example of a focal/tacit shift of the identity of the dream-ego within the space of one dream. This is a recurrent dream of a graduate student. In the dream he found that he was watching a boy watching a river, but suddenly became the boy watching the river. The river then became turbulent and frightening. At the point of maximal fear, the sequence suddenly reversed and he was again himself watching the boy who was watching the river. This strangely symmetrical dream is an excellent example of the shift of the dream-ego from an observing function to identification with the contents personified by the boy, and then a subsequent disidentification under the stress of fearful affect.

In discussing such dream shifts in the language of focal-tacit knowing, several definitions are useful:

Waking-ego is the sense of 'I' inherent in any waking experience. The ego as the centre of consciousness is experienced primarily as a centre of subjectivity. In a subsidiary way, the waking 'I' is tacitly as a centre of subjectivity. In a subsidiary way, the waking 'I' is tacitly identified with the body, relying upon the body for orientation and perception. In a more psychological sense, the 'I' of the *waking-ego* also relies upon an ego-image that involves characteristic patterns of relating to objects that are the substrate of usual forms of response and feeling.

Dream-ego is used for the exactly parallel sense of being a centre of subjectivity within the dream. The dream-ego differs from the waking-ego in several important respects: it can be associated with a number of body-images, and in fact with no image whatsoever. The dream-ego can experience changes and abrupt transitions from one form to another in a fashion that is not experienced by the waking-ego except when bracketed within some form of imaginal activity, as phantasy, day-dreaming, reverie, hypnotic imagery, or active imagination. The dream-ego may behave in a fashion that is more developed or more regressive than the waking-ego. It can have a full range of emotion, but usually seems to lack the capacity for deep ambivalence that can be experienced by the waking-ego (JUNG 3, para. 580). Among the transitions that can be experienced by the dream-ego, one is abrupt awakening from the dream; there is no similar parallel transformation for the waking-ego, excepting the pathological state of narcolepsy, with its rapid transition from the waking state to REM sleep. The most rapid transitions experienced by the waking-ego are changes in emotional tone or in perception. The experiences of the dream-ego are generally compensatory to the waking-ego (JUNG 3, para 693).

The *self* is used here in the traditional Jungian sense as the organising centre of the psyche. it is considered to be

1) the total organised field of the psyche, both conscious and unconscious;

2) the organising centre to which the ego relates as to the central archetype of order (FORDHAM 1), experiencing this symbolic centre in the mandala forms and numinous images; and

3) as the archetypal core of the ego itself, the ego functioning in consciousness as an organising centre reflective of the more comprehensive organisational centering of the self. A significant activity of the self is the formation of dreams, so that not only the context of the dream but the particular rôle assigned to the dream-ego is considered to be a result of the activity of the self.

Centre of subjectivity is a term introduced to refer to the sense of 'I' in the dreaming or the waking state. This sense of identity would seem to me to be a direct reflection of the self as the archetypal core of the ego, whether in the waking or dreaming state.

Complexes are used in the usual sense as collections of related images held together by a common emotional tone. Although reliance upon this traditional definition would make it seem that any image associated with a complex might substitute for any other, it is assumed on the basis of clinical practice that the particular choice of a specific image to represent a certain complex, as the mother complex, would convey some *nuance* of meaning within the structure of that particular dream. This *nuance* of meaning is considered to be a function of the activity of the self. The concept of specific *nuance* accounts for the diversity of images that in a series of dreams seem to represent the same complex. In traditional Freudian dream theory these changing images would be considered to be different *ad hoc* disguises produced by the 'dreamwork' to prevent irruption into consciousness of unacceptable repressed memories.

Ego-image and dominant ego-image are terms introduced in order to speak clearly about the diversity of ego-images that compete for recognition and acceptance by the ego. The terms *ego, shadow,* and *persona* are ways of describing recurrent structures of possible ego-images, although the singular form may be misleading: there is a diversity of personae, shadows, and potential egos. The current dominant ego-image is always under the pressure of individuation.

Complex-structure and *object-relation pattern* are virtually equivalent terms for describing the structure of complexes in an objective language as seen from outside the subject studied (complex structure) or as experienced by the subject when part of the complex-structure constitutes a portion of the identity of his dominant ego-image (object-relation pattern). An example of appropriate use of the terms *complex-structure* would be in describing the structure of complexes in the unconscious of the subject through observation of some objective sample of the subject's psychological productions, as in the Word Association experiment or in viewing the recurrence of similar patterns in a series of dreams. The subject himself, however, would experience the same complex-structure as an object-relation pattern, that is, would experience part of his own dominant-ego identity (and therefore that of significant other persons) as partially influenced by the object-relation pattern in his unconscious mind (of which he is ordinarily unaware). The term *object-relation pattern* is therefore used to speak of a complex-structure that has significant influence on a dominant ego-image and consequently upon significant relations of that dominant ego-image, whether with persons in the outer world or with personified contents of the subject's mind, as in dreams. *Object-relation pattern* is not meant to imply the range of theory, Freudian and Kleinian in origin, that is called 'object-relations theory', although there are similarities that are not central to the present discussion. It would seem that when any complex-structure becomes associated with the dominant ego-images as an object-relation pattern there is a mutual origination of an ego-identity, a shadow identity, a likely persona reflected in a cultural rôle, and expected modes of interpersonal relationship. Any archetypal dominant, as for example that of the great mother, determines a likely form for the ego structure, including patterns of relationship, and constellates specific tasks of development.

The Phenomenology of dreams

Dreaming is such a universal human experience that it is seldom looked at without preconception. Piaget has observed, however, that there appears to be a time in which the developing child experiences the dreams as occuring in the same space and time as ordinary events, much in the form of an hypnagogic (going-to-sleep) or a hypnopompic (awakening) hallucination. Piaget's developmental observation underscores the phenomenological quality of both dreaming and waking experience as *lived occurrences* in which the ego, the centre of subjectivity, may participate or simply observe. In the dream, as in waking life, there are clearly events and causes that appear to be outside the ego but impinge upon it; conversely there are actions by the ego, in the dream or in waking life, that seem to impact upon the (contextual) reality.

Although we may, from the view of waking-ego, describe differences between waking experience and the dream, there is no certainty that the waking-ego has a privileged position, for it seems at times as if the dream-ego experiences the state of the psyche more comprehensively than does the waking-ego to whom it is related. Cocteau's remark that 'The dreamer must accept his dream' emphasises how thrown the dream-ego can be when it finds itself the inheritor of contingencies of which it was not the sole cause. In one of Jung's analogies, the ego is like the hereditary monarch of a kingdom whose boundaries and history he does not entirely know. It is only necessary to remind ourselves that Jung's simile holds equally for the waking-ego and the dream-ego, although the borders of the country surveyed (and perhaps, as we will attempt to show, even the nature of the monarch) may change through influences outside the awareness and power of either ego to alter, this alternation seeming to be evidence for the autonomous activity of the self.

What are the phenomenological differences between the dream-ego and the waking-ego? As far as the archetypal essence of the ego is concerned, there is no difference whatsoever. Some have stated that the 'depth' of feeling and reflection of the dream-ego is less than that of the waking-ego, although this is difficult to substantiate except as a judgement of the waking-ego.

If not in the sense of being a centre of subjectivity, in what do differences lie? Perhaps the primary difference is not in the ego itself, dreaming or awake, but in the way in which the ego experiences its world. Here a distinction is immediately evident: the dream-ego experiences sudden alterations of viewpoint and scene, and may alternately be embodied or disembodied within the dream. Within the dream, scenes change with the rapidity of cinematographic technique without the time and space constraints of the waking world; events may happen outside the range of the expectable—fish swim in the air, small turtles may swallow giant meals, the wind may lift one as a kite, inner thoughts of others may be transparent, and a West Texas horned toad may live in the fire as cheerfully as any alchemical salamander. Perhaps the most extreme dream-event is the ending of the world, an eschatological crisis that fortunately has not manifested in the outer collective world.

In the dream these changes of events outside the dream-ego carry an autonomy equivalent to events in the waking world. It is only through waking reflection or analysis that they are seen to be intimately connected with the processes of individuation of the waking-ego. (I exclude here so-called 'lucid dreams' in which the dreamer is said to be aware of dreaming, or even able to control the course of the dream. New analysands have at times claimed to have this ability, but have never demonstrated it in subsequent dreaming. My speculation is that such claims represent one form of ego-inflation, perhaps non-pathological, and that the phenomena described indicate (1) a possible ability to affect day-residue but not the dramatic structure of the residue in the dream, and/or (2) shifts into non-REM mentation with reverie about the dream.) Although the waking-ego may experience sudden changes in its world, for example, the reappearance of an old acquaintance, one presumed to be deceased, such sudden changes are, in fact, rare. What is common experience both in waking life and in the dream is the rapid shift of emotional tone, which may occur at the moment of a chance remark by a person who is emotionally important. When observed closely, as in the transference/countertransference mode or in the process of group psychotherapy, such sudden emotional changes seem to be related to potential shifts in the tacit boundaries of the currently dominant ego-identity. For clarity it should be remembered that such shifts can be experienced either as positive or negative from the point of view of (1) a regressed object-relation pattern that is competing with a more current identity, or (2) from an emerging identity pattern which has not yet taken a stable and enduring form.

This admittedly incomplete discussion of different modes of experience of the waking-ego and the dream-ego (while both maintain the archetypal sense of being centres of subjectivity) can help us to examine the structure of the dream-ego and its effect upon the alteration of structure in the waking-ego. In this discussion the relevance of Polany's focal-tacit knowing will, I hope, become clear as a useful framework for stating many clinical insights in a more precise form.

Clinical Examples

A middle-aged man with an obsessive-compulsive character structure (which works well for him in his profession) arranged to take a day off from work in order to spend time with his wife on their wedding anniversary. He thus acted in a fashion frustrating to the dominant ego-image of being a continually productive worker. The night before the holiday he had this dream:

> It was in a military school, or the army, talking with another cadet or soldier about a ceremony in which we were to stand in a line while a firing squad shot at us. I remembered that this had happened many times before, and that I had never been hit, but suddenly I realised that it was possible that I might be seriously wounded or killed. The ceremony seemed somehow real and not-real at the time. I decided that my loyalty to the military code was less than my desire to preserve my own safety. With this insight, I simply left the military situation, for which there seemed to be no penalty.

The dream-ego seems to have experienced a significant change in what had been a long-standing pattern. Presumably the possibility of injury had been continually present in previous 'execution', but had not been conscious for the dream-ego. Did the lysis of the dream — leaving the military situation — have impact on the waking-ego that followed the dream?

The analysand described the day after the dream as one in which he did little. Several errands that had been planned in the company of his wife were abandoned by mutual consent, while some were completed. He described his conscious experience of the 'free' day as one of feeling at ease and unregimented but with no sense of exaggerated exhilaration at freedom (which might imply being bound on another level). He said that the most suitable word to describe his state of mind was 'neutral'.

A woman in her late thirties had struggled for years with a severe mother complex. Never being able to elicit from her mother a convincing sense of her mother loving her, she felt unworthy and unable to function in an adult fashion, even though her actual accomplishments were evident, including a

stable marriage, good mothering of two children, and the achieving of an advanced professional qualification. Her extreme unconscious dependence on
her mother was revealed in the following sad dream:

> She had entered a 'mothering contest' at the state fair. She felt she had a good
> chance of winning, because she knew she had been an excellent mother to her two
> children. Then she realised that she could be disqualified, because the judges were to
> assess *how one had been mothered* rather than her own abilities as a mother.

The first clear lysis in the relationship with her mother occurred later when
the mother came for a stay of several days in the patient's home. It was the
first time that the analysand had been able to speak up for her own wants in
the presence of her mother. On the first night of this visit, the patient had
dreamed that she was kissing her maternal grandmother, her mother's
mother. This dream seemed to indicate that her dream-ego had made contact
with a maternal complex (the grandmother) that symbolised a feminine and
mothering relationship earlier and 'deeper' than the pathological image of the
personal mother that had seemed to be the core of her neurosis. When she
awoke, she was able for a number of days to behave as an equal with her
mother, enjoying their relationship for the first time and finding to her surprise that her mother was not formidable at all when the patient was not excessively concerned with her approval.

It is interesting to note that within several days of this successful visit from
the mother, this analysand dreamed of the death of the analyst, 'it felt,' she
said, 'like the death of an esteemed national figure'. She visited my office for a
last time, saw my grave in one of the rooms, and felt that 'the atmosphere was
sunny, not at all morbid'. Perhaps this suggests that with the dimunution of
the excessive dependence on the mother-image she required less of an idealis-
ing transference as a compensating counterweight. I was unable to detect at
the time, or since, any significant change in the analytic, waking, relationship.

Another woman, who also had a trait of a deep self-rejection based on an in-
ternalised object-reaction pattern as a result of a pathological early relationship
with her mother, reported a dream with similar meaning, showing the dream-
ego refusing to consider modifications to the archaic pattern of dependency on
the mother. In her waking life, this dreamer suffered from a severe problem of
obsessive-compulsive scrupulosity, always fearing that she might have done
something wrong and fearing that ultimately she would be sent to hell for her
objectively minor oversights and misdeeds.

She dreamed:

> My husband and I were living at my mother's house, and were sleeping outside
> [the setting already suggests a regressive state, the mother's house, and a potential
> dis-identification from that state — i. e., the 'sleeping outside']. The telephone rang
> and when may husband answered it, it was a wrong number. But I could hear the

voice plainly, and it sounded just like my mother, so I told him to ask. When he asked, the lady on the telephone said that she was not my mother, but that she had this same 'wrong number' many times before [this suggests the motif of synchronicity within the dream, which can raise important theoretical questions]. She said that she had a message for John, and Jean, and Sue and Bill [fictitious names for the dreamer and siblings, but in the dream the correct names were used]. So did NOT [capitalisation from dreamer's written report] take the message, not because *I* was the wrong *receiver*, but because *she* was wrong *sender* (because she was not my mother).

The dream continued immediately with the dreamer meeting a large animal that frightened her, although it was not hostile. She was then followed by a number of other animals (the nature of which she could not specify). They did not seem to be threatening her, although she was afraid of them. She was awakened from the dream by her husband, who heard her making frightened noises in her sleep.

The dreams of these two women show still-active identity patterns based on object-relation structures that reflect archaic parts of early mother-child interaction. Both dreams offer an opportunity for the dream-ego to act within the structure in an affective manner, and thus potentially to change the identity pattern of the waking-ego. In the dream of the state fair mothering contest, no attempt is made to do so and this remembered dream can be considered to offer the classical picture of compensation: the waking-ego, remembering the state of the dream-ego, can reflect upon it as a commentary about its own awakened behaviour. In making such a classic reflection on the compensatory nature of the dream, the waking-ego assumes that it is in some sense identical with the dream-ego, that the 'I' of the waking-ego and the dream-ego somehow refer to the same identity structures.

In the telephone dream of the second patient (who had a clinical picture similar to the first) the dream-ego is faced with three discernible motifs:

1) the setting of living at the mother's house, although married and with her husband;

2) the strange telephone call from someone who sounds like her mother but is not (and the added emphasis of this voice saying that the same thing has happened many times before, i.e., that there may be synchronicity *within the dream* through the mother-sounding-voice repeated by having reached 'by chance' the number of the woman whose voice she resembles); and

3) the sudden appearance of the animals when the message is denied out of apparent loyalty to hearing only what the 'real' mother has to say.

The first of these three motifs (living in the mother's house) could be seen as part of a classic compensation dream. In waking life the ego is not living near the mother, while in the dream she is still at home (with aspects of the setting described later, such as a particular trapeze swing, that suggest a certain time in adolescence). The interpretation of this first motif could be, 'Your dream seems to show you living emotionally with your mother'. This would add emphsis to something already present in the consciousness of the waking-ego: while living in outer life at a great distance from the mother, the ego is still affectively and inwardly identified with the world of the mother. Although the waking-ego has the sense of being a centre of subjectivity, an I-ness, it is not yet a centre of autonomy, the ego-self axis being subordinated to a lesser centre represented by the mother-image.

In the second motif of the dream — the synchronistic 'wrong number' telephone call — the regressed world of the dream-ego is invaded by spontaneous activity of the psyche. Theoretically, the self as fountainhead of the dream has spontaneously injected new possiblities of different object-relation patterns into the mother's house. If it were possible to know what would happen if the dream-ego *had* accepted the call, we could speculate about a change in the waking-ego based upon the action of the dream-ego. Active imagination might have produced some evidence in this regard, but was not utilised with this patient. As it stands, then, we must judge the appropriateness or inappropriateness of the dream-ego's refusing the call by examining internal evidence within the dream. Was her refusal an avoidance of inappropriate influence from outside, or was it an avoidance of new experiences that might have revitalised her individuation? It seems to me that the most consistent reading of the dream suggests a missed opportunity for needed change. The sudden appearance of the animals, and their obvious focus upon the dream-ego in a non-threatening way, suggests that they represent in a different form the message that was refused from the voice that sounded like the mother. She gave no specific images or associations to the animals. Indeed they are not even identified in her memory, so the motif of 'animal' may be amplified in a cultural and archetypal fashion where the appropriate emphasis would seem to be on the animal as a symbol of basic life force, perhaps in the direction of the universally valued 'helpful animal' of fairy tales, the animal form that can do what the hero of the tale cannot directly accomplish. I find nothing in the dream to suggest the dark side of the animal motif as a devouring, rageful life unrelated to the human realm.

The Compensatory Function of the Unanalysed Dream

I have discussed in detail elsewhere (HALL 2, pp. 151—62) the manner in which dreams that have not been analysed nor subjected to reflection may still influence the state of the waking-ego. The dream appears to be a normal psychic product, necessary for the health of the personality. The dream functions in this compensatory and reparative fashion even when not remembered. This may be conceptualised as the action of the dream (of which the activity of the dream-ego is a major factor) influencing the structure of complexes that constitute or influence the waking-ego. Changes may be initiated at many levels from the archetypal objective psyche to the personal unconscious, altering the psychic milieu in which the ego-images occur and perhaps altering the dominant ego-image itself.

The waking-ego inherits any changes the dream causes in its tacit structure and in the structure of complexes that underlie the waking-ego's object-relation patterns. There is thus a continuing dialogue between the waking-ego and the self, mediated partially through the experiences of the dream-ego. In attending to these processes and the relationship of the dream-ego to the waking-ego, it is possible for the analytical psychologist to identify the fine structure of the individuation process as the self complements, compensates, and directly influences the tacit structure of the personality. This micro-process of individuation may be experienced by the waking-ego as moving it more toward balance in its present life situation, but may at times oppose a current adaptation in deference to as yet unrealised tasks of the underlying process of individuation.

One brief example (discussed fully in HALL 2, pp. 157—9 and pp. 172—7) was of a man who seemed to be repeating in a neurotic and compulsive fashion the behaviour of his father in accepting offices in service organisations, only to find the actual work of the office to be a burden. The father had committed suicide at about the same age that the analysand was when he began analysis. In one analytic hour he announced that he had spontaneously changed his pattern, declining such an office several days after he had initially accepted it. He had not himself seen that a dream he told me seemed to show a change in his attitude towards his father; that revealed itself in a changed attitude towards the whole identity structure of the waking-ego, at least to the extent that the waking-ego was tacitly based upon the complex structure pictured in the dream. In the dream the dream-ego watched in a rather passive manner as the father attempted to get the attention of patrons of a coffee house by plying the guitar and singing. When he finally got their applause, he was suddenly blinded and became dependent upon the dream-ego to guide him back to the table. The attitude of the dream-ego was anger and disappointment because now energy would have to be devoted to the care of the disabled father rather than invested in activities such as marriage that were of greater personal interest. It was after this dream that the man 'spontaneously' changed his mind and resigned from the new office.

Although it may be impossible to establish that an *un*-remembered dream is the cause of change in the waking-ego, changes following dreams that were not reflected upon, personally or in analysis, suggest that the change would have occurred even if the dream had not been remembered. In considering the compensatory function of the unremembered dream we are apparently at a boundary of observability similar to that of being unable to know simultaneously the position and the momentum of an electron.

Consideration of the fashion in which the activity of the dream-ego may change the structure of the waking-ego broadens our understanding of the ways in which the compensatory function of dreams functions in the natural process of individuation, even in persons who never recall dreaming but dream (as does everyone) several times each night during the 90-minute REM cycle. In discussing the structure of the compensatory function of dreams, even when unremembered and unanalysed the concept of focal-tacit knowing are particularly useful language.

The Usefulness of Focal-Tacit Knowing

Jungian psychology appreciates the spontaneous activity of the unconscious as an active force within the psyche. The relationship of the ego and the self can stand for the central force and mystery of the individuation process. While the attitude and form of the waking-ego is accessible (within limits) to observation and self-reporting, the activity of the self must remain a more borderline conceptualisation, being inferred (as are archetypes-in-themselves) by the effects that are produced. A major effect of the self is the production of dreams that may be compensatory not only to the current attitude and adaptation of the waking-ego, but that also can influence the ego in a wider sense, involving it in the on-going process of individuation.

Polanyi's epistemology of focal-tacit knowing permits clear description of shifts between the focal knowledge of the ego and the tacit components of that knowledge (ultimately including the body-mind unit) by means of which focal knowledge is contemplated. The search of the waking-ego for a more comprehensive vision of what is known focally leads to the emergence (when the activity is successful) of new and unique ways of comprehending reality in a more complete and satisfying manner. Polanyi seems to rely upon an innate activity of the psyche towards the apprehension of increasingly more comprehensive entities, an activity closely parallel to the activity of the self upon the ego in (1) the individuation process and (2) in the activity of the waking-ego in investigating the nature of reality, as in alchemical lore or in the activity of scientific investigation.

When the focal-tacit activity of the waking-ego's desire to know is focused back upon its own nature, the ego seems to vanish as though over an horizon (SARTRE 6), seemingly revealing its innate emptiness of content and leaving only an inventory of persona attributes that can be catalogued but do not reveal the essence of the sense of subjectivity and autonomy that hallmark the healthy ego. Questions such as, 'what is my real personality?', that are so often asked at the beginning of analysis are never really answered, for to define the 'real' personality would be to identify the innate freedom of the ego again with a particular ego-image, allowing neurotic processes to continue. Although the question of the 'real' personality is never answered in successful therapy, it is transcended: when the ego is truly related to the self (individuating) there is no affective force in the question of defining the 'true' ego-image. The emptiness of which Sartre complained is merely the inability to rely simultaneously upon identical contents in both the focal and tacit compartments of the focal-tacit structure of knowing.

In applying Polanyi's language to dream imagery, it is necessary to make only a few basic contentions:

a) Various psychic contents can be coalesced into a complex. Complexes themselves can be grouped into patterns. Complexes and patterns of complexes can be relied upon tacitly by the ego as a basis for ego-identity.

b) The imagery of dreams reveals focally the content of complexes personified (or imaged) in the dream.

c) Complexes that are imaged in a dream may be within or without the tacit components of the ego; but any complex imaged in a dream is *at that time* in some relationship with the dream-ego (i.e., is to some degree capable of becoming conscious).

d) A complex that is focal to the observation of the dream-ego may be either focal or tacit in relation to the structure of the waking-ego.

e) The ego as a centre of subjectivity is capable of differentation from any specific tacit content with which it is identified, although it is always representative of *some* tacit content, since any observable experience in waking life or in the dream follows the focal-tacit structure of knowing.

Polanyi's concept of focal-tacit knowing permits an increase of precision in clearly differentiating the ego as I-ness (centre of subjectivity) from the contents of the ego. The activity of the dream-ego can then be seen as meaningfully related to all ego activity, awake or asleep, in influencing the complex structures that serve as object-relation patterns for the waking-ego. The ego-self axis can be appreciated as the ego's grounding in the most comprehensive tacit component of the psyche, rather than subordinating the relationship with the self to some less comprehensive cluster, a complex or pattern of complexes, however archetypal the pattern may be. The creation of the dream can be seen as a spontaneous activity of the self to present the ego (in the form of dream-ego) with an opportunity to influence the tacit structure of the waking-ego. The ego related to the self in a responsible manner constitutes the ego-self axis,* the ego then experiencing itself not only as a centre of subjectivity (I-ness) but also as a centre of increasing autonomy, able to take attitudes towards other contents of the psyche under the guidance of the relationship to the self. In the empirical world of everyday reality, this is a furtherance of the process of individuation.

*Note: The term ego-self axis is in some ways unsatisfactory because it can imply or evoke a sense of static mechanical relationship. For the *activity* of the relationship indicated by the term ego-self axis, I prefer the phrase I have coined, 'ego-self spiration', intended to emphasise the dynamic, interactive and necessary relationship of ego and self.

Summary

The dream is conceptualised as the activity of the self assigning the dream-ego a particular rôle (and particular tacit structure) within a dramatisation of complexes (also chosen by the self) that offers the dream-ego an opportunity to influence the tacit structure of the waking-ego furthering (if successful) the process of individuation. This conceptualisation of the dream in terms of focal-tacit knowing permits a further amplification of the principle of the compensatory function of dreams. The dream can be seen as compensatory in three ways, the first two ways constituting the classical view of compensation:

(1) The waking-ego can see in the action of the dream-ego insufficiently recognised aspects of its own waking behaviour. The dream thus appears as a message from the self as dream-maker to the waking-ego.

(2) The dream may appear as a self-representation of the psyche, a revelation that may relate to the activity of the waking-ego or may be relatively independent of such reference (as in objective dreams that aid scientific discovery, seeming to speak about the nature of a more general reality). To the extent that the waking-ego is able to relate this self-representation to its own activity, the self-representation appears compensatory to the limited knowledge of the waking-ego.

(3) The dream assigns the archetypal core of the ego, the sense of I-ness as a centre of subjectivity, to a specific rôle (specific tacit structure) as a dream-ego within a specifically chosen focal dramatisation of other contents of the psyche. The dream-ego is thus offered an opportunity in the dream to influence the patterning of complexes. This is capable of influencing the tacit structure of the waking-ego and can be seen as a third form of the compensatory nature of the dream.

References

1. Fordham, M. (1963). 'The empirical foundation and theories of the self in Jung's works', J. analyt. Psychol., 8, 1.
2. Hall, J. (1977). Clinical Uses of Dreams: Jungian Interpretation and Enactments. New York, Grune & Stratton.
3. Jung, C. G. (1920). 'The psychological foundation of belief in spirits', Coll. Wks, 8.
4. Jung, C. G. (1921). Psychological Types Coll. Wks, 6.
5. Polanyi, M. (1958). Personal Knowledge. Chicago, University of Chicago Press.
6. Sartre, J. P. (1972). The Transcendence of the Ego. New York, Octagon.

(reprinted from The Journal of Analytical Psychology 1982, 27, 239–254 by permission)

Presenting the Singer-Loomis Inventory of Personality

By June Singer (Los Altos, California) and Mary Loomis (Grosse Pointe, Michigan)

The Singer-Loomis Inventory of Personality is designed to measure cognitive styles (Loomis and Singer, 1). The basic assumption of the *SLIP* is that a relationship exists between the manner in which individuals perceive and understand their environments, and the way in which they behave. This premise and the defining categories derive from C. G. Jung's theory of psychological types. The *SLIP* was prepared with the assistance of the Wayne State University Psychology Department and was aided by a grant from the Research Fund of the C. G. Jung Insitute of Chicago. It is being presented for the first time at the Eighth International Congress of the International Association for Analytical Psychology in San Francisco, September, 1980.

Jung (2) defined two basic attitudes — introversion and extraversion — which interacted with four functions — thinking, feeling, sensation and intuition — to form eight psychological types that are common to all human beings. These eight basic categories are being measured in the *SLIP*. Each of the eight categories of cognitive functioning is regarded as a particular cognitive mode, and their unique pattern of development within the individual comprises that person's cognitive style.

According to Jung's theory, introversion and extraversion determine individuals' orientation to their environment. Although both attitudes are present in each individual, there appears to be a biologically determined tendency for one to dominate. The introverted individual emphasizes the internal world of ideas and subjective reactions while minimizing relationships to the external world. The extraverted person emphasizes just the opposite. Value for extraverts lies in objects, or in relationships with people, while their subjective world is of less concern.

Jung hypothesized that the four functions are organized into two function-pairs. The judging function is comprised of thinking and feeling; the perceptual function is comprised of sensation and intuition. Jung specified that the oppositions were bipolar in nature; which is to say that extraversion and introversion were described as mutually exclusive, as were thinking and feeling, sensation and intuition. The assumed oppositions provided the rationale for the construction of two inventories of personality which pioneered in measuring typology in accordance with Jung's theory. These are the Gray-Wheelwrights' *Jungian Type Survey* (GW) (3), and the *Myers-Briggs Type Indicator* (MBTI) (4). Although both of these instruments have generated a substantial amount of research and data, the fundamental bipolar assumption upon which they were based had not been experimentally verified.

In 1976, Singer and Loomis began to consider the importance of investigating the bipolar assumption as utilized in the GW and MBTI. This was in light of the fact that in other psychological research it was being shown that certain fundamental oppositions — or what previously had been believed to be fundamental oppositions — were now yielding to a compromise position. For example, masculinity and femininity could be viewed psychologically as a dichotomy which could merge into androgyny (Bem, 5, Singer, 6). Androgyny was also evidenced in Helson's 1970 study of creative female mathematicians (7). In contrast to their less creative counterparts, creative female mathematicians retained their femininity while admitting masculine characteristics. Creative architects were the subject of Mac Kinnon's 1961 study (8). These individuals were found to be both artistic and intuitive. The creative architects, in addition to being classified as artistic, were seen as enjoying aesthetic and sensuous experiences, which suggests a highly developed sensation function. Yet sensation and intuition are classified as bipolar opposites in Jung's typology.

Why, then, have sensation and intuition, or thinking and feeling, *never* appeared paired as the two most highly developed functions in any profile obtained by inventories measuring Jung's typology? Examining the GW and the MBTI inventories reveals the answer. The inventories are constructed of forced-choice items, which result in a perfect negative correlation between the paired functions. If the test taker chooses one of the two alternative responses to an item, the other is automatically rejected. In talking with people who completed the inventories, the authors learned that many individuals found certain items especially difficult to answer. Either their complaints were that both alternatives seemed equally accurate in describing their preferences or, that both were equally improbable for them. Difficulty in selecting one of the two alternatives also was reported by Sundberg (9). Over half of the graduate students he polled found fault with the MBTI after completing the inventory. In addition, threefourths of his students indicated they would like to argue the meaning of "a lot of the questions." While problems are associated with answering the forced-choice items, less obvious problems are associated with the scoring of those items. In the GW and the MBTI, once a selection has been made, the rejected alternative is ignored. This means that of two highly-likely choices — both almost equally representative of the individual's preference — one is omitted in compiling the profile. Likewise, when there are two highly unlikely choices — neither one being truly representative of the individual's preference — one is given as much weight in scoring as a highly probalble choice.

Because of the distortions inherent in scoring the responses to forced-choice items, the possibility existed that what appeared to be the superior function in the profiles obtained by the GW or the MBTI might be in error. The authors concluded that if they were to test this bipolar assumption to determine whether it was a correct measure of Jung's theory of typology, they would have to measure the functions independently, without forcing a negative correlation. If the bipolar assumption obtained universally, the opposition of the superior and inferior functions should be demonstrable, regardless of the construction of the test items. Further, if the profiles obtained by the GW and the MBTI were not partially artifacts of the forced-choice items, then changing the construction, but not the contents, of the items should not change the profiles.

The GW and the MBTI were reconstructed so that the forced-choice construction was eliminated and items could be scored independently on a scale from *1* to *7*, where *1* was *never* and *7* was *always*. For example, and item such as:

At a party, I
a. like to talk.
b. like to listen.

was replaced by two scaled items separated in the test:

At a party I like to talk.
At a party I like to listen.

The result, which are shown in the table below, demonstrate that many individuals, when given a free choice in responding, showed a different superior function than they did when the forced-choice was required. In addition, in a significant number of cases, the inferior function under the free-choice option did not prove to be the opposite of the superior function.

Table 1: Profile changes when scaled items replace forced-choice items

Number of subjects	GW	MBTI	TOTAL
in the study	120	79	199
Changes in Superior Function	86 (72%)	36 (46%)	122 (61%)
Inferior Function not opposed to Superior	66 (55%)	29 (36%)	95 (48%)

These results demonstrate that the profiles obtained by the GW and the MBTI are partially artifacts of the forced-choice item construction in the inventories. This does not mean that Jung's position on the theoretical opposition of functions is incorrect. It suggests, rather, that for some individuals the opposition of functions may accurately reflect their cognitive styles and personality development, but for other individuals the opposition of functions does not hold. In the profiles of this second group of people, the functions appear to be independent.

In order to assess whether an individual's functions conform to the pattern of bipolar opposition or deviate from it, the SLIP has been constructed to measure the eight cognitive modes independently.

Technical Considerations

Jung's eight basic psychological types are descriptive categories of cognitive functioning. They do not specify which internal processes are involved for the different functions. Nowhere is short term storage or iconic memory mentioned, for example. The SLIP utilizes Jung's descriptive categories. Each of the fifteen questions in this instrument specifies a particular situation constraint. The situations are in accord with the rudimentary taxonomy presented by Pervin in 1976 (10). Each question also specifies an internal affective state for the respondent.

Each individual has the inherent capacity to use all eight cognitive modes. However, because of the interaction between genetic endowment and social reinforcement, some cognitive modes become more highly developed than others. Individuals tend to rely on those modes which have allowed the most successful adaption to their environment. The SLIP profile reveals the relative strengths and weaknesses of the eight cognitive modes at a particular time, for a particular individual. In this respect, the SLIP differs from most other instruments measuring personality factors. It is inappropriate, therefore, to compare a particular cognitive mode from one individual to another.

The fifteen situations comprising the Inventory were selected after a factor analysis led to a revision of the original SLIP, which had consisted of twenty situations (see section of Research, below). An example of the sort of "situation" used in the SLIP follows. Persons taking the Inventory are asked to assign a number on a scaled score for *each* of the eight responses:

Q: I receive an invitation to attend a political rally for a candidate whom I favor. I would

1. *enjoy the party while getting the views of many people to help me make up my own mind.*
2. *throw the invitation away and forget it.*
3. *sit quietly and listen to what the candidate is not saying.*
4. *write a letter saying that while I agree with the principles the candidate stands for, I would rather send a contribution than go to the meeting.*
5. *speculate with others as to how we could influence the public to vote for our candidate.*

6. *go to the rally and offer my services to help design a public opinion poll.*
7. *go and observe the people at the rally and how the event has been managed, because little things often give away what a person is really like.*
8. *volunteer to help in the office preparing mailing or doing other necessary chores.*

Scoring

The Inventories will be machine scored through the Center for the Study of Cognitive Processes, Psychology Department, Wayne State University, Detroit, Michigan 48202. Detailed computerized printouts will be returned for each answer sheet scored. These printouts will include such information for each individual as: the relative strength of the various cognitive modes or functions, the most frequently utilized functions, and the interactions between the functions according to the particular individual pattern of preferences. Each function will be described in the context of the individual's profile. For sample profile, see *Appendix* below.

Research

Factor Analysis

The first version of the Singer-Loomis Inventory of Personality consisted of twenty questions with eight responses to each question. The Inventory was administered to 217 people, all adults, and the results were factor analyzed (Loomis, 11). Five independent factors emerged from the analysis. The first four factors contained both introverted and extraverted responses while the fifth factor consisted almost entirely of extraverted responses. The factor and the amount of variance each explained are shown in Table 2.

Table 1: Factors in the SLIP and the Percentage of the
         Total Variance Each Explained

Factor	Percentage of Total Variance Explained
One-Feeling	8.967
Two-Intuition	8.355
Three-Thinking	6.076
Four-Introverted Sensation	5.750
Five-Extraverted Sensation	4.762
Variance Explained	33.910

The first factor contained items concerned with value judgments, with empathy, and with sympathy. This was labelled *feeling*, and accounted for 8.9 percent of the variance. Half of the items were introverted and half were extraverted. The second factor, explaining an 8.4 percent of the variance, contained items which dealt imagining, speculating, and envisioning. Again, half the items were introverted and half were extraverted. The factor was labelled *intuition*. The third factor, accounting for six percent of the variance, icluded half introverted and half extraverted items dealing with the *thinking* function. The items included responses of systematic planning or logical problem solving.

The fourth factor, also explaining approximately six percent of the variance, contained items which referred to unbiased data-gathering or working with the hands. This was recognized as the non-judgmental *sensation* function. The items were not evenly split between introverted and extraverted responses. Nine of the twelve items comprising this fourth factor were introverted responses, thus the factor was called *introverted sensation*.

The fifth factor, accounting for approximately five percent of the variance, contained items which all related to physical or body sensations. Ten of the eleven items were extraverted and this factor was labelled *extraverted sensation*.

The results of the factor analysis were utilized in revising the original SLIP. First, the five least discriminating questions were eliminated from the current version of the Inventory. Secondly, individual items were examined to determine that their factor loadings are consistent with the scoring of the eight cognitive modes. Also, items were rewritten if they loaded positively on more than one factor. Negative correlations were acceptable and some items did evidence the bipolarity which Jung hypothesized, however they were infrequent. Only four items had negative factor loadings of approximately .3 or greater.

Availability

The Singer-Loomis Inventory of Personality is now available for therapists, educators and other professionals to use with clients. It is hoped that the SLIP will be utilized for research by qualified persons and that the results of such research will be sent to the authors of this instrument. A manual, "About the SLIP," is currently available. This will be revised to include additions based on new research. Any projects using this Inventory may be reported in the forthcoming revised manual, with full credit given to the persons conducting the research.

For further information, please contact the authors: Mary Loomis, Ph. D., 553 University, Grosse Pointe, MI 48230
June Singer, Ph. D., 876 Hoffman Terrace, Los Altos, CA 94022

Singer-Loomis Inventory of Personality
Cognitive Profile Results
Client's Name <u>Sample Sue</u> Examiner <u>Loomis</u> Date Scored _____

Raw Scores
IT *23* IF *26* IS *28* IN *17* ET *19* EF *28* ES *42* EN *27*

Each person utilizes a variety of ways to comprehend reality, both inner and outer. These various ways of comprehending and knowing are cognitive modes. C. G. Jung, in his work, *Psychological Types*, characterized these ways as combinations of "attitude" and "function." The combinations result in eight "types" or "cognitive modes." The uniqueblending of these modes determines a person's "cognitive style." The Singer-Loomis Inventory or Personality is designed to measure the eight distinct cognitive modes of perceiving and judging.

The cognitive style, as determined by this person's responses to the SLIP is shown on the graph below.

```
         Introversion                    Extraversion
4.0

3.5

3.0                                                    **
                                                       **
                                                       **
2.5                                                    **
                                                       **
                                                       **
2.0                         **              **     **  **  **
                            **              **     **  **  **
                            **              **     **  **  **
1.5      **   **   **                 **    **     **  **  **
         **   **   **                 **    **     **  **  **
         **   **   **                 **    **     **  **  **
1.0      **   **   **   **            **    **     **  **  **
         **   **   **   **            **    **     **  **  **
         **   **   **   **            **    **     **  **  **
 .5      **   **   **   **            **    **     **  **  **
         **   **   **   **            **    **     **  **  **
         **   **   **   **            **    **     **  **  **
       ──────────────────────────────────────────────────────
         IT   IF   IS   IN           ET    EF     ES  EN
```

Figure depicting this individual's average scores on the eight cognitive modes
I = Introversion   E = Extraversion
T = Thinking   F = Feeling   S = Sensation   N = Intuition

On this profile, extraversion is dominant. When extraversion is dominant, the individual's primary interest is, "What impact am I making on my world?" Essential decisions and actions are determined by the extravert's relationship with other people. Extraverts cannot ignore objective facts. They have the ability to fit into existing conditions with relative facts. They have many friends. When the extraverted attitude is extreme, an overvaluation of the external world may leave the extravert with only the appearance of being normally adjusted. Extraverts may sacrifice personal preferences and needs, in order to gain success and acceptance in the world. For example, they may be caught in the demands of a continuously expanding business and feel compelled to seize every opportunity to make a profit. This strong outward direction may cause extraverts to fail to consider their own bodies adequately. Simple elementary requirements which are indispensable to physical well-being may be minimized or ignored.

Each person utilizes both introversion and extraversion at different times and in different situations. The conscious awareness of our primary modes of functioning can help us to recognize where we can be most effective, and also when we need to develop alternative modes to adapt to specific situations — or to enhance a general growth pattern.

Function

On this profile, the most highly developed function is sensation. Sensation is characterized by perception via the senses. Attention is paid to detail and small differences can be discriminated with ease. These individuals accept things as they are "right now" and deal concretely with materials at hand.

Cognitive Modes

The combinations of attitudes (introversion and extraversion) and functions (thinking, feeling, intuition, and sensation) represent the cognitive modes shown on the graph.

The leading cognitive mode or "superior function" is extraverted sensation. These people are in touch with the physical aspects of life in themselves and others. They like to work as members of a team, with concrete materials, facts and figures. They have a capacity to assimilate details, even when unrelated, and to store them for future use. They do not fight facts, but are able to accept things as they are and work with them. They are generally unprejudiced, open-minded and egalitarian. They enjoy sharing with others the pleasure of senses: good food, music, active sports, movies, lovemaking and nature's beauty.

The second most highly developed cognitive mode, or "auxiliary function" is introverted sensation.

These people apprehend the background of the physical world rather its surface. What is important to them are the sensory impressions caused by external objects, more than the objects themselves. They have a good memory for detail. Being non-judgmental, they can be guided by what actually happens to them. They may provide a viewpoint that is based on eternal truisms.

The third most highly developed cognitive mode, or "auxiliary function" is extraverted feeling. These people let you know exactly where they stand on an issue and what value they place on people, situations and things. They are open to mutual interchange on many levels, and can respond to others with empathy. They are able to recognize what is appropriate behaviour in a given situation, and if they violate propriety, they do it consciously. Rarely neutral in their judgments about people, they tend to see others as friend or foe. They dislike apathy and want to be noticed and appreciated.

Interactions

An individual may have several well-developed cognitive modes. Generally, they will work together. In fact, the hallmark of a well-adjusted personality is that the most highly developed, or "superior", function is not isolated but works harmoniously with at least one or two other functions. Most frequently this interaction is between the "superior" function and one of the "auxiliary" functions or those that are next most highly developed. The interactions which follow represent the interactions between the most highly developed cognitive mode on this profile and the two "auxiliary" cognitive modes.

With introverted sensation and extraverted sensation, a balance between extraversion and introversion allows these people to appreciate both the external physical world and their own internal personal sensations. These people are able to discriminate fine differences in colors, sounds, and in style and fashion. They note details and remember them. They are aware of the sensations aroused in them by stimulation coming from outside themselves. They enjoy the company of others, especially when they are able to share anything that stimulates the senses, for example: listening to music or eating a good meal, but they also enjoy being alone. The introverted sensation mode provides them with the ability to experience their environment from a unique perspective of their own. They are able to discern a reality behind surface appearances. Since they are not judgmental, they are able to explore the unusual, even the societally unacceptable. They be without a hierarchy of values, and so find it difficult to establish priorities. The intensity of the sensation in the immediate present is of prime importance to them.

Extraverted feeling, extraverted sensation: Since both of the leading cognitive modes, feeling and sensation, are extraverted, these people will work well with others. They are seen by others as warm and sympathetic. They have the ability to see facts and details accurately, to remember them, and to order them. While these people do not often originate projects, they can be enthusiastic in carrying them out, and they are helpful in enlisting the aid of others. They are good in almost any kind of organizational work as well as in the service areas where relationships with people and accurate perceptions are required. Their need for approval from others may be so great that they deny their own inner feelings at times. Because they tend not to consider unexpected eventualities and not to think a problem through before they get started, they are likely to find themselves in compromising positions. They may, however, be able to talk themselves out of these through sheer charm or a display of efficiency.

Creativity

When among the leading cognitive modes, both introversion and extraversion appear, a creative balance is suggested. This is further enhanced when both intuition and sensation, or both thinking and feeling, occur among the most highly developed functions. Creativity appears to be associated with a flexibility in cognitive processes. The combination of these complementary functions seems to associated with an unusual flexibility in using what are normally opposing functions. However, there is the possibility that these functions, although both highly developed, may oppose instead of complementing each other. This would counteract a creative impulse.

Least Developed Cognitive Mode

The least well-developed cognitive mode generally works alone. It tends to appear in times of stress, illness, fatigue, grief, panic, acute disappointment, surprise, when under the influence of toxic substances, or other unusual circumstances. At such times, the usual means of response are often inaccessible to the person and the inferior function autonomously springs into action. All that we have learned fails us and the inferior function seems to have a mind of its own. Under these circumstances, the individual tends to function in a way different from his or her habitual patterns. Those ways of being, which most of the times are repressed or unconscious, tend to remain more primitive than the other functions.

When introverted intuition is the least developed cognitive mode ("inferior function"), these individuals tend to get carried away with a speculation or a project without considering the necessary practical reality or other alternatives. Trusting their own insights, they rarely ask for consultation, consequently they often overlook the essentials to solving their problems. Many of their solutions turn out to be unworkable. When working from this mode, these individuals are unaware of the physical limitations in themselves and others.

Increasing Cognitive Modes

It is important to remember that individuals are most successful in working with their most highly developed cognitive modes. That is, these are the modes that have provided the individuals with their most successful adaptation to the environment. In attempting to increase the modes of functioning which individuals use in their lives, more success will be achieved through the development of those cognitive modes in the middle range. Less success is to be expected through attempting to increase the use of the inferior function.

This completes the individual profile. General characteristics have been discussed, but the specific applications for the individual need to be explored and carefully considered. This may be best done with the help of a professional counselor, psychotherapist, or educator. The applications of this information may extend to many areas such as psychotherapy, educational counseling, vocational counseling, sexual dysfunction counseling, industrial counseling, retirement planning, and matters of personal relationships.

Understanding one's cognitive style makes it possible to see why one does or does not relate well to another person, to a job situation, or to a specific group. It also suggests the kinds of activities in which one is likely to be most successful as well as those in which difficulty may be encountered. This personality profile compares the development of the cognitive modes with one another; it does not compare this person's modes with those of any other person(s). Thus, this is an individual profile, and does not bear any relationship to a standardized profile on a general population.

This individual profile was prepared by Mary Loomis and June Singer, using the *Singer-Loomis Inventory of Personality*

1. Mary Loomis and June Singer. "Testing the Bipolar-Assumption in Jung's Typology," *Journal of Analytical Psychology*, 1980, vol. 25, no. 4, pp. 351—356
2. Carl Jung. *Psychological Types. Collected Works, Vol. 6.* Princeton, N. J., Princeton University Press, 1971.
3. Joseph Wheelwright, Jane Wheelwright, and John Buehler. *Jungian Type Survey: The Gray Wheelwrights Test.* San Francisco, Society of Jungian Analysts of Northern California, 1964.
4. Isabel Myers. *The Myers-Briggs Type Indicator.* Palo Alto, California, Consulting Psychologists Press, 1962.
5. Sandra Bem. "The Measurement of Psychological Androgyny," *Journal of Consulting and Clinical Psychology*, 1974, vol. 42, no. 2, pp. 155—162

6. June Singer. *Androgyny: Toward a New Theory of Sexuality.* New York, Anchor Press/Doubleday, 1976.
7. Ravenna Helson. "Women Mathematicians and the Creative Personality," *Journal of Consulting and Clinical Psychology,* 1971, vol. 36, no. 2, pp. 210—220
8. Donald MacKinnon. "The Personality Correlates of Creativity: A Study of American Architects," in *Creativity.* P. E. Vernon. ed., Baltimore, MD, Penguin Education, 1970, pp. 289—311.
9. Norman Sundberg. "The Myers-Briggs Type Indicator," *Sixth Mental Measurements Yearbook.* O. K. Buros, ed., Highland Park, N. J., Gryphon Press, 1965, pp. 322—325
10. Lawrence Pervin. "A Free-response Description Approach to the Analysis of Person-Situation Interaction," *Journal of Personality and Social Psychology,* 1976, vol. 34, no. 3, pp. 465—474
11. Mary Loomis. *Predicting Artistic Styles from Cognitive Styles.* Unpublished dissertation, Wayne State University, Detroit, 1980.

Images of Madness in Australian Aborigines

By Leon Petchkovsky (Hazelbrook, New South Wales, Australia)

Introduction

The concept of the archetype, it seems to me, loses much of its value if the archetype is not universal. Kingship is patently not universal; Aboriginal societies have thrived without it for 40,000 years. On the other hand, John Perry's accounts of kingship imagery sequences in the acute psychotic process are very compelling, and my filing cabinets contain many case notes of young Australian psychotics of European stock who display very similar image sequences.

How universal then is kingship imagery in psychosis?
1. Do these configurations appear in Aboriginal psychotic persons?
2. If not, then what are the typical image patterns?
3. Are there Aboriginal myths and rituals which have a similar relationship to Aboriginal psychosis that Egyptian/Hebrew/Mesopotamian kingship rituals have to Western psychosis?
4. More generally still, is there a relationship between psychotic imagery and socio-political forms? I.e., if a psychotic Westerner can experience himself as a kingdom in revolution, or a global conflict between communism and democracy, is there an Aboriginal psychotic experience that corresponds to Aboriginal social forms?

In an attempt to answer some of these questions, I made a field trip to the Nothern Territory in May 1980 and I then looked at accounts of myths and rituals of those regions. Professor - John Cawte of the Department of Psychiatry, University of New South Wales, also made available to me case-material of his own. In the course of these investigations, it became apparent that there was another issue inextricably woven with the preceding ones. There was a relationship between the breakdown of the Aboriginal culture and psychotic illnesses among individual Aborigines.

Since this study is a cross-cultural comparison between Western and Aboriginal psychotics, against a frame of reference developed by John Perry, it is important to spell out the details of this matrix in order for this exercise in comparisons to make any sense.

The Meaningfulness of Psychotic Experience

The view that I hold about psychotic processes is encapsulated in the following quotation:

> In the psychotic process called acute schizophrenia, the symbolic concerns in which a person becomes engrossed belong to a subjective reality. Although these concerns are usually totally out of keeping with objective reality, they are meaningful and not merely random disorder. Such ideation may be suppressed by medication, producing a superficial appearance that nomality has been restored. However, if the ideation is given full attention rather than being suppressed, the individual in the psychotic state has an altogether different experience of it that changes the very nature and phenomenology of the psychosis (Perry 7).

Which Psychoses are We Looking at?

The term 'schizophrenia' is a highly contentious one. Karl Leonhard's view, that the 'schizophrenias', like the 'cancers', are not a single disease entity, but many, is one that appeals to me. Furthermore, Leonhard distinguishes (on the basis of some very convincing twin studies) between those 'schizophrenias' with a genetic diathesis and those without (i.e., largely functional ones) (Leonhard 5).

This discussion then, is about the imagery that is found in the acute phase of a functional psychosis (disorders of a purely affective nature excluded).

The Natural Course of Psychosis

Since the advent of the phenothiazines, it has been virtually impossible to study the natural course of psychosis in any phenomenological detail. Jung's meticulous early studies of dementia praecox are therefore particularly valuable; so are Perry's more contemporary observations at Diabasis with unmedicated psychotic persons.

The psychiatrist who eschews facile medication of the psychotic pays the price of commitment to a very demanding doctor/patient relationship whose depth and subtlety is highly reminiscent of the normal mother-baby bonding and nurturing process. (I use the term 'mother' as a metaphor for the rôle of primary care giver and not to designate gender). Jung understood this only too well. After having successfully treated a Russian catatonic schizophrenic girl, he wrote, 'this case was the worst of this kind I have ever treated, but I must confess that I could never make up my mind to treat again a case of such a nature, because I couldn't stand again the strain of such a difficult and dangerous treatment' (unpublished letter to Dr. Kate Haslam, 10th December 1917).

Since the demands of such situations are so extreme, it is not surprising that relatively few data are available of the kind that Perry describes. Nevertheless, a broad consensus is starting to coalesce amongst those people who have had the opportunity to make the kinds of observations I am describing.

Perry sees the psychotic process as a purposeful regression to an experiental state which precedes the rudiments of ego-consciousness. The psychotic's need is for personality growth through what is basically a primordial re-parenting process. The state, which Stanislas Grof calls 'transpersonal' (Grof 3), is one in which the experiential field is filled with archetypal imagery (and which, incidentally, can also be made available during LSD, meditation and ritualistic experiences, to name but a few). If the psychotic experience is adequately related to, the individual does not just recover but grows. If not, chronicity sets in.

The typical syndrome that Perry recognises in acute psychosis in Western people involves an image sequence which he calls the 'Ritual drama of renewal'. Corresponding image sequences can be found in Egyptian, Mesopotamian and Hebrew kingship rituals. This image sequence is described later in this paper. It is, however, important to note that Perry emphasises that,

> In psychotic persons, this sequence apparently represents only among several possible syndromes, such as those of the initiatory or those of the shamanistic class. For example, one patient of mine had the delusion that in an operation a precious stone had been put in her head which gave her magical powers of knowing, hearing, seeing and controlling by telepathy; she did not have any of the usual images of the kingship syndrome just described. Only several years later did I learn that such precious stones are a commonly occuring phenomenon in shamanism in various parts of the world (Perry 6, p. 39).

Imagery of The Ritual Drama of Renewal in The Psychotic Process

Perry's description of the experiential state and the typical image sequence is as follows.

(1) Split self-image
A negative image together with a compensatory over-blown positive image, are presented by the individual (e.g., the person believes himself to be a witch, demon or sinner, as well as a hero, saint or prophet).

(2) The experience of a drama or ritual performance
This would include dancing, chanting, ceremonial motions, as well as experiences of participating in a cosmic drama, of everything being charged with significance, of participation in television, radio, etc. (*Ibid.*, pp. 29–30).

(3) The image sequence of ritual renewal
(This may not be fully developed in any one individual).
   (i) World centre/cosmic axis.
   (ii) Death/dismemberment/sacrifice/the living dead in heaven or hell/
imprisonment as an equivalent of death.
   (iii) Return to beginning/regression/the beginning of time/creation of the
cosmos/Garden of Eden/water of the abyss/early steps of evolution/crea-
tion of planets/oral needs/parent figures.
   (iv) Cosmic conflict/war between good and evil, light and dark, order and
chaos/democracy and communism/Armeggedon and the triumph of the
antichrist/destruction or the end of the world/intrigues, plots spying,
poisoning, all to gain world supremacy.
   (v) Threat of the opposite, fear of being overcome by opposite sex or turned into it; drugs that will turn one into the opposite, supremacy of the
other sex, moves to eradicate it.
   (vi) Apotheosis (royalty, divinity, king or queen, devil or saint, hero or
heroine).
   (vii) Sacred marriage. Royal marriage, incestuous marriage, ritual marriage,
marriage with a god or goddess/as a virgin mother who conceives by the
spirit.
   (viii) New birth of a superhuman child or of oneself (ideas of rebirth,
divine child, infant saviour, prince, reconciler of the division of the world).
   (ix) New society. A new order of society is envisaged, of an ideal or sacred
quality. A new Jerusalem, lost paradise, Utopia, world peace, new age, new
heaven, new earth.
   (x) Quadrated world. A fourfold structure of the world or cosmos is
established usually in the form of a quadrated circle. (Four continents or
quarters. Four political factions or governments or nations; four races or
religions; four persons of the godhead; four elements or states of being).

Imagery of Renewal in Ancient Kingship Myth and Ritual

I will look briefly at the Egyptian rituals for the sake of illustration. There are
very detailed Mesopotamian and Hebrew myths and rituals for a discussion of
which the reader is referred to Perry's *Roots of Renewal* (Perry 7).
   The central Egyptian myth is that of Osiris, who after a conflict with his
brother Set (the personification of evil) was drowned and dismembered. His
wife Isis recovered the pieces (except for the penis) and buried them, thereby
giving him new life as the king of the underworld. His posthumous son
Horus then vanquished Set and became the new king of Egypt, the sky god.
   Osiris was regarded not only as ruler of the dead and personification of the
dead king, but also as a fertility god who granted all life from the underworld,

not only to the deceased in the underworld, but also to the living (the annual flood of the Nile, the sprouting of vegetation, the fertility of men and beasts).

The dead father of the current pharaoh was supposed to become Osiris, the lord of the kingdom of the dead, and the living Pharaoh was enthroned as his son the sky god Horus, lord of the kingdom of the living. The vital forces that gave life to the kingdom were transmitted from the ancestral realms of the dead, through Osiris, in his embrace of his son, the living king, and thus into the realm.

There were several kingship rituals which between them contained the image sequences referred to. The Sed, or 30-year festival, was probably the main enthronement ritual and the most archaic one, and represented a reaffirmation of the living pharaoh as Osiris's son. The ritual contained the following features:

(a) *The world centre* was established at Memphis, the centre of the union of Upper and Lower Egypt, and thus the ordered world.

(b) *Death.* This theme referred the death of Osiris, the death of the Pharaoh, and the flooding of the Nile, thus tying together gods, king and people in an unified cosmos.

(c) *Return to the beginning.* After undergoing baptismal lustrations, the king ritually personified the first creator Atum, standing on the primeval hill as it arose from the waters of chaos.

(d) *Cosmic conflict.* A sacred combat was enacted between the two cities of the delta, representing the stuggle between the forces of death against those of the living. The imagery involved Set, who in the form of a boar, was pitted against Horus, the legitimate heir to the throne.

(e) For a while, the legitimate order was upset, and death and the enemy held the upper hand This was the period of *reversal of opposites.*

(f) *Apotheosis.* But, eventually, Horus prevailed, and the pharaoh was recrowned as victor, the 'Living Horus', at one with Atum, and partaking of the nature of Re, the sun god. The pharaoh performed a dance of circumambulating a representation of the realm.

(g) *Sacred marriage.* The place of this imagery in the Sed ritual is not certain, but at other new year and renewal festivals, there were well documented marital rites.

(h) *New birth.* This part of the rite was primarily to do with the ritual transfiguration of the dead Osiris into the king of the underworld.

(i) *New society.* The Sed coronation rite signalled the creation of a new epoch.

(j) *Quadrated world forms.* 'The representation of the quadrated world recurs throughout the rites. In his baptismal purification rites at the start, the king is given water by the four gods of the cardinal directions. At the enthronement, he is seated four times on four thrones . . . and he is proclaimed to each of the quarters of the world as an arrow is shot by him onto each one' (Perry 6, pp. 84—5).

The Connection Between Individual Turmoil and Collective Imagery

The central task of the psychotic process is to make the transition from internal chaos, conflicts and fragmentation to a personality structure in which a firm ego is in adequate relationship to the other parts of the personality, to other human beings, to the objective world, and to the spiritual world or cosmos through a sense of meaningful participation in the drama of creation. For this process, the kingship imagery is a particularly apt analogue.

According to Perry:

> The natural progress in the evolution of kingship then was the arduous work of realising inwardly that which had been more naively lived out in projected, concrete, externalised form . . . kingship is the natural historical framework and vehicle of this transition from the concretism of the archaic mentality to the spirit quality of the more fully awakened mind of our era. In that older stage of development, man needed to learn self assertion, mastery and purposeful aggression; all that goes into establishing an effective ego-consciousness in a societal context. In the newer, he strove to accomplish an enlightened awareness that would cultivate personal acceptance and affirmation both towards one's self and towards others' selves, in a spirit of non-dominance.
>
> To the question of why kingship motifs should prevail in this particual schizophrenic syndrome, the answer . . . is that the kingship myth and ritual were the vehicle of man's coming to awareness of his spiritual potential as an individual . . . the psychotic, in his reconstitutive process, evidently must travel a similar road from paranoid externalisation and concretising, to an inward realisation of his potential 'individuality' (*Ibid.*, p. 52).

Method

It was hoped that despite the language difficulties and the natural diffidence of the tribal people, the torrential energy of the psychotic process would throw up enough imagery to stick to hospital case records. In April 1980, I obtained permission from the Australian Northern Territory Department of Health to visit the Psychiatric Department at Darwin Hospital, and to examine case records. In general, my hopes proved somewhat ill-founded. The notes on each patient were voluminous, frequently running to two volumes of 500 foolscap pages each, but the munutiae of descriptive phenomenology that I was looking for were not there. I consoled myself with the thought that whatever descriptions of hallucinations and delusions had found their way into the notes had done so on the basis of their vigour. I examined in detail the notes of twelve patients and had the opportunity to interview three of them.

There were also some detailed histories which had been published by Professor John Cawte in his magnificent ethnopsychiatric study *Medicine is the Law* (Cawte 2).

I have drawn on nine of his accounts for this paper.

	1	2	3	4	5	6	7	8	9	i	ii	iii	iv	v	vi	vii	viii	ix	x	xi	xii
1 Split self-idea																▨	▨			▨	
2 Idea of ritual or drama (or ritual enactment	▨		▨	▨											▨	▨			▨	▨	
3 Centre																					
4 Death (or fear of being killed	▨	▨		▨	▨		▨	▨													
5 Return to beginnings (or self or cosmos)															▨						
6 Cosmic conflict world war intercultural clash	▨	▨	▨	▨									▨		▨				▨		▨
7 Threat of the opposite reversal of opposites																					
8 Apotheosis															▨						▨
9 Sacred marriage																					
10 New birth																					
11 New society																					
12 Quadrated world																					
13 Being spoken to by god or ancestral spirits	▨			▨							▨	▨			▨						▨
14 Ideas of sorcery	▨				▨						▨							▨			▨
15 Invasion by spirit of animal	▨		▨	▨	▨													▨	▨		
16 Tribal incest (actual or imaginal)	▨	▨				▨	▨	▨							▨			▨			▨

Table 1

Results

I have tabulated the results. It is clear from my table that while aboriginal psychotic imagery has many features in common with the early stages of the Perry image sequence, the imagery of:
  (7) threat of opposites;
  (8) apotheosis;
  (9) sacred marriage;
(10) new birth;
(11) new society;
(12) quadrated world;
is almost entirely absent in this sample, suggesting that the appropriate paradigm is *not* a kingship one. Moreover, aboriginal psychoses have distinctive features of their own, which I have tabulated at the bottom of Table 1 under:
(13) being spoken to by ancestral spirits;
(14) ideas of sorcery;
(15) invasion by animals or spirits;
(16) tribal incest.
    Perhaps the most remarkable feature to emerge was the frequency with which either the image (or the *actuality*) of tribal incest occurred: there were nine definite instances of this, and a possible tenth.
    Tribal incest refers here to sexual or marital relations between two persons so related that their marriage is prohibited by the tribe. (Adulterous liaisons form the other broad class of prohibited sexual relationship). Broadly speaking, irrespective of whether a particular kinship system is patrilineally or matrilineally determined, marriage is *exogamous,* i.e., to a member of another group, clan, or moiety within the tribe; thus the concept of incest here is very different one from the one Western people are familiar with.
    In summary, this study suggests that Aboriginal psychoses display (i) ideas of ritual or drama; (ii) images of *conflict,* images of *death* or lethal *persecution,* and actual or imaginal *tribal incest.*
    There are two groups of special interest to Jungian analysts from the point of view of imagery: (i) an *animal invasion* group; (ii) a *tribal incest* group. I shall give case histories to illustrate each, but the focus of the paper will be on the last group.
(i) Invasion by animals from the dreaming
(Case description from Professor Cawte's *Medicine is the Law*).
A young Walbiri man, aged 26, went to Lake Nash, to drove cattle, and became acutely disturbed. The Lake Nash culture has a clear belief system to do with invasion by 'wilaiba', a devil animal that enters the victim's body and fills it with bones. The disturbance was severe but brief, diagnostically an acute shock syndrome in the form of *a bouffée délirante aiguë.*
    The patient's verbatim account of the experience follows:

I was sick that Queensland way, really sick. I saw dreaming about animals. These people reckon animals get into people. I went out droving through Alexandria about three years ago. Through to Lake Nash . . . I see old Aboriginal grave. An old man told me, watch out for animal dreaming. That old man's name Eric. Night time holy animal from dreaming come, I feel full inside of animal bones, through legs, belly, chest and head. I get very sick. Holy animal from dreaming . . . they didn't tell me what sort. They got different animals. Wild-looking thing, white colour all over black front and face. Different from dog or cat. Big head, sharp teeth. He didn't eat meat, only people. He got in heart, in belly, in chest, in neck . . . put in bones of man. Then he got out. All night. They take me to doctor man at Dajarra in car belonging to Aboriginal boy. The carry me. Not walk. Not eat. Talk a little. That Eric meet me, bring to camp. Lay me down on tarp [i.e., tarpaulin]. Eric put bushes and branches across his arms, tied on. Then he brushes out bones out of me with branch. I see 'em on tarp. Two big shin bones, old, dry. Big mob little bones. After that, give me blood. Lot of men . . . about twenty . . . cut arms with razor blade and string on arm. Get nearly half bucket full of blood. I drink all, slow. I get right straight away, eat, drink all right.

I pay them all thirty pounds. I stay two weeks at Lake Nash, school teacher bloke, Mr Benjamin, look after me. I won't droving anymore. Might get sick. Eric told me common thing here, animals leave bones in people (Cawte 2, pp. 183—4).

Comment

Central to the experience of serious psychological disturbance, was the feeling of being invaded by a 'foreign' entity, in this case, the 'wilaiba' devil animal.

The invading images need not be 'Aboriginal' ones, as we shall see in the next case.

(ii) An image of intercultural conflict
(Invasion by snake and fish. Case description by Professor Cawte).
These three cases, and his two sons. Professor Cawte comments, 'An attempted transfusion of a personal totem from father to son proved to be incompatible . . . the father became deranged [possessed by a snake] and so did the sons'.

Laraga, aged 60, presented to the local hospital with disturbed behaviour claiming to have been invaded by the rainbow serpent. His younger son Digenda, aged 35, had tried to help him but had become invaded by a fish. The older son Joda, aged 37, then tried to cure them, but in turn became violently disturbed . . . was convinced that his wife and child had been taken by devils. He believed he was talking to God. This surprised the doctors since it was known he had not attended a mission or received instructions in the Christian religion. However, people agreed that such teaching could have been known to him through gossip.

Laraga and Joda were sent to an Adelaide Hospital. Laraga after some time thought the spirit may have left him and be inside Joda. Laraga decided to return to Alice Springs, but to work droving cattle, rather than to hunt with his people. Joda remained in hospital much longer and became catatonic. He was very uncommunicative but was heard saying that a fish was stuck in his throat (*Ibid.*, pp. 176—80).

Here the imagery depicts loss of control over the domestic symbol (the serpent), and invasion by the Christian one (the fish). Fish imagery is not very prominent in Central Australian mythology, and Joda's preoccupation with the Christian God caused some surprise. The imagery parallels the social processes: men caught in the disintegration of their own culture and its invasion by an alien one.

There is, however, an even more fundamental image of cultural disintegration, the image of incest. The fabric of Aboriginal society is the kinship system. Incest disturbs tribal society totally; not only to the furthest reaches of the current kinship network, but backwards in time through outraged ancestors to displeased dreamtime spirits, and forward forever if the incestuous line is allowed to live and breed.

Tribal Incest

Case I. Interviewed at Darwin Hospital by the author
'X'. This 32-year-old man from Elcho Island was admitted to Darwin Hospital with a two-week history of auditory hallucinosis and frightened and aggressive behaviour. On the first morning after his admission he burst into the staff-room looking very wild and restless, and holding an object he had made out of a wooden coat-hanger and several clothes pegs. He sighted down the shaft of this object in a ritualistic fashion but carefully avoided pointing it a me.

During my interview with him later that day (in the form of a Rogerian 'active listening' procedure rather than a structured interrogation), his disturbance abated. He proved to be highly intelligent and articulate man, who, several years earlier, had been a representative at the First National Aboriginal Conference. His first marriage had been a love-match, his wife being of the 'wrong' section. She had developed cancer and died at Darwin Hospital some three years earlier. Since then this man had remarried, this time non-incestuously, but the relationship was an unhappy one. He felt torn between the two cultures. He was not accepted in Western society and desperately craved acceptance from his own people. This was complicated by the fact that he felt he had a mission to bring Christian beliefs to his people but not enough strength to accomplish this.

These details were confirmed by two officers of the Community Welfare Department, one of whom was the patient's brother, and into whose care he was discharged twelve hours later.

Quotations from report (from Officers of Community Welfare Department)

(i) 'X. was the First National Aboriginal conference representative from East Arnhem Land. In this rôle, he faced a tremendous cross-cultural burden in addition to an enormous workload.

'A religious crusade of the fundamentalist type has gripped Elcho Island and for the past two years X. was influenced by this . . . a contributory stress factor . . . his family has not been as supportive as they might have been. I feel he has been encapsulated in an unreal environment (of) . . . religious fanaticism. It would be best ameliorated in a more down to earth environment'.

(ii) 'He needs family support more than what he has been getting . . . this rejection has affected him to the extent of his reaction now . . . my strong recommendation is that he be released to be under control of people who have different views of life than the life he has been involved in . . .' From a report written by his brother.

Case II. 37-year-old man from Melville Island (from hospital records)
This highly intelligent man, a Churchill Fellow, with a history of three admissions over the period 1973—78, had an auditory hallucinosis; he felt that his people were talking hostilely about him and hated him, wanted to kill or poison him, because he has married a girl of the wrong 'section'. Also, his siter and brother were involved in two seperate murders, and Y. felt the relatives of the murdered people would try to kill him under the 'pay-back' system.

Y. stated that the people were continually talking about him. In fact, the community were not discussing him. Nevertheless, the people would not let him have a house or sit on any commitee. Y. drinks occasionally because when he is drunk he cannot hear the voices.

Prior to his admission in 1975, he presented to the nursing sister at Melville Island in great panic, having stripped himself naked, 'to show the people that he was a proper blackfellow all over'. He was convinced he was being poisoned and would only take food from the nursing sister or his wife. In the aerial ambulance, he was screaming and shouting and death-chanting.

Extricating him from Snake Bay for a few days usually relieved Y.'s tension and that of the people.

Case III. 34-year-old man from Bathurst Island with a diagnosis of 'schizophrenic reaction' (from hospital records)
There was a history of two brief admissions preceded by insomnia and hallucinations. The patient heard threatening voices of Tiwi people but said that Tiwi law prevented further elaboration. The voices said they were going to get rid of him because they wanted his wife. They said that his wife is his 'auntie' and that he had therefore broken tribal law. They thought that he was Satan and were using Tiwi needle sorcery to kill him. He had confronted the people about this, and they denied everything. He stopped hearing voices on arrival at the ward.

Case IV. 36-year-old woman from Elcho Island (from hospital records)
This 36-year-old woman initially presented as a puerperal psychosis after her first baby died in 1962. She was involved in a wrong 'section' relationship, and has had psychotic relapses ever since. During her psychotic episodes she presented with aggressive behaviour and regressive phenomena (felt she was three years old), as well as religious mannerisms and posturings (holding her arm up in benediction, talking constantly about God, heaven and happiness). During a psychotic episode in 1967 she refused to attend to her three-month-old baby, or her own needs, and had to be fed. During another episode nine years later, she alarmed other mothers because she took their babies away from their cots to nurse them.

Case V. From Professor Cawte's reports
A 37-year-old full-blood mission-educated aboriginal woman, from one of the broken tribes near Lake Eyre, was near term expecting her seventh child . . . made a suicide threat (very uncommon in outback aborigines) . . . claimed she had caused her mother's death two months before because she had been an adulteress. She presented as puerperal depressive with hallucinations and delusions. Spirit ancestors, 'the voices of my people that's dead and gone', told her what would happen. She would lie awake at night talking to herself, calling out in answer to auditory hallucinations. (It was learned that during the last stage of her pregnancy lightning struck a goanna [a large lizard], whose tail pointed at her belly. She then knew that was *non-tribal.* She wanted to take her children and live with another Aborigine, Harry, who could support her, but the mission explained to her that this would be adultery. After a long illness, she finally resolved the conflict by identification with the Western culture.

The patient was literate, and some of her writings were saved:

> I got married in church and not with a firestick, so I don't think I'll ever see my darling little family again . . . because I went against our law. No one gave me a firestick because I wasn't wanted to marry this man. I don't care now if I dies because I misunderstood the blackfellow ways and got myself into trouble. They've got my blood in a human bone, I found this out in a dream, so there's going to be a war on. My life is kept at Port Augusta in a human bone. My hair was singed and burned at Leigh Creek by some blackfellows to make me mad, found it by my navel, and afterwards I can't hold anything secret. Blackfellow caught me with a whirlwind and made me go mad; and I was told to not to give my mother's name because people might think I am infectious. When Harry couldn't get me in the first place with the whirlwind, he got my mother, so that's what broke me down on mother's day and that's how I know I will never get over my sickness. I was boned in the head when I was small. I can still see the danger ahead. . . . my mother treated me real bad so I got married to this man to get out of trouble but his sisters got very nasty. My mother left the mission *because they called her her father's name (Cawte 2, pp. 3–5).*

Comment

This is a matrilineal culture and the mission must have insisted upon a conventional *patrilineal* restructuring of the tribe to fit in with the Christian ethic.

Discussion

In those last four cases, the imagery of the Aboriginal psyche in disintegration is expressed by the themes of incest and persecution.

There is a small amount of evidence of the death of the hero type of myth, which has a certain likeness to Osiris imagery — the myth of Laindjung — but I have not myself discerned any correspondence between that type of myth and the Aboriginal psychoses which I have as yet encountered. As I have already said, it is incest which threatens the very fabric of Aboriginal society. The dangers it presents are greater than those connected with any other archetypal situation or theme.

There is an incest myth from the Gunwinggu people which clearly expresses the dynamics involved. The account of it which follows is taken from Louis A. Allen's *Time Before Morning*.

Balada, Incest Myth and Associated Ritual

Balada lived in Arnhem Land with his parents. He was as much a part of his country as the trees or stones. When a hawk dropped like a spear through the bright air and bore aloft a goanna writhing in its talons, Balada was elated with the fierce triumph of the bird, but also his stomach shrank against his backbone, for he could feel the nails biting into his own vitals. When he saw the bee, Manjal, busily seeking nectar in the plum blossoms, he spoke to it softly, 'Gather much honey, Manjal', he said watching it wing heavily aloft, 'for I shall share it with you soon'. Then he followed the bee to its nest.

Balada's mother's brother, Awur, was as close to Balada as his father. Awur took Balada to the great tree. In the dreamtime, his first ancestor had turned himself into the tree. To Balada, he said, 'the great tree is sacred to you, for it is the spirit of your father and his father before him . . . to the tree he said 'I have brought the boy, Ngaba, help and protect him'.

Later, Awur was Balada's sponsor in an age-grading ceremony (initiation) that would permit him to marry.

The Ubar ritual required initiates to enter the womb of the mother rainbow serpent (Ngalyod), and then emerge into manhood.

After the initiation, Balada fell in love with Waiula, who was his kin, and therefore forbidden to him. Awur was very concerned and warned him, but the couple eloped. Conflict developed between Waiula's father's kin and Awur's kin. Awur could see that if the couple were not found quickly, there would be bloodshed among the people, whose feelings were running very high. He approached Waiula's father and said 'there will be no killing, I will lead you to Balada'. He had an intuition that Balada would be at the cave of the great tree.

Waiula's father's kinsfolk speared Balada to death, and Balada's kinsfolk speared Waiula. With sorrow, Balada's folk carried his body wrapped in paperbark, to the burial grounds. Closely behind them, Waiula's folk walked, bearing her wrapped body. The bodies became two rocks, so that the people would always remember that wrong unions come to an evil end (Allen 1, pp. 125—9).

Comments

Despite Awur's love for Balada, he decided to betray him when he realised that massive conflict between the two groups is the inevitable consequence of failing to deal with the event of incest.

There is no room in the kinship network for incestuous unions, and they can only be dealt with by death or banishment.

The second kind of myth to consider are creation myths featuring incest. As in other cultures incest is the prerogative of the Gods of spirit beings. The aboriginal creation myths are full of incest.

The Djanggawul Cycle of Incest Creation Myths

This cycle consists of an important series of myths from North Eastern Arnhem Land.

Gangjudingu, the husband of Walu the sun woman, lived with her on an island beyond the mists of the horizon, together with his two sisters. While Walu was away, Gandjudingu committed incest with his two sisters, and was banished by Walu. The brother and sisters, collectively known as the Djanggawuls, set off on their travels to the mainland, creating the water holes and naming the natural features. The children of the incestuous union were the ancestors of the Dua moiety. In their travels, they encountered Laindjung, who was the ancestor of the other moiety (Jiridja).

Julunggul, the rainbow serpent, the father of Gandjudingu, disapproved deeply of his son's incestuous behaviour. Two daughters of the Djanggawul were known as the Wawilag sisters. Boaliri, the younger, and Garangal, the older one, were very powerful beings and travelled together on adventures. Boaliri had an incestuous relationship with a man of her own clan. Garangal was pregnant too, but not incestuously. The two pregnant women gave birth to children, but Julunggul was very displeased, and smelled Boaliri's lochiae, which had polluted his waterhole. He ate up the Wawilag siters together with their babies, even though they were of his own totem. Repentant, he taught the other snakes the stories and ceremonies of the Wawilag sisters (summarised from Allen 1, pp. 43—51, 67—75).

The incest prohibition, as well as preventing the disintegration of the kinship system, has several other closely related functions. These include (i) the development of culture (see the Ngalyod myth, below) and (ii) the maturation of the individual (see Gunapipi ceremony).

Ngalyod, a Gunwinggu Myth

Ngalyod was a mother rainbow serpent. Her people were unhappy despite abundance. She tried to teach them songs and ceremonies but they quickly forgot. An old man had incest with his granddaughter. Ngalyod rebuked him. Later on, a brother cohabited with his sisters; Ngalyod killed him and pronounced, 'brother shall not lie with sister'. As people began to heed her injunctions they began to remember the stories and perform the ceremonies (Allen 1, pp. 76—7).

It can be seen that the Ngalyod story strengthens the incest prohibition in the interests of the development of culture. It also brings to mind Robert Stein's notion that the incest prohibition is a social device for channelling libido into the spiritual realm (Stein 8).

The following account illustrates how the maturation of the individual is aided by a ceremony which helps boys through and past incest dangers.

Gunapipi Initiatory Ceremony

A bullroarer is swung and the women and children run away because Julunggul (the rainbow serpent) is approaching. The novices are taken away from the women, and the women are told that the novices have been swallowed by the snake; the women mourn for their dead sons. Several months later, the neophytes take part in a ritual rebirth from Garangal (the non-incestuous Wawilag sister). They are put in a pit and covered with bark and after several hours the bark is stripped away suddenly, and the boys are confronted with two huge cylindrical representations of Julunggul, which the men push across the trench, terrifying the boys, who are then considered re-born (summarised from Hiatt 4, p. 150).

Incest, particularly mother-child incest, is also an image of *psychological infantilism*. The Gunapipi initiation into adulthood arranges for a 'second' birth' into adulthood, this time non-incestuously.

Discussion

Kinship not kingship

This paper addresses itself to the issue of the central imagery in Aboriginal psychosis. It is decidedly not the imagery of kingship. Two main patterns emerge, an animal invasion pattern, and a tribal incest one, which is the focus of the paper. It has to be borne in mind that Aboriginal psychoses present behaviourally rather than verbally, and that whatever verbal material there is usually needs to be translated. In consequence, more detailed studies are required to establish the coherence and relative frequence of these image patterns. It is unlikely that these are the only common patterns. Nevertheless, I was struck by how often animal invasion or incest appeared in the material, and how they seemed to be mutually exclusive.

In the first syndrome, the individual experiences an invasion by a spirit animal (e.g., the Wilaiba). There is a great struggle between the invading forces and the defending ones, during which the individual feels ill and in great danger of his life. In the second, the experience is again one of great conflict, with fear of death. This time, the threat has come about not because the individual has been invaded by a foreign culture or a spiritual force, but because the incest taboo has been broken, and the kinship network is threatened. Typically, the afflicted person lies in mortal terror that his tribesmen will kill him for this transgression.

In the material collected, there were frequent instances of *actual* incest. However, in most of the reports, the tribal people claimed not to be anxious about that, and it was the individual's *heightened concern* which was judged to be psychotic (at great variance with consensual social reality) by all those involved, black and white. Furthermore, it must be remembered that in the kinship networks of Aboriginal societies, there is usually a class of borderline relationships, involving multiple lineages, where, depending upon which lineage is used to provide the perspective, the relationship can be seen as incestuous or non-incestuous. In practice, tribal consensus detemines the issue. It may well be that in some of the individuals studied, the 'incestuous' relationship was one of these ambiguous ones. The precise details were not available, and must await further study. At this stage, all that can be said is that, in the second group of psychoses, incest seems to be both a precipitant and a core theme.

There are some cases (like case III from Bathurst Island) which feature incest imagery but apparently not actual incest. Knowing the complexity of Aboriginal social networks, I would want to examine the social backgrounds of such individuals in detail, before I could categorically state that no actual incest had occurred. Until then, the issue must remain open whether Aboriginal psychotics can have pure delusions of incest, rather than delusional overconcern about incest.

Myth and Ritual

Are there Aboriginal myths which have a similar relationship to 'tribal incest' psychosis, that kingship renewal myths have to a psychosis of individuation? Yes, up to a point. The myth of Balada spells out clearly the consequences of incest, i.e., disruption of the kinship network. At the level of intrapsychic interpretation of the myth, we could say that a persistent incestuous internal dynamic leads inevitably to images of persecution and the experience of ego death. This myth reads as a good description of the internal prosess of an Aboriginal psychotic suffering from a tribal incest syndrome. Furthermore, it has universal validity as a description of the intolerable anxieties that are generated by incest phantasies.

However, the parallelism breaks down at this point. Whereas there is an opportunity for renewal in the kingship myths, that is not available in the incest myths. Osiris's son Horus re-establishes a kingdom in which the temporal realm is well connected with the sky-world and the underworld (the epitome of individuation), but when Balada and Waiula are killed, they are turned into rocks to remind the people to avoid incest. The focus is on the welfare of the group, rather than the development of individual. What is available is a return to the monolithic security of tribal law. There *are* ritual methods for making contact with the forces of psychological renewal; for instance, in the 'rebirth' experiences of initiation, or in the fertilising thrust the kingship paradigm; nor can I find any myths or rituals in which incest is resolved in any other way apart from the death or expulsion of the offenders, and their transformation into rocks or other natural objects. Psychologically speaking, this would mean that the Aboriginal psychotic can only resolve his conflict in a retrograde manner, either by (i) returning to the tribal ways, or (ii) identifying with the white culture. Unfortunately, the reality is that Australia is inhabited by members of two widely different cultures. In consequence, either solution involves identification with one kind of consciousness at the expense (death) of the other. That in fact is what happens clinically. For instance, tribal incest case I, the man from Elcho Island, recovered from his psychosis by leaving Elcho.

It should be clear by now, that superimposed upon this comparison of myths and madness across cultures, which we have regarded as static for the purpose of exposition, the reality is that both cultures are in transition. Living myth is never static, and hopefully, the poets and visionaries of both cultures are even now dreaming the new Dreaming of resolution.

Psychotic Imagery and Socio-Political Forms

It is no coindence that parallels can be found between social structures and the internal commonwealth. How often it is that socio-political imagery appears in psychotic productions. They are full of espionage, political intrigues, heads of state etc. Conversely, political life mirrors psychopathology, with its dissociations (parties and nations) and its collective psychoses (cold wars, world wars). Most likely, some Russian psychotics have delusions of capitalist invasions, just as some Russian psychiatrists (delusionally?) assume that dissent in a monolithic state *must* be delusional.

These correspondences did not go unremarked in bygone times. I am irresistibly reminded of Goya's etchings of madmen in regalia holding court, and of Jung's schizophrenic woman at the Burghölzli, who would declaim, 'I am Helvetia, made of exclusively sweet butter . . . Naples and I supply the world . . .'

If a psychotic Westerner can experience himself as a kingdom in renewal, or a democracy under attack by communism, then the corresponding Aboriginal experience is that of the fabric of kinship being torn apart by incest, or of an invasion by another culture, as in the Animal Invasion Syndromes.

The archetype of kinship is even more fundamental than the archetype of kingship. The vexatious dichotomies of I and not-I, me and mine versus they and theirs, the perplexing question of, who is my brother? all belong to the archetype of kinship, and refer to intrapsychic realities just as much as social ones. How we answer these questions psychologically determines our sanity ('I am Helvetia'). One has only to reflect upon the relationship between the dream ego and the other figures which appear in the dream to be reminded that these are processes which are familiar to all of us, not just to psychotics and politicians.

The Breakdown of Culture and Psychotic Illness

One can speculate whether, in the original state, before contact with the white culture, there was much psychosis at all among Australian Aborigines. Currently, the incidence seems to be at least as high as in the white population. There were four cases in this series where women carried incestuous pregnancies to term, and then developed puerperal psychoses, in situations where welfare officers and missionaries were insensitive to tribal feelings of abhorrence, and only regarded European definitions of incest as valid.

The men in the series were caught in the same conflict of values. I am inclined to believe that this was at least partly responsible for their psychoses. The issue of aetiology is an important one, and this study was not designed to examine it, though it certainly highlights it. The destruction of culture which is clearly in evidence in many of these case histories is appalling. However, appreciation of the mental hygiene values of traditional ways is mercifully becoming more apparent among professionals who work with the Aborigines. In the meanwhile, we have to await the new dreaming.

Summary

In many acute functional psychoses in Western people, John Weir Perry finds image sequences that are similar to those of the kingship renewal myths and rituals of ancient Egypt, Israel and Mesopotamia.

An examination of the case histories of twenty-one psychotic Australian Aborigines did not reveal these image patterns. A specific Aboriginal pattern did emerge however; the imagery of *tribal incest*, leading to *radical social disruption*; and provoking *deadly retribution*.

Just as violent overthrow of the kingdom is an archetype of psychosis in Western man, so the radical disturbance of kinship structure through incest would seem to be an archetype for Aboriginal psychosis.

Incest is a recurring image in Aboriginal creation myths, and there is a Western Arnhem Land myth (the myth of Balada) which deals specifically with the destructive impact on the kinship system.

References

1. Allen, L. A. (1975. *Time Before Morning*. New York, Thos. E. Cromwell.
2. Cawte, J. (1974). *Medicine is the Law*. Australia, Rigby Ltd.
3. Grof, S. (1976). *Realms of the Human Unconscious: Obsveration from LSD Research*. New York, E. P. Dutton.
4. Hiatt, L. R. (Ed.). (Ed.). (1975). *Australian Aboriginal Mythology*. Carlton, N.S.W., Australian Institute of Aboriginal Studies.
5. Leonhard, K. (1980). 'Contradictory issues in the origin of psychiatry', *Br. J. Psychiat.*, 136, 437—44.
6. Perry, J. W. (1974). *The Far Side of Madness*. New Jersey, Prentice-Hall.
7. Perry, J. W. (1976). *Roots of Renewal in Myth and Madness*. San Francisco, Jossey-Bass.
8. Stein, R. (1974). *Incest and Human Love*. Harmondsworth, Penguin Books.

The Author wishes to thank The Northern Territories Department of Health, and Dr. Lopez and Dr. Wieteska, Psychiatrists, Darwin Hospital.

(reprinted from *The Journal of Analytical Psychology* 1982, *21*, 21—39, by permission)

THEORETICAL EXPLORATIONS

Reassessing Femininity and Masculinity:
A Critique of Some
Traditional Assumptions

By Edward C. Whitmont (New York)

During the early Thirties, Jung made an initial attempt at what he then called a preliminary characterization of the female and male predispositions. He termed Eros the tendency to relatedness, which he deemed fundamentally expressive of the feminine; Logos, spirit, creative and ordering intelligence, and meaning, typified the male attitude. Unfortunately, this first preliminary attempt has been treated in much Jungian literature as though it were the final word for the intervening forty years. Unfortunately, because, in the light of women's increasing awareness of themselves, more and more evidence has been accumulating that the Eros-Logos concept is inadequate for covering the wide range of feminine and masculine dynamics. Moreover, it is also terminologically and psychologically inappropriate.

For one thing, as Hillman has reminded us, mythologically Eros is a male phallic deity. An aggressive hunter, Plato's mighty daimon, the instinctual urge to connect, to touch and possess, he motivates man's urge to connect with man, and his quest for the beautiful, the good, and the divine. He expresses outgoing aggressive libido, striving desirousness, and the insistent urge to join, connect, possess and to penetrate. As patriarchal cosmogonic Eros, the first divinity emerging from the world egg, he is akin to a primordial light or logos manifesting from out of the womb of non-being, a son of the Great Mother. Thence he imposes his own order of connection and desire upon what prior to him was primordial dark void which is also birthing fullness. The birth of Eros is akin in this mythological representation to the biblical "let there be light," that same light which in the Christian version of St. John is from the Logos and is life and love (John 1, Epistle 1, John 4.16) It is thoroughly in keeping with this version that the medieval invocation of Hrabanus Maurus, the "Veni Creator Spiritus," calls upon the Holy Spirit as a male creative entity to "bring light to the sense and love ["*amor*," Latin *eros*] to hearts" (accende lumen sensibus,/Infunde amorem cordibus). Indicidentally, both "*amor*" and "*eros*" are of male gender grammatically.

Looking further into language which in its phonetic and etymological context is more often than not truly expressive of the hidden wisdom of the unconscious, we are struck by the close analogy of Eros, Eris and Ares: love, dissent, and strife. The closeness is as phonetic as it is psychological and mythological.[1]

Indeed, like the Roman Mars, Ares shows his close relation to Eros. Mars *gravidus* represents the life and love engendering genius of spring. And astrologically, Mars expresses both aggressive activity as well as libidinous and erotic desire and sexuality. His symbol, ♂, is an erect phallus.

We see, then, that Eros represents an aspect of the archetypal Yang, outgoing aggressive maleness. The ruthless soldier, striving hero, and frequently equally ruthlessly desirous lover are expressive of the Eros-Ares polarity. By no stretch of the imagination can they be seen as Logos figures.

One of the most typical and at the same time most sublime utterances of Ares-Eros is to be found in Jacob's words as he wrestles with his adversary, the angel, "I shall not let you until you bless me." Thus, at the same time as they are struggling, Jacob craves the angel's blessing.

Eros is the son, Ares the lover of Aphrodite. Together they represent the Twin Suitors, son lovers of the Great Goddess, periodically put to death by one another and reborn, manifesting the life-giving and life-restoring aspects.

Their "crippled" incarnation on earth is the fourth aspect of masculinity: Hephaistos, *homo faber,* man busying himself with making and creating things on earth — the Great Goddess's purported husband, who undertakes to catch her with her immortal lovers in his artifical structures.

It may be argued that, no matter much we "split hairs" about proper terminology and regardless of which mythological name we call it, the Yang-Yin polarity is still of spirit and order versus relatedness. This argument would overlook the fact that words *are* literally Logos, literally indeed. Words, particularly those hallowed by age-old tradition and the power of mythological fantasy, are pregnant with and generate meaning, hence improperly applied have the power to confuse. Moreover, relationship and relatedness, no matter by what name we call them, are by no means typical or exclusive qualities of the feminine any more than spirit is to be considered an exclusively male property.

Relationship is a principle of order — order in space or time. And order pertains to the masculine as well to the feminine principles even though in differing ways. Relatedness, in turn, as psychological concept has come to mean awareness of relationship inter- and intrapersonally. And this includes attraction and connection as much as repulsion, rejection and aggression, mutuality as much as separateness, inner feelings and thoughts as much as outer interaction, rhythmic and lawful order as much as play or even chaotic confusion, discovery of meanings as much as acceptance of meaninglessness.

Relatedness is not to be confused with the longing for personal involvement and empathetic identification which is indeed a quality typical of the feminine consciousness. Such empathetic involvement, however, does not necessarily constitute relatedness at all. Without the inclusion of disjuncture, it may be no more than symbiotic merging and identification — or just sentimental mush.

Relatedness is perception, appreciation, and willingness, as well as ability to receive the other where and how he or she happens to be while still maintaining one's own individual stance and genuine position. It is separateness and encounter in conflict as much as in rapport and communication. It calls for an awareness and affirming acknowledgment of the other in his or her displeasing and unacceptable — no less than in pleasing and acceptable—characteristics. It calls for affirmative awareness and acknowledgement of the nature of the particular relationship itself in its separate, no less than in its sharing, aspect.

Relatedness, therefore, is a conscious achievement that needs to be worked for as an aspect of individuation, by both sexes. Neither relationship nor relatedness can be said to characterize the feminine any more than the masculine consciousness. They comprise the feminine urges to personalization and involvement as much as the masculine drives for distance, control, possession, competition and meaning.

Moreover, in defining the feminine in terms of relatedness primarily, we are wont to overlook its depth dimension, its active, namely, transformative dimension which is quite devoid of any relatedness concern. To equate Yin simply with relationship reduces the feminine to a relatively passive re-active and re-sponding never initiating complex. Such has indeed been the patriarchal cultural bias. The fact is, however, that, prior to working consciously on her relationship problems, the average woman is no more genuinely related than the male who is 'in love,' namely, driven by his erotic libido. By virtue of the cultural training which requires her to be "attentive," "sensitive," and "receptive," she may present the appearance of relatedness; yet, this is but a persona gesture. That impression of seeming relatedness as an *a priori* function of the feminine may also be enhanced by the aforementioned tendency to a more subjective way of reacting by showing emotion (which cultural bias did until now not permit to men), by her tendency to perceive and react in concrete and personal terms, rather than abstractly and impersonally like the male, and by her tendency to nourish, mother, and protect.

Yet unless consciously worked through in respect to the effects all this may have upon the relationship, these tendencies merely serve to make her cloying, self-centered, and possessively, egotistically unrelated in a personal fashion; whereas the corresponding Eros-Ares driven male, self-willed, determined to conquer and to have what he wants, inconsiderate of personal values, is egotistically unrelated in an impersonal way.

The "lover" who is motivated only by his need to conquer and to satisfy his erotic appetites fails to "see" and to accord individuality and human dignity to the object of his desires.

In turn, the over-mothering or over-protective ever-sweet and cloying female likewise acts primarily for the satisfaction of her own needs regardless of those of her partner. By the man she is experienced as suffocating and devouring. His instinctual, more often than not, unconscious response is to "love and leave" her, to take flight after he gets what he wanted and discount her as a person. And indeed she acts out of unconscious possessiveness and the need to express her urge to give and to contain, regardless of whether what she gives is wanted and can be assimilated by the other.

In both cases the lack of distance and appreciation of the other as a separate and different person, with different needs, prevents genuine relatedness. To achieve relatedness the areas of disconnection need to be taken into consideration first. Indeed, unless in touch with her unrelated Yin it is difficult also for a woman to be in conscious relation to her center, the source of instinctual wisdom, hence to achieve genuine relatedness.

If not Eros, what are the archetypal forms of expression of the Yin in both sexes?

Our accustomed definition of Yang and Yin as creative and receptive respectively appears to be too narrow. Perhaps a more adequate rendering might be the idea of exteriorization, diversification, penetration, and external action for Yang and inherence, unification, incorporation, activity and existence for Yin.

Robert Ornstein sees an analogy between the functions of the right and left brain hemispheres and the Yin-Yang dynamic. He presents a tabulation "for purposes of suggestion and clarification in an intuitive sort of way, not as final categorial statement."[2]

Yang	Yin
Day	Night
Intellectual	Sensuous
Time, History	Eternity, Timelessness
Explicit	Tacit
Analytic	Gestalt
Propositional	Appositional
Lineal	Nonlineal
Sequential	Simultaneous
Focal	Diffuse
The Creative: heaven	The Receptive: earth
Masculine	Feminine
Verbal	Spatial
Intellectual	Intuitive
Causal	Synchronistic
Argument	Experience

There is increasing evidence that indeed brain structure and functioning are affected by the preponderance of male or female sex hormones.[3] Whether or not the equivocation of left and right brain scopes for Yang and Yin is or is not an oversimplification remains to be seen. Certainly it is a helpful orientation first guide.

For a more experiental approach and psychological detailing I would like to call first upon a woman's description of her own experience of a Yin dimension which I propose to call "the Medusa aspect" or "transformative dimension." Her account is helpful even though it is of a woman still caught in patriarchy.

As always when one interprets, one tends easily to idealize, and in this instance, to visualize *Yin the Receptive* as something aking to loving motherliness. We start with the mother image in order to actualize the feminine principle, but this is just what we must not do . . . *Yin* is the mother womb of the soul, conceiving and giving birth. Whatsoever falls therein is borne, ripens and is ejected, regardless. It is the everbearing, but also the inert. In conceiving, it remains indifferent, cold and unseeing. It stays immovably on the spot; only in giving birth does it shake and quake like the irrational volcano.

It is in one sense really quite hazardous to realize this, for though the deeply feminine is the center from which all psychic life pours forth just because of its vast inertia it is inimically opposed to all action, all consciousness and development. Just as outer nature, without man's intervention, ceaselessly creates and destroys in unconcerned and senseless continuation, allowing fruits to ripen and decay and animals to live and die, so the feminine without the active intervention of the conscious mind proceeds in an undisciplined and ever life-productive way . . .

This non-humanity is yet a well-spring for human experience, similar to an ancient, sluggish beast which has watched man for thousands of years and now knows everything, long before it occurs . . . This wisdom is not friendly to man, for it never suits a particular time or person but relates solely to the stark, raw everlasting of the unconscious psychic life; and just as organic life never remains static, but goes on relentlessly . . . ever renewing even the organism in the single cell; so the feminine encompasses the whole vibrant ever-new rhythm of psychic activity, the inescapable change of every hardened form. This it contains and destroys all in one. It is unswerving stability and terrifying breakdown. It expresses itself in the sexual demand, in the adaptability of instincts, in shattering emotions and because of its wayward uncontrollability, in a truly devilish wisdom.

In her inmost being every woman is moved by this feminine principle *Yin*. Aside from all she says or does, aside from her most intimate bond to people and spiritual values, it expresses itself in her as something strange and foreign, something "other" that unmistakably goes its own way.

Here she is pushed beyond any need of her own, or the needs of her nearest and dearest, by the compelling necessity of this rhythm. Here she does not recognize outer time and its demands but only the unmistakable signs of an inner ebb and flow. Quite unconsciously and involuntarily this deepest part of her is concerned only with the growth and maturing of life which demands its rights, must demand its rights, whether she wishes it or not.

This is what fundamentally makes women so mysterious to themselves as well as to others. The Yin in them demands the inexplicable and unknowable, pushes on to the next step in the unknown part of life, adds the yet unconscious part to the consciously known; and finds in every situation the germ of the new. It is therefore inexpressible, and all words and explanations can only give an artificial and untrue picture. This great darkness pregnant with life is the reality. To us the darkness seems suspect and morbid, and we turn away from it whenever possible. Therefore the vibrant, living darkness of *Yin* is seldom recognized in its essential meaning by modern cultured women*, in its natural expression of impulsive feelings and emotions which could contact the unknown depths of consciousness. or if it is perceived at all, it is quickly thrust away under the cover of convictions, opinions, concepts and rationalizations that misconstrue and twist the mystery even as it emerges, into being. That which could be understood by experiencing it is cut off, crippled even in embryo. Then the deep substratum of the stream of psychic life is blocked, dammed up, and it floods over in moments of unguarded unconsciousness, in overpowering affects that disturb and twist the meaning of everything around it. Or the *Yin* inserts itself slyly in the conscious and unconscious intrigues and suspicions of women with which they unwittingly poison themselves and those around them.[4]

This dimension clearly alludes not to any Eros quality but rather to a mysterious "womb of the unborn," a material void or emptiness which, nevertheless, is paradoxically also fullness, since it contains in potentia everything that could be; a pregnant sourceground of being as well as dark abyss of non-being, the mystery of Isis as the Great World Mother whose veil no mortal ever can lift, the aboriginal chaos or pleroma, fullness or void beyond and prior to time and space, beyond words, concepts or descriptions. It corresponds to Neumann's transformative aspect of the feminine and is experienced as threatening, devouring and terrifying, certainly by the male, but also largely by women. Therefore I propose to call it "Gorgo" or "Medusa." "Medusa" means ruler or queen and is the dark sourceground aspect of Pallas Athena, who was mythologically the Kore. (Athena was addressed as "Gorgo-like" and as "she who petrifies.")[5]

Medusa and Logos are corresponding female/male opposites. Logos is perceived and valued as creative intelligence and meaningful ordering principle alighting from above; Medusa is depreciated as a seemingly chaotic irrational depth of power unfolding from below, urges that appear to suck, draw, and threaten depersonalization and seeming emptiness that have to be tolerated, suffered, and lived with until they give birth to new forms of life expressions.

And just as Eros-Ares may be seen as the world manifesting incarnation, of the Logos, the "word become flesh," so Medusa manifests in its concrete experiential aspect not only in Pallas-Athena, but in a wide range of female patterns, essentially expressive of a fundamental polarity between Pallas and

---

* Linda Fierz-David is still in the patriarchal age. [Author's Note]

Aphrodite, creative activity, measure, rhythm and concreteness on the one hand, senuous attraction, play, allurement and pleasurable dream on the other; Hera-Hestia, Demeter-Ceridwen, Britomartis-Eve, and the Fates and Norns, on the one side; Astaroth-Artemis, and Lilith-Melusine on the other side. The images of the goddesses or aspects of the manifesting goddess are legion: The great spinner and weaver and measurer of the world web, huntress dancer, the world oriented play of life, joy, attraction, allurement, caring, acculturating, nourishing, supporting, domesticating, civilizing, aesthetic, and artistic but also untamed and untameable wildness, destruction, danger and dread; she is weaver and cutter of the net, the web of destiny, the multicoloured garment of divinity and incarnation. For, unlike the hierarchically divided male Yang, the female Yin remains always the Great Round, the specific aspect reflecting the undivided whole, appearing in innumerable variants.

The allurement, terror, dance, evasiveness, play and dissolution pole I propose to call "Lila," the Sanskrit word for the 'world play.' The feminine principle of order concretized in measure, rhythm, tides and cycles has been mythologically represented by Luna, the moon. Luna supports the claims and needs of reality, is sensitive to its rhythms, adapts to its necessities, nests, grows, nourishes and dies in the here and now. Lila enjoys and deplores, loves and rejects, connects and repels, dances in and plays with reality that is but illusion and makes illusion into reality, Maya. Pallas creates and is ready to strive, indeed fight, for cultural achievement and human dignity. She is concerned with humanizing raw or brutal energy. Medusa is the mystery beyond words.

In terms of archetypal patterns, then, there are four basic ways of developing masculinity, overtly and on the animus level; and there are four ways for femininity and anima tendencies. If we consider the different possibilities of combinations and meanings, a great many different types of men and women can be established, depending upon the way in which both sexes partake of the various elements of both genders. Only the barest outlines are attempted in this description.

The way of Lila is the way of playfulness, charm and attraction, the dance of the senses and of the Muses, artistic or sensuous. She is the crescent moon attuned to beauty, pleasure and enjoyment of the here and now, the play of love and life. She is woman's girlishly youthful aspect, shy like Artemis, touching, escaping yet wanting to be touched, and sensuously allowing like Aphrodite. As Siren, Lorelei, or Circe, she bewitches, allures or gambles with life and reality. As an anima figure she gives lightness, playfulness and poetic inspiration. She may compensate the rigidity of a senex trend or constellate the seduction of the Melusine witch or the Lorelei. In identification she brings out the *puer* the *puella* at their worst.

Luna's feminity is of the full moon, the Demetrian type, the wife, mother, but also with a strong Ares component, the competent administrator and creator of a congenial atmosphere and living space, of home and "soul." She is attuned to the rhythm, tides, needs, and possibilities of concrete life expressions; she has the capacity to structure and order her evironment and she is attuned to people's need and possibilities, aware of measure, limitations, and proportions. Luna has a sense of natural rhythm, tactfulness, and timing, and the capacity for empathy. Her way is the way of attunement, the logic of feeling and of personal responses to needs and possibilities of people and practical, concrete not abstract situations, to the requirements of the moment. She listens, perceives, receives, carries, gestates, reflects, nourishes, and protects. She lives, responds to, and identifies with pattern, process and form and the needs and tides of the body or bodily existence. This is Neumann's elementary aspect of the feminine. As an anima she primarily constellates the maternal, practical and protective dimension. Negatively she constellates the impersonalness of "Natura naturans."

Pallas Athena corresponds to Toni Wolff's Amazon type. She creates the career and pioneer woman but also a Florence Nightingale; she is ready to give battle for the sake of concrete human, not abstract, needs. As an anima figure she may account for idealistic and utopian pipe dreams or brilliant intuitive insights into new creative possibilities and projects.

Medusa is the abyss of transformation, the seemingly chaotic riddle that woman is to herself and to the puzzled man; hers is the dread of unpredictability and seeming emptiness. Her way is the way of the medium priestess or healer but also of the inspired artist. Negatively constellated she can make for an erratic, hysterical, devouring, borderline personality. Yet, we must not forget that Pegasus springs from the heart of the Medusa. Hence the Medusa anima may be met as *femme fatale*, the *"dame sans merci,"* witch or Death hag but also as guardian of the Holy, the *initiatrix and femme inspiratrice*.

Hers is a realm to which every woman and anima must periodically descend for renewal, like the Sumerian Inanna to the death realm of Ereshkigal, her dark sister. When this happens life comes to a standstill according to the myth. Paralysis, inertia, or depression seem to reign. Interest in work and human connections even to those closest to one's heart may be lost temporarily in a haze of indifference. Interestingly enough the myth depicts a conscious and delibrate descent and eventual return for Inanna, the feminine Luna figure, but a sacrificial death as the price for her return for Dumuzi her beloved, an Eros figure.

Apparently the required waiting, the receptive introversion necessary in this phase is somewhat easier for a woman to accomplish than for a man since, by virtue of her Luna side, she is more consciously attuned to her tides including her darkness, than the man. For him the experience is one of temporary "loss of soul," a death-like threat that exacts a sacrifice of Eros, a letting go of one's expectations, demands and desires, the theme of the Buddha's teaching.

For the woman the sacrifice occurs on the animus level by giving up the expectation of having to be the "beloved one" at any price. Instead of endearing herself by sweet compliance as the patriarchal culture has taught her the price for her transformed rebirth is to accept her own reality and to commit herself to what she discovers herself to be even though by the prevailing collective standards this may be held to be ugly and repulsive.

The "Ares" type man or animus is a striving warrior, the "go getter" who sets his goals, relies upon his strength, skill and determination to complete and grab whatever he can get hold of. As an animus quality Ares is the capicity for assertiveness, strength and self-reliance when integrated; cut off from the transformative playful or practical realization aspects of the feminine he operates as unconscious or compulsive hostility and contrariness. Hephaistos is man the maker and builder, striving to make himself immortal in structures, works and empires. As animus he makes for a busybody, restless doer, or practical creativity.

The way of Eros is through desire, through psyche and the Muses. He follows the lead of the anima, either to lose himself in her chaos or playfulness or to concretize and play creatively and find the hidden treasure in the witches' lair. Here we find the dreamer and artist. In combination with Ares he acquires more firmness; with an extreme preponderance of both we may have ruthless desire, greed, power demand and exploitation, ravishers, rapists, Don Juan types, or Hitlers.

As animus, Eros awakens psyche through aspiration, longing and reaching out. He can be a spur to genuine relatedness. In his primitive unassimilated form he demands, expects, desires and must have what he wants. He is sheer possessiveness and greed, a source of endless frustration but also the need to please, to comply and identify with others in order to get one's way.

The preponderance of Logos makes for the scholarly types, the thinker and philosopher. In his more extreme forms he can be quite unrelated both to people and to concrete facts of objects. As animus, Logos aims toward discrimination, discovery of meaning and clarity of thought, or negatively operates as the often described "devil of opinions," as judgmental bias. Logos and Ares make for reformers, searchers and researchers, such as religious revolutionaries. With Logos and Eros we have the mystic, the follower of the way of Christ or of Bhakti Yoga.

We see that each of the types has a positive as well as negative potential. Logos may be discerning wisdom or dogmatic superego; Medusa, intuitive perception of depth or threatening madness; Lila, joyful play or reckless gambling, to mention a few examples. In each type one can discern also what might be considered a growth and renewal or Dionysos-Apollo axis, a daughter-mother or puer-senex polarity. Medusa can appear as young witch or old death hag; Lila is as playful Artemis or has the abundance of Aphrodite: Luna as the urging of spring, the call of youthful expansion, or the maturity of motherhood and the harvest fulfillment. Athena can be the striving artist, or cultural reformer, or the conservative administrator and teacher. Logos can be met in mercurial versatility or Saturnian depth or rigidity; Ares, as *sturm and drang* of heroic outreach, ready to step in where angels fear to tread or as steadfast and patient persistence pursuing and defending a task or cause. Eros can be the onrush of desire and enthusiasm or quiet devotion. Hephaistos may be inventive ingenuity or the master craftsman who catches Ares and Aphrodite in his net joining imaginative beauty with concrete activity.

The reader may have noticed a similarity between these feminine types and those of Toni Wolff (Mother, Hetaira, Medium and Amazon). Wolff's types have been criticized for characterizing the feminine primarily in terms of relationship to the male or masculine, hence making them dependent or secondary to the masculine. Such an approach seems justified and to follow logically as long as the premise holds that the feminine equals Eros which equals relationship or relatedness. This is the assumption which this presentation has undertaken to refute at the very outset. The typology here offered accepts Toni Wolff's intuitive perception yet attempts to characterize the forms of the feminine as autonomous dynamics in their own right, secondary to none and regardless of how they may or may not relate to the masculine. They do, of course, relate to and complement their opposites; but this no more or less than the masculine relates to and complements the feminine. Between these two poles, representing as they do the most basic archetypes, flows incessantly the energy of the life current.

Moreover, in Wolff's typology, the Amazon type is depicted as relatively unrelated. The relatedness urge is credited to the Hetaira. Yet the Hetaira is actually a special instance of Lila who inclines toward a puella woman with a pseudo-related "feminine" persona. In reality it is Pallas who, with her concern for human values, has the more genuine potential for relatedness.

In the light of the above insights, I propose now to reexamine also our ideas about anima and animus as they apply to consciousness and sexual gender.

On the strength of clinical, experience accumulated since the time of their early formulation by Jung, their limitation to the unconscious dynamics of one sex or the other no longer appears quite practical. As Hillman has already suggested, the evidence does not justify the contention that anima exclusively embodies the nonpersonal unconscious of men ans animus of women. Nor can we still uphold the idea or dogma that consciousness in both men and women is masculine and unconsciousness, feminine.[6]

It was during the dominance of the patriarchal, androlatric culture and only in terms of the patriarchy that masculine values, patterns of perception, feeling, and behaviour shaped the structure of consciousness because they were given supreme value. In the patriarchy feminine standards were devalued and rejected hence repressed and reduced to unconscious determinants. Masculinity then represented consciousness.

In our time we witness a re-emergence of feminine Yin and anima qualities in the collective value system. They are becoming cultural determinants again and coshapers of a new consciousness for both sexes. Psychopompic figures appear in unconscious productions as frequently if not more so in feminine shapes as in masculine ones.

Consciousness is difficult to define. The ancient lanuages do not have a definite word for it. In the Latin rootword, *conscientia*, from which both the English and French term are derived, conscience and consciousness are not yet separated. *Conscientia* means joint knowledge, being privy to, having a feeling or sense of. We could formulate it as being in touch with a significance, hence a perception of relationship between a subject and an object. Consciousness is a form of relatedness; relatedness a form of consciousness. This perception of relationship can occur in two ways, in Yang or Yin fashion. The Yang way is the way of the ray and the left hemisphere of the brain, from center to periphery: separative, atomistic, analytical and abstracting. The Yin way, corresponding to right brain activity, draws toward the center, the interior; it moves toward unity, identity, patterns, and analogy. The former represents a male and animus consciousness which we are now more and more recognizing as equal in importance to the analytic leftsided male trend.

Applied to men and women the most we can claim is that, somatically at least, male trends preponderate in men and female ones in women. I do not know whether or not such a preponderance has been established in terms of hemispheric activity and in the ways they 'get in touch with,' relate to the world and themselves. However, even if we do assume a preponderance of Yang and Yin trends psychologically in men or women respectively, these are by no means uniform, as we have seen. While some may be dominants of consciousness, others may remain unconscious in either sex. For example, a woman's conscious attitude may be dominantly determined by Luna and / or Athena. She may be a capable and sensitive administrator or mother. But Logos and even Ares may be additional conscious dominants for her, and Lila, Aphrodite, or Medusa could be buried in her unconscious and operate in anima fashion, namely, as unconscious or even obsessive moodiness. She would then be concerned with meaning, even be wise, but also quite consciously assertive and aggressive and possibly prone to hysterical moods. An Aphrodite Lila woman may be subject to deep depressions or anxieties or become a terror to those around her when obsessed by a Medusa anima's moodiness, in addition to and regardless of a judgmental Logos or self-destructing Ares animus.

A particular man can be an Ares-Lila type in his conscious make-up, a vainglorious aggressive knight of fortune or charming like Chaucer's squire.

> Of his stature he was evene lengthe,
> And wonderly deliver, and great of strengthe.
> And he had been sometime in chevachye

In Flaundres, in Artoys, and Picardye
And born him well, as of so litel space
In hope to stonden in his lady grace . . .
Singing he was or floyting (fluting) all the day
He was as fresh as is the month of May
   Short was his goune, with sleeves long and wyde
   Well coude he site on hors and fair ryde.
               General Prologue, 11. 83—88; 91—94.

But with Logos constellated animus fashion in the unconscious he might also come forth with an opinionated animus dogmatism worthy of the most shrewish 'animus woman.' Or a Logos-oriented scholar may have to contend with a Martian or Hephaistian animus that could make him a cantankerous busybody until, and unless, he manages to integrate this part of his male animus potential.

Masculine traits can also be part of the nonpersonal unconscious potential in men and be obsessive, animus fashion; so can feminine traits in women. Instinct, soul and spirit, anima and animus are archetypal principles that pertain to both sexes equally. Men are not necessarily more spirit oriented than women. Neither do women have a monopoly on soul and instinct. Spirituality as a predominant male characteristic and woman as the embodiment of soul are heirlooms of 19th century romanticism, still dominant in Jung's day but no longer valid in our generation. Women can be and always could be deeply involved with and psychologically determined in their conscious outlook by Logos and out of touch with their affects; men can be immensely sensitive to instinct, feeling, and affect and quite at loss in respect to Logos or for that matter to any other of the masculine archetypes.

Either sex may partake in any of the masculine or feminine determinants in various constellations or degrees, comparable to a zodiacal wheel in which any of its sections can be accentuated to different degrees in different people.

It appears to be impractical—and not born out by contemporary psychological experience in our culture—to limit the concepts of anima and animus to one sex.[7]

In distinguishing anima and animus from shadow, that is, distinguishing as yet unassimilated impersonal potential from the repressed personalized actual habits and tendencies, we will have to be guided by a yardstick other than contrasexuality. The degree of mythologization and relative remoteness of a figure appearing in unconscious material as compared to the comparatively more prosaic personalness of a Jim or Jane, like a neighbor or business acquaintance, points to obsessive or creative potential, that is, to animus or anima rather than shadow.

Jung once exclaimed that theories and terminologies are 'the very devil' in psychology and that, while we cannot do without them, we should not hang on to them beyond the limit of their usefulness. A strict empiricist, he never hesitated to change and readapt his position in the face of new evidence. Now that he is no longer with us, it behooves us to continue in his spirit rather than to adhere to the letter of his word. We are discovering that many gender patterns, which even thirty years ago were considered *a priori* genetically or archetypally prefigurated, have been the result of cultural repressive limitations. Femininity and masculinity are archetypal *a priori* structural patterns of psychic no less than biological functioning. But in respect to identifying their specific contents we still need to retain open minds and be prepared to revise our views.

1 *Areios,* 'devoted to Ares.' *Areious,* 'better than, stouter, braver,' i.e., comparative of "good". *Arete,* 'goodness, excellence.' *Aretao,* to thrive.' (*Ari* and *eri* are equivalent prefixes.) They strengthen the sense of the word, i.e. *erikoos,* 'sharp of hearing.' *Erizeo,* 'to strive'. *Eromai,* 'to inquire, to ask after or for, to petition.' *Eros,* 'desire' or 'love.'

2 Robert Ornstein, *The Psychology of Consciousness* (New York: Harcourt Brace, Inc. 1977). p. 37.

3 This evidence is found in a recent summary in *The New York Times,* Section C (March 25, 1980).

4 Linda Fierz-David, ed. by Psychologische Club: Zürich, "Frauen als Weckerinnen seelischen Lebens," *Die Kulturelle Bedeutung der Komplexen Psychologie* (Berlin: Julius Springer, 1935), p. 490. (This passage was translated by Edward C. Whitmont.)

5 Karen E. Button, "Athena and Medusa," *Anima,* Vol. 5, No. 2. (Spring 1979), 120.

6 I would, in passing, draw attention to the obvious logical contradiction between the contention of unconsciousness being feminine, yet seeing the animus as representing the feminine unconscious; we have conveniently avoided confronting this contradiction—or we have explained it away.

7 Even in the past this practice has often led to such terminological absurdities as "animus of the anima" or to speaking of a man dominated by mother's animus or a woman by father's anima in order to avoid admitting the bona fide animus or anima dynamic as it operated in their own psyches.

(reprinted from Quadrant Vol. 13, No 2. Fall, 1980 pp. 109—122 by permission)

Coupling/Uncoupling

Reflections on the Evolution of the Marriage Archetype

By Robert M. Stein (Beverly Hills)

Behind the human drive toward coupling are images of sacred marriage of a divine couple and the soul's sense of incompletion. As powerful as the human need for coupling is the need to be free and unattached. In other words, the archetype behind the urge to be bound in marriage contains an opposite drive (as do all archetypes) to be unbound and separate. The tension between the needs to be coupled and to be single has become an incresing problem in our times. That the bonds of marriage no longer seem to hold, or at least function creatively to nourish the soul, is largely a consequence of our lack of connection to the changes occuring within the marriage archetype. Our urban-industrial society wreaks havoc on marriage, family and kinship community. As a consequence nuclear families atomize and couples become increasingly dependent on each other and their children for intimacy and security. This dependence has put enormous pressure on the marriage relation to fulfill all needs for intimacy and security, of couse intensifiying the soul's need to be free.

Since the 1960's we have seen sexual freedom, open, multiple or communal marriages, unmarried unions, democratic or patriarchal communes, religious and non-religious communities, explored. And it appears that in spite of the external changes, psychologically the younger generations have encountered the same oppressive patterns in their relationships, and seem just as incapable as older generations of resolving the polarization between the need to be bound and attached, and the need to be free and unattached. The 60's revolution has not reaped many new fruits in marriage and relationship. When tension between the opposites becomes unbearable, separation or divorce is still the prevailing solution.

Let us briefly review some of the ways in which the polarization *within* the marriage archetype has been dealt with historically. In our Western monogamous culture the dominant pattern has been the illicit, extramarital love affair or prostitution. In polygamous cultures, multiple marriages or concubinage, in primitive societies polygamy, ritual orgies, ritual sharing of wives are some of the patterns. Much has been written about comparative cultural

patterns of marriage. My intention is only to show that none of these solutions attend to the soul's need to be separate, free and unattached. An illicit
love affair is eventually as binding and confining as legitimate marriage. The
same can be said for multiple marriages in polygamous culture. Though all
these patterns allow for variations on the theme of coupling, and may relieve
the oppressive tension of the exclusive, monogamous marriage, they hardly
speak to the other pole of the archetype. They do little to heal the split.
Neither does the more modern pattern of sequential marriage and divorce.
The need to be coupled soon returns in full force, and a high percentage of
divorced people remarry.

The Hieros Gamos: Zeus and Hera

The incestuous sacred marriage (Hieros Gamos) between Zeus and Hera
presents a model for human monogamy. It is told that they celebrated their
mating for three hundred blissful years. Only after the royal honeymoon was
over did Zeus begin his wandering infidelities. Hera is recognized in Greek
religion as the Goddess of Marriage, as the guardian of the sacrament of coupling. Her jealousy, wrath and vindictiveness toward her husband's infidelities
with other Goddesses and mortals are well known. To the present day the
myth of unfaithful husband and abandoned, faithful wife, devoted to the sanctity of the marriage bed, continues to be enacted, though changes are evident
as a result of women's liberation and cosmopolitan sexual mores. One argument to support the apparent difference between masculine and feminine archetypes is that women need the stability and security of a permanent relationship in order to raise and educate children. But men seem to have an
equally strong instinctual need to raise and educate children. Studies of
animals with their young suggest it is so for them too. I question the notion
that women are more concerned about permanent coupling than men. Even
among the Olympian deities the Goddesses, including the Mother Goddess,
Demeter, have as much need to be free and uncoupled as do the males. Unless
we believe that Zeus entered into marriage with Hera only in order to satisfy
his lust, we must assume that the great Father God was equally committed to
the Hieros Gamos.[1]

The relation between Zeus and Hera can be viewed from the perspective of
the marriage archetype splitting after three hundred years of blissful union.
Among mortals once the honeymoon is over, typically (archetypally) one
spouse remains secure and content while the other begins to feel dissatisfied
with bondage, unfree to pursue fantasies and desires (sexual and otherwise)
which don't involve the spouse. Jung uses the metaphor of the container and
the contained as a way of viewing this phenomenon. [2] He sees one partner as
having a more complex nature than the other. "The simpler nature works on

the more complicated like a room that is too small, that does not allow him enough space. The complicated nature, on the other hand, gives the simpler one too many rooms with too much space, so that she never knows where she really belongs. So it comes about quite naturally that the more complicated contains the simpler."[3]

The notion of one person as more spiritually developed[4] or psychologically complex than another is such fertile soil for moralistic judgments that I have not found it very helpful. When Jung says, "It is an almost regular occurrence for a woman to be wholly contained spiritually in her husband, and for a husband to be wholly contained, emotionally, in his wife," the concept grows ambiguous.[5] Another objection I have to the container-contained model is that it implies that the simpler nature must become more psychologically aware and developed so the more complex partner will not feel so confined. I agree that a psychologically creative marriage requires the partners to pursue a path of psychological development, but I disagree that marriage or any relationship can contain the soul.

For these reasons I prefer the notion of the split archetype as a way of understanding the soul's inherent need to be both fully coupled (contained) and uncoupled (uncontained). Seen from the perspective of the split archetype, we begin to appreciate how the Zeus-Hera archetypal marriage tends to plunge the feminine into a rigid Senex position and the masculine into the mercurial Puer position. In the traditional monogamous patriarchal marriage, the feminine aspects of the soul become locked into coupling and carrying the responsibility of upholding the sanctity of the marriage bond. The free, unattached creative spirit becomes identified with the masculine, particularly with the eternal young boy, the Puer. As long as the polarity within the marriage archetype remains, the development and creativity of the feminine will remain stifled in both women and men. If the feminine is always a function of a responsiveness to the quick of life, to the movements of the soul in the moment (as I believe it is), to make it the responsible guardian for a rigid patriarchal marriage is surely oppressive to soul and the flow of life.

Philip Slater sees the Zeus-Hera relationship as a reflection of the patriarchal structure of Greek marriage;[6] Kerényi sees the Greek (human) marriage as modeled on the divine Zeus-Hera one.[7] Whichever way we toss this coin, we end up with a pattern of marriage which has prevailed in most cultures. Slater goes so far as to say, "the history of all known civilizations, including our own, is patriarchal."[8] Let me suggest that another archetypal split is there in these opposing views of Slater and Kerényi, important to examine because if the Gods are responsible for determining the patterns of human relationship, it leaves little room for affecting the Gods or archetypes. On the other hand, if archetypes merely reflect human customs and behaviour they are depotentiated and man correspondingly inflated. That human attitudes and behavior can effect transformation within an archetype is essential to an evolutionary perspective and not inconsitent with an archetypal psychology. The danger in this evolutionary perspective is that the great powers which inform and regulate the cyclic patterns of human and cosmic life will be depotentiated, resulting in desacralization of life. Lopez-Pedraza suggests that human nature has two parts, a part that does not change and part that moves.[9] This notion allows for the possibility that archetype and instinct can participate in change while at the same time allowing for the eternal, unchanging nature and power of the Gods. I see the soul's painful struggle with coupling relationships as a challenge to transform the marriage archetype (Zeus-Hera) through a process of deliteralization that will restore the original unity of the instincts to be coupled and uncoupled, but on a new level of consciousness.

Hand in hand with the need to be coupled goes the need to be uncoupled, always there as soon as the coupling instinct moves us toward another person. Seen from this perspective, the freedom the soul needs is to be able to experience being *simultaneously coupled and uncoupled.* Only then are the inherent polarities of the archetype experienced as complementary rather than splitting. How is it possible to experience oneself bound and committed and at the same time separate, free and unattached? Is it possible to honor the traditional marriage vows and still feel free to behave as a single, unattached person?

Some Dynamics of the Monogamous Patriarchal Marriage

In a monogamous culture, by definition, only one marriage at a time is allowed; if I desire to have an intimate relationship with another woman the coupling instinct soon enters and my marriage is immediately threatened. The soul-splitting tension this rather common situation creates can become unbearable and destructive. It results in a holding back in both relationships even if the tension is resolved in the traditional manner by maintaining a dayworld legitimate marriage and going underground with the other person. Even with this resolution the pressure to choose one or the other is always present. For a man this tension is experienced as a terrible pull between two women (internally between two polarized aspects of the feminine), and the fact that the split is *within the marriage archetype itself* gets lost. Instead of dealing with the soul's need to be free and unattached, the split is experienced as being between Wife-Mother and Adventurous, Exciting, Mysterious Other Woman. This tricks each woman into deeper identification with her role, which becomes increasingly oppressive to all parties involved. The phenomenon is similar when it is a woman who takes a lover: Husband becomes identified with Husband-Father, the lover with Adventurous, Exciting, Other Man. This soap-opera pattern has accompanied the marriage commitment for a long time. Because of this, I believe the split within the marriage archetype has been largely overlooked.

Deliteralization and Unifying the Split Archetype

What is missed in the Western love affair as well as in polygamous systems is
the soul's need to be both married and unmarried. If we can now begin to
view the need for extramarital intimacy as arising from this polarization
within the marriage archetype, perhaps something new may emerge. While the
need to feel free and unattached within my marriage may lead me to seek an
intimate involvement with another woman, won't I experience this polarity
with the other woman? If so, won't it be more to the point if I focus on the
split within my soul which has led me toward the other woman in the first
place? I resist being coupled to the other woman as much as I resist being
coupled to my wife, yet experience the desire to be coupled to both. If I can
resolve this conflict in either relationship, it may lead me to a resolution in
the other. If I can experience being bound and coupled, free and uncoupled
with the other woman, perhaps I can achieve that state with the woman to
whom I am literally married. Here is a clue to a possible resolution, a
deliteralization of the marriage bond as well as a deliteralization of the soul's
need to be free and unattached. Let us explore some of the consequences.

By maintaining the connection to both the desire to be coupled and the
desire to be uncoupled, both poles of the instinct (archetype) can be experienced and lived as complementary rather than as divisive opposites. Connection
implies separation. In this instance it means that one separates oneself from
identifying with either the desire to be coupled or uncoupled while maintaining awareness of both needs. This move is an essential step toward deliteralization.

Literalization is the result of identifying with one particular need, feeling, attitude, idea, viewpoint, God, etc. If we identify with the need to be coupled,
fulfillment is only possible through actual marriage (or its equivalent). Only
when this is filled will I become aware of the opposite pole, the need to be uncoupled, which I can also only experience by my identification with its opposite. In other words, if I experience coupling only literally, I experience uncoupling only through the literal act of flight and divorce.[10]

Extramarital Sexuality

Both love and sexuality fare ill under restrictions which limit them to one
primary relationship. As soon as coupling occurs, the need to be free and unbound is close at hand. If the need for extramarital erotic involvement is
primarily an expression of the other pole of the marriage archetype (as I have
suggested) perhaps the vow of sexual fidelity may serve to facilitate rather
than hinder the soul's quest for freedom—which is not necessarily reached
through satifying every impulse and desire. Spiritual freedom, as the great

religions teach, follows the difficult path of being able to let go of worldly and literal attachments. We know how important sexual restrictions have been in the development of culture, and I have no doubt that the universal restrictions on extramarital sexuality were useful for the soul's development. To simply suggest the elimination of sexual restrictions would seem foolhardy.

I think the dialogue and struggle with the archetype, the God, behind the restrictions on extramarital sexual activity are fundamental to soulmaking. For one thing, the desire for fidelity and exclusiveness belongs to the soul's experience of uniting, of coupling, with the beloved. When a culture does not honor this numinous experience, the sacramental mystery of sexual union is profaned. Cultural taboos and restrictions on sexuality originate with the soul's need to sacralize sexuality and life. Still, something seems terribly oppressive to the soul's development in the traditional marriage structure. Something new is needed; I have no doubt that whatever emerges will include a new relationship to the archetype behind the urge for sexual fidelity as well as corresponding changes in the marriage vows and ceremony.

The Church

Marriage, as an institution, is primarily concerned with ensuring the stability and permanence of the relationship, and tends to inhibit or restrain urges toward freedom and uncoupling, so long as it is being determined by the Zeus-Hera archetype. Love is particularly threatening to the exclusivity of the marriage bond because it is a powerful spirit which can not be limited to one relationship. The Church believes that God's nature permeates the world with an all encompassing universal love as well as with an intensely focused love for the particular. Jesus has the capacity to share in both God's universal love (agape) and his special love for the particular individual (eros), but we ordinary mortals seldom have this capacity. For the majority of people marriage is the way. Those chosen to follow the path of agape must forsake that aspect of their natures which binds them to a particular person. The Church seems to believe that when love is consummated in sexual union, the two people are less free to serve God's universal love. Thus, the religious must take a vow of celibacy and not marry to be free to serve the many.

The Church's position here has considerable psychological and empirical validity. Whenever one experiences a strong soul connection with another person, the image of the Hieros Gamos is released. If this union is consummated in the flesh, the soul feels bound to its mate in a sacred marriage which conjures a powerful desire to love and serve the beloved eternally. The body of the beloved is experienced as a sacred, numinous incarnation of God. Lovers experience both an intense love for the God embodied in the beloved, as well as the bliss of God's personal love for them. When lovers merge through erotic union, the soul commits itself forever to serving God through the beloved. For the lover to be cut off from the beloved may seem like being cut off from God. In these notions the Church is expressing a deep understanding of the soul's nature, and the vow of sexual fidelity which incorporates into the marriage ritual is an expression of this wisdom. In the ordination ceremony a priest, in his symbolic mystical marriage to the body of Christ which is his Church, dedicates himself to serving God's love for the Christian community. The religious, just because they are not bound to a particular person, are free to be intimate and loving with many people—free to live the other pole of the marriage archetype in their human relationships.

Sexual Fidelity

Why does love consummated in sexual union seem to bind two people together and make them no longer free? What is there about the coupling instinct which demands sexual exclusivity? Is it possible to transcend these instincts, transform the archetype, so that the soul may live its need to be free, unattached and unencumbered by limitations, on its capacity for love and sexuality? "The pair," as Scripture says, "shall become one flesh." At the moment of union, souls feel bound together in a sacred marriage. The desire to love, cherish, serve, protect and be sexually faithful to the beloved belongs to the total experience. Traditional rituals reflect these human sentiments. In spite of these basic emotions, these psychological truths, which support the traditional marriage vows, it seems essential that modern couples have the freedom to explore other intimate relationships, which may or may not involve sexual intimacy. Won't the soul feel sinful, guilty, if it transgresses the vow of sexual fidelity? I believe that as long as the Zeus-Hera structure of the marriage archetype remains the dominant image of marriage within the soul, the answer is yes. A new image and model is needed that will allow for the possibility of experiencing the Hieros Gamos with more than one person while still honoring the sentiment and psychological truth expressed in the traditional marriage vows.

Much of the suffering one encounters in psychotherapeutic practice relates to the soul's frustration and despair from not being able to unite with its mate. Those who are married tend often to be painfully dissatisfied with the quality of the conjugal connection. Single people long to find their mate or, disillusioned, struggle with their fearful ambivalence about fulfilling the soul's need for coupling. In his book *Marriage, Dead or Alive*, Guggenbühl,[11] speaking of the soul's suffering in marriage, takes the position that marriage is a vessel for salvation, not for happiness and well-being. He believes that individual development may need to be sacrificed for the individuation process which is contained in the marriage relationship. He also states that marriage is *but one* of many paths through which people individuate. Of course each soul must follow a unique path of individuation, but it seems to me that the soul's need for a mate, to be coupled and to share its life with another person, is basic to the human condition and not to be compared with the various paths people must follow for individuation. The fantasy of finding completion through union with another person serves mainly to drive the soul toward its own completion, toward fulfilling its unique destiny. Relationship, love and intimacy, the complexities of human involvements are a *sine qua non* for the soul's development. Attention to relationships, to the care of the love the soul feels toward another soul is, therefore, crucial to everyone's individuation.

Marriage and Community

The marriage archteype is also responsible for binding people together into community through the sacrament of the mystical marriage of God with his faithful followers—for the Jews, for example, the union of Yahweh with Israel, for the Christians the union of Christ with his church. Communal life is not only sustained and renewed by the sacrament of marriage, but really only beginswhen a people are united in a mystical marriage to a common God—the Olympian family did not exist before the Hieros Gamos of Zeus and Hera. *To feel coupled and belonging to a community is, therefore, an even more basic expression of the marriage archetype than the need to feel coupled to another person.* As Jung puts it,

> Everyone is now a stranger among strangers. Kinship libido which could still engender a satisfying feeling of belonging together, as for instance in the early Christian communities—has long been deprived of its object. But being an instinct, it is not to be satisfied by any mere substitute such as a creed, party, nation or state. It wants the *human* connection . . .[12]

Because communal life has broken down for most of us, the modern marriage relation has been burdened with having to carry most of the kinship needs of the soul. To be cut off from its communal roots is perhaps the most threatening experience the soul can have. As long as the kinship libido is primarily attached to one's spouse, the fear of uncoupling will always be greater than the need to change. Since containment in community is so essential to the life of the soul, meeting the challenge of changing the deeply rooted patterns of marriage is overwhelming, and I believe doomed to failure, without communal support, Perhaps small *groups* of people using the archetypal perspective will help deepen our understanding of the sacramental mystery of marriage and sexual union, and facilitate the emergence of communal rituals which will enable the soul to honor its need to be both *free* and *faithful*.

1 In his excellent paper "Hera: Bound and Unbound " in *Spring 1977*, Murray Stein (following Kerényi) presents the thesis that the mating instinct belongs to a feminine aspect of the soul (Hera). His view is that Hera's pain, fury, jealousy, vindictiveness are not owing simply to Zeus's infidelities, but to his not allowing her to fulfill basic need to find "perfection" and fulfillment in *gamos*. He suggests that if Hera's basic need for the Hieros Gamos is fulfilled, her destructiveness can be contained and bound. Besides ignoring the three hundred blissful years Zeus and Hera lived in complete fulfillment of the Hieros Gamos, I find his viewpoint tends once again to attribute the vicissitudes of the soul's passion for union, as well as its painful frustrations and jealous rages in relationships, to the feminine. Such a view keeps women in their traditional role of being responsible for the relationship needs of the soul in marriage. I believe the mating instinct to be primarily informed by the *complete* image of the Hieros Gamos (incest archetype) rather than only one pole of the archetype. (For a more complete study relating the mating instinct to the psychic internalization of the Hieros Gamos and to the incest mystery, see my book *Incest & Human Love: the betrayal of the soul in psychotherapy*. Penguin Books, Baltimore, 1974, now distributed by Spring Publications.)

2 C.G. Jung, "Marriage as A Psychological Relationship," *CW* 17.

3 Ibid., para 333.

4 Ibid., para 331c.

5 Ibid., para 331c.

6 Philip E. Slater, *The Glory of Hera*, Beacon Press, Boston 1971.

7 Carl Kerényi, *Zeus & Hera: archetypal image of father, husband and wife*, Princeton, 1975.

8 Philip E. Slater, *Footholds*, E. P. Dutton, New York, 1977, p. 68.

9 Rafael Lopez-Pedraza, *Hermes and His Children*, Spring Publications, 1977, p. 89.

10 Nathan and Sandra Schwartz, in a paper titled, "On the Coupling of Psychic Entropy and Negentropy," *Spring 1970*, also develop the view of a split in the marriage archetype, but imagine the split in terms of "profane time" and its entropic, disordered correlate, and the unifying order of "sacred time."

11 Adolf Guggenbühl-Craig, *Marriage—Dead or Alive*, Spring Publications, 1977.

12 C.G. Jung, "Psychology of the Transference," *CW* 16, para 445.

(reprinted from Spring 1981 by permission)

Symbolic Psychotherapy, a Post-Patriarchal Pattern in Psychotherapy

An Interpretation of the Historical Development of Western Psychotherapy through a Mythological Theory of History[1]

By Carlos Byington (Rio de Janeiro)

To Erich Neumann In Memoriam

Jung's concept of the individuation process should be used inside a broad archetypal theory of individual and collective development if we do not want to use archetypal psychology to feed a cancer of Western culture which is the dichotomy between human being and nature, psyche and matter, individual and society, as well as between psychology and sociology, and between the psychological individual's stadial development and history. Archetypal psychology has gone beyond psychoanalysis through Jung's concept of the collective unconscious. Archetypes encompass personal experiences inside general human patterns of development including those of the Oedipus Complex as described by Freud and those that belong to the child-breast relationship as described by Melanie Klein. Unless, however, we realize the prospective funtioning of archetypes in structuring evolutionary patterns of collective consciousness, the backbone of history in all cultures, the patterning of collective consciousness by the cultural aspect of the Self will remain unconscious and unknown.

One of the most important theoretical inferences from Freud's discoveries of unconscious processes is that consciousness is not the master in its own house. In a famous passage, he states that this is the main resistance to an acceptance of the extistence of unconscious processes, comparable to the historical resistances to Copernicus's discovery that the Earth was not the center of our planetary system and to Darwin's theory of evolution, through which it became clear that our species had not been a primary creation but had appeared after thousands of others[3]. It seems that this is the same resistance that prevents many to accept the evolutionary approach to archetypal individual and collective development. It is as if the ego would thus try to limit and control the concept of the archetype in the time dimension of consciousness to avoid the fact that the archetype is permanently structuring and transforming consciousness. To keep the concept of the archetype in a timeless dimension is to preserve its "eternal mystery", and although true in one sense this idea may be used as a defensive rationalization. In fact, we experience the "eternally-mysterious" dimension of the archetype much more when we become conscious that we are transforming and becoming, day and night. As we strive both consciously and unconsciously towards the human goal, we experience with force the immutability of the archetype.

Erich Neumann contributed greatly to the subject of archetypal evolution by bringing Bachofen's theory[4] that a matriarchal mythological stage preceded the patriarchal stage into archetypal psychology[5]. Developing the research of these two pioneers, I feel we can identify two further patterns that are post-patriarchal. If we believe that the mythological stadial development of cultures ends up in the patriarchal stage, we cannot understand such cultures as the Egyptian, Indian, Greek, Chinese, and Western Culture after Christ, from a mythological evolutionary perspective. We are left with the notion of the individual process as a process by which each individual, in the second stage of life, differentiates himself from collective consciousness and tries to follow his path toward wholeness, while collective consciousness remains stationary in the patriarchal cycle. In this view, members of a culture may individuate, but the culture itself is not subject to the direct patterning of archetypes. Viewing ourselves this way, we become alienated and unconscious of the structuring function of the cultural Self and cannot consciously engage ourselves with the cultural conditions.

The same dire consequences which follow alienation from the individual soul, stressed again and again throughout Jung's works, can occur when alienation from the collective soul takes place. In this sense, modern man is not only in search of an individual soul but also of a collective soul. In fact, there can be no sound development of the individuation process without also conscious direct and creative participation in the archetypal development of collective consciousness.

Symbols of the Self cannot be seen as true images of totality if this totality is not also situated in the cosmic dimension, i.e., related somehow to the universe. Therefore, there must not be any difference between the concept of the Self and the concept of universal totality which corresponds to the concept of an all encompassing deity or universal principle. In this sense, the patterning function of the archetype of the Self must be seen all the way from the deintegration of galaxies, to planetary systems, to cultures, to individuals, to organisms, to molecules and atoms. The archetypal function of modern art and science is not to perpetuate the man-world dichotomy, but to enable us to perceive phenomena more readily as a differentiation of the universal Self. This is what the theories of Teilhard de Chardin[6] and of Martin Heidegger[7] have conceived. To be complete, consciousness of the individual soul must be accompanied by consciousness of the cultural or collective soul and finally of the universal soul. To avoid metaphysical, philosophical, scientific, political and psychological dissociation and alienation, these concepts must never be envisaged separated from one another. Every time we consider the concept of the Self as an individual or partial phenomenon, we incur a dissociation and become blind to the light which permeates and links up all parts of the universe meaningfully. As Indian mysticism has expressed "God is only one, but throughout time the sages have given Him many names". Libido is psychic energy which is but one of the many forms of cosmic energy. Consciousness is archetypally related to light because both are phenomena which interrelate things meaningfully, and they are but two forms of universal interrelationship, being themselves interrelated.

From atoms to galaxies, we find different expressions of centroversion through which partial phenomena, be they electrons or stars, are meaningfully related to a center which can be thought of as an image of the universal Self and its principle of organization. Such reasoning allows us to speak of more than one self as, for instance, the individual self, the therapeutic self and the cultural self. This, however, should not prevent us from seeing all these organized forms of being as expressions of the universal Self. All these expressions will present central images, whether as the nucleus of atoms, stars or cells, or as the central star of a planetary system like our Sun, or as the nucleus of our planet, the government of our country or the therapeutic coniunctio of the analytical transference. These centers are an expression of the organizing aspect of the archetype of totality and, because of this, they have many phenomena in common which interrelate them meaningfully, as, for instance, the phenomenon of gravitation. These interrelating phenomena must be searched for carefully for us not to associate these various expressions of the universal Self in an undiscriminated way. It is interesting that the discovery of these interrelationships sometimes comes about long before distinct knowledge of the phenomena they interrelate. Darwin, for instance, discovered the meaningful interrelationship of species, through his idea of evolution, long before Mendel discovered genes. Before Darwin, it was clear only that members of the same species were interrelated; it was quite unthinkable that all biological forms of life were interrelated. Yet creation myths had, in many ways, expressed this idea from beginning of human culture.

The archetype is the gene of psychology through which not only we formulate the patterning of the universe but also the patterning of the mind and of culture. This pattern is not only structural (diagram 2) but also evolutionary (diagram 1). There is a common manifestation between the expression of the individual self and the collective self which is the symbol. Myths are one of the most basic forms of the meaningful interrelationship of symbols within the collective self and therefore, they are a fruitful way of evisaging the structure and evolutionary pattern of the collective self and of

THE ARCHETYPAL DEVELOPMENT OF THE PERSONALITY
THE FOUR ARCHETYPAL CYCLES

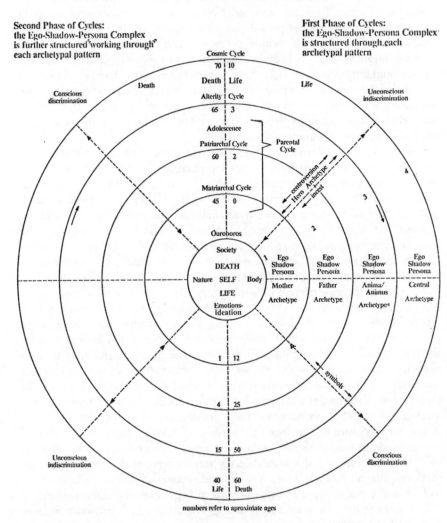

Second Phase of Cycles:
the Ego-Shadow-Persona Complex
is further structured "working through"
each archetypal pattern

First Phase of Cycles:
the Ego-Shadow-Persona Complex
is structured through each
archetypal pattern

numbers refer to aproxiniate ages

From Diagram 1 in
Carlos Byington, The Archetypal Development of the Personality

perceiving the way through which it is related to the individual self. This fact led Jung to speak of the individual myth referring to the process of individuation[8]. Therefore, Neumann's choice of the mythological matriarchal and patriarchal stages described by Bachofen[9] as patterns also for individual psychic development was a very significant step to propitiate our consciousness of the interrelationship of the individual and collective Self. We shall follow this path beyond the patriarchal pattern in order to conceive a mythological theory of history which will allow us to interrelate meaningfully the development of society and the individual in all their development archetypal patterns.

The process of individuation described by Jung in the second half of life may be seen as a process of relatively successive stadial developments passing through the confrontation with the shadow, the anima/animus archetypes and ending in the mid-point personality stage where the archetype of the Self becomes dominant.[10].

The research of Michael Fordham describing ego formation through deintegration of the Self[11] and of Erich Neumann describing the matriarchal and patriarchal stages in ego formation[12] allowed us to see archetypal development of the personality also in the first half of life.

In this paper, I try to present a general theory of development of the individual and of culture; so that we may situate the process of individuation as described by Jung inside the historical development of any given culture and interrelate them meaningfully, in the political as well as in all human dimensions. For this to be done, we must consider certain concepts which will assemble individual and social occurrences in a meaningful and interrelated way. These concepts can be grouped into the following items:

1. The transformation of Neumann's archetypal phases into cycles which encompass childhood and adult life.

2. The conception of two post-patriarchal cycles structuring ego and collective consciousness which I have named the Alterity Cycle and Cosmic Cycle.

3. The formulation of a separate pattern for the *archetypal pole* and for *the conscious pole* of every archetypal cycle inside the ego-Self Axis (diagram 2).

3a. The recognition that these patterns may be constelled in many different historical situations independently of the dominant cycle in that period.

3b. The recognition that in every archetypal cycle all psychic phenomena including archetypes and all social functions and institutions will be affected characteristically by the dominant archetypal pattern.

3c. Every archetypal cycle, having a distinct conscious pattern, will forcibly have too a characteristic Weltanschauung. The necessary pattern to perceive the psychic process of differenciation and transformation of the individual self and the collective self in all archetypal cycles is the cosmic archetypal pattern of consciousness.

3d. Interpretation is a psychic function which associates psychic phenomena meaningfully and, therefore, also has a distinct and characteristic form in every archetypal pattern of consciousness. Interpretation in the patriarchal pattern associates symbols to specific references and is, therefore, causal and reductive. Interpretation in the post-patriarchal alterity pattern is exercised through the amplification of the prospective-creative-revealing characteristic of symbols. This fact differentiates enormously psychotherapeutic theory and technique based on the patriarchal pattern from that based on the post-patriarchal alterity pattern. I avoid the polarity analytical-synthetical used by Jung to study this phenomenon[13] because reduction is not a phenomenon which occurs by analytical decomposition. The term "psycho-analysis" was used by Freud throughout his work meaning both examination or exploration and analytical decomposition as understood in the natural sciences. I do not think it possible for a symbol to be analytically decomposed as understood in this sense and, therefore, I use the term "analysis" meaning the examination of the symbol.

4. The concept of the symbol as the intermediator between the archetype and consciousness introducing prospectively new ways of being which become existential process.

4a. The main function of the symbol is existential creativity.

4b. The process of compensation is secondary and subordinate to the primary, life-creating function of the symbol.

4c. The transformation process of a symbol into the extistential process includes its passage from image into number and word. Image-word and image-number are polarities of the symbolic dimension.

4d. The interpretation of symbols inside the patriarchal pattern reduces them to signs because if refers them to specific causes codified from theory. This transforms psychotherapists into "head shrinkers" because such psychotherapeutic procedure reduces psychic processes to certain dimensions of the personality. I have referred throughout the paper to dichotomies as a cancer of Western mind because they are a degenerate fixation of the patriarchal pattern of discrimination. The patriarchal pattern separates the polarities of a dimension creating fixed polar discriminations to deal with reality. Right and wrong, good and bad are dogmatically preestablished. Although rigid, the patriarchal pattern is very useful and necessary for the mind to deal with new territory as well as to structure itself. If archetypal fixations occur and the patriarchal pattern is not transcended into the alterity pattern, discriminations will degenerate into dichotomies which will become every time more rigid, inadequate and unproductive. In this manner, dichotomies corrode our transformation into the alterity pattern and thus prevent our archetypal development and creative experience of the living symbol.

4e. The interpretation of symbols based on the alterity pattern links consciousness creatively to the Self and leaves "the symbol as the best expression of itself"[14]. Interpretation is therefore, the science and art of dealing with

THE EGO-SELF STRUCTURE

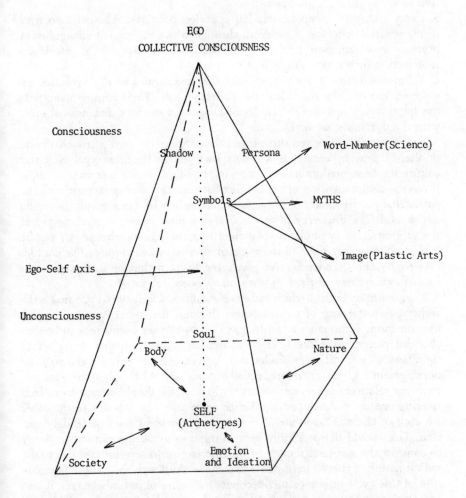

DIAGRAM 2 in Carlos Byington, "The Archetypal Development of the
                         Personality".

symbols. Symbolic interpretation, through leaving the symbol as it is, enhances the prospective function of symbols, whereas reductive interpretation restrains their creative power.

5. Every archetype is bipolar and has countless polarities. The main polarity of the central archetype is life-death through which it patterns all significant psychic transformation producing symbols which express the life-death-resurrection or transformation motif.

6. Diagrams 1 and 2 are respectively the structural and the evolutionary representation of the individual and collective Self. Their common image is the spiral which links up the circles of Diagram 1 in three dimensional form with the pyramid-cone of Diagram 2.

7. Special emphasis is given throughout the paper to the post-patriarchal cycle or alterity pattern because, as will be shown, this is the archetypal cycle our culture has been predominantly "working through" in the past two millenia. From the comprehension of the conflict between the alterity pattern with the patriarchal pattern much of the archetypal conflicts of western culture can be understood. The discovery of the process of individuation in psychology and the application of symbolic development in archetypal psychotherapy can be understood as expressions of the cycle of alterity of our culture. The conflict between symbolic and reductive psychotherapy can thus be seen as the conflict of two archetypal patterns with many historical parallels.

8. The great many decades which make every individual archetypal cycle makes the archetypal patterning of consciousness through the cycles a very complex phenomenon. Although we can frequently observe the dominance of one archetypal pattern over the field of consciousness, other patterns are acting simultaneously in different shades and degrees. All patterns are essential for development and are, therefore, equally important. Although archetypal patterns are relatively sequential and evolutionary, we should refrain from considering one more developed and better or in any way superior to the other for each of them is "absolutely" needed to perform its own particular function. This should be specifically kept in mind to avoid the cultural tendency to consider the matriarchal cycle or the matriarchal pattern inferior due to the radical nature of the Western patriarchal cycle. Although the radical implantation of this cycle in our culture accounts for many of our advantages, it also accounts for many of our disadvantages and, therefore, cannot be relied upon to explain the nature of other archetypal cycles, above all the matriarchal cycle and the matriarchal pattern which it has repressed so much. Let us now try to amplify some of these themes.

Employing Neumann's concept of the ego-Self axis[15], we can describe an archetypal pattern for both ends of this axis in each archetypal stage. The ego pole of the ego-Self axis does not occupy only, therefore, the center of consciousness but may present all nuances of consciousness varying from the symbolic state still indiscriminated to intense discrimination of the symbol. By discrimination, I mean the identification of the various polarities present in the symbol as well as relating them to the other discriminated polarities already present in consciousness. The ego complex may be seen as inseparable from the shadow and the persona which present, as much as the ego, a typical pattern in each of the archetypal stages of development. The ego-shadow-persona complex presents, then, typical patterns in the second half of life which are just as important for ego development as are the archetypal patterns identified by Neumann in the first half of life.

I have amplified Neumann's matriarchal and patriarchal phases of personality development into archetypal cycles with two phases which cover the whole life cycle of the archetype. In the first phase, the ego is structured through the archetype and in the second phase the ego is further structured actively "working through" the archetypal pattern during many decades. In the matriarchal cycle, for instance, the ego is first structured through the primary relationship and very soon a part of it begins to enter the second phase, beginning maternal activities which will "work through" the patterning of the mother archetype. This further structures the ego and encompasses, during many decades, activities such as childbirth, raising children, taking care of one's home, one's body, one's interests and all maternal caring for, which everyone carries out so frequently (diagram 1). Any fixation in the first phase of an archetypal cycle will inevitably bring about typical disturbances in the second phase of that cycle. Post-partum psychosis, for instance, must be studied as a severe disturbance of the second phase of the matriarchal cycle where we frequently find the emergence of intense fixations which have occurred in the first phase of this cycle.

The anima/animus archetypal cycle structures consciousness with the capacity to relate on equal terms to "the other" in general. After firmly deintegrating from the Self in the patriarchal cycle, and separating from the parental cycle in adolescence, the ego, through the anima/animus pattern, is structured to relate creatively to "the other" in general on equal terms as in Buber's I-Thou relationship[16]. "The other" may be the shadow, the wife, the profession, society, the unconscious in general, nature, the body, etc. The openness and creative relationship to otherness which characterizes this cycle of development have led me to name it the cycle of alterity. This is the consciously creative life stage when the ego, firmly established, participates through symbols and imagination actively in the creative work of the Self. In marriage, in professional life and through relationship in general, the ego sacrifices systematically its acquired position to transform itself creatively through the encounter with otherness. The cycle of alterity is basically oriented by the synchronicity principle.

The creative encounter with otherness is not compatible with causality and reduction. Because the symbol can in this state of consciousness be experienced as the best expression of itself and not be manipulated by omnipotence and magic amidst the principle of fertility and desire of the matriarchal cycle or limited by reduction and causality amidst the repressive organizing principle of the patriarchal cycle, the cycle of alterity expresses the first truly symbolic stage of consciousness. In the cycle of alterity, consciousness is for the first time able to open up for the whole range of meanings encompassed by a symbol without losing its identity. The human encounter with the living symbol will frequently bring consciousness back into states of unconscious indiscrimination but the strong sense of identity structured into consciousness will allow it to go through these states of unconsciousness and come back transformed and again discriminated without "acting out" unconsciousness all around itself (as we see in acute psychotic behavior).

In the last cycle of archetypal development, consciousness is directly structured through the central archetype and the ego sacrifices all bondages including those with the body. The ego thus prepares itself for Nirvana (freedom from polarities) and accompanies the soul in its full experience of wholeness. Due to the transcending nature of these experience which include the sacrifice of bodily and social existence, I have called this last life cycle, the cosmic cycle of the archetypal development of the personality (diagram 1).

The matriarchal pattern of conscious development is binary and is inspired in the satisfaction of desire or the principle of fertility of the mother archetype. Good is that which in that particular moment satisfies desire, lust and growth. The matriarchal pattern is frequently exercised in magic. Because the ego is not sufficiently differentiated to deal with both polarities of one dimension simultaneously, it experiences each polarity in a separate situation and functions in the either-or pattern. Due to this relatively small differentiation of the ego, the persona and the shadow also are not clearly discriminated in this cycle.

This relative smaller deintegration of the ego in the matriarchal cycle as compared to the greater deintegration of the ego in the patriarchal cycle should not be considered an inferior state of consciousness. Although it has many disadvantages inherent in the either-or (binary) pattern which occurs as a result of the great proximity of the ego to unconscious processes, this same proximity offers many advantages. This nearness of consciousness to the latent Self endows consciousness with great sensitivity to creative phenomena in the sensuous, practical, feeling-intuitive fertility aspects of survival. The psychic body roots (diagram 2) of consciousness are so near to the Self that bodily symptoms become the expression of an infinitely sensitive radar of awareness. The prospective function of symbols is so much more acutely sensed by matriarchal consciousness that it frequently acquires the capacity of divination and oracular prophecy. This characteristic of matriarchal consciousness is probably the explanation for the fact that most spontaneous intuitive perception (usually called e.s.p., extra-sensorial-perception) occurs in the mother-son or mother-daughter relationship.

The patriarchal pattern is ternary and is based on formulations once established and used from then on as undisputable truth. The ego is capable of a triangular relationship confronting both polarities or dimensions simultaneously, as long as they have been discriminated beforehand and dogmatically codified, as for instance, the function of father and mother in the Oedipal triangle. The persona and the shadow are here distinctly differentiated. This dogmatic structure of consciousness is maintained through the principle of repression which is characteristic of the dogmatic authority principle of the father archetype and which establishes reduction and causality as patterns to deal with in reality.

The patriarchal cycle of personality development has many advantages over the matriarchal cycle due to its greater deintegration from the Self. Herein however, lie also its disadvantages. Greater deintegration allows consciousness fixed discriminations which are used by memory to codify consciousness and plan behaviour. The patriarchal pattern allows the ego to function as bulwark against disorganized chaotic unconsciousness and endows the personality with the capacity to maintain tradition without ritual and behaviour logically coherent with former attitudes. Exactly these characteristics acquired through greater ego deintegration, however, can be very disadvantageous for intelligent behaviour because, as we know, in the same way in which too much sun may be life destroying and create deserts, so also too much planned computerized behaviour may miss completely the swift turns of life and originate void efficiency. Thus, logic and highly organized consciousness, presenting regularly the highest I.Q.'s may, under unforeseen circumstances, originate the most inadequate unintelligent and absurd behaviour.

One of the most important aspects of the evolutionary cycles of the archetypal development of the personality (diagram 1) is that only the appearance and stadial dominance of cycle are sequential. The structuring function of archetypal cycles is during a great period of life simultaneous. Although there are dominant archetypal patterns for every life stage, other patterns continue to function and structure consciousness. It is important to realize that what we call simply "the ego" is one of the most complex structures of the psyche, presenting in one day just about every archetypal pattern one can think of.

The relative simultaneity of the matriarchal and patriarchal cycles of consciousness allows us to conceive a larger parental cycle of consciousness which collides fully with the alterity pattern in the turmoil characteristic of the crisis of adolescence. Many aspects of the personality including those which are called primary identities, including sexual identity, depend not only on how the implantation and initial phase of the archetypal cycles have taken place but also fundamentally on the interrelationship of the matriarchal and patriarchal patterns which will form the parental archetypal coniunctio. From the nature of this coniunctio and its relative harmonies and disharmonies will depend

greatly the individual and cultural identity, the polarizing conflicts of the phase
of adolescence and the implantation and development of the cycle of alterity
and its coniunctio. The radical and intensive implantation and development of
the patriarchal cycle in western culture has contributed greatly to the radically unilateral identity of man and woman in our culture and the implantation
of a parental coniunctio of a highly unilateral, rigid and repressive nature expressed exuberantly in the marriage institution. This has affected adversely the
whole individuation process in western culture, as well as its crisis of
adolescence and the development of its alterity cycle.

   The development and identity of man and woman, as is well known, is intensely conditioned by cultural tradition. This tradition, however is archetypally rooted in the relative identification of woman with the matriarchal
and man with the patriarchal pattern. In fact, many characteristics of the
matriarchal and patriarchal archetypal images which represent these archetypal patterns have their origin in physical characteristics of man and
woman. However, in the same way that each individual cell has double paired
chromosomes, so each individual psyche also has the parental pair of mother
and father archetypes. Up to the patriarchal cycle, man and woman's identities are much conditioned by and subordinated to the social constellation
and interrelationship of matriarchal and patriarchal cycles of their particular
culture. Man and woman's psychic identities are also basically conditioned to
their different archetypal development for only man must undergo a transsex-
ual passage in the primary relationship to structure sexual identity. The
relative identification of woman with the matriarchal and man with the
patriarchal pattern and vice-versa tends to become an absolute one in a radical
collective patriarchal cycle such as we find in western culture. It is in the
alterity cycle that man and woman can structure their full identity encompassing in their personality the creative interaction of opposites.

   Ego post-patriarchal deintegration from the Self and the social birth of the
phenomena of individuality and democracy are parallel occurrences. By individuality, I mean the possibility for each person to develop his/her own personality in relationship to society and government which means to say that individuality is an individual and a social phenomen at the same time. Individuality is phenomenon of the alterity pattern. The fact that many people
participate in competitions for a winner to appear is a patriarchal
phenomenon which prepares for individuality through group rules of competition. In individuality proper, however, competition is a mere reference to
differentiate oneself and seek one's own goal through the process of individuation. The predetermined goal in the process of development is a characteristic
of the patriarchal pattern.

   It is only with the alterity pattern and individuality that the ego is able
to relate directly to the Self, and the individual with his group in a creative,
imaginative and democratic relationship of government. It is only then that

the ego will be able to face dialectically the shadow and the archetype in himself and others, including his individual self and his cultural self expressed somehow in his government. It is at this stage of conscious development, when the anima and animus archetypes become dominant, that the dialectical interplay of the matriarchal and patriarchal patterns come fully into consciousness and we become able to participate creatively in the interplay of opposites. Only then do we realize that this dialectical duality exists in us, in other people, in therapy and in government. This pattern of consciousness which brings knowledge of creative polarity is essential for consciousness to become responsible for development before individual and collective development i.e. vis-a-vis individual and social History.

Until the alterity pattern becomes dominant in consciousness, the identity of man and woman is mostly conditioned by the interplay of the parental coniunctio in one's particular culture. From alterity onwards, we start to be able to participate in the cultural forces of the parental coniunctio and become conscious of men and women's duality as the fundamental human quaternio.

Most women and men build up their identity basically through the cultural parental coniunctio. Women identify predominantly with the matriarchal side and men with the patriarchal side of the cultural parental coniunctio. Many deviate from this norm and may come to suffer from a disturbance of social identity. These people will only be able to go through their identity problem through the creative development of polarities in alterity, when the individual identity of every man and woman can be fully searched for and developed through the patterns of relationship of the anima-animus archetypes. It is the process of individuation in the alterity cycle of individual development and collective development in our culture which will some day create the post-patriarchal model for sexual identity which is being searched for so intensely in our time. This model is defensively built for instance, when each sex tries to build an identity through differentiation or imitation of the other sex, for, in such circumstances, the patriarchal pattern is not really transcended. The new collective post-patriarchal identity model of man and woman will be created through their interrealtionship inside the quaternary cross pattern of alterity.

The alterity pattern is quaternary and is inspired by the need and capacity to participate directly in the creative organization of the central archetype. This activity is only possible if consciousness is able to realize that creativity cannot have a preestablished codification of polarities and must allow the symbolic discrimination into polarities to occur always inside to the context of the moment. Nothing is either good or bad, right or wrong beforehand. If something is good or bad, right or wrong will be decided according to the situation of all other polarities inside the dynamic totality of a particular context. This situation is completely creative and exactly because of its intense creativity, it might become easily confused, i.e., very indiscriminated as to the identity of every part in the context. This is so because when consciousness deals with polarities creatively, it never ceases to be itself a creative polarity in permanent transformation inside the ego-Self Axis. Therefore, if consciousness does not discriminate its own polarities at the same time that it deals creatively with any other polarity, it will be liable to confuse its polarities with other polarities which is exactly what happens in the matriarchal pattern. In this situation, alterity cannot be exercised and regression into the matriarchal pattern is practically inevitable. Therefore, in the same way that adult love has as its shadow the permanent threat of regression and incest, so the alterity pattern is permanently threatened by regression into the matriarchal pattern.

When the ego is still deintegrated from the Self, and its sense of individual identity is weak, as happens in the matriarchal cycle, the confusion between its polarities (ego-shadow, ego-persona, ego-archetype) is not so serious to impair development as it would be in the post-patriarchal cycle. This is so because when the ego is still very near to the total personality or Self, its motivations tend to coincide basically with the need to grow. The situation is different when consciousness is firmly deintegrated from the Self and confuses its own polarities with any polarities it deals with creatively. When the ego is firmly deintegrated, it becomes a strong center of power and its needs and intentions may vary greatly from those of the whole personality. Therefore, when such an ego acts through the matriarchal pattern, it might do so regressively leading to indiscrimination and omnipotence which can intensely impair the development of the whole personality.

Therefore, consciousness in the alterity pattern must function inside a quaternary system of reference in which the dynamic polarities of conscious identity are experienced creatively and simultaneously with the creative experience of any polarities of otherness. For this to happen, it is necessary that the ego be strong and firmly able to discriminate polarities creatively and at the same time be endowed with the amount of generosity necessary to sacrifice its dogmatic power position through the patriarchal cycle and not impose itself dogmatically whenever confronting the other. In the beginning of alterity, creativity will naturally discover and confront the repressed shadow of the patriarchal cycle in order to ransom the repressed contents of the personality. Later on, creativity will continue to participate naturally in the growth process through discovery. The more it is practiced, the more centroversion, i.e., the organizing creative activity of the central archetype, is experienced and the ego becomes a conscious worker dedicated to the service of the transforming whole. When he understand deeply the alterity pattern, the Messianic cross becomes one of its most natural and expressive symbols.

In the cycle of alterity, the motif of redemption of the oppressed becomes an underlying theme which will be more or less pronounced proportionately to the intensity of the preceding patriarchal cycle. Redemption of the oppressed is here a part of the sacrifice and salvation motif which encompasses the acquisition of the creative participation in the transforming whole. Sacrifice is present as part of the rite of passage of every archetypal phase and cycle. The voluntary sacrifice of the Son, however, as the Messianic redeemer of the oppressed, represents the rite of passage of an intensely radical patriarchal cycle into the cycle of alterity.

I use Freud's basic duality of the life and death instincts (17) not as instincts and not as a dichotomy, but as the basic dialectical duality in the central unity of the Self. Every archetypal cycle experiences this duality as it passes from one of its phases to the next and from one cycle to the following(18). Because of this, the death-resurrection motif is an essential symbol in archetypal psychology which emerges greatly into consciousness in the alterity cycle due to its direct participation in archetypal creativity (diagram 1).

Archetypal cycles overlap and consciousness functions with relatively developed parts in various cycles simultaneously as we can easily understand from diagram 1. The occurrence of specific archetypal cycles does not exclude the constellation of any archetype whatever to face existential demands. Archetypal cycles of development must be carefully discriminated from archetypal patterns. A situation might have to be faced, for instance, with the patriarchal pattern to avoid either chaotic or matriarchal regression even though the patriarchal cycle has been transcended. Under such circumstances, we cannot consider this situation regressive.

Whenever I refer to matriarchal regression in individual or collective consciousness, I am not underestimating the importance of the matriarchal cycle or undervaluing those cultures where the matriarchal pattern is dominant. *By matriarchal regression I definitely do not imply that dominantly matriarchal cultures are underdeveloped or regressed.* I use the expression "matriarchal regression" referring to individual or collective instances of intense indiscrimination of patriarchal, alterity or cosmic consciousness when the matriarchal pattern is adopted regressively, i.e. inadequately. In such instances, when we do not have matriarchal rites in a matriarchally organized culture to orient our consciousness, we tend to act regressively, i.e., without those discriminations which we normally have at our disposal. The same thing happens with the patriarchal pattern when it is adopted regressively. Sometimes it is a "reculer pour mieux sauter" but sometimes it is a "reculer pour ne pas savoir comme sauter," i.e. regression into the patriarchal pattern because of not wanting to go through the anxiety of transformation to deal adequately with reality inside the new archetypal alterity pattern. Patriarchal regression is a very common regression in international politics today as each time more and more people and countries in the world want to transcend the patriarchal cycle into the alterity of individual and collective consciousness.

The main function of the central archetype is centroversion, i.e., the creative centralized organization of the archetypal development of the personality through symbols. The compensatory function of the central archetype is reactive to ego development and is, therefore, secondary to the creative function of the central archetype.

Incest is here envisaged as the sexual expression of a wider phenomenon which is the degeneration of the personality or culture through any activity which should be done in a new way in development and is instead practiced in an old way. It is the evolutionary archetypal aproach to individual and collective development which allows us to see the incest motif as part of the larger degeneration motif. Whenever there is psychic life, individual or collective, there is development and wherever we find psychic development we find the threat of remaining too much in archetypal patterns which must be transcended. In those cases, individual and social decay will be one of the most common expressions of this degeneration. Sexual intercourse with parents or near relatives may be a symbol of degenerative archetypal activity. Because consciousness relates directly to its uroboric origin in the alterity cycle, consciousness continues to use the incest taboo and other rituals to avoid degeneration but does it in a much more discriminated way it did with the repressive method of the patriarchal pattern.

Imagination like all other psychic functions is exercised in a very different way inside different archetypal patterns. The imagination in the alterity pattern must be differentiated from the imagination used to apply the precodified commandments of the patriarchal pattern (causality) and from the imagination of the fulfillment of fertility and of desire of the matriarchal pattern (magic). Creative imagination is the main way through which the ego deals with the Self in the alterity pattern. Active imagination is one of the ways to exercise the creative imagination. Other ways are found in all forms of conscious symbolic creative expression. The creative imagination of alterity is essentially linked to the archetypal development of the personality inside the anima-animus archetypal patterns through the creative phenomonon of synchronicity.

In the cycle of alterity, the ego participates through symbols directly in the creative activity of the Self and, therefore, synchronicity becomes its main principle of relationship. Causality is quite insufficient to express a creative direct relationship between ego and Self because it functions reductively. Only synchronicity can express fully the quaternary alterity pattern because it is able to preserve conscious identity and conscious centroversion simultaneously (Jung's midpoint personality). This is why we can experience the all-encompassing center in synchronistic phenomena and at the same time deal with the relationship of the whole to the parts and the parts among themselves. This is what gives causal knowledge a relative value in the alterity cycle, losing the almost absolute value it had in the patriarchal cycle. For this reason synchronicity is, quite understandably, the basic conscious structuring principle in the alterity pattern.

In order to really transcend the patriarchal pattern, the psyche must be seen archetypally to avoid unilaterality and reductivism which are the "avant garde" of patriarchal repression. The coniunctio archetype is expressed in the alterity cycle through the anima-animus archetypes and encompasses in this stage more than ever union and separation without which the alterity pattern cannot be exercised. The union-separation of polarities to take place freely, as it must be, in the creative expression of the alterity pattern, can only be conceived when psychic activity is seen as an expression of wholeness through its parts. Jungs's concept of libido as simply psychic energy, without being unilaterally reduced to any particular function, is fundamental to liberate psychic creativity so that the alterity pattern can be exercised. However, as the psyche is here conceived as a development of the cosmos, in the way seen by Chardin (19, it is necessary for us to perceive wholeness expressing itself concretely and immediately around us to become conscious in the clearest possible ways of the formation of psychic symbols through their roots in totality. For this to happen, libido or psychic energy must be conceived as an expression of universal energy.

Neumann described the relationship of the child with the body, society, nature and self as the four basic experiences of the primal relationship (20). I have substituted "emotions and ideation" instead of "Self" for two main reasons. First, because all roots of consciousness originate on the Self to form symbols. Secondly, because if we situate "Self" separately from nature, society and body, we would fall head on into the mind-world dichotomy and build archetypal psychology in a basically dissociated way which would result in many inevitable dissociations later on. These four basic experiences can thus be seen as the 4 basic columns or functions of the ego-Self Axis not only in the primal relationship but in all other archetypal cycles as well. In fact, these four columns forming the ego-Self Axis may be seen as the structural foundation of archetypal psychology (diagram 2). Only, however, if we situate methodologically our observing conscious standpoint on the cosmic pattern can we perceive this *structural* foundation (diagram 2) inseparable from the four *evolutionary* Cycles (diagram 1) as the *structural-evolutionary polarity of psychological archetypal development.*

Although *these four columns of the ego-Self Axis are always present and active in all archetypal development,* they sometimes influence symbol formation unequally. It is at times important to consider that the body is more dominant in the matriarchal pattern and cycle, society in the patriarchal pattern and cycle, emotions and ideation in the alterity pattern and cycle and nature in the cosmic pattern and cycle.

Symbols are initially predominantly unconscious, i.e. indiscriminated in the unitary reality. If their root springs dominantly from the body-dimension of the Self, symbols tend to appear in their initial stage through some form of bodily expression as was first observed in hysterical conversion by Breuer and Freud (21). If their root springs dominantly from the nature-dimension of the Self, they tend to appear first through fantasies involving nature as happened in the natural Sciences and in the religions which include nature-spirits called animism by Tylor (22). If the roots of a symbol spring dominantly from the social dimension in the ego-Self axis, this symbol tends to be expressed mainly through the interpersonal relationship and appear initially in the symbiosis-autism type of relationship (23). Now if, however, a symbol is primarily embedded in the dimension of ideation and emotions of the Self, it will tend to appear as inflation (24).

All four types of initial indifferentation of a symbol may be at the core of omnipotent behavior. These four ways are the natural paths of symbols from the initial stage of archaic indifferentation, i.e., "confusion" and ambiguity, towards increasing discrimination as they approach the center of consciousness. A symbol is always composed of image-word and number and is always somehow conscious and unconscious in different degrees. The more the unconscious characteristics of symbols predominate, the more their image content will also predominate. Artists express symbols mostly as they emerge and, therefore, the creativity of art is very near to the image, to unconscious indiscrimination, ambiguity and without practical usage. Scientists on the other hand, "work-through" symbols mostly as they approach the center of consciousness, and, therefore, the creativity of science is very near to mathematics, conscious discrimination and practical usage. These two types of creativity are parts of the creativity of the ego-Self Axis and serve to structure individual and collective consciousness. Fixations in development, therefore, tend to be expressed through symbols still very indiscriminatedly and can be much more easily expressed through artistic means than through well discriminated discourse. This explains why artistic expressive techniques have intensified so much our capacity to constellate symbolic unconscious material in therapy. Due to the fact that many people in this field today are artists, not fully trained in science, i.e. trained sufficiently in organized knowledge and in depth psychology, we can also understand why so much of the constellated unconscious contents is not sufficiently "worked through". This fact undermines psychological growth in psychotherapy and propitiates regression into orthodox theory and technique. Such scientifically unprepared therapists may lead analysands into intense indiscrimination, even into psychotic reactions. Intense "working through" of symbols into discrimination is, therefore, indispensable for individual and cultural development. *Fixations may occur indistinctly with symbols which originate predominantly in any one of the four columns.* One may suffer from a paranoid idea, or acrophobia, or obsessive jealousy or bodily symptom and each of these forms will be a symbol still indiscriminated due to a fixation predominant in the development of one of the four roots of the ego-Self Axis.

It is through the alterity pattern that the ego is able to relate to the Self directly through symbols and, it is through the cosmic pattern of consciousness that all other pattern can be archetypally studied, interrelated and formulated in many cultural ares such as, for instance, archetypal psychology, archetypal anthropology and archetypal history. Any such archetypal formulation tries to envisage the developmental interrelationship of archetypal fields meaningfully as an expression of the overall organizing activity of the archetype of the Self. In order to encompass such different fields of development, the concept of the central archetype must be enlarged. It is necessary to amplify the concept of the Self to encompass cosmic anthropology in which the human phenomenon is conceived as part of cosmic development. To do so, the central archetype must be conceived as the organizing principle of the universe, not only as an imago of the universal deity, but as the very same concept of the deity itself.

Archetypal or Mythological History

Bachofen and Morgan among many others have described matriarchal cults associated with matrilineal genealogy and marriage patterns which would have preceded patriarchal societies like ours. Engels described the development of family, state and property from matriarchal into patriarchal societies (25). Neumann studied the mythological patterns of matriarchal and patriarchal mythologies, following Bachofen, and became the first follower of Jung to see the mythological historical foundations of western consciousness although, as pointed out by Giegerich (26), without linking this development to historical events, i.e., to western history itself.

Developing Neumann's research, we can conceive not only Neumann's matriarchal and patriarchal phases of collective development as cycles, as already described for individual development, but we can also conceive the alterity and cosmic cycles as stages of cultural development. Individual and collective development may be seen, in this manner, to interrelate meaningfully, allowing us the conception of an archetypal social psychology (27).

Applying these concepts to the development of our culture and studying our patriarchal-Messianic mythology as related in the Old and New Testaments, we find the transition from our matriarchal into our patriarchal cycle to be abundantly represented in the Exodus. There follows an extensive symbolical and concrete description of the implantation of the revealed patriarchal pattern in the remaining books of the Pentateuch. The decline of the patriarchal pattern and the rise of the Messianic myth appear already in many books of the Old Testament and are fully related in the New. This makes it possible to formulate further a mythological theory of history and apply it extensively to Western culture. In the same way which symbols structure individual consciousness through the various archetypal patterns of the ego-Self axis, so myths structure the cultural development of collective consciousness. The difference is that, instead of decades, collective consciousness is structured and "works through" myths during centuries and millenia.

A historical archetypal view of Christianity and the myth behind it gives us a very different perspective from the one given to us by factual history. In fact, through archetypal history we realize how much Christianity as a historical religion and all Christian institutions live still very much inside the patriarchal pattern and lag behind in the historical implantation of the myth. For this reason, it seems more clarifying to substitute the usual denomination of the Judeo-Christian tradition by the patriarchal-Messianic myth. Of course modern Judaism does not correspond to the patriarchal pattern, not does Christianity to the Messianic myth. Many important works in our culture, like those of Nietzsche, for instance, have ignored this and have confused intensely the Messianic myth with Christian institutions, creating enormous confusion through lack of discrimination (28). We find, generally, that the more one is educated by Christian institutions, the more one tends to confuse them with the Messianic myth.

Our Messianic myth reveals through the mystery of the Trinity the way through which the heroic Son creates the symbolic path for our culture to go beyond the patriarchal pattern, sacrificing and submitting acquired conscious power to the creative transformation of dialectically confronting polarities inside the quaternary pattern of alterity. The heroic quest is to sacrifice all power obtained through the repressive attitude of the patriarchal pattern and search for a creative relationship between consciousness and the self.

The implantation of the patriarchal cycle in our culture can be symbolically centralized in commandments dogmatically revealed in stone and the myth of Isaac which equates disobedience with filicide. It is in this mythological patriarchal context that ritual circumcision, representing the convenant between man and the deity, may be seen as the symbolic threat of filicide and castration which established repression as the main organizing principle of the ego-Self axis in the patriarchal cycle of western culture. The Messianic hero refrains from oedipic parricide and, on the contrary, totally confirms the authority of the father. "Think not that I have come to abolish the Law and the Prophets; I have come not abolish them but to fulfil them. For truly, I say to you, till Heaven and Earth pass away, not an iota, not a dot will pass from the Law until all is accomplished". (Mt 5:17). This Messianic myth totally confirms the authority of the Father, i.e. establishes as an undisputable fact for consciousness the existence of the patriarchal cycle for individual and collective development and only in this way really opens the symbolic path to transcend it through the death-resurrection motif. This transcendence is actualized in the new dialectical creative relationship (the coniunctio of the anima-animus archetypes) constellated from then on in the ego-Self axis as an essential condition for salvation, i.e., the transformation of the patriarchal cycle into the alterity cycle of the archetypal development of Western culture.

Historically, this is so true that, with the intense accumulation of atomic weapons, which today is already 60 times as much as necessary to destroy human life on Earth, our species does not stand much chance of survival if we continue dealing with conflicting polarities essentially through repression.

A mythological theory of history is necessary for us to accompany the creative function of the central archetype in our culture and understand further the gains and difficulties of the historical implantation of mythological, i.e., symbolic salvation. It is such an archetypal historical reasoning which allows us to link synchronistically the decline of the Roman Empire, the decline of our patriarchal cycle and the first millenium of alterity "working through" the mythological sacrifice of collective consciousness to admit the necessity to redeem its repressed and opressed polarities. Jungian typology, when applied to archetypal history, may help us to understand the "working through" of the Messianic alterity pattern in the introvert-feeling-intuitive functions mainly experienced in monastic life and in the ritual of the mass. This typological approach guides our understanding to accompany our transition into the second phase of the alterity cycle of our culture, extraverting collective consciousness through thinking and sensation into the gigantic creative eruption of the Renaissance to encompass nature into alterity and salvation. It is possible to draw from this fact the hypothesis that individual and collective consciousness pass historically from the feeling and intuitive functions into thinking and sensation to absorb archetypal patterns. Willeford's idea of the primacy of the feeling function in ego development supports this hypothesis[29].

One fundamental fact in archetypal development is that the psyche relies on the initial phases of development to go further. Whenever it has great difficulties in one cycle, it falls back on the preceding pattern to help structure the new stage. It looks sometimes as if it were only a regression, but it is also, as Jung pointed out frequently, a "réculer pur mieux sauter" (a retreat to go further). This happened from the 4th Century onwards, when Christianity became definitely institutionalized and began to rely every time more on the patriarchal pattern.

The negation of the alterity pattern through the patriarchal pattern can be archetypally understood through the archetype of denial which is expressed in the Messianic myth through the treason of Judas and the denial of Peter. The latter becomes the church-founder and, therefore, the main apostle of the institutionalization of the myth and, at the same time, he is the apostle who denies the Messiah three times before the new day. This means archetypally that the myth was to be negated many times through the very rock on which it stood, before it definitely structures collective consciousness with the new alterity pattern.

"During the first three centuries of the Church, there is not trace of any official persecution, and the early Fathers, especially Origen and Lactantius, reject the idea of it. Constantin, by the Edict of Milan (313), inaugurated an era of official tolerance, but from the time of Valentinian I (321—375) and Theodosius I (346—395) onwards, laws against heretics began to appear, and increased with astonishing regularity and rapidity."[30].

We must reason archetypally to accompany the creativity of the central archetype during the cultural mutation which occurs during the transcendence of one archetypal cycle over another. Christianity faced the cultural task of transforming the patriarchal ternay dogmatic repressive pattern into the quaternary creative alterity pattern through the Messianic myth of salvation. Sin, crime, madness and creativity, as well as all psychic functions and institutions had to be conceived in a different conscious pattern which would completely change the patriarchal Weltanschauung of western collective consciousness. All polarities had to be rediscriminated in the new pattern guided by the all-encompasing and fundamental life-death polarity which is being radically changed by the "working through" of the death-ressurrection motif in our Messianic myth. If we still cannot even conceive all this today, much less carry it on, we can easily imagine how Western collective consciousness was overburdened with the gigantic task imposed on it by the collective unconscious in the first millenium of institutionalized Christianity. Patriarchal repression increased progressively through an ambiguous Christ-Devil polarity which served to torture, burn and strangle people on one side but on the other professed salvation continuously and practiced it ritually through the mass. This paradox can be understood by a theory of mythological history which sees the myths of a culture above and below the historical development of its institutions. It is this archetypal view of history which can understand how Christian philosophy, during centuries so well embedded in introverted Platonism, began to turn into extraverted Aristotelianism to be crowned in the Summa Theologica (1266—1273) of St. Thomas Aquinas in the same century that Pope Gregorius IX recommended confiscation of property, banishment and even death in the Inquisition[31].

As creativity increased to extravert into all activities in the Renaissance to an astonishing degree, collective consciousness could not change proportionately into the alterity pattern and began to present many instances of chaotic indiscrimination and regression into the matriarchal pattern. The liberation of sexuality for profound individual love led frequently into sexual orgies and even into loss of sexual identity. The explosion of creative reasoning to discover the world became frequently a path leading into magic, divination, and superstition frequently feeding the hunger for knowledge and salvation with indiscriminated lust, illusions and quackery. Mystical creativity became many times a way into heresy and psychosis. Young and still indiscriminated sciences were easily confused with science fiction. Culture bordered chaos and the patriarchal pattern was reactively reintensified more than ever. The creative urge of alterity, however, was too strong and could not be contained be repression. Extravert creativity was lived from then on through science apart from religion bringing an enormous dissociation to our culture. This is the deep materialist wound we carry since the Renaissance which the Messianic myth is everyday more pushing to heal.

The Renaissance explosion of creativity and its repression by the patriarchal pattern seen archetypally explains to us that scientists were not at all materialists when they turned their creativity to nature but were genuinely living religiously the salvation of nature from the sameness and stagnation it had been condemned by the patriarchal pattern because dissociated from wholeness. The Renaissance scientist was truly engaged in extraverted mysticism. He was fascinated by the synchronistic discovery in nature of the same creative dimension he had come to know in his soul and which could lead it to salvation, i.e., to understand the meaningfulness of psychic creative development throughout life. He discovered and marvelled that his Messianic call had led him towards nature synchronistically proving the existence of an organizing principle in the world to be tested cosmically and used to develop consciousness through the same search for truth and knowledge he had learned to live innerly. This fact shows that the natural sciences are the result of an expansion of consciousness in the second phase of our cycle of alterity and that materialism was not created by science and must be mainly associated with the repressive attitude of the church, although this repressive attitude of the church was the consequence of its resorting to the patriarchal pattern to avoid matriarchal regression and even cultural chaos. It is necessary to admit that this repressive attitude is one of the nuclei of our fixation in the first phase of development of the alterity cycle of Western culture, through which our historical dissociation grew into materialism.

Renaissance scientists had a mystic experience of wholeness through which the principle of salvation, experienced introvertedly through discrimination of the opposites (sin-atonement, evil-good, conscious-unconscious and wrong-right), was also valid extravertedly (error-truth, wrong-right, ignorance-knowledge). This was all the more fascinating because nothing was codified beforehand and everything had to reveal itself creatively through the confrontation of polarities. This propitiated collective consciousness to experience, more and more, truth at the objective level as a duality in unity[32]. Western science served as a long initiation rite of cultural preparation to confront the duality of the subject (the One) with the duality of the object (the Other) to live the quaternary alterity pattern as modelled by the cross symbol in our culture. Alchemists were not simply projecting inner unconscious contents onto matter. This is a formulation based on the subject-object, psyche-matter dichotomy. Alchemists were preparing through symbolic indiscrimination, the way to discover that metals could be transformed like the soul, and, therefore, could be redeemed through knowledge from stagnation. The alchemical Opus is psychic not because it is "projected outside" but because it is expressed both through inside and outside. When this idea is fully developed, it becomes clear that the natural sciences are an expression of our Messianic myth, which constellated salvation of the world proportionately to the intensity of repression constellated in our patriarchal cycle. In spite of the dissociation of the Renaissance, the Messianic myth continued to express itself and become more and more institutionalized through the church and through western humanism, even though many times under the cover of materialism as, for instance, in Communism.

Archetypes and all psychic functions appear differently in every archetypal cycle. The child and hero archetypes, for instance, are significantly different in every cycle of development. There is the child of care and love in intimate physical closeness in the matriarchal cycle, the child of direct spiritual guidance in the patriarchal cycle, the child of creative transformation inside wholeness in the alterity cycle and the child leading to eternal communion in the cosmic cycle. The hero archetype although always present, since *we never find archetypal development without heroism on the part of the ego,* also varies significantly in every cycle. It is fundamentally important for archetypal psychology to differentiate the dragon slashing-liberating hero of the matriarchal cycle, the discovering, conquering and codifying hero of the patriarchal cycle, the sacrificial polarity-confronting and creatively-transforming hero of the alterity cycle and the contemplative hero who lead away from polarities into conscious realization of life as an expression of universal wholeness in the cosmic cycle. To negate heroism in any phase of archetypal development favours regression. In the same way, to continue cultivating the heroic pattern of the archetypal phase, which is passing away, favours tradition excessively, stagnation, regression and degeneration. Therefore, one of the great development challenges of our culture is to favour the anti-hero trend against the patriarchal heroic pattern but to cultivate with the same intensity the heroic pattern of the alterity cycle.

Another great misunderstanding of our culture, which has been helped greatly by the Renaissance dissociation, is the incomprehension of the heroic pattern of our Messianic myth. Christ as hero is the redeemer of patriarchal elitism, prejudice, inequality and repression, guiding Western consciousness to learn how to sacrifice the ego power acquired in the patriarchal cycle to become able to relate creatively to all other polarities including the central archetype. This heroic pattern guides the ego to have such trust in the creative organizing capacity of the Self that it can frequently sacrifice its acquired position and dies as a thesis confronting antithesis in order to participate glorified in the creation of a new synthesis.

Our Messianic heroic pattern guides the consciousness of men to face their shadow in their submissive, dissimulated, stagnating, omitting, aggressive, cowardly, parasitic, false, arbitrary, prepotent, elitistic, incestuous attitudes covered up by the law and order of patriarchal repression. Mary Magdalene, as an anima figure, represents the dedication and inspiration we acquire when we realize that the confrontation with the repressed shadow or unknown sides of life lead to greater consciousness and deeper relationship with wholeness even when we have to pass through the death of our former identity.

In the same way, our messianic heroic pattern guides the consciousness of modern woman to face her shadow and develop her animus in the individuation process, engaging herself simultaneously in the social development of the alterity pattern. Christ as an animus figure leads a woman's consciousness to face its polarity confrontation and active creative transformation. Mary Magdalene as a heroic figure leads a woman's consciousness to face its prostitute shadow expressed through seductive, envious, aggressive, passive, cowardly, exhibitionistic, omitting, manipulating, impotent attitudes as an institutionally commercialized object of desire and to seek a redeeming participation in wholeness[33].

Another great failure of discrimination of our culture, which greatly hinders our relationship with the central archetype through our Messianic myth, is the idea that this myth is trinitarian, idealistic, masculine and unilateral, having to be complemented somehow by the feminine, by nature, by the body or by social commitment. This misunderstanding originates in the already mentioned confusion between the institutions and the myth, between factual and archetypal history. Our Messianic myth occurs through the transforming mystery of the Trinity inside the quaternary pattern of wholeness. The myth encompasses all polarities and does not exclude anyone or anything from salvation, as its development into the Renaissance shows. The Apostles are 12 men from different parts of patriarchal society representing patriarchal collective consciousness but it is women who experience the ressurrection and communicate it to men who do not believe them. "But in the first day of the week at early dawn, they went to the tomb, taking the spices which they had prepared. And they found the stone rolled away from the tomb but when they went in, they did not find the body. While they were perplexed about this, behold, two men stood by them in dazzling apparel; and they were frightened and bowed their faces to the ground; the men said to them why do you seek the living among the dead? Remember how he told you while he was still in Galilee, that the son of Man must be delivered into the hands of sinful men and be crucified and the third day rise? And they remembered his words and returning from the tomb they told all this to the eleven and to all the rest. Now it was Mary Magdalene and Joanna and Mary, the Mother of James, and the other women with them who told this to the apostles; but these words seemed to them an idle tale and they did not believe them." (Lk 24: 1—11).

Symbolically, the cross is the mandala symbol of totality which expresses the transforming power of the myth. Only defensive unconsciousness can state that this myth lacks evil or concrete-bodily-sensuous commitment. To state it in this manner is to deny once more the myth and to do it, one has to overlook the obvious fact that our Messianic myth is exactly a myth of incar-

nation, temptation, sacrifice and salvation and because of it, its cross is not only an idea but carries the body of the Messiah nailed onto it. When we realize
this and associate it to the fact that the hero leads collective consciousness to
transformation, we are ready to understand that our Messianic cross carries
the body of Western consciousness which is searching for redemption from
the sin of patriarchal repression and ignorance in the social, political,
economical, psychological, artistic, sexual, ecological and religious dimensions
of our culture.

With these considerations in mind, we can understand that the decay of the
West[34] must not necessarily be the decline of our culture but the decline of its
patriarchal cycle with which we do not have necessarily to identify. In the
decline of the traditional values regarding crime, error, sin, honor, authority,
courage, sexual identity, freedom, property, tradition, fatherhood,
motherhood, honesty, aggression, coherence, respect, consideration and love,
we may see the death of their dogmatic, elitistic and oppressive discriminations inside the patriarchal pattern which open the way for their discrimination into a free, creative and equalitarian discrimination in the alterity pattern.
Through archetypal history, we also understand that the cultural movements
synchronistically occurring in the world today, which include the active social
participation of the Catholic church, correspond to the institutionalization of
the Messianic myth still underway. The women's rights movements, racial
and sexual strivings for equality, the transformation of the family and marriage patterns, the economical and political struggle of the oppressed,[35] the
ecological movement, the new relationship with the body, the development of
existential philosophy, the appearance and astounding growth of immunology
and the late developments in psychotherapy may all be synchronistically
related to the implantation of alterity through our Messianic myth.

All social activities express an archetypal transition when seen through long
periods of development. These include forms of government, artistic expression
and even all forms of social play. When we study the history of games, as for
instance, tennis, football, soccer and baseball, comparing them not only with
how they were played in the past but also with the games and deadly tour-
naments which preceded them historically, we clearly realize how they are expressing and implanting the alterity pattern in collective consciousness. This
application of an archetypal theory of history may thus encompass all factual
transformation including Marx's theory of historical development of society
through economic class struggle[35] as one of the expressions of our cycle of
alterity. In all these phenomena we may discriminate the new alterity pattern
frequently still mixed with the traditional patriarchal pattern, as for instance,
when Marxism reduces causally the dialectical transformation of society to
economical polarities and ignores dialectical polarities in the political and in
all other cultural dimensions, thus falling into economical reductivism. We
also see the patriarchal pattern in Marxist dialectics when the working class is

stimulated to obtain power repressively instead of fighting for the transformation of the pattern of relationship in society.

These countless changes in our culture show us, from the archetypal historical point of view, that during the past two thousand years, our collective consciousness "worked through" the notion that the oppressed must be faced and redeemed and that its next great age will be to deal creatively with Otherness. Astrologically, we can than say that the aeon of Pisces transformed our collective consciousness to acknowledge as a necessity the confrontation of the shadow and the redemption of the oppressed, whereas the aeon of Aquarius will continue to transform our consciousness, in the second phase of our cycle of alterity, through the anima/animus and coniunctio archetypes, to deal more and more creatively with otherness, including interspatial contact with other forms of life.

Archetypal Psychotherapy

With the greater development of Western consciousness through the natural sciences, a greater deintegration of our ego allowed the rediscovery and study of psychic phenomena more separated fron traditional discriminations and, therefore, more liable to accurate observation.

It is a synchronistic event that Mesmer entered Paris in the same day as Pinel and a year before the French Revolution[36]. Mesmerism in the 18th Century was to be the precursor of hypnotism in the 19th Century and of psychoanalysis in the 20th Century, and I think, we may add, very probably of archetypal psychology in the next Century. Indeed, when we study the archetypal pattern of consciousness in these forms of psychotherapy, we realize that they are following the archetypal patterns shown in diagram 1. In fact, it seems that all developing psychic activity seens to follow this pattern. We must understand, however, that in this case we do not have cycles of development but simply the same stadial succession of archetypal patterns.

Hypnotism with its either-or, conscious or unconscious activity and its ritualistic procedure corresponds to the little developed ego of the matriarchal pattern. Psychoanalysis has expressed greatly the patriarchal pattern. The parricide-incestuous shadow, the anxiety of castration in men and penis-envy in women, the repetition-compulsion pattern, the repressive pattern to deal with incest, the formation of the superego and the dogmatic transformation of symbols into signs through reduction are a combination of consequences and concepts of the patriarchal pattern of consciousness. This pattern is also present in the technique where the analyst-analysand relationship is powerfully assymetrical and characteristically marked with patriarchal elitism (I am sound—you are neurotic); prejudice (my claims are interpretations—your claims which disagree with mine are resistances); and repression (I sit and see—you lie down and don't see).

However, it was just such a patriarchal pattern which allowed the analyst's ego to deal with the ego and shadow of the analysand simultaneously, i.e., in the same state of mind of the analyst-analysand relationship, forming the ternary pattern of therapeutic relationship which Freud described in the transference phenomenon and which opened the field of dialectical relationship to Western consciousness.

Jung's concepts of the psyche and its development could not possibly come to terms with psychoanalysis because they are mostly situated in the alterity pattern. His concept of libido springs from the notion of psychic reality as a unique reality which is only possible when the ego transcends the patriarchal pattern and experiences the Self directly through the anima/animus and coniunctio patterns. Only in the alterity cycle of life, therefore, can consciousness experience the central creative capacity of the Self, perceive and describe the archetypal world, realize that a symbol is the best expression of itself, treat polarities symmetrically and with equal rights, accompany psychic development through symbolic creativity of dreams, admit the creative involvement of the analyst's unconscious as well as the analysand's and see transformation through creative confrontation of thesis and antithesis to become synthesis. The alterity pattern has also been present in analytical psychology's technique from the beginning in the analyst-analysand equal confrontation and in the many expressive techniques including drawing, painting and active imagination. Jung's discovery of the archetypal transference was also a major step in archetypal psychotherapy. "Thus the encounter with anima and animus means conflict and brings us up against the hard dilemma in which nature herself has placed us. Whichever course one takes, nature will be mortified and must suffer, even to the death; for the merely natural man must die in part during his own lifetime. The Christian symbol of the crucifix is therefore a prototype and an 'eternal' truth. There are medieval pictures showing how Christ is nailed to the Cross by his own virtues. Other people meet the same fate at the hands of their vices. Nobody who finds himself on the road to wholeness can escape that characteristic suspension which is the meaning of crucifixion for he will infallibly run into things that thwart and 'cross' him: first, the thing he has no wish to be (the shadow); second, the thing he is not (the 'other', the individual reality of the 'You'); and third, his psychic non-ego (the collective unconscious). This being at cross purposes with ourselves is suggested by the crossed branches held by the king and queen, who are themselves man's cross in the form of the anima and woman's cross in the form of the animus. The meeting with the collective unconscious is a fatality of which the natural man has no inkling until it overtakes him. As Faust says: —'You are conscious only of the single urge/Oh may you never know the other'".[37]

However, with the relative liberation of psychotherapy from the repressive, reductive and dissociating patriarchal pattern, an avalanche of creativity invaded this field. The liberation-redemption of the body through psychodrama, the intuitive perception of psychic creativity's role in development, as well as the extension of therapy into marriage, family, and social group created a new world difficult to discriminate. Such creativity confused theory and technique to such an extent that even the conscious-unconscious polarity which is fundamental to orient development became neglected and indiscriminated. With it, the transference concept which was perhaps the greatest discovery of modern psychotherapy began to be disregarded, neglected and even expressively denied.[38] The result of this overlowing creativity is that just as in the Renaissance, psychotherapy is becoming a chaotic field much too often subject to either chaotic indiscrimination, matriarchal regression or defensive reactivation of the patriarchal pattern, i.e., of orthodoxy.

The "crucial" point which has been neglected seems to me to be the permanent discrimination of the defensive from the creative transference both of analyst and analysand which must be carefully "worked through" as conscious and unconscious polarities of both analyst and analysand engage themselves in the quaternary cross pattern of alterity to initiate the conscious-unconscious or "night-sea" journey of transformation. It is fundamentally important to differentiate and discriminate the ego-shadow and ego-archetype polarities of both the analyst's and analysand's personalities, which means to deal with neurotic fixations and defenses simultaneously and as effectively as with new creative tendencies. Only the careful and precise discrimination of the defensive (repetition compulsion) and the creative (prospective) transference allows us to work more and more with symbolic development as the expression of archetypal psychotherapy without regression into the guru, shamanic and magic psychotherapeutic relationship of the matriarchal pattern which is not liable to scientific observation.

Symbolic development, with direct participation of the analyst using all available expressive techniques, allows for a creative development of psychotherapy where both analyst and analysand participate[39]. The importance of training analysis and the training program during which expressive techniques are learned as means of symbolic expression side by side with neurotic and psychotic psychopathology, cannot be overstressed. The knowledge of psychopathology and of the creative process must be equally balanced because their interrelationship involving analyst and analysand forms the developmental quaternary cross pattern of post-patriarchal psychotherapy where the dialectic interchange between good and evil, shadow and archetype, art and science must be carefully considered and "worked through" in the process of transformation, i.e. salvation.

Those who blame Descartes for the dichotomies of western collective consciousness have misread into his work our cultural split and difficulty to conceive science and religion together as did the Renaissance scientists[40]. The Cartesian coordiates used the cross-pattern mandala to relate image and number allowing collective consciousness to study image-space scientifically, i.e. mathematically. It is this same cross-pattern mandala which we need to relate scientifically, in a dialectical relationship, ego-persona-shadow-archetype of analyst and analysand, inside the therapeutic self, through which the symbol will show meaningfully the link between image and word, unconscious and conscious processes. This is the quaternary cross pattern of alterity which structures consciousness to face symbols and be continually transformed by them towards psychic growth and healing guided by the principle of synchronicity.

1 Summary of a 76-page paper[2] written for the VIII International Congress of Analytical Psychology. San Francisco, September 2-9-1980.

2 This paper is a summary of two books in preparation which contain ideas developed since my graduation from the C.G. Jung Institute, Zürich, in 1965, with the thesis "Genuiness as Duality in Unity". One of the books in preparation is "The Archetypal Development of the Personality" to which belong Diagrams 1 and 2 in this summary. The other book is "The Cycle of Alterity of Western Culture. An Interpretation of Our Messianic Myth through a Mythological Theory of History", where I expand Bachofen's and Neumann's idea of mythological History beyond the Patriarchal Cycle in the way referred to in this paper.
I wish to thank Mr. David Philip Butler for his revision of part of the English manuscript.

3 Sigmund Freud (1920). *Além do Principio do Prazer.* Rio de Janeiro, Edição Standard, Imago Editora, 1976, vol.-18, pag. 73

4 Johan Jakob Bachofen (1861). *Myth, Religion and Mother Right.* New York, Bollingen Series no. 84, Princeton University Press, 1973.

5 Erich Neumann (1949). *The Origins and History of Consciousness.* London, Routledge and Kegan Paul Ltd., 1954.

6 Teilhard de Chardin (1956). *La Place de l'Homme dans la Nature.* Paris, Ed. du Seuil, 1956.

7 Martin Heidegger (1926). *Sein und Zeit.* Tübingen, Niemeyer Verlag, 1926.

8 Carl Gustav Jung (1959). *Erinnerungen, Träume und Gedanken.* Rascher Verlag, 1967, pag. 10.

9 Johan Jakob Bachofen (1861). *Myth, Religion and Mother Right.* New York, Bollingen Series no. 84, Princeton University Press, 1973.

10 Carl Gustav Jung (1934). *Relationship between the Ego and the Unconscious.* London, Routledge and Kegan Paul, Coll. Works, vol. 7 part. 2, pag. 171, 1945.

11 Michael Fordham (1969). *Children as Individuals.* London, Hodder and Stoughton Ltd., 1969, pag. 104.

12 Erich Neumann (1959). *The Child.* New York, Putnam's Sons, 1973, chapter 4 and 5.

13 Carl Gustav Jung (1943). *The Psychology of the Unconscious.* Coll. Works, London, Routledge and Kegan Paul, 1953, vol. 7, pg. 128—140.

14 Carl Gustav Jung (1920). *Tipos Psicológicos*, Rio de Janeiro, Zahar Editores, 1967, Definiçoes.
15 Erich Neumann (1959). *The Child*. New York, Putnam's Son, 1973, pg. 20.
16 Martin Buber (1913). *Eu e Tu*. Rio de Janeiro, Cortez & Moraes Ltd.
17 Sigmund Freud (1920). *Além do Principio do Prazer*. Rio de Janeiro, Edição Standard, Imago Editora, vol. 18, pgs. 68—73.
18 Carlos Byington (1979). "Aspéctos Arquetípicos do Suicídio", *Boletim de Psiquiatria SP*, 1979, vol. 12, no. 1—4, pg. 13—40.
19 Teilhard de Chardin (1956). *La Place de l'Homme dans la Nature*. Patris, Ed. du Seuil, 1956.
20 Erich Neumann (1959). *The Child*. New York, Putnam's Sons 1973, pg. 26.
21 Joseph Breuer und Sigmund Freud in *Estudos sobre a Historia*. Rio de Janeiro, Edição Standard, Imago Editora, 1978, vol. 2.
22 Edward Burnett Tylor (1871). *Primitive Culture* in Encyclopedia Britannica, *Animism*, London, 1961.
23 José Bleger (1967). *Simbiose e Ambiguidade*. Rio de Janeiro, Livraria Francisco Alves Editora S.A., 1977.
24 Edward F. Edinger (1972). *Ego and Archetype*. Baltimore, Penguin Books Inc. 1974.
25 Friedrich Engels (1884). *A Origem da Familia da Propriedade Privada e do Estado*. Rio de Janeiro, Ed. Civilizaçao Brasileira, 1977.
26 Wolfgang Giegerich. *Spring*. "Ontogeny versus Phylogeny?" New York, Spring Publications, 1975.
27 Carlos Byington (1979). *As Bases Arquetípicas de uma Psicologia Social*. Lecture in Escola Paulista de Medicina, Sao Paulo, Nov. 9, 1979. Unpublished.
28 Friedrich Nietzsche (1885). *Der Antichrist*. Munich, Wilhelm Goldmann Verlag, 1964.
29 William Willeford (1976—77). "The Primacy of Feeling", J. Analyt. Psychol., 1976, vol. 21, no. 2 and 1977, vol. 22, no. 1.
30 *Inquisition*. H.C. Lea (1888). *History of the Inquisition in the Middle Ages* in Encyclopedia Britannica, London, 1961.
31 *Inquisition*. Encyclopedia Britannica, 1961.
32 Carlos Byington (1965). *Genuiness As Duality in Unity*. Diploma Thesis of the C.G. Jung Institute in Zürich, 1965.
33 Carlos Byington (1979). *Jocasta e Clitemnestra. Incesto e Homicidio no Inconsciente da Mulher Ocidental*. Palestra na 2a. Reuniao Latino-Americana de Mulheres Universitarias, Rio de Janeiro, Dez. 10, 1979, Unpublished.
34 Oswald Spengler (1917). *A Decadência do Ocidente*. Rio de Janeiro, Ed. Zahar, 1964.
35 Carlos Byington. "Uma Leitura Arquetípica da Luta de Classes". in *Psicanálise e Política*, Rio de Janeiro, Bloch Editores, 1980, pgs. 201—221.
36 Gregory Zilboorg and George W. Henry (1941). *A History of Medical Psychology*. New York, W. W. Norton & Co; Inc., 1941, pg. 342.
37 Carl Gustav Jung (1945). *Psychology of Transference*. London, Routledge and Kegan Paul, 1954. Coll. Works, vol. 16, pp. 470.
38 Robert Stein (1973). *Incest and Human Love*. Baltimore, Penquin Books Inc., 1974, pg. 157.
39 Carlos Byington (1979). *Perspectivas Arquetípicos da Relação Terapêutica*. Palestra no Centro de Psiquiatria do Hospital das Clinicas. Sao Paulo, Sep. 27, 1979, Unpublished.

40 René Descartes (1641). *Meditations Touchant La Premierè Philosophic.* Geuvres et Lettres. Bibliotheque de La Pleiade. Paris, Librairie Gallimard, 1958. Meditation cinquième ". . . Mais quand bein même je dormirais, tout ce qui se présente à mon esprit avec evidence, est absolument véritable. Et ainsi je reconnais très clairement que al certitude et la vérité de toute science dépend de la seule connaissance du vrai Dieu."
Bible Quotations—Revised Standard Version. New York, Thomas Nelson and Sons. 1952.

Jung and The Emerging New Consciousness

By Fred Blum (Hemel Hempstead)

I.

A central theme in Jung's thought is the movement from a mode of awareness which is dominated by the collective unconscious to individual personhood. This movement characterizes not only the evolution of humankind from the *participation mystique* of archaic man to a conscious differentiated awareness of modern man, but also the growth and the development of the individual to that personhood which is the fruit of the process of individuation. This central Jungian theme had a clear awareness of the critical nature of the transformations of consciousness which characterize our time.

I am intentionally speaking of "our" time though Jung was born over 100 years ago, and though his own creative insights therefore predate by one to two generations the developments of our present time. It is all the more noteworthy that Jung did in fact foresee well over half a century ago the crisis of our own time and the potentialities—as well as the dangers—which accompany it. An example of his foresight can be found in his essay on "The Spiritual Problem of Modern Man." In this essay, first written in 1928 and expanded in 1931, Jung fully recognized the "precarious situation" in which the Western World now finds itself spiritually.[2] At the same time he clearly stated that we are "at the threshold of a new spiritual epoch."[3]

Skaken by the first World War which he deeply experienced as a symptom of the death of a civilization, he could see through the outer trappings which were meant to protect the Western world from "the abyss" which was opening up before it. "Western man", Jung said, "lives in a thick cloud of incense which he burns to himself so that his own countenance may be veiled from him in the smoke."[4] These words written half a century ago were prohetic of the present moment, when the smoke is losing its power to hide the true predicament we face.

II.

Jung pioneered a new awareness which we who are actually living at a turning point in history, can now see more clearly in its basic structure and outline. In order to put Jung's insights into a clear perspective, we must examine them in a very broad historical context.

Graph 1

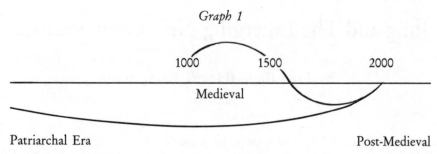

Patriarchal Era   Post-Medieval

Mode of Consciousness

Graph 1 shows two waves coming to a breaking point at our time. One wave encompasses the whole patriarchal era; another, shorter one, starts about A. D. 1000 with the medieval world. It breaks around 1500 to usher in what we usually call "modern times", beginning with the Renaissance, Reformation, and the Enlightenment and culminating in the Industrial Revolution, which is really just concluding. I shall call this period simply the "postmedieval" era, which is now coming to an end. The "new spiritual epoch" which we are just entering will be referred to as the "New Era".

Im am primarily concerned with the transitions that have occurred in the "shorter wave" of this graph, and Table 1 indicates the characteristics of the evolutionary process within this move from medieval to post-medieval, to New Era consciousness.

Table 1

Medieval mode of consciousness	Postmedieval mode of consciousness	Consciousness of the New Era
symbol	sign	
substance	form	
quality	quantity	
emotion	thought	
subject	object	synthesis of
inner	outer	essential features
spirit	matter	of
soul	psyche	medieval and
group	individual	postmedieval
values	facts	modes of consciousness
faith	science	
absolute	relative	
teleology	causality	
eternity of time	clock-time	

The medieval mode of consciousness was symbol-centered in the sense in which Jung understood the meaning of the religious symbol expressed a deeper reality of life. It was an inner-directed world in which the spirit was central and faith dominated human consciousness. The quality and substance of things was experienced strongly. Time was more alive as eternity than as the movement of a clock.

The postmedieval mode of consciousness arose by relegating the world of the middle ages to a "secondary or tertiary"[4] reality and giving primary importance to those aspects of reality neglected in the medieval world.[5] This was dramatically illustrated by the replacement of the symbol by the sign, a transformation which radically changed the whole world view of Western man. Consciousness was identified with a rationality whose clearest expression is the mathematical sign which defines the "real" world which postmedieval man explored. This was a world of scientifically observable facts—a world which could be reduced to quantitative calculations applied to material bodies moving according to clock-time in outer space. It was also a world which reduced personhood to the psyche of an individual existing in isolation. Causality rather than teleology became the dominant way in which the relationships between objects were explained.

The new era into which we are moving is essentially a synthesis of the two aspects of reality which were dominant in the medieval and postmedieval modes of consciousness. Such a synthesis amounts to a "rediscovery" of these aspects which were neglected in the postmedieval era an activation of the "transcendent function" capable of creating a new, higher unity between the truths revealed by the postmedieval and the medieval modes of awareness.

III.

Jung's life work was oriented toward an overcoming of the kind of rationality which was essentially outer-object oriented and which left the inner world in darkness, making postmedieval man " hopelessly unconscious."[6] An essential need of what is called "modern man" was a transformation which was to result from "turning his attention from outward material things to his own inner processes."[7] Jung noted the "widespread and ever-growing interest in all sorts of psychic phenomena" almost half a century before it became—in "our" time—an obvious phenomenon.[8] He clearly realized that "the gods whom we are called upon to dethrone are the idolized values of our conscious world."[9]

Jung did not reject such positive achievements of the post-medieval world as a truly scientific approach to life, but he realized that the kind of science which belongs to the new era must be radically different from the science of the postmedieval era. He referred specifically to Einstein's relativity theory as an example of a radical transformation of our world view from determination and materialism to a new synthesis of spirit and matter, of inner and outer, subjective and objective, soul and body: "spirit is the life of the body seen from within, and the body the outward manifestation of the life of the spirit."[10]

The quest for a new synthesis was a central theme in Jung's life. He knew that such a synthesis had to be anchored in the universal ground of humankind's "one" psyche. He said explicit: "The psyche is not individual, but is derived from . . . humanity . . . in some way or other we are part of a single all-embracing psyche . . ."[11] Such an understanding of the psyche is in sharpest contrast to that of John Locke—the philosopher par excellence of the postmedieval era, who reduced the soul to a "tabula rasa," a film that is sensitive to the impressions of the outer world. Locke assumed that the environment molded the psyche of isolated individuals in the image of the culture to which they belonged. It is not accidental that Locke considered the dream as belonging to a reality which was incompatible with and totally separate from the objective factual world of postmedieval man.[12]

The synthesis which Jung strove to realize encompassed the essential reality of the postmedieval as well as of the medieval world. His attitude towards the medieval world view was as discriminating as his attitude toward the postmedieval world view. He accepted certain aspects and rejected those incompatible with "the intensive and extensive consciousness"[13] needed today. He rejected in particular the collective identifications which underlay the medieval understanding of faith, of the absolute, etc. But he was deeply influenced by some aspects of medieval thought, such as alchemy.

The radical transformation of consciousness which his own understanding of reality implied can best be illustrated by his understanding of the significiance of synchronicity.[14] An example of synchronicity given by Jung was the appearance of a scarabacid beetle at the window the very moment when a patient told him of a dream in which a golden scarab appeared as a symbol of transformation. Other examples include the precognition of events which in fact happen later in time, and knowledge (e.g. through a dream) of events which happen far removed in space. Rhine's parapsychological experiments provide another example.[15] The common characteristic of synchronistic events is that they "relativize" time and space in the sense of happening independently from our understanding of three-dimensional space and one-dimensional clocktime.[16] They relativize, therefore, the fundamental understanding of reality as consisting of objects moving in space—the very foundation of the principle of causality which is the basic principle of understanding the postmedieval world. Synchronicity indicates, therefore, "an acausal connecting principle." It opens our awareness to a reality which postmedieval man could not grasp but which was alive in the medieval world view. Jung understood this reality with the help of the empirical scientific tools of the postmedieval world—again using the synthesizing approach which characterizes the whole thrust of his activities.

The outstanding characteristic of the reality which the synchronistic principle opens up is that it is a wholistic order which has a deeper meaning revealing itself in a coincidence of inner-subjective-personal and outer-objective-
universal events. It thus brings into unity a world view essentially concerned
with outer-objective and a world view concerned with inner-subjective aspects
of life.

IV.

The wholistic nature of the newly emerging consciousness expresses itself in
different ways. The very fact that the new consciousness is a synthesis of the
medieval and the postmedieval world views indicates its comprehensiveness. But
since the medieval world view is in its essential structure close to the Eastern
world view, the new consciousness also amounts to a synthesis of many aspects
of Eastern and Western dimensions of awareness. It is not hard to document
the importance which Jung attached to an understanding of the East.

As we look again at Table 1 we realize the fundamental transformations
which are necessary to bring the salient features of the medieval and
postmedieval consciousness into unity. Aspects of reality which have so far
been experienced as opposites and indeed constitute opposite world views
have to be brought together in a new wholeness. This is only possible as two
movements occur in our psyche: (1) a movement into that depth where we
find the universal archetypal reality, and (2) a further differentiation of our
consciousness.

The movement into depth amounts to a movement to that reality which
though universal manifests itself at different stages of the evolutionary process
and in different cultures in different ways. We move, so to speak, to the
universal building stones for historically and culturally different world view.
Unless we move into this depth, no genuinely new synthesis can develop, but
only a mixing-up of various aspects of different cultures. Jung warned
repeatedly against simply accepting aspects of the Eastern world view without
integrating them into our Western heritage. The dangers of a false pluralism at
one extreme and a monolithic unity at the other are real dangers in the current period of fundamental transformation of consciousness, for now the opposites of medieval-postmedieval and East-West must be brought into a
new—a higher—unity.

The unity of the newly emerging consciousness is a multidimensional one.
This means that the various dimensions—symbol/sign, quality/quantity, in-
ner/outer—can be brought into harmony if we recognize their true universal
meaning. This recognition is only possible when we become able to differentiate between what is universal and in this sense timeless and eternal on the
one hand and what is time- and culture-bound and in this sense unique on

the other hand. This differentiation, which was not possible before the insights of depth psychology became available to us, is the key to an understanding of the structure and dynamics of the newly emerging consciousness.

Until now the universal reality and its unique expressions were more often than not intermingled. Historically or culturally unique phenomena were given universal sanction, the partial truth of different scientific or religious insights were given absolute universal sanction. As regards the Western world the culture- and time-bound synthesis of Rome, Athens and Jerusalem which was an essential aspect of the Christian achevement was intermingled with Christianity's universal timeless aspects. The time- and culture-bound aspects were sanctioned by giving them universal meaning.

In the newly emerging consciousness we can differentiate between the universal core and essence of all manifestations of life and the historically, culturally as well as personally unique expressions which the universal archetypal reality takes on. This differentiation leads to a new dynamic process of development. To differentiate the universal and the (historically, culturally and personally) unique opens the way to the source or centre of life. The new wholeness implies, therefore, a new centredness, namely a centredness in what is essentially universally human. This is tantamount to centredness in the divine core of our life—and of all life.

By speaking about a universal centre, I mean to indicate that the deeper universal reality of life is structured, that is has a pattern, and that it constitutes an order. Synchronicity reveals that this order has a meaning transcending the often apparently meaningless events of daily life. Synchronicity also gives evidence that the meaning of our personally unique life, our destiny, is interwoven with a transpersonal ultimate reality. There is a link between the subjective and objective, the inner and the outer, or in other words, a link between the universal eternal and the uniquely personal. In the newly emerging consciousness we can become aware of this linkage without identifying the universal with the unique. We can be conscious of ourselves as members of a particular group, culture or civilization, conscious of our personal uniqueness while also being conscious of the peculiarity of other time and civilizations. Such consciousness is rooted in the universal common ground of all life and thus lends to a new and deeper relatedness. This is a precondition for the new wholeness becoming a living experienceable reality.

To understand this new wholeness we must mention a final characteristic of the newly emerging consciousness. I already mentioned and showed in graph I that two movements come together in our time: the end of the postmedieval era and the end of a much longer epoch, the patriarchal age. Today we are again becoming aware of the significance of the feminine. The appreciation of the feminine is a crucially important aspect of Jung's psychology, and it is not accidental that Neumann understood the sculptures of Henry Moore as heralding the rediscovery of the feminine archetype in our time. This development opens the potentiality of a new unity of the masculine and the feminine in a deeper and higher synthesis. The new wholeness is based on a recognition of the universal masculine and feminine principles and a clear differentiation between what in a universal sense is truly feminine and truly masculine and what particular cultures or civilizations consider masculine and feminine. Jung's work is permeated by such a search which is bound to give to the feminine a new significance—after thousands of years of its dominance by the patriarchy.

A deep transformation is necessitated by a recognition of the feminine and its inclusion on equal terms into a new unity with the masculine. When this need is placed against the depth of transformation necessary to bring the medieval and the postmedieval world into a unity, we begin to see what a far-reaching transformation is truly necessary to bring the potentialities of this new era of human development into the reality of a new consciousness.

V.

In concluding I want to raise a question: what does the emerging new consciousness mean for Jungian psychology? The constant growth of interest in Jung is a clear indication that he has a growing relevance for our time. His thought indeed pioneered a new era of human development. But just as Jung developed his ideas all through his life, so we, who stand on his shoulders, have an obligation to develop the insights which he passed on.

I can in this paper briefly indicate the direction of this development. It requires first of all a reconsideration of the meaning of the concept of the archetype and of the unconscious. Jung used these concepts in quite various ways; they need to be clarified and his thought made more systematic. There is also a need for a new differentiation between the universal eternal and the various time- and space-bound manifestations of the universal reality. Though a world view based on the causal understanding of material bodies moving in outer space is inadequate neither do human beings live only in a reality of a meaning and order which is both cosmic and unique. The universal-eternal interacts with the reality of space (different nations, civilizations) and the reality of time (different stages of human development). It is imperative that we differentiate more clearly than Jung did between what we may call the human collective unconscious and the culturally and historically determined, social, collective unconscious.

In the process of such a differentiation, Jungian insights could become the foundation of a more encompassing—and more integrated—understanding of the human psyche and of the human community. Because Jung penetrated to the depth of the newly emerging consciousness, his insights can readily provide the framework for integrating many insights of other schools which, because they are more limited in their grasp of reality, cannot provide the framework for the necessary integration.

Since the new era is an era of the Holy Spirit, the ultimate integrating principle of a further differentiated and more encompassingly integrated Jungian psychology will be the universal-cosmic reality of that Spirit which gives an ultimate meaning and unity to life and finds expression in infinite personally and culturally unique ways. This Spirit transcends the manifestation of archetypes because it emanates from that universal eternal source of our life which Jung knew personally. We know from his autobiography about the personal knowledge Jung had of this eternal source, but as a doctor living in the postmedieval world of science, he could not make such knowledge the cornerstone of his writing. He consciously accepted the limitations of an empiricism which could not do full justice to the whole and hence to the essential core of his being. But in the newly emerging consciousness the full significance of his work can be realized.

1 C.G. Jung, *Collected Works*, vol. 10, pp. 74—94.
2 *Ibid.*, p. 89
3 *Ibid.*, p. 91
4 *Ibid.*, p. 89
5 John Locke, *An Essay Concerning Human Understanding*, Book II, Chapter VIII, Everyman's Library, Dent & Son, London 1967.
6 C.G. Jung, *Collected Works*, vol. 10, p. 82
7 *Ibid.*, p. 83
8 *Ibid.*
9 *Ibid.*, p. 88
10 *Ibid.*, p. 94
11 *Ibid.*, p. 86, see also p. 88
12 John Locke, *op. cit.*, Book II, Chapter 1, p. 83
13 C.G. Jung, *Collected Works*, p. 75
14 *Ibid.*, *vol. 8, pp. 419—519*
15 *Ibid.*, pp. 432, 450, 523 ff.
16 *Ibid.*, p. 456 (archetype of order), p. 457 (quality of being), p. 452 (equivalente of meaning), p. 450 (total situation).

View Point from New Zealand

By Dorothea Norman Jones (Wellington, New Zealand)

Jung has said that the land influences the people who live on it. I spent my first 17 years in New Zealand before I left for 40 years to work in Britain, India and Africa. I have been back for twelve years, and I have been interested in the people who have lived on it for the last 150 years, the period since it was first settled by Europeans.

It is a very austere land, much occupied by mountain ranges and volcanoes in the North, with rocky coasts and the sea never far away.

In Europe I always feel that the land is friendly to human beings and that the mountain villages seem as though they belong. In India I felt the land was actually hostile to human beings and would like to destroy them. In New Zealand I feel the land is quite indifferent to human beings. It is as if the mountains look down on the human life and simply do not notice it. The mountains endure depredations such as the burning off of their forests and consequent erosion and flooding as though they will always be there and human life will pass away.

There is a marvellous "untouched by man" quality about some of the mountains where man has actually never been. Snow peaks in the South Island with names such as Chaos and Cosmos have this quality.

This character of the land and the extreme isolation of the islands of New Zealand from the rest of the world have had a strange effect on the people. You really feel you are on the edge of the world and may drop off. The recent airplane disaster in Antarctica, in which a DC-10 on a science flight to the Antarctic crashed on Mt. Erebus with the loss of over 250 New Zealanders, English, Americans and Japanese, made that feeling even stronger.

You cannot get further away from the rest of the world. Although air travel is very quick now, and you can be on the other side of the world in 30 hours or so, it is still very expensive. Easy going and coming is only possible for the young who can work their way round the world. The majority of the young do seem to do this in the late teens and twenties. But for the rest of the people a trip away is the ambition of a life time which most can only do when they retire.

And so the whole culture shows the effects of this isolation. Both Europeans and Maoris, who form perhaps more than 10% of the population, have lost their original culture, and the country is in the early and painful stages of evolving a new culture of its own.

New Zealanders of European origin—English, Scottish, Irish and Danish—have now lived there for 5 generations, as have some Chinese. In the last 30 years there have been many Dutch settlers and refugees from Europe.

The Europeans who arrived in the early and middle part of the last century, those pioneers who burnt off the forests and broke in the land, seem to have been people well rooted in family life, firmly supported by the culture of the land they came from. But with each succeeding generation, the supporting structure seems to have become weaker and people more rootless, and I think the quality of mothering has progressively declined. The fifth generation has been left very uncertain of who they are.

This may explain strangely immature state of many of New Zealand's young men of European descent. In spite of being married, they seem to be fixed in an adolescent state. They have time only for rugby or other sport and spend their time drinking with the boys in the pub and are never at home. They do not seem able to mature into responsible husbands and fathers, and so even if the marriage does not break up, lonely wives have to be both mother and father to the children. I have often wondered why so many of the women between 40 and 50 look so masculine, and why maternal looking women in this age group seem so rare.

I asked one or two experienced psychotherapists about this and they said two factors may be responsible.
(1) The economic depression of the late 1920's and early 1930's led to a "failure of nerve" in many men who found themselves unable to fulfill their expected roles as successful breadwinner.
(2) The 1939—1945 War effectively removed man men, so that the women had to function as solo parents.

Perhaps as a consequence of these factor, women became managing and masculine looking; their femininity receded. This had a profound effect on the children: the girls found femininity much devalued and the boys remained dependent and immature. One might expect this consequence when the image of a good father is entirely absent from the family, and the mother is a woman whose mothering qualities, if ever there, have been suppressed by the need to act as a controlling father. In turn, the immature men have become absent fathers and the girls who failed to find their femininity have become unmaternal, managing mothers. This does not, of course, apply to the whole population, but is a definite trend.

The Maoris, on the other land, have lived in New Zealand for six or seven centuries, since their ancestors made the great, three week long journey by canoe from Polynesia, a tremendous feat of navigation, to the land of the Long White Cloud where they settled mainly in the warmer North Island. They were able to retain their tribal structure well, until the last thirty years when, for the first time, Maoris began coming into towns and working in mainly unskilled occuptaions. Though from earliest times there have been distinguished Maori members of Parliament and even Cabinet Ministers and orators.

In the last century there were battles about land. The Maoris have a great reverence for nature. They revere mountains and trees and rivers, and the tradition of good mothering; and the family, being the great concern of Maori women, is traditionally strong. But this family is a very extended family, and the *marae* is a sort of tribal home where all members of the tribe belong and to which they are always welcome to return. There, the Elders are greatly respected. At a family gathering, all sleep on mattresses on the floor of the *marae*, and there is a great feeling of belonging together.

The younger Maoris have suffered a great loss of such roots by leaving the tribal lands and coming into big cities to find work. In the cities they are often lonely and get into trouble with drink and bad company. Of late years there have been great numbers of unemployed young Maoris and the emergence of gangs and warfare. The Maori Elders themselves are making determined efforts to create urban *maraes*, places in cities where young lost Maoris can feel at home.

The treatment of the subject of death varies much in the two cultures. People of European origin are tending to handle the subject of death in a more and more unnatural way, trying to banish it and ceasing to make it part of living. I have had to treat many seriously disturbed children years after the death of the father because his death had not been treated in the right way at the time. Perhaps, if he had died in the night, the body had been whisked away by the undertaker before the child woke in the morning, and the child had never been able to believe that he was really dead. He suspected that mother was telling lies and found her someone to be very frightened of.

The Maoris, on the other hand, have a very satisfactory ritual, the Tangi. The body of the dead man lies among them for two or three days while the members of the tribe assemble from everywhere. They hug and kiss the dead man and weep over him and make speeches to him: they say all that is in their hearts to him, and hug and kiss and weep over each other before the burial and the great feast.

English people coming out to settle in New Zealand, having been told that it is just like England, feel strange and only then begin to realize how much they have been supported by their own tradition and culture, when it is no longer there. There is more sun, higher wages and life is easier, but so much is missing in the psychic atmosphere. Yet the absence of tradition and the small population (just over three million) would make new ideas about social experiments possible in a way that could never be possible in older countries with larger populations, if any one had any new ideas. Superficially, the culture seems a very materialistic one, unleavened by spiritual influences in the cities and towns. However, in quiet backwaters one finds many individuals who have retreated from this kind of world and who live by very different values.

As the only Jungian analyst in New Zealand, I find that the average New Zealander has deep suspicions about the shadow side of life and denies this side in every possible way. Expressions of anger are unacceptable socially, and what your neighbors think of you very much governs what you do. People are surprised and bewildered by the outbreaks of violence and gang warfare, and call for more law and order to suppress them.

In fact, New Zealanders of European origin find it very hard to believe that there is an unconscious at all. This perfectly understandable in view of a past when the settlers were occupied with felling trees and making pasture land and only had time for practical considerations. Even among present day New Zealanders there is a tendency to disparage any kind of intellectual activity. Most of my analytic patients have been people from England, Europe or United States of America or New Zealanders who have lived in these contries. One could say that Jung's description of how man of this age is more and more out of contact with his unconscious is well illustrated in New Zealand.

But in spite of the fact that the Behaviourist school has dominated the teaching of psychology there for a long time, I have lately been delighted to find that young psychiatrists and students of all kinds are, on their own, finding what they seek in Jung's ideas.

Self-Realization in the Ten Oxherding Pictures

By Mokusen Miyuki (Montebello, California)

In my paper entitled, "A Jungian Approach to the Pure land Practice of *Nien-fo*," I challenged the prevailing psychological view of Eastern religions as aiming at the "dissolution," or at least the "depotentiation," of the ego.[1] I argued that the Pure Land Buddhist practice of *nien-fo* (the mental and/or verbal recitation of Amitabha's name), for example, aids the individual to strengthen, rather than dissolve, the ego through the integration of unconscious contents. In this paper, I would like to further support this point by examining the Zen tradition's *Oxherding Pictures*.[2] These pictures are products of the Zen "mind" and express in an art form the experience of *satori* of Zen enlightenment. Since enlightenment is a psychological reality *par excellence*, these pictures can be analyzed by employing Jungian methodology and conceptual framework, and by viewing them as portraying what C. G. Jung calls "the individuation process."

On the Texts

Although only a few sets of the *Oxherding Pictures* exist today, in the past there must have been several sets of pictures—and those of various numbers. The variety of sets can be inferred from the fact that there are records of differing "verses" which accompany such pictures.[3] The Zen scholar D. T. Suzuki has made two sets of the *Ten Oxherding Pictures* which are wellknown in the West: namely, the set whose accompanying ten *Prefaces* and *Verses* were written by the twelfth century Zen master Kuo-an and another earlier version to which the Zen master Pu-ming wrote the ten accompanying *Verses*.[4] The version by Kuo-an has enjoyed wide acceptance in Japan while the one by Pu-ming was popular in China.[5]

Pu-ming's *Ten Oxherding Pictures* portrays a wild, black ox that becomes increasingly white as the pictures proceed. These pictures are entitled: (1) Undisciplined, (2) Discipline Begun, (3) In Harness, (4) Faced Round, (5) Tamed, (6) Unimpeded, (7) *Laissez Faire*, (8) All forgotten, (9) The Solitary Moon, and

(10) Both Vanished. Evidently, the emphasis in these pictures is placed upon the gradual achievement of *satori* (Zen enlightenment), which is shown by the progressive whitening of the black ox. The concept of whitening that which is black is based on the Buddhist doctrine of *tathagatagarbha*, the realization of the Buddha-nature, or the genuine self, which is obscured by the dark side of the personality.

According to Ts'u-yüan, who wrote the *Preface* to Kuo-an's version, Kuo-an was not satisfied with the idea of gradual whitening of the ox, nor with the gradual, progressive liberation of the Buddha-nature; thus, he presented his experience of *satori* in a different manner. His pictures are entitled: (1) Searching for the Ox, (2) Seeing the Traces, (3) Seeing the Ox, (4) Catching the Ox, (5) Herding the Ox, (6) Coming Home on the Ox's Back, (7) The Ox Forgotten, (8) The Ox and the Man Both Forgotten, (9) Returning to the Origin, Back to the Source, and (10) Entering the City with Blissbestowing Hands. The notion expressed in these pictures is the sudden gain or loss of one's genuine self, as symbolized by the ox.[6]

Zen's "Mind" and Jung's "Psyche"

The Oxherding Pictures have also been referred to as the *Mind-ox Pictures,* thus indicating that the ox, or the genuine self, in the picture represents the Zen concept of "mind."[7] In Chinese Buddhism, the term "hsin," "mind," which also refers to the "heart" or essence, has been used interchangeably with the term "hsing," which means 'nature or essence.' Accordingly, in Zen the psychic reality connected with the word "mind" is that of *satori* in the sense of "seeing one's own nature" (*chienshing*). A famous Zen tenet illustrates this connection:

> A special transmission outside the scriptures,
> Not depending upon letters,
> Pointing directly to the Mind (literally "human mind")
> See into Nature itself and attain Buddhahood.[8]

In this tenet the word, "mind," "nature," and "Buddhahood" are all used to express different aspects of one and the same reality; namely, *satori.*

The view of *satori* implied in the pictures of both Pu-ming and Kuoan is to be understood in terms of the doctrine of *tathagatagarbha,* or the realization of the Buddha-nature. This doctrine assures the possibility of universal enlightenment and has become basic to the so-called "sinified Buddhism," such as Hua-yen, T'ien-t'ai, Ch'an (Zen in Japanese), or Ch'ing-t'u (Pure Land). For instance, Chih-yen (602-668 A.D.), the third patriarch of Hua-yen Buddhism, viewed the Buddha-nature as having a tripartite character: (1) the Buddha-

1. Undisciplined

2. Discipline Begun

3. In Harness

4. Faced Round

5. *Tamed*

6. *Unimpeded*

7. *Laissez Faire*

8. *All Forgotten*

9. The Solitary Moon

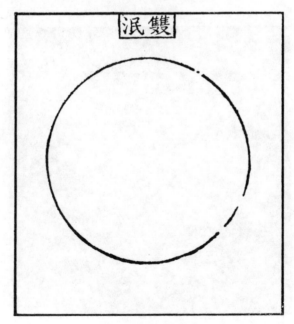

10. Both Vanished

1. Searching for the Ox

2. Seeing the Traces

3. Seeing the Ox

4. Catching the Ox

5. Herding the Ox

6. Coming Home on the Ox's Back

7. The Ox Forgotten

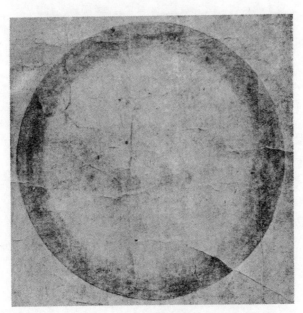

8. The Ox and the Man Both Gone Out of Sight

9. Returning to the Origin

10. Entering the City

nature itself, the genuine essence which is universally ever-present in all beings, although it is in a state of dark ignorance and passion obscured and defiled; (2) the Buddha-nature as the driving force, *(yin-chu)*, or the fundamental urge to realize itself through the practice of *prajna* (wisdom) and *samadhi* (concentration); and (3) the Buddha-nature as perfectly realized through practice.[9] In Zen, as mentioned above, both terms "mind" and "nature" are used interchangeably in designating the Buddha-nature. Hence, the Zen concept of "mind" refers to something quite different from the Western concept of the word.

Jung was well aware of the fact that the Eastern concept of "mind" is radically different from that in the West. He states: "In the West, 'mind' is more or less equated with consciousness, whereas in the East the word 'mind' is closer to what the West refers to as the unconscious."[10] Jung seems to imply here that in the East the word "mind" designates what he means by the "psyche", or the psychological process which includes both conscious and unconscious. Were this so, the Zen concept of mind could be taken as equivalent to Jung's concept of the total psyche, of the Self.

Jung explains the relationship of consciousness to the unconscious as follows: "Consciousness, no matter how extensive it may be, must always remain the smaller circle withing the greater circle of the unconscious, an island surrounded by the sea; and like the sea itself, the unconscious yields an endless and self-replenishing abundance of living creatures, a wealth beyond our fathoming."[11] From this viewpoint, then, the *Oxherding Pictures* can be understood as depicting the attempt of the oxherd, or the ego, to creatively relate itself to the inexhaustible treasure of the "mind-ox," or the unconscious. In Kuo-an's version, however, this confrontation of the ego with the unconscious ceases with the seventh picture wherein an "individuated man" is portrayed. Accordingly, the last three pictures by Kuo-an can be taken as decribing the life of the genuine man, or the individuated ego, working in the service of the Self in and through common, daily activities.

Self-Realization

In writing about individuation, Jung states: "Individuation means becoming a single, homogeneous being, and, in so far as 'individuality' embraces our innermost, last, and incomparable uniqueness, it also implies becoming one's own self. We could therefore translate individuation as 'coming to selfhood' or 'Self-realization.'"[12] The German term Selbstverwirklichung, which is translated here as "self-realization" in English, indicates the psychological urge of the Self to realize itself—the Self being the center and the whole circumference embracing both conscious and unconscious psyche. This point is clarified by Edward F. Edinger when he states: "Individuation seems to be the innate urge of life to realize itself consciously. The transpersonal life energy in the process of self-unfolding uses human consciousness, a product of itself, as an instrument for its own self realization."[13]

According to Jung, therefore, individuation begins with the innate urge of the Self for realization, regardless of the conscious will or external situation. To become "a single, homogenous being" is not something the ego can create at will. Being driven by the Self's urge, it becomes possible for the ego, the center of the conscious personality, to evolve. Jung states: "The ego stands to the self as the moved to the mover, or as object to subject, because the determining factors which radiate out from the self surround the ego on all sides and are therefore supraordinate to it. The self, like the unconscious, is an *a priori* existent out of which the ego evolves. It is, so to speak, an unconscious prefiguration of the ego. It is not I who create myself, rather I happen to myself."[14] This fundamental urge of self-realization as basic to the creative life of the individual as well exemplified in Jung's *Memories, Dreams, Reflections* which begins with the following statement: "My life is a story of the self-realization of the unconscious. Everything in the unconscious seeks outward manifestation, and the personality too desires to evolve out of its unconscious condition and to experience itself as a whole."[15]

The innate urge for self-realization has been designated in Buddhism as that aspect of the Buddha-nature which, to use Chih-yen's conception, is manifested as the driving force to realize itself. The Buddha-nature is always present as Kuo-an states in his *Preface* to the first picture: "The beast has never gone away, and what is the use of searching for him" (p. 129). In Kuo-an's version, the eternal presence of the Buddha-nature as the Self's urge to realize itself is symbolized by the circle, which conveys the idea of the non-beginning and non-ending quality of eternity, represents the everpresence of the Buddha-nature in which Zen practice takes place.

Once the innate urge of the Self to realize itself is activated, the Self relentlessly imposes on the ego the task of integrating the dark side of the psyche, or the unconscious. For, as "the smaller circle within the greater circle of the unconscious,"[16] the ego is constantly conditioned by Self as the determining factor for its existence and development. Since the Self is the paradoxical totality in which the opposites such as conscious and unconscious, light and darkness, good and evil, are united, there is no conscious realization of totality without integration of the opposite. Jung states: "Whenever the archetype of the self predominates, the inevitable psychological consequence is a state of conflict . . . and man must suffer from the opposite of his intention for the sake of completeness."[17] The ego, thus endangered by the demand of *the Self's urge to realize itself, is depicted in Pu-ming's version of the Oxherding Pictures* by the gradual process of whitening, that is, the depotentiating and integrating the wild black ox as the symbol of the overwhelming energy of the unconscious.

Self-realization, or the ego's encounter of the archetype of the Self is not a neutral experience. As a numinous experience, it exercises a powerful influence on the shaping or rehaping of conscious contents. Jung states: ". . . the archetypes have, when they appear, a distinctly numinous character which can only be described as "spiritual," if "magical" is too strong a word. Consequently this phenomenon is of the utmost significance for the psychology of religion. In its effects it is anything but unambiguous. It can be healing or destructive, but never indifferent, provided of course that it has attained a certain degree of clarity."[18]

Edward F. Edinger characterizes the development of the ego in its confrontation with the Self as a circular process of alternating ego-Self separation and ego-Self union. He states: "Indeed, this cycle (or better spiral) formula seems to express the basic process of psychological development from birth to death."[19] In this manner, the progressive differentiation of the conscious life takes place continually throughout life as the result of the conscious assimilation of the unconscious contents, or the enrichment of consciousness by the integration of the unconscious. The idea of the progressive enrichment of the conscious life is evidently depicted by Pu-ming, as mentioned above, by the gradual process of whitening, or integrating, the wild black ox, or the unconscious. It is also indicated by Kuo-an in the tenth picture of his version of the Oxherding Pictures. In this picture, "Entering the City with Bliss-bestowing Hands," the scene of an old man meeting a young boy in the market place is portrayed, showing thus that the individual old man, or the matured consciousness, acts for the further enrichment of conscious life in and through common activities, such as meeting or greeting people on the street. With this last picture, the development of the ego reverts to the ordinary life depicted in the first picture but on a richer level of consciousness.

Psychologically speaking, the circle symbolizes the temenos, the magic circle, or the protective function of the Self. The ego consciousness, as mentioned above, constantly faces the danger of being assimilated by the menacing energy of the unconscious. If it is to resist assimilation and be protected from the danger of fragmentation or disintegration, it is of prime importance for the ego to be strengthened by integrating the unconscious contents. In self-realization, the acted Self which is the paradoxical totality, provides the ego with the strength and stability for its development while it simultaneously imposes on the ego the task of integrating the dark side of the personality. The protective function of the Self is indicated, in Kuo-an's version of the Oxherding Pictures, by the circle in which each of the ten pictures are depicted, representing thus the ever-presence of the Buddha-nature, of the Self, which provides the practitioner with the strength and stability. The square in which Pu-ming portrayed each of the ten pictures in his version can also be taken as showing the utmost importance of the integration of the unconscious into consciousness, being supported by Self's protective function.

In Zen practice, the archetype of the Self is projected onto the master as the ideal self-image; hence, the encounter of the ego with the Self takes place, as projected on the master-disciple relationship. Accordingly, Zen emphasizes the importance of meeting the "right" master for the disciple in seeking for a genuine realization of *satori*. The encouragement as well as the admonition of the master provides the disciple with the *temenos* within which the latter's psychological security is gained. Being thus protected from an unconscious outburst and disintegration, the disciple can attempt to creatively relate himself to the treasure house of the Buddha-nature or the unconscious.

Jung has observed that in the numinous experience, or the confrontation with the Self, mandala symbolism often emerges in the manifested unconscious materials, such as dreams, psychic episodes, myths, fairytales, and such religious depictions as the *Oxherding Pictures*.

Self-Realization in the First Seven Pictures of Kuo-an

According to Jung, a mandala is a symmetrical structure consisting of ternary or quaternary cominations which are concentrically arranged. The ternary combinations symbolize the dynamic process of development or growth, whereas the quaternary configurations represent a static structural wholeness, or completion.[20] Jung's observation about the combination of the numbers three and four can be seen in the first seven pictures in Kuo-an's *Ten Oxherding Pictures*. Were it possible for us to understand the third picture, "Seeing the Ox," as representing the Zen "goal" of "seeing into Nature itself,"[21] then, the fourth picture, "Catching the Ox," can be taken as representing attained wholeness or completion. Since self-realization is cyclic or spiral, as symbolized by the empty circle, the achieved totality is both the end and the beginning. Thus, as soon as the fourth state is realized, a new struggle begins on a higher level of consciousness. The new process thus initiated in the fourth picture reaches its culmination in the sixth picture, with the seventh picture, as the fourth of this second series, depicting the completion of the second ternary process. Therefore from the first to the third picture with the fourth as the completion, and the process from the fourth to the sixth picture with the seventh as a second completion. Since the number seven comprises the union and totality of the ternary process and the quaternary completion, the seventh picture can be taken as portraying a final accomplishment.

The view that the seventh picture of Kuo-an's version is symbolic of the completion of the process is supported by the title. "The Ox Forgotten, Leaving the Man Alone." In the preceding pictures, individuation or self-realization— in terms of the dialectical confrontation of the ego (the oxherd) and the Self (the ox)—has led the individual to experience a transformation of personality symbolized as "the Man." Kuo-an states in his *Verse:* "Where Lo!

the ox is nor more [in Sanskrit, literally "emptied"]; the man alone sits serene-
ly" (p. 132). Thus, the ox, the Self, has "emptied" itself to become the "man"
With this seventh picture, the oxherding scenes cease and the "man" is
depicted instead of the ox. In Pu-ming's version, this individuated man is portrayed in the ninth picture, entitled "The Solitary Moon."

In Kuo-an's *Ten Oxherding Pictures*, therefore, *satori* as the on-going process
is depicted as three sets of processes; namely, the initial process from the first
to the third picture with the fourth as the completion; the continuing process
from the fourth to the sixth picture with the seventh as a second completion,
which is followed by the life of the "individuated ego," or the "Self-centered
ego," the ego which functions in the service of the Self, portrayed from the
eighth to the tenth pictures. This third process reverts to the first pictures as a
third completion, returning thus to the "beginning" on a different level of
consciousness.

Self-Realization in The Last Three Pictures of Kuo-an

The genuine "man" in the seventh stage must face, and struggle with, another
serious problem, or *duhkha* ("dis-ease"), precisely because this is the final state
of achievement for the ego that has attempted conscious assimilation or unconscious contents. At this stage, individuation as the confrontation of the ego
with the Self ceases as such; for, as far as the ego is concerned, there are no
resources to draw upon in order to effect any change regarding the realization
of the next stage. This stage can manifest as the perilous state of psychic stagnation against which it is said that the ego has no means to cope. This danger of
psychic stagnation has been recognized in Buddhism and designated as "the
danger of the Bodhisattva, or [of] the seeker for the ultimate enlightenment,
sinking into *śunyata*, or "emptiness."

According to the *Daśabhumi-sutra*, the "*Sutra* of the Ten 'Stages,'" which
describes the ten stages of the Bodhisattva's spiritual progress, the Bodhisattva
faces the danger of "sinking into *śunyata*," especially follows the realization of
the truth of "Interdependent Origination" at the sixth stage.[22] Since no means
is available for the ego to overcome this psychic danger, the leap from this
state to the next is no longer felt as an activity of the ego. Thus, the
Daśabhumi-sutra metaphorically speaks of the transition from the seventh
stage, "Far-going," to the eighth, "Immovable," as follows: A sleeping man
sees himself in a dream trying desperately to cross a raging torrent and to
reach the yonder shore. His hopeless attempt awakens him. Once awakened,
he finds himself free from all dis-ease *(duhkhas)* of worry, despair, frustration,
or agony. The *sutra* describes this experience of *satori*, or awakening, as
"without merits" *(anabhogatas)*.[23] The phrase "without merits" refers to the
psychological condition wherein self-realization rakes place so as the ego

comes to function in an "ex-centric" manner in the service of the Self. Jung refers to this psychological state as "an ego-less mental condition," "consciousness without an ego," or the like, which is also expressed by St. Paul as the state in which "It is no longer I who live, but Christ who lives in me" (Galatians 2:20).[24] The Daśabhumi-sutra maintains, therefore, that the practice of the ten paramitas, or "perfections," in this eighth stage—as well as the last two stages—is carried out in and through the realization of the Buddha's wisdom and compassion. In other words, in these three last stages, the Bodhisattva is in the service of, and in perfect unison with, the spontaneous manifestation of the activity of the Buddha's wisdom and compassion. The expression "without merits" designates this "Self-centric" functioning of the psyche in self-realization.[25]

In the eighth picture, the "Self-centric" functioning of the psyche is symbolized by the empty circle. As mentioned above, the circle in which each of the ten pictures is portrayed represents the ever-present activity of the Buddha-nature, or the Self in which Zen practice is pursued. Therefore, the "empty circle" of the eighth picture can be taken as depicting the fully manifested activity of the Buddha-nature, or the Self, in the conscious life of the practitioner whose ego functions in the service of the Self. This is to say, in this "Self-centric" condition of the psyche, the individual experiences the paradoxical state/process of simultaneous occurrence of emptying/fulfilling, or negating/affirming, in regard to the psychological life. The ego is emptied by the very act of the Self realizing, or fulfilling, its urge. To put it differently, in facing the emptying activity of the Self's urge, the ego is forced endlessly and relentlessly to sacrifice whatever it has achieved. Yet, his sacrifice of the ego is, at the same time, the fulfillment of the urge of the Self, or the genuine man.

Accordingly, this ego-sacrifice in the sense of Self-fulfillment must not be confused with ego-dissolution or ego-depotentiation. On the contrary, the integrated ego is strong and flexible enough to develop the attitude of listening in order to function harmoniously with the Self. The ego thus strengthened can function in unison with, and in the service of, the Self. Therefore, the word "forgotten" used in Kuo-an's title, "The Ox and the Man both Forgotten," designates the emptying activity of the Buddha-nature, or the Self; which is supraordinate to the function of the ego. Hence, once the "Self-centric" functioning of the psyche takes place, the "ego-centric" functioning of the psyche is "forgotten" or has disappeared, what is overcome is not the ego itself but the function of the ego which is to be characterised as "ego-centric." In Buddhism the term "ego-centric" is used to describe the ego's appropriating orientation which is conditioned by the darkness of ignorance and the egoistic passionof defilement and which, accordingly, obscures the genuine activity of the Buddha-nature. In the Taoist tradition, the word "forgotten" (wang) has been used synonymously with wu-wei, "non-doing" or "letting something be," or *tsu-jan*, *"naturalness"* or *"being through itself." Therefore, the word "forgotten" indicates the psychological condition of "being emptied" (kung, śunyata)* wherein the ego is opened to the service of the activity of the Self, the matrix of life.

The last two pictures of Kuo-an's version continue to describe the "Self-centric" functioning of the psyche. For the individuated ego, or the ego functioning in the service of the Self, neither the human world nor the natural world are experienced as alien to itself. Both nature and human activity become authentic to the genuine man. He experiences both as the Buddha-nature realizing itself in different modalities. Psychologically viewed, the experience of the Buddha-nature, or the Self, in nature and human relationship can be understood as paralleling the archetype of the Self which is sometimes associated with synchronistic or parapsychological effects. In the *Preface* to the ninth picture, "Returning to the Origin, Back to the Source," Kuo-an states: "From the very beginning, pure and immaculate, the man has never been affected by defilement" (p. 133). This "original so-ness" refers to the universal presence of the activity of the Buddha-nature, or the Self, which realizes itself in and through the receptive, flexible ego. The same idea of "naturalness" is also referred to in the last line of Kuo-an's *Verse:* "Behold the streams flowing—whither nobody knows; and the flower is red on its own accord." The Chinese term *tsu*, "of its own accord," is used as a compound, *tsu-jan*, in Taoist thought, meaning "naturalness" occurring as the creative spontaneity of nature, within and without. In other words, *tsu-jan* can be taken psychologically as the living reality of self-realization, or the creative urge of the Self manifesting itself in nature.

The living reality of the Self is also experienced in human affairs as interpersonal relationships. This is the theme of the last, or tenth, picture in Kuo-an's version, entitled "Entering the City with Bliss-bestowing Hands." Carrying a gourd he [the old man] goes into the market, leaning against a staff he comes home. He is found in company with wine-bibbers and butchers, he and they are all converted into Buddhas" (p. 134).

It should be noted here that the old man depicted in the picture has a belly protruding like that of the so-called laughing Buddha. D. T. Suzuki interprets this emphasis on the belly as showing the significance of "diaphragmatic thinking," or "a sort of 'thinking' which is done with the whole body or the whole 'person.'"[26] This man embodies what Lin-chi (d. 866) calls "the total action of total being."[27] A man who "thinks" thus goes anywhere he likes and makes all sorts of friends as a manifested activity of *śunyata*, which is symbolized by the gourd he carries. In other words, this man is the genuine man in and through whom self-realization, or emptying/fulfilling activity of the Buddha-nature, takes place. Tsu-te, the author of the *Six Oxherding Pictures*, depicts in the last, sixth, picture the life of the genuine man, or the Self, as a person who can function as a total being, or the Self, by playfully assuming any *saṁsaric* form of existence, depending on the circumstances in which he finds himself.[28] This playfulness is, psychologically understood, "an ego-less" or the "Self-centric" condition of the psyche wherein self-realization takes place. In Buddhism, it is the play of the Bodhisattva who, out of selfless compassion, mingles with sentient beings in suffering in order to liberate them. In this manner, this last picture merges with the first picture on a different level of consciousness.

Summary

Psychologically, the *Oxherding Pictures* can be taken as portraying in an art form what Jung calls individuation. Our study, employing Jung's concepts and methodology, has afforded us a psychological understanding of Zen *satori* (enlightenment) in terms of self-realization, or the urge of the Self to realize itself. The essential feature of *satori* does not consist in ego-transcendence or ego-negation, but rather in a life-long process which demands that the ego make ceaseless efforts towards the integration of the unconscious contents. The ego thus enriched and strengthened through the assimilation of the unconscious is freed from "egocentric" ways of functioning, which are conditioned by the darkness of ignorance and passion. Consequently, the ego can attain an attitude which allows it to function in an "ex-centric" manner in perfect unison with, and in the service of, the Self. This state can be designated as "Self-centric." Lin-chi calls it "the total action of the total being," or the Self realizing itself in its totality.

1 J. Jacobi, *The Way of Individuation,* trans. R. F. C. Hull (New York: Harcourt. Brace & World. Inc., 1967), p. 72. J. Henderson, "The Jungian Orientation to Eastern Religion" (taped lecture. Los Angeles: C. G. Jung Insitute, 1975). See M. *Miyuki, "A Jungian Approach to the Pure Land Practice of Nien-fo," The Journal of Analytical Psychology* (London: The Society of Analytical Psychology), Vol. 24, no. 3 (July 1980), pp. 265—274.

2 This article is a further elaboration of the paper entitled "Selbstverwirklichung in the Ten Oxherding Pictures," presented at the Eighth International Congress of International Association for Analytical Psychology. San Francisco. September 1980.

3 Various number of the *Verses* which accompany *The Oxherding Pictures* are found in the *Zoku zokyo* as follows: Kuo-an's *prefaces* and *Verses* to *The Ten Oxherding Pictures* (1. 2. 113. pp. 459a—460b and 1. 2. 116, pp. 489a—b); Pu-ming's *Verses* to *The Ten Oxherding Pictures* (1. 2. 113, pp. 461a—462a), which are followed by those of many other masters who also wrote their *Verses* to accompany the pictures used by Pu-ming. Hence the popularity of Pu-ming's version is undeniable. The last of these masters in Chü-che, who also wrote the ten verses to *The White Ox Pictures* (1. 2. 113. pp. 470b—471a). There are also two other masters' *Verses* to *The Oxherding Pic-*

tures: namely, the *Verses* for *The Six Oxherding Pictures,* composed by Tsu-te Hui-hui of the twelfth century (1. 2. 116. pp. 489b—490a) and the *Verses* for *The Four Oxherding Pictures* (1. 2. 137. pp. 210a—b) by Hsüeh-ting, a contemporary of Kuo-an. These different *Verses,* composed by the five zen masters, to *The Oxherding Pictures* of various numbers are translated into English by Zenkei Shibayama. See *The Zen Oxherding Pictures,* Commentaries by Zenkei Shibayama and Paintings by Gyokusej Jikihara (Osaka: Sogensha, 1975). For an English translation and exposition of *The Six Oxherding Pictures,* see Z. *Shibayama. The Six Oxherding Pictures,* trans. Sumiko Kudo (Kyoto(?): The Nissha Printing Co., Ltd. No date).

4 For the English of both Kuo-an's and Pu-ming's texts, I have used D. T. Suzuki's translation in his *Manual of Zen Buddhism* (London: Rider and Company. 1950), pp. 127—144. Suzuki's translation of Kuo-an's text with his discussion is also found in his article, "The Awakening of a New Consciousness in Zen," in *Man and Transformation.* Bollingen Series xxx 5 (New York: Pantheon Books, 1964). pp. 179—202. For another translation and discussion of Kuo-an's version, see M. H. Treavor, tr. *The Ox and His Herdsman: A Chinese Zen Text* (Tokyo: Hokuseido Press, 1969).

5 Yanagida Seizan, "Ni-hon zen toku-shoku" (Characteristics of Japanese Zen), in Ogisu Jundo, ed., *Zen to ni-hon bun-ka sho mon-dai* (Problems of Zen and Japanese Culture), Kyoto (Heirakuji shoten, 1969), pp. 79—84.

6 *Zoku zokyo* 1. 2. 113. p. 459a.

7 Z. Shibayama, *The Six Oxherding Pictures,* pp. 3—4.

8 See D. T. Suzuki, *Studies in Zen* (London: Rider and Company, 1955). p. 48.

9 Chih-yen. *Hua-yen ching K'ung-mu chang* (The Essentials of the *Hua-yen Sutra).* Taisho 45 p. 549b—c.

10 C. G. Jung. "On the Tibetan Book of the Great Liberation," *Psychology and Religion: West and East. The Collected Works of C. G. Jung* (hereafter abridged as CW) 11 (New York: Pantheon Books. Inc., 1958). par. 774.

11 C. G. Jung. *The Practice of Psychotherapy,* CW 16, par. 366.

12 C. G. Jung. *Two Essays on Analytical Psychology,* CW 7, par. 266.

13 E. F. Edinger, *Ego and Archetype* (Baltimore, Maryland: Penguin Books Inc., 1973). p. 104.

14 C. G. Jung, *"Transformation Symbolism in the Mass." CW 11. par. 391.*

15 C. G. Jung, Memories, Dreams, Reflections, recorded and edited by Aniela Jaffe: trans. Richard and Clara Winston (New York: Pantheon Books, 1961). p. 3.

16 See the footnote 11 above.

17 C. G. Jung, *Aion,* CW 9, ii, par. 123.

18 C. G. Jung, "On the Nature of the Psyche," *The Structure and Dynamics of the Psyche,* CW 8, par. 405.

19 Edward F. Edinger, *Ego and Archetype,* p. 5.

20 Ibid., p. 188. For a discussion on the mandala symbolism of the ternary process and quaternary completion in the major teachings of Buddhism, see M. Miyuki, "The Ideational Content of the Buddha's Enlightenment as *Selbstverwirklichung" (to be published in the anthology entitled Buddhist and Western Psychology,* edited Nathan Katz, Shambhala/Great Eastern).

21 See D. T. Suzuki, *Studies in Zen,* p. 48.

22 *The Daśabhumisvaro nama mahayanasutram,* edited Ryuko Kondo (Tokyo: The

Daijyo Bukkyo Kenkyu-kai. 1936). p. 119. The first seven stages are the stages in which the Bodhisattva's realization in the eighth stage is also suggested by its name, i.e., "Immovable" *(acala)*, which indicates that the Bodhisattva firmly establishes himself in Buddha's wisdom and compassion.

23 Ibid., p. 135.

24 See C. G. Jung, "On 'The Tibetan Book of the Great Liberation'," CW 11, par. 744. Also see C. G. Jung. "Forward to 'Introduction to Zen Buddhism'," CW, par. 890.

25 The ninth stage is called "Excellent Wisdom" *(sadhumati)*. At this stage the Bodhisattva attains the four wisdoms of non-hinderances by which he can preach the profound *dharma* of the Buddha. The tenth stage is called "Dharma-*Cloud*" *(dharma-megha)*. At this stage of the final realization, the Bodhisattva bestows Buddha's wisdom and compassion, or an abundance of *dharma* like rain on all sentient beings in order to liberate them the *samsaric* existence of suffering and sorrow.

26 D. T. Suzuki, "The Awakening of a New Consciousness in Zen." in *Man and Transformation. p. 201.*

27 *Lin-chi, Chen-chou Lin-chi Hui-chao ch'an-shih yü-lu* (The Dialogues of the Zen Master Lin-chi Hui-chao), Taisho 47, p. 501b.

28 See Z. Shibayama, *The Six Oxherding Pictures, pp. 44.*

(reprinted from Quadrant, volume 15, Spring, 1982 pp. 25—46 by permission)

Analytical Psychology and Political Terrorism

By Guiseppe Bartalotta (Rome)

"Sweet revolution I wish my woman's tears would change into bullets"

This sentence was written on the wall of a school in Milan soon after the death of the political leader Aldo Moro. It was the hottest moment of terrorism in Italy.

Only a medieval witch or a ferocius Medea of today with a "negative animus", could have wanted to transform her feminine tears into instruments of death. Tears according to our culture, are a female expression of the human soul, because a man who cries is not very manly. The graffito I have quoted leaves us terrified and astonished, yet also nailed down by a question: where may the light be in this enormous shadow, where is the opposite pole in this contradiction?

When I actually started writing this paper, I felt less confident of being able to deal with such a burning issue than when I advanced my proposal to the Committee. One had to take into consideration a phenomenon that at first sight looked more like a psychopathological product than a human and historical communication with dynamic meaning for others. At that moment I remembered this sentence by Jung: "To meet oneself is the most disagreeable thing; one escapes from symbolic images as one gradually projects one's own unconscious onto them."

Now the figure of the devil is an extremely precious property and very likeable. As a matter of fact, until it wanders outside ourselves, like a roaring lion, one knows where evil is; evil in in the devil, that personal demon which has always existed under this or that guise. With the development of consciousness after the Middle Ages, the devil was slowly eliminated. In his stead we have made diabolical figures of a series of men, to whom we are glad to yield our shadow. With what delight, for example, do we read newspaper articles concerning crimes. An inveterate criminal becomes a popular fellow because it makes the conscious of others much lighter, since it is now known where evil is."[1]

This sentence encouraged me to continue.

Before tackling the subject of terrorism from the point of view of psychological dynamics, it is necessary to mention the sociology of this problem.

Terrorism is a universal phenomenon of recent years, bursting into bloody war-like forms of revolt in the western world. Now we must ask ourselves when and how terrorism was born and above all who the terrorists are.

The origin of the contemporary wave of terrorism can be found in the year 1968: the youth who were revolting in European and American universities made it clear that in a sick society they did not want to reform only their schools. They felt it was necessary to better the overall society's "quality of life". The political choice the students made was inspired by Marxism, and particularly by leaders such as Marcuse, Adorno and Sartre. At the same moment in history many young groups, in Europe, joined in with the struggles of workers. Young people discovered that alienation was not only the alienation of working relationships, as in Marx, but that there were also other forms of human alienation. There was social conditioning which through the family, mass media, religion, controlled the free realization of man. Young people opened a new horizon for social evolution: if up to now the fights had always been vertical between a subordinate class and an hegemonic class, the social fights were now going to be horizontal, occurring within the same social class. Ethnic minorities, feminists, homosexuals, young people, indeed all the sub-cultures, organized their own fights. Politicians were then obliged to take an interest in the problems of all these sub-groups. It had been discovered that politics concerned not only economics but also the private life of people.

There are many sociological hypotheses as to the reasons and ways terrorism was born out of this movement. I will briefly mention the more important.

1. Industrialization and consumerism have caused processes in society known as atomization and *anomie*.

2. The decline of religious authority with the secularization of society has been accompanied by a loss of faith in many human values that have guided people for centuries. The juvenile revolt searched for a new set of human values in social justice, which demanded a passionate striving for liberation from old social structures.

3. Young people were often giving vent to frustation when joining in the revolt; they had not found jobs in proportion to their qualifications.

4. The revolution demanded complete devotion, and it raised expectations that great radical changes in society would occur. The new faith played on the interest in the possibility of change that has always fascinated young people.

5. Lack of confidence in the parliamentary democracy caused many young men to believe that economic power controlled the political parties. So they organized their own political groups outside traditional political parties to avoid the social control which does not allow a real democracy.

All these factors led to the formation of terrorist groups, which are still very much with us today. I will try now to analyse what the personality and the motivations of a terrorist are likely to lie.

1. A typical terrorist is born in a middle-class family, his intelligence is above-average, his education is on a university level.

2. Generally he has a good religious background, a basic marxist ideology and middle-class behaviour.

3. Women terrorists, less in number than men, have more courage and take greater risks.

So the psychological motivations and the expectations of a young man who joins a terrorist group can be found in the following:

1. The need for liberation from a repressive society which finds its preservation and financial coercion by employing the mass media, religion, the school, and the police.

2. The need for an individual experience outside mass consumerism. Such individual experience is generally found by using drugs and belonging to religious or political groups.

3. The adhesion to an ideology which generally projects the myth-man, fighting for a future of freedom and social fairness, a future in which a man can realize himself freely.

4. A religious outlook on life which has on one hand the polarization of good and evil and on the other a need for absolute and transcendental belonging. Young people see in terrorism, as in the new ideologies and religions, the possibility of realizing a society ruled by new ethical values.

After these preliminary sociological remarks, is it possible to hypothesize a Jungian interpretation of terrorism?

I think that a Jungian interpretation of terrorism must refer to "puer" and "Shadow" themes. But though it is possible to refer to the "puer" theme at the very first moment of juvenile revolt, the psychodynamics of terrorism really refer to the "shadow" theme as well, including the individual shadow and the archetypal shadow.

In Italy, the first important political groups that later acted out terrorism were born in the University of Trento. Trento is a fairly small country town in the most Catholic region of Italy. Trento was the town where the Catholic "Council of Trento" was held in 1563. Here the "Counter-Reformation" was born; here was born the big reactionary reply of the Catholic Church to the Renaissance and to Luther. Nearly four hundred years later in 1962, a few years before the youth revolt of 1968, the University of Social Sciences was founded in Trento: this was the very first University course Italy had ever had in Social Sciences, and it led to a cultural development as important as that which the Council of Trento set off in 1563.

The first counter culture groups were born in those years. Curcio, one of the most important first leaders, along with other young people organized the Trento "Counter University", using a name which recalls the earlier "Counter Reformation".

The "Counter University" (or "Negative University", as it was also called) was a regular course of study in which the lectures of the Trento University teachers could be criticized in a dialectic form. Curcio said: "We launch the idea of a Negative University in the State Universities themselves, which reaffirms in a way antagonistic towards teaching the necessity of theoretical and dialectic thinking, in order to denounce what mercenary barkers call reason".[2]

This Negative University of Trento University, attended by intelligent and diligent students, coincided in time with the world youth revolt which was contesting prevailing ideologies and art. These were the years that a counter-culture was developing; every aspect of human evolution, every value and opinion that had been valid up to that moment was contested. The world has certainly changed after the juvenile revolt.

Men like Pope John XXIII, Kennedy, and Khruschev seemed to understand the times. But did common people, political and economic power, put themselves in front of the youth revolt giving it the critical attention they would give a big shadow, that they recognized as theirs, in which everyone could find the reflection of his own evil. Even today do people put themselves in front of terrorism with such critical attention?

It is very difficult to think of terrorism as having something to do with ourselves, as our shadow; it is much easier to resolve the problem with the police and the law. Jung says: "In reality, however, the acceptance of the shadow-side of human nature verges on the impossible. Consider for a moment what it means to grant the right of existence to what is unreasonable, senseless, and evil! Yet it is just this that the modern man insists upon. He wants to live with every side of himself to know what he is. That is why he casts history aside. He wants to break with tradition so that he can experiment with his life and determine what value and meaning things have in themselves, apart from traditional presuppositions."[3]

Certainly a life which thinks poorly of history is an alienated life. Man is his own history; history is the result of the great contradictions born in man and in his own nature. Terrorism, like all sorts of evil which pass through the mind and the heart of man, is born and lives in the same man. Terrorism is born in this very society, not on Mars; it is born in the middle-class which has been the dominant one in the last two centuries. I quote from Jung again:

"Whether primitive or not mankind always stand on the brink of actions it performs itself but does not control. The whole world wants peace and the whole world prepares for war, to take but one example. Mankind is powerless against mankind, and the gods, as ever, show it the ways of fate. Today we call the gods "factors", which comes from "facere", "to make". The makers stand behind the wings of the world-theatre. It is so in great things as in small. In the realm of consciousness we are our own master; we seem to be the "factors" themselves. But if we step through the door of the shadow we discover with terror that we are the objects of unseen "factors."[4] Jung is a pessimist about political people and power minded-people. We can be sure that the political and economic power finances and takes advantages of terrorism for its own interest.

If we believe in the psychic dynamics formulated by Jung, if we believe in the Jungian hypothesis of correlative opposites, in which each attitude finds its own opposite in an endless process, we must also believe that the same law regulates the great anima of humanity.

I remind you that terrorists are human beings, almost always intelligent and cultured people with the same human training and feeling as other people. I repeat that terrorists are living among us, among the middle-class, which hold the reins of power. Certainly many terrorists are psychopathic or neurotic people, but that only brings them nearer to the dynamics and contradictions of the deepest unconscious.

Jung said: "To go mad is no art. But to take out the wisdom from madness is the height of all art. Madness and not intelligence is the mother of the sages."[5]

"To take out the wisdom from madness": This is the bold duty of psychotherapy. In our every day work as analysts we all have to experience madness not as arbiters or judges but as partakers of the great contradictions of the human soul. With the same attitude both analysts and citizens could confront terrorism. All of us then would meet that big shadow with the same humility that we use every day meeting our own personal shadow. We don't understand, but we can learn to understand the message it bears within. Jung warns: "The light God bestrides the bridge-Man from the day side; God's Shadow, from the night side. What will be the outcome of this fearful dilemma, which threatens to shatter the frail human vessel with unknown storms and intoxications? It may well be the revelation of the Holy Ghost out of man himself. Just as man was once revealed out of God, so, when the circle closes, God may be revealed out of man."[6]

Can we search even for God in terrorism, can we search for a light in a shadow so great in this century of big interrogatives about human destiny? Anyway we all must confront ourselves with the great shadow of terrorism.

In old Rome, at a corner of a bridge, there is a tablet in memory of a girl, Giorgina Masi, twenty years old, killed there by police in May 1977, during a demonstration of young extraparliamentary people. On this tablet there is written some poetry by an unknown woman. It reads:

If the revolution of October
had been of May
If you still lived
If I had not been impotent
in front of your enemy
If my pen had been my winning weapon

courage born of anger strangled in the throat
If to have known had become our force
If the flowers we gave
to your courageous life and our death
least became garlands
in the struggle of all us women
If . . .
It would not need words to try to affirm life
but life itself and nothing more

I would like to continue this thought If . . . each of us, men and women, had written down his or her own act of courage, a commitment to a confrontation we were no longer able to put off, then that memorial tablet, that death, more or less similar to many others, would have been avoided. Of course, such poor words as mine would have made no sense today (if indeed they have made sense) for true life needs no words.

1 Über die Archetypen des Kollektiven Unbewußten Eranos Jahrbuch 1934 Thein Verlag Zurig 1935, p. 200
2 A. Silj Mai più senza fucile Vallecchi 1979, p. 43
3 C. G. Jung, The Collected Works Ed. 1973 vol. 11, p. 342
4 C. G. Jung, The Collected Works Ed. 1973 vol. 9/1, p. 25
5 Über den indischen Heiligen Vorwort zu H. Zimmer "Der Weg zum Selbst" Herausgegeben von C. G. Jung Rascher Zurig 1944, p. 14
6 C. G. Jung, The Collected Works Ed. 1973 vol. 11, p. 186